We All Lost the Cold War

PRINCETON STUDIES IN
INTERNATIONAL HISTORY AND POLITICS

Series Editors
John Lewis Gaddis · Jack L. Snyder · Richard H. Ullman

We All Lost the Cold War

• *RICHARD NED LEBOW AND JANICE GROSS STEIN* •

PRINCETON UNIVERSITY PRESS

PRINCETON, NEW JERSEY

Library of Congress Cataloging-in-Publication Data

Lebow, Richard Ned.
We all lost the Cold War / Richard Ned Lebow and Janice Gross Stein.
p.   cm. — (Princeton studies in international history and politics)
Includes index.
ISBN 0-691-03308-0
ISBN 0-691-01941-X (pbk.)
1. Cold War. 2. United States—Foreign relations—Soviet Union.
3. Soviet Union—Foreign relations—United States. 4. Cuban Missile
Crisis, 1962. 5. Israel-Arab conflicts. 6. Jewish-Arab relations—1973–
7. Nuclear weapons. 8. Nuclear warfare. I. Stein, Janice Gross. II. Title. III. Series.
D849.L425   1993
327.73047—dc20   93-14206

This book has been composed in Laser Sabon

Princeton University Press books are printed on acid-free paper and meet the guidelines
for permanence and durability of the Committee on Production Guidelines for Book
Longevity of the Council on Library Resources

Second printing, and first paperback printing, 1995

Printed in the United States of America

3   5   7   9   10   8   6   4

To my parents,

who taught me to care about the past,

and to my sons,

who taught me to care about the future.

JGS

To all the courageous people

who protected me from the Nazis

and arranged my escape from occupied Europe,

and to the wonderful parents

who adopted me in America.

RNL

• C O N T E N T S •

To THE "WINNERS" go the spoils—and the opportunity to impose their version of history on events. Across the political spectrum, Americans have concluded that resolve and strength "won" the Cold War and "defeated" the Soviet Union. Deterrence and its twin strategy of compellence have been given credit for restraining Soviet aggression, for convincing Khrushchev to withdraw Soviet missiles from Cuba, for preventing Soviet military intervention in the Middle East in 1973, and for the collapse of the Soviet empire.

This book challenges all these claims. We contend that the strategies of deterrence and compellence were generally more provocative than restraining and that they prolonged rather than ended the Cold War. This central theme is documented through a detailed reconstruction of the calculations of Soviet and American leaders in the Cuban missile crisis in 1962 and the crisis in the Middle East in 1973. These two crises provide a window on the broader relationship between the superpowers. Drawing on new evidence of the calculations of Soviet and American leaders, the book advances an interpretation of the impact of nuclear threats and nuclear weapons radically at odds with the conventional wisdom.

Our analysis is historical but has important implications for contemporary foreign policy. Although the Cold War is over, its "lessons" survive. The final three chapters of the book explore the links between past and present and propose a very different set of lessons. We urge greater appreciation of the risks of threat-based strategies and greater attention to the clarification of interests and reassurance when adversaries are driven by need rather than opportunity.

We circulated drafts of the manuscript to friends and colleagues and received helpful suggestions for refinement of the central argument of the book. We also got extensive criticism, less about the details of the study and rather more about its principal thesis. American scholars and policymakers whose world view was shaped by the Cold War found it difficult to believe that the strategy of deterrence provoked rather than restrained in 1962, was irrelevant in 1973, and prolonged the Cold War. Russians who are now deeply critical of Soviet policy echoed these views. We received the same response, but in reverse, from Russians at the other end of the political spectrum who blame the United States for the long Cold War. Needless to say, our thesis is also anathema to American "revisionists" who also hold the United States primarily responsible. They all see the conflict between the superpowers as a Manichaean struggle between good and evil. The book portrays the Cold War as a contest between insecure, competitive, and domestically driven leaders with competing conceptions of security. We hope that the new evidence we have gathered for this book will speak clearly to the reader.

Our individual and collective research has attempted to reconstruct the calculations of all parties to a conflict. Only by understanding the perspectives of all sides, could we capture the origins, dynamics, and resolution of a conflict. This commitment to multiple imaging made it impossible to study the relationship between the superpowers because so little good evidence was available about the calculations that lay behind key Soviet foreign-policy decisions. We recognized nevertheless that our analysis of deterrence and other strategies of conflict management was incomplete as long as we could not assess their impact on the superpower relationship during the Cold War. *Glasnost* and the subsequent collapse of the Soviet Union created the political environment that gave us access to Soviet documents and policymakers.

The other requisite for scholarship is funding. The Carnegie Corporation of New York provided a generous stipend to Ned Lebow, and Janice Gross Stein was fortunate to receive a Connaught Senior Research Fellowship from the University of Toronto. Both authors benefited from support from the United States Institute of Peace and the Canadian Institute for International Peace and Security. We lament the dissolution of the Canadian Institute, which contributed so much to research and scholarship. We are especially grateful to David Hamburg and Fritz Moser of the Carnegie Corporation, Samuel Lewis of the United States Institute of Peace, and Geoffrey Pearson, former director of the Canadian Institute, for their personal and intellectual interest in our work.

Much of the evidence for this book comes from interviews. We are deeply grateful to the many former American and Soviet officials who generously shared their time and experience with us. We are also indebted to those who helped to arrange these interviews. We want to thank the John F. Kennedy School of Harvard University for organizing a series of conferences on the Cuban missile crisis that brought scholars together with American, Soviet, and Cuban policymakers. In Moscow, we are grateful to Georgi Arbatov and the late Vadim Bogdanov, director and deputy director of the Institute of the United States and Canada, and to Andrei Melville and Aleksandr Nikitin, director and deputy director of the Soviet Peace Committee, for arranging our many visits to the then Soviet Union and facilitating our meetings with key Soviet officials.

The Soviet interviews were initially made possible by the personal intervention of President Mikhail Sergeevich Gorbachev. He had become interested in crisis management in the mid-1980s. At the time, President Ronald Reagan was committed to the development and eventual deployment of a ballistic missile defense. Gorbachev was publicly committed to oppose any such deployment, and worried that the superpowers were on a collision course. To learn more about how an earlier acute confrontation had been resolved, he asked for the record on the "Caribbean crisis" only to be told that there was none. He then asked Ambassador Aleksandr Alekseev, who had been Khrushchev's representative in Havana in 1962, to put together a short history of that crisis on the basis of interviews. After reading this document, Gorbachev admitted to having spent a restless night and told the Politburo the following day that "The world had almost been blown up because two boys were fighting in the schoolyard over who had the bigger stick." Gorbachev subsequently instructed Soviet officials to cooperate with Western scholars who were attempting to reconstruct the "Cuban missile crisis" from the Soviet perspective.[1] He was also gracious enough to consent to an interview.

We also want to acknowledge the assistance of colleagues who, despite their busy schedules, read all or part of innumerable drafts of the manuscript or provided us with documents. The constructive criticism of Michael Brecher, George Breslauer, John Lewis Gaddis, Alexander L. George, Robert Glasser, James Goldgeier, Franklyn Griffiths, Robert Herman, Walter Isaacson, Robert Jervis, Murrey Marder, Jack Snyder, Blema Steinberg, Thomas Risse-Kappen, William Taubman, Yaacov Vertzberger, and David Welch significantly improved the quality of the book. Anatoliy Dobrynin's cable, which appears in the appendix, is courtesy of NHK.

Very special thanks go to four individuals who played a central role in this project. McGeorge Bundy, Oleg Grinevsky, Raymond A. Garthoff, and William A. Quandt in the first instance provided us with detailed information about the crises in which they participated. They also helped to arrange interviews with officials in the United States and the Soviet Union. Finally, all four read the manuscript as scholars and provided insightful criticism.

We want to thank our research assistants, Stephen Bernstein, Amir Hashemi, David Eichberg, Kirsta Leeburg, Linda White, administrative assistant Elaine Scott, and Sandra Kisner, Anita Tilford, Kendall Stanley, Marian Reed, and Hyla Levy. Their frequent trips to libraries, careful checking of references, typing, and photocopying saved us many hours of labor. They all responded to our frequently irritable requests with unfailing good humor and patience.

This book is the most recent product of a collaboration that began with *Psychology and Deterrence*, published in 1985. Drawn together by a common research agenda and complementary regional expertise, the authors have become each other's toughest critics. To the surprise of our colleagues, who know our determined personalities, our collaboration has been harmonious. Indeed, we no longer know who thought of what idea or wrote which paragraph. We both nevertheless want it known that any questionable arguments in the book are the responsibility of the other.

Richard Ned Lebow
Janice Gross Stein
Pittsburgh and Toronto
January 1993

AFL-CIO	American Federation of Labor-Congress of Industrial Organizations
ASW	Anti-submarine warfare
CIA	Central Intelligence Agency
CINCLANT	Commander in Chief, Atlantic
CINCLANTFLT	Commander in Chief, U.S. Atlantic Fleet
CINCUSNAVEUR	Commander in Chief, U.S. Naval Forces Europe
DEFCON	Defense Condition
DIA	Defense Intelligence Agency
Ex Comm	Executive Committee of the National Security Council
FBI	Federal Bureau of Investigation
ICBM	Intercontinental ballistic missiles
IDF	Israel Defense Forces
INF	Intermediate nuclear forces
INR	Bureau of Intelligence and Research
IRBM	Intermediate range ballistic missile
JCS	Joint Chiefs of Staff
JFK	John F. Kennedy
KGB	Komitet Gosudarstvenney Bezopasnosti; Committee on State Security (Soviet)
MAC	U.S. Military Assistance Command
MAD	Mutual assured destruction
MRBM	Medium range ballistic missile
MIRV	Multiple independently targetable reentry vehicle
NATO	North Atlantic Treaty Organization
NIE	National Intelligence Estimate
NORAD	North American Air Defense Command
NSA	National Security Agency
NSC	National Security Council
OAS	Organization of American States
SAC	Strategic Air Command
SALT	Strategic Arms Limitation Talks
SAM	Surface-to-air missile
SDI	Strategic Defense Initiative
SECDEF	Secretary of Defense
SG(A)	Special Group (Augmented)
SHAPE	Supreme Headquarters Allied Powers Europe
SLBM	Submarine launched ballistic missile
SRF	Strategic Rocket Forces
START	Strategic Arms Reduction Talks
TASS	Soviet News Agency

UN	United Nations
USCINCEUR	Commander in Chief, U.S. European Command
USSR	Union of Soviet Socialist Republics
WSAG	Washington Special Action Group

We All Lost the Cold War

Introduction

THE COLD WAR IS OVER. Within a brief period of two years, the political map of Europe changed beyond recognition: the Berlin Wall came down, Germany was reunified within the North Atlantic Treaty Organization (NATO), communist governments were ousted in Eastern Europe, and the Soviet Union disappeared. Even before the Berlin Wall was demolished in November 1989, many analysts in the West had declared the Cold War over and the United States its winner. This judgment quickly became conventional wisdom.

The consequences of more than four decades of intense Soviet-American rivalry warrant a more sober assessment. The Cold War had no winners, only losers. There is no dispute that the Soviet Union lost: the USSR has disappeared and its communist government is no more. This judgment leaves two intriguing and important questions unanswered. Did the Soviet Union lose because of the strategies the United States used to wage the Cold War? What were the consequences for the United States of the strategies it used during the Cold War? The first question is the central concern of this book. The second question is more easily answered: the United States paid a heavy economic, diplomatic, and moral price for the long and bitter Cold War.

The growing national debt, decaying infrastructure, and large trade imbalance are all attributable in part to decades of excessive military spending. Three years after the Cold War ended, 60 percent of the discretionary federal budget outlays still went to national defense and the livelihood of one of every twenty American workers depended directly on defense spending.[1] Until the Clinton administration, over 30 percent of the approximately $150 billion government and industry spent every year on research and development was related to defense.[2] This large expenditure had little spin-off for commercial product development and is one important reason why American industry has become increasingly less competitive.[3]

The competition between the superpowers during the Cold War also ensnared the United States in costly worldwide commitments made in the expectation that they would promote and preserve its reputation as a reliable ally. Successive administrations created and maintained a worldwide network of alliances in the global struggle against communism. The most successful was NATO; it proved extraordinarily effective in reintegrating Germany into the European community. In other alliances, authoritarian "kleptocrats" used American aid and arms to enrich themselves and suppress domestic opponents. When these regimes were challenged from within or without, the United States often came to their defense in the belief that the credibility of the United States in the global competition with the Soviet Union was at stake. Military involvement in Vietnam was a national disaster.

The foreign policy of the United States during the Cold War also undermined its moral stature. In 1945, American troops were welcomed everywhere as liberators. Democratic forces around the world looked to the United States for political support and economic assistance. After the Cold War began, Washington increasingly shifted its support to repressive regimes to prevent the spread of communism. In South Korea, southern Africa, Chile, Central America, and the Caribbean, Democratic and Republican administrations alike kept corrupt governments in power. By the end of the Cold War, the United States was widely regarded as a powerful obstacle to democratic change. At home, in the name of security, successive presidents concentrated power in the executive and shrouded their, at times, unconstitutional actions in secrecy. National security was also invoked by the Federal Bureau of Investigation (FBI) and the Central Intelligence Agency (CIA) to violate the civil liberties of American citizens during the McCarthy era and the Vietnam War.

It would be satisfying to know that these heavy costs in lives, treasure, and legitimacy kept the peace between the United States and the Soviet Union. Throughout the long years of the Cold War, the United States relied heavily on threat-based strategies to restrain the Soviet Union. Deterrence was used to prevent aggression that could provoke a serious crisis, and its sister strategy, compellence, was often used to manage crises once they erupted. Deterrence is widely credited with preventing war between the superpowers and teaching Soviet leaders that aggression would not pay. The central argument of this book is that this claim is unfounded.

We argue that the strategies of deterrence and compellence provoked at least as much as they restrained. The buildup of arms and the use of threats had complex but generally harmful consequences for the relationship between the two superpowers. Often, they elicited the kind of behavior they were intended to prevent. The Cuban missile crisis was the direct result of the heavy-handed practice of deterrence by both superpowers. In October 1973, Brezhnev's attempt to compel the United States provoked a worldwide alert of American strategic and conventional forces.

We examine the impact of deterrence and compellence in detailed studies of the two most acute Soviet-American confrontations of the last quarter century: the Cuban missile crisis of 1962 and the crisis in the Middle East in 1973. We demonstrate the largely pernicious consequences of threat-based strategies in both cases. In the Cuban missile crisis, the reality of nuclear deterrence and the fear of war it inspired nevertheless had a positive impact on the resolution of the crisis. In our reconstruction of both crises, we explore the contradictory consequences of nuclear threats and nuclear weapons.

These two crises provide a window on the broader relationship between the United States and the Soviet Union during the Cold War. We examine the immediate impact of deterrence and compellence in the two crises and their long-term impact on the broader relationship between the superpowers. We contend that the strategy of deterrence prolonged the Cold War and helped to extend the life of communism in eastern Europe and the Soviet Union. We agree with George Kennan that the primacy of military over political policy in the United States during the Cold War delayed rather than hastened the great changes that finally overtook the Soviet Union.[5] By looking through the window of these two crises at the broader superpower relationship, we can learn lessons that will be applicable to the prevention, management, and resolution of international conflict beyond the Cold War.

A WINDOW ON THE COLD WAR

The choice of the Cuban missile crisis needs little justification. It is universally recognized as the most acute confrontation of the Cold War. At the time, John F. Kennedy estimated the likelihood of war to be "somewhere between one out of three and even."[6] Nikita Khrushchev was equally pessimistic. A week after the crisis, he told newsmen in Moscow that "we were on the edge of the precipice of nuclear war. Both sides were ready to go."[7]

The missile crisis was not an isolated event. It was the most dangerous of a series of crises that threatened the peace between the superpowers in the late 1950s and early 1960s. The origins of the Cuban missile crisis illuminate the dynamics of superpower rivalry and the ways in which conflicting interests, mutual insecurities, and threat-based strategies can provoke war-threatening confrontations.

The Cuban missile crisis is also important because of the influence it had on subsequent American thinking about national security. It spawned or confirmed lessons about crisis prevention and management that continue to shape American thinking and policy. The most important of these is the belief that resolve discourages aggression and accommodation invites it. The missile crisis appeared to illustrate both sides of the coin of resolve. Its origins were attributed to Kennedy's alleged failure to demonstrate resolve; his self-imposed restraint at the Bay of Pigs, his performance at the Vienna summit, and his failure to interfere with the construction of the Berlin wall, were all thought to have convinced Khrushchev that he would meet with no resistance if he sent missiles to Cuba. Kennedy's unquestioned resolve during the crisis that followed has long been credited with persuading Khrushchev to withdraw the missiles.

New evidence challenges these interpretations. It suggests that Khrushchev's determination to send missiles to Cuba was not the result of his low estimate of Kennedy's resolve; rather, he decided to deploy them secretly out of respect for that resolve. His decision to withdraw the missiles was conditioned almost as much by the expectation of gain as it was by the fear of loss. Kennedy made an important concession to Khrushchev through a secret "back channel," and considered a further concession if necessary to end the crisis. The "hidden history" of Cuba also reveals that the efforts of both sides to manipulate the other's perception of its interests and resolve were largely unsuccessful. These findings challenge some of the most fundamental axioms of the American approach to crisis prevention and management.

Before the era of *glasnost*, this kind of book would have been impossible to write.[8] Nikita Khrushchev's heavily edited memoirs and a sampling of the letters he wrote to John F. Kennedy were the only firsthand accounts of Soviet policy in the missile crisis. The few published Soviet histories of the crisis were propagandistic and of limited value. Our analysis of the missile crisis is made possible by a cornucopia of new information that has only recently become available.

Hundreds of declassified documents from the National Security Council, State and Defense Departments, and CIA have been released, as well as transcripts of some of the secret tape recordings President Kennedy had made of the deliberations of his advisory group, the Executive Committee of the National Security Council (Ex Comm).[9] On the Soviet side, we have Khrushchev's correspondence with Fidel Castro during and immediately after the crisis and some of the cable traffic between the Soviet embassy in Washington and Moscow. Cuba has released militia reports, correspondence, and drafts of the Soviet-Cuban treaty negotiated on the eve of the missile deployment.

New insight into the crisis has also been provided by the oral testimony of the participants. The Sloan Foundation sponsored two retrospective seminars in January and June 1983.[10] In March 1987, the Sloan Foundation and the Carnegie Corporation sponsored a more ambitious two-and-a-half day conference attended by scholars and former Kennedy administration officials.[11] Four subsequent conferences in Cambridge, Moscow, Antigua, and Havana, provided the opportunity for Soviet and Cuban officials to discuss the missile crisis with their American counterparts.[12] These encounters were triumphs of *glasnost*; leaders who twenty-five years earlier had regarded one another as implacable foes, sat down at the same table, shared their memories of events, and together sought to understand the decisions that had brought the world to the brink of nuclear holocaust.

In the United States, we conducted extensive interviews with Secretary of State Dean Rusk, Secretary of Defense Robert McNamara, Secretary of the Treasury C. Douglas Dillon, National Security Advisor McGeorge Bundy, Special Counsel to the President Theodore C. Sorensen, Under Secretary of State Chester Bowles, and Press Secretary Pierre Salinger. We also interviewed many lesser known but influential political, military, and intelligence officials from the Kennedy years.

In Moscow, we spoke to key officials from the Khrushchev period and individuals who, through their family relationships, were well-informed about the "Caribbean crisis." These include Ambassadors Leonid M. Zamyatin and Oleg N. Grinevsky, members of the foreign ministry crisis action group; Anatoliy F. Dobrynin, Ambassador to the United States; Aleksei I. Adzhubei, Khrushchev's son-in-law, political confidant, and former editor of *Izvestiya*; Ambassador Georgiy A. Kornienko, Dobrynin's assistant during the crisis; Georgi A. Arbatov, director of the Institute of USA and Canada; Gen. Valentin Larionov, Adm. Nikolai Amelko, Anatoliy A. Gromyko, son of Foreign Minister Andrei A. Gromyko; Sergei N. Khrushchev; and Sergo Mikoyan, a Latin American expert and son of Khrushchev's deputy prime minister, Anastas I. Mikoyan. We also drew on interviews with other Soviet officials conducted by our colleagues.[13]

We analyzed a second Soviet-American crisis to control for the idiosyncracies of Cuba. The most serious superpower crises of the postwar period were over Berlin in 1948–49 and 1959–62, and the crisis that erupted in the Middle East in 1973. The first Berlin crisis occurred at the beginning of the Cold War at a time when the United States had a monopoly on nuclear weapons. In the second round of Berlin crises, from 1959 to 1962, both superpowers had significant nuclear capabilities, but, for much of this period, Khrushchev and Kennedy were in power. A comparative analysis of the missile crisis and Berlin would have been unrepresentative of Soviet-American interaction in crisis during the Cold War. The crisis in 1973 seemed a more appropriate choice. It reflects a different style of crisis management in Moscow and in Washington, but includes a strong nuclear threat, and in contrast to the Cuban missile crisis, took place in an era of strategic parity and superpower détente.

Many policymakers and scholars view the outcome of the crisis in 1973 as confirmation of the most important lessons of the missile crisis. They have argued that American resolve, communicated through a worldwide alert of American strategic and conventional forces and a naval deployment in the eastern Mediterranean, deterred the Soviet Union from sending military forces to Egypt. After the crisis, the American national security establishment was even more convinced that threats backed by demonstrable and usable military force are effective instruments of crisis management. Once again, this conclusion is inconsistent with the evidence.

Like the Cuban missile crisis, the crisis in 1973 is a useful vehicle for analyzing the broader sweep of Soviet-American relations. The years preceding the crisis were marked by the beginnings of détente between the superpowers, the development of norms of competition in regions of disputed interest, and an explicit attempt to spell out procedures to prevent nuclear war. The difference in the context of the two crises could not be sharper, but the more benign environment of 1970–73 was not sufficient to prevent the outbreak of a serious crisis between the two superpowers.

Only in the last few years has new evidence become available about the background, development, and resolution of the 1973 crisis. We have interviewed Egyptian, Israeli, American, and Soviet officials. In Egypt, these include President Anwar el-Sadat, members of his staff, and senior Egyptian military officers, some of whom were in the Crisis Operations Center during the October War. Egyptian officials spoke frankly about their decisions and also about Soviet policy toward Egypt before and during the war. In Israel, the late Chief of Staff David Elazar, as well as officials in Military Intelligence and in the Ministry of Foreign Affairs, provided valuable evidence. Interviews with Golda Meir, prime minister of Israel at the time, Moshe Dayan, then the minister of defense, and Simcha Dinitz, Israel's ambassador to Washington, were very helpful in reconstructing the relationship between Israel and the United States on the eve of the war, after the Syrian-Egyptian attack, and during the crisis that followed.

Key American officials are now willing to speak much more freely about their estimates of Soviet intentions at the time. Secretary of State Henry Kissinger, CIA Director William Colby, and Chairman of the Joint Chiefs William Moorer provided invaluable reconstructions of American policy during the crisis. We also interviewed members of the National Security Council staff and senior officials in the State and Defense Departments and the CIA.

In the past, very little was known about Soviet thinking during the crisis. No documents were available, and Soviet officials with access to the Brezhnev Politburo did not discuss the crisis other than to repeat standard Soviet interpretations. After *glasnost*, a number of influential and knowledgeable officials from the Brezhnev period consented to be interviewed. These included Ambassadors Anatoliy Dobrynin and Leonid Zamyatin, who was Brezhnev's chief spokesman and at his side during his talks with Henry Kissinger in Moscow. Ambassadors Georgiy Kornienko and Victor Israelian were part of a crisis action group created by Foreign Minister Anatoliy Gromyko that attended Politburo meetings and implemented its political directives. Ambassador Israelian shared with us his extensive and detailed notes of those meetings. These notes recorded the conversations among Politburo members and provided a unique and invaluable body of evidence.

We also benefited from discussions with Aleksandr Kislov, Deputy Director of the Institute of World Economy and International Relations and a leading expert on the Middle East; Vadim Zagladin, deputy director of the International Relations Department of the Central Committee in 1973; Georgi Arbatov, director of the Institute of USA and Canada, who was with Brezhnev for part of the crisis; and Anatoliy Gromyko, who was in the Soviet Embassy in Washington during the October War and had access to the relevant cable traffic between Moscow and Washington in the crucial thirty-six hours of the crisis. Adm. Amelko and Gens. Larionov and Yuri Yakovlevich Kirshin shared with us their knowledge of Soviet military preparations and attitudes, based on their experience and their research in the relevant Soviet military archives.

Although most American and Soviet documents are still classified, we have a rich body of interpretative evidence from both sides. It permits us to explore superpower interactions in the crisis in 1973 in a way that has never before been possible. We are therefore able to offer new propositions about the origins of crisis, the dynamics of escalation, and the strategies and mechanisms that resolved the crisis. We recognize that some of the conclusions that we draw from the new evidence will be controversial, but we hope that our analysis will provoke a rethinking of some of the most cherished assumptions about the impact of deterrence and compellence on crisis prevention and management.

How Reliable Is the Evidence?

Our analysis of Soviet policy and many of our conclusions about Soviet-American interaction rely on information supplied by Soviet officials. How credible are their accounts of Soviet policy? When Soviet officials first began to talk about the Caribbean crisis, Ray S. Cline, CIA Deputy Director for Intelligence from 1962 to 1966, charged that their revelations were propaganda, intended to mobilize support for Gorbachev's foreign policy.[14] Cline accused Soviet officials of presenting a false picture of Khrushchev's motives, and of exaggerating the risks of war, in the expectation that this would be grist for the mill of the American antinuclear lobby.

Before *glasnost*, Soviet analyses of foreign policy were notoriously self-serving. The first revelations about the missile crisis were superficially consistent with Gorbachev's foreign-policy objectives. There are nevertheless good reasons for taking the testimony of Soviet officials seriously.

The context in which Soviet officials granted these interviews is important. If they had begun to talk about the crises in 1962 and 1973 in the Brezhnev era, when the substance and process of Soviet foreign policy was a tightly guarded state secret, their motives and information would have been suspect. Instead, they began to speak openly only in the era of *glasnost*, when such behavior was no longer extraordinary, but part of a broader attempt by reform-minded officials and intelligentsia to reevaluate the Soviet past. Our most recent interviews were conducted in the post-Soviet era—we were in the office of a senior diplomat when the building and the foreign ministry was taken over by the Russian government. Former officials of a former country no longer have a party line to defend.

Soviet officials first answered our questions when the Soviet Union was still in existence. Much of what they said was deeply embarrassing to the Soviet image at home and abroad. Revelations about Soviet military weakness and how it frightened Soviet leaders, about Khrushchev's and Brezhnev's emotional instability, or how the Soviet military shot down an American U-2 aircraft in violation of their standing orders, paint a picture of the Soviet Union of the 1960s and 1970s as an insecure, bungling, irresponsible, and badly governed country. It is difficult to see what propaganda advantages Soviet leaders could have expected to gain from such confessions.[15]

The ongoing revision of Soviet history cannot be understood as a piecemeal response to propaganda needs of the moment. This is not to suggest that the glimpses we have been given of the substance and process of Soviet policy from Stalin through Brezhnev have been unrelated to political agendas. Gorbachev used *glasnost* to mobilize popular support against the conservatives at every level of the party and government bureaucracy that opposed and resisted his reforms. Greater Soviet openness about the past also helped to convince Western publics of Gorbachev's sincerity. Gorbachev and some of his advisors may have viewed their critical examination of the Soviet past as costs to be borne in pursuit of important domestic goals. Others embraced *glasnost* as an end in itself. They were committed to transforming the Soviet Union into a more open society.

The possibility that some testimony may have been motivated by a political agenda does not mean that it is false. It is possible, and probably likely, that some officials chose to talk about the two crises, because the facts of the cases, as they understood them, provided support for policies they favored. This was certainly true of some former Kennedy officials, who provided new information about American policymaking in the missile crisis at the Hawk's Cay Conference in March 1987. They were motivated in part by their political concerns. Critical of the Reagan administration's pursuit of military superiority, they wanted to use the lessons of the Cuban missile crisis to help expose and publicize the dangers of Reagan's policies. Few challenged the credibility of their testimony.

Before *glasnost*, Soviet officials repeated the party line in public and in private. The officials that we spoke to disagreed about important details and argued among themselves, sometimes in our presence, about their respective interpretations of events and the validity of their information. It would have been very difficult and enormously time-consuming for the Soviet government to have orchestrated and staged these kinds of historical debates for purposes of propaganda. It is unlikely that they could have done so convincingly. Soviet officials displayed the same mixture of knowledge and ignorance, and insight and confusion, as their American counterparts. We believe that most of these officials, Soviet and American, told the truth as they understood it. Their understanding may be flawed, but it is not dishonest.

Perhaps the most telling evidence is the reluctant confirmation of some of the most important Soviet revelations by American officials. At the Moscow Conference, Anatoliy Dobrynin revealed that he and Attorney General Robert Kennedy had worked out a secret arrangement for the withdrawal of the American Jupiter missiles from Turkey.[16] Traditional American accounts had denied that there was any such agreement and maintained that Dobrynin was merely "informed" by Robert Kennedy on the evening of 27 October that the United States had intended all along to remove the Jupiters. Dobrynin's statement elicited a startling admission from former presidential special counsel Theodore Sorensen. Robert Kennedy's manuscript, *Thirteen Days*, he explained, was "very explicit that this [the missile trade] was part of the deal; but at that time it was still a secret even on the American side." Kennedy was assassinated before his memoir was published and Sorensen was asked to review it for accuracy. "I took it upon myself," he confessed, "to edit that out of his diaries, and that is why the ambassador is somewhat justified in saying that the diaries are not as explicit as his conversation."[17]

The Dobrynin-Kennedy exchange is only one instance of synergism between officials from Moscow and Washington. Officials often confirmed the testimony of their allies and former adversaries, or provided information that we used to elicit new evidence in subsequent interviews. In those instances where testimony about the facts are contradictory—as distinct from differences of opinion about motives—we acknowledge the discrepancies and weigh the evidence carefully. Even when officials proved to be wrong, they appear to have been honestly misinformed.

The general reliability of the evidence from Soviet officials does not mean that we accepted what they said at face value. As with their Western counterparts, the accuracy and value of recollections varies from person to person and issue to issue. Officials may have only limited knowledge about certain events, may have seen only some of the relevant documents, or reported what they had heard indirectly. People also find it difficult to reconstruct with precision the evolution of policy that was formulated many years before. Their memories are sometimes influenced, consciously or unconsciously, by their political or personal agendas, or by the human tendency to impose more order on events in hindsight than existed at the time.

These problems cut across national boundaries. Most of the Ex Comm, including some of Kennedy's closest foreign-policy advisors, did not know about the agreement on the Jupiter missiles or about Kennedy's willingness to consider further concessions. The president carefully hid this information from them. Some of what they did know, they kept secret to protect the late president's reputation, or because they were disturbed by its wider implications. We encountered the same problem of compartmentalized information on the Soviet side. Policymaking under Khrushchev and Brezhnev was secretive, and nobody had detailed knowledge of the whole process. More often than not, officials had bits and pieces of specialized information that had to be pieced together with other testimony to reconstruct critical decisions.

Soviet officials also varied in their openness. Sergo Mikoyan and Aleksandr Alekseev, who devoted their careers to furthering Soviet influence in Latin America, were reluctant to volunteer information that they thought might embarrass Fidel Castro or strain Soviet-Cuban relations. What they said is generally accurate as far as we can determine, but Mikoyan and Alekseev at first withheld important information that subsequently came to light and is damaging to Castro.

In the autumn of 1990, *Khrushchev Remembers: The Glasnost Tapes*, was published.[18] It is based on portions of Khrushchev's tape-recorded memoirs that did not appear in the earlier two volumes of *Khrushchev Remembers*, published in the 1970s. Khrushchev's son, Sergei, had withheld segments of the transcription that he thought likely to create problems for the family or the Soviet Union.[19] The last volume includes Nikita Khrushchev's description of the cable he received from Castro at the height of the crisis that pleaded with him to launch a preemptive nuclear strike against the United States if it attacked Cuba.[20] The Cuban government was enormously displeased, and insisted that publication of the cable was "intended to serve the sinister purpose of fanning anti-Cuban hysteria in the United States and around the world." In response to *The Glasnost Tapes*, the Cuban government published the five cables exchanged by Castro and Khrushchev between 26 and 31 October, along with official commentary. The cables largely confirm Khrushchev's allegation.[21]

A more serious danger than deliberate distortion is contamination. Some Soviet officials and scholars have read much of the Western literature on the two crises. Aleksandr Kislov and Victor Israelian, for example, acknowledge that they have read Henry Kissinger's memoirs carefully. Former Soviet officials can unwittingly confirm Western interpretations by repeating them back to Western scholars.[22] This kind of "echoing" may have occurred at the Cambridge Conference in October 1987. Fedor Burlatsky suggested that Khrushchev came away from the Vienna summit with the impression that Kennedy was weak, vacillating, and not courageous enough to oppose a missile deployment in Cuba.[23] For many years this has been the conventional wisdom in most American analyses of the crisis. There are good reasons for rejecting this interpretation, as chapter 4 demonstrates. It seems likely that Burlatsky, who barely knew Khrushchev, absorbed the idea from the Western books and articles he read and injected it into the play he wrote about the missile crisis.

The problem of contamination may become more pronounced in the future as many Russian historians and social scientists reject the orthodox interpretations of their former country's history and foreign relations. Some Russian scholars, deeply antagonistic to communism, have adopted the traditional Western point of view that assigns to the Soviet Union primary responsibility for the Cold War.[24] Russian scholars will continue to be influenced by Western interpretations until they gain access to the many Soviet archives that are still closed.

Because critical Soviet documents remain classified, Western students of Soviet foreign policy are forced to rely more heavily than usual on the oral testimony of former Soviet officials. Some scholars have questioned the value of history constructed on the basis of what they deride as hearsay.

They contend that oral history is a poor substitute for written sources and contemporary documents.[25]

We recognize the limitations of oral history and lament the incomplete documentary record on both crises. Some documentation has become available, and more may be released in the future. Foreign ministry and military officials who have looked through the relevant Soviet archives report a general dearth of the kind of material we would most like to see: notes and summaries of Politburo meetings, records of conversations between and among key policymakers, and the working documents of advisory groups set up to assist crisis management. The central archives of the Soviet Communist Party that were opened on 2 March 1992 did not contain the minutes of Politburo meetings during the Khrushchev and Brezhnev eras.[26] Most files of the International Department of the Central Committee remain classified.

Even when all the government and party records are released, they will not provide the basis for a complete reconstruction of either crisis. The deployment of missiles in Cuba was shrouded in secrecy, and no written records were kept by the handful of officials involved in its planning and initial implementation.[27] In 1973, Brezhnev made all the important decisions in consultation with the Politburo or a very small circle of advisors.

The problem of documentation must be put in comparative perspective. Western scholars never complained about the use of interviews to reconstruct the American side of the Cuban missile crisis. In the years when few American documents were available, studies of the crisis relied on the memoirs and oral testimony of Kennedy administration officials. The first prominent study, by newsman Elie Abel, was based almost entirely on his talks with administration officials.[28] Subsequent accounts made use of the histories *cum* memoirs of Theodore Sorensen and Arthur Schlesinger, Jr., Roger Hilsman, and then of the posthumously published memoir of Robert Kennedy.[29] Graham Allison's *The Essence of Decision*, for fifteen years considered the standard account of the crisis, used the same sources.[30] The only important documents available to American scholars and journalists were sanitized copies of some of the messages exchanged by Kennedy and Khrushchev.[31] Western officials and scholars nevertheless wrote histories of the crisis and drew policy lessons.

In recent years, hundreds of documents pertinent to the Cuban missile crisis have been declassified. These documents, especially the transcripts of some of the secret Ex Comm tapes, are of enormous importance. None of these documents contains the most important new evidence about Kennedy's decisions during the crisis. The compelling evidence comes from the recent revelations of former American officials, the same kind of source we have used to reconstruct Khrushchev's decisions. The documents offer no hint that, unknown to the Ex Comm, Kennedy engaged in back-channel negotiations with Khrushchev, made a secret concession on the Jupiter missiles in Turkey, and considered a further concession if that became necessary to resolve the crisis. For obvious reasons, the president and the few officials he confided in made sure that there was no documentary record. A history based only on the documents would be very misleading.

Extraordinary secrecy also surrounded the Bay of Pigs invasion. Within the CIA, the Deputy Director of Intelligence Ray S. Cline and his directorate were not informed about the operation.[32] Secretary of State Dean Rusk remembers that he was not allowed to consult the department's Bureau of Intelligence and Research, that almost certainly would have provided him with a critical evaluation. He was also prohibited from discussing the operation with senior officials at State. This secrecy, Rusk insists, "made it very difficult for historians to reconstruct the Bay of Pigs operation, particularly its planning, because very little was put on paper. [Allen] Dulles, [Richard] Bissell, and others proposing the operation briefed us orally." The written records do not include even the substance of these conversations.[33]

The missile crisis may be an unusual case. President Kennedy struggled to find the political room to reconcile the competing demands of foreign and domestic policy. He consequently kept some of his actions and decisions secret not only from the public but from many top government officials. He deliberately misled some of his most trusted officials and advisors like Dean Rusk to protect them and himself from subsequent congressional inquiries.

No such secrecy was necessary in 1973. Even so, when the documents are released, they will be misleading. Kissinger frequently had different versions of documents prepared for different audiences and rarely put anything on record from his extensive back-channel discussions. Future scholars, Kissinger noted, will have "no criteria for determining which documents were produced to provide an alibi and which genuinely guided decisions."[34] The documentary record is not only misleading but frequently incomplete. The most important decisions grew out of informal conversations among officials that were not recorded. When the documents are released, they will tell only part of the story. We cannot be confident of our understanding and interpretation of critical foreign-policy decisions during the Cold War when they are based largely, or entirely, on the written record.

THE LESSONS OF HISTORY

At the height of the American commitment to Star Wars, General Secretary Mikhail Gorbachev called for the record of the Caribbean crisis because he hoped that an analysis of its lessons would help him to deal with Ronald Reagan.[35] In 1990, President George Bush modeled his unsuccessful attempt to coerce Saddam Hussein to withdraw the Iraqi army from Kuwait on Kennedy's success in compelling Nikita Khrushchev to withdraw Soviet missiles from Cuba.[36]

As these examples suggest, the missile crisis has been an important source of learning for American and Soviet leaders about crisis prevention and management. For Americans, it confirmed the lesson of Munich: weakness and vacillation encourage aggression, and capability and resolve deter. For Soviets, it underlined the need to achieve and maintain strategic equality with the United States to avoid being victimized by a predatory adversary.

The lessons of Cuba were reconfirmed for Americans by the crisis in 1973. Once again, the Soviet Union seemed intent on challenging the United States, on this occasion by sending military forces to Egypt. Secretary of State Henry Kissinger believed that Moscow had been restrained in 1962 by the American strategic alert, and ordered a worldwide alert of American strategic and conventional forces in October 1973 to forestall Soviet intervention. Kissinger attributed Soviet restraint to American deterrence.[37]

It was no accident that the crises of 1962 and 1973 appeared to validate the lessons of Munich. In the absence of direct evidence about Soviet motives and calculations, American officials and foreign-policy analysts interpreted Moscow's policies in both confrontations in accord with their assumptions. They assumed that Soviet leaders were aggressive and attributed whatever restraint they showed to American military capability and resolve. The efficacy of deterrence and its sister strategy, compellence, was confirmed tautologically.

New information about the missile crisis emerged when the political agendas of those who knew began to change. The first opening was Robert Kennedy's memoir, written in support of his bid for the presidency.[38] More information became public in the 1980s, in response to Ronald Reagan's policies toward the Soviet Union. Kennedy administration officials attending the Hawk's Cay Conference in 1987 expressed concern that Reagan and his advisors had "overlearned" the lesson of Cuba. At one of the lunches, a prominent Republican and former cabinet member in the Kennedy administration confessed that he never thought he would live to see the day "when the White House, not the Kremlin, posed the greatest threat to the peace of the world."[39] Robert McNamara expressed the hope that American policymakers would act more cautiously if they knew just how difficult crises like the Cuban missile crisis were to control.[40]

In the Soviet Union, revelations about the missile crisis may initially have been motivated by the desire to mobilize support in the West for arms control. The Soviet delegation to the Cambridge Conference, the first occasion at which Soviet officials spoke freely about the crisis, was headed by Georgiy Shakhnazarov, a Gorbachev advisor and confidant, who spoke of the need to educate the American public about the dangers of nuclear confrontation.[41] But willingness to speak openly about the past was also part of a broader attempt by reform-minded officials to discredit the foreign and strategic policies of Brezhnev. Like its American counterpart, the traditional Soviet interpretation of the missile crisis had been used to justify those policies.

Historical "lessons" cast long shadows. They help define the problems policymakers identify as critical, and the range of strategies they consider appropriate. If the lessons leaders learn are wrong, superficial, or applied inappropriately, they will not be good guides to policy. They can blind leaders to the underlying dynamics of a conflict and create false expectations that strategies that worked in the past will succeed once again.

We can do nothing about the lives and resources expended in the course of the long struggle between the United States and the Soviet Union. However, the lessons we learn from the Cold War are still within our control. With evidence now available, we can more confidently reconstruct and reinterpret its history and reevaluate the policy lessons it generated or confirmed. Better history can produce better lessons. In this way, we can all still win the Cold War.

PART ONE

The Cuban Missile Crisis, 1962

Missiles to Cuba: Foreign-Policy Motives

In our discussions and exchanges on Berlin and other
international questions, the one thing that has most
concerned me has been the possibility that your government
would not correctly understand the will and determination
of the United States.

—*John F. Kennedy* [1]

THE DEPLOYMENT OF MISSILES to Cuba came as a rude shock to the Kennedy administration. Senior officials had reasoned that Khrushchev would have to be completely irrational to challenge the United States in a region where it possessed overwhelming military superiority after President Kennedy had made clear that the introduction of offensive weapons was unacceptable to his administration.[2] Ever since the crisis, Western analysts have speculated about Khrushchev's motives for sending missiles to Cuba and his reasons for believing that the United States would tolerate them.[3]

For many years, Soviet officials were extremely reticent to talk about the "Caribbean crisis." As close an ally as Fidel Castro received no answers when he questioned Leonid I. Brezhnev, Aleksei N. Kosygin, and other Politburo members about Khrushchev's goals and calculations.[4] Only with *glasnost* did knowledgeable Soviets become willing to discuss the Khrushchev era. They affirm that the missile deployment was conceived by Khrushchev and carried out on his orders. The Presidium, the highest organ of the Communist Party in 1962, discussed and approved the initiative, but its authorization was largely pro forma because Khrushchev was powerful enough to impose his policy preferences on the Party and government.[5] Our analysis accordingly focuses on Khrushchev, his motives and expectations, and the pressures—foreign and domestic—that he faced.

Knowledgeable associates of the former Soviet leader attribute the missile deployment to two immediate foreign-policy concerns: Khrushchev wanted to prevent an American invasion of Cuba, and to offset American strategic superiority. He also sent missiles to Cuba to subject the United States to the same kind of close-range nuclear threat that the Jupiter missiles, then being deployed in Turkey, posed to the Soviet Union. In chapter 2 we analyze these foreign-policy objectives. In chapter 3 we look at the domestic context of the missile decision and argue that Khrushchev's commitment to economic and political reform provided an equally strong incentive for him to send missiles to Cuba. In chapter 4 we examine Khrushchev's reasons for believing that the deployment would succeed.

Khrushchev's foreign policy cannot be understood in isolation from its broader international setting. In particular, it is necessary to consider American foreign policy and its consequences for the Soviet Union. Our narrative traces these links with regard to Cuba, the strategic balance, and Khrushchev's concern to achieve "psychological equality."

THE THREAT FROM CUBA

Fidel Castro's embrace of communism and subsequent alignment with the Soviet Union made Cuba a major battlefield of the Cold War. Like Berlin, that other flashpoint, Cuba was a beleaguered outpost within the other side's sphere of influence. The Soviet Union was unprepared to abandon Cuba, just as the United States was unwilling to give up its precarious position in Berlin. Both superpowers regarded the other's outpost as an affront and a danger.[6]

In April 1961, anti-Castro refugees, trained and supported by the United States, carried out an abortive invasion of Cuba at the Bay of Pigs (Playa Giron).[7] In the seventeen months between the Bay of Pigs and the missile crisis, American policy toward Cuba was shaped by anger, domestic politics, and broader foreign-policy concerns. The administration, the CIA, and the military were keen to avenge the Bay of Pigs. The president was subjected to mounting pressure to invade Cuba from the Congress and some of the most powerful members of the media. Kennedy also considered it essential to display firmness toward Cuba to offset whatever impression of weakness his refusal to commit American forces to the faltering Bay of Pigs invasion had conveyed to Khrushchev. For all three reasons, the White House searched for ways to overthrow Castro that did not involve direct American military intervention. The president ruled out an invasion as too costly, certain to antagonize European allies, contrary to America's traditions, and too likely to provoke a wider confrontation with the Soviet Union.[8]

Kennedy accepted full responsibility for the abortive invasion, a gesture that muted some of the criticism of his leadership.[9] Cuba nevertheless became the administration's "political Achilles' heel."[10] Public-opinion polls revealed mounting frustration and anger at Castro's durability and Moscow's alleged use of Cuba as a base to spread subversion in the Caribbean. Kennedy's critics assailed his apparent reluctance to deal decisively with Castro, and the Republicans, sensing a Democratic vulnerability, announced that Cuba would be "the dominant issue" of their 1962 congressional campaign.[11]

The media assault on the administration grew in intensity during the summer of 1962 and reached a peak in September and October, in response to the ongoing and well-publicized Soviet military buildup in Cuba. Conservative newspapers and magazines gave prominent coverage to the exploits of anti-Castro refugees and Republican protests against the administration's failure to check the mounting Soviet military presence in the Caribbean. *Time*, in the vanguard of these attacks, heaped abuse on Kennedy. A 14 September editorial insisted that "the U.S. simply cannot afford to let Cuba survive indefinitely as a Soviet fortress just off its shores and a cancer throughout the hemisphere."[12] A week later, *Time*'s cover story, on the Monroe Doctrine, featured pleas by prominent Republicans for a blockade or invasion of Cuba. "Just Get It Over With," a subhead proclaimed. *Time* dismissed Soviet warnings that an invasion could lead to nuclear war as nothing more than a bluff.[13]

Sentiments also ran high in the administration. "We were hysterical about Castro," Secretary of Defense Robert S. McNamara remembered.[14] Under Secretary of State Chester A. Bowles described the National Security Council (NSC) meetings of 20 and 22 April at which the Bay of Pigs failure was discussed as "emotional" and "almost savage."[15] The consensus was "to get tough" with Castro and "teach him a lesson." "Emotions ran almost as high at subsequent meetings."[16]

Bowles thought that the Bay of Pigs was a "humiliating" defeat for Kennedy and had temporarily "shattered" his self-confidence.[17] Ray Cline, the CIA's Deputy Director for Intelligence, who regularly briefed the president on Cuban developments, thought the Kennedy brothers were "deeply ashamed" by their failure at the Bay of Pigs and "obsessed with the problem of Cuba." "They were a couple of fighting Irishmen who felt they had muffed it, and they vented their wrath on Castro for the next two years."[18]

Robert Kennedy took the setback very personally. He repeatedly voiced his desire for revenge to CIA and top administration officials. According to Arthur Schlesinger, Jr., he was "filled with inchoate urgencies" and ready to do anything to prevent his brother from suffering another setback.[19] Brig. Gen. Edward G. Lansdale, the administration's expert on guerrilla warfare, was impressed by the desire of both Kennedys "to bring Castro down." He was certain "that they had that emotion in them until they were both killed. But Bobby felt even more strongly about it than Jack. He was protective of his brother and felt his brother had been insulted and dishonored by the Bay of Pigs. He felt the insult had to be redressed rather quickly."[20]

In this charged atmosphere, Bowles' advocacy of nonviolent measures elicited anger and derision. The president rejected his counsel out of hand. "There can be no long-term living with Castro as a neighbor," he insisted.[21] Kennedy was more receptive to the recommendation of the Taylor Commission to increase harassment of Cuba and other communist regimes in the Third World.[22] He ordered the Defense Department to expand its capability for paramilitary operations. Goaded by Robert Kennedy, Gen. Maxwell Taylor began to explore the possibilities of organizing Cuban exiles for covert hit-and-run attacks against Cuba.[23] On the political front, the administration, with full support of Congress, took steps to isolate Cuba politically and economically.[24]

Laos and Berlin

The Bay of Pigs was only one of the events that heightened the administration's concern about Castro. In March of 1961, the Soviet Union began an airlift to resupply pro-communist Pathet Lao forces in Laos. In April, just a week before the Bay of Pigs, the Soviet Union achieved a stunning first in space by putting cosmonaut Yuri Gagarin in orbit around the earth. In June, Khrushchev presented Kennedy with a blunt ultimatum on Berlin. These developments, but especially the threat of a new Berlin crisis, created a siege mentality in the White House.

Kennedy had come to office deeply troubled by the Soviet Union's new assertiveness. He suspected that Khrushchev's growing bellicosity reflected the Soviet leader's conviction that the "correlation of forces" was shifting in his country's favor. Khrushchev claimed that the Soviet rate of industrial growth had surpassed that of the United States. The Soviet space program had achieved a series of stunning firsts, and the Strategic Rocket Forces (SRF) had begun to deploy intercontinental ballistic missiles (ICBMs) capable of striking the United States. In the Third World, many anticolonial movements had adopted Marxist rhetoric and looked to Moscow for support. Communist or pro-communist governments had come to power in Vietnam, Guinea, Indonesia, and Cuba, and seemed to presage the passage of much of Africa and Asia into the socialist camp.

On the eve of Kennedy's inauguration, Khrushchev made a widely publicized speech in which he announced that "there is no longer any force in the world capable of barring the road to socialism." Pointing to recent anti-imperialist triumphs in Vietnam, Algeria, and Cuba, he observed that the current state of world affairs had "greatly exceeded the boldest and most optimistic predictions and expectations." He went on to hail "national-liberation wars" as the wave of the future and promised support for such uprisings "whole-heartedly and without reservation."[25]

Khrushchev's speech made a profound impression on the new president who took it as an "authoritative exposition of Soviet policy." He discussed the speech with his staff and read passages from it to the NSC. He ordered the CIA to prepare a detailed analysis of the text and sent the analysis and the speech to fifty top administration officials with instructions to "read, mark, learn and inwardly digest."[26] At their June summit, Kennedy complained bitterly to Khrushchev about the speech and warned that Soviet support of national-liberation movements would lead to "a direct confrontation" between the superpowers.[27]

Kennedy interpreted the growing Soviet involvement in Laos as Khrushchev's first attempt to put his strategy into practice.[28] When the Pathet Lao launched a new offensive on 26 April, the NSC held "a long and confused session" and debated immediate intervention. Kennedy was reluctant to send American forces into combat but considered it essential to convince Khrushchev that the United States would not abandon Laos.[29] He put American forces on alert and ordered ten thousand Marines in Okinawa to prepare to move out at a moment's notice.[30]

The danger passed. A few days later, opposing Laotian forces negotiated another cease-fire. On 12 May, Soviet and American representatives met in Geneva to establish the ground rules for a neutral Laos. Kennedy and his advisors attributed this favorable outcome to the administration's toughness coupled with its willingness to leave the Soviet Union a face-saving escape route.[31]

In June, Kennedy met Khrushchev in Vienna and was presented with an ultimatum on Berlin. Khrushchev warned that the Soviet Union would sign a separate peace treaty with East Germany if the Western powers did not consent to a German treaty and give up their occupation rights in Berlin. If the West tried to shoot its way into Berlin, Moscow would come to the assistance of its fraternal ally. "No force in the world," Khrushchev proclaimed, "would prevent the USSR from signing a treaty."[32]

Secretary of State Dean Rusk described the Vienna summit as "a brutal moment" for Kennedy. Khrushchev had set out to intimidate him and "the experience sobered and shook" the young president.[33] Kennedy came away convinced that Khrushchev doubted his willingness to defend Western commitments and interests. He became more obsessive about demonstrating resolve and more fearful about the consequences of a showdown. He told newsmen about Khrushchev's demands and spoke of his determination to stand firm. "The prospects for nuclear war," he warned, "were now very real."[34]

Kennedy returned to Washington concerned that he had "less than six months to prepare for a possible nuclear war over Berlin." Assistant Secretary of the Navy Paul B. Fay, a wartime friend, received a phone call to ask if he had built a bomb shelter for his family. "No," he answered, "I built a swimming pool instead." "You made a mistake," Kennedy replied. "And he was dead serious," remembered Fay.[35] According to *Time*'s White House sources, Kennedy brooded about the dangers of war, "became moody, withdrawn, often fell into deep thought in the midst of festive occasions with family and friends."[36]

By temperament a man of action, Kennedy coped with his postsummit anxiety by taking charge of the administration's political response to Khrushchev. He "saturated" himself with the details of the problem. He reviewed the military contingency plans of NATO and the Joint Chiefs of Staff (JCS), found them wanting, and dictated changes. He ordered a rapid military buildup of American forces in Germany.[37] Convinced that Khrushchev would be more impressed by action than rhetoric, he asked Congress for an additional $3.25 billion military appropriation, standby authority to call up the reserves, and a temporary tax increase to pay for these measures. By late fall, the armed forces had been increased by some three-hundred thousand men, and forty-thousand additional troops had been dispatched to Europe.[38]

The Berlin crisis came dangerously close to a flashpoint in mid-August when the East Germans began to construct a wall to seal off their sector of the city. To test Soviet intentions and demonstrate Western resolve, Kennedy ordered fifteen hundred American soldiers in armored vehicles to pass through the East German checkpoints on the autobahn to Berlin. Vice-President Lyndon Johnson and retired Gen. Lucius Clay, commander of American forces during the 1948–49 crisis, were sent to Berlin to publicize the American commitment to defend the city.[39] The president estimated the chances of a nuclear exchange to be about one in five.[40]

Focus on Castro

The Bay of Pigs assumed new significance in the president's mind as he anticipated a confrontation with the Soviet Union. He wondered if his refusal to commit American forces to the invasion had encouraged "Khrushchev to assume that he was dealing with a weak and vacillating new American president" who could be intimidated "by taking a harsh position, particularly in regard to Berlin."[41] He worried that Khrushchev would assume that he would back down again rather than commit American forces to combat. The president, Arthur Schlesinger, Jr. remembered, wanted "to dissuade the communists from regarding restraint as evidence of weakness."[42]

One way to send this message, Robert Kennedy insisted, was to increase the pressure on Castro. The attorney general had been pushing for an offensive against Castro since the debacle at the Bay of Pigs.[43] He turned to the CIA for assistance. Anxious to regain its lost prestige, the Agency was extremely receptive to Kennedy's overtures. "We wanted to earn our spurs with the President," Richard Helms remembered.[44] The Agency proposed that a campaign of sabotage be carried out by anti-Castro refugees. Robert Kennedy and Latin American experts at the State Department preferred to build a revolutionary movement within Cuba. In late August, a compromise was reached. The Cuban Task Force, which included Richard Bissell from CIA, George Ball from State, and Richard Goodwin from the White House, recommended to the president that he follow both approaches.[45]

President Kennedy remained committed to the overthrow of Castro from within and ordered greater support for indigenous Cuban resistance forces. In November, he asked Edward G. Lansdale, a veteran organizer of anti-guerrilla efforts in the Philippines and Vietnam, to take command of an operation "to help Cuba overthrow the Communist regime."[46] Kennedy insisted that "Operation Mongoose," as this effort became known, be "kept in a low key" to conceal American involvement as much as possible. Large-scale operations would attract public attention and jeopardize efforts to secure the release of Bay of Pigs veterans still in Cuban prisons. To make sure his instructions were followed, he set up a new review committee, the Special Group (Augmented) [SG(A)], headed by Maxwell Taylor, to oversee all covert operations against Cuba.[47]

Lansdale and Robert Kennedy ignored the president's orders to keep operations low-key.[48] The attorney general told Mongoose planners in January 1962 that "no time, money, effort—or manpower is to be spared."[49] The CIA took these instructions to heart and set up "Task Force W" with a budget of over $50 million a year. Within months, Miami became the largest CIA station in the world with six hundred full-time officers directing an expatriate force of about three thousand Cubans. Task Force W purchased or rented over a hundred "safe houses" and proprietary fronts, operated its own fleet of fast-attack craft, and ran a small air force. In the summer of 1961, JM WAVE, the code-word designator for the Miami operation, prepared to stage commando raids against Cuban sugar mills, oil refineries, chemical plants, and military installations. The few operations it mounted failed.[50]

The CIA tried to eliminate Castro. With the assistance of the Mafia, the Agency organized a series of assassination attempts. Bad luck, incompetence, and likely Mafia betrayal foiled plots to dispose of Castro by poisoned food and drink and exploding cigars. The assassination attempts were briefly suspended after the Bay of Pigs, but reactivated by the CIA's Deputy Director for Plans, Richard Helms, possibly with the knowledge and approval of Robert Kennedy.[51] The Agency outdid itself the second time around. It tried poison pills in April 1962, a three-man hit squad in June, a diving suit contaminated with tuberculosis bacilli in August, and in January 1963, it proposed placing a rare sea shell, filled with explosives, in waters where Castro dived. The Cuban leader survived all these attempts. Discouraged by the Agency's record of failure, Helms terminated the assassination program in February 1963.[52]

The Contradictions of Cuban Policy

The covert operations against Cuba were equally disappointing. "Operation Mongoose wasn't worth a damn," McNamara opined.[53] Arthur Schlesinger, Jr. complained that it "expended its efforts on trivial, aimless, mindless, pinprick sabotage"[54] "All it accomplished," the CIA's Ray Cline admitted, "was to make Castro beholden to the U.S.S.R."[55]

Mongoose was based on a political contradiction. The CIA's Board of National Estimates had told the president that it was extremely unlikely that Castro could be overthrown by clandestine operations.[56] National Security Advisor McGeorge Bundy pointed out to John McCone, Director of CIA, that a campaign of paramilitary harassment made sense only if it was the prelude to an invasion.[57] But Kennedy and McNamara were strongly disinclined to invade and had made their opposition clear to the CIA.[58] Robert Kennedy and Gen. Lansdale, and the CIA on Lansdale's instructions, remained committed to large-scale covert operations against Cuba.[59]

Operation Mongoose risked sending the wrong message to Moscow. If the operation was untraceable to the United States, as Kennedy insisted it had to be, it could not possibly signal resolve. If Castro and Khrushchev realized, as they were bound to, that Washington was behind the attacks, they would likely view them as a prelude to invasion. The administration would incur the wrath of Havana and Moscow for an unintended threat. Kennedy authorized and persevered with Mongoose in the face of these inconsistencies. His emotional need to strike out against Castro was exceptionally strong. In Bundy's view, the covert operations were "a psychological salve for inaction."[60]

The assassination plots were also riddled with contradictions. In the judgment of the CIA's Board of Estimates, Castro's elimination would accomplish little. Assassination would make him a martyr to the Cuban people and bring Ernesto Che Guevara, Raúl Castro, or some other hard-liner to power.[61] At least one administration insider claims that Kennedy spurned assassination for moral as well as practical reasons.[62] However, Robert McNamara maintains that it is "almost inconceivable" that Helms would have attempted to assassinate Castro without the approval of senior White House officials.[63] McNamara and his colleagues nevertheless deny any knowledge of the assassination attempts.[64]

A third contradiction in American policy concerned the ongoing military preparations for an invasion of Cuba. In response to White House directives, the Pentagon prepared contingency plans for air strikes and ground assaults against Cuba, all of them with American forces. The plans were tested in a series of large-scale and well-publicized exercises. In April, the Marines carried out an amphibious assault, *Lantphibex I-62*, against the Puerto Rican island of Vieques.[65] In late April and early May, exercise *Quick Kick*, sent 79 ships, 300 aircraft, and more than 40,000 troops against the southeastern coast of the United States to simulate an invasion of Cuba.[66] *Jupiter Springs*, held in the summer, practiced the airborne component of a Cuban assault. *Swift Strike II*, conducted in the Carolinas in August, involved four Army divisions and eight tactical air squadrons, some seventy-thousand personnel, in a simulated limited war. The Pentagon billed it as "the largest peacetime war games in United States military history."[67]

On 19 April, as the Bay of Pigs invasion was being overwhelmed on the beaches, a "gloomy meeting" of top political and military leaders considered and rejected the possibility of using American forces to topple Castro.[68] Arthur Schlesinger, Jr., who attended the Cuban task force meetings in May, reports "complete agreement against any thought of direct intervention." McGeorge Bundy recalled that "We were unsure of our next move. The only thing we really did know was that we did not want an enlarged version of the Bay of Pigs. We were not going to repeat that exercise by adding a zero and throwing in the American Army."[69] Defense Secretary McNamara insists that the administration "had *absolutely no intention* of invading Cuba."[70] "The military prepared its contingency plans—that's its job," he explained, "but those plans were never entertained seriously by me or by the president."[71]

Domestic politics also played a role. By late summer, the president had become even more concerned about Cuba. Burgeoning Soviet arms shipments and Republican charges that he was not doing enough to get rid of Castro convinced him to give greater latitude to Lansdale. On 23 August, he ordered Taylor, chairman of the SG(A) to develop "with all possible speed" the Mongoose option for provoking an uprising in Cuba. He requested the Defense Department to accelerate their contingency planning in response to reports of increased Soviet arms shipments to Cuba and the remote possibility that Moscow might introduce nuclear weapons capable of attacking the United States.[72] Subsequent directives in September and early October instructed Lansdale to consider "new and more dynamic approaches," and ordered the Defense Department to be ready to blockade Cuba and carry out air strikes against Soviet surface-to-air missile (SAM) sites on the island.[73]

Kennedy's instructions to the Defense Department were a hedge against the unpleasant possibility that Soviet involvement in Cuba would compel him to consider military action. The military planning and exercises that followed did not indicate any commitment to attack Cuba then or later.[74] In the president's mind, their principal purpose was intimidation. Many officers nevertheless hoped that the Caribbean buildup was a prelude to invasion. Once their forces were in place they actively sought the go-ahead from the White House.[75]

To mask preparations for scenarios the military might be ordered to execute, Adm. Robert L. Dennison suggested that the press be told that they were part of *Phibriglex-62*, another large Marine amphibious exercise scheduled for mid-October. Reporters were duly informed that the Marines would hit the beaches and liberate the Puerto Rican island of Vieques from an imaginary despot named Ortsac—Castro spelled backward.[76] Neither the Cuban nor the Soviet leaders were fooled. Like Operation Mongoose and the assassination plots, the military buildup and exercises sent the wrong message to Havana and Moscow.

THE THREAT TO CUBA

Almost every Soviet official who claims any knowledge of the missile deployment insists that one of its important objectives was to protect Fidel Castro and his revolution. Officials close to Khrushchev report that he was politically and personally committed to maintaining and fostering the development of socialism in Cuba.

Soviet Involvement in Cuba

Serious Soviet interest in Cuba began only after Castro came to power. We "had no idea," Khrushchev later wrote, "what political course his regime would follow." Soviet Latin American specialists knew that Che Guevara was a communist, and Raúl Castro, too, but that he kept it a secret from his brother. Khrushchev's son-in-law and *Izvestiya* editor, Aleksei I. Adzhubei, at first thought Castro "an ordinary American dictator," who had already gone "to bow down to Washington and meet with Nixon."[77]

Soviet-Cuban relations grew closer after the visit of Deputy Prime Minister Anastas I. Mikoyan to Havana in February 1960 in response to an invitation from Fidel Castro. Mikoyan was "truly charmed by the wit and courage of Fidel" and returned a great supporter of his revolution. Khrushchev's daughter Rada and her husband, Adzhubei, also visited Cuba and came home with glowing reports.[78] Diplomatic relations were soon established, and when the United States cut off Cuba's oil supply, the Soviet Union helped by supplying much needed petroleum products. This aid put a heavy burden on Soviet shipping and forced the government, Khrushchev admitted, to buy additional tankers from Italy.[79]

As Cuba moved toward socialism, Washington's hostility became more pronounced. Castro's show trials of Batista stalwarts, nationalization of businesses, including American enterprises, restrictive policies toward landowners, and appointment of communists to government positions led to American political and economic pressure on Cuba and a not so secret effort to train anti-Castro refugees for a possible invasion.[80] Castro became increasingly concerned about security and asked Moscow for arms.[81] "We gave them tanks and artillery and sent them instructors," Khrushchev acknowledged.[82] By the time of the Bay of Pigs, Castro had publicly declared his intention of putting Cuba on the road to socialism, and the Soviet Union was committed to supplying economic and military aid.

Khrushchev derived enormous personal satisfaction from his assistance to Cuba. By helping Castro, whom he viewed as "a modern-day Lenin," he felt that he was doing something of great historical importance that would earn him a prominent place in the pantheon of socialist heroes.[83] Khrushchev "was really a romantic in that matter," Alekseev remembered.[84] He took pride in the realization that Soviet aid had enabled Cuba to survive "right in front of the open jaws of predatory American imperialism."[85] Anastas Mikoyan also had a sentimental attachment to Cuba. After the missile crisis, he confided to Dean Rusk: "You Americans must understand what Cuba means to us old Bolsheviks. We have been waiting all our lives for a country to go Communist without the Red Army, and it happened in Cuba. It makes us feel like boys again!"[86]

The Soviet Union also had more tangible foreign-policy reasons for supporting Cuba. Khrushchev recognized that "Cuba's very existence is good propaganda for other Latin American countries, encouraging them to follow its example and to choose the course of Socialism." But if Cuba fell to the capitalists after the Soviet Union had declared its support, it would have "a devastating effect on the revolutionary world movement." Close relations with Castro were also useful in the ideological struggle with the People's Republic of China; Moscow could demonstrate that it was not a "paper tiger" but a worthy leader of the communist world.[87]

Khrushchev probably made up his mind to send missiles to Cuba in May 1962, during a state visit to Bulgaria.[88] While in Bulgaria, he claimed:

> one thought kept hammering away at my brain: what will happen if we lose Cuba? I knew it would have been a terrible blow to Marxism-Leninism. It would gravely diminish our stature throughout the world, but especially in Latin America. If Cuba fell, other Latin American countries would reject us, claiming that for all our might the Soviet Union hadn't been able to do anything for Cuba except to make empty protests to the United Nations.[89]

Khrushchev Comes to Cuba's Defense

The Bay of Pigs and the harassment of Cuba that followed convinced Khrushchev that Kennedy would mount a second invasion, this time with American forces. "I was haunted by the knowledge that the Americans could not stomach having Castro's Cuba right next to them. They would do something. They had the strength, and they had the means."[90] In Vienna, six weeks after the Bay of Pigs, Khrushchev confronted Kennedy with his suspicion. Kennedy sought to reassure him and admitted that the Bay of Pigs invasion had been a mistake.[91]

The prospect of another assault on Cuba continued to trouble top Soviet officials throughout the summer and fall of 1961.[92] Khrushchev told his Kremlin colleagues "that it would be foolish to expect the inevitable second invasion to be as badly planned and as badly executed as the first. I warned that Fidel would be crushed if another invasion were launched against Cuba and said that we were the only one who could prevent such a disaster from occurring."[93] During the crisis and afterward, Khrushchev insisted that he sent missiles to Cuba to "restrain the United States from precipitous military action against Castro's government."[94]

Soviet Views of the Threat

Until 1987, the only independent account of Khrushchev's motives came from Finnish President Urho Kekkonen, who had visited Moscow in October 1962. The day before Kennedy proclaimed the quarantine, Kekkonen had a long talk with Khrushchev, who told him that he had expected the United States to invade Cuba in late August or early September, but now believed there would be no attack.[95] Khrushchev did not tell Kekkonen about the missiles but may have been expecting that their presence would deter an American attack. Kekkonen's account tallies with a contemporary American intelligence report that Cuban military officers had feared an attack all summer long but thought the danger had passed in September.[96] It also fits with an off-the-record account of Soviet policy given by Deputy Prime Minister Mikoyan to President Kennedy several weeks after the crisis. Mikoyan assured Kennedy that the missiles had been purely defensive and justified by the threats of invasion voiced by Richard Nixon and American generals.[97]

Former Soviet officials insist that the Soviet leadership as a whole believed that Kennedy would try to reverse the humiliation of the Bay of Pigs. Oleg Troyanovsky, one of Khrushchev's chief foreign-policy aides, reports that "we received an enormous amount of information on the intentions of the United States to launch a second attack on Cuba."[98] Sergo Mikoyan reported that his father, regarded within the leadership as an authority on Cuba, believed that a second "invasion was inevitable, that it would be massive, and that it would use all American forces."[99] Former Foreign Minister Andrei Gromyko described the missile deployment as the result of "the very sharp, aggressive stand of the [Kennedy] administration concerning the new Cuba, and . . . the Cuban leadership."[100] Khrushchev told Gromyko about his plan to send missiles to Cuba aboard a flight home from Sofia, Bulgaria in May 1962. Khrushchev had insisted that "it is essential to deploy a certain number of our nuclear missiles there. This alone can save the country [Cuba]. Last year's failed assault isn't going to stop Washington."[101]

Georgiy N. Bol'shakov, a KGB officer, and Khrushchev's "back channel" to Kennedy, told the same story. During a return visit to Moscow in the late summer of 1962, Khrushchev sought him out to talk about the United States. Khrushchev spoke about Cuba and his belief that Kennedy would mount a second invasion. Asked for his opinion, Bol'shakov concurred, and emphasized the political pressures on the president since the Bay of Pigs to take action against Cuba. Yes, Khrushchev interrupted, and "he wouldn't mind getting revenge."[102]

Sergei Khrushchev also says that Cuba was very much on his father's mind in the spring and summer of 1962. He had one reason for installing the missiles: "the defense of Cuba from the possible landing by U.S. troops."[103] He expected that the missiles, once operational, "would force Kennedy to choose between accepting Cuba or fighting a nuclear war." As a reasonable man, he could only choose the former.[104] "Nikita Sergeevich was convinced that missiles were necessary to do the job because Cuba was too far away to help by conventional means."[105] Marshal Malinovsky had warned him that an American invasion "would take only a few days, and, even with all its enthusiasm, the Cuban army would not be able to deal with it."[106]

The fullest account of Khrushchev's concern about Cuba has been provided by Aleksandr Alekseev in his memoir of the crisis. A KGB officer, Spanish Civil War veteran, and chief of the Latin America department of the

KGB's First Chief Directorate, Alekseev was sent to prerevolutionary Cuba under cover as a journalist. He quickly established a close relationship with Fidel Castro.[107] At Castro's request, Khrushchev appointed him ambassador. Khrushchev summoned Alekseev to his Kremlin office in May and questioned him for more than an hour about Cuba and its revolution. Four days later, Alekseev attended a second meeting in the Kremlin at which the missile deployment was discussed by top Soviet leaders. Khrushchev insisted that conventional weapons alone "could hardly stop an aggressor." He expressed his "absolute conviction" that the Kennedy administration was planning a second invasion "in revenge for its defeat at the Bay of Pigs" and could only be stopped by the threat of nuclear war.[108]

Soviet officials offer several reasons why Khrushchev thought a second invasion almost certain. Capitalism in the United States could not tolerate a socialist state in the Western hemisphere. The industrial and financial elite was implacably hostile to Cuba and worked through the Pentagon and CIA to engineer Castro's overthrow. They used the media to whip up anti-Communist passions and generate pressure on the president to take action.[109] And Kennedy himself, as Khrushchev explained to Bol'shakov, was hankering for revenge for the Bay of Pigs.

Khrushchev and other Soviet leaders regarded American policy toward Cuba in the year after the Bay of Pigs as unambiguous proof of Washington's hostile intentions. The administration's successful attempt to expel Cuba from the Organization of American States (OAS) was seen as political preparation for an invasion. So too were the administration's widely publicized charges that Castro was spreading communism throughout the hemisphere. This was propaganda designed to garner public and foreign support for military action. Most telling of all were the assassination attempts and covert operations that the CIA mounted against Castro. Their only purpose could be to destabilize his regime as a prelude for invasion.[110]

Moscow's assessment was reinforced by repeated Cuban warnings. According to Gen. Fabian Escalante, the Cubans kept their Soviet comrades fully informed about Washington's military preparations and covert operations against their economy and government. Jorge Risquet, a Politburo member and long time associate of Fidel Castro, reports that "For us there was no doubt" that the United States was preparing a military assault. "It was a logical political conclusion."[111]

Many Soviet and Cuban leaders remain convinced that the United States had been poised to attack Cuba. At the 1987 Cambridge conference, Soviet officials expressed their belief that Kennedy would have invaded Cuba if he had not been deterred by the missile deployment. Robert McNamara insisted that Kennedy had not intended to invade Cuba and was reluctant to do so even at the height of the missile crisis. Well before the Soviet conventional arms buildup in Cuba, the president had concluded that an invasion would be prohibitively costly.[112]

There was incredulity on both sides. Some of the former American officials, knowing how adamantly opposed Kennedy had been to a second Cuban invasion, found it hard to believe that Khrushchev and his advisors could have worried so much about Cuba's security. The dialogue is revealing. It demonstrates how leaders expect adversaries to assess their intentions accurately, even though they are routinely bewildered by their adversary's behavior but do not hesitate to put the worst possible construction on it. This process of false attribution and its nearly catastrophic consequences for Soviet-American relations is now recognized by at least some of the participants on both sides.[113]

> MIKOYAN: I think all the participants in the discussion agreed that the United States was preparing for the liquidation of the Castro regime.
>
> SORENSEN: But I remember that your father referred to Richard Nixon's threats to Cuba at the time, even though Nixon wasn't part of the government. I recall that President Kennedy thought this showed a remarkable misunderstanding about the American government.
>
> MIKOYAN: But there were invasion plans.
>
> MCNAMARA: Let me say that we had *no* plan to invade Cuba, and I would have opposed the idea strongly if it ever came up.
>
> SORENSEN: Well, that's the wrong word.
>
> MCNAMARA: Okay, we had no *intent*.
>
> SHAKHNAZAROV: But there were subversive actions.
>
> MCNAMARA: That's my point. We thought those covert operations were terribly ineffective, and you thought they were ominous. We saw them very differently . . . I can assure you that there was no intent in the White House or in the Pentagon—or at least, in *my* Pentagon—to overthrow Castro by force. But if I were on *your* side, I'd have thought otherwise. I can very easily imagine estimating that an invasion was imminent.
>
> SHAKHNAZAROV: I do not wish to turn the meeting into reciprocal accusation. I am inclined to believe you had no plan. But surely this is very important for lessons.
>
> SEVERAL VOICES: Yes, certainly.[114]

OVERCOMING STRATEGIC INSECURITY

The second proximate cause of the missile crisis was the pervasive sense of strategic insecurity felt by both superpowers in the early 1960s. First the United States, then the Soviet Union, worried that its adversary had achieved a significant strategic advantage that it would try to exploit for political gain. In their efforts to protect themselves against nuclear blackmail, Washington and Moscow only exacerbated one another's insecurity. Their reciprocal initiatives culminated in the Soviet attempt to deploy ballistic missiles secretly in Cuba.

Khrushchev's Bluff

The Soviet Union launched its first ICBM in August 1957, and its first satellite, the famous *Sputnik*, in October. In the aftermath of these triumphs, Soviet leaders began to deny that the West any longer possessed a strategic advantage.[115] In March 1958, Khrushchev told a French journalist that the Soviet Union had broken out of "capitalist encirclement" and that it was "no longer clear who encircles whom."[116] By 1959, Khrushchev and Defense Minister Marshal Rodion Malinovsky were loudly proclaiming Soviet strategic superiority.[117] In January 1961, he insisted that nuclear war, while devastating to both sides, would result in certain victory for socialism.[118]

Khrushchev's depiction of the strategic balance was based on extravagant claims about the size and accuracy of the Soviet ICBM force.[119] Three days after the first *Sputnik* was lofted into orbit, Khrushchev confided to James Reston of the *New York Times*: "We now have all the rockets we need: long-range rockets, intermediate-range rockets and short-range rockets."[120] In January 1959, he told cheering delegates to the Twenty-first Party Congress that serial production of ICBMs had begun.[121] In November, he boasted that Soviet factories "were turning out missiles like sausages." Two months later, he announced that the USSR led the world "in the creation and mass production of intercontinental ballistic rockets of various types."[122] In a January 1961 address to the Supreme Soviet—the speech that so disturbed Kennedy—Khrushchev reiterated his by now routine assertion of strategic superiority and went on to insist that the economic balance was also tipping in favor of socialism.[123]

The View from Washington

Sputnik shattered American complacency about technological superiority. Soviet achievements in space and Khrushchev's claims about the number and accuracy of its missiles aroused widespread concern among Americans and Europeans that they would soon become vulnerable to a devastating nuclear attack.

Western anxieties were further exacerbated by Khrushchev's increasingly belligerent rhetoric. In the Taiwan Straits and Berlin crises, he threatened the West with nuclear destruction.[124] In July 1959, at the height of the Berlin crisis, he warned Ambassador Averell Harriman that if the United States tried to maintain its position in Berlin by force, Soviet missiles would "fly automatically."[125] Khrushchev's challenge to Berlin and stepped-up support for Third World liberation movements coincided with Soviet claims of strategic superiority. American officials interpreted these actions as an expression of Khrushchev's belief that the correlation of forces increasingly favored the Socialist camp.

This view of Soviet foreign policy received official sanction in a special interagency report prepared at the president's request. The covering letter, signed by Dean Rusk, Robert McNamara, CIA Director John McCone, and Chairman of the Joint Chiefs Lyman Lemnitzer, advised that Soviet successes in space had had a chilling effect on American opinion and had given Khrushchev the confidence "to confront us with continuing political pressure, subversion and various forms of unconventional warfare." It warned of the possibility that Khrushchev would overplay his hand as Soviet military strength increased. Even a temporary Soviet advantage would bring about "a dangerous change in the calculus of risks."[126]

THE "MISSILE GAP"

Sputnik aroused the same level of concern in the United States as had the Soviet detonation of an atomic device eight years earlier. Military officers, journalists, and alarmed Congressmen demanded urgent measures to keep the Soviet Union from gaining any strategic advantage. President Eisenhower was not persuaded by these alarums, but a more impressionable Congress forced him to accept a severalfold increase in the number of planned ICBMs. The air force, still dissatisfied, lobbied for a much larger missile force.[127]

Presidential hopefuls in both parties made the "missile gap" a campaign issue and promised to restore America's strategic edge. Cassandra-like predictions of strategic vulnerability were common in Kennedy's campaign speeches.[128] On 23 January 1960, he criticized the Eisenhower administration for its failure to keep abreast of the Soviet Union and warned that the United States was becoming "second in space—second in missiles."[129] In August, he told a convention of Veterans of Foreign Wars that "the missile gap looms larger and larger ahead."[130] In New York, in September, he called for a strategic buildup: "We must step up crash programs to provide ourselves with the ultimate weapons—the Polaris submarines and Minuteman missiles—which will eventually close the missile gap."[131] Ten days after his inauguration, Kennedy delivered a somber State of the Union message to Congress. He offered an alarming assessment of the military situation and spoke of the urgent need to reevaluate the country's defense strategy.[132]

Less than two months later, Kennedy announced the largest and fastest peacetime military buildup in the nation's history. He asked Congress for some $17 billion in supplemental appropriations to increase the number and production rates of the Polaris submarines and land-based Minuteman missiles. To guard against a Soviet surprise attack, he placed 50 percent more of the Strategic Air Command's (SAC) bombers on fifteen-minute standby alert and ordered a 50 percent increase in the number of Polaris submarines on station by the end of 1964. In May, he pressed Congress for a shelter program as a form of "survival insurance" against fallout. Concern that the impending showdown in Berlin might lead to nuclear war led him to renew his request for fallout shelters in July.[133]

American assessments of the strategic balance bore little relationship to reality. From its first ICBM deployments in 1959, the United States fielded missiles at a faster rate than the Soviet Union. Around the time the first 4 Soviet SS-6 ICBMs were deployed in Plesetsk, between the fall of 1960 and the spring of 1961, the United States had 27 operational Atlas D ICBMs and three Polaris submarines carrying a total of 48 missiles (SLBMs). By the end of 1962, the American strategic arsenal had jumped to 200 operational ICBMs and nine Polaris submarines with 144 SLBMs.[134] The Soviets, by comparison, had 20 to 35 operational ICBMs and no long-range SLBMs.[135]

When Kennedy took his oath of office in January 1961 the intelligence community was deeply divided on the question of the missile gap. The December 1960 National Intelligence Estimate (NIE) had concluded that there was no evidence that the Soviet Union was engaged in a crash effort to build ICBMs. American intelligence had not detected any new missile bases in addition to the two it already knew about. But the NIE still showed the Soviets ahead in numbers; they were thought to have 35 to 150 operational ICBMs. Projections of future deployments were more uncertain, ranging from the Army-Navy low of 50 ICBMs by mid-1963, to an Air Force high of 600 to 800.[136]

The new president was given a copy of the December 1960 NIE, and kept abreast of later intelligence about the Soviet ICBM force. It would have been politically embarrassing to have admitted at the outset of his presidency that he had been mistaken in his campaign charges that the Eisenhower administration was allowing the Soviet Union to pull ahead in missiles. Kennedy avoided reporters who questioned him about the missile gap. Secretary of Defense McNamara was not as astute. In a background briefing on 6 February 1961, he told newsmen that the superpowers had "about the same number of ICBMs at present—not a very large number." To McNamara's chagrin, the *Washington Post* quoted his estimate. Newspapers around the country picked up the story and some accused the administration of duplicity about the missile gap.[137]

Opinion within the intelligence community remained divided well into the spring of 1961; the June NIE still referred to a missile gap.[138] By early September the CIA had "positive" intelligence that Moscow would deploy only a small force of SS-6 ICBMs. The September NIE lowered the number of operational missiles and the projection of those to be deployed.[139] On 5 September, McNamara shared the new intelligence with the Senate Foreign Relations and Armed Services Committees. Meeting jointly in executive session, the senators were treated to a detailed description of the Soviet strategic order of battle. The Soviet strategic arsenal, McNamara admitted, was neither as large nor increasing as rapidly as had been supposed. The nuclear capabilities of the United States surpassed those of the Soviet Union "roughly by a factor of two."[140]

The new intelligence was the result of photographic reconnaissance satellites; the first successful mission, Discoverer 14, was sent over the Soviet Union in August 1960. More Discoverers were sent into orbit before the end of the year, and their photographic capsules were successfully recovered. Four more capsules were recovered between mid-June and September 1961. They are said to have provided detailed coverage of the Soviet SS-6 base at Plesetsk.[141] Their photographs confirmed reports by Oleg Penkovskiy, a turncoat colonel in Soviet military intelligence, that the SS-6 would only be deployed in small numbers because of its operational inadequacies.[142]

THE "MISSILE GAP" EXPOSED

In the fall of 1961, the administration sent a blunt message to Moscow: the United States possessed strategic superiority. President Kennedy took this unusual step in the hope that it would moderate Khrushchev's alarming bellicosity.

The immediate catalyst for the administration's decision was Moscow's announcement on 30 August that it would soon start a new series of nuclear tests. Only two months before in Vienna, Khrushchev had promised Kennedy that his country would not be the first to resume testing. Soviet Foreign Minister Andrei Gromyko had repeated the promise to Dean Rusk.[143] Kennedy's reaction "was one of personal anger at the Soviets for deceiving him and at himself for believing them."[144]

The Soviet announcement prompted a series of emergency meetings at the White House.[145] Robert Kennedy remembered them as "the most gloomy meetings . . . since early in the Berlin crisis." There was a consensus that Khrushchev had resumed testing "to try to intimidate the West and neutrals."[146] Presidential advisor Arthur Schlesinger, Jr. characterized his behavior as "brinkmanship with a vengeance" and worried that "it may get us very close indeed to war."[147] John J. McCloy, in charge of disarmament negotiations in Geneva, admonished Kennedy "to show now that he was capable of hard and tough leadership—that he could not continue to stand by and let the communists kick us in the teeth."[148]

Khrushchev proceeded to rub salt in American wounds. He jubilantly proclaimed to the delegates of the Twenty-Second Party Congress that the Soviet Union had developed a 100-megaton bomb and would probably detonate a 50-megaton weapon at the end of the current round of nuclear tests.[149] Between 1 September and 4 November, the Soviets exploded at least thirty nuclear devices, most of them in the atmosphere. A 30-megaton explosion on 23 October touched off a storm of protest. Jawaharlal Nehru of India and Kwame Nkrumah of Ghana, leaders sympathetic to the Soviet Union, added their voices to the general condemnation of the Soviet test series.[150] Brushing aside an 87–11–1 appeal of the United Nations General Assembly to postpone the promised 50 megaton blast, Khrushchev ordered the test on 31 October, the final day of the Party Congress.[151]

On 17 October, in the same speech announcing his intention to explode a 50-megaton bomb, Khrushchev boasted once again of the growing power of the socialist camp.[152] The next day, *Pravda* and *Izvestiya* published the full text of Khrushchev's Report to the Central Committee with its assertion "that the forces of socialism . . . are more powerful than the aggressive imperialist forces."[153] These statements, coming hard on the heels of the nuclear tests, convinced Kennedy and his advisors of the need to do something dramatic to disabuse Khrushchev of his illusions regarding the military balance.

After consulting with McNamara, Rusk, National Security Advisor McGeorge Bundy, and CIA Director Allen Dulles, Kennedy decided to tell Khrushchev that American intelligence had discovered just how few ICBMs the Soviet Union had been able to field.[154] Deputy Secretary of Defense Roswell Gilpatric, scheduled to give a speech to the Business Council in Hot Springs, Virginia on 21 October, was chosen to deliver the message.[155]

Gilpatric began his speech by stressing the president's determination to possess strategic forces that could sustain a first strike and still inflict "unacceptable losses" on an enemy. He described the "quick-fix" measures the administration had put into effect to strengthen its military position in Berlin and demonstrate its intent to resist Soviet aggression against that city. Behind these steps, Gilpatric declared, lay resolution and confidence based on "a sober appreciation of the relative military power of the two sides." In a pointed reference to Khrushchev's well-publicized claims of superiority, which he dismissed as "extravagant," he assured his listeners that the Soviets also knew the truth.[156]

Gilpatric went on to describe the major components of America's strategic arsenal and to contrast them to the weapons available to the Soviet Union. The comparison was revealing. The destructive power available to respond to a Soviet surprise attack "would be as great—perhaps greater than—the total undamaged force which the enemy can threaten to launch against the United States in a first strike." The United States had "a second strike capability which is at least as extensive as what the Soviets can deliver by striking first." "We are confident," Gilpatric concluded, "that the Soviets will not provoke a major nuclear conflict."[157]

To make sure Moscow got the message, the Defense Department told reporters that the speech had been cleared "at the highest level."[158] The next day, Secretary of State Dean Rusk endorsed Gilpatric's remarks on television and assumed coresponsibility for the speech. He explained that the favorable strategic balance was one important reason why the administration was able to confront the Soviets in Berlin from a position of strength. "Mr. Khrushchev must know that we are strong, and he does know that we are strong," Rusk insisted, despite his public attempts to deny this reality.[159] Deputy Assistant Secretary of Defense Paul Nitze took Soviet Ambassador Mikhail Menshikov to lunch at the Metropolitan Club and warned him that "there would be nothing left of the Soviet Union" after an American nuclear strike.[160]

On 8 November, Kennedy reviewed the history of the missile gap at his press conference. He told newsmen that his campaign charges about Soviet strategic superiority were based on the information available to him at the time. Reality turned out to be different; "based on our present assessments and our intelligence we . . . would not trade places with anyone in the world."[161] A few days later, McNamara told reporters that the American nuclear arsenal was "several times that of the Soviets."[162] Kennedy is reported to have shown Gromyko the actual satellite photographs of Soviet missile sites to support his assertion that the Soviets had deployed only a few ICBMs.[163]

The View from Moscow

During the summer of 1962 President Kennedy told James Wechsler of the *New York Post* that only "fools" could believe that victory was possible in nuclear war. What worried him was that Khrushchev might interpret his reluctance to wage war as a symptom of an American loss of nerve. The time might come when he would have to run the supreme risk to convince Khrushchev that conciliation did not mean humiliation. "That son of a bitch won't pay any attention to words," Kennedy complained on another occasion. "He has to see you move."[164]

Khrushchev did pay attention to Kennedy's words—just as Kennedy did to his. And contrary to the president's expectation, his words conveyed enormous threat. The strategic and political implications of the American message were staggering. Almost overnight the Kremlin was confronted with the realization that its nuclear arsenal was not an effective deterrent.

THE SOVIET DILEMMA

Soviet ICBMs were all but useless. Their sizeable force of medium- and intermediate-range missiles (MRBMs and IRBMs) could strike at targets in Western Europe but did not have the range to reach the United States. Their small fleet of long-range bombers was slow and outdated and could not be counted on to penetrate American air defenses. The missile gap could eventually be closed by a crash program to develop more effective second-generation ICBMs and perhaps a submersible delivery system. This effort would be extremely costly and, more importantly, it would do nothing to solve the immediate problem of acute strategic inferiority and the likelihood that American leaders would exploit this inferiority for political purposes. Missiles in Cuba would help to reduce the impact of strategic inferiority.

The twenty-four R-12 MRBMs and sixteen R-14 IRBMs earmarked for Cuba represented at least a doubling of the Soviet nuclear-strike capability against the United States, and there is no reason to believe that the buildup would not at some point have gone beyond forty launchers. Some administration officials and military analysts worried that these missiles would have given the Soviets a limited first-strike capability.[165] Their concern seems misplaced as both the MRBMs and IRBMs were more inaccurate and cumbersome than was generally recognized at the time.[166] There can be no question, however, that Soviet missiles in Cuba, some with limited mobility, would have greatly complicated any American first strike and correspondingly reduced the American military's confidence in its ability to carry out such an attack.[167] Surviving missiles, most likely the thousand-mile range MRBMs, could have been used against cities in the southeastern United States and were so targeted, Khrushchev subsequently revealed.[168]

The Kennedy administration's public disclosure of the strategic imbalance also created serious political problems for the Soviet Union and its leader. Khrushchev's claims of strategic superiority had provided the Kremlin with a new foreign-policy instrument.[169] Khrushchev had exploited his country's putative advantage in a crude and opportunistic way in an unsuccessful attempt to weaken the Western alliance and its links to Berlin.

With his bluff exposed, he could no longer play this game. It was now possible that Kennedy would use his undeniable strategic advantage to try to intimidate the Soviet Union and its allies. The Soviet response to the Gilpatric speech was prompt. The next day, 23 October, Marshal Malinovsky delivered an angry address to the Twenty-Second Party Congress that referred specifically to Gilpatric's claim of American strategic superiority. "What is there to say to this latest threat, to this petty speech?", Malinovsky asked. "Only one thing: The threat does not frighten us."[170] But Moscow was chastened.[171]

Khrushchev became more cautious in his rhetoric. In a widely publicized speech in March 1962, his first reference to the strategic balance in many months, he observed that the United States had lost its nuclear monopoly. This was a return to the argument the Soviet Union had made five years earlier when its strategic capability was extremely limited.[172] In a major speech in July, Khrushchev remained on the defensive. He dismissed American claims of superiority as "groundless." Recalling that the Soviet Union had ultimately defeated Hitler, he insisted that numerical comparisons were poor predictors of the outcomes of wars.[173]

Soviet sensitivities to nuclear intimidation were further exacerbated by "an incautious interview" that the president gave to Stewart Alsop in March 1962.[174] Kennedy explained to Alsop that the United States had always regarded its nuclear arsenal as retaliatory. "But Khrushchev must *not* be certain that, where its vital interests are threatened, the United States will never strike first. In some circumstances," he explained, "we might have to take the initiative."[175] Khrushchev responded with a speech in which he accused Kennedy of making "an unwise statement."[176] The Soviet press condemned Kennedy's remark as a crude attempt at blackmail.[177] In a subsequent speech, Khrushchev accused Kennedy of initiating "a sinister competition as to who will be first to start such a war."[178]

OVERCOMING STRATEGIC VULNERABILITY

Beyond all of the circumstantial evidence linking the deployment of missiles to Soviet strategic vulnerability, there is the direct testimony of Soviet bloc officials. In November 1962, Anastas Mikoyan stopped in Washington on his way back from Cuba and gave a briefing to Warsaw Pact ambassadors. He explained the missile deployment as an attempt to defend Cuba *and* equalize the strategic balance of power.[179]

Fidel Castro also maintained that the deployment was motivated by broader strategic objectives. Soviet leaders had explained to the Cubans that by accepting the missiles "we would be reinforcing the socialist camp the world over."[180] According to Castro, Khrushchev "was obsessed by the idea of achieving a certain parity."[181] Emilio Aragonés, an aide to Che Guevara and member of the Cuban Central Committee in 1962, confirms Castro's account. The Central Committee was unanimous in its decision to accept the missiles, "but we six, and especially Fidel Castro, were sure that we were doing this . . . not so much to defend Cuba as to change the correlation of forces between capitalism and socialism." Aragonés insists that Cuba could have been defended more effectively by conventional weapons.[182]

Khrushchev made a guarded admission in his memoirs that the missiles were intended to do more than deter an American invasion. "In addition to protecting Cuba," he wrote, "our missiles would have equalized what the West likes to call 'the balance of power.' "[183] Other Soviet officials also stress this motive.

Sergo Mikoyan believes that "Khrushchev saw his missiles as defensive and necessary to offset your strategic advantage."[184] "Our 'pentagon' thought the strategic balance was dangerous, and sought parity." Khrushchev was also "very concerned about a possible American attack. He worried . . . that somebody in the United States might think that a seventeen-to-one superiority would mean that a first strike was possible."[185]

Georgiy Shakhnazarov, formerly the private secretary to Mikhail Gorbachev and a Central Committee member, contends that Khrushchev was even more intent on redressing the strategic imbalance than he was on protecting Castro. Khrushchev, he says, worried about the military consequences of American superiority "because there were circles in the United States who believed that war with the Soviet Union was possible and could be won." He hoped to use the missiles "to publicly attain parity" at minimal economic cost."[186] Gen. Dimitri A. Volkogonov insists that there is ample documentation in the Ministry of Defense archives to sustain Shakhnazarov's claim that the military, and Defense Minister Malinovsky, were fearful of an American first strike.[187]

Sergei Khrushchev acknowledged that Soviet political authorities were also troubled by American strategic superiority. "It naturally tormented our leadership a great deal. Because we were actually subject to a possible strike of American missile forces, and aviation forces, and we had nothing with which to respond." However, Khrushchev maintains that his father was more worried about the political consequences of the imbalance. "He believed that all the intercontinental missiles, and all the submarine-based missiles which were in existence, were a sufficiently menacing force to prevent the possibility of a first-strike from the United States." Narrow strategic calculations did not influence his decision to send missiles to Cuba.[188]

"Many Soviet generals," Ambassador Leonid M. Zamyatin explained, "did fear an American first strike. Khrushchev did not take their concerns seriously." Otherwise "he would never have placed missiles in Cuba where they could provide the pretext for such a strike." According to Zamyatin, a member of the foreign ministry's working group on the "Caribbean crisis," Khrushchev worried that Kennedy would exploit American nuclear superiority for coercive ends; "this is what *he* had tried to do in the aftermath of *Sputnik*." He interpreted American claims of strategic superiority "as presaging an intensified campaign of intimidation." If the Soviet Union could equalize the strategic balance by sending missiles to Cuba, it would be in a much better position to cope with this threat.[189]

ARMS AND TENSIONS

It is apparent that neither superpower foresaw the consequences of its strategic saber rattling. At least some Soviet diplomats worried that Khrushchev's bluffs would backfire, but they worried even more about the consequences of telling him so. An exception was Kirill V. Novikov, who spoke out at a 1959 Central Committee discussion of strategic arms policy. "We are provoking an arms race with the United States," he warned, "and one in which we will be the big losers given American technological prowess." The response was hostile. Marshal Malinovsky chided him for being afraid of the Americans. Efim P. Slavsky, Minister of Medium Machine Construction (responsible for the nuclear weapons program), and Serbin I. Dimitrievitch, Director of the Central Committee's Department for Military Industry, scoffed at Novikov's assertion. Slavsky then made one of the most ironic predictions of the Cold War. An arms race, he insisted, "would benefit the Soviet Union because it would bankrupt the United States."[190]

American expectations were equally far from the mark. Although none of the Soviet officials we interviewed identified the Gilpatric speech as a catalyst of the missile deployment, they all contended that Kennedy's strategic buildup and threatening rhetoric greatly exacerbated Soviet insecurities and contributed to Khrushchev's decision to send missiles to Cuba. American attempts to constrain Soviet aggressiveness through demonstrations of military capability and resolve backfired. They made a provocative foreign policy *more* rather than less attractive to Khrushchev because of the expected short-term costs of living with American strategic superiority.

There is a double irony here. The American buildup and assertions of superiority that Khrushchev found so threatening were unnecessary. Defense Secretary McNamara had advocated a rapid expansion of American strategic forces in response to intelligence estimates of the Soviet Union's capability to produce and deploy ICBMs. In 1987, he explained to Soviet officials:

> The procurement lead time was roughly seven years. So in 1961, we were ordering forces based on the force we thought you would have in 1968. And we based our estimates on what we called the "worst case" estimate. And therefore, we based it on capabilities. We didn't know your intentions. We estimated

your capability to produce. So eight years in advance, we estimated that capability, and we bought weapons in anticipation of that. That was why the forces developed as they did—and it was very dangerous, for both of us, because it led to this constant imbalance, which you might well have interpreted as showing signs of aggression.[191]

After the missile crisis, McNamara sent a memorandum to the president in which he argued that the administration's strategic buildup might have frightened Soviet leaders. "You put those two things together: a known force disadvantage that is large enough in itself to at least appear to support the view that the United States was planning a first-strike capability and, secondly, talk among U.S. personnel that that was the objective—it would have just scared the hell out of me!"[192]

Some of McNamara's former colleagues have since come around to his point of view. Arthur Schlesinger, Jr., adamant at the time about the need to deal with Khrushchev from a position of strength, now thinks that the buildup "sent the wrong message to Moscow" and "compelled Khrushchev to start worrying about the Soviet missile gap."[193] McGeorge Bundy acknowledges that the administration was "inattentive" to Khrushchev's fear of the possibly crippling consequences of strategic inferiority. Bundy believes that Khrushchev's concern was aggravated "by his Marxist-Leninist outlook and its emphasis on the correlation of forces as the determinant of international issues."[194] Fewer strategic forces might have bought more security.

TIT FOR TAT

The Soviet test of an ICBM in August 1957 triggered American fears of a missile gap and led to accelerated efforts to develop and deploy American ICBMs. In the interim, the United States resorted to "stopgap" measures to protect the West in the years during which the Soviets were expected to have a strategic edge.

One such measure was the stationing of MRBMs in Europe, where they could target Eastern European and Soviet cities. The primary purpose of the missiles was political: they were intended to reassure Western Europeans of Washington's commitment to their defense. Intermediate-range Thor missiles were deployed in Great Britain, and medium-range Jupiters in Italy. Turkey also agreed to host a squadron of Jupiters.

The Soviet Union denounced the forward deployment of American missiles, but was especially vocal in its opposition to the Jupiters earmarked for Turkey. Khrushchev was deeply offended by the prospect of nuclear-armed missiles just across the Black Sea and sent Soviet missiles to Cuba to even the score.

The View from Washington

The idea of stationing Jupiter missiles in Europe originated in the Eisenhower administration. It was supported by the Pentagon and Supreme Headquarters Allied Powers Europe (SHAPE), who wanted to target ballistic missiles against Soviet MRBMs, air bases, staging areas, and logistical complexes in Eastern Europe and the Soviet Union.[195] Secretary of State John Foster Dulles supported the proposal because he thought it would strengthen deterrence and allied interdependence. Dulles and Eisenhower saw the Jupiters as an interim measure until the United States could deploy ICBMs on its own territory.[196] The Jupiters were vulnerable to air and ground attack but the military did not consider this a serious drawback. They reasoned that the Soviet Union would be incapable of coordinating simultaneous attacks against European and North American missile and air bases. Former Air Force Chief of Staff, Gen. Nathan Twining described the Jupiters' vulnerability as a virtue; an attack against them would provide SAC with early warning of an impending nuclear attack against the United States.[197]

The proposed deployment met unexpected resistance from the European allies; they wanted reassurance but not at the price of becoming targets for Soviet missiles. Italy was finally persuaded to accept the Jupiters; Turkey did so willingly.[198] In October 1959, the Turkish government formally agreed to host a squadron of Jupiters. In June 1960, Turkey and the United States signed a second accord about the details of the deployment.[199] Turkey would own the missiles, and the United States would own and control the warheads. Soldiers from both countries would man the missile sites. The Jupiters could only be launched by order of the commander of SHAPE, an American, with the concurrence of both governments.[200]

President Eisenhower, never very enthusiastic about the missiles, began to have serious second thoughts about deploying them so close to the Soviet Union. In June 1959, when missiles for Greece were under discussion, he warned Under Secretary of State Douglas Dillon that Khrushchev would almost certainly regard the deployment as extraordinarily provocative— "just as we would if he put missiles in our backyard." In what proved to be a remarkably prescient observation, Eisenhower wrote: "If Mexico or Cuba had been penetrated by the Communists and then began getting arms and missiles from them, we would be bound to look on such developments with the gravest concern." In this circumstance, "it would be imperative for us to take positive action, even offensive military action."[201]

Eisenhower became increasingly uneasy about the deployment in Turkey. On his instructions, Secretary of State Christian Herter requested the NATO Council in December 1960 to rescind its approval. Herter told the Council that the Jupiters were obsolete, vulnerable, and could only be used for a first strike. They invited Soviet preemption.[202] Herter's plea was rejected because the Turkish and Italian governments were strongly opposed to reopening the question of the missiles.

The controversy spilled over into the Kennedy administration. Three weeks after his inauguration, Kennedy was presented with a Congressional report, two years in the making, that was highly critical of a European missile deployment. The Ad Hoc Subcommittee of the House Joint Committee on Atomic Energy recommended against construction of the five projected Jupiter sites in Turkey. In lieu of the missiles, it recommended that a Polaris submarine with sixteen IRBMs, operated by U.S. personnel, be dedicated to NATO.[203] In a closed session of the Senate Foreign Relations Committee, Senator Albert Gore (D-Tenn.) characterized the Jupiters as "the kind of provocation which needs to be considered very carefully." "I wonder," he mused, "what our attitude would be if warheads should be attached to [Soviet] missiles in Cuba."[204]

In light of all this criticism, President Kennedy asked for an internal review of the deployment to Turkey in April 1961. The review was carried out by representatives of State, Defense, and the CIA. There was a near-consensus in State and Defense that the Jupiters were militarily useless for anything but a first strike.[205] CIA Director John McCone described the Jupiters as worthless and had earlier urged President Eisenhower to reconsider the deployment.[206] National Security Advisor McGeorge Bundy thought their warheads "worse than useless."[207] Secretary of State Dean Rusk remembered that "we joked about which way those missiles would go if we fired them."[208] Their warheads were "duds." The missiles were also extremely vulnerable. They were deployed aboveground and their thin aluminum skins were easy targets for a marksman. Rusk was told "any casual traveler with a .22-caliber rifle could shoot holes in the missiles from an adjacent highway and put them out of action."[209]

There was additional opposition to the Jupiters on political grounds. Roving Ambassador Averell W. Harriman, who had opposed the missiles in Turkey from the beginning, warned that they would cause trouble with Moscow because they would be "humiliating to Soviet pride."[210] On his own initiative, Rusk tried to talk Turkish Foreign Minister Selim Sarper out of the deployment in April 1961. Sarper explained that it would be embarrassing for the Turkish government to reverse its position because it had just attained legislative approval for its contribution to the cost of the Jupiters. Turkish morale would be adversely affected by withdrawal of the missiles unless some other weapons system was substituted in its place. The two men agreed that this would not be possible until the spring of 1963 when Polaris submarines would become available.[211]

Khrushchev spoke out repeatedly against the deployment and complained to Kennedy about it on three occasions during their private talks at the Vienna summit.[212] He charged that the American military buildup in Turkey posed a serious threat to Soviet security.[213] In September 1961, Khrushchev told *New York Times* correspondent C. L. Sulzberger that he was very unhappy about "what is going on in Turkey. She is our neighbor, but you have stationed your bases there and threaten us from those bases. You have set up bases in Greece as well." Khrushchev pointed out that the Soviet Union was "displaying self-restraint and patience with regard to those countries" and urged the United States to act according to the same principles.[214]

Despite opposition to the Jupiters at home and abroad, the administration's internal review, completed shortly after the June summit, urged the president to persevere with the deployment. Acknowledging that the missiles were militarily worthless, the cover letter to the review warned "that, in the aftermath of Khrushchev's hard posture at Vienna, cancellation of the IRBM deployment might seem a sign of weakness." Turkish opposition to cancellation and Gen. Norstad's belief that the missiles were militarily useful also had to be considered.[215] Kennedy was persuaded by the political argument, and decided to go ahead with the deployment in the hope that another demonstration of American resolve would make Khrushchev more cautious in his approach to Berlin.[216]

In early 1962 Kennedy began to question his decision. His second thoughts appear to have been a response to mounting opposition to the weapons in the Congress and administration.[217] A National Security Action Memorandum drafted less than a month before the missile crisis indicates presidential interest in removing the missiles.[218] McGeorge Bundy, who authored the Memorandum, reports that on 23 August the State Department asked the American ambassador in Ankara what could be done to secure Turkish agreement to cancel the deployment. No answer had been received at the time of the crisis. "For a year and a half," Bundy reported, Kennedy knew that "the Turkish missiles could be removed only over the resistance of both the Turks and Washington's custodians of NATO solidarity (of whom, in one mood, he was the foremost). He had not pressed the matter home."[219]

The View from Moscow

Khrushchev was pleased by Kennedy's victory over the "son-of-a bitch" Nixon, but did not expect a Democratic victory to result in any fundamental reorientation of American foreign policy.[220] He nevertheless toyed with the idea of reaching an accommodation with the new administration. If successful, it would demonstrate the validity of his foreign policy and strategic doctrine, strengthen his hand at home, and provide the justification for a major shift in resource allocation.

The Bay of Pigs convinced Khrushchev that Kennedy was not interested in détente. So did his performance in Vienna. Khrushchev was impressed by Kennedy's knowledge of international affairs and commitment to peaceful coexistence, but disappointed by his desire to protect colonialism by freezing the status quo in the Third World. "This was absolutely unacceptable."[221] On the afternoon of 3 June, when the two leaders met for a private talk,

Khrushchev brushed aside Kennedy's complaints about Cuba with the rejoinder that American weapons in Turkey posed a greater threat to the Soviet Union. Twice more that afternoon, he returned to the subject of the American missiles in Turkey. On the last occasion, which followed an animated discussion of Taiwan, he warned Kennedy that "the U.S. had surrounded the USSR with bases" and that "this was very unwise and aggravates relations."[222] He returned home disappointed that Kennedy "wasn't willing to go much beyond the basic point" of preventing war, and convinced that for the moment détente was an unrealistic goal.[223]

Khrushchev made many subsequent references to the Jupiters.[224] During the crisis, Khrushchev complained about the missiles to visiting American businessman William E. Knox.[225] On 27 October, in a long private letter to Kennedy, Khrushchev defended the missiles in Cuba as a justifiable response to the Jupiters in Turkey. American policies had exposed the Soviet Union to enormous dangers:

> you have surrounded the Soviet Union with military bases, surrounded our allies with military bases, set up military bases literally around our country, and stationed your rocket weapons at them? This is no secret. High-placed American officials demonstratively declare this. Your rockets are stationed in Britain and in Italy and pointed at us. Your rockets are stationed in Turkey.
>
> You are worried over Cuba. You say that it worries you because it lies at a distance of ninety miles across the sea from the shores of the United States. However, Turkey lies next to us. Our sentinels are pacing up and down and watching each other. Do you believe that you have the right to demand security for your country and the removal of such weapons that you qualify as offensive, while not recognizing this right for us?
>
> You have stationed devastating rocket weapons, which you call offensive, in Turkey literally right next to us. How then does recognition of our equal military possibilities tally with such unequal relations between our great states? This does not tally at all.[226]

Khrushchev's plea for equality was not an ex post facto rationalization. He had made the same argument to Kennedy at Vienna and to other high-placed Americans before the crisis. He was less troubled by the military implications of the Jupiters, than by the political inequality they represented. Khrushchev, his son insisted, did not view the missiles in Turkey as a new military threat "because the Soviet Union had been surrounded by U.S. Air Force bases since 1945." It was the *uselessness* of the weapons that offended him.[227] Khrushchev had made this point to Richard Nixon during the vice president's July 1959 visit to the Soviet Union. The missiles could only be used as first-strike weapons, he complained. "If you intend to make war on us, I understand; if not, why do you keep them?"[228]

Lenin's concept of the "correlation of forces" was central to Khrushchev's understanding of East-West relations. He took the gradual evolution of

American foreign policy toward grudging acceptance of the Soviet Union as proof of this principle. Eisenhower had sought improved relations because of "our economic might, the might of our armed forces, and that of the whole socialist camp." "By the time Kennedy came to the White House and we had our first meeting in Vienna, there had already been a shift in the balance of power. It was harder for the U.S. to pressure us than it had been in the days of Dulles and Truman. It was for this reason that Kennedy had felt obliged to seek an opportunity to reach some kind of agreement."[229]

American pronouncements of strategic superiority in the fall of 1961 had a chilling effect on Khrushchev. They compromised his strategy, based as it was on convincing the United States of the Soviet Union's growing military and economic power. If American leaders had moderated their policies because of Moscow's impressive military and economic achievements, they would now revert to a more aggressive policy in recognition of the Soviet Union's strategic weakness and vulnerability.

Khrushchev's understanding of the correlation of forces was not mechanistic. He was sensitive, as Gen. Volkogonov put it, to "the purely psychological element" of security.[230] Changes in the military-economic balance were necessary but insufficient conditions for foreign-policy change. Leaders had to recognize that a shift had occurred before they adjusted their policies. The capitalist world had been slow to acknowledge the progress made by the Soviet Union because of its visceral dislike of socialism. Vivid demonstrations of Soviet power were necessary to bring capitalist conceptions in line with reality. The Soviet detonation of a nuclear device in 1949 and the launching of the first *Sputnik* in 1957 had captured the attention of the West. Soviet leaders recognized that both events had compelled American leaders to take the Soviet Union more seriously.[231]

Even before his strategic bluff was exposed, Khrushchev was convinced that the United States still regarded the Soviet Union as a second-rank power. This is why Eisenhower and the CIA had dared to send U-2s over the Soviet Union, and why Kennedy was proceeding with the deployment of the Jupiter missiles. These were blatant attempts to intimidate the Soviet Union. Khrushchev believed that American presidents would not behave this way if they came to regard the Soviet Union as an equal superpower.

Khrushchev understood that the United States was in many ways a more powerful country, but he thought that American leaders exaggerated their relative advantage and failed to appreciate the true power of the socialist camp.[232] This power was only partly due to tangible economic and military accomplishments; it was also the result of the commitment to Marxist principles of progress and social organization. These principles were ultimately responsible for the Soviet Union's impressive achievements and made it an attractive model for many newly independent countries. Khrushchev also gave great weight to the equalizing role of nuclear weapons; their unheralded destructiveness gave the superpowers a de facto veto over one another's existence. Khrushchev was convinced—and the missile crisis would prove him right—that American strategic superiority did not alter this fundamental political truth.

To change American policy it was necessary to change American conceptions of the Soviet Union through "a striking demonstration of Soviet power." Aleksandr Alekseev reports a revealing conversation with Khrushchev in the latter's Kremlin office in May 1962. In explaining the missile deployment to a small circle of top officials, Khrushchev emphasized the need to defend Cuba. He also spoke of his intention to hold the United States hostage to the threat of nuclear destruction. "Inasmuch as the Americans already have surrounded the Soviet Union with a circle of their military bases and missile installations of various designations, we should repay them in kind, let them try their own medicine, so they can feel what its like to live in the nuclear gun sites."[233]

This was the deeper political purpose of the missiles in Cuba. By making Americans feel vulnerable to nuclear attack, Khrushchev hoped to achieve, in the words of Georgiy Kornienko, a greater degree of "psychological equality" with the United States.[234] As Leonid Zamyatin understood his policy, Khrushchev "thought he could reshape the political outlook in Washington and thereby lay the groundwork for a more equal and cooperative relationship."[235] Khrushchev sent missiles to Cuba to protect against loss, but also to make gains. They were to serve as the catalyst for the détente that he saw as critical to the success of his efforts to transform the Soviet Union economically. Following the missile deployment, Khrushchev intended to launch another peace initiative on Berlin and Germany to pave the way toward Soviet-American rapprochement.[236]

Kennedy and the Ex Comm never seriously considered the possibility that the missiles in Cuba might be a response to the Jupiters.[237] The only senior American official known to have made this connection was Ambassador Harriman. "In my judgment," he wrote the president on 22 October, "Khrushchev has been under great pressure from his military and from the more aggressive group to use Cuba to counter U.S. action and to offset the humiliation to which they consider they have been subjected by nuclear bases close to their borders." This pressure was "aggravated by our placing Jupiter missiles in Turkey."[238] None of the Kennedy principals remember the Harriman memorandum, nor is there any evidence that it influenced the president.[239]

Today, Kennedy officials view the Jupiters differently. McNamara, Rusk, Bundy, and Sorensen all consider the Jupiters to have been provocative and unwise. Kennedy went ahead with the deployment, they maintain, because of his belief that Khrushchev would misinterpret cancellation as lack of resolve. Kennedy worried that restraint on his part would encourage Khrushchev to challenge Western interests in Berlin. In practice, the Jupiter deployment was the catalyst for a more serious challenge.

ACTION AND REACTION

Students of deterrence distinguish between general and immediate deterrence. General deterrence relies on the existing power balance to prevent an adversary from seriously considering a military challenge because of its expected adverse consequences.[240] It is often a country's first line of defense against attack. Leaders resort to the strategy of immediate deterrence only after general deterrence has failed, or when they believe that a more explicit expression of their intent to defend their interests is necessary to buttress general deterrence. If immediate deterrence fails, leaders will find themselves in a crisis, as Kennedy did when American intelligence discovered Soviet missiles in Cuba. General and immediate deterrence represent a progression from a diffuse if real concern about an adversary's intentions to the expectation that a specific interest or commitment is about to be challenged.

Both forms of deterrence assume that adversaries are most likely to resort to force or threatening military deployments when they judge the military balance favorable and question the defender's resolve. General deterrence pays particular importance to the military dimension; it tries to discourage challenges by developing the capability to defend national commitments or inflict unacceptable punishment on an adversary. General deterrence is a long-term strategy. Five-year lead times and longer are common between a decision to develop a weapon and its deployment.

The origins of the missile crisis indicate that general deterrence was provocative rather than preventive. Soviet officials testified that the American strategic buildup, deployment of missiles in Turkey, and assertions of nuclear superiority, made them increasingly insecure. The president viewed these measures as prudent, defensive precautions against perceived Soviet threats. His actions had the unanticipated consequence of convincing Khrushchev of the need to protect the Soviet Union and Cuba from American military and political challenges.

Khrushchev was hardly the innocent victim of American paranoia. His unfounded claims of nuclear superiority and nuclear threats conveyed an enormous sense of threat and were the catalysts of the American strategic buildup and deployment of the Jupiters. Kennedy's decisions to persevere with the Jupiters and inform the Soviet Union about the true state of the strategic balance were the direct consequence of Khrushchev's ultimatum on Berlin. In attempting to intimidate their adversaries, *both* leaders helped to bring about the kind of confrontation they were trying to avoid.

Kennedy later speculated, and Soviet officials have since confirmed, that American efforts to reinforce deterrence encouraged Khrushchev to stiffen his position on Berlin.[241] The action and reaction that linked Berlin and Cuba were part of a larger cycle of insecurity and escalation that reached well back into the 1950s, if not to the beginning of the Cold War. The Soviet

challenge to the West in Berlin in 1959–61 was motivated primarily by Soviet concern about the viability of East Germany and secondarily by Soviet
vulnerability to American nuclear-tipped missiles stationed in Western Europe. The American missiles had been deployed to assuage NATO fears
about the conventional military balance on the central front, made more
acute by the creation of the Warsaw Pact in 1955. The Warsaw Pact, many
Western authorities now believe, represented an attempt by Moscow to consolidate its control over an increasingly restive Eastern Europe.[242]

The Cold War began as a struggle for influence in Central Europe in the
aftermath of Germany's defeat. The superpowers, guided by incompatible
visions of security, sought to incorporate as much of Europe as possible in
their respective spheres of influence when it became apparent that their goals
could not be achieved through collaboration. The division of Europe into
opposing alliance systems that had at their disposal the most advanced conventional and nuclear weapons was a response to the insecurity and fear of
war that the Cold War generated on both sides. General deterrence, initially
a result of superpower tensions, had become by 1960 an important source
of conflict in its own right.

Missiles to Cuba: Domestic Politics

*I am a child of two epochs. One man inside me
understood something and the other shouted something
completely different.*

—Nikita S. Khrushchev[1]

By 1962, Khrushchev was extremely frustrated by the apparent failure of many of his key domestic programs. To sweep away the obstacles that he believed stood in the way of their success, he took dramatic and risky action. The missile deployment was one of these actions; its most important purpose was to compel the United States toward a political accommodation with the Soviet Union. An accommodation would strengthen Khrushchev's hand at home and free scarce economic resources for agricultural and industrial development. The first part of the chapter examines the domestic context of the missile deployment and the links between Khrushchev's domestic and foreign policy.

The chapter goes on to assess the relative importance of domestic and foreign objectives in Khrushchev's decision to send missiles to Cuba. Even the most cursory analysis indicates that Khrushchev's foreign policy was poorly conceived; his objectives were incompatible with one another and with a missile deployment. These contradictions are partially explained by Khrushchev's need to respond to diverse problems. They also reflect deeper contradictions within Soviet society that Khrushchev was unwilling to recognize and incapable of addressing.

DOMESTIC POLITICS AND MISSILES IN CUBA

The son of impoverished peasants, Khrushchev had grown up in a small village and worked in a coal-mining town in the Donets Basin. He joined the Communist Party after the revolution and rose rapidly through the ranks of the local and regional Party organizations. In 1938, he became Stalin's viceroy in the Ukraine where he gained a reputation as an efficient and innovative administrator who had a serious interest in agriculture. Yugoslav communist Milovan Djilas, who visited the Ukraine shortly after the war, observed that Khrushchev was the only leader who "openly brought out shortcomings" of the collective farms and examined the "daily life of the Communist rank and file and the citizenry."[2]

After Stalin's death, Khrushchev triumphed over his most immediate rival for power, Georgiy Malenkov, by opposing reductions in defense spending and negotiations with the West.[3] His opposition gained him the support of conservatives who helped to remove Malenkov from the leadership. Khrushchev then reversed himself and adopted some of Malenkov's policies. Claiming that nuclear weapons had revolutionized modern warfare, he reduced the size of the armed forces and repudiated the Leninist-Stalinist line that war between opposing social systems was "fatalistically inevitable." In its place, Khrushchev proclaimed the doctrine of "peaceful coexistence" that looked forward to a peaceful worldwide evolution toward socialism. The unassailable strength of the socialist camp would deter imperialist aggression.[4]

On the domestic front, Khrushchev presented himself as a radical reformer who sought to revitalize agriculture, make industry more efficient, and produce more consumer goods for the masses. Agriculture was a disaster; it had been nearly destroyed by Stalin's forced collectivization of the 1930s and the years of bad management that had followed. The 1953 harvest produced less than half the grain of 1913, the last prewar and prerevolutionary growing season. Livestock also remained below prerevolutionary levels. The food-distribution system was so primitive that a significant percentage of every year's meager harvest rotted before reaching market.[5]

Khrushchev openly condemned the Party's "lordly and bureaucratic attitude toward the village." Many officials, he charged, were ignorant of the details of farming and unresponsive to local needs and advice; they were the principal impediment to agricultural progress. Khrushchev tried to restructure the Party's relationship to the peasantry. He decentralized authority by abolishing Machine Tractor Stations and distributing their machinery to collective and state farms. He called for the formation of local organizations to propose initiatives from below and to put pressure on the Party to respond.[6] In industry, too, he hoped to combat inefficient and debilitating "rule by fiat" and "commandism" through broadened political participation and decentralization of authority.[7]

At the same time that he encouraged local initiative, Khrushchev sought to reform the Party through successive purges. Careerists were to be replaced by younger, more dedicated "idealists" who would transform the Party into a vehicle for progress. Khrushchev never articulated a concept of the institutional evolution of the Soviet Union, but he seems to have anticipated "a withering of the state process" and a sharp reduction in police and management functions. The Party would remain and probably expand in size because of its critical role in managing a modern economy.[8]

De-Stalinization was the centerpiece of Khrushchev's populist strategy. His dramatic exposé of the crimes of Stalin and the rehabilitation of millions of Stalin's victims were intended to undermine the legitimacy of Khrushchev's opponents and encourage an increasingly critical public attitude toward the "bosses" who stood in the way of change. Like Mikhail Gorbachev a generation later, Khrushchev cultivated the image of himself as a pragmatic problem solver who would stimulate productivity and economic growth by mobilizing the masses. Those around him believe that he "saw his own destiny as that of giving peace and prosperity to the Soviet people."[9] His memoirs and casual conversations bespoke this concern.[10]

There was also an element of political calculation in Khrushchev's attack on Stalin. For several years, he adroitly exploited the discontent of newly mobilized intellectuals and Party activists to intimidate his opponents and keep his rivals off balance by shifting the popular agenda to suit his political needs. The younger party secretaries, whose rise to prominence Khrushchev encouraged, had little if any direct involvement in Stalin's crimes. They were natural allies in Khrushchev's fight against the old guard.[11]

Khrushchev's break with Stalinism at home and abroad was an enormous gamble. If his policies succeeded, the Soviet economy would grow stronger and more efficient. Détente with the West would free scarce capital, material resources, and labor for economic development. Khrushchev's political standing would be correspondingly enhanced. His policies were anathema to a substantial majority of the upper levels of the Party and government. Conservatives, military officers, and other officials with a vested interest in the Cold War, were strongly opposed to any opening to the West and the institutional and budgetary changes that came in its wake.[12] In December 1959, Khrushchev created a new branch of the armed forces, the Strategic Rocket Forces (SRF), to emphasize his growing reliance on nuclear deterrence. Two months later, he used his burgeoning détente with Eisenhower to justify a one-third reduction in the Soviet armed forces.[13] Together with his political rivals, many leading military officials were ready to exploit any of Khrushchev's failures to undermine his authority.[14]

Khrushchev's attempt to explore the possibilities of a limited accommodation with the West also provoked the uncompromising ideological hostility of Soviet conservatives. They ridiculed the notion that the capitalists could have any serious interest in improving relations with the Soviet Union. The People's Republic of China voiced the same criticism. The Chinese leadership excoriated Khrushchev's doctrine of "peaceful coexistence" and charged that Eisenhower would exploit his gullibility to the detriment of the entire socialist camp.[15]

According to Aleksei Adzhubei, Khrushchev was willing to run the risks of détente because he was convinced that President Eisenhower was sincere in his professions of good will toward the Soviet Union. Khrushchev distinguished between Eisenhower, whom he described as "an honorable man," and his administration's unpalatable policies. These he attributed to the Rasputin-like influence of John Foster Dulles.[16] In his memoirs, Khrushchev says that his initial high regard for Eisenhower was in part due to Stalin, who spoke frequently "about Eisenhower's noble characteristics" in conversations with his inner circle. Stalin, had "always stressed Eisenhower's decency, generosity, and chivalry in his dealings with his allies."[17]

The Spirit of Camp David

Khrushchev's opening to the West was initially reciprocated. Cold War tensions eased, and President Eisenhower invited him to visit the United States. Khrushchev remembered his sense of elation—and also his foreboding—on the eve of his departure. He was troubled by Eisenhower's decision to receive him at Camp David, a place neither he nor the Soviet embassy had heard about before. "One reason I was suspicious," Khrushchev confessed, "was that I remembered in the early years after the Revolution when contacts were first being established with the bourgeois world, a Soviet delegation was invited to a meeting held someplace called the Prince's Islands. It came out in the newspaper that it was to these islands that stray dogs were sent to die. . . . I was afraid maybe this Camp David was the same sort of place, where people who were mistrusted could be kept in quarantine." Upon his arrival in the United States, he was greatly relieved to be received with full honors and delighted to discover that it was a sign of special favor to be invited to Camp David.[18]

This passage is one of many in Khrushchev's memoirs that reveals his acute concern about avoiding humiliation. His concern seems to have had both personal and political roots. As the peasant leader of a quasi-pariah socialist country, he was doubly insecure in his dealings with the West and its more worldly and seemingly self-confident leaders.[19] On many occasions, his insecurity led him to infer insults when none were intended. Before coming to the United States, he worried about being received with the proper protocol. Although reassured by the American ambassador that he would be treated as a head of state, Khrushchev still fretted about discrimination he might encounter. He admitted to being "very sensitive" on this score and unwilling to tolerate "even a hint of anti-Sovietism."[20]

The other face of Khrushchev's insecurity was his desire for approval and delight in acceptance. He was particularly responsive to flattering and gracious treatment. Egyptian journalist Muhammad Haykal remembers that Khrushchev was so overwhelmed by his regal welcome in Cairo that "there were tears in his eyes."[21] He was equally thrilled by his red-carpet treatment in Washington and the many courtesies extended to him in the United States. "It made me immensely proud; it even shook me up a bit." Standing on the podium at Andrews Air Force Base, the Soviet visitors "felt pride in our country, our Party, our people, and the victories they had achieved. We had transformed Russia into a highly developed country."[22]

Khrushchev regarded his visit as a "colossal moral victory" for socialism.[23] "Who would have guessed," he told his Kremlin colleagues, "that the most powerful capitalist country would invite a Communist to visit? This is incredible. Today they *have* to take us into account. It's our strength that led to this—they have to recognize our existence and our power. Who would have thought the capitalists would invite me, a worker? Look what we've achieved in these years."[24]

Khrushchev was deeply moved when "Ike" called him "my friend."[25] On his arrival home, he treated the crowd at the airport to a rambling description of his trip that was full of praise for the American president. Khrushchev described in detail his visit to the Eisenhower farm, how he had "made friends with the President's grandchildren," and learned of their desire to visit Russia. "Eisenhower sincerely wanted to liquidate the Cold War and improve relations between our two countries" but, he warned, "not all Americans think like Eisenhower." Powerful interests in the United States "want to continue the Cold War and the arms race." It was not clear "whether the forces supporting the President can win."[26]

Camp David and the limited détente it symbolized paved the way to a four-power summit and Khrushchev's invitation to President Eisenhower to visit the Soviet Union. The Soviet media mobilized public support for the president and the spirit of Camp David. This was hardly necessary; casual discussion with Russians indicated enormous enthusiasm for Eisenhower and the prospect of a thaw in East-West relations. "Wherever I went in Russia," *Newsweek*'s correspondent wrote, "the ordinary folk have been filled with great expectations by the Eisenhower-Khrushchev talks. And they give the credit for what they believe is a great change in the Cold War to Nikita Khrushchev. Make no mistake about it. Khrushchev has never been so popular in the U.S.S.R."[27]

On the Defensive

Khrushchev was out of the Soviet Union for the better part of February and March 1960 and did not return to Moscow until 3 April. In his absence, opposition forces in the Party, KGB, and military were in close contact and prepared to confront Khrushchev with their demand that he end his search for détente with the United States.

Between 4 and 9 April, Khrushchev's foreign policy was subjected to stinging criticism in the Presidium. Defense Minister Rodion Malinovsky objected to the troop reductions he had pushed through the Presidium in January, arguing that they would be interpreted as weakness in the West. KGB Chairman Aleksandr N. Shelepin charged that Khrushchev's encouragement of free thinking would lead people to reject communism. Other Presidium members complained that the relaxation in international tensions ushered in by Camp David had aroused false expectations that the Cold War would end and allow greater liberalization at home.[28]

Khrushchev's adversaries returned to their earlier accusation that détente with the West was doomed to failure. They pointed to the recent statements by Western leaders that suggested unwillingness to compromise on Berlin. For Khrushchev and other Soviet leaders, the key issue in East-West relations was Germany and the status of its former capital. At Camp David, where Khrushchev and Eisenhower agreed to the Paris summit, that troubled and divided city was at the top of their agenda. During the fall and winter of 1959–1960, Khrushchev defended his foreign policy on the grounds that it would lead to progress on Berlin. However, opposition from West German Chancellor Konrad Adenauer compelled a frustrated Eisenhower to adopt a more uncompromising position on Berlin. Soviet leaders were apprised of this shift by the KGB, who learned about it from their well-placed moles in the government of the Federal Republic of Germany.[29]

Khrushchev understood that he was isolated and vulnerable. On 9 April, his situation was made even more difficult by the successful overflight of the Soviet Union by an American U-2 reconnaissance aircraft. Early that morning, the U-2 had taken off from Peshawar, Pakistan and had flown a northeasterly course to the city of Semipalatinsk and then west over two of the Soviet Union's most important missile test sites at Sary Shagan and Baykonur before turning south and back to it base at Peshawar.[30]

The United States had been sending U-2s on intelligence missions over the Soviet Union since July 1956. Soviet leaders had fumed quietly about the violation of their air space and their inability to bring down these high-flying spy planes. *PVO Strany*, the air-defense command, had standing orders to shoot down any U-2s that overflew the Soviet Union and had recently been provided with the new SA-2 missile, designed for that purpose. On 9 April, at 4:47 A.M. local time, the U-2 was picked up by Soviet radar 250 kilometers into Soviet air space en route to Semipalatinsk. High-altitude fighter aircraft were scrambled but required instructions from the air base at Semipalatinsk to vector them to their target. The existence of this base was officially secret, and the request for the fighters to make radio contact and land at the base had to be approved by Moscow. By the time this authorization came, the U-2 was long out of range. At Sary Shagan, there was an SA-2 battery, but the commander of the battery and his troops were away from their posts attending a political course on Marxism-Leninism. The U-2 then passed over the SA-2 test site at Baykonur, but no launches were planned that day and all the missiles were in storage almost 100 kilometers away.[31]

Khrushchev was "completely beyond himself in rage." In October 1959, he had asked the West to "take no action" before the summit that would "worsen the atmosphere" and "sow the seeds of suspicion." Instead, the United States had given his domestic adversaries the opportunity to intensify their criticism. Khrushchev speculated that perhaps the plane had been sent on its provocative mission by the CIA and American military without the president's knowledge.[32]

On 10 April, Khrushchev left Moscow for a "holiday" at Gagra on the Black Sea. He remained out of the public eye for two weeks. His whereabouts were announced only on 20 April, an unusual time lag for the Soviet press of the time. He failed to return to Moscow for the long-planned celebration of the ninetieth anniversary of Lenin's birth on 22 April.[33] Soviet sources report that Khrushchev remained almost alone at Gagra, out of communication with Moscow, in a foul mood, and planning his next move.

Khrushchev emerged from his isolation on 25 April to make a long speech in Baku. In a veiled reference to the U-2, he expressed "alarm" at the strikingly "negative aspects" of Western policy in recent weeks. Soviet foreign policy, he left no doubt, would also become more intransigent. He rejected the disarmament plan the Western powers had recently tabled in Geneva and reverted to a much harder line on Berlin. He warned that the Soviet Union would sign a separate peace treaty with East Germany if the four-power negotiations failed and the West would lose its access to Berlin "by land, water, or air." The speech was widely regarded as Khrushchev's toughest in several months.[34]

Events at home and abroad compelled Khrushchev to abandon, at least for the time being, his policy of accommodation with the West. His speech in Baku was the opening salvo of a new, harsher line. It was intended to send a strong message to militants in Washington and to his critics in the Presidium. Upon his return to Moscow, Khrushchev instructed Foreign Minister Gromyko to have his Berlin task force prepare for renewed confrontation.[35]

On the day Khrushchev delivered his Baku speech, CIA Director Allen Dulles and Deputy Director of Plans Richard Bissell convinced Eisenhower to send another U-2 over the Soviet Union to photograph Plesetsk, where intelligence sources indicated the first operational ICBMs were being deployed.[36] That flight, on May Day 1960, was brought down by Soviet air defenses over Sverdlovsk (now Ekaterinburg), in Central Russia.

Col. Gen. Georgiy Mikhailov, a former staff officer of *PVO Strany*, reports that several missiles were fired at the U-2. The first exploded near the high-flying plane and caused it to lose altitude. The pilot, Francis Gary Powers, bailed out. The second missile hit the descending U-2. The third missile destroyed a Soviet MiG-19 that had been scrambled to intercept the American plane. Colonel Mikhailov and his colleagues were dumbfounded when they saw the quality of the pictures produced by the U-2's cameras; they had nothing remotely as good.[37]

The United States at first denied that it had engaged in spying and then reversed itself when the Soviets showed journalists the remains of the aircraft. What made Khrushchev apoplectic was the Associated Press bulletin on 9 May announcing that the U-2 had been sent "under President Eisenhower's general orders" and the suggestion that "such flights may continue until Soviet leaders open their borders to inspection."[38] Khrushchev was convinced that the flight was "an affront orchestrated by the president himself."[39] "By sending a plane on an espionage mission," he told journalists, "the American militarists have placed me, the man responsible for arranging the visit of the United States President to the USSR, in a very difficult position."[40]

The downing of the U-2 and Eisenhower's response acutely embarrassed Khrushchev. Soviet militants affirmed their earlier warnings that Eisenhower's interest in rapprochement was insincere. Mao Tse-Tung expressed the pious hope that the U-2 would wake up "certain people" who harbored the illusion that Eisenhower was a "lover of peace."[41] At a reception in Moscow, Khrushchev dragged American Ambassador Llewellyn Thompson into a side room and complained to him that "This U-2 thing has put me in a terrible spot. You have got to get me off it."[42]

Under heavy criticism for his policy of accommodation, Khrushchev used the U-2 incident to retract his invitation to Eisenhower to visit the Soviet Union and to justify confrontation at the Paris summit.[43] At the opening session of the summit, on 15 May, and at a press conference the following day, Khrushchev bitterly criticized the United States, its policy of aerial spying, and the president's connivance with the CIA. The summit collapsed and with it, the "spirit of Camp David."

Economic Problems

Khrushchev's economic reforms were also running into serious difficulty and mounting criticism.[44] The Virgin Lands program was becoming expensive and increasingly unproductive. Collective and state farm output was decreasing. Low prices for meat and dairy products failed to compensate collective farms for the cost of production and encouraged them to slaughter their cattle and withhold their produce from the market. In the industrial sector, the growth of heavy industry slowed, and the growth of light industry and the rate of capital investment came to a halt. Inflationary pressures triggered worker riots in the fall and winter of 1959–1960.[45]

Confronted with failure at home and abroad, Khrushchev underwent a sharp change of mood in 1960. His earlier predictions of economic bounty were replaced by a somber pessimism. He retreated from his commitment to light industry and consumer goods and called for more investment in heavy industry and agriculture. He allocated more funds to the Virgin Lands program and increased his pressure on local cadres to adopt low-cost but unrealistic agricultural practices. He intensified his purge of regional party organizations and sought to establish greater central control; in 1960–1961, he retired almost 40 percent of the Party's professionals. Through doctrinal changes and rhetoric he tried to intensify the conflict between local party officials and the masses.

Soviet military and foreign policy underwent a parallel shift in 1960–1961. To placate his opponents, Khrushchev reluctantly suspended the previously announced commitment to reduce the Soviet armed forces by one-third.[46] He also temporarily retreated from his preference for minimal deterrence in favor of the combined arms offensive to which most of the military was committed.[47] His economic programs required a reduction in international tension, but Eisenhower's response to the U-2 ruled out the possibility of détente. Khrushchev was also under mounting pressure from militants to display uncompromising toughness to the capitalist world. His bellicose rhetoric and rocket rattling, challenges to the Western position in Berlin, and resumption of nuclear testing were a response to this pressure. The return of the Cold War was a sign of Khrushchev's weakness, not of Soviet strength, as Kennedy and his advisors supposed.[48] According to Castro, Khrushchev continued to be obsessed by the goal of accommodation. "He was constantly talking about this, constantly talking about peace, constantly talking about negotiations with the United States, trying to do away with the Cold War, with the arms race and so on."[49]

Missiles to the Rescue

Khrushchev's response to his mounting domestic and foreign problems had been largely ineffective. The structural problems bedeviling Soviet agriculture and industry could not be solved by political mobilization and party purges; they also antagonized the cadres upon whom he ultimately depended for support. Intensified confrontation with the West brought an equally negative return; it exacerbated American anxieties and prompted Kennedy's accelerated strategic buildup, which the Soviet Union found very costly to match. Khrushchev would now resort to more intense intimidation. He would send missiles to Cuba to coerce the United States into making an accommodation with the Soviet Union.

From 1960 on, Khrushchev was a leader on the defensive who responded in increasingly impulsive and ineffective ways to the deepening crisis. He grew bitter and more authoritarian toward his colleagues, presenting them with one fait accompli after another.[50] In domestic and foreign policy he was drawn to grand and risky ventures that held out the prospect of recouping his losses and preserving his authority. "With things still going poorly," his son admits, "Khrushchev grasped at straws."[51] None of these initiatives were carefully thought through or implemented with proper supervision and care. They led to the major policy failures that precipitated his removal from power in October 1964.[52]

Khrushchev's most ambitious domestic initiative was the costly expansion of the Virgin Lands program. In 1954, he had convinced the collective leadership that the country's agricultural problems could be alleviated by cultivating unused lands in Siberia and Kazakhstan that had been left "to the rabbits and wild goats." The government authorized the planting of over 70 million acres of new land, a goal that was exceeded in the course of the next several years. The program made sense as a short-term measure designed to boost grain output for a few years to buy time to reform and modernize Soviet agriculture.[53] In 1958, Khrushchev boasted that within three years the Soviet Union would overtake the United States in the production of meat and milk, and would be able to buy all its grain from collective farms at a cheaper price.[54]

The first harvests were encouraging, although production per acre was well below that of traditional areas. The initial success was due in large part to exceptionally good weather that facilitated a bumper crop in 1958. Agronomists advised Khrushchev against overreliance on the new lands because of their vulnerability to windstorms and extreme variations in temperature and rainfall. Critics warned that successive yearly planting would exhaust the thin top soil and bring inhospitable alkaline soil to the surface. Continuous cropping and insufficient fallow could turn whole provinces into giant dust bowls.

Khrushchev brushed aside these criticisms and dramatically expanded the scope of the program in the autumn of 1961. He called for the intensive cultivation with spring wheat of another 27 million acres of new land. The program was carried out at enormous cost to investment in traditional agriculture. As critics had predicted, output steadily declined in the new lands and also fell off in the "black earth" region of the Ukraine, the country's bread basket, because funds for fertilizer and irrigation had been siphoned off to pay for Khrushchev's experiment. In 1963, there was a catastrophic crop failure and the Soviet Union was forced to import grain from abroad at great expense.[55]

The missile deployment was the international analogue of the Virgin Lands expansion.[56] Beyond its immediate objectives, the missile deployment, like the Virgin Lands program, was an attempt by an increasingly frustrated leader to preserve his domestic programs and ultimately, his political authority. Chapter 4 documents how the planning and implementation of the missile deployment were characterized by the same impulsive emotional commitment and disregard for professional advice that led to disaster in the Virgin Lands.

Both policy initiatives were quintessential Khrushchev. He spurned incrementalism in favor of radical solutions. In response to setbacks, he pushed ahead with even more dramatic and risky policies that held out the prospect of enormous gain—and risked equally staggering loss. De-Stalinization, the Virgin Lands program, the chemical industry expansion, and the challenge to the West in Berlin all had these characteristics. They required the coercion of foreign adversaries or domestic opponents and, when they failed, made Khrushchev vulnerable to charges of authoritarianism.[57]

Reinforcing Objectives?

Knowledgeable Soviets disagree about the relative importance of the foreign-policy motives that prompted the missile deployment. Sergei Khrushchev, Georgiy Kornienko, Aleksandr Alekseev, and Sergo Mikoyan, maintain that, above all, Khrushchev acted to protect Cuba from invasion. Fidel Castro, Georgiy Shakhnazarov, and Dimitri Volkogonov are convinced that his primary concern was to redress the strategic imbalance. Aleksei Adzhubei and Leonid Zamyatin contend that Khrushchev was intent on achieving "psychological equality" to compel a fundamental shift in American foreign policy.

Khrushchev is probably responsible for this divergence of opinion. He was anxious to build support for the missile deployment and is likely to have used different arguments with different people. "He was very astute," Castro observed. "He was capable of talking about an issue in one set of terms, while thinking about it in other terms."[58]

Sergo Mikoyan's information comes largely secondhand from his father. The elder Mikoyan was deeply involved in Soviet-Cuban relations and was Khrushchev's special emissary to Fidel Castro. He was committed to defending Cuba from American attack but was dubious about the feasibility and consequences of a secret missile deployment.[59] In speaking to him, and to Ambassador Alekseev, Khrushchev would almost certainly have stressed the deterrent value of the missiles and his concern for Cuban security.

Because of his military background and access to documents in the Ministry of Defense archives, Gen. Volkogonov is more sensitive to the military problem posed by American strategic superiority in 1962. Defense Minister Malinovsky and Marshal Sergei S. Biryuzov, the recently appointed commander of the SRF, favored the installation of missiles in Cuba because they were anxious to reduce Soviet strategic vulnerability. In speaking to the military, Khrushchev would have emphasized this objective to enlist their support.

As editor of *Izvestiya* and political confidant of his father-in-law, Adzhubei was privy to many of Khrushchev's thoughts about foreign and domestic policy. It is not surprising that he has a different understanding of Khrushchev's motives, one that emphasizes the links between foreign and domestic policy and the broader political objectives the missile deployment was intended to serve.

It is possible, even likely, that Khrushchev made no effort to evaluate the relative importance of the diverse objectives he sought, since he regarded them as mutually reinforcing. We can nevertheless speculate that his first priority was to rescue his domestic reforms; he was deeply committed to them, personally and politically. He saw détente as critical to the success of his domestic program, and all three of his foreign-policy objectives were intended to facilitate détente by convincing the Kennedy administration that the Soviet Union was a superpower deserving of respect.[60]

Many American students of the crisis have imputed far-reaching offensive objectives to Khrushchev.[61] They surmise that the missiles were intended to undermine NATO, foster communist revolution in Latin America, and compel Western concessions in Berlin. Soviet officials insist that Khrushchev envisaged the missile deployment as a purely defensive action. Adzhubei admits that Khrushchev found the Berlin problem "extraordinarily irritating," but he does not believe that it motivated his decision to send missiles to Cuba.[62] Andrei Gromyko contends that there was no direct connection between the deployment of the missiles and Germany.[63]

Soviet officials contend that Khrushchev wanted to keep Cuba well-insulated from Berlin. The morning after Kennedy announced the blockade, East German leader Walter Ulbricht reportedly telephoned Khrushchev to suggest that he make American recognition of East Germany a condition for withdrawal of the missiles from Cuba. Khrushchev rejected this request, much to Ulbricht's annoyance.[64] Later that day, First Deputy of Foreign Affairs Vasiliy A. Kuznetsov suggested that Khrushchev respond to the American pressure on Cuba with Soviet pressure in Berlin. "Khrushchev replied quite harshly, saying that we did not need that kind of advice."[65]

The secret missile deployment that was considered offensive by the Americans was regarded as defensive by the Soviets. Soviet officials who agree that the missiles represented a serious challenge to the Kennedy administration contend that undeniably coercive means were intended to advance legitimate, defensive purposes.[66] In 1961, Khrushchev told representatives of the British Labour Party that the Soviet decision to resume testing was meant "to shock the Western powers into negotiations over Germany and disarmament."[67] Some Soviet officials maintain that this was also a primary objective of Khrushchev's challenges to the West in Berlin in 1959 and 1961.[68] Even though Khrushchev's goals were defensive, the relationship between the ends he sought and the means he chose was fraught with contradiction.

CONTRADICTIONS

Foreign-policy analysts expect statesmen to have consistent preferences and to choose policies most likely to advance their preferences. Khrushchev violated both these expectations. He did not choose the appropriate means, given his ends, nor did he recognize the contradictions among his objectives. The missile deployment threatened some of his most important foreign-policy goals. It was a singularly inappropriate means of advancing his proclaimed objectives. The secret deployment of missiles raised rather than lowered the risks of an American invasion of Cuba. It was also illusory for Khrushchev to believe that a missile deployment would compel the United States to move toward détente.

Castro insisted that Cuba could have been best protected by conventional forces. Marshal Malinovsky rejected the feasibility of defense with conventional forces; he contended that American forces could overrun Cuba in a matter of days.[69] Malinovsky may have overestimated American military capability—the Pentagon expected a more prolonged and costly struggle. More important, Khrushchev discounted, or failed to consider, the deterrent role of Soviet conventional forces in Cuba. Even if he doubted the efficacy of conventional defense, he could have tried to exploit the deterrent value of Soviet conventional forces.

When the Kennedy administration sent additional forces to Berlin in response to Khrushchev's ultimatum, it publicized the arrival of reinforcements. The purpose was to reassure West Berliners that the United States was committed to their defense, but also to send a political message to Moscow about American resolve to defend Berlin. Khrushchev believed that Kennedy was as committed as he was to avoiding a superpower war; he should have reasoned that the planned forty-five-thousand (actual forty-two-thousand) Soviet forces in Cuba, many more troops than the West maintained in Berlin, would have served as an effective "tripwire" deterrent.[70] A tripwire strategy would have required fewer forces and would have put significantly less pressure on Kennedy to respond. By shrouding the conventional deployment in Cuba in secrecy, Khrushchev sacrificed whatever deterrent value this forty-two-thousand-man force might have possessed.

An even more serious contradiction is that in the short term—and that is what mattered to Castro and Khrushchev—the missiles were irrelevant to deterrence. In his memoirs, Khrushchev acknowledged he was in a great hurry to deploy the missiles "because we expected there was not much time before the Americans repeated their invasion."[71] Cuban and Soviet intelligence agencies predicted that an American attack was most likely to come in September or October 1962; afterward, the probability of invasion would decline.[72] Khrushchev was advised that the danger was greatest in the late summer. On 15 October, the day before Kennedy announced the discovery of missiles in Cuba, Khrushchev told Finnish President Urho Kekkonen that he had expected the United States to invade in late August or early September, but now believed there would be no attack.[73]

The first missiles in Cuba did not achieve emergency operational capability until the middle of October and were not expected to be fully operational until sometime in December. If all had gone according to plan, the Americans would have been informed of the missiles in the middle of November, well *after* the invasion threat had peaked. The missiles could not possibly have deterred an attack in September and October if their presence was unknown to the Kennedy administration![74]

Under these conditions, the missiles were a dangerous liability to the Soviet Union and Cuba because American military action against Cuba could have unwittingly triggered a nuclear war. Had the United States attacked in late October, thinking it would meet opposition only from conventional forces, many of the missiles would have been operational and some might have been armed with nuclear warheads.[75] Depending on the command and control procedures in effect, missile crews about to be overrun could have received orders—or acted on their own authority—to launch their weapons against the United States. The destruction of one or more American cities would have generated enormous pressure on the president for a massive retaliatory strike against the Soviet Union.

Reality could have emulated fiction. In Stanley Kubrick's 1964 movie, *Dr. Strangelove*, the Soviet Union perfects a doomsday device in the form of "dirty" bombs designed to explode automatically and poison the planet's atmosphere with radiation if the Soviet Union is attacked. Moscow's objective is to deter an American attack by making it suicidal. The doomsday machine cannot be disabled; otherwise it would lack credibility. Soviet leaders make a fatal error: they turn on the device *before* they notify Washington of its existence. B-52 bombers from the Strategic Air Command attack the Soviet Union because of an error in their "Fail-Safe" system, and the world is destroyed. Like Kubrick's Russians, Khrushchev could have paid a tragic price for weapons that he had sent to Cuba. As long as they were unknown to the Americans, they had no deterrent value, only the potential to destroy Cuba and the Soviet Union.

If we relax or abandon the assumptions that Khrushchev chose policies most likely to achieve his preferences, and that his preferences were consistent, we can better understand his behavior. Cognitive psychologists argue that human beings tend to avoid "trade-offs" among important values. Rather than recognize that one policy may advance important objectives at the expense of other valued goals, people are more likely to see their choices as supportive of all their objectives. As they move toward a decision, they may alter some of their earlier expectations or establish new estimates to strengthen the case for their preferred course of action.[76]

The failure to recognize trade-offs leads advocates of a policy to advance multiple, independent, and mutually reinforcing arguments in its favor. They become convinced that the policy in question is not only preferable to other alternatives but that it can achieve all their goals. Opponents similarly attack a policy as ill-considered in all its consequences. Ordering cognitions in this way helps people to make difficult or costly choices because nothing need be sacrificed. The world is rarely as neatly ordered or benign. Important decisions almost always involve conflict among values, sometimes requiring major trade-offs.

Khrushchev's decision reflects this kind of cognitive blindness. Not only was his choice of a missile deployment inconsistent with his objectives, but his objectives were contradictory. Khrushchev was moved by foreign-policy interests to defend Cuba, by strategic considerations to develop a second-strike capability, by domestic circumstances to seek détente, and by his emotions to seek revenge. Revenge and détente were contradictory, but Khrushchev convinced himself that all these goals were compatible. In the face of contrary predictions by his experts on the United States, he persuaded himself that the missiles could be the catalyst for détente.[77] Psychological research suggests that people are most likely to deny trade-offs when their competing objectives are extremely important.[78] Khrushchev was caught in precisely this kind of dilemma.

Khrushchev's decision to send missiles to Cuba was not an isolated instance of cognitive distortion. His policy toward Cuba was also inconsistent with his broader goal of détente. Communist Cuba had become a thorn in the side of the United States and a highly charged foreign-policy issue for most Americans. Khrushchev's support of Castro angered Americans across the political spectrum and generated pressure on the Kennedy administration to pursue a more militant policy toward both Cuba and the Soviet Union. The highly visible Soviet military presence in Cuba added insult to injury. Khrushchev had important reasons for wanting to support Cuba, but he could not do so *and* hope to improve relations with the United States.

Khrushchev's foreign policy was riddled with contradictions. His primary objective was clear: accommodation with the West based on the recognition of the Soviet Union's coequal status as a superpower. However, many of his most prominent actions—the ultimatums to the West on Germany, the construction of the Berlin Wall, and support of revolutionary forces in the Third World—made this goal more difficult to achieve. These actions were prompted by other goals and needs. The ultimatums on Berlin and the Wall were attempts to save East Germany and defuse militant critics in Moscow. Increased aid to the "progressive forces" of the world was intended to spread Soviet influence to new regions and to demonstrate the Soviet Union's bona fides as a revolutionary power in its struggle with China for the loyalty of the world's communist parties.

Khrushchev failed to think through the implications of his foreign policy. He refused to make trade-offs among competing and contradictory objectives and convinced himself that a policy of confrontation would advance all his goals. He miscalculated badly. His challenge to the West's position in Berlin, the Middle East, and Southeast Asia intensified the Kennedy administration's perception of threat and made it less rather than more willing to compromise on Berlin and other critical issues on Khrushchev's foreign-policy agenda. The missile deployment provoked a war-threatening crisis that ended in a humiliating defeat for the Soviet Union and seriously eroded Khrushchev's authority at home.

Khrushchev's domestic policy was characterized by the same conceptual confusion and inconsistency. He never developed a comprehensive strategy of reform. His political and agricultural reforms were piecemeal and at times contradictory. In the Virgin Lands program and expansion of the chemical industry, he pursued unrealistic objectives that wasted scarce resources and weakened his political standing. His policy of de-Stalinization and mobilization of the masses competed with his insistence on discipline and the primacy of the Communist Party. Khrushchev ultimately chose to impose severe limits on liberalization, even though these restrictions curtailed individual initiative as a creative force for change.

Khrushchev's failure to match means to ends and to make hard choices among ends almost certainly had deeper political and personal causes. His policy objectives, foreign and domestic, were in the last resort incompatible with a Stalinist political system committed to the global advancement of Soviet-style socialism. A product of that system, Khrushchev could not bring himself to do more than criticize and disavow its most egregious excesses.

He was careful to attribute the crimes of Stalin to his personality, not to the Leninist political system that Khrushchev had spent his adult life trying to impose on the country. "Father never took the final step," Sergei Khrushchev admitted; "the stereotypes laid down in the thirties were just too strong."[79]

Intellectually and emotionally, Khrushchev was unprepared to recognize that rigid, authoritarian political and economic structures could not achieve a better-fed and more secure society. In the final analysis, the deployment of missiles in Cuba can best be understood as an illusory attempt to avoid this deeper, underlying contradiction that was far too threatening for Khrushchev to confront.

Why Did Khrushchev Miscalculate?

The Americans are going to have to swallow this the same
way we have had to swallow the pill of the missiles in Turkey.

—Nikita Khrushchev [1]

Khrushchev possessed [a] rich imagination and when some
idea gripped him he was inclined to see in its implementation
an easy solution to a particular problem, a sort of cure-all.

—Oleg Troyanovsky [2]

THIS CHAPTER reconstructs Khrushchev's calculations on the eve of the Cuban missile deployment. It addresses what has always been one of the most puzzling questions about the crisis: why did Khrushchev think that the United States would accept Soviet missile bases in Cuba?

Most Western analysts have argued that Khrushchev went ahead with the deployment because he did not believe that Kennedy would discover the missiles before they were operational or risk war to remove them once they were. We contend that Khrushchev had no good reasons to suppose that Soviet missile bases could be constructed secretly in Cuba, or that the United States would tolerate the missiles. Like many leaders before and since, Khrushchev indulged in wishful thinking. He was driven by political need and anger and wanted to believe that his bold challenge would succeed. Once committed to the deployment, he became insensitive to warnings from Soviet foreign-policy experts that it was likely to provoke a serious confrontation with the United States. Kennedy's attempts at deterrence failed because Khrushchev was blind to American interests and signals.

KENNEDY'S WARNINGS

In the fall of 1962, President Kennedy responded to congressional and public concern that the Soviet Union might send missiles to Cuba with a series of stern warnings. On 4 September, he drew a distinction between "offensive" and "defensive" weapons and put Khrushchev on notice that "the gravest issues" would arise if the United States acquired evidence of "offensive ground-to-ground missiles or of other significant offensive capability either in Cuban hands or under Soviet direction and guidance."[3] On 7 September, he requested and quickly received congressional approval for standby authority to call up one-hundred-fifty-thousand reservists.[4] At a 13 September press conference, he promised to take whatever action was necessary to ensure that no offensive weapons were installed in Cuba.[5]

The president reinforced these public warnings with private messages to the Kremlin. He sought to dissuade Soviet leaders from dismissing his threats as idle campaign rhetoric. On 4 September, Robert Kennedy met with Soviet Ambassador Anatoliy Dobrynin to tell him that his brother would not tolerate offensive weapons in Cuba.[6] Two days later, Theodore Sorensen repeated the message to Dobrynin, adding that in his judgment the November congressional elections would not inhibit the president's freedom of action in foreign policy.[7] Under Secretary of State Chester A. Bowles also stressed Kennedy's resolve to Dobrynin when the two men met on 13 October.[8]

Khrushchev gave every indication that he recognized the American strategic interests and Kennedy's political needs. In April, well before the president's warnings, Khrushchev sent him two reassuring letters. His letter of 22 April could not have been more specific. "We do not have any bases in Cuba," and he declared, "we do not intend to establish any."[9] On 4 September, Ambassador Dobrynin called on Robert Kennedy to relay a confidential promise from Khrushchev not to create any trouble for the United States during the election campaign.[10]

On 11 September, the Soviet government issued an official response to Kennedy's warnings. It made no commitment to refrain from introducing missiles into Cuba—this would have been too abject an act of submission. The statement declared that the Soviet Union had no need to station any retaliatory weapons to defend Cuba.[11] Two days later, Dobrynin explained the Soviet position to Chester Bowles and emphatically denied that his government had any intention of deploying missiles in Cuba.[12]

On 22 October, almost a week after the Americans had discovered the missiles, the administration received another reassuring message, this time from Georgiy N. Bol'shakov, a counselor at the Soviet embassy and managing director of *Soviet Life*. Just back from talks in Moscow with Khrushchev and First Deputy Prime Minister Anastas I. Mikoyan, Bol'shakov conveyed the Soviet leader's personal promise that "no missile capable of reaching the United States would be placed in Cuba."[13] Bol'shakov, a high-level KGB operative, served as an unofficial channel of communication between Kennedy and Khrushchev. Between April 1961 and December 1962, he carried more than forty private letters between the two leaders. The letters addressed a number of delicate issues including Laos, Berlin, and Soviet-American plans for a Vienna summit. Kennedy had come to rely on this back channel and was deeply offended that Khrushchev used a trusted messenger to deceive him.[14]

Public and private Soviet assurances conveyed the impression that Khrushchev understood the gravity of the American warning. However, in May, Khrushchev had decided to send missiles to Cuba. His assurances were designed to lull the Kennedy administration into inaction until the missiles were in situ and operational. They were also intended to provide a political justification for the missiles when Khrushchev announced their presence in Havana in November.

COMPETING EXPLANATIONS

Western scholars have put forward two contrasting explanations for Khrushchev's behavior. The most widely accepted is that Khrushchev was convinced that the missile deployment would succeed because Kennedy lacked the will to oppose it.[15] Proponents of this explanation maintain that Kennedy's youth and personality conveyed the impression of inexperience and indecision, and that his refusal to commit American troops to the faltering Bay of Pigs invasion, his poor performance at the Vienna summit, and his failure to prevent construction of the Berlin Wall, conveyed lack of resolve.[16]

Scholars have also faulted Kennedy's practice of deterrence; they do not believe that he effectively communicated his opposition to Soviet missiles in Cuba. Graham Allison, author of what was for many years the definitive study of the crisis, stressed the low-key nature of Kennedy's warnings, his acceptance of the Soviet conventional buildup in Cuba, and the timing of the president's statements; all this gave the impression that his warnings were aimed at domestic political critics, not the Russians. "Even up to the day of discovery," Allison insisted, "a man in Moscow, listening to the array of messages emanating from Washington, could have had grounds for reasonable doubt about the U.S. government's reactions."[17]

The charge that Kennedy's vacillation encouraged Khrushchev to send missiles to Cuba originated with the president. From the moment he assumed office, Kennedy worried about his reputation for resolve. He confided his concern to friendly journalists. Elie Abel, then with the National Broadcasting Company, recalled a conversation with the president in September 1961, just after the Berlin Wall went up. Abel declared his interest in writing a book about the president's first year in office. Kennedy discouraged him. "Who would want to read about disasters?" After the Bay of Pigs and the Berlin wall, Khrushchev probably thought him a "pushover."[18] During the Berlin crisis, Kennedy voiced the same concern to James Wechsler of the *New York Post*. He worried "that Khrushchev might interpret his reluctance to wage nuclear war as a symptom of an American loss of nerve." The time might come, he told Wechsler, that he would have to run "the supreme risk" to convince Khrushchev that conciliation did not mean humiliation. "If Khrushchev wants to rub my nose in the dirt, it's all over."[19]

The president's concern for his reputation was shared by his advisors and shaped their understanding of the missile deployment. Theodore Sorensen reports that the favored theory of the Ex Comm was that the missiles were a test of America's will:

> Khrushchev believed that the American people were too timid to risk nuclear war and too concerned with legalisms to justify any distinction between our overseas missile bases and his—that once we were actually confronted with the missiles we would do nothing but protest—that we would thereby appear weak and irresolute to the world, causing our allies to doubt our word and to seek accommodations with the Soviets, and permitting increased communist sway in Latin America in particular.[20]

The president also thought in these terms. In his nationally televised address proclaiming the naval "quarantine" of Cuba, he told the American people that the missiles represented a challenge that had to be answered "if our courage and commitments are ever to be trusted again by friend or foe."[21]

An alternative explanation for the missile deployment also starts from the premise that Khrushchev erred in his judgment. But it shifts the onus for that miscalculation from Kennedy to Khrushchev. Because the Soviet leader regarded the missile deployment as the only means of coping with serious strategic and political threats, he deluded himself that it would succeed. He became correspondingly insensitive to information that indicated he was courting disaster.[22]

Were the reasons attributed to Khrushchev by the first interpretation plausible? The evidence suggests that Kennedy's age, performance in Vienna, and decision not to commit American troops to the Bay of Pigs, gave no reasonable grounds for doubting the president's resolve.[23]

The myth has grown up that Khrushchev did not take Kennedy seriously because of his youth.[24] Ambassador Dobrynin's predecessor in Washington, Mikhail Menshikov, was struck by the youthful appearance of both Kennedy brothers and referred to them as "boys in short trousers" in at least one of his cables to Moscow. A hardliner who wanted Khrushchev to pursue a more militant policy toward the United States, Menshikov routinely dismissed Kennedy's warnings as mere bravado.[25]

Khrushchev did comment on Kennedy's age on several occasions during the Vienna summit, but never suggested that his youth implied weakness.[26] Khrushchev's remarks indicate that he may have viewed Kennedy as less predictable, less compromising, and more concerned with establishing a reputation for himself than an older president would have been. During the missile crisis, he told American businessman William Knox that the blockade was an act of "hysteria." "The president was a very young man," younger than his son. He "was confident that Eisenhower would have done things differently."[27]

The widely credited story that Khrushchev took Kennedy's measure in Vienna and found him wanting originated with James Reston of the *New York Times*. Three-and-a-half years after the summit, he proposed it as an explanation for the Soviet decision to send missiles to Cuba. Reston was careful to point out that his hypothesis was speculative and based on the president's somber mood following his meeting with Khrushchev.[28] Abel and others treated the proposition as incontrovertible fact.[29]

All eyewitness accounts of the summit report plain speaking between the two leaders with neither man giving ground.[30] Arthur Schlesinger, Jr., described the conversations as "civil but tough." He insists that there is no truth to "the legend that Khrushchev browbeat and bullied Kennedy at Vienna."[31] Kenneth O'Donnell, a political and personal confidant of the president, tells the same story, as do Dean Rusk and knowledgeable Soviet officials like Ambassador Georgiy M. Kornienko, who ridicules the notion of Kennedy as a weak president.[32] That "doesn't fit at all with my impression of how Khrushchev perceived Kennedy."[33]

Khrushchev told reporters that Kennedy was tough, especially on the question of Berlin.[34] He confided to Kornienko that he had been right in his assessment of Kennedy as "a really intelligent, extraordinary politician."[35] According to Sergei Khrushchev, "Father returned to Moscow after the summit with a very high opinion of Kennedy. He saw him as a worthy partner and strong statesman, as well as a simple, charming man to whom he took a real liking."[36] Speaking of the summit in his memoirs, Khrushchev remembered Kennedy as a refreshing change from Eisenhower because of his thorough preparation, frankness, and the verve with which he argued his case. "This was to his credit and he rose in my estimation at once. . . . He was, so to speak, both my partner and my adversary."[37]

The third and most commonly cited justification for Soviet doubts about American credibility is Kennedy's refusal to commit American forces to save the Bay of Pigs invasion.[38] It is certainly conceivable that Khrushchev interpreted the president's restraint as a failure of nerve, but his remarks indicate that he also regarded it as an act of courage. In their private discussions in Vienna, Kennedy confessed that the Bay of Pigs had been a mistake. Khrushchev was supportive. He told the president that he respected his explanation and valued his frankness. Afterward, he told his son how he was struck by the contrast between Kennedy's willingness to admit his mistake and Eisenhower's refusal in 1960 to apologize for the U-2 overflight of the Soviet Union.[39]

The Bay of Pigs disaster had made Cuba the administration's "political Achilles heel."[40] Khrushchev did not have to be an especially astute student of American politics to recognize that Kennedy could not afford another fiasco in Cuba; he was under pressure to honor his well-publicized commitment to keep Soviet missiles out of Cuba.

Those who blame the crisis on Kennedy's failure to develop an adequate reputation for resolve ignore the occasions when Kennedy successfully demonstrated strength. Berlin in 1961 is the most striking example. In July, Ambassador Menshikov advised Moscow that the Kennedy brothers' tough words on Berlin could safely be ignored. When the moment of decision approaches "they will be the first to shit in their pants."[41] But Kennedy did not behave in accord with Menshikov's prediction. He rejected Khrushchev's demands outright and reinforced the American garrison in Berlin. His unyielding defense of Western access rights to Berlin compelled Khrushchev to retreat from his challenge and should have strengthened his estimate of the president's resolve—and led him to question the judgment of his representative in Washington. So too, should Kennedy's success in using the threat of American military intervention in Laos to compel communist-backed forces to accept a cease-fire.[42] Khrushchev, not Kennedy, bore the primary responsibility for his miscalculation of the likely consequences of sending missiles to Cuba.

THE DECISION

Khrushchev's colleagues respected his "sharp political skills" but regarded him as "very emotional and impulsive."[43] "He made decisions first and thought about them, if at all, later," lamented Anatoliy Dobrynin. Georgi Arbatov offered Khrushchev's 1960 Berlin ultimatum as a case in point: he threatened to sign a separate peace treaty with East Germany without informing the Presidium, foreign ministry, or armed forces.[44] Soviet and Cuban officials contend that Khrushchev acted just as impulsively when he decided to send missiles to Cuba. He committed himself to the plan before consulting any of his foreign-policy advisors.[45]

The idea of a missile deployment may have been planted in Khrushchev's head in September 1959 by AFL-CIO leader Walter Reuther. In San Francisco, on his visit to the United States, Khrushchev entered into a heated discussion with American labor leaders. He complained bitterly about the American missile and military bases ringing the Soviet Union. "Who prevents you," Reuther broke in, "from deploying missiles in Canada or Mexico?" Soviet officials traveling with Khrushchev were struck by the suggestion.[46]

In his memoirs, Khrushchev says that he conceived of the missile deployment during a state visit to Bulgaria in the middle of May 1961.[47] "I didn't tell anyone what I was thinking. I kept my mental agony to myself. But all the while the idea of putting missiles in Cuba was ripening inside my mind."[48] According to Fedor Burlatsky, Khrushchev had a big lunch at the Bulgarian seashore resort of Varna (or in the Crimea, in another version of the story) and fell asleep in a deck chair with the book he was reading spread on top of his ample belly. He awoke late in the afternoon and extolled the tranquillity of the scene to Defense Minister Rodion Ya. Malinovsky, seated in a nearby deck chair. Malinovsky reminded Khrushchev that beyond that "tranquil" horizon the Americans were deploying missiles armed with nuclear weapons aimed at the Soviet Union. Khrushchev became angry and expressed his desire to send missiles to Cuba to "get even" with the Americans for their "intolerable provocation."[49]

Interviews with Soviet officials indicate that Khrushchev may have sounded out some of his senior advisors about a missile deployment in late April and early May, before his trip to Bulgaria. Sergo Mikoyan believes that his father, recognized as something of an expert on Cuba, was the first to be approached. The Khrushchev and Mikoyan houses were adjacent, and the two men used to walk a lot and discuss foreign affairs.[50]

Khrushchev told Mikoyan that he intended to install a small number of medium-range missiles in Cuba "very speedily," and would not reveal their presence to the United States until after the November congressional elections. Mikoyan was incredulous. He expressed doubts that the missiles could be deployed secretly, and warned that their discovery was likely to provoke a crisis with the Kennedy administration. Khrushchev disagreed. He expected that the missiles in Cuba "would be received in the United States as the Turkish missiles were received in the Soviet Union."[51]

Khrushchev also confided his plan to send missiles to Cuba to Gromyko, Malinovsky, Presidium member Frol R. Kozlov, and Marshal Sergei S. Biryuzov, the recently appointed commander of the Strategic Rocket Forces. Gromyko, Malinovsky, Mikoyan, Kozlov, and Biryuzov discussed the missile deployment with Khrushchev at his home and in his garden without any note-takers present.[52] Khrushchev then raised the matter in the Presidium. He told its members that it was "a very complex question, and that the consequences of that step were difficult to evaluate immediately." He asked that discussion be postponed "until the next meeting."[53]

When the Presidium reconvened, Khrushchev went into more detail about the proposed deployment and a lively debate ensued. Mikoyan had serious reservations. He worried about the reaction of the United States and warned that the proposed deployment would be "a very dangerous step." After the meetings, Presidium members returned home with Khrushchev and "sat till late at night" discussing the implications of sending missiles to Cuba.[54]

Khrushchev put Malinovsky in charge of developing the operation and for reasons of security insisted that only a small circle of people be told of the plan.[55] The defense minister was a reluctant supporter of a secret missile deployment.[56] Marshal Biryuzov was extremely enthusiastic and impressed by the deterrent potential of Soviet missiles in Cuba.[57] Mikoyan was openly skeptical. He questioned Khrushchev's assumption that the missiles could be shipped to Cuba, transported inland, and deployed in the field without being detected by the Americans. He was also dubious about Fidel Castro's willingness to allow missile bases in Cuba because of the risks. In response to Mikoyan's objections, Khrushchev proposed that Marshal

Biryuzov go to Havana to investigate the feasibility of a secret deployment. He would carry a letter, Khrushchev announced, "in which I shall ask Fidel's opinion."[58]

Gromyko maintained that he also expressed reservations about sending missiles to Cuba when Khrushchev first broached the idea to him on the plane ride home from Bulgaria. He warned "that putting our nuclear missiles in Cuba would cause a political explosion in the United States." Khrushchev made light of the risk and told Gromyko that he would ask the Presidium to discuss the possibility of sending missiles to Cuba at its next meeting.[59]

Sometime after the second Presidium meeting, Khrushchev summoned Aleksandr I. Alekseev, ambassador designate to Havana, and Sharaf R. Rashidov, a candidate member of the Presidium and First Secretary of the Uzbek Communist Party to his Kremlin office. Alekseev and Rashidov were to be part of the delegation to Havana. In the presence of Mikoyan, Gromyko, Malinovsky, Kozlov, and Biryuzov, Khrushchev grilled the two men about Cuba, its leadership, and defense capability. "And suddenly the question was asked," Alekseev remembered, "the unexpected nature of which rooted me to the spot. Khrushchev asked me, how in my opinion, Fidel would react to a proposal to deploy our missiles on Cuba. Having overcome with difficulty my confusion, I expressed doubt that Fidel would agree to such a proposal." Marshal Malinovsky was certain that he would and drew an analogy between Cuba and Republican Spain, which had openly sought Soviet military assistance.[60]

Khrushchev stressed to the group how critical it was to prevent the United States from attacking Cuba. He expressed his

> absolute conviction that in revenge for its defeat at the Playa Girón [the Bay of Pigs], the Americans will undertake an invasion of Cuba. It is necessary to raise the price of a military adventure against Cuba to the highest level, to equalize the magnitude of the threat to Cuba to the threat to the United States. Logic suggests that such a means could only be the deployment of our missiles with nuclear warheads on the territory of Cuba.[61]

A consensus was reached to send Rashidov, Biryuzov, and Alekseev to Havana to see if the Cubans were willing to accept Soviet missiles, and if they were, to explore if and how they could be installed secretly. Before the three men left for Cuba, they were summoned to Khrushchev's country dacha, to meet with all of the Presidium members in Moscow at the time. At this meeting, Alekseev insists, "complete unanimity prevailed."[62]

On 30 May, a delegation of agricultural experts, led by Presidium member Rashidov, arrived in Havana for a well-publicized visit.[63] The delegation included Marshal Biryuzov and Gens. Ushakov and Ageyev, traveling under assumed names.[64] As he was not yet accredited as ambassador, Alekseev went along as an advisor to the embassy. At a reception for the visitors, Alekseev took Raúl Castro aside and confided to him that "Our delegation wants to discuss the question of defense, and between us, Engineer Petrov is not Engineer Petrov, he is Marshal Biryuzov of the Strategic Rocket Forces." Castro promised to arrange a meeting with his brother, which took place that evening.[65]

At this meeting, Rashidov handed Khrushchev's letter to Fidel Castro. Alekseev, translating for Rashidov, explained the Soviet government's concern that Cuba was about to be attacked by the United States. Khrushchev was prepared "to assist Cuba in fortifying its defense capability, even to deploy on its territory Soviet intermediate-range missiles, if our Cuban friends consider it useful to them to deter a potential aggressor." Castro "fell to thinking," and then said: "If this will serve the socialist camp, and if it will hinder the actions of American imperialism on the continent, I believe that we will agree. But I will give you an answer only after I consult with my close comrades."[66]

The next day Alekseev and Rashidov met with both Castro brothers, Che Guevara, President Osvaldo Dorticós Torrados, and Blas Roca. The Cuban leaders agreed to host the missiles. Marshal Biryuzov and Gens. Ushakov and Ageyev then entered into discussions with their Cuban colleagues about camouflage and other details of the deployment.[67]

Between the two meetings, the Cuban leaders met among themselves to discuss Khrushchev's proposition. All six members of the Central Committee favored the deployment on the grounds that it would help "change the correlation of forces between capitalism and socialism." Rashidov had insisted that the missiles were meant to protect Cuba, but the Central Committee agreed this could be done more effectively with conventional forces. "We didn't really like the missiles," Castro confided. "If it had been a matter only of our own defense, we would not have accepted the deployment of the missiles here." The Central Committee was concerned that the missiles would turn their country into "a Soviet military base" and damage their image throughout Latin America. They felt they had no choice but to go along with Khrushchev's request. "We could not refuse," Castro explained, because "we were already receiving a large amount of assistance from the socialist camp."[68]

The Cubans worried at first about the likely American reaction. Castro admitted that his "unlimited confidence" in the Soviet Union led him to downplay this concern. The Soviets, he convinced himself, must know what they were doing because they "had decades of experience in diplomatic, international, and military matters." Castro was also influenced by Khrushchev's strategic claims, and counted on the Soviet Union's nuclear prowess to deter an American attack against the missiles in Cuba. Most of all, Castro was impressed by Khrushchev. "In Nikita's public rhetoric you could see— you could detect—confidence, certainty, and strength. . . . So what was really protecting us," Castro reasoned, "was the global strategic might of the USSR, not the rockets here." It was "Soviet will, Soviet determination, Soviet global might."[69]

Mikoyan, who had expected Castro to reject the missiles, was amazed; he subsequently acknowledged that he had "underestimated Fidel's capacity to take risks." Mikoyan was still worried about the problem of secrecy, and was unimpressed by Marshal Biryuzov's claim that there were places in the mountains where the Americans would never discover the missiles. He thought Biryuzov was "a fool."[70]

Khrushchev convened a meeting of the Presidium on 10 June. Biryuzov and Alekseev described their talks in Havana, and Biryuzov assured the Presidium that the missiles could be installed secretly. "They would look like palm trees" to American reconnaissance aircraft.[71] Khrushchev agreed that the deployment could be carried out secretly "if we acted very carefully and did not send immediately a stream of ships." He would announce the presence of the missiles to the world in Havana on 6 November.[72] The Presidium approved the deployment and the plans for its implementation that had been prepared by the Ministry of Defense.[73]

Khrushchev had intended to send only a small number of missiles to Cuba, but the Ministry of Defense plan called for 24 R-12 launchers with 36 SS-4 MRBMs and 6 training missiles, 16 launchers for 24 SS-5 IRBMs, and nuclear warheads for all the operational missiles. Also to be sent were four motorized rifle regiments, two air-defense missile divisions comprising 24 missile sites, two regiments of tactical cruise missiles, a regiment of 40 MiG-21 aircraft, a regiment of 33 Il-28 light bombers, an Mi-8 transport helicopter regiment, a transport air squadron, and a coastal defense force consisting of land-based missiles, a squadron each of surface ships and submarines, and a brigade of missile launching patrol boats. By mid-October, the total deployment would reach forty-two-thousand of the planned forty-five-thousand men. Khrushchev approved this plan despite his earlier insistence that a large-scale movement of men and matériel would threaten the security of the operation.[74]

On 2 July, Raúl Castro, the Cuban defense minister, arrived in Moscow for two weeks of talks. During his visit, Soviet and Cuban officers worked out many of the details of the missile deployment. Khrushchev attended two meetings of their working group, on 3 and 8 July. The first step, everyone agreed, was to install a dense network of SA-2 SAMs to provide perimeter and point air defense of Cuba and of the MRBMs and IRBMs that would be stationed at San Cristóbal, Sagua la Grande, Guanajay, and Remedios. Before the end of the month, the first ships laden with military equipment had departed for Cuba.[75]

Castro, Malinovsky, and Biryuzov, with Alekseev once more acting as translator, drafted an agreement to govern the deployment. The Soviet Union was to have custody over the missiles and missile sites at all times, although Cuba would continue to exercise sovereignty over the sites. The SAMs would be manned by Soviet forces. Moscow would assume all the costs of the deployment and agree to renegotiate it after five years. Everything was to be in place by November. Had the crisis not intervened, Khrushchev would have traveled to Havana sometime that month for a public ceremony at which he and Castro would have signed the treaty and announced the presence of the missiles.[76]

In early August, Castro made some changes in the draft treaty. He sent it back to Moscow on 27 August with Che Guevara and Emilio Aragonés, who were to discuss the proposed changes with Khrushchev.[77] The major point of contention was secrecy. The Cubans wanted the treaty and the missiles made public from the outset. "We had every sovereign right to accept the missiles," Castro insisted. "We were not violating international law. Why do it secretly—as if we had no right to? I warned Nikita that secrecy would give the imperialists the advantage."[78] Guevara and Aragonés told Khrushchev about the mounting anti-Cuban sentiment in the United States and the serious possibility that Kennedy might react violently to a secret fait accompli. The Cuban leadership thought an attack on Cuba more likely still if the administration discovered the missiles before they were fully operational.[79]

Khrushchev made light of the Cuban concerns. "You don't have to worry," he assured them, "there will be no big reaction from the U.S. And if there is a problem, we will send the Baltic Fleet." "When he said that," Aragonés exclaimed, "Che and I looked at each other with raised eyebrows. But, you know, we were deferential to the Soviets' judgments because, after all, they had a great deal of experience with the Americans, and they had superior information than we had."[80]

Fidel Castro was unhappy with Khrushchev's insistence on secrecy and appears to have dropped a hint about the impending deployment in a 26 July speech.[81] This displeased Khrushchev, who reiterated his insistence that the communiqué of the August Soviet-Cuban talks in Moscow remain secret. Khrushchev never signed the draft treaty; he may have refused out of concern that Castro would make it public.[82]

Khrushchev remained confident. He brushed aside the misgivings of Mikoyan, Gromyko, Castro, and Polish leader Władyslaw Gomułka, whom he let in on the secret sometime during the summer. When Gomułka expressed concern about the political consequences of the deployment, Khrushchev assured him that all would turn out well. He told Gomułka the story of a poor Russian farmer who lacked the money to buy firewood for the winter. He moved his goat into his hut to provide warmth. The goat was incredibly rank but the man learned to live with its smell. "Kennedy would learn to accept the smell of the missiles."[83]

WHY WAS KHRUSHCHEV SO CONFIDENT?

Khrushchev was optimistic that the United States would accept the missiles for several reasons. Foremost in his mind was the fundamental similarity between the installation of Soviet missiles in Cuba and American missiles in Turkey. The general secretary had been deeply offended by the proposed deployment of the Jupiters and had repeatedly protested against them. He had not interfered with their installation. He expected the same response from Kennedy. For Khrushchev, his son explained, the missiles in Cuba were a Soviet "tit" for an American "tat."[84]

The link between the missiles in Turkey and Cuba was privately acknowledged by the Kennedy administration. Late in the summer, some of Kennedy's advisors considered the possibility that Khrushchev would announce that he was sending missiles to Cuba in response to the American missiles then going into Turkey. Theodore Sorensen and McGeorge Bundy believe that the president would have found it extraordinarily difficult to have opposed an open deployment. During the crisis they thought frequently about the precedent set by the Jupiters. They worried that world opinion would be receptive to the Soviet claim that the missiles in Cuba were a legitimate response to the Jupiters in Turkey.[85]

Khrushchev's confidence also derived from his expectation that the missiles could be kept secret until they were operational. This would be after the off-year elections in November, and, he told members of the Presidium, "electoral tensions [will] have eased."[86] Once the deployment became a fait accompli, the missiles would represent the status quo, and the onus of changing it would shift to the Americans. The cost of attacking the missiles after they were operational would also increase dramatically. "My thinking went like this," Khrushchev wrote in his memoirs. "If we installed the missiles secretly and then if the United States discovered the missiles were there after they were already poised and ready to strike, the Americans would think twice before trying to liquidate our installations by military means."[87]

Khrushchev counted on the deterrent value of uncertainty. Because the president could not be sure that all the missiles would be destroyed in a first strike, he would hesitate to attack for fear that any surviving missiles would be launched against American cities. The administration did in fact calculate its response on the basis of a conservative worst-case analysis. Although there was no firm evidence of nuclear warheads in Cuba, everyone assumed that they were there. As Robert McNamara put it: "We couldn't take the chance of being wrong, so we worked on the assumption throughout the crisis that at least some missiles were operational and armed with nuclear weapons."[88]

Aleksei Adzhubei contends that there was another reason for his father-in-law's unwarranted optimism: his belief "that Kennedy recognized that there could be no winners in a nuclear war."[89] Kennedy was tough, but committed, just as he was, to keeping their competition peaceful.[90] Adzhubei believes that the critical event in shaping Khrushchev's judgment was Kennedy's cautious policy during the Berlin crisis in 1961. The most dangerous moment of that confrontation came on 27 October, when American bulldozers, tanks, and jeeps advanced to challenge the Soviet checkpoints at the border between the two Berlins. They encountered Soviet tanks that had been lying in wait on side streets. The jeeps passed through the Soviet checkpoints but quickly retreated to the Western sector when they spotted advancing Soviet tanks and infantry. The forces of the two sides spent a tense night with their tanks facing one another at point-blank range. The next morning, Marshal Ivan S. Konev called Khrushchev to report that the opposing forces were only five meters apart and that war seemed imminent. Khrushchev ordered him to withdraw the Soviet tanks and redeploy them on side streets. Within twenty minutes, he learned "to his great relief" that the Americans had withdrawn in response.[91]

Khrushchev's order to Konev was given in response to a back-channel communication from Kennedy proposing a mutual disengagement.[92] The encounter "convinced Khrushchev that Kennedy was as committed as he was to avoiding war." Before the Berlin standoff, Adzhubei maintains, Khrushchev feared war and Western intentions. Afterward, he feared only Western intentions. Khrushchev's "near certainty" that Kennedy would not start a war was "the most fundamental reason" for his belief "that it would be safe to send missiles to Cuba."[93]

Aleksandr Alekseev also stressed Khrushchev's faith in Kennedy's good judgment. In his discussions with Alekseev, Khrushchev "expressed confidence that the pragmatic Americans would not be so bold to take an irrational risk—exactly as we now are not able to take any measures against the American missiles in Turkey, Italy, and the F[ederal] R[epublic of] G[ermany], which are directed against the Soviet Union." Kennedy and other "sober-minded politicians in America should reason just as we do today."[94]

THE FLAWS IN KHRUSHCHEV'S REASONING

None of the reasons that Khrushchev gave for his expectation that Kennedy would accept the missiles withstand close scrutiny. They are all based on unrealistic or contradictory assumptions.

There were important differences between the missiles in Cuba and Turkey that made it inappropriate for Khrushchev to predict the American response to Soviet missiles in Cuba on the basis of his response to the American missiles in Turkey. The Soviet missiles would cause a grave domestic political problem for President Kennedy; the Jupiters had no such consequences for Khrushchev. The Kennedy administration also took a different view of the foreign-policy consequences of the two deployments. Khrushchev's action struck them as especially ominous because of its likely repercussions in Europe. The Ex Comm transcripts make clear that for Kennedy, the important link was not between Cuba and Turkey, but Cuba and Berlin.[95] This association generated an imperative for action that rivaled the domestic pressures on the president to confront Khrushchev. If Kennedy retreated from his public commitment to keep Soviet offensive weapons out of Cuba, he expected America's adversaries and allies to doubt his resolve to defend substantively more important commitments like Berlin.

Khrushchev failed to consider another critical and obvious difference between the missiles in Turkey and Cuba. The United States had installed its missiles openly.[96] The Soviet Union deployed its missiles secretly, after promising that no missiles would be sent to Cuba. Khrushchev's duplicity shocked and infuriated the president, who "was personally deceived."[97] Anger was also a significant factor in the Ex Comm's initial reaction to the missiles.[98] According to Bundy, "The intensity of the American reaction in October was very largely a function of the deception."[99]

The president and Ex Comm were also disturbed by the more general implications of Soviet duplicity. Khrushchev's deceit seemed to indicate his total disregard for the accepted rules of superpower politics; it confirmed the American image of him as wild and unpredictable. There was a consensus that Khrushchev had to be taught a lesson to prevent him from becoming even more aggressive and irresponsible. He had to be convinced of the administration's determination to honor and defend its commitments.[100]

Khrushchev's reliance on secrecy was misplaced. He had insisted on secrecy because he was certain that Kennedy would never accept a public deployment. Sergei Khrushchev explained that his father expected Kennedy to send the American navy to interdict Soviet freighters transporting the missiles to Cuba. He also worried that the announcement of a Soviet-Cuban defense pact would serve as the catalyst for an American invasion of Cuba. He intended to inform Kennedy about the missiles only after they were deployed and operational.[101]

Khrushchev's belief in the need for secrecy is inconsistent with his analogy between the missiles in Cuba and Turkey. If Kennedy would accept the missiles in Cuba because he, Khrushchev, had exercised restraint in Turkey, then there was no need for secrecy. Khrushchev's repeated and emphatic opposition to an open missile deployment indicates that on at least one level he recognized that there were fundamental differences between the two deployments.

Khrushchev's belief that Kennedy would not accept an open missile deployment is ironic. The administration was convinced that Khrushchev sent missiles to Cuba because he did not believe that Kennedy had the resolve to oppose the deployment. Soviet and Cuban officials suggest that Khrushchev insisted on a secret deployment because he had no doubts whatsoever about Kennedy's resolve. If Khrushchev had thought Kennedy weak and irresolute, he might have acceded to Castro's request for an open deployment and there might not have been a crisis.

Bundy and Sorensen contend that the president would have found it extremely difficult to threaten force if the missile deployment had been announced publicly. A forceful response would have been more difficult still if Khrushchev had announced his intention to send missiles to Cuba *before* the September warnings. Kennedy would have found Soviet missiles in Cuba extraordinarily embarrassing but might only have protested verbally, as Khrushchev had when the Jupiters went into Turkey. Khrushchev seriously misjudged the American reaction.

Khrushchev erred further in assuming that operational missiles would deter the administration from threatening military action against them. The

CIA reported that all twenty-four MRBM launchers became operational during the course of the crisis. There is no reason to suppose that the administration would have acted any differently if the missiles had been discovered a week or two later, when more of them would already have been operational and possibly armed with nuclear warheads.[102]

Khrushchev was also wrong in his expectation that the missiles could be deployed secretly. Soviet shipments to Cuba were carefully monitored by American intelligence, and this coverage was increased in the summer of 1961 in response to the Soviet conventional arms buildup on the island. Special efforts were made to detect the transport or arrival of Soviet missiles and related equipment. Because of this extraordinary surveillance, Soviet missile bases were discovered on 14 October by a U-2 reconnaissance aircraft while they were still under construction.[103]

Khrushchev's optimism was not grounded in reality. Above all, it ignored the domestic political costs to Kennedy of allowing the missiles to remain in Cuba, even if their presence only came to light after the congressional elections. Public concern about Cuba became most acute during the late summer and early fall of 1962, in response to the Soviet military buildup in Cuba and Republican charges that the administration was not doing anything to prevent Soviet penetration of the hemisphere. This was a month or two after Khrushchev made his decision to send missiles to Cuba. However, there were repeated and dramatic indications of extraordinary public pressure on the administration before Khrushchev's decision to send missiles to Cuba. Since the Bay of Pigs in April 1961, Cuba had constantly been in the headlines, and the columns of Washington's leading journalists should have left no doubt in any Soviet leader's mind that the president could not afford another defeat over Cuba. Khrushchev was remarkably well informed about American politics; many of his earlier decisions revealed a reasonably sophisticated grasp of American electoral politics.

In his memoirs, Khrushchev acknowledged the critical importance of public opinion in presidential elections. During the 1960 campaign, the White House had asked him to release U-2 pilot Francis Gary Powers. Khrushchev told the Central Committee:

> If we release Powers now it will be to Richard M. Nixon's advantage. Judging from the press, I think the two candidates are at a stalemate. If we give the slightest boost to Nixon, it will be interpreted as an expression of our willingness to see him in the White House. This would be a mistake. . . . Therefore, let's hold off on taking the final step of releasing Powers.[104]

In Vienna, Khrushchev told Kennedy that the Soviet Union had voted for him "by waiting until after the election to return the pilots." Kennedy agreed.[105]

Khrushchev had an earlier revealing encounter with Republican vice-presidential candidate Henry Cabot Lodge. On a visit to Moscow during the 1960 campaign, Lodge attempted to reassure Khrushchev that Soviet-American relations would not suffer if Nixon were elected. As Khrushchev tells it,

Lodge insisted that "Nixon was not really the sort of man he deliberately appeared to be at election rallies." He urged the Soviets not to pay attention to the campaign speeches. "Remember, they're just political statements. Once Mr. Nixon is in the White House I'm sure—I'm absolutely certain—he'll take a position of preserving and perhaps even improving our relations."[106] Khrushchev was unconvinced; the candidates' speeches reflected a "substantial difference in the shading of their political characters."[107]

Khrushchev's evident sensitivity to the nuances of presidential politics makes his willingness to dismiss Kennedy's very specific warnings as campaign rhetoric all the more enigmatic. If he had refused to interpret Nixon's speeches in this light—after being urged to do so by his running mate—why would he do so with Kennedy's warnings when all private communications from the president's emissaries emphasized the seriousness of his intent? Kennedy's warnings should also have sounded an alarm because they came hard on the heels of reports from Ambassador Dobrynin in Washington about "the political and press excitement" in the United States regarding Cuba.[108] The contradiction between Khrushchev's grasp of American politics and his expectations on the eve of the Cuban deployment defies simple explanation.

So, too, does Khrushchev's apparent certainty that Kennedy would respond to the missiles in a rational and unemotional way. The president and his advisors were outraged by the discovery of the missiles. It provoked the same kind of hostility and resentment that the Jupiter deployment in Turkey had aroused in Khrushchev. Kennedy's response to the missiles in Cuba, like Khrushchev's response to the Jupiters, was strongly influenced by anger. It is remarkable that Khrushchev, who sent missiles to Cuba at least in part out of anger, was blind to the possibility that the same emotion could influence his adversary's response.

REASONS OR RATIONALIZATIONS?

Were Khrushchev's arguments about why the United States would accept Soviet missiles in Cuba the basis for his decision, or were they rationalizations he invoked to convince himself and others of the wisdom of a policy to which he was deeply committed? The way in which the decision was made strongly suggests that they were rationalizations.

Secrecy

Although Khrushchev regarded secrecy as essential, he never seriously investigated its feasibility. His complacency was all the more remarkable because he had originally planned a small missile deployment; he feared that a larger, more elaborate operation would telegraph his intentions to the Americans. But the generals had insisted that a small, symbolic deployment was militarily useless. They committed Khrushchev to a much larger operation that would send a veritable "stream of ships" to Cuba, just what he had hoped to avoid.[109] The troop transport alone involved 85 merchant marine ships that made 185 trips to Cuba. The ships sailed from seven ports on the White, Barents, Baltic, and Black seas.[110]

Khrushchev had also been warned by Anastas Mikoyan that American intelligence would almost certainly discover the missiles before they became operational. Marshal Malinovsky had disagreed. He "was sure it could be done speedily and that if it was camouflaged it would not be discovered."[111] To placate Mikoyan, Khrushchev asked Marshal Biryuzov, commander-in-chief of the Strategic Rocket Forces, to investigate this question during his stay in Cuba. To no one's surprise, Biryuzov, a committed supporter of the plan, reported back to Moscow that the missiles could be deployed secretly.[112]

Khrushchev placed great store in the opinion of Gen. Issa A. Pliyev, an elderly officer whose chief claim to fame was that he had led the last major cavalry charge in history, in August 1945, against the Kwantung Army in Manchuria. At Malinovsky's suggestion, he had been summoned from an unimportant post in the Caucasus to command the Soviet expeditionary forces in Cuba.[113] He knew little about modern warfare and nothing about American intelligence capabilities, but he quickly agreed with Biryuzov that the missiles would look like palm trees to American aircraft.[114] Khrushchev accepted their judgment and never asked for the opinion of intelligence officers in a position to offer professional assessments of American capabilities.[115] He was absolutely convinced that the missiles would not be discovered.[116]

Khrushchev's trust in Malinovsky, Biryuzov, and Pliyev was misplaced. The Kennedy administration had made no secret about its efforts to monitor military developments in Cuba. The detailed reports made public during the summer indicated that American intelligence was monitoring the weapons entering Cuba as part of the Soviet conventional buildup. After Kennedy's warnings in early September, Moscow had to assume that Washington was watching shipments to Cuba even more closely than before.[117] Cuban and Soviet intelligence was fully acquainted with the surveillance potential of U-2 aircraft. Soviet experts had examined the camera in the U-2 shot down in May 1960 and had prepared an extensive report on its capabilities. Khrushchev had grudgingly admitted that the photographs it took were remarkably clear.[118]

Ambassador Kornienko reports that he knew "through a back channel that not a single specialist who had any relation to this [operation] believed that it could be done secretly."[119] Adm. Nikolai Amelko, at the time deputy to the chief of the general staff, was adamant about the impossibility of a secret deployment. At every stage of the journey, he insisted that the missiles were visible to American satellites or spies. They were first brought down river by barge to the Black Sea port of Odessa for reloading onto ocean-going vessels. They caused a stir in Odessa, where "Everybody was talking about missiles being sent overseas." The next stage of their journey was from Odessa to Cuba, aboard merchant ships used in the Baltic lumber trade. Sending these ships to Cuba was anomalous and "should have alerted the American navy that something was up." Finally, the missiles were vulnerable to detection when they were unloaded at Cuban ports and transported to their bases. "It was," Amelko insisted, "a crackpot scheme."[120]

Oleg Troyanovsky, one of Khrushchev's principal foreign-policy advisors, was also deeply troubled by the assumption that such an enormous operation could be kept secret from the Americans. Sometime toward the end of September he summoned the courage to express his disbelief to Khrushchev when the two men were alone in the latter's study. Khrushchev brushed aside his objections with the rejoinder that it was now "too late to change anything." "I had the feeling," Troyanovsky remembered, "of a man in a car which lost control, gathered speed, and rushed God knows where."[121]

Implementation

The deployment "was a *top* secret."[122] A decision was made at the outset to send all messages by hand. There was no use of radio. By the time of Raúl Castro's visit in July, some members of the Presidium were discussing the operation, but without writing anything down.[123] Later on, only the highest commanders in the military were told of the plan. Soviet military personnel and technicians sent to Cuba were not informed of their destination until after their ships passed through the Straits of Gibraltar. They brought with them everything required by standard operating procedures. For soldiers, this included winter clothes and skis.[124] The Soviet navy was equally ill-informed. Merchant marine ships, used to transport the missiles, received their orders through a separate chain of command. Adm. Amelko insists that top naval officers knew nothing about the missile deployment "until Kennedy announced the blockade."[125]

Knowledge that Cuba was being carefully watched led Soviet political and military authorities to take extraordinary measures to mask the missile deployment. Despite his concern for secrecy, Khrushchev left the operational details to the military and made no effort to satisfy himself that they had taken all possible precautions. However, he did attend two meetings of the Cuban-Soviet military planning group.[126] His laissez-faire approach stood in sharp contrast to the effort Kennedy and McNamara made to oversee every relevant detail of the blockade.

The Soviet military and merchant marine handled all but the last part of the deployment successfully. The transport of missiles to Cuba and to their bases in the hinterland went undetected. The first medium-range missiles arrived on the wide-hatched freighter *Omsk* on 8 September; more came a week later on *Poltava*. By mid-October, forty-two of the planned sixty combat missiles had reached Cuba.[127] The missiles and related equipment were off-loaded at night under cover of darkness. During the day, Soviet military and construction crews wore colorful sport shirts to disguise their identities.

The Cubans went to extraordinary lengths to facilitate the deployment. The land surrounding the missile sites was cleared of inhabitants and hundreds of families had to be relocated. "We had to negotiate with them, give them land, give them advantages—and all of this secretly," Castro explained, "because we couldn't explain what this was for." Security was almost impossible to maintain because of the large troop movements, and there was talk of missiles. When the missiles arrived, they were huge and difficult to conceal. "There were all sorts of leaks." The government responded by trying to put any citizen who knew or suspected something in isolation.[128]

At the missile sites, Soviet military authorities made a fatal mistake: they failed to mask construction work until *after* the sites were discovered by the Americans.[129] Scanning the film of countryside around San Cristobal, American photo-intelligence analysts spotted military vehicles and tents that suggested preparatory work for an SA-2 SAM site. They then identified six long canvas-covered objects, which they estimated to be more than sixty feet long. Comparison with side view photographs of the Soviet SS-4 missile taken at Moscow parades permitted positive identification.[130]

The Soviet military also erred with respect to the method and timing of construction. If Soviet construction crews had worked only at night and had camouflaged the launcher sites during the day, their activities would have been much more difficult to detect. The SA-2 missiles should have been deployed before any construction work began. They would have made American high altitude overflights of Cuba extremely difficult and hazardous.[131] The SA-2 network did not become operational until after construction of the MRBM and IRBM bases had begun and some of the MRBMs were operational.[132] President Kennedy found this inexplicable.[133]

Western analysts attributed these anomalies to poor planning and organizational rigidity. They speculated, and Soviet generals now confirm, that because of the overriding concern for secrecy, the units involved in the deployment were given information on a need-to-know basis.[134] Rigid compartmentalization hindered overall coordination and seems to have accounted for the inverse order in which the SAM and MRBM sites were constructed. It also reinforced the already strong organizational tendency to do things by the book. The missile sites were laid out in the same way they were in the Soviet Union. Superfluous equipment like tanks and anti-tank missiles was also deployed, not because it could protect the missiles from American attack, but because it was standard equipment for Soviet regiments.[135]

Beyond these coordination problems, the Soviet effort was hindered by arrogance. Soviet generals were overconfident and unwilling to seek or listen to the advice of Cuban officials prepared to help them. This was a costly mistake and "absolutely Russian," Sergo Mikoyan admitted. "We never asked Fidel about camouflage," and he was dismayed. Castro later insisted that the missile sites could have been better disguised as agricultural projects."[136]

Dissent

Khrushchev consulted very few officials before committing himself to the missile deployment. Anatoliy Dobrynin, the man on the spot in Washington, was neither consulted nor informed about the missiles.[137] He learned about them from Dean Rusk an hour before the president's speech announcing the blockade.[138] Dobrynin knew more about the Kennedy administration than any other Soviet official and could have been consulted without compromising security. Khrushchev's failure to solicit his views suggests that he was not seriously interested in exploring Kennedy's likely response to the missiles.

Khrushchev's response to dissent was equally revealing. By making his commitment to the missile deployment very clear, he discouraged subordinates from raising objections. Andrei Gromyko said nothing further after his airplane discussion with Khrushchev and remained silent throughout the Presidium meetings.[139] Khrushchev made no attempt to draw him out even though he had extensive knowledge of the United States; Gromyko had served in Washington from 1940 to 1948, and had visited the country many times since. Once the deployment was approved, Gromyko put his career ahead of his country's interests. He supported the initiative and on the eve of the crisis cabled Khrushchev from Washington that Kennedy would not raise any serious objections to the missiles.[140]

Oleg A. Troyanovsky was more courageous. He read most of the foreign-policy documents brought to Khrushchev's attention, but learned only belatedly of the first secretary's intention to deploy nuclear missiles in Cuba. He was definitely taken aback with this information, "because being someone knowledgeable of U.S. affairs, and realizing the importance of such a step, I knew this would entail serious consequences." Troyanovsky's colleagues in the Secretariat told him "that there was no sense in discussing this because the decision had been made and a change in the decision would be impossible." He nevertheless found an appropriate time to talk to Khrushchev, who insisted that the Soviet Union had the right to send missiles to Cuba because "we were surrounded by U.S. military bases and U.S. missiles. Against this logic, what was I to say, especially since I really did not expect a change in the decision that had been made? That was the end of our discussion."[141]

Deputy Prime Minister Mikoyan was in a better position to speak out. Khrushchev regarded him as a loyal colleague and friend. He took his opinions seriously and often used him as a sounding board on issues of foreign policy. "We would always talk things through and even argue quite a bit," Khrushchev later confessed.[142] Mikoyan had a reputation as a moderate. He had vigorously opposed Soviet intervention in Hungary and had been against the "hard policy in Berlin" in 1961.[143]

It was because of Mikoyan's doubts that Castro would host Soviet missiles that Khrushchev sent Biryuzov and Alekseev to Havana. He was less responsive to Mikoyan's concern that the missiles would be discovered by the Americans and provoke a crisis. To the best of our knowledge, Khrushchev never questioned Malinovsky's and Biryuzov's assurances that the missile bases could be kept secret. He neither probed the reasons for their confidence nor sought independent advice from intelligence officials or military officers knowledgeable about camouflage.

Khrushchev also rode roughshod over dissent. At the Presidium meeting on 10 June, members had to indicate their support for the proposed deployment. Col. Gen. Semyon Pavlovich Ivanov, Secretary of the National Defense Council, went around to collect their signatures, but not everyone signed. Some of the secretaries of the Central Committee refused, as did Mikoyan. Gen. Anatoliy Gribkov explained: "In our country we had the following norm: if you agreed with a certain document, you would write down that you were in favor. Not all were in favor, but a great many did sign." Ivanov reported to Khrushchev "that a number of comrades did not want to sign." Khrushchev sent Ivanov back to them and when approached with Khrushchev's demand for their compliance, everyone signed. "So there was no real unanimity on the Soviet side either, despite the fact that there is a signed document."[144]

Détente

The most striking evidence of Khrushchev's failure to think through the consequences of his policy was his illusory expectation that the missiles would serve as a catalyst for superpower accommodation. Soviet officials report that Khrushchev believed that Soviet-American relations would *improve* after Kennedy was informed of the missiles. Khrushchev was convinced that the Americans respected power and would moderate their hostility when they were forced to accept the Soviet Union as a military equal. It was by no means self-evident that the missile deployment would compel a shift in the American estimate of the military balance. And to the extent that the administration felt threatened by the missiles, it was at least as likely to exploit its conventional superiority in and around the Caribbean to destroy them or compel their withdrawal. Khrushchev's plan was as flawed in its conception as it was in its implementation. In a classic example of diplomatic understatement, Anatoliy Dobrynin called it "not well thought through."[145]

LOOKING BENEATH THE SURFACE

Fedor Burlatsky maintains, and we agree, that Khrushchev's behavior was not rational. "There are some *irrational* reasons—psychological or emotional reasons. We must research this case from both points of view."[146]

Our analysis should begin with the combination of strategic and political needs that made the missile deployment so attractive to Khrushchev. As he saw it, the missiles were necessary to protect Cuba, reduce the Soviet Union's crippling strategic inferiority, and compel the United States to moderate its hostility toward the socialist camp. All three objectives were central to the attainment of his domestic agenda. Khrushchev was "absolutely convinced," Aleksei Adzhubei explained, that "we could not negotiate successfully with the United States over Cuba, or any other matter, without first taking practical action to improve our military position."[147]

When leaders feel compelled to challenge important adversarial commitments, they frequently convince themselves that their action will succeed in the face of contradictory evidence.[148] Because they see their challenges as necessary and feel powerless to back down, they expect their adversaries to acquiesce. Under these conditions, wishful thinking can impair the judgment of otherwise sensible leaders and lead them to seriously flawed assessments of adversarial responses.

For psychologists, wishful thinking is a form of "bolstering." People are most likely to bolster decisions that risk serious loss. They exaggerate the expected rewards of their chosen course of action and suppress their doubts. They may also try to avoid anxiety by insulating themselves from information that indicates their choice may lead to serious loss.[149]

Bolstering serves a useful psychological purpose by helping people move toward commitment and cope with the doubts and internal conflict that risky decisions generate. Bolstering is detrimental when it discourages a careful evaluation of alternatives or realistic assessment of the risks associated with a preferred course of action. It lulls people into believing that they have made good decisions when they have avoided a careful appraisal of their options. People who bolster become overconfident and insensitive to the information that is critical to the evaluation of their policy.[150]

Nikita Khrushchev's decision to send missiles to Cuba displays strong evidence of bolstering. He sent missiles to Cuba to prevent serious foreign and domestic losses. He saw no other way of coping with these threats and was thus strongly motivated to believe that the deployment would succeed. He refused to take seriously the possibility that the missiles would be discovered by the Americans before they were operational or that Kennedy would threaten or use force to remove the missiles if he learned of their presence.

Bolstering helps to explain Khrushchev's premature commitment to the deployment. He informed his colleagues of his decision, he did not ask for their advice. When he told Gromyko about his plan on their return flight from Bulgaria, Gromyko "had a definite feeling that he had no intention of changing his position." According to Gromyko, his warning that the missiles would cause "a political explosion" in the United States did not please Khrushchev. After some reflection, "Khrushchev terminated the discussion by announcing his intention to bring the matter before the Presidium."[151] Anastas Mikoyan had the same impression; Khrushchev had made up his mind and "was not at all pleased" by his doubts.[152]

Khrushchev's premature commitment to the missile deployment was most likely a response to the anxiety it aroused. Rather than recognize the attendant risks, Khrushchev tried to avoid thinking about them. He assured himself and everyone else that there was nothing to worry about. This kind of behavior is a classic manifestation of bolstering. So, too, was Khrushchev's response to dissent, failure to involve himself in the details of implementation, and insensitivity to warnings from the United States once he was committed to the deployment.

Khrushchev's bolstering was facilitated by the Soviet political system; the powerful general secretary could brush aside criticism and intimidate dissenters by merely expressing a strong opinion. When he was removed from power, Khrushchev was charged with having "undervalued other Presidium members," behaving "tactlessly" toward them, and "disdaining their views."[153] But Khrushchev, too, was a victim of the system. In the absence of any constitutional guarantees to office, Khrushchev, and Brezhnev after him, were driven to accumulate as much power as possible to protect themselves against challenges to their leadership. Vadim Zagladin, a top advisor to Brezhnev and Gorbachev, maintains that this kind of "leadership from above" was also responsible for "the disastrous intervention in Afghanistan."[154]

After making stressful decisions, people tend to upgrade the appeal of their chosen course of action and downgrade that of rejected alternatives. By convincing themselves that there were overwhelming reasons for deciding as they did, they boost their confidence in their course of action, which in turn enables them to maintain their commitment.[155] Such "post-decisional rationalization" is dysfunctional when confidence is unwarranted or makes people insensitive, as it did Khrushchev, to the kinds of problems their policy is likely to encounter. Once they have committed themselves, people often try to cope with residual anxiety by practicing "defensive avoidance." They do their best to insulate themselves from information that suggests their policy may not succeed. When confronted with critical or threatening information, they deny, discredit, distort or otherwise explain it away.[156]

Defensive avoidance helps to explain Khrushchev's dismissal of Kennedy's warnings in September. As precise as those warnings were, they came *after* Khrushchev had committed himself to the missile deployment and was therefore unreceptive to information that challenged its feasibility.

When Gromyko described Kennedy's warnings to the leadership, Khrushchev recalled that "We listened to him but went on with the operation."[157]

Wishful thinking, overconfidence, and insensitivity to threatening information help explain why Khrushchev committed himself prematurely to the missile deployment, failed to think through its implications, and remained committed in the face of Kennedy's warnings. Anger also played a role.

Khrushchev made little attempt to hide his feelings. He gave vent to anger and joy in Presidium meetings, diplomatic forums, and in private encounters with ordinary citizens and other world leaders. Andrei Gromyko complained that he "had enough emotion for ten people—at a minimum."[158] Khrushchev's outbursts reflected his personality, especially his tendency to equate his honor and self-esteem with the fortunes of the Soviet state. Because he internalized his country's triumphs and failures, they were more keenly felt, and more likely to be expressed in emotional outbursts.

Khrushchev's reaction to the U-2 was a striking example of his propensity to personalize events. He was humiliated and enraged by the intrusion of the spy planes. He also felt "impotent" because the air defense command was unable to prevent repeated penetrations of Soviet airspace.[159] In May 1960, when a U-2 was finally brought down by a new missile, Eisenhower accepted personal responsibility for the flight, but insisted that "such flights may continue until Soviet leaders open their borders to inspection."[160] The president's public statements exposed Khrushchev to rebuke and ridicule from his domestic adversaries and the Chinese.

Khrushchev felt betrayed by Eisenhower's "two-faced policy."[161] In Paris to attend the four-power summit, he denounced Eisenhower in violent terms to British Prime Minister Harold Macmillan. Macmillan was struck by Khrushchev's intensely personal portrayal of the incident. In a private meeting, the Soviet leader complained "that his *friend* [bitterly repeated again and again], his friend Eisenhower had betrayed him."[162] He told Macmillan and French President Charles de Gaulle that he would not be satisfied until he had "Eisenhower's apology for what he had already done and his assurances that it wouldn't happen again." Both leaders tried without success to convince Khrushchev that it was unreasonable to expect a great power to apologize for spying; insistence on an apology would break up the summit. Khrushchev was unyielding. "My anger," he wrote, "was building up inside me like an electric force which could be discharged in a great flash at any moment."[163]

The Jupiters rekindled Khrushchev's unresolved emotions about the U-2. The Americans had again ignored Soviet sensitivities in their quest for unilateral advantage. The perceived purpose of the missiles, like the U-2 flights before them, was to intimidate Soviet leaders by making them feel vulnerable to attack. Khrushchev, according to Leonid Zamyatin, was "deeply angered" by the Jupiters.[164] In the words of Aleksei Adzhubei, he was "furious" and "itching for revenge."[165]

Khrushchev acknowledged his desire for revenge in his tape-recorded memoirs. "The Americans," he observed bitterly, "had surrounded our country with military bases and threatened us with nuclear weapons, and now they would learn just what it feels like to have enemy missiles pointing at you; we'd be doing nothing more than giving them a little of their own medicine. And it was high time America learned what it feels like to have her own land and her own people threatened."[166]

Emotional arousal inhibits the desire and ability to think clearly. Khrushchev's anger may have helped to blind him to the consequences of his choice and contributed to his wishful thinking. It could also have prompted his premature commitment to the missile deployment in April or May, and explain why he made no serious effort to explore the problems and implications of his policy and brushed aside objections from advisors whose opinions he was otherwise disposed to take seriously. Kennedy's September warnings provoked another outburst of anger. Khrushchev told the Presidium: "What made the Americans think they had such a unilateral right? After all, America used our neighbor's territory to station its rockets. Now that we were doing the same, they were threatening us with war. It angered us and we agreed that we would continue to pursue this policy."[167]

The relative importance of anger and perceived political need in Khrushchev's decision to send missiles to Cuba is difficult to assess; their behavioral consequences were the same. We suspect that Khrushchev was moved by both anger and need, and that they made him insensitive to the warnings of friends and the threats of adversaries. Irrespective of their relative impact, it is Khrushchev, not Kennedy, who bears the onus for the miscalculation that provoked the most acute crisis of the Cold War.

COULD KENNEDY HAVE DONE MORE?

Kennedy has been criticized for not warning Khrushchev earlier about his unwillingness to tolerate offensive weapons in Cuba.[168] Critics assume that Khrushchev might have reconsidered his plan if he had been warned in the spring of 1962, before he had committed himself to the missile deployment. We can only speculate about how Khrushchev would have responded to deterrence before he had made his decision.

Earlier warnings might have punctured Khrushchev's illusions and forced him to confront some of the dangerous consequences of the deployment of missiles to Cuba. It is also possible that deterrence would have failed for the same reasons that the warnings of his own advisors had so little impact. Khrushchev was angry and had compelling domestic and foreign-policy reasons for deploying the missiles. He might have discounted warnings issued in May just as he did Kennedy's warnings in September.

Kennedy's critics not only assume that Khrushchev would have responded positively to earlier warnings, they argue that by the spring the president should have been sensitive enough to the possibility of a Soviet missile deployment in Cuba to have issued those warnings. Just how reasonable was it to have expected Kennedy to have warned Khrushchev in April, May, or early June?

Immediate deterrence requires a defender to make or reinforce a commitment when there is some evidence that it might be challenged. Before the Soviet conventional buildup began in the summer of 1962, no one in Washington had reason to suppose that Moscow might consider sending missiles to Cuba capable of attacking the United States. Even in September McGeorge Bundy explains, "We did not expect Khrushchev to put missiles in Cuba, which accounts for the relatively untroubled way in which we wrote our warnings in September."[169]

When the Soviet conventional arms buildup in Cuba assumed major proportions, Kennedy put Moscow on notice that certain categories of weapons would be unacceptable. The timing of his public and private warnings was dictated by events. It is unreasonable to have expected him to have issued stern warnings against a provocation that neither he nor his advisors considered a remote possibility.[170] A strategy that requires leaders to warn adversaries in detail against any provocation that they can imagine would in any case be ineffective; adversarial leaders would routinely discount such warnings because so often they would apply to challenges that they were not considering.

DETERRENCE AND CRISIS PREVENTION

In chapter 2 we examined the role of general deterrence in Soviet-American relations on the eve of the Cuban missile crisis. We found that deterrence was provocative instead of preventive. Soviet officials testified that the American strategic buildup, missile deployment in Turkey and assertions of strategic superiority exacerbated their insecurity. President Kennedy considered all these actions as prudent, defensive measures against Soviet threats, especially in Berlin. Instead of restraining Khrushchev, they convinced him of the need to do more to protect the Soviet Union and Cuba from American military and political challenges. Through their avowedly defensive actions, the leaders of both superpowers made their fears of an acute confrontation self-fulfilling.

In this chapter we analyzed the practice and failure of immediate deterrence to prevent a Soviet missile deployment in Cuba. It illustrates another fundamental problem of deterrence: the inability or unwillingness of leaders facing serious domestic and foreign problems to engage in a comprehensive and open-minded assessment of the expected costs and benefits of a challenge. Khrushchev made only the most cursory examination of the feasibility of sending missiles to Cuba and its likely impact on the United States. He committed himself to the deployment before consulting with the intelligence experts and foreign-policy advisors who could have helped him to make a more informed judgment. He then sought out confirming opinions and discounted information that indicated that the deployment might fail and provoke a crisis. Khrushchev's behavior bore little relationship to the expectation of rational decision making that lies at the core of deterrence theory and strategy.

Chapters 2 and 3 offer vivid testimony to the ways in which American and Soviet general deterrence helped provoke the most serious crisis of the Cold War. Leaders of both superpowers overplayed their hands. Their military buildups and deployments, claims of strategic superiority, and threatening rhetoric aroused their adversary's fear and anxiety and provided Khrushchev with strong incentives to send missiles to Cuba. They were also a root cause of the wishful thinking that led him to dismiss or discount the technical and political obstacles that threatened the deployment's success.

Kennedy's critics accuse him of not practicing deterrence early or forcefully enough. They allege that his failure to commit American forces at the Bay of Pigs, his poor performance in Vienna, and failure to prevent the construction of the Berlin Wall, convinced Khrushchev that he could act with impunity in Cuba. We have shown that Kennedy's attempts to demonstrate resolve, not his apparent irresolution, prompted Khrushchev's decision to send missiles to Cuba. Immediate deterrence failed at least in part because Kennedy practiced general deterrence too forcefully.

Why Did the Missiles Provoke a Crisis?

*If I point a pistol at you like this in order to attack you, the
pistol is an offensive weapon. But if I aim to keep you from
shooting me, it is defensive, no?*

—*Nikita S. Khrushchev* [1]

*You see, we had already staked out a public position
on the issue: if the Soviet Union does anything to threaten the
safety of the United States or Latin America, we cannot
tolerate it. . . . We felt the same way* you *would feel if
we put missiles in Finland.*

—*McGeorge Bundy* [2]

THE DISCOVERY of Soviet missiles in Cuba created a crisis for the Kennedy administration.[3] A week later, Kennedy's proclamation of a limited naval "quarantine" of Cuba triggered a crisis in Moscow. There is nothing puzzling about the Soviet reaction to Kennedy's speech: it issued a direct challenge and raised the prospect of an American attack against Cuba and Soviet forces stationed there. Considerable controversy surrounds the Kennedy administration's reaction to the missile sites; critics contend that Soviet missiles in Cuba did not threaten any vital American interest and that it was irresponsible for the president to risk war to remove them. This chapter examines this controversy; it looks at why the discovery of the missile sites constituted a crisis for the Kennedy administration.

The traditional interpretation of the crisis, enshrined in the writings of administration insiders Theodore C. Sorensen and Arthur M. Schlesinger, Jr. and newsman Elie Abel, depicts the missiles as an intolerable provocation.[4] The president had to compel the Soviet Union to withdraw the missiles to defend the balance of power, preserve NATO, and convince Khrushchev and the world of American resolve. Sorensen, Schlesinger, and Abel laud the "quarantine" as the optimal strategy, hail the outcome of the crisis as an unqualified American success, and attribute it to Kennedy's skill and tenacity.

The revisionist interpretation, associated with the writings of journalist I. F. Stone and historians Ronald Steel and Barton Bernstein, maintains that Kennedy needlessly risked war for domestic political gain. Revisionists condemn the blockade as irresponsible and attribute the peaceful resolution of the crisis to Soviet moderation and American good luck.[5] New evidence permits us to reevaluate these competing claims. It indicates that both interpretations are overdrawn and one-sided. Kennedy opposed the Soviet missiles for domestic and foreign-policy reasons.

DOMESTIC POLITICS

Revisionists accuse the president of risking the peace of the world to advance his political career. I. F. Stone, the most prominent early revisionist, distinguished sharply between presidential political and American national interests. The former might be well served by a crisis, but the latter required compromise and diplomacy. Kennedy chose confrontation because it was more likely to get the missiles out of Cuba before the November congressional election. "There was no time for prolonged negotiation, summit conference, or U[nited] N[ations] debates if the damage was to be undone before the election. Kennedy could not afford to wait."[6]

Sorensen, Schlesinger, and more recent defenders of the traditional interpretation deny that Kennedy or his principal advisors were influenced in any way by domestic political considerations.[7] "I've listened to the tapes of the October 27th [Ex Comm] meetings," McGeorge Bundy exclaimed, "and I can say with a high degree of confidence that I don't think there was any worry of that kind whatsoever. I have no recollection of anyone voicing any fear of being lynched over the affair in Cuba."[8] Sorensen insists that the president chose the blockade over the air strike in full recognition that it would adversely affect his political standing. "JFK at the time was convinced his course would hurt his party in the elections." He recognized that the air strike would "be a swifter and more popular means of removing the missiles before Election Day."[9] Dean Rusk's revelation that late in the crisis Kennedy considered concessions to Khrushchev is cited as further proof by traditionalists of the president's willingness to incur severe domestic political costs.[10]

The evidence supports the claim of the revisionists that domestic considerations shaped Kennedy's response to the missiles. The president's objective, however, was to avoid loss, and not, as most revisionists allege, to make political gains for himself or his party. Some former administration officials now acknowledge this truth.

"Once they [the missiles] were there," maintains John Kenneth Galbraith, Kennedy's ambassador to India, "the political needs of the Kennedy administration urged it to take almost any risk to get them out."[11] According to Dean Rusk, the administration "would have been discredited" in the eyes of the public if it had accepted Soviet missiles in Cuba.[12] Roger Hilsman, then head of the State Department's Bureau of Intelligence and Research, argues that Kennedy had helped to create his political predicament. He had used Cuba to great effect in his campaign against Richard Nixon, asking over and over why a Communist regime had been allowed to come to power just ninety miles off the coast. Then came the Bay of Pigs and the Soviet military buildup. The president was "peculiarly vulnerable on Cuba."[13]

Rusk and Hilsman argue that Kennedy was responding to more than just electoral pressure. If the administration had tolerated the missiles, Hilsman explains,

> it would be faced with a revolt from the military, from the hardliners in other departments, both State and CIA, from not only Republicans on Capitol Hill but some Democrats, too; that it would be faced with all this opposition at home just at the time that it would be undergoing deep and very dangerous challenges from the Soviets brought on by the alteration in the balance of power wrought by their successful introduction of missiles in Cuba, and which might well put the United States in mortal danger. This was why the Administration was in trouble.[14]

Domestic and foreign-policy considerations combined to propel Kennedy into a showdown with Khrushchev.

Theodore Sorensen now acknowledges the existence of these political factors but does not consider them significant. He insists that the pressures pushing Kennedy toward a confrontation were always offset by those pulling him in the opposite direction.[15] Public opinion was divided over the blockade. Many Americans believed that the president was needlessly courting nuclear war, but the overwhelming majority supported the president. There was also a vocal minority who thought his policy too weak. Kennedy was surprised and angered when he heard this kind of complaint from prominent Democrats, senators whom he briefed about the crisis before announcing the blockade. Richard Russell of Georgia criticized the blockade as a halfway measure that would arouse allied opposition without forcing the withdrawal of the missiles. J. William Fulbright of Arkansas, chairman of the Senate Foreign Relations Committee, joined Russell in calling for an invasion of Cuba.[16] Only the previous month, the Senate had adopted a joint congressional resolution by an overwhelming 86–1 vote, calling for the use of force, if necessary, to halt Cuban aggression and communist subversion in the Western hemisphere.[17]

Kennedy indicated that domestic politics were very much on his mind. On the morning of 16 October, shortly after being informed of the discovery of the missile sites, he summoned Kenneth O'Donnell to the Oval office. "You still think that fuss about Cuba is unimportant?" he asked his special assistant and appointments secretary. "Absolutely," O'Donnell replied. Kennedy showed him the photographs. "You're an old Air Force bombardier. You ought to know what this is. It's the beginning of a launching site for a medium-range ballistic missile." "I don't believe it," O'Donnell exclaimed.

"You'd better believe it," Kennedy admonished him. "It was taken Sunday, and checked and rechecked yesterday. We've just elected Capehart in Indiana and Ken Keating will probably be the next president of the United States."[18]

Kennedy's concern about the domestic political implications of his policy resurfaced a week later. On Wednesday morning, 22 October, the day the quarantine went into effect, the navy reported that Soviet ships were still steaming toward the blockade line. The Kennedy brothers walked together to that morning's Ex Comm meeting. Robert Kennedy reported that his brother turned to him and said: "'It looks really mean, doesn't it? But then, really there was no other choice. If they get this mean on this one in our part of the world, what will they do on the next?' 'I just don't think there was any choice,' I said, 'and not only that, if you hadn't acted, you would have been impeached.' The President thought for a moment and said, 'That's what I think—I would have been impeached.'"[19]

Was Kennedy seriously worried about impeachment? His remarks to his brother can be read as a frank admission of political vulnerability. They might also represent post-decisional rationalization.[20] Kennedy had opted for a risky course of action, one he knew could escalate to war. Any responsible leader in this situation would have second thoughts about the wisdom of his policy. Risk, uncertainty, and self-doubt generate anxiety. To cope with it, people convince themselves that their chosen course of action will be more successful than originally anticipated and that the costs and drawbacks of any alternative would be correspondingly higher. The president's comment may have been intended to reduce his anxiety and buttress his commitment; we must be cautious about accepting it at face value.

Even if we accept that Kennedy's concern about impeachment might have been exaggerated, his comment still reveals sensitivity to the domestic implications of his policy. The core of the problem was Kennedy's prior public commitment to keep "offensive weapons" out of Cuba. If he now accepted the missiles, McGeorge Bundy reasoned, Republican opponents would have brought a triple indictment against him: "You said it wouldn't happen, and you were wrong; you said you would know how to stop it if it did happen, and you don't; and now you say it doesn't matter, and it does."[21] In the wake of this criticism—and public grumbling by dissatisfied generals—the administration would suffer severe political consequences.

Defense Secretary Robert McNamara remembers that "right from the beginning, it was President Kennedy who said that it was *politically* unacceptable for us to leave those [Cuban] missile sites alone."[22] McNamara made the same point to the Ex Comm during its first day of deliberations: "I'll be quite frank," he announced to the group. "I don't think there is a military problem here . . . this, this is a domestic political problem."[23] Not everyone agreed. Some participants insisted that the missiles would upset the strategic balance.[24] Nobody challenged McNamara's contention that the president faced a serious domestic political problem.

In 1987, Theodore Sorensen made a revealing admission about the calculations that led to Kennedy's warnings to Moscow in September. They were issued on the assumption that the Soviet Union had no intention whatsoever of sending missiles to Cuba.[25] The purpose of the warnings was to deflect Republican charges that the administration was "soft" on Cuba. By appearing to stand up to Khrushchev and Castro, Kennedy could convey the appearance of toughness without risking confrontation abroad—or so he thought.

Sorensen's remarks, and those of other administration officials, make it apparent that Kennedy tried to walk a fine line between the Scylla of domestic political loss and the Charybdis of military action. By drawing the line at the introduction of "offensive weapons," for example, missiles, bombers, and submarines, he in effect told Khrushchev that he would not oppose the continuing buildup of Soviet conventional forces in Cuba. This was a major concession, given public and congressional opposition. Kennedy was willing to expose himself to considerable recrimination at home in the hope of forestalling a serious confrontation with the Soviet Union. To seek such a conflict in the hope of personal or political gain would have been as unacceptable to him as it is to the revisionists.

THE NEED TO DISPLAY RESOLVE

Traditionalists maintain that Khrushchev sent missiles to Cuba because he doubted Kennedy's resolve. It was therefore imperative to demonstrate to Khrushchev that the administration would not be coerced. Revisionists portray Kennedy's concern for resolve as neurotic and deny that it was necessary to meet the foreign-policy objectives of the United States.

Proponents of both interpretations agree that Soviet missiles in Cuba did little or nothing to alter the military balance. The Joint Chiefs of Staff and Ex Comm militants thought differently; they worried that the missiles would make the United States significantly more vulnerable to a Soviet attack.[26] Defense Secretary McNamara rejected this argument. He maintained, and the president agreed, that the missiles would make no difference because the United States was already targeted by ICBMs deployed in the Soviet Union. American intelligence expected the Soviet ICBM force to grow substantially in the course of the next few years whether or not there were any missiles in Cuba. "A missile is a missile," McNamara exclaimed, "It makes no difference whether you are killed by a missile fired from the Soviet Union or from Cuba."[27]

Kennedy, Rusk, and McNamara were concerned about the foreign-policy consequences of the missiles. The president believed that "The Soviet move had been undertaken so swiftly, so secretly and with so much deliberate deception—it was so sudden a departure from Soviet practice—that it represented a provocative change in the delicate status quo."[28] Dean Rusk was convinced that "If we allowed deployment of Soviet missiles just ninety miles off our coast, American credibility would have been destroyed, and there would have been a devastating psychological impact on the American people, the Western hemisphere, and NATO."[29] The consensus of the Ex Comm, Arthur Schlesinger reported, was "that while the missiles might not have had much effect on the overall U.S.-Soviet military balance, they had a considerable effect on the world *political* balance." They would permit the Soviets "to act with impunity in the very heart of the American zone of vital interest—a victory of great significance for the Kremlin, which saw the world in terms of spheres of influence and inflexibly guarded its own."[30]

Neither the president nor the Ex Comm were persuaded that Khrushchev's challenge had defensive purposes. They discounted the possibility that the Soviet buildup in Cuba, conventional and nuclear, was intended to protect Cuba from American attack.[31] The Ex Comm also considered and rejected the "strategic fix" hypothesis.[32] At the first Ex Comm meeting, Secretary of State Dean Rusk brought up CIA Director John McCone's hypothesis "that Khrushchev may feel that it's important for us to learn about living under medium range missiles." His observation elicited no response.[33]

Administration officials reasoned that the missile deployment was offensively motivated. Dean Rusk speculated that Khrushchev had put missiles into Cuba to compel American concessions on Berlin and, if that failed, to provide the security umbrella he needed to take decisive action against the Western presence in that city.[34] Under Secretary of State George Ball viewed it as an attempt to augment Soviet strategic capabilities and possibly to compel American concessions.[35] President Kennedy thought Khrushchev sought multiple ends: he wanted to raise doubts about America's commitment to defend Europe; encourage revolution in the Third World, especially in Latin America; and heal the rift between the communist giants by giving lie to Chinese charges that the Soviet Union was an ineffectual "paper tiger."[36] Kennedy suspected that Khrushchev intended to announce his fait accompli in a speech at the United Nations in which he would make "cocky demands on Berlin and other matters."[37]

These interpretations cast the Soviet initiative in a particularly threatening light. Worse still, they seemed to indicate Soviet lack of respect for American capability and resolve. In its first assessment, the CIA advised the White House that Khrushchev had felt free to challenge the United States because he believed that the balance of military power was shifting in favor of the Soviet Union.[38]

At the outset of the crisis, Ambassador Charles "Chip" Bohlen, one of the Ex Comm's two Soviet experts, invoked an adage he attributed to Lenin: "If you strike steel, pull back; if you strike mush, keep going."[39] According to this hypothesis, widely accepted within the Ex Comm, Khrushchev doubted American resolve because of the widespread abhorrence of war and obsession with affluence. This is why the president had refused to commit troops to the Bay of Pigs landing or to oppose the construction of the Berlin Wall. In the words of Arthur Schlesinger, Jr., "the missiles represented the supreme probe of American intentions. No doubt, a 'total victory' faction in Moscow had long been denouncing the government's 'no win' policy and arguing that the Soviet Union could safely use the utmost nuclear pressure against the United States because the Americans were too rich or soft or liberal to fight."[40]

We feared that "Khrushchev's successful gamble might well have tempted him toward further adventures," McGeorge Bundy reported.[41] According to Robert McNamara, "There was the risk that if we did not respond forcefully in Cuba, the Soviets would continue to poke and prod us elsewhere. And what if the next prod came around Berlin, which had been driving Khrushchev nuts for years? If that happened, than the risk of disaster would go way up, relative to Cuba."[42] Berlin was uppermost in the president's mind. If they got away with the missile deployment, "they [would] start getting ready to squeeze us in Berlin," he warned the Ex Comm on 16 October.[43] A week later, Sander Vanocur, who covered the White House for NBC, walked through the Cabinet Room after an Ex Comm meeting and observed that the president had written on his yellow legal pad: "Berlin . . . Berlin . . . Berlin . . . Berlin. . . ."[44]

Revisionists are unpersuaded by these arguments. They believe that Kennedy's policies reflected his personal insecurity. I. F. Stone alleges that Kennedy blockaded Cuba to prove his machismo. The "eyeball to eyeball" confrontation it provoked "was the best of therapies for Kennedy's nagging inferiority complex."[45] Ronald Steel also stressed Kennedy's obsession with his image and his irrational fear that Khrushchev would never take him seriously again if he backed away from his pledge to keep Soviet missiles out of Cuba.[46]

Revisionists are right in sensing something extraordinary about Kennedy's belief that Khrushchev saw him as weak and irresolute. Soviet testimony indicates that Kennedy misjudged his adversary. The missile deployment was neither opportunity-driven nor prompted by lack of respect for Kennedy's resolve. It was not Kennedy's performance in Vienna, acceptance of the Berlin Wall, or failure to commit troops to the Bay of Pigs that led Khrushchev to send missiles to Cuba, but Kennedy's deployment of Jupiters in Turkey, proclamations of strategic superiority, and political-military pressures against Castro.[47]

Kennedy's failure to grasp Khrushchev's motives was due in part to the misleading historical analogy he and his advisors drew between Nazi Germany and the Soviet Union. The two dictatorships shared much in common in the Stalin-Hitler years; they were expansionist regimes governed by a mix of propaganda and terror. On the eve of World War II they had conspired to divide Eastern Europe between them. Postwar American policymakers assumed that the Soviet Union, like Nazi Germany, was driven by its ideology and bent on world domination. Hitler, Stalin, and Khrushchev were all consummate opportunists, constantly probing for weak spots in their adversaries' defenses in the hope of expanding their influence and territory.[48]

Kennedy saw the Soviet Union through the prism of the 1930s. His world view had been shaped by the fiasco of appeasement. His father, Joseph Kennedy, had served as ambassador to the Court of St. James on the eve of the war, and had been an outspoken partisan of appeasement. The twenty-three-year-old Kennedy lived with his parents in England while he expanded his Harvard senior thesis into a book. *Why England Slept* was a stunning indictment of England's lack of preparedness and of the political and moral bankruptcy of appeasement.[49] The young Kennedy's personal involvement with this issue, his political opposition to his father, and the death of his older brother in the war that appeasement helped to bring about made him more committed than most to "the lesson of Munich" and its application to Soviet-American relations.

In fairness to Kennedy, his predisposition to draw parallels between Nazi Germany and the Soviet Union was greatly abetted by Khrushchev's bullying speeches, boasts of superiority, and crude displays of force. His aggressive posturing evoked memories of Hitler and aroused fear of another war. In hindsight, it is apparent that many of Khrushchev's bellicose displays were intended to mask Soviet inferiority or to impress the Chinese. Kennedy and his advisors could not know that these factors motivated Khrushchev's behavior.

Neither the analogy to the 1930s nor Khrushchev's threatening behavior can fully account for Kennedy's doubts about his reputation for resolve. There *was* something neurotic about the president's confessions to administration officials and friendly newsmen that his foreign policy was a string of "disasters" and encouraged Khrushchev to believe that he was a "pushover."[50] The Bay of Pigs was admittedly a disaster, but the Vienna summit and the Berlin crisis could only be so interpreted by a president who distorted reality to confirm his unjustified fears. Kennedy had been resolute in Vienna. Khrushchev had told journalists how impressed he had been by his firmness and grasp of the issues.[51] Kennedy had been unyielding on Laos and Berlin. He had successfully exposed Khrushchev's bluff to sign a separate treaty with East Germany. It was odd that the president worried that his refusal to tear down the Berlin Wall would be seen as a sign of cowardice; its construction was a confession of communist weakness. Kennedy's acceptance of the Wall represented a statesmanlike decision to eschew a confrontation in the heart of Europe.

Kennedy's insecurity seriously distorted his understanding of Khrushchev. His faulty historical analogy encouraged him to see Khrushchev as aggressive and opportunistic. His doubts about himself led him to exaggerate the extent to which Khrushchev saw opportunities to exploit. These distortions were complementary and combined to produce a seriously flawed understanding of Soviet foreign policy.

Kennedy's image of Khrushchev was also self-justifying. He analyzed successive encounters with Khrushchev in terms of the assumptions he made about himself and Khrushchev's understanding of him. In doing so he confirmed tautologically the validity of those assumptions. This process blinded him to the possibility that Khrushchev could respect his resolve but act aggressively for defensive reasons.

In evaluating Kennedy's concern for establishing a reputation for toughness, we need to distinguish between Soviet-American relations before and after the discovery of Soviet missiles in Cuba. Even if Khrushchev's decision to deploy the missiles had little or nothing to do with his assessment of Kennedy's resolve, Kennedy's failure to take a firm stand against the deployment could have raised doubts about that resolve. In this respect, the missiles were very different from the Bay of Pigs or the Vienna summit. The implications of both for the president's credibility were marginal at best; it was not at all obvious how, if at all, his credibility was engaged. In Cuba, Kennedy had publicly drawn a line and had staked his reputation on its defense. To have accepted Soviet missiles in Cuba would have exposed his well-publicized commitment as a bluff.

The domestic costs of accepting the missiles would also have been high. The administration would have been crippled and the Republicans might have won control of Congress in November. Kennedy's willingness to accept these losses to avoid the risks of a Soviet-American crisis would have communicated a clear and dangerous message to Khrushchev. It could have encouraged him, as Kennedy feared, to encroach further on American interests in the expectation that he would not meet serious resistance. Above all else, the president and his advisors wanted to discourage a new challenge in Berlin where they believed the risk of escalation was far greater than in Cuba. The revisionists are wrong to dismiss the serious international implications of the deployment just as the traditionalists err in ignoring its domestic political consequences. Both concerns were very much on the president's mind.

WHY THE BLOCKADE?

Kennedy supporters praise the "naval quarantine"—really a limited blockade—of Cuba as a judicious and successful choice. Revisionists contend that it unnecessarily risked war for a goal that could have been achieved by diplomacy. Critics on the right, the "hawks," contend that an air strike would have been a better choice. Some of them believe that Kennedy should have exploited the opportunity provided by the Soviet missiles to invade Cuba and overthrow Castro. We address the criticism of the hawks elsewhere in this volume. Here, we examine the controversy between traditionalists and revisionists and the reasons why Kennedy chose the blockade in preference to a secret diplomatic overture to Khrushchev.

The documents and oral testimony of Ex Comm participants indicate that Kennedy had two objectives: to get the missiles out of Cuba and to demonstrate resolve to Khrushchev. A secret overture, even if it led to the withdrawal of the missiles, would not convey resolve. This was necessary, the president was convinced, to forestall another challenge in Berlin. He opted for a full-fledged confrontation in full recognition that it entailed a serious risk of war. As Dean Rusk put it, "If we don't do this, we go down with a whimper. Maybe it's better to go down with a bang."[52]

The question of resolve was also at the heart of the debate between advocates of the blockade and the air strike, the two most attractive options on the Ex Comm's menu. The air strike appealed to many of Kennedy's advisors because, unlike the blockade, it would get rid of the missiles, not just put pressure on Khrushchev to remove them. The air strike was also a more dramatic demonstration of resolve. The Ex Comm's final draft scenario for the air strike described its message of resolve as its principal advantage. By carrying out his pledge to eliminate offensive weapons in Cuba, the president "shows that [the] U.S. has [the] will to fight and to protect vital interests (of great importance vis-à-vis Berlin)." The air strike, the document acknowledged, "may force Khrushchev to react strongly and could result in some type of war."[53] The blockade was less likely to provoke a war and, for this reason, conveyed less resolve.

The president faced a difficult choice. A few Ex Comm members, including former Secretary of State Dean Acheson and Assistant Secretary of Defense Paul Nitze, denied his need to make any trade-off; they did not believe Khrushchev would retaliate against an American air strike even if it killed hundreds of Soviet military personnel. Acheson advised that "We should proceed at once with the necessary military actions and should do no talking."[54]

Most of the Ex Comm worried that Khrushchev might choose or be forced to respond to an air strike with military action of his own. They were concerned, as Dean Rusk warned his colleagues on 16 October, that they were "facing a situation that could well lead to general war."[55] The Ex Comm struggled with the pros and cons of the air strike and the blockade. Uncertainty about the effectiveness and consequences of both options resulted in long and torturous deliberations. Many Ex Comm participants changed their mind at least once during the week it took to reach a near-consensus in favor of the blockade.

The president was among those whose preferences changed. At first, he was drawn to the air strike, but upon reflection rejected it as too risky. He opted for the blockade because it conveyed resolve without resorting to violence and was less likely to provoke military escalation. In his mind, it represented a compromise between the imperatives for action, which pushed him up the ladder of escalation, and the risks of a confrontation, which pulled him down.[56]

The Ex Comm's Soviet experts, Charles "Chip" Bohlen and Llewellyn

"Tommie" Thompson, argued unsuccessfully for a private overture to Khrushchev. During the Ex Comm discussions on the second and third day of the crisis, Bohlen suggested that Kennedy send a letter to Khrushchev asking him to withdraw the missiles and proceed with a blockade, air strike, or invasion, only if Khrushchev refused. "No one can guarantee," he wrote the president, "that withdrawal can be achieved by diplomatic action—but it . . . seems essential that this channel be tested before military action is employed."[57]

For two days, Kennedy's advisors tried unsuccessfully to draft a letter to Khrushchev. They were unable to find language that would express indignation and demand the withdrawal of the missiles without provoking the crisis the letter was meant to avoid.[58] But this is not the only reason why Kennedy rejected Bohlen's proposal. He did not believe that a letter, no matter how well drafted, would convince Khrushchev to halt work at the missile sites and remove the missiles. "We couldn't imagine," McGeorge Bundy told Soviet officials many years later, "your obviously adventurous leader backing off from a move of this seriousness if we merely confronted him privately."[59] To get the missiles out, Kennedy and most of his advisors believed, it was necessary to threaten military action. If so, they reasoned, it was better to present Khrushchev with a fait accompli than an ultimatum that would allow him time to prepare a countermove.[60]

Revisionists fault Kennedy for not following the advice of Bohlen and Thompson. Ronald Steel believes that Kennedy should have "used traditional diplomatic channels to warn the Russians that he knew what they were up to, and thus give them a chance quietly to pull back." He could have communicated with Khrushchev through Georgiy Bol'shakov and Soviet Foreign Minister Andrei A. Gromyko, who visited the White House on 18 October, three days after the president had learned of the missiles in Cuba.[61] Walter Lippmann argued that Kennedy should have confronted Gromyko with the facts, giving "Mr. Khrushchev what all wise statesmen give their adversaries—the chance to save face."[62]

At issue is not Kennedy's ability to communicate with Khrushchev but the likelihood that a purely diplomatic initiative would have convinced the Soviet leader to withdraw his missiles.[63] None of the revisionists offer any reason to support their expectation that Khrushchev would have responded positively. One possible argument, and it seems implicit in Lippmann's formulation of the problem, is that backing down in response to a private rather than a public ultimatum, would have been less costly and hence more attractive to Khrushchev. It might also be supposed that a secret letter outlining the consequences to Khrushchev of the missile deployment might have encouraged him to reconsider his policy.[64]

We will never know if secret negotiations could have prevented a crisis. It is possible that Khrushchev might have been persuaded by a combination of threats and promises to dismantle the Soviet missile bases under construction in Cuba. We think it more probable that he would have rejected Kennedy's demand and have insisted that the missiles were necessary to protect Cuba from an American invasion. He would have tried to drag out his exchange of notes with Kennedy as long as possible to gain time for the missiles to become fully operational.

When he decided to send the missiles to Cuba, Khrushchev did not consider the domestic political pressures that would make the missiles unacceptable to Kennedy. Nor is there any evidence that he considered the important differences between openly deploying missiles in Turkey and secretly installing them in Cuba after giving the administration assurances to the contrary. Knowledgeable Soviet officials agree that Khrushchev's failure to grasp these consequences was the result of anger and wishful thinking.[65]

Khrushchev's emotional commitment to the missile deployment made it unlikely that a letter, or even an exchange of letters, would have led him to reconsider. We know that he discounted Kennedy's public and private warnings of 4 and 13 September, both of which should have made it clear that Washington would not tolerate the introduction of ballistic missiles into Cuba.[66] There is little reason to suppose that he would have responded differently to subsequent warnings and threats not backed up by observable military preparations.

Backing down in response to a secret ultimatum from Kennedy would also have created very serious problems for Khrushchev with two important constituencies: Fidel Castro and the Soviet officials whose support he relied on to maintain his authority. Castro welcomed the missiles and bitterly opposed their withdrawal.[67] Other Soviet militants felt the same way, and almost certainly would have accused Khrushchev of cowardice and of betraying Cuba. In the next chapter we argue that the crisis and the threat of war were probably necessary to convince Soviet hard-liners that Khrushchev had no choice but to remove the missiles, or have them removed by the United States. The crisis also eased the political consequences for Khrushchev by enabling him to secure a pledge not to invade Cuba from Kennedy and a private commitment to withdraw the American Jupiter missiles from Turkey some time after the Soviet missiles left Cuba.

It is possible, but unlikely, that Kennedy would have promised not to invade Cuba in the absence of a crisis. It is extremely unlikely that he would have consented to withdraw the Jupiters on Soviet demand. That concession was a secret move by a president anxious to avoid further military escalation that he believed could lead to war. Because the noninvasion pledge came late in the crisis, most Americans did not view it as a concession by a weak and irresolute president but as a statesmanlike gesture to end the confrontation by allowing a defeated adversary to save face. They knew nothing about the promise to remove the Jupiters, not made public until years later.

There is also the question of Kennedy's objectives to consider. Removing the missiles was Kennedy's primary objective. He also wanted to teach Khrushchev a lesson, something unlikely to be accomplished by quiet diplomacy. For this, he needed a dramatic public confrontation.

Time Pressure

Definitions of international crisis emphasize the perception of threat, heightened anxieties of war, and the limited time leaders have to respond to the threat.[68] Traditionalists and revisionists agree that time pressure was acute in the missile crisis but advance divergent explanations for why this was so. Traditionalists insist that the United States had to act before the Soviet missiles in Cuba became operational and made military action against them prohibitively costly. Revisionists contend that Kennedy had to remove the missiles before the November congressional elections. The evidence indicates that the president felt pressed for altogether different reasons.

In his widely acclaimed biography of John F. Kennedy, Arthur Schlesinger, Jr. reported that at the outset of the crisis the CIA had estimated that the Soviet missiles would be on pads and ready for firing in about ten days. According to Schlesinger, "The deadline defined the strategy."[69] The president and his advisors had to destroy, neutralize, or remove the missiles before they became operational and threatened to rain nuclear destruction on American cities. At the very first Ex Comm meeting, on the morning of 16 October, the president acknowledged this pressure. "I don't think we got much time on these missiles," he complained. "So it may be that we just have to, we can't wait two weeks while we're getting ready to, to roll."[70]

Robert McNamara has challenged this depiction of American policy. He insists that neither he nor the president was overly concerned about the operational status of the missiles. "I know that the later writing on the subject makes it sound like an important issue, but it had no effect on my decisions."[71] McGeorge Bundy explained that there was great concern about the missiles during the first week of the crisis. The concern was most pronounced among the Ex Comm hawks: Chairman of the Joint Chiefs Maxwell Taylor, former Secretary of State Dean Acheson, Secretary of the Treasury C. Douglas Dillon, CIA Director John McCone, and Assistant Secretary of Defense Paul Nitze.[72] The Ex Comm tapes reveal that Kennedy and McNamara also felt this way on the first day but quickly came to the realization that it was not a critical policy consideration.[73] They authorized further reconnaissance missions primarily to satisfy Ex Comm hawks and the joint chiefs.[74]

McNamara offered two reasons for his and the president's lack of concern. The first was intelligence information indicating that some of the missiles were operational as early as 15 October, although the CIA was unsure if those missiles had nuclear warheads.[75] The second was the need for caution: "We couldn't take the chance of being wrong, so we worked on the assumption throughout the crisis that at least some missiles were operational and armed with nuclear weapons."[76] For Kennedy and McNamara, knowledge that more missiles would soon come on line did not alter the fundamental fact that Khrushchev had some capability to launch a nuclear attack against the United States from missile bases in the Soviet Union and Cuba from the very beginning of the crisis.

Recently released CIA reports support McNamara's claims about the status of the missiles. On the morning of 19 October, only three days after the president learned of the missile sites, the CIA advised the White House that two MRBM launch sites with their sixteen R-12 missile launchers had an emergency operational capability. The MRBMs had a range of eleven-hundred nautical miles and could be launched within eighteen hours.[77] Bad weather grounded photoreconnaissance aircraft on 20 October. The next day's overflights discovered, and the president was quickly advised, that eight to twelve MRBM missiles had full operational capability.[78] By 23 October, the CIA had identified six MRBM sites. Four were presumed to be fully operational, and the two others were suspected of having some emergency capability.[79] On 27 October, the CIA reported that by the next day all six MRBM complexes would have achieved full operational status; their twenty-four MRBMs could be launched within six to eight hours, and a second salvo of twenty-four missiles within another four to six hours.[80] The White House never had a "window of opportunity" that would close when Soviet missiles came on line. From the beginning, the situation was one of gradually diminishing advantage because at least some missiles became operational shortly after their discovery.

McNamara maintains that the significance of missile readiness was political; it provided the militants with a rationale for military action against Cuba. According to George Ball: "The air strike advocates were using the issue of the missiles becoming 'operational' to buttress their case for urgency." It was the most powerful argument they could make against the blockade, before and after its implementation.[81] McNamara regarded the arguments as an attempt to justify a policy hardliners wanted for other reasons. Those who argued for an air strike on the grounds that it was necessary to keep the missiles from becoming operational "*continued* to favor it after it became clear that the missiles *were* operational."[82]

If there was no deadline imposed by the missiles, why did the president feel that he was acting under such extreme time pressure? Everyone agreed that during the first week of the crisis the sense of urgency was the result of the need to keep the discovery of the missiles in Cuba secret until the administration was prepared to respond. "There was a real concern," Douglas Dillon explained, "to control the agenda and keep it from being set by some newspaper."[83] George Ball thought the consequences of a leak would have been horrendous: "I'm just trying to think how we could have held off for three, four, or five days with the country screaming at us, when are you going to react, what are you going to do, with speeches in the Congress, with resolutions being passed, with demonstrations in the streets, the place would have been—the country would have been up in arms."[84] Dean Rusk worried that news of the missile sites "could lead to panic and confusion and even a mass exodus from our cities."[85]

A leak would have been politically damaging to the president. It would have generated enormous public and congressional pressure for immediate military action.[86] It could also have impaired the quality of the American response. In the week between the discovery of the missiles on 16 October and the administration's announcement of the quarantine on the twenty-second, the president and Ex Comm had time to consider the pros and cons of several different courses of action.[87] Advocates of the air strike and blockade agree that their free-wheeling debate led to a more informed decision. It also permitted the administration to orchestrate the political and military details of its strategy in a manner that would not otherwise have been possible. "The greatest lesson I took out of this," McNamara told George Ball, "is the increasing soundness of the decision with the passage of time."[88]

There was another critical consideration for the president: his need to gather support for the blockade from the cabinet, joint chiefs, and his own advisors. Kennedy was blunt about this need. On 22 October, he convened a full meeting of the National Security Council (NSC) to brief its members about the naval quarantine that he would announce that evening in a special televised address to the nation. Turning to the domestic aspects of the crisis, he stressed how important it was for the NSC to sing "one song" and to "make it clear that there was no difference among his advisors about the proper course to follow."[89] Kennedy was about to initiate a war-threatening confrontation with the Soviet Union. To make credible demands on Moscow, he needed bipartisan support. If his policy failed, and the crisis moved toward war, he would need this backing even more.

The issue of internal support became more critical during the second week of the crisis. The transcripts and participant accounts of the Ex Comm meetings make it apparent that the proponents of military action had agreed to the blockade in return for a tacit commitment that the president would carry out an air strike and possibly an invasion, if the blockade failed. As the week wore on, the pressure for an air strike mounted.[90] The principal advocates of the air strike—Paul Nitze, Douglas Dillon, and John McCone—became increasingly outspoken and critical of the blockade.[91] On the morning of 27 October, the joint chiefs unanimously recommended immediate military action to the president. "Time was getting a little tight," they warned, because of the impossibility of keeping military forces at full-alert status indefinitely.[92] The consensus had broken down. The president, Sorensen admits, was "under *tremendous* pressure at this point."[93]

Sorensen insists "that the President was determined *not* to step on that ladder of escalation at all."[94] He chose the blockade because it finessed his need for choice. But when the blockade appeared to have failed, the militants pressed for an air strike, and Kennedy found it increasingly difficult to avoid committing himself to a fight or a trade. Either policy involved serious political costs. It would also shatter the fragile unity of the Ex Comm and make it impossible for the administration to speak in one voice to the Congress and American people.

THE DANGER OF ESCALATION

The traditional and revisionist interpretations address only the domestic and foreign-policy costs of accepting Soviet missiles in Cuba. Both interpretations fail to consider the possible costs of doing something to get the missiles out. These costs were very much on the president's mind.

Kennedy was sensitive to the likelihood that the Republican opposition—and Democrats like Senators Russell and Fulbright, who clamored for an invasion of Cuba—would turn on him the moment American military operations ran into serious opposition. He may have remembered the fate of his Democratic predecessor, Harry S. Truman. Ohio Senator Robert A. Taft, leader of the Republican opposition, initially supported Truman's decision to come to the aid of South Korea. Within weeks, Taft and other Republican senators were derisively referring to the conflict as "Truman's War."[95] Truman's subsequent decision to cross the thirty-eighth parallel and occupy North Korea was primarily a response to domestic political pressures.[96] But as soon as Douglas MacArthur's advancing forces encountered Chinese forces and made an ignominious and costly retreat, the Republicans turned on Truman and successfully made his conduct of the Korean War a major campaign issue.[97]

Kennedy's desire to avoid this kind of political trap was an important reason for rejecting an air strike. So, too, was his concern that American military action would compel Soviet retaliation and trigger a spiral of escalation that could lead to thermonuclear war. During the second week of the crisis, escalation appeared no more acceptable than capitulation. This unpalatable choice pushed the president to find an alternative. His and Khrushchev's skill in finding one is the subject of the next chapter.

The Crisis and Its Resolution

I'm not a czarist officer who has to kill myself if I fart at a masked ball. It's better to back down than to go to war.

—Nikita S. Khrushchev [1]

The Cuban missile crisis reminds me of two boys fighting in the schoolyard over who has the bigger stick.

—Mikhail S. Gorbachev [2]

THE OUTCOME of the missile crisis has traditionally been regarded as a triumph of American coercive diplomacy.[3] John F. Kennedy exploited his country's nuclear superiority and conventional superiority in the Caribbean to impose a limited blockade of Cuba. He also prepared to mount an aerial offensive and invasion of Cuba. Confronted with superior force and resolve and offered the face-saving concession of a pledge not to invade Cuba, Khrushchev reluctantly agreed to remove the Soviet missiles. This explanation of Khrushchev's retreat captures only a small part of the much more complex calculus of both leaders.

The Cuban missile crisis is like the proverbial onion whose layers need to be peeled away one by one. In this chapter we begin by exposing the first and most visible layer: threats of force and their impact on both leaders. We argue that Kennedy's blockade and implicit threat of direct military action against Cuba had important consequences. By generating strong *mutual* fears of war, they prompted major concessions by *both* sides.

Khrushchev agreed to remove the missiles in return for a public pledge from Kennedy not to invade Cuba and a private promise to remove the American Jupiter missiles from Turkey sometime after the crisis. The outcome was a compromise. If Khrushchev had "hung tough" for a while longer, Kennedy would probably have agreed to a public exchange of missiles. To the public, who knew nothing of Kennedy's secret concession, the crisis was an unalloyed American triumph.

The second layer of the onion is domestic politics. Khrushchev and Kennedy worried deeply that concessions would undercut their political authority. As the crisis intensified, both leaders devoted considerable effort to finding ways of insulating themselves from the domestic costs of concession. It is no exaggeration to say that they became coconspirators; they cooperated to find ways of making concessions while conveying the appearance of resolve.

The third and deepest layer of the onion is mutual learning and reassurance. Each leader viewed the other's behavior as extraordinarily threatening because it appeared to be directed toward purely aggressive ends. They were both reluctant to make concessions for fear they would be interpreted as signs of weakness and encourage further challenges.

The missile crisis and the palpable threat of war it raised, helped both sides to break through some of the barriers of mistrust that divided them. Through letters and back-channel contacts, Kennedy and Khrushchev developed some insight into the interests, insecurities, and constraints that shaped one another's policies. Each leader succeeded to some extent in reassuring the other about the defensive nature of his motives. This significantly reduced the perceived cost of concession. This process and its broader implications are the subject of chapter 12.

THE ONSET OF THE CRISIS

For the United States, the crisis began on 16 October, when President Kennedy was informed of the discovery of missile sites in Cuba. The night before, the CIA had notified several high-ranking administration officials about the missiles, but National Security Advisor McGeorge Bundy decided not to tell the president until the following morning. He wanted to protect the secret and was concerned that late-night telephone calls or meetings would alert the press. Bundy also reasoned that his boss would profit from an undisturbed night of sleep.[4]

During the week the Ex Comm debated and prepared the administration's response to the missiles, Khrushchev assumed that all was going according to plan.[5] On Thursday, 18 October, Soviet Foreign Minister Andrei Gromyko, in the country for the opening of the United Nation's General Assembly, came to the White House to talk about Berlin and Cuba. Gromyko assured Kennedy that the Soviet Union would do nothing in Berlin before the congressional elections; afterwards, there would have to be some dialogue. He complained about the American threat to Cuba, and justified the Soviet decision to send soldiers and technicians to the island as a defensive and precautionary measure.[6]

From his rocking chair, Kennedy disavowed any intention to invade Cuba and told Gromyko that the Soviet arms shipments had seriously aroused American opinion. He was under pressure to take firmer measures against Castro. He read aloud his 4 September statement warning that the introduction of offensive weapons into Cuba would have the gravest consequences for Soviet-American relations. Gromyko repeated the assurances that his government had already given the administration. The Soviet foreign minister left the White House in a jovial mood and told reporters that his discussion with the president had been "useful, very useful."[7]

Kennedy was not so buoyant. He told Dean Rusk and Llewellyn Thompson that perhaps he had made a mistake by not telling Gromyko that he knew about the Soviet missiles in Cuba. Both men assured him that he had acted wisely by keeping the knowledge to himself. Moscow should be told nothing until the president had decided on an appropriate response; premature disclosure would give Soviet leaders a tactical advantage. That evening, Dean Rusk hosted a dinner for Gromyko at the State Department and steered the conversation away from Cuba. He and his guest became embroiled in arguments over Berlin and about who had started the Cold War.[8]

Gromyko later claimed that he felt extremely uncomfortable about repeating Khrushchev's assurances because the Soviet deception was likely to provoke a serious crisis. His conversation with Kennedy "was perhaps the most difficult I have had with any of the nine presidents with whom I had dealings in my forty-nine years of service."[9] Khrushchev had no such misgivings; he was delighted with Gromyko's performance. The Soviet foreign minister, he boasted, had "answered like a gypsy who was caught stealing a horse. 'It's not me and it's not my horse. I don't know anything.'"[10]

Gromyko's cables to the Presidium tell a different story. They did not emphasize the administration's concerns but rather downplayed them. Soviet "boldness" in Cuba, he advised, had compelled Washington to rethink its plans for invading Cuba. The anti-Cuba campaign had been scaled down in its intensity, and the press was now in an uproar about Berlin. "The purpose of this change in American propaganda was to divert attention from Cuba, not without the White House doing its share."[11] Gromyko told Ambassador Anatoliy F. Dobrynin that he was pleased with the results of his meetings with Kennedy and Rusk. Dobrynin, who had no inkling that Soviet missiles were being deployed in Cuba, was surprised that Kennedy had not pressed Gromyko harder on this question given the administration's obvious concern. In retrospect, he thinks this was a great mistake on Kennedy's part.[12]

Gromyko's attempt, as Dobrynin put it, "to play down" Kennedy's opposition to Soviet missiles in Cuba helped to lull Khrushchev into believing that all was well. Gromyko's colleagues maintain that his cable was very much in character. As one of them put it, "he stayed in power for so long because he told his superiors only what they wanted to hear." Gromyko's willingness to pander to Khrushchev had a chilling effect on his subordinates. They often felt constrained from reporting the truth as they understood it for fear that it would offend and embarrass Gromyko.[13]

The View from Moscow

On Monday, 22 October, Soviet officials learned that something extraordinary was afoot in Washington. That morning's *New York Times*, which was on the newsstands the evening before, reported a crisis atmosphere in Washington, a major military buildup in the Caribbean, and the expectation that the president would address the nation on television.[14] At 6:00 P.M., one hour before the president was to go on the air, Dean Rusk briefed Ambassador Dobrynin about the contents of his speech. Dobrynin refused to believe that his country had sent missiles to Cuba. When Rusk showed him the U-2 photographs, "he aged ten years before my eyes." Dobrynin left the meeting "badly shaken."[15]

In Moscow, Khrushchev scheduled a late-night meeting of the Presidium. It was held in a large hall in the Kremlin, two rooms away from Khrushchev's study. In attendance were all the Presidium members in Moscow, alternate members, Central Committee Secretaries, and many top officials from the foreign and defense ministries. About a hour before Kennedy spoke, at 2 A.M. Moscow time, the text of his speech was transmitted to the foreign ministry by the American embassy. It was relayed by telephone to Oleg Troyanovsky at the Kremlin, who provided an on-the-spot translation of relevant passages for the Presidium.[16]

Kennedy's announcement of the "quarantine" was seen to leave room for political maneuver, "the more so because the President called the blockade a 'quarantine' which created an illusion of still greater vagueness." Because it contained no ultimatum or direct invasion threat, the speech encouraged the illusion that Kennedy might yet accommodate himself to the presence of the missiles.[17]

Following a lengthy discussion, Khrushchev decided on the broad outlines of a reply and instructed Deputy Foreign Minister Vasiliy V. Kuznetsov to have his staff submit a final draft the next day.[18] Khrushchev recommended to everyone present that they spend the night in the Kremlin so that foreign correspondents would not get the impression that Soviet leaders were anxious or frightened.[19] This was a futile ruse. Ambassador Foy Kohler cabled Washington that "the remarks of almost every Soviet official" made it clear that the Soviet leadership was really "shaken."[20]

Khrushchev subsequently acknowledged that the entire Soviet leadership was under great stress.

> I remember a period of six or seven days when the danger was particularly acute. Seeking to take the heat off the situation somehow, I suggested to the other members of the government: Comrades, let's go to the Bolshoi Theater this evening. Our own people as well as foreign eyes will notice, and perhaps it will calm them down. They'll say to themselves, 'If Khrushchev and our other leaders are able to go to the opera at a time like this, then at least tonight we can sleep peacefully.' We were trying to disguise our own anxiety, which was intense.[21]

Another indication of stress was Khrushchev's inability at first to come to grips with the gravity of the situation. Soviet officials report that it took two or three days for him to confront the reality that if he did not remove the missile the Americans almost certainly would.[22] Vasiliy Kuznetsov dismissed Khrushchev's blistering messages to Kennedy on 23 and 24 October as attempts to conceal his confusion. Without any guidance from the Kremlin, the foreign ministry was unable to act. This put Ambassador Dobrynin in a particularly difficult position. He received no response to his cable describing his talk with Robert Kennedy in the Soviet embassy on the evening of 23 October. In the absence of instructions, Dobrynin could not acknowledge Kennedy's assertion that there were Soviet missiles in Cuba. He nevertheless hastened to inform Moscow of the gravity of the situation and of the possibility that the United States would attack Cuba.[23]

Soviet Policymaking

Crisis policy was made by Khrushchev in consultation with a group of top officials. They included President of the Supreme Soviet Leonid I. Brezhnev, Prime Minister Aleksei N. Kosygin, First Deputy Prime Minister Anastas I. Mikoyan, First Deputy Foreign Minister Vasiliy Kuznetsov, Foreign Minister Andrei A. Gromyko, Secretary of the Central Committee Leonid F. Ilychev, Chairman of the Committee on State Security (KGB) Aleksandr N. Shelepin, Minister of Defense Marshal Rodion Ya. Malinovsky, Commander of the Strategic Rocket Forces Marshal Sergei S. Biryuzov, Director of the Central Committee's Department for Relations with Socialist Countries Yuri Andropov, Khrushchev foreign-policy aide Oleg Troyanovsky, Presidium members Petr N. Demichev, Frol R. Kozlov, Boris N. Ponomarev, Dimitri S. Polyansky, and Mikhail A. Suslov. Pavel Satyukov and Aleksei Adzhubei—editors-in-chief, respectively, of *Pravda* and *Izvestiya*—and various officials from the Central Committee and foreign ministry were also invited to some of the meetings at which the crisis was discussed.

Khrushchev conferred with these men individually, in small groups, and in full Presidium sessions. These meetings generally took place in his Kremlin office, but sometimes at his home or the suburban government mansion in Novo-Ogarevo.[24] He also consulted with allied leaders. He corresponded almost daily with Fidel Castro but did not inform him of his negotiations with President Kennedy.[25] Critical decisions and letters to Kennedy were approved by the Presidium but in every case reflected Khrushchev's will.[26]

Khrushchev had two working groups assisting him. The first, in the Central Committee, was led by Andropov. The second, in the foreign office, reported to Gromyko. It was composed of Andrei M. Alexandrov-Argentov, Felix N. Kovaliev, Lev I. Mendelevich, Mikhail N. Smirnovsky, and Leonid M. Zamyatin, with Oleg Grinevsky as its secretary. Both groups saw Khrushchev's correspondence with Kennedy and Castro and relevant embassy cables. Alexandrov was, inter alia, responsible for liaison between the KGB and foreign ministry, and did his best to ensure that relevant information collected by the KGB was made available to both groups.[27]

There was no firm division of labor, although of the two groups the one in the Central Committee was the senior. Andropov and Gromyko kept in close touch. Gromyko often passed on memorandums and drafts from the foreign-ministry to the Central Committee group. But sometimes he submitted them directly to Khrushchev. The foreign-ministry group reworked and polished drafts of Khrushchev's letters to Kennedy. Unlike other Soviet leaders, Khrushchev drafted much of his own correspondence. During the missile crisis, he dictated letters to Kennedy. Some of them were ten pages and "long-winded and rambling." The foreign office group worked hard to transform them into coherent and succinct letters for his approval.[28]

Neither working group staffed options the way the Ex Comm did; this was simply not done in the Soviet Union. Officials waited for their superiors to choose a policy line and only then responded with more detailed studies or plans for implementation. "The game in the Soviet foreign ministry," according to Ambassador Grinevsky, "was to guess the policy choices that would be made and be ready to respond." Most of the staff papers analyzed American policy and intentions; this was a much safer enterprise.[29]

In their meetings, members of both groups did not hesitate to discuss the key questions of the crisis. What was the risk? How should the Soviet Union respond to the blockade? How could war be avoided? How can Khrushchev retreat and save face? The foreign-ministry group had lengthy private discussions about what would happen if the United States attacked the missiles or invaded Cuba, possibilities considered very likely. By Thursday, the third day of the crisis, there was a consensus within the group that the missiles would have to be withdrawn. There were significant disagreements about how to respond to an American attack against the missiles or Cuba. Some officials maintained that the Soviet Union should do nothing, that the loss of Cuba, galling as it would be, was still preferable to World War III. Others believed that the Soviet Union should take military reprisals of some kind.[30]

The Soviet Dilemma

Khrushchev was in a thoroughly unenviable position. The missiles in Cuba were vulnerable to American attack, as was the Castro regime. If Kennedy used force—and his public commitment to remove the missiles and extensive military preparations made that a real possibility—Khrushchev knew that he could protect neither the missiles nor the Cuban government.[31] Prudence dictated accommodation. But to withdraw the missiles in response to American threats would entail serious political and foreign-policy costs.

If he pulled the missiles out, Khrushchev would appear weak and indecisive at home and abroad. His domestic political opponents would brand him as the author of an impractical and provocative scheme. Militants would accuse him of losing his nerve. Sergei Khrushchev says his father "did *not* want to run the blockade, but the Soviet Union would have experienced a national humiliation if he had failed to challenge it." Khrushchev reluctantly ordered a ship to proceed to Cuba, fully expecting the Americans to fire on it. "He was surprised by Kennedy's restraint and wisdom when the navy did not sink it. Kennedy rose in his esteem. Nikita Sergeevich thought that this was one of the most dangerous moments of the crisis."[32]

Khrushchev also faced a delicate situation with Castro, whom Khrushchev thought "a young and hotheaded man." When Khrushchev announced that he would withdraw the missiles in return for an American promise not to invade Cuba, Castro was adamantly opposed.[33] "You don't know Americans," he told Alekseev and Mikoyan. "Any agreement with them is just paper. . . . They only understand the language of force."[34] Khrushchev had to consider the possibility that Castro would refuse to cooperate with a decision to withdraw the missiles and seriously complicate his relations with the United States.

Even if Castro did not block withdrawal of the missiles, he might still excoriate Khrushchev for cowardice in the face of American threats. Cuban disenchantment with Khrushchev would be exploited by China, intent as it was on convincing other communist parties that the Soviet Union was a "paper tiger." Cuban and Chinese criticism would greatly intensify Khrushchev's political embarrassment at home.

Collectively, the expected costs of retreat provided a strong incentive for Khrushchev to stand firm and deny the dangers that lay ahead. To Khrushchev's credit, he did not succumb to wishful thinking a second time. He had persevered with the missile deployment in the face of warnings from his foreign-policy advisors and President Kennedy. The American blockade and the mounting preparations for an invasion of Cuba soon brought him back to reality. Aleksei Adzhubei reports that his father-in-law slowly came to the realization that "he had put himself out on a limb that Kennedy would saw off unless he climbed down." Once Khrushchev overcame his anger, he sought to end the crisis peacefully "with the maximum possible result for *us*."[35] His biggest worry "was that the American military would force Kennedy into attacking Cuba before some kind of acceptable accommodation could be found."[36]

Khrushchev's Strategy

As much by default as by design, Khrushchev pursued a two-pronged strategy. By appearing tough and uncompromising, he tried to extract concessions from Kennedy in return for withdrawing the missiles. At home, he sought to convince his Presidium colleagues that failure to remove the missiles would provoke an American invasion of Cuba.

Khrushchev implemented his strategy with considerable skill. To keep the pressure on Kennedy, Soviet work crews stepped up the pace of construction at the Cuban missile sites.[37] In Europe, Soviet and Warsaw Pact Armed forces announced an alert.[38] The Ministry of Defense canceled all leaves and deferred the impending release of troops in the Strategic Rocket Forces, Air Defense Forces, and submarine fleet.[39] In Hiroshima, the head of the Soviet news agency TASS announced that American ships would be sunk if they attacked Soviet ships.[40] Khrushchev's public statements and messages to Kennedy were equally uncompromising. He rejected the president's demand that the Soviet missiles be withdrawn as "arbitrary," and denounced the Cuban blockade as an illegal "act of aggression" that was "pushing mankind toward the abyss of a world missile nuclear war." He warned that Soviet ship captains had orders not to tolerate "piratical actions of American ships on the high seas" and would defend themselves if necessary.[41] By Wednesday morning, 24 October, *Gagarin* and *Komiles*, two Soviet merchantmen, were only a few miles from the blockade line.[42]

Khrushchev was all bluster in his interview with William Knox, President of Westinghouse International. In Moscow on business, Knox was summoned to the Kremlin on Wednesday and subjected to a three-hour harangue. Khrushchev told him that Soviet ships would challenge the blockade and Soviet submarines would sink American destroyers if they interfered with Soviet shipping. He warned Knox that he would not be the first to fire a nuclear weapon but "if the U.S. insists on war, we'll all meet together in hell."[43] Dobrynin gave the same message to Robert Kennedy on 23 October. He told the attorney general that "our captains had an order to continue their course to Cuba, for the action[s] of President Kennedy were unlawful." His answer "made Kennedy a bit nervous."[44] In retrospect, Dobrynin considered this to have been the tensest moment of the crisis. He watched on television as the first ship reached the blockade line and remembered breathing "an enormous sigh of relief" when it was allowed to pass through.[45]

Despite his threats, Khrushchev was careful not to provoke a military clash. Within hours of learning about the blockade, he ordered Soviet ships en route to Cuba to stop and the sixteen carrying arms to return to the Soviet Union. Soviet admirals advised him that there was no chance of running the blockade or of opposing the Americans at sea. The Soviet navy had few surface ships in the Atlantic and only the submarines normally on station. The Americans, Khrushchev was told, had mustered overwhelming naval and air forces at short notice.[46]

All sixteen vessels with military cargoes, including five carrying missiles and one suspected of transporting nuclear warheads, turned back after the quarantine was announced and before it went into effect.[47] Two of the ships that turned back, *Poltava* and *Kimovsk*, had been the prime targets for boarding. *Kimovsk* was a large-hatch ship that had previously delivered military equipment to Cuba. *Poltava*, designated by the American navy as its "first target," was thought to be carrying nuclear weapons.[48] The ships that halted, tankers and freighters with nonmilitary cargoes, stood dead in the water, some of them for two days, and then resumed their journey toward Cuba. No Soviet ship reached the quarantine line until Thursday, 25 October.

Khrushchev's strategy was risky. In the hope of extracting concessions from the Americans, he rejected their demand and raised the threat of war. He assumed that Kennedy was as anxious to avoid a military clash as he was. If the president wanted to exploit the missile deployment as a pretext to invade Cuba, Khrushchev's truculence would backfire. So could the round-the-clock work on the missile sites. Khrushchev may have hoped that fully operational missiles would deter an American attack. Some of his advisors worried that stepped-up efforts to ready the missiles could provoke an attack from an administration anxious to prevent the United States from becoming more vulnerable to nuclear attack.[49]

Even if Khrushchev's judgment of Kennedy was correct, it was not clear how far the president could be pushed before he would feel compelled to attack either the missiles or Cuba. Military action by either side could set in motion an unstoppable spiral of escalation. In his messages to the president, Khrushchev repeatedly warned of this danger. Timing was everything. Khrushchev had to remain uncompromising long enough for Kennedy to soften his terms, but not so long that he despaired of negotiating an acceptable settlement and succumbed to the mounting pressures to order an air strike or invasion.

THE VIEW FROM WASHINGTON

On Monday evening, 22 October, President Kennedy proclaimed a "naval quarantine" to prevent the further shipment of offensive weapons to Cuba. To enforce what was in effect a partial blockade, the U.S. navy put 183 ships into the Caribbean and Atlantic sea lanes. Naval aircraft flew hundreds of sorties to spot, identify, and plot the course of every vessel approaching Cuba from the mid-Atlantic. The army and air force prepared for military action against Cuba. The assembled invasion force included five Army and one Marine divisions—more than 140,000 troops—supported by 579 ground- and carrier-based combat aircraft. American strategic forces were also brought up to an unprecedented state of readiness, Defense Condition (DEFCON) II. Many more nuclear armed B-52 bombers went airborne and as many ICBM missile silos as was possible were raised to full-alert status.[50]

The President's Dilemma

By Saturday, 27 October, the prospect of war weighed heavily on Kennedy's mind. The blockade had done nothing to stop construction at the missile sites; American intelligence reported that Soviet construction crews were working around the clock to make the sites fully operational. Khrushchev appeared interested in resolving the crisis, but in return for withdrawing the Soviet missiles in Cuba, he insisted that the United States give a formal pledge not to invade Cuba and remove its Jupiter missiles from Turkey. When the Ex Comm adjourned that afternoon, the president passed out sealed envelopes to all the participants. Inside were instructions for them and their families if they and other top officials should have to evacuate

Washington in the next day or two for an unspecified wartime command center.[51] Kennedy estimated that the odds of the Soviets starting a war were "somewhere between one out of three and even."[52]

Kennedy had chosen the blockade over the air strike because he regarded it as less risky. A vocal minority in the Ex Comm had favored an air strike and pressed for it now that the blockade seemed to have failed. Paul Nitze, John McCone, Douglas Dillon, and Maxwell Taylor all urged an air strike on the grounds that the blockade had done nothing to stop construction at the missile sites. McNamara remembers that "Taylor was *absolutely convinced* that we had to attack Cuba."[53] Some advocates of the air strike thought it should be limited to the Soviet missiles and their bases. Others wanted to go after a wide range of military and economic targets as well. All were convinced that Khrushchev would not dare respond to an air strike with military action of his own.[54]

The air force steadfastly opposed a limited or so-called "surgical" air strike, and demanded an attack of some 500 sorties against the missiles preceded by a "softening up" strike of 1,190 sorties against related military targets. This was to be followed by six more days of massive strikes. The bombing was expected to prepare the way for the invasion the joint chiefs insisted would have to follow a day or two later. The chiefs advised Defense Secretary McNamara that the invasion would lead to "a bloody battle" in which the Cuban and Soviet forces would sustain "heavy casualties." All the preparations for the air strike and invasion were ordered to be in place by Monday, 29 October.[55]

The Ex Comm transcript for 27 October indicates that not everyone was as sanguine as the hawks. Some officials voiced concern that even a limited air strike would provoke some kind of Soviet reprisal, most probably against Berlin or the Jupiter missile bases in Turkey. McNamara was absolutely convinced of this and said so three times during the course of the day's deliberations.[56] He subsequently reaffirmed his belief "that if we initiated military action, *something* would follow. There would have been a Soviet response *somewhere*—and that was simply unforeseeable. I didn't expect a strategic exchange, but I just didn't know where things would go."[57] Dean Rusk thought that Khrushchev would have "serious problems controlling his own Politburo [sic]."[58] Llewellyn Thompson worried that Khrushchev was sufficiently impulsive to order some kind of military retaliation that "would result eventually, if not immediately, in nuclear war." Thompson, whose judgment on Soviet matters carried great weight with the president, had warned earlier that the prestige and honor of the Red Army would require retaliation if the United States killed Soviet military personnel in Cuba.[59]

McNamara described the most likely scenario of tit-for-tat escalation. The United States would strike Cuba and have to follow with an invasion. The Soviet Union would respond by attacking the Jupiter missiles in Turkey.

That would compel American retaliation against Soviet air and naval bases in and around the Black Sea. "That was the *minimum* response we would consider, and I would say that it is *damned dangerous.*"[60] The president agreed. The consequence of an air strike, he warned "is going to be very grave [words unclear], and very bloody."[61]

The Search for a Compromise

Early accounts of the crisis portray Kennedy as prepared to order an air strike if the blockade failed to achieve its purpose.[62] Fortunately, it did not prove necessary; on Sunday, Khrushchev agreed to remove his missiles in return for a pledge not to invade Cuba. Khrushchev's "capitulation" is generally attributed to Kennedy's resolve and his willingness to make a "face-saving" concession on Cuba.

Aleksandr Fomin, KGB station chief in Washington, had suggested a non-invasion pledge as a possible means of resolving the crisis. Khrushchev had also asked for such a pledge in his Friday letter to the president. These communications set the stage for Robert Kennedy's meeting with Soviet Ambassador Anatoliy Dobrynin on Saturday evening, 27 October. At this meeting, Kennedy presented Dobrynin with a de facto ultimatum. As one Kennedy confidant put it: "He told the Ambassador that we would remove the missiles from Cuba if we did not hear by the following day that the Russians were willing to remove them."[63] Kennedy also carried a conciliatory message from the president: a letter offering an American pledge not to invade Cuba in return for withdrawal of the Soviet missiles in Cuba. Students of the crisis have generally regarded the Kennedy-Dobrynin meeting as the catalyst for Khrushchev's decision, made the following day, to accept Kennedy's terms for ending the crisis.

Robert Kennedy's memoir sheds some light on his Saturday night meeting with Dobrynin. That morning, the White House had received a message from Khrushchev demanding the removal of the American missiles in Turkey as a quid pro quo for withdrawal of the Soviet missiles in Cuba.[64] The president instructed his brother to tell Dobrynin that he would not withdraw the Jupiter missiles under Soviet pressure but "had ordered their removal some time ago, and it was our judgment that, within a short time after this crisis was over, those missiles would be gone."[65] The attorney general brandished a stick as well as holding out a carrot. He told Dobrynin that pressure was mounting within the government for military action to remove the missiles and that his brother could not hold out much longer. The ambassador "should understand that if they did not remove those bases, we would remove them."[66]

The president had not in fact decided what to do if Khrushchev spurned his offer. He was very reluctant to attack Cuba and was contemplating further concessions if they were necessary to end the crisis. On 24 October, Dean Rusk, acting on presidential instructions, cabled Raymond Hare, the

American ambassador in Turkey, that the administration was considering removal of the Jupiter missiles. Hare was asked to evaluate the political consequences for Turkey of several different scenarios, including "outright removal" of the Jupiters.[67] He reported back on 26 October that Turkey would "deeply resent" any sacrifice of its interests "to appease an enemy," and advised that if the administration decided to remove the Jupiters, it do so on a "strictly secret basis with the Soviets."[68]

From the very outset of the crisis the Kennedy brothers had recognized the need for compromise. On Sunday evening, 21 October, a day before the quarantine speech, Robert Kennedy confided to Arthur Schlesinger, Jr. that "We will have to make a deal in the end."[69] That morning, the president expressed the same opinion to British Prime Minister Harold Macmillan.[70] The most salient bargain was an exchange of missiles: Soviet missiles in Cuba for American missiles in Turkey.

The Ex Comm discussed the possibility of an exchange of missiles almost from the beginning of their deliberations; on Wednesday morning, 19 October, the president had posed the question of removing the Jupiters.[71] Robert McNamara and Assistant Secretary of State Harlan Cleveland had argued that some kind of trade would be necessary to get the missiles out of Cuba. McNamara had suggested "that we might have to withdraw our missiles both in Italy and Turkey." He even conceded that the United States might ultimately have to abandon Guantanamo.[72] United Nations Ambassador Adlai E. Stevenson had urged the president to consider such a deal when he was first informed about the discovery of Soviet missile bases.[73] Averell Harriman also favored a missile trade as a face-saving way out of the crisis for Khrushchev. On Wednesday, 22 October, he advised the president that it might help Khrushchev to overcome military opposition to withdrawal of the missiles and facilitate a "swing" toward improved relations with the United States. He wrote a second memorandum on Friday.[74]

On Saturday morning, the president weighed the pros and cons of an exchange of missiles before the Ex Comm. He worried that Khrushchev's insistence on a missile trade would be very difficult to oppose. "We're going to be in an insupportable position, if this becomes his proposal."[75] Kennedy also became increasingly open about his disenchantment with military action as the day wore on. He was troubled by the likely domestic and foreign-policy repercussions of an air strike that led to an invasion of Cuba, as the joint chiefs insisted it must. He told the Ex Comm: "We can't very well invade Cuba with all its toil, and long as it's going to be, when we could have gotten them [the missiles] out by making a deal on the same missiles in Turkey. If that's part of the record I don't see that we'll have a very good war."[76] "When the blood starts to flow," he warned, public opinion at home and in Europe would turn against a president who had gone to war for the sake of "obsolescent missiles." How could he convince the American people that a missile trade was a sensible action *before* the fighting began? It would be seen as a sellout to the Soviet Union.[77] "If we take no action or if we take action," the president opined, "they're all going to be saying we should have done the reverse."[78]

The "hawks" were horrified by the prospect of a missile trade, but other key members of the Ex Comm, in continuous session that afternoon, expressed guarded support. Dean Rusk and George Ball thought that a trade could successfully be explained to the Europeans. Theodore Sorensen had submitted a memorandum to the president making the same argument.[79] Robert Kennedy spoke in favor of a trade. As he and Rusk were almost always on opposite sides, the fact that they now advocated the same course of action was significant. Rusk and Bundy believe that the president was strongly influenced by their concurrence.[80]

The Ex Comm adjourned after agreeing on a reply to Khrushchev, the famous Trollope ploy.[81] Kennedy would ignore Khrushchev's morning message demanding withdrawal of the Jupiter missiles and respond instead to his message of the previous evening, proposing withdrawal of the Soviet missiles in Cuba in return for an American pledge not to invade Cuba.[82] The president's letter, drafted by Sorensen and Robert Kennedy, insisted on "appropriate United Nations observation and supervision" of the withdrawal of the missiles. It made no mention of the Jupiters.[83]

The Secret Deal

After the Ex Comm meeting, the president and eight Ex Comm members (Dean Rusk, Robert McNamara, Robert Kennedy, McGeorge Bundy, Theodore Sorensen, George Ball, Roswell Gilpatric, and Llewellyn Thompson) reconvened in the Oval Office to discuss the contents of an oral message that Robert Kennedy would convey that evening to Ambassador Dobrynin. The attorney general was tapped for this task on the advice of Llewellyn Thompson, who thought the use of such an unusual channel for the president's message would give it special salience in Moscow. "The Russians having a conspirational tone of mind," Dean Rusk explained, "we thought they would pay more attention to what Bobby was saying more than anyone else short of the President himself."[84]

McGeorge Bundy recalls that the first part of the message "was simple, stern, and quickly decided—that the time had come to agree on the basis set out in the president's new letter: no Soviet missiles in Cuba, and no U.S. invasion. Otherwise future American action was unavoidable."[85] Rusk proposed that Kennedy should tell Dobrynin that the administration would not enter into an explicit arrangement about the Jupiters, but that the president was determined to remove them after the Soviet missiles came out of Cuba. His suggestion was quickly accepted by the group and approved by the president with the caveat that no one outside the assembled group be told anything about this part of the message. Robert Kennedy was to stress the need for secrecy to Dobrynin; the Jupiters would not be withdrawn if Moscow made any mention of the president's promise.[86]

The meeting in the Oval Office lasted only about twenty minutes. Bundy believes that it was significant that Rusk had authored the proposal regarding the Jupiters. Everyone thought of him as "NATO's representative" on the Ex Comm. When Rusk made it clear that he regarded the Jupiters as "a phony issue" and did not believe their removal would cause a serious problem for Turkey or the European allies if it was put properly, it "made it easier for the rest of us to support it."[87]

Rusk returned to his office at the State Department. From there he telephoned Robert Kennedy to emphasize again that he convey the impression that the United States would not enter into an agreement concerning the Jupiters. The president's intention to remove them was "a piece of information" that was being passed on to the Soviets. Kennedy told Rusk that he had just talked to Dobrynin who, when told that the missiles in Turkey were coming out, exclaimed: "This is a very important piece of information."[88] The air force had been working hard to deploy the Jupiters, and the first missile had become operational on the day Kennedy announced the quarantine. As far as we know, the Soviet Union had no evidence that the administration had previously tried to halt or slow the deployment and any claim to this effect by Robert Kennedy would have been regarded as a rather transparent attempt to save face. From Moscow's perspective, a promise to remove the Jupiters was a concession, and an important one.

Protecting the President

When the Jupiters came out of Turkey six months later, there was speculation that there had been a secret understanding with Moscow. The administration was publicly outraged. In January 1963, Dean Rusk assured the Senate Foreign Relations Committee that no "deal" or "trade" had directly or indirectly been made with regard to the Jupiter missiles.[89] McNamara told the same thing to the House Appropriations Committee.[90]

"We misled our colleagues, our countrymen, our successors, and our allies," McGeorge Bundy admitted many years later. "We denied in every forum that there was any deal, because the few who knew about it at the time were in unanimous agreement that any other course would have had explosive and destructive effects on the security of the U.S. and its allies."[91] In a jointly authored *Time* magazine article in 1982, McNamara, Rusk, Ball, Gilpatric, Sorensen, and Bundy argued that any disclosure of the full contents of Kennedy's discussion with Dobrynin would have been "misread" as a "concession granted in fear at the expense of an ally."[92] McNamara insisted that even a secret trade would have set a dangerous precedent. "If they [the Soviets] could get away with that, what else would they do? We saw in Berlin the previous years that they would go just as far as they thought they could. There was a slicing of the salami; slice by slice they were moving ahead, or trying to." Kennedy and his principal advisors believed that "it was absolutely essential" that "we not convey to the

Soviets the impression that we either were weak or would behave in a weak fashion."[93]

The Kennedy inner circle was so worried about the consequences of publicity that they rewrote history. In their public accounts of the crisis, administration officials and journalists to whom they confided reported that the president had ordered the Jupiters out of Turkey *before* the crisis.[94] Roger Hilsman, head of State Department intelligence, described an August National Security Action Memorandum that allegedly had ordered the missiles removed.[95] In his best-selling book, newsman Elie Abel described how Kennedy told Under Secretary of State George Ball in August 1962 to "press the matter" with Turkey even at "some political cost to the United States."[96] The president, Abel contended, assumed that the missiles had been withdrawn and was furious to learn from Khrushchev that they were still there.[97]

The State Department was made the scapegoat. According to Robert Kennedy's memoir, Dean Rusk failed to persuade the Turkish government to agree to the removal of the missiles. The president then ordered them out, but the State Department failed to push the matter in the face of vigorous objections from Turkey. Kennedy described his brother as the unwitting victim of State's duplicity. "The president believed he was president and that, his wishes having been made clear, they would be followed and the missiles removed. He therefore dismissed the matter from his mind. Now, he learned that the failure to follow up on this matter had permitted the same obsolete Turkish missiles to become hostages of the Soviet Union."[98] Arthur Schlesinger, Jr. repeated the story in his 1978 biography of Robert Kennedy.[99]

These accounts are inaccurate and misleading. In chapter 2 we described how Kennedy had persevered with the deployment of the Jupiter missiles in spite of the misgivings of former President Eisenhower and many senior national security officials.[100] Kennedy did *not* order the missiles withdrawn prior to the crisis, although he had expressed interest in finding some way of halting the deployment. The National Security Action Memorandum to which Hilsman refers merely instructed the Defense Department to look into the question of "what action can be taken to get [the] Jupiter missiles out of Turkey?"[101]

Kennedy's surprise and anger at learning that the missiles had not been removed is a myth. A National Security Action Memorandum drafted less than a month before the crisis reveals that he knew that the missiles were still in the process of being deployed in Turkey.[102] Dean Rusk and George Ball confirm that Kennedy knew about the missiles; Rusk had briefed him about Turkish opposition to their removal, and he had accepted the need for delay. Rusk denies that the president expressed any anger toward him then or later in the crisis.[103]

McGeorge Bundy, author of the August National Security Action Memorandum, tells the same story. His memorandum, sent out on 23 August, had asked what could be done to get the missiles out of Turkey, but no decision had been taken before the crisis. "For a year and a half," Bundy remembered, Kennedy knew that "the Turkish missiles could be removed only over the resistance of both the Turks and Washington's custodians of NATO solidarity (of whom, in one mood, he was the foremost). He had not pressed the matter home." The president later regretted his failure to act and was extremely annoyed during the crisis when the Jupiters appeared to stand in the way of a settlement. "In his anger he once or twice expressed himself as if he had given orders that had not been obeyed. But it was not so."[104]

The "disinformation" campaign served its purpose; it allowed the president to make a critical concession beyond the glare of publicity. On 29 October, McNamara ordered the Jupiters in Turkey dismantled. The following March, the State Department reluctantly confirmed press reports that the missiles were being removed.[105] Seven years after the crisis, the State Department story helped to defuse the revelation in Robert Kennedy's posthumous memoir that the president had indeed made a concession on the Jupiters to the Soviet Union.[106]

A More Secret Deal

Khrushchev subsequently acknowledged the "deal" he had struck with Kennedy over the Jupiters: "President Kennedy told us through his brother that in exchange he would remove missiles from Turkey. He said: 'If this leaks into the press, I will deny it. I give my word I will do this, but this promise should not be made public.' He also said that he would remove the missiles from Italy and he did that."[107]

Anatoliy Dobrynin confirms Khrushchev's account. Robert Kennedy never told him, as alleged in his memoir, that the Americans had been planning all along to remove the missiles. The president committed himself to their removal when Dobrynin and Robert Kennedy agreed that a concession on the Jupiters might help resolve the crisis. On Monday, 29 October, Dobrynin handed Kennedy a confidential letter from Khrushchev to the president summarizing his understanding of the arrangement. The attorney general read the letter and Dobrynin said: "'Yes, we agree to remove our missiles in exchange for a firm pledge not to attack Cuba, and also with [the] full understanding that the American missiles would be removed from Turkey.'" Kennedy explained to Dobrynin "that it would be very hard for them to accept this promise publicly." Implementation would also take time; the Jupiters had been authorized by NATO, and NATO would have to approve their withdrawal. "He would require time for that. But he would give his word, on behalf of the president, that they would guarantee to remove them within some 3, 4, or 5 months."[108]

Ambassador Dobrynin's recollections elicited a startling admission from Theodore Sorensen. Kennedy's memoir, he explained, was "very explicit that this [the withdrawal of the Jupiters] was part of the deal; but at that time it was still a secret even on the American side." Kennedy was assassinated before his manuscript was published, and Sorensen was asked by the publisher to review it for accuracy. "I took it upon myself to edit that out of his diaries, and that is why the ambassador is somewhat justified in saying that the diaries are not as explicit as his conversation."[109] Kennedy's disingenuous description of the State Department's duplicity may have been another example of Sorensen's "creative editing."

Sorensen insisted that the administration had refused to sign a letter drafted by Dobrynin describing the president's promise to withdraw the Jupiters as part of the arrangement reached by the two governments. The eight members of the Ex Comm who had met in the Oval Office to give Robert Kennedy his instructions were reconvened by the president and collectively "decided not to accept that letter but to return it to the Soviets as though it had never been opened."[110]

Ambassador Dobrynin revealed that he had had three secret meetings with Robert Kennedy during the acute phase of the crisis. The first meeting was at the Soviet embassy on Tuesday, 23 October, the day after the president had proclaimed his quarantine. The two men met alternatively at the Soviet embassy and the Justice Department "in the small hours of the night" or occasionally in the morning. The conversations were "animated" and "tough." "Robert Kennedy was . . . emotional; it was not so easy to conduct a discussion with him. But, all the same, within reasonable limits, we conducted these conversations."[111]

According to Dobrynin, the critical meeting took place on Saturday evening, 27 October, at the Justice Department. Kennedy spoke at length about the threat to American security represented by the Soviet missiles in Cuba. Dobrynin emphasized Cuba's legitimate concern for its security and how it was threatened by the United States. Acting on his own initiative—he had no relevant instructions from Moscow and did not even have the text of the message that Khrushchev had sent that morning to the president—he raised the question of the Jupiters in Turkey and the danger they posed to the Soviet Union. "You installed these weapons near our borders. So how come you raise such a racket about missiles in Cuba?" Kennedy replied:

> If that was the only obstacle to the settlement . . . the President saw no insurmountable difficulties that could stand in the way. The main difficulty for the President was public discussion of the question concerning Turkey. The siting of missile bases in Turkey was a result of a formal decision adopted by the NATO Council. For the President to announce now by unilateral decision the withdrawal of the missile bases . . . would mean dealing a blow to the whole structure of NATO and the position of the United States as the Organization's leader at a time when it was already wrestling with many decisive issues, as the Soviet government undoubtedly knew.
>
> Nevertheless, President Kennedy was ready to come to terms with Khrushchev on this issue as well. It would probably take four or five months for the United States to withdraw its missiles from Turkey. This was the minimum time which the U.S. administration would require with due regard to the proce-

dure existing within NATO. The exchange of opinion of the whole Turkish aspect of the problem could be continued through himself, Robert Kennedy, and the Soviet Ambassador. Right now, however, there was nothing the President could say publicly about Turkey in that context. Robert Kennedy warned that what he was telling me about Turkey was strictly confidential and was known in Washington to just another two or three people besides his brother and himself.[112]

Dean Rusk's Revelation

For many years, Dean Rusk protected an equally explosive secret about the events of Saturday night. After Robert Kennedy had left the Oval Office for his meeting with Ambassador Dobrynin, discussion turned to the question of how the administration could mask the withdrawal of the Jupiters. When the other officials departed, Rusk stayed behind for a private talk with the president. Kennedy wondered what he would do if Khrushchev failed to accept the terms outlined in his letter and his brother's conversation with Ambassador Dobrynin. Kennedy again voiced concern that an attack on Cuba would rapidly escalate into a Soviet-American war. To forestall this, he was willing to consider ending the crisis on Khrushchev's terms: a pledge not to invade Cuba and a public missile trade. "It was clear to me," Rusk recalled, "that President Kennedy would not let the Jupiters in Turkey become an obstacle to the removal of the missiles sites in Cuba because the Jupiters were coming out in any case."[113]

Rusk suggested a face-saving way for Kennedy to agree to Khrushchev's demand for a public missile exchange. Rather than replying directly to Khrushchev, he should agree to a proposal embodying Khrushchev's conditions that United Nations' Secretary General U Thant would be asked to put forward in his own name. Andrew Cordier of Columbia University could be used to approach U Thant; he had only recently left the United Nations and had a close relationship with the secretary general. Kennedy agreed, and dictated a short draft proposal calling on the superpowers to withdraw their missiles in Turkey and Cuba. Rusk was to assure Cordier that Kennedy would respond affirmatively to the proposal, but Cordier was not to put it in the hands of U Thant until he received a further signal from Rusk. The signal never came because the next day Khrushchev indicated his willingness to settle on the basis of the terms Robert Kennedy had discussed with Dobrynin.[114]

It is possible that the Rusk-Cordier initiative was only an option being explored by the president. It cannot be considered conclusive proof that he had rejected an air strike in favor of an exchange of missiles. However, it certainly suggests that he was leaning in this direction. It is significant that Kennedy instructed Rusk to give Cordier a copy of the proposed statement for U Thant. This entailed some risk of a leak, a risk the president presumably would only have assumed if he was serious about the stratagem. Otherwise, Rusk could have contacted Cordier, but not have given the president's proposal to him.

Another indication that Kennedy was unwilling to attack Cuba is his response to the downing of Major Rudolf Anderson, Jr.'s U-2 by a Soviet SAM on the morning of 27 October. Kennedy decided against a retaliatory strike despite his apparent support for such an attack on Tuesday and the "almost unanimous agreement" in the Ex Comm that an attack should be launched the next morning.[115] Reluctance to use force was also apparent in his failure to order preparations for the larger air strike against Cuba the joint chiefs were demanding. McNamara insists that "if President Kennedy were going to strike on Monday or Tuesday, then he would have told *me* about it so that we could make the necessary preparations. He hadn't told me, so I don't think he *was* going to strike."[116]

Dillon, Sorensen, and Bundy also think it very unlikely that Kennedy would have ordered an air strike. His initial response to a negative reply from Khrushchev, Bundy and McNamara argue, would have been to extend the blockade to petroleum products and other items vital to the Cuban military and civilian economy. McNamara and Bundy favored this option, and Bundy believes that the "turn of the screw" would have won out in the end.[117] Dean Rusk disagrees; he thinks that Kennedy would have activated the Cordier channel before Tuesday, the day American forces were expected to be ready to invade Cuba.[118]

What would have happened if Kennedy had gone ahead with the United Nations initiative? Early in the crisis he had voiced the opinion that a deal on the Jupiters "could break up the [NATO] Alliance by confirming European suspicions that we would sacrifice their security to protect our interests in an area of no concern to them."[119] This was an extreme prediction, but not a surprising one; the president offered it as a justification for why he should *not* agree to a missile trade. NATO would have survived, but American prestige assuredly would have suffered.

The president's other foreign-policy concern, that a concession would encourage more aggressive Soviet efforts to communize Latin America, was also exaggerated. It rested on two false assumptions: that a major purpose of the missiles was to provide a strategic shield behind which Soviet and Cuban agents could spread revolution in the Western hemisphere, and that Khrushchev had risked the deployment because he doubted Kennedy's resolve. For the president and the Ex Comm, this was the most serious cost, given their understanding of Khrushchev and the Soviet Union.

The domestic repercussions of a public missile exchange would also have been serious. It would have provoked a bitter schism in the Ex Comm. This is certainly one reason why Kennedy chose to keep his plan secret from the hawks. He also kept it secret from the six officials with whom he had discussed his brother's meeting with Dobrynin—and all of them favored removal of the Jupiters. Rusk was something of an outsider in the Ex Comm; he had not participated in many of its deliberations because of his need to represent the government at previously arranged state functions where his absence would have been noticed. He also had a well-deserved reputation for probity.

There was substantial opposition to Kennedy's policy. Dean Acheson had left the Ex Comm in protest against Kennedy's choice of a blockade over an air strike. The four remaining hawks, Paul Nitze, Douglas Dillon, John McCone, and Maxwell Taylor, had agreed to the blockade in return for what they considered a promise by the president to use force if necessary to remove the missiles. They pressed vigorously for an air strike when the blockade appeared to have failed. So did the joint chiefs—this is why Kennedy had excluded them from the Ex Comm.[120] The hawks felt betrayed when they learned after the event that Robert Kennedy had promised Dobrynin that the Jupiters would be withdrawn.[121]

Acheson later voiced public criticism of Kennedy. The hawks and the chiefs kept their disappointment to themselves.[122] They might not have remained silent if Kennedy had agreed to an eleventh-hour deal, brokered by the United Nations, to trade the American missiles in Turkey for their Soviet counterparts in Cuba. A quarter-century after the event, the revelation that the president had contemplated such a trade stunned veterans of the Ex Comm. Douglas Dillon was "really shocked." "I had no idea," he exclaimed, "that the President was considering such a thing. If we had actually followed through on it, and publicly traded missiles, it would have been a terrible and totally unnecessary mistake."[123] McGeorge Bundy, a belated convert to the blockade, was "profoundly depressed" by the news.[124]

If the exchange had been public, the Ex Comm hawks and the chiefs would have been encouraged to voice their opposition by Republican senators, like Kenneth Keating of New York. Journalists and congressmen, disappointed that Kennedy had not used the crisis as a pretext to overthrow Castro, would also have attacked the administration. An alliance of governmental and congressional critics could have been politically devastating to the president. Kennedy's political advisors had warned him earlier that a trade was out of the question. Kennedy's apparent willingness to consider an exchange despite its expected foreign and domestic costs reflected his belief that an air strike would lead to a costly conventional conflict with Cuba, and quite possibly to an even more costly war with the Soviet Union. In justifying his decision not to authorize an air strike in retaliation for the downing of the U-2, Kennedy told the Ex Comm: "It isn't the first step that concerns me, but both sides escalating to the fourth and fifth step—and we don't go to the sixth because there is no one around to do so."[125]

More Protection

Kennedy did not live long enough to write his memoir of the crisis. Had he survived, it is possible that he would have agreed with the analysis offered many years later by his secretary of defense. According to McNamara, everything "added up to one unequivocal conclusion: We had to get the missiles out of Cuba, but we had to do so in a way that avoided both the political consequences of appearing weak—as we would appear if we publicly traded missiles—and also avoided unacceptable risk of military escalation. In other words, we had to force the missiles out of Cuba, without forcing the Soviets to respond in a way that could have led us all into disaster. And let me tell you, that was no easy task."[126]

Kennedy's solution to this problem was to disaggregate interest from appearance.[127] His interest and his country's were best served by withdrawing the Jupiters in return for the Soviet missiles in Cuba. Knowledge of the trade had to be kept from the allies and the American people, and, as McNamara indicated, from most of the Ex Comm and the military. Kennedy was careful to limit the discussion of what his brother would tell Dobrynin about the Jupiters to the "rump" Ex Comm that met secretly in the Oval Office. This group also prepared a cover story to explain and justify the subsequent dismantling of the missiles.

Saturday night's Oval Office meeting contained an element of deception. The president led Rusk and the other officials present who would have opposed an explicit missile trade to believe that this would not occur. Robert Kennedy was instructed to tell Dobrynin that the missiles were coming out and that he was merely passing on this "piece of information" to the ambassador. Dean Rusk, who was most insistent that there be no appearance of giving in to Soviet blackmail, telephoned the attorney general afterward to make sure that he put the matter to Dobrynin in accordance with his instructions.[128]

When the meeting in the Oval Office finished, Kennedy did not know that Khrushchev was as anxious as he was to end the crisis. His only communication from Khrushchev had been his tough, unyielding message, received that morning. The day's events had made the president increasingly pessimistic about finding a peaceful solution to the crisis. Unsure of what was happening in Moscow, he considered making a further concession. With Dean Rusk, he searched for a way to make that concession possible by minimizing its adverse political consequences.

THE VIEW FROM MOSCOW

The first sign of Soviet interest in an accommodation came on Thursday, 25 October. Soviet diplomats, who had been silent since the proclamation of the blockade, hinted that Moscow might be prepared to accept some kind of compromise settlement to end the crisis.[129] The next day Aleksandr Fomin, a Soviet embassy official known to head KGB operations in the United States, telephoned John Scali, ABC's State Department correspondent, to request an urgent meeting. Over lunch, Fomin suggested that his country might be willing to dismantle and remove its missiles under United Nations' supervision and pledge never to reintroduce them in return for a public American guarantee not to invade Cuba. Scali rushed to the State Department where Dean Rusk instructed him to tell Fomin that the administration saw "real possibilities" in the proposal but that "time is very urgent." Fomin assured Scali that his message would be rushed "to the very highest levels" of the Kremlin.[130]

The Fomin-Scali exchange was followed by a long letter from Khrushchev that proposed a settlement similar to the one worked out by Fomin and Scali. He proposed that "we, for our part, will declare that our ships, bound for Cuba, will not carry any kind of armaments. You would declare that the United States will not invade Cuba with its forces and will not support any sort of forces which might intend to carry out an invasion of Cuba. Then the necessity for the presence of our military specialists in Cuba would disappear." This message was received at the State Department on Friday evening and greeted with a great sense of relief. For the first time, Robert Kennedy noted, the president expressed some optimism about the outcome of the confrontation.[131]

The American press was given only excerpts from the Khrushchev letter. Taking their cue from the White House, they portrayed the message as extremely emotional in tone. In his biography of Kennedy, Arthur Schlesinger, Jr. described the Friday message as "hysterical."[132] For Theodore Sorensen, it was "long, meandering [and] full of polemics."[133] Elie Abel called it "the nightmare outcry of a frightened man."[134] Dean Rusk says that "its distraught and emotional tone bothered us, because it seemed that the old fellow might be losing his cool in the Kremlin."[135]

These accounts are misleading. The message, only fully declassified in 1973, struck a very personal tone. Khrushchev did not address the particulars of the crisis as much as he discussed his reasons for sending missiles to Cuba. The letter also warns of the danger of war and the difficulty both leaders would have in controlling events if there was a violent encounter along the blockade line.[136] It is possible that some administration officials misread Khrushchev's sensible fear of runaway escalation as the overly emotional response of a frightened man.

The Friday Message

Ex Comm officials and historians agree that this message was a critical turning point. It was the first sign that Khrushchev was prepared to consider the removal of the Soviet missiles. Soviet evidence indicates Khrushchev moved toward a settlement in two stages.

On Wednesday, 24 October, Khrushchev had sent another letter full of bravado to Kennedy. He accused the United States of "banditry" and warned again that Soviet ship captains would not recognize the blockade.[137] The following day he received a short and firm reply in which the president referred to the Soviet leader's earlier assurances that no offensive weapons would be sent to Cuba and insisted that the Soviet government take steps to permit a "restoration of the earlier situation."[138] Khrushchev understood that the missiles would have to be withdrawn. He ordered a new letter drafted that linked the possibility of a withdrawal of missiles in Cuba to an American pledge to refrain from military action against Cuba and to withdraw its missiles in Turkey.[139]

A draft letter was prepared by the foreign-ministry working group and presented to Khrushchev on Thursday evening. In the meantime, intelligence reports arrived indicating that an American invasion of Cuba was imminent. Soviet and Cuban intelligence had been monitoring the American military buildup in and around the Caribbean and warned that an attack could come within the next ten hours.[140] The Soviet embassy in Washington had reached the same conclusion. They had also received a direct warning from an American journalist, who alleged that he had been invited to go to Florida that night to join the invasion force.[141] Khrushchev did not put much trust in intelligence reports, but he could not afford to ignore them.[142]

Khrushchev's overriding concern was to prevent an invasion of Cuba. He worried that fighting in Cuba would quickly lead to a Soviet-American war. In light of the threatening information he had received, he dictated a new letter that made no mention of the Jupiter missiles and insisted only on a pledge not to invade Cuba. In return, he advised Kennedy, Soviet ships would not carry any armaments to Cuba. He told his colleagues that "we could come back to the issue of the Turkish missiles at another time, but for the moment, the most important thing was to stop the invasion."[143]

Khrushchev's Friday letter spoke eloquently of the danger of war and of the impossibility of stopping it once it began. He warned that an attempt by the American navy to stop a Soviet ship could be the catalyst for a superpower war. The letter went on to point out that the threat of armed attack "has constantly hung, and continues to hang" over Cuba. Khrushchev's fear of war was real but diffuse.[144]

The Saturday Message

Before he had received any reply to his Friday letter, Khrushchev sent another message to Washington. This letter, drafted on Saturday morning, upped the ante: in addition to a pledge not to invade Cuba, the United States would also have to remove its missiles from Turkey.[145]

Khrushchev's Saturday message and its relationship to Friday's message and the Fomin probe has been one of the great mysteries of the crisis. The Ex Comm was disturbed by the Saturday message because it appeared to disavow the Friday proposal. Ex Comm officials speculated that there had been a failure in communication or, more alarming, that Khrushchev had been overruled by hard-liners in the Presidium.[146]

One piece of the puzzle is now clear. Aleksandr Fomin was acting on his own initiative. He had no instructions from senior officials in the KGB to make contact with the administration or to explore the possibility of a compromise settlement. His report on his conversations with John Scali was not received in Moscow in time to influence Khrushchev's Friday message. Kennedy and the Ex Comm were wrong to read that message as a proposal based on the Fomin "feeler."[147]

There is no evidence the Saturday cable was a response to pressure from Soviet militants to stand firm in the face of American blackmail.[148] Marshal Malinovsky had been a lukewarm supporter of the missile deployment but nevertheless opposed withdrawal of the missiles for the first few days of the crisis. He was concerned about the consequences of American strategic superiority and reluctant to give up weapons that would partly redress this imbalance. He also opposed retreat in the face of American threats. By Thursday, he, too, had come to the conclusion that the missiles would have to be withdrawn to save Cuba. He spoke in support of Khrushchev's proposed letter to Kennedy offering to withdraw the missiles in return for a pledge not to invade Cuba. Malinovsky's views were important to other officials because so many of their arguments on both sides of the issue hinged on military calculations or scenarios.[149]

One important reason for Saturday's cable was concern in Moscow that Friday's cable had been insufficient. It had proposed that Soviet ships would not carry any kind of armaments to Cuba in return for a promise from the United States not to invade Cuba. It had not contained a promise to remove the missiles already in Cuba, and Khrushchev and his advisors felt the need to specify their willingness to do this.[150] A second reason was Khrushchev's belief that Kennedy was prepared to remove the American missiles in Turkey.

Walter Lippmann, arguably the best-connected journalist in Washington, proposed in the *Washington Post* on Wednesday, 25 October, that the administration make a "face-saving" concession to Khrushchev. The United States should agree to dismantle the Jupiter missiles in Turkey in return for Soviet withdrawal of their missiles in Cuba. Turkey was comparable to Cuba because it "is the only place where there are strategic weapons right on the frontier of the Soviet Union." Lippmann did not believe that either deployment was of much military value; they "could be dismantled without altering the world balance of power."[151]

Lippmann was not the first journalist to suggest a trade; similar proposals had been made in European and American newspapers. It had also gained attention at the United Nations where a number of nonaligned countries had cosponsored a resolution calling for a mutual withdrawal of missiles from Cuba and Turkey.[152] On Wednesday, 24 October, Max Frankel of the *New York Times* reported that the administration did not believe that the two deployments were equivalent but was "mindful of the appeal of the argument." On Thursday, Frankel wrote that there was considerable "unofficial" interest in a trade in the Ex Comm. The Frankel story had an air of authenticity because his column on Wednesday had described in considerable detail the course of the Ex Comm's deliberations in the week leading up to the blockade decision. This information could only have been obtained from an inside source.[153]

Georgiy Shakhnazarov contends that a missile trade appealed to Soviet leaders as a face-saving way to end the crisis. They also saw an exchange as symbolic recognition by the United States of the right of socialist countries "to equal security."[154] Impressed by Lippmann's reputation and stature, officials in the Washington embassy read his column as a trial balloon inspired by the White House. They cabled their analysis to Moscow, and a second message was hurriedly drafted for Khrushchev's approval by the foreign ministry. Saturday's message was intended to flesh out Friday's offer and to extract another concession that would make an accord more beneficial to the Soviet Union and easier to justify for Khrushchev.[155]

Khrushchev seems to have sent his Saturday message in ignorance of the consternation it would cause in Washington.[156] He also failed to realize how it would anger Fidel Castro, who concluded that Moscow was bargaining away Cuba's security. Sergo Mikoyan called the message "a big mistake."[157]

One problem with this explanation is timing. The Lippmann column appeared on Thursday morning, and a cable summarizing its content and significance would have reached Moscow that evening. If the foreign ministry considered the cable so important, it would have been on Khrushchev's desk by Friday morning at the latest. Khrushchev would thus have read the cable, or at least have been apprised of its contents, before he wrote his message on Friday. That message made no mention of a missile trade.[158]

It is possible that it took a day for Soviet diplomats in Washington to reason through the implications of the Lippmann column. At a gathering of Eastern European diplomats on Friday, 26 October, Dobrynin brought up Lippmann's proposal for a missile swap and asked his colleagues if it "should be regarded as an indirect suggestion on the part of the White House."[159] Even if Khrushchev had a timely report, he may have been overwhelmingly preoccupied with the prospect of an invasion of Cuba. On Thursday and Friday, Moscow received numerous indications that an American attack against Cuba was imminent. Khrushchev was desperate to prevent an invasion and may have been unwilling to complicate the prospect of an agreement by asking the United States for an exchange of missiles as well as a promise not to invade Cuba.

Ambassador Georgiy Kornienko believes that the timing of Khrushchev's message can be explained by information he received on Saturday indicating that President Kennedy would not attack Cuba for another few days. Kornienko says that he was the source of this intelligence. He had lunch on Thursday with William Rogers, the journalist who had earlier warned of the impending invasion. Rogers had not flown to Florida. The military was ready to go, he insisted, but the president felt the need to convince the world that he had no choice but to invade. Kennedy would make another attempt to negotiate a settlement. Kornienko immediately cabled a report to Moscow, but the cable was delayed in transmission and subsequently held by Gromyko and Kuznetsov. It finally reached Khrushchev on Thursday evening, along with other information indicating that an invasion was at least forty-eight hours away. Khrushchev felt a sense of relief and told his colleagues: "Let's go back to the letter that also included Turkey."[160]

Kornienko's explanation requires Khrushchev to have changed his estimate of American military intentions three times in as many days. On Friday, he was supposedly alarmed about the prospect of invasion, on Saturday, to have decided that his concern was exaggerated, and on Sunday, when he rushed to accept Kennedy's proposal for ending the crisis, to have once again become convinced that an attack was imminent.

It seems unlikely that Soviet intelligence estimates would have been so unequivocal about American intentions *and* have changed so rapidly and repeatedly. The administration's intentions were unknown to Moscow— they were also unknown in Washington because Kennedy had made no decision. The best Soviet and Cuban intelligence could do was to try to infer American intentions from the nature and readiness of American military preparations. These preparations indicated a steady buildup of ground, naval, and air forces; nothing about the buildup or movement of American forces suggested that a decision to invade had yet been made, or that it had been made and postponed. According to Gen. Anatoliy Gribkov, military intelligence on 26 October indicated that American forces were likely to invade Cuba the following night.[161] Oleg Grinevsky confirms that Khrushchev and the Presidium "expected an attack against the missiles." "Their fear was constant, and did not diminish on Saturday or Sunday."[162] Oleg Troyanovsky maintains that on Saturday Moscow was *more* worried about the possibility of invasion and regarded it as imperative to table a proposal acceptable to the Americans.[163]

It is also hard to believe that Khrushchev changed his mind about something so important on the basis of a story from an American journalist. And all the more so when previous intelligence from that source had been so obviously wrong. Rogers had not gone to Florida the night before as he said he would, there had been no invasion on Thursday, and at lunch that day, without identifying his source, he told Kornienko a new story.

A Missed Opportunity

It took a minimum of eight to ten hours to communicate between Washington and Moscow. All cables needed to be encoded; this was a time-consuming procedure if the cables were as long as Dobrynin's report of his conversation on Friday night with Robert Kennedy. Western Union was the only telegraph service available to the Soviet embassy in Washington. In Moscow, an incoming cable would be sent to the foreign ministry where it was decoded by hand, typed, and brought to Gromyko or his assistants. In special cases, handwritten drafts would be rushed to Gromyko's office and read aloud to him. "All of this took a very long time," Georgiy Kornienko remembered.[164]

Dobrynin reported that the embassy regularly made frantic telephone calls to Western Union when they had priority cables. The telegraph agency would send an old man on a bicycle. "We gave him the cables. And he, at such speed—and we tried to urge him on—rode back to Western Union where the cable was sent to Moscow." From today's vantage point, Dobrynin mused, "it all seems rather colorful, but at the time it was no joke. This was a nerve-racking experience, we sat there, wondering if he would be fast enough to deliver the important communication."[165]

Messages between Khrushchev and Kennedy were also subject to long delays, in part because of the need to translate them. Impressed by the urgency of the situation, and disturbed by the twelve-hour delay in the transmission of his Friday message, Khrushchev took the extraordinary step of having his Saturday message broadcast by Radio Moscow. Picked up by the wire service, it came across the White House ticker at 10:17 A.M. Saturday morning, which was 5:17 P.M. Moscow time.

Because of the twelve hours it took to translate and transmit Khrushchev's Friday message, it reached the White House too late for the president and Ex Comm to prepare a response that day.[166] McGeorge Bundy believes that if Khrushchev's letter "had reached us even a few hours earlier, we would have been able to reply on Friday."[167] The American response would have been in Khrushchev's hands on Saturday morning.

Unfortunately, Khrushchev's Friday message was delayed, and his message on Saturday caused consternation in Washington. Khrushchev's apparent about-face confused the Ex Comm and contributed to the heightened sense of threat its members felt that morning. It delayed the American reply to the Soviet leader's Friday message because the president and his advisors spent much of Saturday trying to make sense of the two communications and work out an appropriate response.

Why the Settlement on Sunday?

Western students of the crisis argue that the threat of an American attack against Cuba convinced Khrushchev that he had no choice but to withdraw the missiles. Khrushchev's messages on Friday and Saturday indicate that he was prepared to remove the missiles. Soviet fear of war explains the substance of Khrushchev's Sunday message but not its timing.

The climactic day of the crisis, Saturday, 27 October in Washington, was Saturday evening and Sunday morning in Moscow. On Saturday morning, Khrushchev and 23 officials left the Kremlin for the governmental mansion in Novo-Ogarevo, not far from Khrushchev's suburban dacha. Among the 23 were Presidium members, associate members, and some of their principal deputies.[168]

Throughout the day, Khrushchev conferred with senior officials while their deputies waited in an ante room with military and intelligence officials. From time to time, Presidium members would come out of the inner room to relieve the tension or draw a glass of tea from the samovar. Khrushchev and his colleagues were desperately trying to guess American intentions. Would the United States attack the missile sites, invade Cuba, or possibly launch a nuclear strike against the Soviet Union? There was a strong feeling that they should do nothing to provoke any kind of American attack.[169]

Until Saturday, the Presidium was divided between those who favored accommodation and those who wanted Khrushchev to stand firm. There were sharp disagreements about how the Soviet Union should respond to any attack against Cuba. Several scenarios were discussed, including an attack against West Berlin and an air strike against the American missiles in Turkey. By Saturday, Presidium members recognized that the military options were limited and likely to provoke further escalation. However, the consensus on a political accommodation did not congeal until that afternoon. By the end of the day, Soviet officials focused their attention on defusing the crisis.[170]

At 3:00 A.M. Sunday, Khrushchev summoned key officials to his dacha for a meeting that began at about 4:00 A.M. Over glasses of tea, Gromyko, Ilychev, Troyanovsky, Kuznetsov, and Malinovsky discussed the need to end the crisis.[171] The tension was "phenomenal." Many members of the Presidium considered it possible, even likely, that Kennedy would attack the Soviet Union as well as Cuba. They reasoned that the Americans, recognizing that an attack on Cuba would provoke a Soviet-American war, would attempt to destroy the Soviet Union at the outset.[172]

This somber mood was attributable in the first instance to word of Dobrynin's conversation with Robert Kennedy on Saturday evening. Khrushchev and his colleagues also had reports of well-advanced American preparations for an air and ground assault against Cuba, and cables from Washington and Havana warning of imminent military action.[173]

Robert Kennedy had met Dobrynin at the Justice Department at 7:45 P.M. Saturday. The attorney general told the ambassador that "the Cuban crisis was fast going from bad to worse." An unarmed American reconnaissance aircraft had been shot down over Cuba and the military was demanding retaliation. "But to answer fire with fire would mean provoking a chain reaction that would be very difficult to stop." The president needed to continue surveillance flights as they were the only way to obtain timely information about the state of readiness of the missile sites.[174]

Kennedy impressed upon Dobrynin the mounting danger of war. Soviet missiles in Cuba were unacceptable to the United States; they would be attacked if they were not withdrawn. "Hot heads" in the government were clamoring for an immediate assault, and the destruction of the U-2 had made it more difficult to ignore their demands. The president would have no choice but to retaliate if another aircraft were shot down. Dobrynin insists that Kennedy gave him no ultimatum, but "stressed the importance of receiving an answer on Sunday. So I conveyed this to Moscow."[175]

The two men also discussed the Jupiters. The attorney general "confirmed the agreement with the president to remove the missiles from Turkey." Dobrynin was told that he could convey this assurance to his government along with the president's insistence that "it cannot be made part of a package and publicized." The missiles would have to be withdrawn according to "standard NATO procedures." Kennedy gave the ambassador a telephone number to reach him at the White House if he had any news to report from Moscow. "He was very nervous throughout our meeting," Dobrynin remembered. "It was the first time I had seen him in such a state."[176]

Dobrynin returned to the Soviet embassy and asked Georgiy Kornienko to help him draft a cable to Moscow. Robert Kennedy had said that the president was prepared "to make an arrangement." Kornienko pulled out a copy of Webster's and the two men read through the several meanings of "arrangement." The first one was agreement, which could be translated as *soglasheniye*. They agreed that this might be misunderstood in Moscow because it implied a formal understanding. Another possibility was mutual understanding, best conveyed by the Russian *vzaimoponinaniye*. This they judged a bit weak. They finally agreed on *dogovorionnost'*, which meant that the two sides agreed. Dobrynin and Kornienko thought the president's concession very helpful, but had no idea how Moscow would respond.[177]

Dobrynin's cable arrived at the foreign ministry early Sunday morning. Vladimir Suslov, one of Gromyko's assistants, read it over the telephone to Oleg Troyanovsky at the Khrushchev dacha, who took extensive notes that he read to the Presidium. According to Troyanovsky, the import of Dobrynin's cable was clear. "Although strictly speaking, the words of [the] younger Kennedy could not be described as an ultimatum, he made it clear that the U.S. government was resolved to get rid of the missile bases even by bombing them if it came to that." Everybody understood "that the answer to the Kennedy message had to come in less than 24 hours, that we should not delay, and that we should give a very precise answer."[178]

Khrushchev had also received disturbing messages from Havana.[179] On Friday, Ambassador Alekseev had described Castro as "very optimistic, exuding optimism. He knew for sure nothing would happen." That night, he was "wavering" and worrying about an American attack, "He even asked me to take him down to the bunker, to the bomb shelter, fearful as he was of a bombing strike." There, between 2:00 and 6:00 A.M., Alekseev helped Castro draft a letter to Khrushchev.[180] In it Castro warned that some kind of attack against Cuba "is almost imminent within the next 24 or 72 hours." The most likely possibility was an air strike against the Soviet missiles "with the limited objective of destroying them." An invasion was "less probable although possible."[181]

Alekseev cabled Castro's letter to Moscow along with his own analysis of the situation. The contents of both cables were described to Khrushchev and later to the Presidium. Troyanovsky, read the Castro cable to Khrushchev over the telephone, who interrupted several times and asked Troyanovsky to repeat the most important passages. Troyanovsky felt that Khrushchev was less troubled by Castro's plea for a nuclear strike if Cuba was attacked than he was by the Cuban leader's belief that an air raid against the missiles "was practically imminent."[182] Castro's warning was reinforced by "snowballing" reports from Soviet intelligence warning that bombing raids were set for 29 or 30 October unless some accommodation was reached with the president."[183] For Khrushchev and other Soviet leaders, these reports encouraged the most ominous interpretation of Robert Kennedy's demand that the United States receive an answer to the president's Saturday message within 24 hours.[184]

Another report of imminent invasion came from Aleksandr Fomin. It described his meeting with John Scali on Saturday afternoon.[185] Earlier that day, Dean Rusk had summoned Scali to his office to tell him about Khrushchev's Saturday morning message. Rusk asked him to go back to Fomin and ask what had happened. Scali was furious because he thought he had been used to carry a purposely misleading message to the administration. He accused Fomin of "a stinking double cross" and told him that a missile exchange was totally unacceptable. Scali exceeded the instructions he had received from Rusk. He told the KGB boss that the administration was "absolutely determined to get those missiles out of there." "An invasion of Cuba," he asserted, "is only a matter of hours away." The two men met again on Sunday after Khrushchev had announced his decision to withdraw the missiles. Fomin reported that he had been instructed to thank Scali "and to tell you that the information you supplied was very valuable to Khrushchev in helping make up his mind quickly." He added with a smile, "And that includes your 'explosion' of Saturday."[186]

The "state of alarm" created by the cables from Dobrynin, Castro, and Fomin was compounded by a false report. At Novo-Ogarevo, where Khrushchev and his entourage had moved sometime that morning, Army Gen. Semyon Ivanov, Secretary of the Defense Council, was called to the telephone and told that a message had been received that Kennedy would give another nationally televised address at 5:00 P.M. Moscow time. "Everyone agreed that Kennedy intended to declare war, to launch an attack." A telegram was immediately sent to the Washington embassy for verification. "We had the feeling then that there was very little time to unravel what was taking place."[187]

Khrushchev's anxiety was further aroused by two events that took place on Saturday morning. At 10:30 A.M., a U-2 operated by SAC overflew the Chukotski Peninsula in eastern Siberia. The pilot radioed for assistance and fighter aircraft were sent to help. Soviet MiGs scrambled from a base near Wrangel Island, but the U-2 was escorted home without any shots being fired.[188] Soviet generals advised Khrushchev that the plane could have been on a last-minute intelligence mission in preparation for an American nuclear attack.[189] At almost the same time, Major Anderson's U-2 was shot down over Cuba by a SAM missile. Khrushchev was horrified. He initially assumed—incorrectly—that the Cubans were responsible and that his trigger-happy ally had given the "militarists at the Pentagon" the pretext they needed to push Kennedy into a Cuban invasion. He wrote to Castro and pleaded with him to "show patience, firmness and even more firmness."[190]

By all accounts, Khrushchev hastened to accept Kennedy's terms to forestall an American attack against Cuba—and perhaps against the Soviet Union as well.[191] His extreme anxiety was apparent in a telephone call to First Deputy Foreign Minister Vasiliy V. Kuznetsov, made shortly after being apprised of the two U-2 incidents. Kuznetsov and his deputy Mendelevich had left Novo-Ogarevo earlier that morning for New York and the United Nations. Khrushchev reached them at Vnukovo-2, Moscow's main military airport, before they boarded their plane. When Kuznetsov hung up the phone, he "looked extremely distressed, the color drained from his face, and he left without saying a word to anyone." Khrushchev had told him: "The situation is very bad. I'm not sure you will be able to land safely in the United States."[192] That evening, an agreement with Kennedy in hand, a much relieved Khrushchev told the Presidium that "The world [had] hung on a thread."[193]

Khrushchev was willing to settle on Sunday for positive reasons as well. Kennedy was prepared to issue a pledge not to invade Cuba in return for withdrawal of the Soviet missiles under United Nations' supervision. Dobrynin's cable made it apparent that he would also remove the Jupiter missiles from Turkey sometime after the crisis so it would not look like part of a "package deal." Khrushchev and his inner circle were convinced that this was the president's "last concession." They agreed that they should send Kennedy an affirmative reply.[194]

Kennedy's concessions were very important to Khrushchev. He considered them an important victory for the Soviet Union and one that enabled him to withdraw with honor. The Kennedy administration may have regarded the pledge not to invade Cuba as a low-cost concession; Khrushchev and his colleagues did not. They believed that the United States was preparing a second invasion to avenge the Bay of Pigs and that it had been prevented by the missile deployment. As late as 1987, high-ranking and well-informed Soviet officials were still convinced that the United States had been planning an invasion, and greeted with disbelief the assertions of Robert McNamara and McGeorge Bundy that the administration had rejected pleas for another invasion.[195]

For Khrushchev, the withdrawal of missiles from Cuba in exchange for the removal of the Jupiters from Turkey was "extremely welcome."[196] One of his most important reasons for sending missiles to Cuba was to change the political context in Washington by exposing the United States to the same kind of close-range nuclear threat faced by the Soviet Union. Khrushchev hoped that the missiles would make the Kennedy administration more respectful of legitimate Soviet security concerns and more willing to reach a political accommodation. This in turn would free scarce resources and manpower for domestic development. By forcing the Americans to accept the link between the Jupiter missiles in Turkey and the missiles in Cuba, Khrushchev thought that he had taken a great step toward "psychological equality" with the United States. He hoped that after the crisis, he and Kennedy could go forward on a variety of fronts to restructure superpower relations.

American concessions were also important to justify the withdrawal of the Soviet missiles to the Cubans and Soviet militants. Khrushchev had the authority to withdraw the missiles without their consent, but to preserve that authority in the long term he needed to isolate the hard-liners and convince his remaining colleagues that he had made the right decision. It was particularly important that he appear to have made the right decision because he had committed the Soviet Union to the missile deployment. The ensuing crisis with the United States and the need to withdraw the missiles under the threat of war were *his* policy failures.

Khrushchev later told Norman Cousins, the editor of *Saturday Review*, that the last holdout to a compromise was the Soviet military.[197] "When I asked the military advisors if they could assure me that holding fast would not result in the death of five hundred million human beings, they looked at me as though I was out of my mind, or, what was worse, a traitor. . . . So I said to myself: 'To hell with these maniacs. If I can get the United States to assure me that it will not attempt to overthrow the Cuban government, I will remove the missiles.'"[198] Khrushchev accentuated the positive side of the agreement to its critics. "I told my comrades, 'We achieved our goal. Maybe the Americans have learned their lesson. Now they have the time to think it over and weigh the consequences.'"[199]

Sunday's Radio Message

At 10:00 A.M. on Sunday, Khrushchev created two working groups to prepare a positive reply to Kennedy's letter. The first, headed by Andropov and Gromyko, drafted a message to be delivered to the American embassy. The second, headed by Leonid Ilychev, was to write a message for immediate broadcast over Radio Moscow. Khrushchev took this extraordinary step because he was anxious to respond as quickly as possible, before Kennedy was supposed to go on television that night. He worried that a message sent through official channels might not arrive before what he took to be Robert Kennedy's 9:00 A.M. Monday (Washington time) deadline.[200]

To observe proper protocol, the "official" message had to be delivered first. Mikhail Smirnovsky, chief of the foreign ministry's Department of

United States Affairs, went by limousine to the American embassy a half-hour before his colleagues bound for Radio Moscow. The embassy was almost unapproachable. It was surrounded by hundreds of demonstrators—all mobilized by the KGB—and chanting "hands off Cuba." By the time the police cleared a path for Smirnovsky's limousine, the Radio Moscow broadcast had already been monitored by embassy officials. Smirnovsky was embarrassed to have to present a message that had already been broadcast to the world.[201]

The delegation sent with Ilychev to Radio Moscow also ran into difficulty. The elevator was held open pending their arrival, and they were whisked inside and up to the broadcast studio. There was no announcer to be found. One finally arrived when Leonid Zamyatin was on the verge of reading the message himself. The announcer wanted to study the text "so he could read it with the right emphasis." Ilychev cut him short and ordered him to read it right away. " 'Time is of the essence,' he said. 'If you make a mistake, just read it again.' "[202]

The dispatch of the two delegations did little to relieve the tension at Novo-Ogarevo. Soviet officials were confused, uncertain, and fearful. The only Presidium member who appeared calm was Leonid Brezhnev. At the height of the discussion, he came out of the inner sanctum to check on the fortune of his favorite soccer team, CSK. He was annoyed that the deputies were discussing the crisis and not listening to the match on the radio.[203]

While they were waiting for Kennedy's reply to the radio message, a cable arrived from the KGB in Washington. From the time Kennedy had announced the quarantine of Cuba, the KGB had put him under intensive surveillance. They now reported that he had gone to church. Khrushchev and his colleagues argued about the significance of the report. Some Presidium members feared that it was a prelude to a nuclear attack; the president had gone to church to pray before giving the order to destroy the Soviet Union. Mikoyan thought that Kennedy was probably as confused as they were and was praying for divine guidance. Some suggested that the church visit was disinformation, a deliberate attempt by the Americans to mislead Soviet leaders. Mikoyan observed that this made no sense: how could the Americans plant the story about Kennedy's visit to church as a deliberate deception, when they could not know how it would be interpreted? One or two others challenged the validity of the report on different grounds. "The KGB has been wrong about everything else," they insisted. "Why should we believe them now when they tell us the president has gone to church?"[204]

Khrushchev's message announcing that the Soviet Union would withdraw its missiles from Cuba was rebroadcast over American radio at 9:00 A.M. Washington time.[205] McGeorge Bundy telephoned the good news to the president. Kennedy prepared to go to 10:00 mass at St. Stephen's Church. Bundy waited for him at the door of the residential quarters of the White House to give him the text of the message as he left for church. When Kennedy returned, Mrs. Bundy had arrived with their children, and Robert Kennedy, in an ebullient mood, passed out chocolates.[206] In Moscow, the tension finally eased when Kennedy's positive response to Khrushchev's message was picked up on the radio. They celebrated with vodka, not chocolate.[207]

Keeping the Agreement Secret

Sometime late on Sunday, Khrushchev sent a confidential letter to Ambassador Dobrynin in Washington summarizing their agreement on the Jupiters. In it, he deferred to the president's insistence that the matter be handled confidentially by the attorney general and Soviet ambassador. Dobrynin was unable to present the message to Robert Kennedy until he returned from New York on Monday evening. Dobrynin pointed out that Khrushchev had written the letter on Sunday agreeing to withdraw the missiles from Cuba "with the prior arrangement about Turkey in mind." Kennedy agreed that this was also his understanding. The ambassador gave Kennedy a copy of the letter. Kennedy "accepted it without comment." The following day he returned and said, "No, we would rather not keep this; we are giving it back to you." He repeated that the administration was committed to their arrangement, but declined to accept the letter. "Kennedy did not want any paper to that effect in his files."[208]

Khrushchev accepted this informal pledge. By then he, too, had considered it preferable to a public American commitment to withdraw the Jupiters. Fidel Castro was vehemently opposed to an exchange of missiles because it made Cuba look like a Soviet pawn. He reacted very strongly to Khrushchev's letter of the twenty-seventh asking Kennedy to withdraw the missiles from Turkey. Khrushchev began to appreciate that Kennedy had done him a favor by insisting on a secret "arrangement."[209]

FROM ADVERSARIES TO ALLIES

Our analysis indicates striking parallels between Kennedy and Khrushchev. Both adopted rigid positions at the outset of the crisis and gradually became more moderate and ready to compromise. Their emphasis shifted from winning to resolving the crisis in a way that would not undermine their authority at home or abroad. Khrushchev's threatening rhetoric on Wednesday and Thursday was intended to impress the United States and his Soviet colleagues with his resolve; it probably also reflected his anger and frustration. On Friday and Saturday, Khrushchev, like Kennedy, became more Machiavellian in dealing with his colleagues. He too wanted to build and hold together a coalition to support the concessions necessary to end the crisis.

The two leaders moved toward compromise for essentially the same reason. Kennedy feared that escalation would set in motion a chain of events that could lead to nuclear war. Khrushchev's concession makes it apparent that he was also committed to keeping the peace. Khrushchev subsequently paid a heavy political price for his Cuban policy; Soviet officials agree that his decision to send missiles to Cuba which then had to be withdrawn contributed to his removal from power in October 1964.[210]

Most Americans believe that the crisis was resolved because the Soviet Union backed down. Dean Rusk's famous quip, "we're eyeball to eyeball, and I think that the other side just blinked," is often quoted as a pithy illustration of this supposed truth.[211] However, the revelations by Sorensen and Rusk about the concession Kennedy made on the Jupiters and the further concession he contemplated, make it apparent that when Kennedy and Khrushchev were "eyeball to eyeball," both leaders blinked.[212] They did so out of a wholly commendable fear of war and its consequences.

The resolution of the missile crisis stands in sharp contrast to its origins. The confrontation occurred because of the inability of either superpower to empathize with its adversary and to predict its likely response to their actions. In Moscow, lack of empathy was compounded by overconfidence. Khrushchev made no serious effort to ascertain how the United States was likely to respond to the missile deployment. He neither solicited nor listened to the views of his best-informed foreign-policy experts. Khrushchev ignored Clausewitz's dictum that leaders should consider carefully the last step before taking the first.

The crisis was resolved because both leaders rejected any course of action they suspected would lead to an unstoppable spiral of military escalation. Their mutual commitment to settle the crisis peacefully, even at the price of major concessions, grew in intensity as the crisis deepened. Khrushchev and Kennedy became progressively less interested in winning and more committed to resolving the crisis. They devised a public-private arrangement designed to protect each of them against political reprisal from allies and domestic adversaries.

Diplomacy triumphed over force because of mutual learning. Three reinforcing factors were responsible. Most importantly, leaders had time to learn. Kennedy and his advisors had time to cool their anger and formulate policy in terms of a broader conception of the national interest. Khrushchev was able to overcome his initial shock and approach the crisis with a sense of sober realism. He gradually came to appreciate how isolated the Soviet Union was and how vulnerable he was politically. He was apparently surprised by the uneasiness of many of his Eastern European allies; Janos Kadar of Hungary was outspoken in his concern about the consequences of escalation.[213] Fedor Burlatsky believes that Khrushchev was also influenced by Soviet public opinion. The Soviet people were "very afraid of the dangers of war" and Khrushchev knew that "Society did not support in their hearts [his] adventurous actions."[214]

Learning was also facilitated by the information each leader received during the crisis. Kennedy's correspondence with Khrushchev prompted him to revise his conception of the Soviet leader and his objectives. Kennedy developed a new understanding of Khrushchev as a leader who had bungled into the crisis and was desperately searching for a way to retreat without losing face. This understanding made it much easier for Kennedy to make the concessions necessary to end the crisis. He no longer thought that Khrushchev would interpret a concession as weakness and respond by becoming more aggressive. Instead, he expected Khrushchev to see his concessions as proof of his commitment to avoid war and to reciprocate with concessions of his own. Kennedy was also able to develop a more accurate estimate of domestic and allied opinion and concluded that a compromise would be acceptable to NATO.

Khrushchev also rethought his understanding of Kennedy. The president's success in restraining the American military impressed him. "After the crisis," Sergei Khrushchev remembers, his father "was very interested in cooperating with Kennedy. He had been burned by his experience with Eisenhower. Khrushchev believed that Kennedy could control the hard-liners who would try to sabotage a new détente."[215] What impressed Khrushchev even more, Aleksei Adzhubei explained, was Kennedy's commitment to restraint. "He had us by the balls and didn't squeeze."[216] After Cuba, Khrushchev's attitude toward the West and Kennedy changed markedly. Some of his former associates believe that if Kennedy had not been assassinated in November 1963 and Khrushchev not removed from office in October 1964, the Cold War might have ended much sooner than it did.[217]

A third stimulus to learning was the threat of war. By Saturday night, war was no longer an abstract concept but a real fear. McNamara recalls that when the Ex Comm meeting ended on Saturday evening, he returned to the Pentagon and watched a spectacular sunset over the Potomac. He wondered how many more sunsets he was destined to enjoy.[218] Soviet accounts reveal that Khrushchev and his advisors suffered from similar angst. There is an old saying that nothing so concentrates the mind as the thought of execution. In this instance, it inspired a creative search for accommodation as the would-be victims sought desperately to cheat the hangman.

PART TWO

The Crisis in the Middle East,

October 1973

The Failure to Prevent War, October 1973

*I don't see any contradiction between détente and our attempt
to separate Egypt from Moscow. Détente did help to split
Egypt from the Soviets. And it made crisis management
easier. I don't see any contradiction.*

—*Henry Kissinger* [1]

*The Soviet leadership, particularly Brezhnev, had no strategy,
no political line. What was our line, to strengthen our relations with the United States or to strengthen our relations
with the Arabs and the progressive forces? The two principles
were contradictory. We never recognized this.*

—*Victor Israelian* [2]

THE CRISIS between the United States and the Soviet Union at the end of the
October War in the Middle East was the most serious since 1962. The Soviet
Union threatened that it might act unilaterally to stop the fighting between
Egypt and Israel. The United States then attempted to deter Soviet intervention through a worldwide alert of its strategic and conventional forces. This
was the only time, since 1962, that strategic forces had been alerted during
a crisis between the superpowers.

The crisis developed in stages. It grew out of the bitter Arab-Israel conflict
that once again exploded into war in October 1973. The Soviet Union and
the United States first failed to prevent the war, then airlifted massive
amounts of military equipment to their allies, and finally were unable to stop
the fighting in the Middle East before it led to their most intense confrontation since 1962. In this chapter we explore the first in this series of failures:
the inability of the United States and the Soviet Union to prevent a war
among their allies. We examine the puzzling contradictions in Soviet and
American strategies of crisis prevention.

The crisis at the end of the October War in 1973 took place in a context
that was strikingly different from 1962. Before the missile crisis, a spiraling

process of threat and counterthreat had fueled distrust, fear, and mutual expectations of an impending confrontation. There was acute tension in the relationship between the two superpowers over Berlin and Cuba. Striking asymmetries in the strategic balance had heightened the sense of Soviet vulnerability and contributed to Khrushchev's decision to deploy the missiles in Cuba.

Conditions were dramatically different in 1973. Rough strategic parity prevailed between the two superpowers. Neither felt the acute sense of political and strategic vulnerability that had contributed so significantly to the crisis in 1962. In a period of growing détente, Soviet and American leaders had met successfully at two summits, communication between them was frequent and direct, and they had begun to discuss some informal rules to avoid a war-threatening crisis in their relationship. The context of their relationship was far less threatening than it had been eleven years earlier.

The improvement in superpower relations made mutual assessment of intentions easier. Soviet and American leaders had met several times. They knew one another better and, consequently, each was less prone to miscalculate the other's intentions. Years later, former Secretary of State Henry A. Kissinger observed: "I do not share the negative evaluation of [General Secretary Leonid] Brezhnev today. Brezhnev understood the big picture and was eager for arms reductions. [Foreign Minister Andrei] Gromyko and I were friends. We liked each other and worked well together."[3] Both sides were persuaded that neither wanted war, and both were sensitive to the risk of escalation inherent in their competition in the Third World. Their much improved relationship was not enough, however, to prevent a serious crisis between the superpowers.

THE VIEW FROM CAIRO AND JERUSALEM

The crisis between the United States and Soviet Union arose out of a war between their allies. To understand their failure to prevent a crisis, we must first examine the origins of the war and the calculations of leaders in Cairo and Jerusalem.

The roots of the war in October 1973 can be traced back to an earlier, unplanned war in 1967. Israel defeated the Egyptian, Syrian, and Jordanian armies and, in the course of the war, captured the Sinai peninsula, the Golan Heights, the West Bank of the Jordan, and East Jerusalem. After the war, the intelligence services of the United States, the Soviet Union, Egypt, and Israel all agreed that Egypt's military capability was inferior to that of Israel; Egypt could not recapture the Sinai in a general war.

Israel's continuing occupation of the Sinai was an intolerable humiliation to Egyptian leaders. In an attempt to compel Israel to withdraw its forces, President Jamal ab'dul al-Nasir initiated a war of attrition across the Suez Canal in March 1969. In the course of that war, Moscow sent twenty-thousand combat and support personnel to Egypt, Soviet forces assumed responsibility for the defense of Egyptian air space, and Soviet pilots engaged in dogfights with Israel's aircraft over the Suez Canal. The war ended in stalemate in August 1970.

The protracted and costly war settled little. Egypt and Israel read the results of the war differently. Both sides claimed victory even though both had suffered serious losses. Although Egypt had failed to compel even a partial withdrawal by Israel, its leaders insisted that they had won a significant victory because they had neutralized Israel's air superiority over the canal zone. Nevertheless, the high political, economic, and psychological costs of the continued occupation of the Sinai led Nasir's successor, Anwar el-Sadat, to search desperately for a strategy to compensate for Egypt's military inferiority.[4]

In February 1971, in a departure from past practice, the new president offered to sign a peace agreement with Israel in return for a full withdrawal of Israel's forces.[5] Although Sadat explicitly rejected the normalization of relations between Egypt and Israel, he expressed interest in a diplomatic resolution of the conflict. Two years of indirect bargaining with Israel through the United States produced no tangible results. Israel's leaders saw little reason to make concessions.

Israel's politicians and generals, with few exceptions, insisted that they had prevailed in the War of Attrition.[6] Israel had shown itself capable of withstanding significant military pressure in a long war and had resisted Egyptian as well as international pressure to withdraw from the Sinai without compensating political concessions. Some of Israel's leaders recognized the growing frustration of Arab governments, but, in response, placed an even heavier emphasis on the importance of military superiority as the basis of deterrence.[7]

Throughout most of 1972, Egypt's military command insisted that a general attack was impossible until the Egyptian air force acquired advanced medium- and long-range bombers that could strike at Israel's airfields. This Egyptian estimate was known to Israel's intelligence and became the basis of its estimate of the likelihood of attack. The operating assumption of Israel's military intelligence was that Egypt would not attack until the Egyptian air force could strike at Israel in depth and at Israel's airfields in particular. Syria was expected to attack only in conjunction with Egypt.[8] Air superiority was a basic principle of Israel's strategic planning and, consequently, its leaders were receptive to an evaluation by Egypt that emphasized the deterrent effectiveness of Israel's air force.

Military Intelligence in Israel considered an Egyptian attack unlikely before 1975, and Israel's leaders therefore saw no military or diplomatic imperative for accommodation. Their confidence in deterrence blinded them to the intense pressures on President Sadat and to his growing desperation. Israel's leaders did not use the time provided by deterrence to push the process of negotiation forward. Deterrence became a substitute for diplomacy.

President Sadat was pessimistic about the prospects of diplomacy. He feared that if the military and diplomatic stalemate were not broken, the cease-fire along the canal would become permanent and Egypt would be unable to reverse the status quo. He worried that the postponement of military action month after month would lead to explosive domestic consequences, an alarming deterioration of Egypt's position in the Arab world, and serious decline in domestic morale.[9] Pessimistic about the prospects of negotiation, but alarmed by the growing costs of inaction, President Sadat turned his attention to the creation of a military option that would compensate for Egypt's military inferiority. He dismissed the generals who opposed military action and appointed as chief of staff Gen. Saad el-Shazly, the leading proponent of a limited military attack across the canal.[10]

The purpose of an attack, under the cover of dense antiaircraft defenses, was the deliberate creation of an international crisis. The president of Egypt intended, through the use of conventional force against Israel for limited military objectives, to provoke a crisis between the superpowers and thereby to inflate the costs to them of perpetuating a status quo that he found intolerable. Sadat hoped to change the political context of the Arab-Israel conflict and to demonstrate to the superpowers that continued immobility could be dangerous to them, not only costly to him. The president hoped to push the United States to committing itself to a diplomatic resolution of the Arab-Israel conflict. To implement his strategy, President Sadat desperately needed sophisticated military equipment from the Soviet Union. From 1971 on, he repeatedly and insistently demanded arms from Moscow.

SOVIET FOREIGN-POLICY OBJECTIVES

To understand the Soviet response to Arab demands, and their failure to prevent the Egyptian and Syrian attack, we first examine the broader context in which policy developed. We look at the tension between their foreign-policy objectives of détente and support for anti-imperialist forces in the Third World, then at the impact of domestic politics on foreign policy, and finally at the decision-making style of Leonid Brezhnev. We then interpret Soviet policy toward its Arab allies as the result of these three vectors that varied in intensity and immediacy.

The Struggle against "Imperialism"

The Soviet leadership saw the Middle East as a critical arena in the world-wide struggle against imperialism. Ever since 1955, when Nikita Khrushchev agreed to sell arms indirectly to Egypt, Cairo had been one of the Soviet Union's most important allies in the "anti-imperialist struggle." Khrushchev supported military and economic assistance to the "progressive forces" in the Third World who were inspired by the Soviet model of development. He also favored assisting those "bourgeois" nationalist leaders who were committed to the defeat of Western hegemony in the Third World, the "weak link" in the imperialist chain.[11]

President Nasir of Egypt was considered the preeminent leader in the Arab world and a prominent figure in the nonaligned movement that was performing a historic role in the defeat of imperialism. Egypt was important to the Soviet Union because of its leadership in the Arab and the Third World; in the worldwide struggle between socialism and imperialism, support for progressive regimes like Nasir's Egypt could first restrain and then eliminate imperialist influence in the Middle East.[12]

Khrushchev's successors continued to emphasize the need for the unity of all "progressive" forces against "reactionary" forces in the Arab world and global imperialism. Brezhnev and his colleagues extended political support to a new revolutionary Ba'athist regime that came to power in Damascus in February 1966 and increased military assistance to Egypt and Syria. The relationship with President Nasir remained close despite tensions that grew from his repression of Egyptian communists. In a discussion with party leaders Walter Ulbricht of East Germany and Władysław Gomułka of Poland in April 1967, Brezhnev described the difficulties that the Soviet Union faced in Egypt. The USSR had succeeded in "partly pushing the Americans out of the Near East" because of its "consistent application of the Leninist principle of seeking temporary allies." "Nasser [Nasir]," he admitted, "is highly confused on ideological questions but he has proved that we can rely on him. If we . . . want to achieve progress, then we must also accept sacrifices. One sacrifice we bear is the persecution of Egyptian Communists by Nasser. But, during this phase, Nasser is of inestimable value to us."[13]

The Soviet commitment to Egypt and Syria deepened in the wake of the disastrous Arab military defeat in June 1967. To reinforce the capacity of its Arab allies to resist the "forces of imperialism," the Soviet Union massively rearmed Egypt and Syria and, in the spring of 1970, sent Soviet combat forces to Egypt to help defend its air space during the War of Attrition. When Nasir died just after the fighting stopped, the Soviet Union moved quickly to cement its relationship with his successor, Anwar el-Sadat. As long as Soviet-American competition remained acute, military and diplomatic support of Egypt as part of a global struggle against imperialism created no ideological, political, or diplomatic difficulties for Brezhnev and his colleagues.

Détente with the United States

At the beginning of the 1970s, the relationship between the Soviet Union and the United States began to improve considerably. At the Twenty-Fourth Party Congress in April 1971, General Secretary Brezhnev announced a "peace program." Soon afterward, the superpowers agreed to measures to reduce the risk of nuclear war through mutual notification and consultation in the event of a nuclear accident, and to modernize the hot line with satellite transmissions. In May 1972, Brezhnev and President Richard M. Nixon met in Moscow, where they signed the first important strategic arms-limitation agreement and discussed, among other issues, the prevention of war-threatening crises in their relationship. After the summit, Brezhnev spoke publicly of the "restructuring" (*perestroika*) of Soviet-American relations and of the "channeling" of international conflict to reduce an uncontrolled arms race and the threat of thermonuclear war.[14]

In the spirit of "détente," the two leaders attempted to develop some general principles and informal rules to govern their relationship and prevent crises. They negotiated the Basic Principles Agreement in 1972 and then, at the urging of the Soviet Union, the Agreement on Prevention of Nuclear War.[15] The latter agreement, reached at their summit meeting in June 1973, was most directly relevant to crisis prevention; it required both sides to "immediately enter into urgent consultation with each other and make every effort to avert this risk," if their direct relationship or relations with other countries "appear to involve the risk of a nuclear conflict."[16]

The Soviet leadership regarded these agreements as significant achievements and gave them great prominence in their press and commentaries. Brezhnev referred to détente as "the most remarkable turnaround in all post-war history."[17] Georgi A. Arbatov, the founding Director of the Institute of the United States and Canada in the Soviet Academy of Sciences and a close advisor to Brezhnev during this period, observed:

> It [is] possible to say that an historically significant turn has become evident in relations between the USSR and the USA. Its essence is a transition from the "cold war" to relations of genuine peaceful coexistence, signifying not only the absence of war but also the easing of tension, the normalization of political relations, the solution of emerging problems by negotiation, and the development of mutually advantageous cooperation in many spheres.[18]

The importance of coequal superpower status and the prevention of nuclear war were repeatedly emphasized by Soviet leaders.[19] From Moscow's perspective, these agreements formalized the new status of the Soviet Union as the political and military equal of the United States. Especially important to Moscow was the second article of the Basic Principles Agreement, that referred to the "recognition of the security interests of the parties based on the principle of equality and the renunciation of the use or threat of force," and the recognition "that efforts to obtain unilateral advantages at the expense of others, directly or indirectly, are inconsistent with these objectives."[20] To members of the Politburo, these agreements symbolized American acceptance of the Soviet Union as a global power. Soviet leaders expected mutual restraint, American recognition of Soviet political as well as military parity in areas of joint interest, and further progress on arms control. As an equal, the Soviet leadership expected to participate fully in the resolution of major international conflicts.

Soviet leaders also alluded to the "historic significance" of the agreement to prevent nuclear war. Leonid M. Zamyatin, an official of the Ministry of Foreign Affairs who subsequently headed TASS, issued a statement in

Brezhnev's name following the signature of the agreement: "The crux of this agreement is to rule out the possibility of nuclear war between the United States and the Soviet Union. It also sets the aim of excluding an outbreak of nuclear war between either of the parties and other countries."[21] In the months that followed, Soviet commentators continued to give great prominence to the agreement, its irreversibility and permanence, and its contribution to the prevention of nuclear war.[22]

Soviet analysts referred explicitly to the contribution the agreement would make to crisis prevention. One commentator noted approvingly that the agreement could be considered a "code of nuclear conduct."[23] Georgi Arbatov was more restrained. He observed that the agreement was only a first step that would have to be followed by others if the risk of nuclear war were to be reduced. The general relationship between the two countries would have to continue to improve to facilitate "the prevention of new conflicts and crises and the creation of a mechanism that would make [it] possible in a timely way to resolve emerging problems through negotiation."[24]

Soviet strategic parity with the United States made détente politically possible. Newly confident of Soviet capacity to compete, Brezhnev promoted détente insofar as it simultaneously reduced the risk of nuclear war between the two superpowers and formalized the status of the Soviet Union as the equal of the United States. As the Soviet Union achieved strategic equality, its interest in reducing the risk of nuclear war grew commensurately. In Arbatov's opinion, strategic parity made it imperative for both sides to make every effort to prevent the outbreak of nuclear war.[25] The two were closely linked.

In explaining détente, Soviet commentators insisted that the Basic Principles Agreement was the result of the changing and positive "correlation of forces" between the United States and the Soviet Union. Soviet analysts saw the agreement as American political recognition of Soviet strategic parity. They drew the corollary lesson that threats or use of military force under the condition of strategic parity would be foolhardy.[26] The favorable change in the "correlation of forces," Soviet leaders argued, ended Soviet inferiority and denied the United States the capacity to impose its will through nuclear blackmail or position-of-strength diplomacy.[27] The political benefits of U.S. strategic superiority had been neutralized.

The development of détente with the United States should have created a dilemma for Soviet leaders. The pursuit of competitive advantage in the Third World as part of the global struggle against imperialism could jeopardize the improvement of relations with the United States. In the worst case, wars in the Third World could lead to pressure for superpower military intervention to rescue an ally on the verge of defeat. When both the Soviet Union and the United States sought to make gains at the other's expense, military intervention by one could provoke a crisis with the other.

Soviet leaders and analysts generally rejected any contradiction whatsoever between détente and support for progressive forces in the Third World.

On the contrary, they argued that the twin principles of the nonuse of force and peaceful coexistence created more favorable conditions for national liberation struggles.[28] Soviet commentators vigorously denied that the new agreements with the United States forged an understanding between capitalism and socialism that precluded support for national liberation struggles in the Third World. Détente and the prevention of crises that could escalate to nuclear war did not hinder Soviet capacity to support its allies in the Third World. The Basic Principles Agreement explicitly stated that it did not affect any obligations that either power had undertaken toward their allies. Brezhnev insisted that cooperation with the United States need not and would not dampen the conflict between opposed social systems nor retard the world revolutionary process.[29] In his public statements, Brezhnev denied any trade-off between Soviet obligations to regional allies and global crisis prevention.

The Domestic Objectives of Détente

Brezhnev and Prime Minister Aleksei Kosygin, like Khrushchev, supported détente in part to help the faltering Soviet economy. In the period of political succession after Khrushchev's ouster, the collective leadership made few choices among priorities at home or abroad. Rather, Brezhnev met the important priorities of all the senior Politburo members—Aleksei Kosygin, Nikolai Podgorny, and Mikhail Suslov.[30] Soviet leaders spent heavily on agriculture, housing, and consumer goods to push the economy ahead on a wide front. At the same time, they funded all the military services, built up Soviet strategic capability, and increased their capacity to project conventional forces in areas they considered especially important.[31]

By the end of the decade, the high rate of spending across the board had begun to strain the resources of the Soviet economy. As early as April 1970, Brezhnev referred to the "difficulties, inadequacies, unsolved problems" of the Soviet economy.[32] Brezhnev also spoke more pessimistically than he had a few years earlier of the renewed capacity of imperialism to compete. The Soviet Union had succeeded in competing economically with capitalism, but the cost was heavy.[33] Although the Soviet Union had achieved great success, imperialism nevertheless still had the capacity to "adapt" to new conditions and to reorganize and compete.[34] Arbatov, a "reformist" thinker, argued that the scientific and technological revolution had allowed imperialism to reduce labor costs, increase productivity, and create more room for "social maneuver," including higher wages, improved management practices, and the simultaneous growth in military spending and living standards.[35]

The promise of technology transfer to generate innovation at home was one of the factors pushing Brezhnev toward détente with the United States. Although serious economic reform was not on the agenda of the regional Party leaders and national government officials who controlled the Central Committee, economic performance was a central concern. Détente appealed to ministry leaders in the industrial sector and some regional party leaders, who were attracted by the prospect of foreign technology and investment, and to ministerial and Party leaders responsible for agriculture who hoped to import cheap grain. Foreign Ministry officials, as well as scientific and cultural members of the Central Committee, were natural constituents of détente. Outside the obvious coalition were party leaders responsible for ideology and military leaders responsible for defense. They were most strongly committed as well to the support of "progressive forces" in the struggle against imperialism.

Despite the reservations of some members of the Politburo and the Central Committee, the General Secretary abandoned the policy of "selective détente" with Western Europe that attempted to split Washington from its allies, and embraced "détente" with the United States. Arms-control agreements with the United States would bring increased trade, credits, and the transfer of technology.[36] In part because détente served important domestic as well as foreign-policy objectives, Brezhnev and his colleagues were reluctant to face the contradiction between the pursuit of détente and the traditionally important support of "progressive" forces to defeat imperialism.[37]

THE DOMESTIC POLITICS OF FOREIGN POLICY

Brezhnev did not exercise the undisputed authority in the Politburo that Khrushchev did before the Cuban missile crisis. After Khrushchev was ousted in 1964, leadership was collective. Partly in reaction to Khrushchev's "erratic" style, his successors were determined to provide more stable and predictable leadership. Analysts of Soviet politics generally agree that the four most important members of the collective leadership in these early years were Brezhnev, Kosygin, Podgorny, and Suslov.

During the period of political succession, Brezhnev struggled to build authority and consolidate power.[38] To shape a consensus on disputed issues, at times he had to compensate some of his colleagues with concessions that were important to them. Brezhnev was strongly committed to the support of "anti-imperialist forces" battling capitalism in the Third World, as was Suslov who was in charge of party ideology. Podgorny supported "selective détente," a broad international coalition of capitalist governments and Third World forces to resist American imperialism. Only Kosygin urged economic cooperation with the United States to improve economic performance in the Soviet Union.[39] The need to build consensus frequently led to compromise and fragmentation in Soviet foreign policy.[40]

Most observers of Soviet politics concur that by 1971 the succession struggle was largely over and that Brezhnev was far more than first among equals. The general secretary, who had then become personally committed to détente with the United States, had built a broad consensus in the Politburo in its favor. Members nevertheless disagreed about the kind of détente that was appropriate and the specifics of policy. Brezhnev's peace program, announced at the Twenty-Fourth Party Congress in April 1971, was not approved until the Plenum of the Central Committee that November. As Georgiy Kornienko, then the head of the American desk in the Ministry of Foreign Affairs, observed, "There was a common consensus about détente, with differing opinions about concrete issues. The concept of détente was accepted by everyone. There was only disagreement on specific questions."[41] Victor Israelian, then the head of the Department of International Organization in the ministry, noted that although discussion always concentrated on specific issues, "There were shadings of opinion about détente within the Politburo. There were different approaches, not divisions within the Politburo."[42] These differences focused largely on the scope and occasionally on the timing of cooperation with Washington. Opposition to increasing trade with the United States, for example, lasted well into 1973.

The visit of President Nixon to Moscow, scheduled for May 1972, was preceded by a secret trip by Henry Kissinger, then national security advisor to President Nixon, to Moscow in April. Kissinger observed that

> Leonid Brezhnev, when I met him, was clearly the leading Soviet figure. But equally he was obviously not yet in complete charge. . . . Even in his first encounter with me, he left the impression that he was expounding the agreed position of a collective to which he was under some obligation to report back. . . . Brezhnev, it seemed, had authority to add nuances to an agreed position, but could not make radical shifts on his own. . . . At the same time, Brezhnev left the impression that if convinced that a change was necessary, he would be able to carry the Politburo with him.[43]

Leonid Zamyatin agreed with this analysis. He observed that "Although the Politburo was not deeply divided about détente before the Moscow 1972 summit, nevertheless Brezhnev was very cautious and often afraid to take major decisions, especially foreign-policy decisions by himself. Major foreign-policy initiatives always required something of a consensus in the Politburo. Without one, there would be no decision."[44]

After the United States resumed the bombing of Hanoi and mined the harbor of Haiphong, there was some opposition to proceeding with the planned summit in Moscow. On 9 May, Brezhnev convened a meeting of the Politburo to consider whether to cancel the summit. Foreign Minister Andrei Gromyko, KGB head Yuri Andropov, International Department head Boris Ponomarev, Kornienko, and Arbatov, as well as other experts and consultants attended. Some members demanded that the meeting be canceled. They believed, Arbatov recalls, that "if we agreed to go through with the summit we would be politically humiliated and would lose our authority in the eyes of the world, particularly the Communist world, and with liberation movements."[45]

A protracted debate preceded approval of the summit. The preeminent concern was the impact of cancellation on the new Soviet agreements with the Federal Republic of Germany, which were to be ratified by the Bundestag. Some of the Soviet leadership realized that a deterioration in relations with the United States could harm the prospect of ratification that, as Arbatov observed, was already threatened by active opposition within Germany.[46]

Once the Soviet leadership decided not to cancel the summit, Brezhnev convened a plenum of the Central Committee to approve the decision. Although Brezhnev had made the decision, he wanted to share the responsibility. The fear of appearing insufficiently "revolutionary," Arbatov noted, was a constant concern of the Soviet leadership: "an insufficiently firm class attitude might cause opposition forces to coalesce within the Party and provide a pretext for an attack against the leadership."[47] The plenum approved the forthcoming summit and the policy of détente, and Podgorny and Kosygin accompanied Brezhnev to most of the summit sessions.

In an unusual display during the summit, Podgorny openly challenged Brezhnev.[48] Indeed, during their meetings, Brezhnev repeatedly told President Nixon how difficult it had been to proceed with the summit.[49] This kind of dissent in the spring of 1972 could have fractured the consensus that was necessary to sustain the Soviet commitment to détente. Soviet officials insist, however, that the influence of those opposed to proceeding with the summit was not great. Podgorny and Petr Shelest were the most senior members of the Politburo who opposed proceeding with the scheduled visit by Nixon. Shortly afterward, Shelest was removed from his position as party leader in the Ukraine, paving the way for his expulsion from the Politburo in April 1973.[50]

Podgorny was more senior and more troublesome. He opposed the summit in part because it would compromise Soviet credentials with "progressive" forces in the Middle East.[51] Yet his influence was limited. Leonid Zamyatin described the role of Podgorny during this period:

> Podgorny was a public representative of the Soviet Union and largely a figurehead. He was a "gray" cardinal. His influence on Brezhnev was indirect. He had a very limited mind and pretended to have more influence than he did. At one point I asked Brezhnev what Podgorny was likely to say about an initiative under discussion. Brezhnev answered: "Why would you ask him?" Brezhnev said that the only time Podgorny got him to agree to anything was on their drives to their dachas. Brezhnev loved to drive his cars very fast. Podgorny would sit next to him on the front seat talking the entire time. Brezhnev said that he would sometimes agree to his requests just to get him to stop talking.[52]

Israelian confirmed that although Podgorny was an opponent of Brezhnev, the General Secretary had little difficulty in neutralizing his opposition. "Podgorny competed personally with Brezhnev, not on the basis of ideological differences. Podgorny pretended that he was an equal. He would telephone Brezhnev from his dacha in the country, offer advice and make Brezhnev furious. But Podgorny was not tough. Although he supported the Arab case, he never wanted to make any risky moves. Brezhnev had no difficulty dealing with him."[53] The opposition of those who advocated the postponement of the summit posed no serious threat to Brezhnev's authority.[54]

In the spring of 1973, changes in the Politburo increased Brezhnev's authority. For the first time since he had consolidated his leadership, Brezhnev was finally able to remove two of his opponents in the Politburo, Petr Shelest and G. I. Voronov, and appoint three new members who brought expertise and new channels of professional advice with them.[55] In April 1973, Andrei Gromyko, Minister of Defense Andrei Grechko, and Yuri Andropov, were promoted to full membership.

Gromyko, who had been extensively involved in negotiations with the United States, was a strong supporter of détente. "Gromyko was the father of détente," Leonid Zamyatin explained. "He believed that the key to better relations with the United States was equality in strategic arms. This would provide a framework for détente and better relations."[56] After he was appointed to the Politburo, Gromyko's role in foreign policy became paramount.

Grechko was "a tough guy, a typical soldier, a representative of the military," who believed that the greater the Soviet military advantage, the more cooperative the United States would become.[57] He was also actively involved in discussions with Arab leaders about their military needs and negotiated agreements on transfer of military equipment.

Andropov was a reformer but a somewhat reserved supporter of détente.[58] He was "lukewarm" in his support of détente with the United States, Israelian observed. "At times, he played Gromyko's card and at times he played Grechko's hand."[59] Zamyatin similarly noted that "Andropov was particularly well-informed about the West and much closer to Gromyko in his policy preferences. He had some hesitations, however, about détente."[60] Andropov was generally cautious, Arbatov observed, in order to avoid confrontation with his colleagues.[61] On balance, the changes in the membership of the Politburo in the spring of 1973 apparently deepened the consensus in favor of détente and strengthened Brezhnev's authority. As Israelian noted, "In 1973, Brezhnev was completely in charge. He was the decisive man."[62]

Staff work and policy formulation for the Politburo also became more supportive of détente. The International Department of the Central Committee traditionally played a significant role in the preparation of papers for the Politburo on foreign policy. There was always competition between the foreign ministry and the International Department.[63] Headed by Boris Ponomarev, a protégé of Suslov, its analyses were supportive of activism in the Third World. As détente gathered momentum, the work of the department broadened to include contact with political and economic leaders in the West.[64] Secretary Ponomarev and the first deputy chief, Vadim Zagladin, traveled repeatedly to Western Europe and the United States. Inevitably, the scope of its reports to the Politburo broadened and built support for détente among those most committed to active support of progressive forces in the Third World.[65]

Two other changes occurred which strengthened the consensus in favor of détente. When Andrei Gromyko was promoted to full membership in the Politburo, the Foreign Ministry had the capability to feed analysis and policy recommendations directly to the inner core of policymakers. Their analyses were generally more pragmatic than those of the International Department and strongly supported détente. During this period as well, Georgi Arbatov, a protégé of Andropov, gained personal access to Brezhnev. A leading "reformist" thinker and a supporter of détente under Khrushchev, he transmitted his views directly to the General Secretary. By the spring of 1973, Brezhnev had access to a more diversified and supportive stream of policy advice than he had had a year earlier.[66]

Brezhnev's authority among his colleagues was also strengthened by the obvious and visible progress of détente. Trade agreements were signed with the United States and the Federal Republic of Germany, and after a poor harvest the year before, 1973 promised to bring a bumper crop. Brezhnev's strategy of using foreign economic reserves as a motor of Soviet development appeared to be vindicated. He was consequently less concerned about and less dependent on the approval of skeptics in the Politburo in early 1973 than he was in the spring of 1972.[67]

Brezhnev was clearly the preeminent leader by 1973. In sharp contrast to the previous year, for example, during the preparatory talks in Moscow for the summit in San Clemente, Brezhnev alone conducted almost all the negotiations; only highly technical subjects were left to Foreign Minister Gromyko.[68] "Brezhnev was at the height of his powers," Arbatov maintained, "sure of himself, satisfied with his policy. It was at least a year before he became sick. There could be different opinions, but Brezhnev was in full control. They [the Soviet Politburo] ruled by consensus. He [Brezhnev] was not a dictator, but he was always able to get the consensus he wanted."[69]

Brezhnev's authority was greater and the consensus in favor of détente was broader in 1973 than it had been a year earlier. Nevertheless, he still had to fashion a consensus within the Politburo on Soviet policy in the Middle East. Brezhnev had to craft a coalition among those who favored détente at some cost to Soviet support of allies in the Third World, those who favored military aid to Arab leaders, and those who were ideologically committed to support the struggle against imperialism in the Third World. To do so, the Soviet leader reaffirmed his support for allies in the worldwide struggle against imperialism. He thereby preserved his revolutionary credentials and compensated some of those who were naturally outside the coalition in favor of détente.[70]

Brezhnev's Decision Making

Brezhnev tried to soften the differences among his colleagues, engineer a compromise, and reward those whose demands remained unmet. The General Secretary acknowledged that the Politburo worked by consensus and avoided votes wherever possible.[71] His preferred style of decision making was to share responsibility. His style fit nicely with the wishes of his colleagues who, above all, wanted to avoid the erratic and unpredictable excesses of Khrushchev's foreign policy. In his careful, cautious, almost "gray" style, Brezhnev was the obverse of his predecessor.

Brezhnev was particularly supportive of the demands of the military when he attempted to create a consensus on policy. As second secretary of the Central Committee, he had supervised the defense industry for several years. "From his first days in office," Arbatov observed, "Brezhnev treated the military as a very important power base. For him that alone was reason enough to give the military virtually anything it asked for. I think his earlier activities as Central Committee secretary of defense industries must have contributed significantly to this attitude. From then on, he was under the strong influence of our defense-industry officials."[72]

At Politburo meetings, Brezhnev often waited until most of his colleagues had spoken and only then intervened to craft a consensus that was frequently not apparent to others around the table. "Brezhnev's great strength," Israelian observed, "was that he was a master at building a consensus."[73] To build a consensus, Brezhnev often masked sharp and difficult trade-offs among alternatives. At times, therefore, Soviet policy was an unstable and incoherent compromise.

Brezhnev's style of leadership reinforced his personal reluctance to face and make hard choices. Soviet officials who observed Brezhnev's leadership allege that he was disinterested and at times poorly informed on the substance of policy. Fedor Burlatsky suggests that Brezhnev saw himself as an expert in "organization and psychology," and that he had little interest in the complexities of policy.[74]

> He [Brezhnev] blew with the wind and he was conservative by nature. He had no real expertise on domestic or foreign policy. . . . Unlike Khrushchev, Brezhnev never spoke first at leadership meetings; usually he spoke last. He would see what others had to say and shape his remarks accordingly. If the group had misgivings or was divided, he would just put off a decision. He was a sort of Soviet Tory, but without the high cultural level of British Tories.[75]

Andrei Gromyko, a member of the Politburo from April 1973, described Politburo discussions chaired by Brezhnev as a shambles, as did Victor Israelian.[76] Kornienko observed that Brezhnev had very few foreign policy ideas of his own: "Until he became ill, Brezhnev had good common sense, but he would not initiate policy. He would only veto proposals if he felt somehow that they would cause trouble."[77] Kissinger noted as well that Brezhnev was "disorganized."[78] This style of leadership likely contributed to contradiction and fragmentation in Soviet foreign policy.

MOSCOW'S RESPONSE

The change in the Soviet relationship with the United States created a dilemma for Moscow in its relationship with Egypt and with other "progressive" regimes in the Third World. President Sadat had largely given up hope of a diplomatic settlement of the Arab-Israel conflict and was determined to go to war to create the crisis the Soviet Union wanted to avoid. Sadat proclaimed 1971 "the year of decision" and repeatedly asked for the delivery of sophisticated military equipment, especially long-range bombers. He met with little success.[79]

At first, the Soviet leadership denied President Sadat the diplomatic and military support he needed to go to war. Following the inconclusive termination of the War of Attrition between Egypt and Israel in August 1970, the Soviet Union repeatedly warned Sadat against the use of military force to recapture the Sinai peninsula. Instead, Soviet leaders urged a diplomatic solution, much to the annoyance and frustration of Egyptian officials.

Nikolai Podgorny, the Chairman of the Supreme Soviet and a senior member of the Politburo, visited Cairo in May 1971. He persuaded Sadat to sign a formal Treaty of Friendship and Cooperation with the Soviet Union and promised that military supplies would be forthcoming. At the same time, he urged Sadat to avoid a war that Egypt could not win. He also pressed Egypt's president to refrain from participation in any negotiations sponsored by the United States; he assured Sadat that, with the passage of time, international pressure would force Israel to withdraw.[80] Mahmoud Riad, at one time the foreign minister of Egypt, testified that "Clearly, the Soviets favored a diplomatic solution and if Egypt opted for a military one, they did not want any part in adopting such a decision." A decision for war, Podgorny made clear, "would be Egypt's alone."[81]

In the spring of 1972, Soviet policy changed. From February through December, Moscow's strategy can best be described as "hedging." For the first time, a communiqué released at the end of a visit by Sadat to Moscow in February 1972 did not call for a peaceful settlement of the Arab-Israel conflict. In April, at the end of another visit by Sadat to Moscow, the communiqué was even clearer: "Arab states . . . have every justification *to use other means* for the return of the Arab lands seized by Israel."[82] Although they continued to press for a diplomatic solution to the conflict and to caution privately against war, Soviet leaders publicly acknowledged the Arab right to use force.[83]

Soviet officials also informed Sadat in March 1972 that they would require payment in full and in hard currency for all arms deliveries.[84] This demand effectively quadrupled the price of the equipment that Egypt had requested. Evgueny Pyrlin, the deputy director of the Middle East division in the Soviet Foreign Ministry in 1973, considered the request reasonable; the advanced electronic equipment and interceptors Egypt was asking for were not yet widely available to Soviet armed forces.[85] Soviet officials were also well aware of the limited resources that Egypt had when they insisted on payment in hard currency.[86] Given Egypt's economic crisis and its shortage of hard currency, Soviet leaders considered it very unlikely that Sadat would be able to pay for the military equipment he needed to go to war from Egyptian resources alone.

The Soviet demand for payment in hard currency reduced the impact of the cessation of public warnings against war. Some of what Soviet leaders gave with one hand, they took away with the other. Despite Soviet insistence on hard currency for arms shipments, the public acknowledgment of Egypt's right to use force nevertheless represented a shift in Soviet strategy.

Frustrated by the lack of diplomatic progress and the limits imposed by the Soviet Union, President Sadat decided on a dramatic step. In July 1972, he asked Soviet military personnel in Egypt to leave. He did so to remove the constraint on military action imposed by the presence on the ground of Soviet personnel and to increase the pressure on Moscow to supply the sophisticated military equipment Egypt needed to go to war. Expulsion of Soviet advisors also made it easier for Sadat to secure the hard currency from conservative Arab leaders that he needed to pay for Soviet military equipment.[87] In the fall of 1972 and the spring of 1973, Sadat then pushed the Soviet leadership, insistently and hard, to deliver the sophisticated military technology he had repeatedly asked for in the past. His demand was strongly supported by Ambassador Vladimir Vinogradov in Cairo, who insisted that acquiescence to the Egyptian request would pave the way for the return of Soviet military experts to Egypt.[88]

Sadat's actions sharpened the Soviet dilemma. If Soviet leaders did not provide Egypt with the military equipment it requested, they would antagonize their most important ally in the Middle East. If they acceded to Sadat's request, they would make it possible for Egypt to go to war; only the absence of sophisticated weapons constrained Cairo from attacking Israel. A war between Egypt and Israel could provoke a crisis with the United States and jeopardize their burgeoning détente with Washington.

In early 1973, Moscow began to supply Egypt with the military equipment that it previously had been unwilling to sell. Soviet leaders no longer hedged. Brezhnev, with the assistance of Gromyko and Grechko, evidently developed a three-track strategy. The Soviet Union decided early in 1973 to accelerate arms deliveries to Cairo to restore its relationship with Sadat and the Egyptian military. At the same time, it continued to urge Egypt privately to seek a diplomatic solution to the conflict. Soviet leaders also took an unusual step; they warned the United States that war was imminent if the diplomatic stalemate continued. They hoped simultaneously to prevent a crisis with Washington, forestall an Egyptian turn to the United States, and restore the Soviet position in Egypt.

In February 1973, Sadat's national security advisor Hafiz Isma'il traveled to Moscow to meet with Brezhnev.[89] The meeting was followed by one between an Egyptian military delegation, headed by Field Marshal Ahmad Isma'il, and Soviet Defense Minister Andrei Grechko. The Soviet Union agreed to accelerate delivery of medium-range bombers and missiles. The tone of Soviet policy pronouncements also changed significantly. Official commentators now declared that "The Arab governments have the complete right to use any form of struggle in the liberation of their occupied territories."[90]

To minimize the contradictions in Soviet strategy, Brezhnev and Gromyko tried to preserve their relationship with the United States by warning that there would be war in the Middle East unless progress was made in resolving the Arab-Israel conflict. When Kissinger came to Moscow in May 1973 to prepare for the forthcoming summit, Brezhnev told him of the growing likelihood of war and "hinted" at the increasing difficulty he was experiencing in restraining his Arab allies.[91] At the summit meeting in San Clemente in June, Brezhnev suddenly forced an emotional one-and-a-half-hour discussion of the Middle East at an unscheduled late-night meeting. He warned Nixon that, without at least some kind of informal agreement on the principles of a solution, he "could not guarantee that war would not resume."[92]

Aleksandr Kislov was unequivocal in his assessment of the deliberate character of the warning: "The war was the result of a great mistake and intellectual failures. Brezhnev told Nixon during his visit to the United States that there would be war in the Middle East if there was no change in Arab-Israeli relations. This was an intentional warning. Nobody in Washington or Tel Aviv wanted to believe this."[93] By telling the United States that war was likely, Soviet officials maintain, they explicitly fulfilled their responsibilities toward the United States with respect to crisis prevention.[94]

When Soviet leaders were informed by Syria and Egypt on 4 October that they intended to attack in a few days, they sent Soviet transport planes to Damascus and Cairo to evacuate the families of military advisors.[95] The airlift of Soviet dependents was ordered by Grechko and approved by Brezhnev and Gromyko.[96] When the Soviet military made no effort to camouflage the airlift, an infuriated President Sadat concluded that the withdrawal of Soviet families was meant to warn the United States that war was imminent.

Soviet officials disagree on whether the airlift was a deliberate signal to Washington. "We withdrew all our dependents seventy-two hours before the war began," Aleksandr Kislov explained. "We didn't tell you [the United States] explicitly why we did this, but we didn't conceal it either. We expected you to pick up the signal. It is true that we didn't want to risk the lives of our dependents. But, war was impossible to miss."[97] Gromyko put greater emphasis on protecting the lives of Soviet citizens. He informed his staff on 4 October that war was imminent and that Soviet dependents would be airlifted from Cairo and Damascus. One of his aides warned Gromyko that the airlift would signal Arab intention to go to war. Gromyko replied that undoubtedly it would, but that the lives of Soviet families were more important.[98] Either Soviet officials deliberately warned the United States or they did not care if Washington drew the correct conclusions.

All the Soviet warnings went unheeded by the United States. Even if American officials had understood the signals, they still would have perceived a fundamental contradiction between détente and Soviet support of a surprise attack by Egypt and Syria against Israel. Warning the United States of war did not remove the fundamental contradictions in Soviet policy. The decision to accelerate arms deliveries to Egypt was the critical step in the process that led to war in the Middle East and a crisis between the United States and the Soviet Union. Why did Soviet leaders pursue a contradictory and self-defeating strategy?

WHY DID SOVIET LEADERS FAIL TO MAKE THE HARD CHOICES?

The pattern of Soviet policy became progressively less coherent. Brezhnev and his colleagues began by strongly opposing Egyptian and Syrian plans to go to war but then gave their Arab allies the tools they needed to fight even though they privately opposed war. Soviet policy toward their Arab allies also became less compatible with détente as their relationship with the United States improved.

The Soviet Union responded three different ways at three different times to President Sadat's insistent and repeated demands for arms. In 1971, the Soviet leadership strongly opposed Egypt's intention to go to war and delayed the shipment of sophisticated equipment to Cairo. This decision was consistent with Brezhnev's "peace program" and emerging détente with the United States. In the spring of 1972, Moscow demanded payment in hard currency for all arms deliveries but moderated its public opposition to a use of force. It is especially anomalous that Soviet strategy changed just before the scheduled summit between General Secretary Brezhnev and President Nixon in Moscow. At precisely the moment when the promise of détente was growing, Brezhnev inched closer to supporting Egyptian action that could imperil détente. In early 1973, Soviet strategy changed again. Moscow continued to urge Egypt privately to seek a diplomatic solution to the conflict but began to supply its Arab allies with the military equipment that they needed to wage war. Soviet leaders made this decision when détente was flourishing.

In 1971, Soviet leaders responded to an immediate and pressing problem when they decided to oppose war and delay shipment of sophisticated military equipment to Cairo. Brezhnev and his colleagues repeatedly cautioned against war primarily because they were deeply pessimistic about Arab capability to win against Israel. Soviet military advisors, present in large numbers since March 1970, had little confidence in their Egyptian counterparts, and warned repeatedly of the disastrous consequences of military action by Egypt.[99] Opposition to war nevertheless severely complicated the Soviet relationship with Egypt.

Soviet leaders were also increasingly disturbed by Sadat's actions at home and abroad, but they still hoped to preserve their increasingly shaky relationship with Sadat. In the nine months since Nasir's death, Sadat had begun to privatize the Egyptian economy, to purge pro-Nasirites from the party, the government, and the military, and to establish diplomatic contacts with the United States. Soviet leaders distrusted Sadat and questioned his loyalty to the Soviet Union. To cope with an unreliable Sadat, Brezhnev hoped to strengthen the relationship with Egypt through a formal treaty of cooperation and vague promises of military aid, even while he continued to oppose war. To neutralize the dissatisfaction of Politburo members who were committed to the support of Egypt and Syria, Brezhnev sent the visible and articulate Podgorny, a proponent of strong ties to the Arab world, to negotiate with Cairo.[100]

Soviet policy was an unstable compromise that, at best, bought time. Podgorny made only vague promises of military assistance but warned Egypt both against a use of force and against the diplomacy of the United States. Such advice was inherently incredible in Cairo and provoked further frustration in Egypt.

In the spring of 1972, Soviet policy became far more contradictory. Brezhnev moderated his public opposition to a use of force by Egypt as détente with the United States was developing, yet made the purchase of Soviet arms far more expensive for Cairo. In large part because Soviet leaders hedged, policy pulled in several competing directions at once.

Moscow's insistence on hard currency was designed to make Sadat a more quiescent ally.[101] Leonid Zamyatin explained:

> There were three reasons why we changed our arms policy, insisting on cash rather than payments in credits that we extended. The first and most important of these was to try to make Sadat more pro-Soviet. If he had become more pliant in his foreign-policy line, we would have extended arms credits. The second reason was that Egypt had cut back on the supply of goods, especially cotton, to the Soviet Union. We wanted to signal our displeasure. Finally, there were nasty disagreements about the quality of Soviet military equipment. The Egyptian military constantly complained about its quality and insisted that several fighter crashes were the result of the bad aircraft we supplied. We sent

a special commission to investigate and discovered that the problem was the Egyptian pilots. In one case, the pilot hadn't removed the chocks before take-off, in another case he violated elemental rules of flight. Relations deteriorated rapidly between the two militaries.[102]

Soviet leaders wanted to teach Sadat a lesson but also to preserve their relationship with Egypt. The Soviet relationship with Arab states was important in the global struggle to preserve and promote Soviet influence against imperialism. The Politburo responded to Egypt's growing frustration by dropping its public opposition to war.

Soviet-Arab relations also played in the politics of the Politburo in the spring of 1972.[103] Policy changed before the scheduled summit in Moscow, when Nixon's visit was the subject of considerable controversy within the Politburo. Brezhnev may well have needed to co-opt and compensate critics by increasing Soviet support of Egypt in order to silence opposition to the summit. It is likely that Brezhnev built support for the forthcoming summit by reassuring the skeptics that détente would not compromise Soviet support of its allies in the Third World. The need to build consensus helps to explain the hedging in Soviet strategy toward Arab governments in the spring of 1972, and the nascent contradiction between Brezhnev's policies toward the United States and toward Egypt.[104]

Domestic politics does not help to explain the far more acute contradictions in Soviet strategy in 1973. Brezhnev was at the height of his power. Détente, his most important accomplishment in foreign policy, was flourishing. Trade was no longer an issue in the politics of the Politburo and the success of détente lent even greater authority to his leadership. If policy toward Egypt and Syria in 1972 had been driven in part by the need to fashion consensus and co-opt critics, these imperatives were far less important in 1973.[105] Under these circumstances, policy should have been more coherent and less segmented. It was not. Rather, the contradictions became more acute in 1973.

A look back at the trajectory of Soviet policy toward the United States and the Arab-Israel conflict suggests a puzzling pattern. In 1971, when Brezhnev was still consolidating his authority and détente was in its early stages, Moscow warned Egypt strongly against war and delayed the shipment of military equipment that Sadat urgently requested. In 1973, when Brezhnev was at the height of his powers and détente was progressing well, Brezhnev and Grechko sold Egypt the armaments that made war possible. We must look beyond domestic politics for a satisfactory explanation of the contradictions in Soviet policy.

The Soviet decision to sell Egypt the equipment it needed to go to war and to support publicly the use of force against Israel was in large part a response to the immediacy of the threat of Egypt's defection to the United States.[106] Egyptian leaders have suggested that, humiliated by the expulsion of their advisors, Soviet leaders reconsidered their policy and decided to supply the arms that Cairo had long demanded. According to Ismail Fahmy, the Egyptian Under Secretary of State for Foreign Affairs: "Clearly, the Soviets had got the message that they could not take Egypt for granted and had to take positive measures to maintain good relations."[107]

Soviet leaders were both angered and humiliated by the expulsion of their military advisors from Egypt, but they worried that Sadat would turn to the United States for help in pressuring Israel to return the Sinai.[108] This expectation was not unreasonable; Sadat did begin private exploratory discussions with Henry Kissinger through a back channel. Pyrlin explained that

> The KGB had copies of practically all the confidential documents that the United States and Egypt exchanged, including the personal secret messages between Presidents Nixon and Sadat. The volume of information in the possession of Soviet intelligence demonstrated that the "game" Mr. Sadat was playing with the United States was very serious. . . . Soviet intelligence information was very alarming, offset only by the optimistic cables of Ambassador Vinogradov in Cairo about the constant interest of President Sadat in developing better relations with the USSR, especially in the military field. . . . Besides, there was in the Soviet leadership very influential people like Boris Ponomarev [candidate-member of the Politburo and Head of the International Department of the Central Committee] who constantly insisted that the pro-American zigzags of President Sadat were tactical maneuvers, that Sadat was and would be a "friend and brother" of Soviet leaders. Under their influence, the Soviet leadership was convinced that Egypt could be brought back into the orbit of Soviet policy.[109]

In making the critical decision to supply the arms that made war not only possible but probable, Brezhnev and his colleagues responded to the most immediate imperative of preventing the defection of an ally.

We have explained the three critical decisions—to deny Egypt military and diplomatic support in 1971, to hedge in the spring of 1972, and to sell Egypt the equipment it needed to go to war in early 1973—as the result of foreign-policy or domestic considerations. Neither explanation accounts completely, however, for the general pattern of sharpening contradiction between core Soviet foreign-policy objectives. Over the long term, Brezhnev could not pursue détente and simultaneously give Egypt the military equipment that would enable Sadat to create the international crisis that the General Secretary wanted above all to avoid.

Domestic and foreign-policy considerations need to be supplemented by psychological considerations. Soviet leaders denied the need to make hard choices between their competing goals. Denial operated at several levels. Egyptian officers have speculated that Soviet military and civilian officials, even after the arms began to flow, underestimated Egyptian determination and capacity to go to war.[110] Although it is easy to understand how the Soviet military underestimated the Egyptian capacity to fight, given the past performance of the Egyptian army and the badly strained relations between

Soviet and Egyptian military personnel, it is more difficult to understand how they underestimated Egypt's commitment to go to war.

After the war, Soviet analysts referred to the obvious evidence of Egyptian intentions. "When I visited Egypt in May 1973," Kislov acknowledged, "there was open talk of war. War was impossible to miss."[111] Yevgeny Primakov admitted in retrospect that the diplomatic deadlock in Egypt and Syria had generated an acute political crisis in both countries.[112] Yet, the Politburo did not draw the obvious conclusions. "Grechko had the mistaken idea," Pyrlin observed, "that President Anwar Sadat would surely consult with Soviet military experts and political leaders before the beginning of large military operations against Israel."[113] At most, Soviet leaders warned in general terms of an inevitable explosion if the stalemate continued. To manage the contradictions in their strategy, Soviet leaders were motivated to underestimate the desperation of President Sadat and his determination to break through the impasse Egypt confronted.

The consensual style of Brezhnev's leadership and the working habits of the Politburo made evaluation of the painful trade-offs among policies even more unlikely. The inner group of Politburo members that dealt with foreign policy toward the Middle East consisted of Brezhnev, Gromyko, Andropov, and Grechko, joined at times by Suslov and Podgorny who had a strong interest in the Third World.[114] The poles of the spectrum were defined by Grechko who argued for speedy rearmament of Egypt and by Gromyko who urged a diplomatic solution.[115]

Grechko faced no dilemma.[116] More skeptical of détente, he favored the resumption of military supplies to Egypt to regain the strategic and political advantages the Soviet Union had lost in the Middle East. Grechko and Dimitrii Ustinov argued that the relationship with Egypt provided tangible benefits that would be lost if Moscow refused to supply Egypt with at least some of the equipment it was requesting.[117] After President Sadat notified the Soviet Union in December 1972 of his decision to extend the five-year agreement granting the Soviet Union naval facilities in Egypt, the military became even more determined advocates of supplying Egypt with some of the advanced equipment it had requested.[118]

It was Brezhnev, Andropov, and Gromyko who faced the difficult trade-off between Soviet interests in the Middle East and crisis prevention.[119] They confronted the dilemma in large part because Egyptian objectives were not only different from but diametrically opposed to their interest in détente with the United States. Sadat's strategy was one of deliberate crisis creation. Soviet leaders resolved the contradiction between support of a regional ally and promotion of détente largely by denying the inherent dilemmas. "The official conception at the time," Pyrlin explained, "was that the delivery of arms to nonaligned countries, especially those in conflict with the imperialist powers or their clients, as Egypt was in confrontation with Israel, had no relationship to Soviet-American détente."[120]

Brezhnev also seemed to have convinced himself that additional arms supplies would make it easier for the Soviet Union to restrain Egypt even as it restored the Soviet reputation and position in the Middle East.[121] Soviet leaders expected that the increase in Egyptian dependence on the Soviet Union for essential military equipment would increase their influence on critical decisions in Cairo.[122]

Certainly, Soviet leaders continued to warn vigorously of the dangers of the initiation of hostilities. On at least four occasions in 1973 before the Egyptian attack in October, Brezhnev warned Sadat against the use of force. The president of Egypt subsequently acknowledged that "some of the [arms] deal began reaching us after the Field Marshal's [Ahmad Isma'il's] return in February. We were happy that our relations would return to normal. But the USSR persisted in the view that a military battle must be ruled out and that the question must await a peaceful solution."[123] Soviet warnings did not have their intended effect. President Sadat gave them little weight.[124] He chose rather to interpret the flow of military supplies as the best measure of Soviet policy. As Sadat remarked, "It looks as if they want to push me into a battle."[125]

Soviet leaders seriously underestimated the desperation of President Sadat, his inability to tolerate the continuation of the status quo, and his pessimism about the possible benefits of diplomacy.[126] Sadat was alarmed by the deepening détente between the superpowers and its capacity to freeze an unacceptable status quo between Egypt and Israel.[127] He was "shocked" by the communiqué Brezhnev and Nixon issued at the end of their summit meeting in 1972.[128] He suspected that they had agreed to perpetuate the status quo in the Sinai in order to promote détente.[129] Ismail Fahmy told Sadat "that the superpowers were contributing to the maintenance of 'no peace, no war' because a permanent settlement of the Middle East had low priority for them. Détente was likely to make this priority even lower, as the two superpowers would now be preoccupied with safeguarding their rapprochement. As a consequence, the Soviets would become even more reluctant to provide Egypt with the arms it needed for a new confrontation with Israel."[130]

Brezhnev may also have overestimated Soviet capacity to limit the scope of the war and stop the fighting short of an Arab defeat, should Soviet warnings fail and Egypt go to war.[131] A crisis with the United States was most likely if the Soviet Union intervened to prevent the military defeat of its allies. In an interview in the spring of 1973, President Sadat revealed that he had reassured Soviet leaders that Egypt would "not drag the Soviet Union into a war with the United States," nor would he expect Soviet soldiers to die for Egypt.[132] This reassurance should not have carried great weight with Soviet leaders, given their low estimate of Egyptian military capability.

Soviet leaders had no basis to expect that they could control their ally after Sadat had expelled Soviet advisors. They also had little reason to anticipate that once war started, they would be able to stop the fighting before their allies asked for Soviet help. Soviet reasoning can best be explained by wishful thinking in the face of a difficult policy dilemma. It was particularly characteristic of Brezhnev, Israelian observed, to engage in wishful thinking.[133]

Soviet leaders were caught between two unpleasant options: antagonizing their most important ally in the Middle East or increasing the risk of crisis and confrontation with the United States. When people are confronted with a painful choice, they generally pay more attention to minimizing immediate and certain loss in comparison to longer-term, less certain costs.[134] The damage to the Soviet Union of refusing to supply Egypt was obvious, tangible, and immediate. Moscow would lose valuable naval facilities in Egypt, and more important, the reputation of the Soviet Union as a reliable ally would be compromised. Soviet leaders chose to avoid immediate damage and to deny the longer-term adverse consequences that were highly probable.

Denial was made much easier by the two long-standing strains of "expansionist" and "reformative" internationalism that dominated Soviet thinking about relations with the United States.[135] Brezhnev avoided the contradictions in Soviet policy by separating Soviet policy at the global and regional levels. Soviet policy was "reformist" toward the United States and "expansionist" in the Middle East. From 1970 on, the Soviet Union struggled to prevent the loss of a valuable ally in the Middle East within the broader context of an attempt to promote "progressive" forces that would defeat imperialism throughout the region. "We wanted both to protect our clients, and expand our influence," Gen. Yuri Yakovlevich Kirshin noted. "We had an expansionist policy in the Middle East."[136] Brezhnev selectively combined the two tendencies to argue that military and economic cooperation with the United States could proceed without inhibiting the revolutionary process in the Third World and the broader conflict between the two social systems.[137] His approach can be described as "expansionist détente."[138]

The Soviet policy of arming Egypt but cautioning its leaders privately against military action, and warning the United States that an explosion was imminent in the Middle East in order to protect détente, was unrealistic. It failed because leaders in Moscow did not face critical trade-offs. Brezhnev and the Politburo chose to avoid short-term losses with their Arab allies in the unreasonable expectation that they could avoid long-term losses in their relationship with the United States. Victor Israelian put it bluntly, "The Soviet leadership, particularly Brezhnev, had no strategy, no political line. What was our line, to strengthen our relations with the United States or to strengthen our relations with the Arabs and the progressive forces? The two principles were contradictory. We never recognized this."[139] Denial and wishful thinking about their relationships abroad led to a critical failure by the Soviet leadership to face and make the hard choices. This failure would ultimately bedevil their relationships both with the United States and with Arab governments.

AMERICAN FOREIGN-POLICY OBJECTIVES

Within the framework of détente, Washington attempted to exclude the Soviet Union from the core of the Middle East. President Nixon and Henry Kissinger, the president's national security advisor, relied on deterrence to prevent an Arab attack against Israel and waited for Arab governments to appreciate that only Washington could break the diplomatic logjam. To understand this response, we look first at what the United States wanted to accomplish through détente with the Soviet Union.

Détente

When President Nixon took office in January 1969, he acknowledged that the United States had lost its strategic superiority. Washington needed "sufficiency" to ensure that it could defend its interests and commitments abroad and a different kind of relationship with the Soviet Union that would minimize the consequences of the loss of American strategic superiority.[140] Arms-control agreements that would limit the buildup of missiles were now an imperative of the nuclear age.

Nixon and Kissinger were convinced that the arms race was the symptom rather than the cause of conflict between the superpowers.[141] The president at first linked movement on arms control to progress toward a settlement in the Middle East and Vietnam.[142] Nixon and Kissinger attempted to create a closely linked mixture of incentives that would induce the Soviet Union to act with greater restraint, especially in areas of contested interest. If the United States were successful, a new, more stable international order could gradually replace the intense competition of the Cold War. As part of this strategy, Nixon and Kissinger emphasized the importance of economic agreements that would provide the incentives for Soviet restraint, strategic agreements that would reduce the risk of nuclear confrontation, and agreement on norms and informal rules that would govern competition in areas of mutual interest.[143]

Domestic public opinion in the United States, as well as the Soviet leadership, rejected the "linkage" of strategic arms negotiations to political problems in the superpower relationship. Public opinion considered arms control too important to be made hostage to other issues, and the Soviet leadership rejected linkage as blackmail. By 1971, the administration had decoupled arms control from Soviet concessions in the Middle East and Vietnam. On the contrary, in a strategy of reverse linkage, Nixon made secret trade concessions to facilitate a limited arms-control agreement.[144]

Even though "linkage" proved to be unworkable, Nixon and Kissinger nevertheless valued détente because it gave the Soviet Union a stake in international order and was a step toward Soviet restraint in the Third World. "Progress in one area," Kissinger observed, "adds momentum to progress in other areas. By acquiring a stake in this network of relationships with the West, the Soviet Union may become more conscious of what it would lose by a return to confrontation."[145] Détente was part of a step-by-step process to enmesh Moscow in a web of relationships that would gradually restrain its aggressiveness.

Unilateral Gain

Nixon and Kissinger attached far less symbolic or substantive importance to the principles enunciated in the agreements signed at the two summits than did their Soviet counterparts. Washington had inserted the clause enjoining the search for unilateral advantage into the Basic Principles Agreement.[146] Yet, the United States concentrated on excluding the Soviet Union from diplomacy between Arabs and Israelis and from any future peace settlement. As Kissinger candidly acknowledged, "I said in 1969—and all hell broke loose—that we must expel the Soviet Union from the Middle East. And we did it."[147] The United States did not acknowledge Soviet "equality," as it had committed itself to do at the summit in 1972, but deliberately sought gains at Soviet expense in the Middle East.

Kissinger confessed to his amazement that Sadat had expelled Soviet military personnel without asking for a quid pro quo from the United States.[148] Once Soviet personnel were gone and at no cost to the United States, he was determined not to permit their return. Although Nixon and Kissinger hoped that détente would create incentives for Soviet restraint, they felt free themselves to attempt to make gains at Soviet expense in the Middle East. Their double standard in the evaluation of Soviet and American behavior was explicit. Kissinger put it bluntly:

> Our policy [was] to reduce and where possible to eliminate Soviet influence in the Middle East . . . under the cover of détente. . . . Détente was not a favor we did the Soviets. It was partly necessity; partly a tranquillizer for Moscow as we sought to draw the Middle East into closer relations with us at the Soviet's expense; partly the moral imperative of the nuclear age.[149]

Some Soviet officials acknowledged that the recognition of the equality that they considered so important was not forthcoming from the United States. "We understood that détente was a limited process," Vadim Zagladin observed. "It primarily concerned arms control. Other fields of international relations were not discussed. In the Middle East, the United States was unwilling to talk."[150]

In describing his secret trip to Moscow in April 1972 to prepare for the summit, Kissinger revealed his lack of understanding of the symbolic importance of equality to Soviet leaders:

> Equality seemed to mean a great deal to Brezhnev. It would be inconceivable that Chinese leaders would ask for it. . . . To Brezhnev it was central. . . . He expressed his pleasure when in my brief opening remarks I stated the obvious:

that we were approaching the summit in a spirit of equality and reciprocity. What a more secure leader might have regarded as a cliché or condescension, he treated as a welcome sign of our seriousness.[151]

If Kissinger had genuinely understood the psychological and symbolic significance of political equality to Brezhnev, he should have anticipated the damaging consequences to Soviet-American relations of his exclusionary strategy in the Middle East.

WASHINGTON'S RESPONSE: DETERRENCE AND DELAY

By arming Egypt, the Soviet Union made possible another round of war between Egypt and Israel. Although war was possible, however, it was not inevitable. Even as late as the spring of 1973, President Sadat expressed interest informally in an interim agreement along the Suez Canal, tied to a phased final settlement of the conflict.[152] However, the United States made little effort to break the diplomatic impasse between Egypt and Israel after Secretary of State William Rogers' attempt to mediate a limited agreement along the Canal failed in 1971. American officials felt no pressure to begin another round of negotiations because they considered a war between Egypt and Israel so unlikely. President Nixon was preoccupied with Watergate, and Kissinger was confident that Israel's unquestioned military superiority would deter an Arab military attack. His confidence in deterrence blinded him to Sadat's growing desperation and made him insensitive to Soviet warnings of an impending war.

Deterrence

Following Egyptian and Soviet violations of the American-brokered cease-fire that ended the War of Attrition in 1970, the United States agreed in December 1971 to supply Israel with new Phantom and Skyhawk aircraft over the course of the next three years. This agreement was the first long-term arrangement on military sales between Washington and Jerusalem. The supply of sophisticated aircraft further increased American and Israeli confidence in Israel's military superiority and its capacity to deter an attack. As we have seen, Israel's military intelligence was persuaded that Egypt would not attack until the Egyptian air force could strike at Israel in depth and at airfields deep behind the lines, and that Syria would attack only in conjunction with Egypt.[153] This judgment was shared by military intelligence in both Moscow and Cairo, and their lack of confidence in Egyptian military capability was known to both Jerusalem and Washington.[154]

When President Sadat expelled Soviet military personnel in July 1972, Israeli and American confidence in deterrence increased. Neither Jerusalem nor Washington understood that Sadat had asked Soviet advisors to leave because he was determined to go to war. In a detailed analysis prepared for the president, Kissinger did observe that the departure of Soviet personnel could reduce Soviet ability to restrain Egyptian military action in the future.[155] But his emphasis was on the weakening of Egyptian military capability.

Confidence in deterrence made American leaders insensitive to a series of warnings from Moscow that a crisis was brewing. In his meeting with Kissinger in Moscow in May 1973 to prepare for the forthcoming summit, Brezhnev warned that war was likely and that it was increasingly difficult to restrain Arab leaders.[156] At that time, large military maneuvers by the Egyptian army were in progress, and Israel had mobilized some of its reserves in response. On his return from Moscow, Kissinger directed the staff of the National Security Council to develop a contingency plan for a war between the Arabs and Israel. The study concluded that the Egyptian army was engaged in maneuvers and discounted the likelihood that Egypt intended to attack.[157]

At the summit meeting in San Clemente, Brezhnev warned again, intentionally, that war was likely in the absence of diplomatic progress. He insisted that war could be averted only if the United States and the Soviet Union agreed on a set of governing principles for the resolution of the conflict. Kissinger described the warning by Brezhnev as an outburst, probably "as much from frustration as from conviction." He added that Brezhnev "must have heard the same Egyptian threats as we had and may have shared our own estimate that such an effort was bound to end in Arab defeat. He knew that our ally was militarily stronger and that we held the diplomatic keys to a settlement."[158] Kissinger subsequently admitted that "we dismissed this [the warning] as psychological warfare because we did not see any rational military option that would not worsen the Soviet and Arab positions."[159]

The United States also missed the signal built into the Soviet airlift of its personnel three days before the war. Years later, Kissinger admitted somewhat ruefully:

> I do find it credible now that Brezhnev tried to warn us at San Clemente and through their open airlift. The warnings were probably meant. We missed those warnings. I regard [our flawed evaluation of the meaning of the airlift] as one of our biggest intelligence failures. We thought there was another quarrel between the Soviets and their Arab allies. But, why should they take their dependents out from both [Cairo and Damascus] at the same time. We missed it.[160]

American leaders were insensitive to evidence that war was imminent in the Middle East because of their exaggerated confidence in Israel's military superiority as a deterrent. Looking only at the military balance, they discounted Sadat's frustration with the ongoing diplomatic impasse and the intolerably high cost of the status quo. Rather than preventing war, confidence in deterrence blinded the United States to the frustration of Egypt and its incentives to go to war.

Delay

The second component of American strategy, a deliberate strategy of diplomatic delay, emerged even before the expulsion of Soviet personnel from Egypt. At the beginning of the Nixon administration, Secretary of State Rogers had been given primary responsibility for the Middle East, while Kissinger worked closely with the president on Vietnam and Soviet-American relations. Rogers pushed hard, first for a comprehensive settlement of the Arab-Israel conflict and then, when that proved impossible, for an interim agreement between Egypt and Israel that would open the Suez Canal. Kissinger was skeptical of the likelihood of any agreement as long as the Soviet Union remained deeply entrenched in the Arab Middle East. He advocated delay until Egypt reversed its alliance with Moscow and moderated its demands. Unlike Rogers, who focused primarily on reducing regional tensions, Kissinger viewed the Arab-Israel conflict in terms of its broader implications for Soviet-American competition in the Third World.

The division over strategy was exacerbated by personal and institutional rivalry between the two men. President Nixon vividly describes each man's opinion of the other: "Rogers felt that Kissinger was Machiavellian, deceitful, egotistical, arrogant, and insulting. . . . Kissinger felt that Rogers was vain, uninformed, unable to keep a secret, and hopelessly dominated by the State Department bureaucracy."[161] As Kissinger noted wryly:

> Middle Eastern policy was controlled by the State Department. As a Jew, I was thought to be prejudiced. At State, there was a procedural approach which was bound to fail. Without Nixon and me, it didn't have the energy. Nixon supported them, but it was the wrong approach, without energy.[162]

The president was made acutely uncomfortable by the rivalry between his two advisors and was frequently reluctant to overrule one in favor of the other. Consequently, Middle Eastern policy, like its Soviet counterpart, at times lacked coherence and coordination.

After Rogers failed, in the summer of 1971, to conclude an interim agreement between Egypt and Israel to reopen the Suez Canal, diplomatic efforts were largely frozen. By the end of 1971, Kissinger's strategy of deadlock and delay was consistent with the president's preferences. The United States was entering an election year and the president wanted the Middle East kept quiet until the elections were over.[163]

At the summit meeting in Moscow in May 1972, Kissinger pretended to engage in joint discussions with Foreign Minister Gromyko about the principles of a settlement in the Middle East. Kissinger's strategy of diplomatic deadlock was deliberate. He is surprisingly candid in his memoirs about his tactics. "In order to waste as much time as possible in my meeting with Gromyko, I made Gromyko repeat some of his formulations over and over again so that I could 'understand them better.'"[164] The practical consequence of his discussions with Gromyko "was to confirm the deadlock."[165]

Confident of Israel's military superiority and its capacity to deter, Kissinger argued that Washington could afford to sit back and wait for the right political preconditions. "Our objectives were served," he observed, "if the status quo was maintained until either the Soviets modified their stand or moderate Arab states turned to us for a solution."[166]

After the congressional elections in November 1972, Secretary Rogers was increasingly a lame duck, and Kissinger and Nixon shaped Middle Eastern diplomacy. Ironically, Kissinger's influence grew as the relationship between Egypt and the Soviet Union became increasingly strained. Once Egypt had expelled Soviet personnel, stalemate should no longer have been desirable; it had achieved its purpose of rupturing the relationship between Egypt and the Soviet Union. By the end of 1972, Kissinger had the ear of the president and the opportunity he had long been seeking to move ahead forcefully in secret negotiations with Egypt.

Kissinger did become informally involved in Middle East diplomacy. He participated in separate back-channel negotiations with Anatoliy Dobrynin, the Soviet ambassador to Washington, with Simcha Dinitz, Israel's ambassador, and in the spring of 1973, with Hafiz Isma'il, President Sadat's national security advisor. The State Department was informed that the talks with Hafiz Isma'il were taking place and was permitted to send Alfred (Roy) Atherton, deputy to Assistant Secretary of State for Near Eastern and South Asian Affairs Joseph Sisco, as an observer to the discussions.[167] Atherton gave only a very limited briefing on his return to the department. As one official of the Department noted wryly, "He [our observer] was under a 'wrap' from Henry."[168] Often the State Department was not informed of the results of these conversations and proceeded independently in its effort to get presidential approval for negotiations between Egypt and Israel.

President Nixon, once the elections were over, began to push for a more active effort at a settlement of the Arab-Israel conflict. Although he shared Kissinger's perspective on the Middle East as an arena of Soviet-American competition, concurred with the attempt to exclude the Soviet Union, and agreed that Arab states would have to moderate their demands before a settlement was possible, the president was nevertheless concerned that the conflict would explode if a settlement were not reached. In preparation for Hafiz Isma'il's visit to Washington in February 1973, Nixon pencilled a note on the margin of a briefing paper prepared by Kissinger: "this year I am determined to move off dead center. . . . This thing is getting ready to blow."[169] Nixon was even more direct in his notes in his diary written at the same time: "I spoke to Henry about the need to get going on the Mideast. I am pressing him hard because I don't want him to get off the hook with regard to the need to make a settlement this year. . . . What he's afraid of is that Rogers et al., will get a hold of the issue and will try to make a big public play on it and that it will break down."[170]

The crisis over Watergate began to develop in Washington at about the same time, and the president's attention was focused on the Senate hearings and the damning revelations of John Dean. Distracted, Nixon did not prod his national security advisor. Kissinger was convinced that Egypt had no military option and, therefore, "no choice but to await the American diplomatic initiative."[171] He again chose to delay further in order to moderate President Sadat's terms for a settlement. The meetings between the two national security advisors were unproductive.

On 15 May 1973, Secretary of State Rogers proposed a new American initiative. He made his proposal at a time when the Egyptian army was engaged in extensive military maneuvers and Israel had ordered a limited mobilization of reserves. The secretary suggested an "exploratory" effort that would help to stabilize the region even if it did not succeed. Publicly, the United States would promote a limited agreement on the canal, but privately it would try to organize direct Egyptian-Israeli talks on a broader agenda. Kissinger still saw no urgency for crisis prevention through diplomatic action in the Middle East. He persuaded the president to discourage Rogers from engaging in any diplomacy to break the deadlock.[172] Kissinger was planning a major diplomatic initiative after Israel's elections in late October and was, in the meantime, "stalling."[173]

The strategy of deliberate delay contributed significantly to the failure to prevent war. Diplomatic deadlock increased Sadat's frustration and left him no option but a war against Israel. Kissinger thought that a desperate Sadat would recognize the critical role of the United States, abandon his alliance with Moscow, and give Washington the political advantage at the expense of the Soviet Union in the Middle East that it wanted. Kissinger actively tried through delay and deadlock to produce desperation in Egypt. Confident in deterrence, he did not give much weight to the possibility that Sadat, despairing of diplomatic progress, might attack.

THE FAILURE TO PREVENT WAR

The strategies of both superpowers were fatally flawed. Although the dilemmas they confronted were substantially different, components of their strategies were strikingly similar. The United States and the Soviet Union significantly underestimated the intensity of Sadat's motivation to attack and misread his strategy. Vulnerable to growing domestic political opposition at home and pessimistic about the direction of international political trends, the president of Egypt saw little option but a limited attack to create an international crisis. The relative military balance was only one, and not the most important, component in his broader strategic calculation.

Miscalculation

In deciding to supply Egypt with medium-range bombers and missiles while warning against war, Soviet leaders overestimated their capacity to control their ally. They should not have made this mistake. They had good access to Egyptian leaders and independent sources of intelligence in the country. In

Kislov's judgment, the signs of war in Egypt were so obvious that they could not be missed.[174] Soviet leaders denied the painful choice they confronted between immediate loss of an important regional ally and the longer-term risk of crisis with the United States. In effect, they wished it away.

The United States miscalculated for quite different reasons. In their critical misjudgment, American officials were heavily influenced by the similar miscalculation of Israeli military intelligence.[175] But they were exposed repeatedly to Soviet warnings, which Israel's leaders were not. How can their miscalculation be explained? An important factor was the almost reflexive confidence of Kissinger and, to a lesser extent, Nixon in the relative military balance as a necessary and sufficient basis for successful deterrence and crisis prevention. They ignored Soviet warnings in part because they were blinded by their misplaced confidence in deterrence.

The Irony of Détente

The emphasis by both superpowers on the competitive dimension of their relationship was also an important component in the failure to prevent war. Within the broader context of the worldwide struggle to defeat American imperialism, the Soviet Union sought to avoid the immediate loss of its most important ally in the Middle East to Washington. The two tendencies of "expansionist internationalism" and "reformative internationalism" had long existed in Soviet thinking about its relationship with the United States.[176] Brezhnev selectively combined these two strains to craft a strategy of "expansionist détente" that would allow him, he hoped, to achieve Soviet objectives with the United States and in the Arab world. Soviet leaders denied any contradiction between détente with the United States and the defeat of American "imperialism" in the Third World.

The United States attempted to reverse Egypt's pattern of alliance with Moscow and score competitive gains. Years later, Kissinger explicitly rejected any contradiction between détente and expulsion of the Soviet Union from the Middle East:

> I don't see any contradiction between détente and our attempt to separate Egypt from Moscow. Détente did help to split Egypt from the Soviets. And it made crisis management easier. I don't see any contradiction.[177]

Kissinger denied the trade-offs and chose to exploit détente and the ambiguous and limited understanding on crisis prevention reached at the summit a year earlier as a cover for exclusion of the Soviet Union.

Each side saw the other's gain as its loss and its gain as the other's loss. In this respect, Nixon and Kissinger were very much like Brezhnev and his colleagues. In both capitals, preeminent leaders denied the inherent contradictions of their strategies. They all interpreted détente selectively as they competed with each other. Moscow saw détente as an opportunity to preserve and promote its influence and constrain the United States, whereas

Washington treated détente as a cover in the search for unilateral gain in the Middle East and as a constraint on Soviet behavior. Neither considered how détente might limit their own behavior.[178]

United in their mutual fear of nuclear war, the United States and the Soviet Union nevertheless disagreed sharply on what they expected of one another and what was appropriate. Each hoped that in the context of strategic parity, détente would constrain adventurous behavior by the other. The Soviet Union saw détente and the accompanying agreements as an opportunity to limit the American propensity to engage in nuclear blackmail and to resort to military force in the Third World, whereas the United States saw détente as a constraint on aggressive Soviet action. Détente and the accompanying agreements on basic principles and crisis prevention masked profound if unarticulated disagreement about appropriate limits of superpower behavior in the Third World and, in so doing, created unrealistic expectations about the limits of competition.[179]

Denial in the face of unpleasant alternatives and the use of a double standard in evaluating the behavior of others are quite common. The impact of the two together is pernicious. Denial prevents leaders from confronting the contradictions of their strategy until the crisis is upon them. A double standard of the kind used by Soviet and American leaders to evaluate the other's behavior sets the stage for disappointment when behavior defies expectations. This in turn encourages distrust, which can badly damage a relationship. This is precisely what happened after the United States and the Soviet Union failed to prevent war in the Middle East.

Confronted by President Sadat, whose strategy was one of deliberate crisis creation, neither Soviet nor American leaders faced up to the difficult and painful choices inherent in an effective strategy of crisis prevention. Neither set of leaders was willing to forego immediate political loss or sacrifice political benefit in the Middle East to reduce the risk of war in the region and serious crisis between the Soviet Union and the United States. What is especially damning, is not that they tried and failed, but that neither set of leaders seriously tried.

The Failure to Limit the War:
The Soviet and American Airlifts

When the war started, Sadat pressed us hard to honor our
agreements and then to accelerate deliveries as early as October 8. A decision was made in the Politburo to go along.

—*Victor Israelian*[1]

We would pour in supplies. We would risk a confrontation.
I wanted a demonstrative counter to the Soviet airlift. . . .
Once a stalemate had become apparent . . . we moved
decisively, even brutally, to break it.

—*Henry Kissinger*[2]

ON OCTOBER 6, 1973, at 1:55 P.M., 240 Egyptian planes crossed the Suez
Canal to bomb command posts, airfields, and radar installations of the Israel Defense Forces, and 1,848 artillery guns opened fire along the entire
front. Syrian forces attacked simultaneously across the Golan Heights. War
in the Middle East had begun. Although they had failed to prevent war, the
United States and the Soviet Union could still have prevented a serious crisis
in their relationship if they had limited the war before their allies risked
serious defeat.

At the beginning of the war, both Moscow and Washington expected
Arab armies to be badly defeated. Both superpowers wanted to avoid a rout
of Arab armies in part because they feared it could provoke a crisis in their
own relationship. Moscow wanted to forestall any request for military intervention from its Arab allies and the consequent risk of confrontation with
the United States. "It should be clear," Brezhnev told his colleagues at a
Politburo meeting, "that Soviet involvement on behalf of the Arabs in the
war would mean a world war."[3] In the first two days of the fighting, *Pravda*,
which usually spoke for Brezhnev, warned again and again of the dangers
of escalation.[4]

Richard Nixon and Henry Kissinger, newly appointed as secretary of
state, also worried about the consequences if Arab armies were badly
routed. They initially were confident of Israel's capacity to defeat Arab ar-

mies once it mobilized its reserve forces and recovered from the initial surprise. Then, Kissinger argued, "The Middle East may become . . . what the
Balkans were in Europe in 1914, that is to say, an area where local rivalries
. . . have their own momentum that will draw in the great nuclear powers
into a confrontation."[5]

Soviet and American leaders wanted to prevent a crushing Arab military
defeat not only to avoid a crisis in their relationship. Moscow wanted to
forestall damage to its reputation as a reliable ally to states in the Third
World; once war had started against their wishes, Soviet leaders wanted
above all to avoid loss. Nixon and Kissinger looked forward to playing a
dominant if not exclusive role in postwar negotiations; they hoped to make
gains. It would be much easier for the United States to monopolize postwar
diplomacy if Arab armies were not humiliated on the battlefield. Almost as
soon as the fighting began, Kissinger saw the war as an opportunity to exclude the Soviet Union from its diplomatic aftermath.

Wars can be limited in their objectives, scope, and duration. The superpowers could not have determined the objectives of their allies in the Middle
East, but they could have affected the scope and duration of the fighting if
they had restricted the quality and quantity of the military supplies that they
sent to their allies. Egypt, Syria, and Israel were fighting an intense war that
consumed vast amounts of military equipment at an unprecedented rate.
The Soviet Union and the United States were the exclusive suppliers of the
heavy military equipment that all three combatants desperately needed if
they were to continue fighting for more than a week. The superpowers were
consequently well positioned to limit the scope and duration of the fighting.
They missed the opportunity. At the end of the first week of the war, both
the Soviet Union and the United States were airlifting massive amounts of
military equipment to the Middle East.

We first examine why the superpowers missed the opportunity to restrict
the supplies they sent to their allies. The next chapter looks at why they
could not stop the fighting between their allies before it provoked a serious
crisis between them. These two failures are interconnected: their failure to
restrict the scale of their airlifts made termination of the war far more difficult. We analyze how and why the two superpowers pursued contradictory
and self-defeating strategies of crisis prevention.

The View from Moscow

The Soviet Air- and Sealift

Arab armies achieved major military successes in the first twenty-four
hours of the fighting. The Egyptian army quickly crossed the Suez Canal,
burst through Israel's Bar-Lev Line, and put substantial forces on the east
bank of the canal. The unexpectedly easy crossing gave President Sadat an
enormous psychological and political victory in the Arab Middle East.
Syrian forces advanced rapidly to the edge of the Golan Heights and were

only hours away from crossing the borders of 1967 into Israel's populated Hula Valley.

A small group of Politburo members met on the evening of 6 October, a few hours after the fighting began.[6] This informal but select group, chaired by Brezhnev, would meet regularly throughout the first week of the war. Present were Andrei Gromyko, the foreign minister; Yuri Andropov, the head of the KGB; Andrei Grechko, the defense minister; Mikhail Suslov, in charge of ideology; occasionally Aleksei Kosygin, the prime minister; as well as Konstantin Chernenko, who acted informally as secretary.[7] They were assisted by a staff of four officials from the Foreign Ministry—Vasiliy Kuznetzov, the deputy foreign minister; Georgiy Kornienko, the head of the American desk; Mikhail Sytenko, the head of the Middle Eastern division; and Victor Israelian, the director of the Department of International Organizations—organized as a special working group. These sessions were not formal Politburo meetings. The choices made at these meetings nevertheless carried the weight of Politburo decisions.[8]

At the end of the first week of the war, at a meeting of the Politburo on 12 October, Brezhnev suggested that the procedure be changed. He set up a special Commission of the Politburo on the Middle East, which was chaired by Suslov and included Gromyko; Andropov; Grechko; Boris Ponomarev, the head of the International Department of the Central Committee; and K. F. Katushev, responsible for policy toward communist parties abroad. The Commission was supposed to review the documents and discuss the issues and then forward their recommendation to the Politburo. Although the commission met several times, its role was secondary. Throughout the war, all important decisions were made at Politburo meetings, at informal meetings chaired by Brezhnev, or in telephone conversations among Brezhnev and Gromyko, Andropov, and Grechko.[9]

The Soviet military did not anticipate the early battlefield successes of Arab armies.[10] "Grechko believed," observed Evgueny Pyrlin, the deputy chief of the Middle East division of the Soviet Foreign Ministry, "that without the assistance of Soviet military experts and their direct participation in military operations, Egypt could not cross the Suez Canal and mount an offensive in the Sinai desert."[11] The meeting on 6 October began with a military briefing by Gen. Viktor Kulikov, the chief of staff. His briefing that night was characteristic of his reports over the next several days; he generally emphasized the failures of the Arab armies and the large losses of personnel and equipment. His expectation was that Arab victories were temporary and that Egypt and Syria would lose as soon as Israel mobilized its forces. The impression was created, Israelian observed, that the military leadership of Egypt and Syria was inept.[12]

Officials from the Foreign Ministry were also surprised that Egyptian forces had crossed the canal. Victor Israelian, who attended almost all of the meetings of the Politburo once the war began, noted that, "From the very beginning of the war, our mentality and expectation was: 'this is a lost war.' Even Grechko was surprised."[13]

As soon as the war began, Soviet officials began to organize a massive airlift of military supplies to Syria and Egypt, in anticipation of their needs. On 9 October, the fourth day of the war and the first day of the airlift, Soviet transport planes flew only to Syria; the military situation had deteriorated rapidly as Israel concentrated its counterattack on the northern front and pushed Syrian forces back to the cease-fire lines of 1967 on the Golan Heights.

Within a day, Soviet Antonov-12s and the huge Antonov-22s began flying to Egypt as well, and a large scale sealift began at the same time. By 12 October, the Soviet Union was flying 60 to 90 flights per day to Syria, Egypt, and Iraq. By the end of the war, American intelligence estimated that 934 Soviet flights had airlifted fifteen-thousand tons of equipment, and the sealift had added another eighty-five-thousand tons on 30 ships.[14]

The Soviet Union also made other contingent military preparations in connection with the air- and sealift. On 9 October, naval surveillance of the U.S. Sixth Fleet was tightened. The next day, 10 October, three of the seven Soviet airborne divisions, already at increased combat readiness, were placed on ready-to-move status.[15] After a bombing raid by Israel sank a Soviet merchant ship, *Ilya Mechnikov*, in the Syrian port of Tartus, a Soviet destroyer was sent northeast of Cyprus to protect Soviet merchant vessels approaching the combat zone.[16]

Why the Airlift?

The massive transfer of military supplies by air and by sea is one of the most controversial components of Soviet policy during the war. Some military analysts estimate that without this massive resupply, Egypt could have fought for only five days. Syria was even more dependent on resupply.[17] Soviet motives in supplying its allies are the subject of considerable debate.

Some analysts of Soviet policy have speculated that the airlift was a response to the accidental bombing by Israel of a Soviet cultural center in Damascus.[18] Aleksandr Kislov, a senior Soviet expert on the Middle East, denied that the airlift was a response to the bombing and the death of Soviet civilians: "The beginning of the airlift was purely coincidental with Israel's attack on our cultural center. It took several days to organize and planning began with the outbreak of the war."[19]

Soviet leaders decided to airlift supplies to their allies for several closely related reasons. First and foremost, they received an urgent request from President Sadat; at the beginning of the war, Sadat "begged" for the airlift.[20] Israelian explained that "we had a series of bilateral agreements with the Arabs. At the beginning of 1973, Sadat asked us to accelerate arms deliveries. We agreed. The Ministry of Defense dealt with this. When the war started, Sadat pressed us hard to honor our agreements and then to accelerate deliveries. A decision was made in the Politburo on 8 October to go along."[21] Kislov explained that Brezhnev saw little choice but to respond favorably to the Egyptian request. The Soviet Union could not afford to "abandon" Syria and Egypt; its reputation as a reliable ally was at stake.[22] Soviet leaders reasoned as well that the airlift would increase their leverage with Egypt and Syria when it became necessary to press forcefully for a cease-fire.[23]

Soviet military experts also anticipated substantial Arab reverses as soon as Israel was able to mobilize its full complement of reserves. Grechko and Gen. Viktor G. Kulikov supplied Politburo members with extensive data on the extent of Arab losses, but when asked about Israeli losses, Kulikov "could not answer this question in any intelligible way."[24] After 11 October, when Syria began to suffer serious military reverses, the airlift became even more important. The Soviet Union's reputation as a reliable arms supplier was at stake once the fighting began.[25]

From Moscow's perspective, the airlift was also a substitute for the Soviet forces that might otherwise be needed to prevent an Arab defeat.[26] Soviet civilian leaders were pessimistic about Arab military prospects, and the briefings that they received from the military deepened their concern. Soviet leaders reasoned that the resupply of arms would reduce rather than increase the likelihood of confrontation with the United States. If Arab armies could hold their positions on the battlefield, they were less likely to require and request Soviet military intervention. It was Soviet intervention that was most likely to trigger a crisis with the United States.[27]

Finally, the airlift met domestic political needs. A refusal to mount the airlift would have angered those in the Politburo who defended Arab interests and, more generally, supported "progressive forces" in the Third World. Grechko, Andropov, and Suslov strongly supported rearmament of the Arabs.[28] They were among the colleagues that Brezhnev consulted most frequently. A rejection of Sadat's request would have fractured the consensus within the Politburo that Brezhnev valued so highly.

When they agreed to Sadat's request for an airlift, Soviet leaders saw no inconsistency between crisis prevention and their obligations to their regional allies. The airlift would enhance their reputation in the Middle East as a reliable ally and military supplier. A few Soviet leaders initially saw some opportunity to make gains. "The first successes of Egyptian and Syrian military forces," Pyrlin explained, "were interpreted as a victory of Soviet weapons. Grechko argued that this advantage must be exploited, that Israel with all its American military equipment would be humiliated both politically and militarily, and that America's position in the Middle East would be damaged."[29] Others reasoned differently; they argued that supplying weapons might help to prevent an Arab military defeat and thereby forestall a request for Soviet forces. Soviet leaders were wrong on both these issues.

We argue in the next chapter that the airlift strengthened the resolve of Sadat and President Assad of Syria to continue the fighting and made a cease-fire more difficult, not easier, to achieve. Soviet officials did not appreciate how the massive supply of military equipment would strengthen Egyptian and Syrian political independence and reduce their incentives to end the fighting. Soviet leaders also misunderstood how the airlift would be interpreted in Washington. A few Western observers of Soviet foreign policy saw the airlift as a defensive action designed to prevent Soviet losses in the Arab world.[30] This was certainly not the interpretation of the most important policymakers in Washington. As the airlift gathered momentum, Nixon, Kissinger, and other senior officials saw Soviet resupply of Egypt and Syria as a direct challenge to the United States. Soviet leaders badly misjudged the consequences of the airlift on both the political independence of their allies in the Middle East and crisis prevention.

Moscow's Dilemma

On 10 October, Kissinger proposed that the Soviet Union curb its airlift in exchange for American restraint in supplying Israel.[31] The secretary called Soviet Ambassador Anatoliy Dobrynin "to say that we were aware of the 'very substantial' Soviet airlift, which was 'not helpful.'" Kissinger concluded their conversation by warning that the Soviet airlift would "force us to do at least the same."[32]

The trade-off between crisis prevention and supply of allies was now clear. This was the only opportunity the two superpowers would have to restrict the scope of their military supplies and reduce the risk of escalation. The appeal came at a time of relative symmetry on the battlefield. Syrian forces had been pushed back across the lines that Israel had held before the war began, but Egypt was holding its gains along the canal.[33] If Soviet leaders had given priority to crisis prevention, this would have been the opportune moment for them to reach an agreement with the United States.

A decision to curb the airlift would have involved undeniable costs. It was more difficult—and compromising—for the Soviet Union to limit its ongoing airlift than for the United States to refrain from beginning a military airlift. Soviet leaders did not consider the two actions equivalent.[34] Yet, the refusal to agree to such an arrangement was also costly. If the Soviet Union refused to restrict the scope of its resupply, the response in Washington was predictable.[35] Kissinger had warned Dobrynin explicitly that the United States would match the Soviet airlift.[36] A full-scale American airlift would strengthen Israel's military capability and increase its capacity to defeat Arab armies. A confrontation between the United States and the Soviet Union would then become more likely.

The Soviet leadership now faced a decision with no good choices. It responded to these dilemmas by ignoring the trade-offs and treating the problem as technical and almost routine. Israelian reports that "Kissinger's proposal was discussed by the Politburo but it was rejected. It did not get much attention. It did not become a big issue. We took note of Dobrynin's information, but Politburo members considered that we had contractual obligations to sell arms and we were selling them."[37]

Brezhnev and his colleagues had reasoned that there was no direct conflict between their military obligations to their allies and the prevention of a crisis with the United States. They had no expectation that Arab armies would prevail and thought therefore that their resupply of Arab armies would stabilize the battlefield. In part because they did not have good information on Israel's military losses and thought that Israel's military capability was so superior, the Politburo had not expected that the United States would find it necessary to match its action. Once the United States made clear that it would do so unless the Soviet Union limited the scope of its airlift, this set of assumptions was no longer reasonable. An American airlift could well tip the balance in favor of Israel and produce the defeat of Arab armies that the Soviet Union wanted to avoid. Instead of facing the trade-offs and reevaluating their assumptions, Soviet leaders ignored the conflict among their objectives.

Ironically, at the end of the war, Brezhnev did more than Kissinger had asked, but he did it too late. On 24 October, when Egypt's armies were trapped and desperate, he stopped the Soviet airlift completely as a deliberate signal of Soviet willingness to cooperate with the United States in ending the fighting. American officials misunderstood the message and interpreted the cessation of the airlift as the freeing of the necessary transport aircraft for a possible deployment of Soviet troops.[38] Instead of signaling Soviet interest in cooperation, the cessation of the Soviet airlift contributed to an acute crisis with Washington.

THE VIEW FROM WASHINGTON

Henry Kissinger was extraordinarily influential in shaping Washington's response to the outbreak of the war. He was secretary of state to a beleaguered president increasingly distracted by an acute political crisis at home. As soon as the fighting began, a high-level interdepartmental group of officials met to monitor developments, review contingency plans, and coordinate policy. The Washington Special Action Group (WSAG) was generally chaired by Kissinger and included his deputy, Brent Scowcroft; James Schlesinger, the secretary of defense; Adm. Thomas Moorer, the chairman of the Joint Chiefs of Staff; William Colby, the director of the CIA; Kenneth Rush, the deputy secretary of state; and Alfred (Roy) Atherton, the deputy assistant secretary of state for Near Eastern and South Asian Affairs. Staff members from the National Security Council, the State Department, and the Pentagon attended as they were needed.[39]

Kissinger regarded the Soviet airlift very differently than did Moscow. It was not a defensive action but "the beginning of a protracted duel in which Washington and Moscow, each protesting its devotion to cooperation, sought to weaken the other without risking an open confrontation."[40] He speculated about why the Soviet Union had launched its airlift: "Was the [Soviet] purpose to stoke the fire of conflict, or to support a client and keep a Soviet hand in the postwar negotiations? Was it to encourage Arab intransigence, or to establish Soviet bona fides for a peace effort? Were they helping their most hard-pressed associate to keep it from collapsing, or were they encouraging a new onslaught?"[41] The answer was academic because neither offensive nor defensive Soviet purposes were acceptable to Nixon and Kissinger. They were determined to limit Soviet influence in the Middle East and exclude Moscow from any postwar negotiations.

American Restraint

In the first week of the war, despite the Soviet airlift, the American response was restrained. American officials were confident that Israel would win a quick military victory once its reserve forces were fully mobilized and committed to battle. "The best result," Kissinger told Secretary of Defense Schlesinger, "would be if Israel comes out a little ahead but got bloodied in the process, and if the U.S. stayed clean."[42]

On the first day of the war, 6 October, Israel requested an increase in supplies of ammunition. At the first WSAG meeting, Deputy Secretary of State Kenneth Rush and Secretary of Defense James Schlesinger opposed sending any supplies to Israel immediately. "Defense wants to turn against the Israelis," Kissinger later told White House Chief of Staff Alexander Haig, who was with Nixon in Key Biscayne, Florida.[43] The WSAG decided on a "low profile;" items in the pipeline would be shipped to Israel but any additional requests would be handled on an almost routine basis.[44]

The following evening, Kissinger told Israel's ambassador in Washington, Simcha Dinitz, that Israel could use unmarked El Al commercial planes to pick up eighty Sidewinder missiles and bomb racks during the night at Oceana Naval Base in Norfolk, Virginia.[45] Later that night, Schlesinger inquired whether Kissinger was willing to use U.S. aircraft; "No," Kissinger replied, "they are coming here."[46]

On 9 October, American officials began to question their earlier expectation of a quick, crushing Israeli victory. They learned that a large Israeli counterattack against Egyptian forces the previous day had failed to dislodge Egyptian armies. Israel's military attaché in Washington told Kissinger that Israel had suffered over a thousand casualties, and had lost five-hundred tanks and forty-nine aircraft, heavy losses for the Israel Defense Forces (IDF). Ambassador Dinitz asked for an urgent meeting with Kissinger to press for accelerated deliveries of weaponry.

After the initial reverses on the battlefield, Defense Minister Dayan ordered an operational check of missiles capable of delivering nuclear weapons.[47] The CIA picked up some activity and a day later, William Colby handed Henry Kissinger an update on Israel's nuclear capability.[48] Prime Minister Golda Meir considered the situation so desperate that she asked Dinitz to arrange a secret visit to Washington so that she could meet personally with President Nixon to impress upon him Israel's urgent need for American military aid.[49] Kissinger rejected the proposal; since her visit could not be kept secret, the United States "would be forced to announce a massive resupply policy, destroying any possibility of mediation. The Arab world would be inflamed against us. The Soviet Union would have a clear field."[50]

Kissinger convened a meeting of the WSAG to consider options ranging from continuation of the low-profile resupply to a full-scale military airlift. He then met privately with the president who, in response to the unexpected information of Israel's battlefield losses, instructed Kissinger to inform Israel that its losses in matériel would be replaced and asked Kissinger to work out the logistical details of resupply.[51] Nixon gave no direct instructions to Secretary of Defense James Schlesinger; Israel was expected to use its own limited airlift capability.[52] "With this kind of movement," Schlesinger told Kissinger, "we won't be able to keep it quiet." "It is extremely important," Kissinger insisted, "to keep it as low-key as we can."[53]

On 10 October, the National Security Council asked the Department of Transportation to charter civilian planes to fly consumables to Israel.[54] The attempt to charter commercial aircraft proved to be very difficult and met with little success. On 11 October, Assistant Secretary of State Sisco told Kissinger that none of the charter companies were willing to assume the risks of ferrying equipment to Israel.[55] Kissinger then instructed the Pentagon to charter transport planes for Israel to use, and President Nixon ordered Kissinger to tell Schlesinger "to speed it up."[56] At a meeting with a distressed Ambassador Dinitz on 12 October, officials of the Department of Defense offered replacement of three F-4 Phantom aircraft every two days.

Why American Restraint?

The measured American response can be plausibly explained in the first instance by the bureaucratic struggle between the State Department and the Pentagon in the absence of the president. Nixon was distracted by a serious domestic political crisis: in the midst of growing domestic turmoil over Watergate, Vice President Spiro Agnew had resigned, and President Nixon went into seclusion at Camp David until he announced the appointment of Gerald Ford on 12 October. His domestic problems were further magnified that same day by a court order to release nine tapes requested by Special Prosecutor Archibald Cox in connection with his investigation of Watergate. The conflict over the airlift was resolved only by the personal intervention of President Nixon when he returned from Camp David.

For three days, as the administration struggled with the logistics of chartering cargo aircraft, serious divisions continued among senior officials in Washington about the scope and timing of an airlift to Israel. Kissinger and Schlesinger each accused the other of responsibility for the delay in getting supplies to Israel.[57] Peter Rodman, special assistant to Henry Kissinger, claims that the charters were deliberately delayed by the Pentagon: "Bill Clements [the assistant secretary of defense] was dragging his feet. Henry did not blame [Secretary of Defense] Schlesinger, but the Pentagon bureaucracy."[58] Nevertheless, Rodman acknowledged, "Kissinger did make some remarks that fueled the controversy. I can remember him saying: 'The fact that Israel is dependent upon us doesn't hurt us.'"[59]

Kissinger did press the Pentagon to get the chartered aircraft in the air or find some way to get the necessary supplies to Israel. He met with little success. Joseph Sisco remembered a tense encounter with Pentagon officials:

> I went with Henry to the Pentagon and got into a shouting match with them, as did Henry. I said to him: "We're not going to move these people. You have got to get on the telephone with the president."[60]

The chartering of civilian aircraft to fly cargo to Israel was proceeding very slowly, in large part because the logistical and technical problems were serious.[61] When asked directly who was responsible for the delay in the airlift, Kissinger discounted the logistical problems and blamed the Pentagon bureaucracy. "Clements was not enthusiastic about it," he insisted, "and didn't use any ingenuity to make it happen."[62]

More important than logistical difficulties or bureaucratic bungling were American objectives. Washington, like Moscow, hoped to prevent a humiliating Arab defeat and a confrontation between the superpowers. Some American officials considered that restraint in the pace of military resupply would make it easier to persuade Israel to end the war before it won the military victory they anticipated. The prospect of an early cease-fire was also a consideration. Secretary of Defense James Schlesinger explained after the war: "The United States, delayed, deliberately delayed the start of its resupply operations, hoping that a cease-fire could be implemented."[63]

A final consideration was the prospect of some cutback in Soviet resupply. Kissinger supported restraint throughout the first week in order "to bring about a moderation in the level of outside supplies that were introduced into the area."[64] He explicitly warned Moscow that the Soviet airlift would provoke a similar response from Washington.[65] If Moscow did not reduce its airlift, Kissinger's intention to match Soviet actions was apparent.

The American Airlift

When the effort at agreed limits with the Soviet Union and a cease-fire in the war failed, some senior American officials began to favor quick resupply of Israel. On 12 October, Ambassador Dinitz reported that Israel's supplies were running so low that Israel's offensive against Syria would have to be slowed and the military front with Egypt would be jeopardized.[66] This analysis had contradictory implications: it seemed to reduce the danger of a confrontation with the Soviet Union because an Arab military defeat was not imminent, but suggested that, without large-scale resupply, Israel would not win the limited victory that Nixon and Kissinger wanted.

Late on 12 October, in response to the adverse reports from Israel, Schlesinger became convinced that if the United States were going to resupply Israel, it should use its own military aircraft. The chairman of the Joint Chiefs of Staff, Adm. Thomas Moorer, also supported the use of American military transport to airlift equipment to Israel.[67] A military airlift would be efficient and easier to control.

Kissinger, on the other hand, gave priority to political considerations rather than efficiency. He opposed a highly visible military airlift to Israel, in order, in his words, "to preserve Arab self-respect."[68] Shortly after midnight, Kissinger talked to Haig on the telephone.

> HAIG: He's [Schlesinger] ready to move MAC [U.S. Military Assistance Command] aircraft in there immediately. I think that would be foolish.
>
> KISSINGER: That would be disaster, Al. How can he fuck everything up for a week—he can't now recoup it the day the diplomacy is supposed to start. . . . You know goddamn well they didn't try [to charter civilian aircraft].
>
> HAIG: We do have the option of sending some American planes in there. I think that's a high risk for us.
>
> KISSINGER: I think it's stupid.[69]

Late in the evening of 12 October, after yet another meeting with a desperate Dinitz, Kissinger telephoned Schlesinger. Kissinger claims that after checking with the president's chief of staff, Alexander Haig, the two men decided on three steps: ten C-130 transport aircraft loaded with ammunition would be sent directly to Israel, the United States would use military transport to fly consumables to the Azores for El Al to pick up, and they would continue to press for charters.[70]

Schlesinger maintains that after Kissinger called, he went to his office at the Pentagon, consulted with his senior officials, and decided on a direct military airlift. Schlesinger phoned Haig to clear his decision with Nixon, because he did not "trust" Kissinger. Only after it had been cleared, did he phone Kissinger to inform him that three giant C-5As would fly directly to Israel.[71]

Concerned about Arab reaction, Schlesinger and Kissinger recommended to the president that not more than three C-5A transports be used to resupply Israel.[72] Nixon overruled them both. "My reaction was that we would take just as much heat for sending three planes as for sending thirty. . . . Goddamn it, use every one we have. Tell them [the Pentagon] to send everything that can fly."[73] President Nixon ordered an open and large-scale military airlift to Israel. The president subsequently explained that what mattered was not the number of aircraft, but making the airlift "work."[74]

Why the Airlift?

Nixon was sensitive to Israel's dilemma. Egypt's armies were firmly entrenched on the east bank of the canal, Israel's offensive against Syria had stopped when Damascus was within range of its artillery, and Israel was urgently requesting resupply. The president still wanted to prevent a crushing Arab military defeat, but, like Kissinger, he also wanted at least a limited

victory by Israel to reinforce Moscow's inability to promote Arab interests.[75] The needs of Israel, while important, were nevertheless clearly secondary to the growing contest with the Soviet Union.

President Nixon ordered the full-scale military airlift primarily because of
Soviet actions and his concern for reputation and resolve. Once he defined
Soviet actions as a challenge, he saw no alternative but to meet that challenge. Nixon hoped to prevent a crisis with the Soviet Union by firmly reinforcing reputation, resolve, and commitment.

Kissinger was surprised that the president had moved so quickly and decisively in ordering such a large airlift.[76] He agreed, nevertheless, that the
decisive consideration was the Soviet failure to cooperate in the limitation of
the war. American intelligence was monitoring the Soviet air- and sealift
closely and was alarmed by its scope and scale.[77] At first, administration
officials had interpreted the airlift as a response to the deteriorating military
situation on the Syrian front. The Soviet refusal to curb its airlift once both
fronts seemed to have stabilized suggested to Kissinger that Moscow was
trying to exploit the war to make offensive gains.[78] This judgment was reinforced by Egypt's failure to agree to a cease-fire and the subsequent announcement by the Soviet Union that it would agree to a cease-fire only if it
were linked to a withdrawal by Israel to the lines of 4 June 1967. Soviet
policy was now seen as a clear violation of the norms of détente.[79]

Kissinger, like Nixon, acknowledged that competition with the Soviet
Union had moved to a new level of intensity: "The die was now cast: matters
had reached a point where maneuvering would be suicidal and hesitation
disastrous. . . . We would pour in supplies. We would risk a confrontation.
I wanted a demonstrative counter to the Soviet airlift. . . . Once a stalemate
had become apparent . . . we moved decisively, even brutally, to break it."[80]

The airlift provided badly needed military assistance to Israel. By the end
of the war, the Military Assistance Command had moved eleven-thousand
tons of supplies, forty F-4 Phantoms, thirty-six A-4 Skyhawks, and twelve
C-130 transports.[81] For the administration, however, the primary purpose
of the airlift was to send a strong signal to Moscow. The Soviet Union,
Kissinger is reported to have said at a meeting of the WSAG, should be "run
into the ground" to demonstrate that the United States could outperform it
as a military supplier, even at the risk of confrontation.[82] The war in the
Middle East had become as much a contest between the United States and
the Soviet Union as a battleground between Arabs and Israelis.

A MISSED OPPORTUNITY

The large-scale resupply by the United States and the Soviet Union of their
allies was a principal cause of the dangerous confrontation between them at
the end of the war. The key decision, which Soviet leaders treated as routine,
was the Soviet refusal to limit arms shipments to Egypt and Syria in return
for a promise of American restraint. The United States then met the chal-

lenge it saw by airlifting larger quantities of arms more quickly to Israel.[83] Once Israel knew that it would receive the supplies it needed, it took the offensive and its military success against Egypt led to the kind of lopsided outcome both superpowers wanted to prevent.

As the first C-5 transport touched down in Israel on 14 October, an armored battle initiated by Egypt in the Sinai ended with a significant Israeli victory. The following day, Israel began an offensive against Egyptian forces on the east bank of the canal that permitted Israeli armor to cross the canal and turn the tide of the war. The airlift was important to Israel, but not so much because of the military equipment it brought. The equipment did not arrive in time to affect the outcome of the crucial battles on the fourteenth and fifteenth of October.[84] The scope and pace of the resupply and the assurance that supplies would be fully replenished did give Israel's military commanders the confidence they needed to take the offensive. Five days later, the Egyptian army faced a desperate situation.

How could both sets of leaders have so badly misjudged the consequences of the military resupply of their allies? The obvious explanation is the strategic logic created by the demands of their allies. It is possible that the Soviet Union reacted primarily to Syrian military losses, whereas the United States reacted to Israeli losses on the Egyptian front.[85] Instead of concentrating on the gains each of their allies had made, both Moscow and Washington responded to their losses and moved to reinforce the military capability of the weak. This explanation, although certainly valid to a degree, is not wholly convincing.

Soviet leaders expected Arab military reverses from the outset of the fighting, when they made their decision to accelerate arms deliveries.[86] They refused to curb their airlift, however, in exchange for an American promise of reciprocal restraint. Their logic is difficult to understand: a large-scale American airlift could only strengthen Israel's capacity to defeat Arab armies.

The power of the weak over the strong is even less persuasive as an explanation of American behavior. It has been suggested that Israel's nuclear alert blackmailed the United States into resupplying Israel with military equipment.[87] A more restrained version of the same argument suggests that some American officials worried that the weakness of their ally might lead to "desperate" action. Prime Minister Meir had written to Nixon of the threats to Israel's survival and warned that "Israel might have to use every means" under the circumstances. At his meeting with Kissinger late in the evening of 12 October, Dinitz delivered a note that warned of "very serious consequences" if the United States did not immediately begin shipping critically needed military equipment.[88]

The evidence does not sustain the proposition that Washington was blackmailed. Both Dinitz and Kissinger insist that Dinitz made no mention whatsoever of Israel's nuclear capability, much less its readiness to use nuclear weapons if its survival were at stake.[89] CIA Director William Colby confirmed that Israel's nuclear capability played no role in discussions of the airlift. "There was no nuclear blackmail. There was no emphasis on it in any of the discussions. Our intention was to get the airlift going. No blackmail was needed. They [Israel] were in a tough situation, the balance of forces was overwhelmingly against them. At most, the question of Israeli nuclears was in the back of our head, but it didn't influence our judgment."[90] Officials in Washington generally did not fear an escalation to the nuclear level unless Israel found itself in a desperate situation where Arab armies threatened Israel's civilian population.[91]

Washington also did not respond quickly to Israel's military reverses. Despite the pleas of Prime Minister Meir and Ambassador Dinitz, it took more than seventy-two hours for the United States to organize a full-scale military airlift. When Dinitz was still hinting broadly at escalation, Kissinger favored only a limited airlift. This response was not consistent with officials who were blackmailed by their ally's weakness.

Soviet and American leaders miscalculated in part because they did not think through the consequences of their decisions. Moscow did not consider carefully just how much military aid would permit their allies to defend themselves but would not provoke the United States to match their airlift. Washington did not think through how much aid was necessary to permit Israel to win a limited victory without giving it the capability to inflict a crushing defeat on Arab armies. American military aid gave Israel's army the confidence it needed to go on the offensive against the Egyptian army. The tide of the war turned because of Israel's military strategy and serious Egyptian mistakes, but the airlift was a crucial psychological prerequisite for offensive action by the IDF. Even had officials in Washington thought through the problem much more carefully than they did, it was unrealistic of them to think that they could calibrate military aid to precise battlefield results.

Soviet and American leaders were naive as well in their expectation that the resupply of their allies would enhance their control. Sadat complained bitterly about the pace and supply of Soviet military equipment.[92] Egyptian officials alleged that many of the earlier planes arrived half empty and some contained tents and canteens.[93] The Egyptian military reacted with annoyance rather than gratitude. More important, the flow of military supplies emboldened Egypt and Syria to resist insistent Soviet pressures for a ceasefire. The miscalculation was even sharper in Washington's case: once the tide of battle turned, Washington found it nearly impossible to stop Israel's army on the move. Control of their allies, difficult at best, became even more precarious.

Soviet and American leaders also had a poor understanding of how their actions would be understood by one another. Brezhnev and his colleagues considered the airlift as a legitimate action to help allies who were militarily inferior. Nixon and Kissinger saw the "massive" Soviet airlift as a direct challenge to the United States. The Politburo, even after it was told directly, did not consider the large-scale American airlift as a response to their own.

Rather, Soviet leaders thought it unnecessary and provocative. Brezhnev spoke of "frenzied activity" by the United States, and Gromyko considered the airlift the result of "the activation of Zionists in the country."[94]

Finally, leaders in the United States and the Soviet Union miscalculated because they avoided the difficult choices they faced for as long as they could. Psychological explanations of foreign policy predict that when leaders confront unpleasant and painful trade-offs, they deny the contradictions. Despite explicit warnings from Kissinger, leaders in Moscow misjudged the likely American reaction to a continuation of the Soviet airlift. When they were finally forced to face the painful trade-off by the American request to curb their air- and sealift, Soviet leaders ignored the complexity of the problem, treated the choice as simple and routine, and, with almost no consideration, decided to continue their large-scale airlift. Nixon and Kissinger also denied the contradiction between their regional and global interests. Only a firm demonstration of resolve in the Middle East, they argued, would prevent a crisis with the Soviet Union.

When they confront difficult and dangerous choices, leaders need to overcome their doubts and uncertainty. Accordingly, they may also convince themselves that there is no alternative to the strategy they have chosen.[95] They persuade themselves that they have chosen the best possible policy on all counts; the policy they have chosen will enhance all their important values.[96] Kissinger described the airlift to Israel in precisely this way. "But we had no alternative anyway," he wrote in his memoirs. "If the Soviet-armed states won, the Soviets would control the postwar diplomacy."[97] Kissinger convinced himself that he had no choice but the option that offered some prospect of preventing Soviet gain. Denial and wishful thinking can have pernicious consequences. They make leaders insensitive to evidence that their preferred policy can have adverse consequences.

The psychological explanations that predict denial and wishful thinking when leaders can find no "good" option do not tell us which option leaders are likely to choose. To understand why leaders chose the strategies they did, we must look at their dominant political beliefs. The American decision to demonstrate resolve by matching the Soviet air- and sealift is not surprising. It was consistent with Nixon's and Kissinger's deeply held beliefs about the importance of clear commitments and firm demonstrations of resolve.[98] These central beliefs outweighed their confidence in the vague norms of restraint that they had negotiated with Moscow; they had sought détente with Moscow in part because it provided the cover for a strategy of unilateral advantage. Insofar as Kissinger and Nixon saw any contradiction at all between crisis prevention and the demonstration of resolve through a matching airlift, predictably their long-standing belief in the value of reputation and resolve prevailed.

Soviet leaders were similarly unrestrained by the norms of competition implicit in their agreements with Washington when these norms competed with their desire to restore their reputation as a reliable ally and arms supplier. The Soviet emphasis on the compatibility of détente with support for "progressive forces" dominated, reinforced by the fear of appearing insufficiently "revolutionary."[99] Indeed, it removed the contradiction between crisis prevention and Soviet "obligations" to Egypt.

The Soviet and American failure to restrict the scope of supplies to their allies and thereby to prevent an escalation of the fighting is alarming. It is alarming because Moscow and Washington began with two critical advantages that are so often absent: the context was right, and they broadly agreed on the tactical objective of the war. Both sets of leaders had taken the first controversial steps to détente, and both wanted, for reasons of their own, to prevent an overwhelming Israeli military victory. Both sets of leaders then confronted pressing demands from their allies, which created painful policy dilemmas between the imperatives of crisis prevention and their interests in the Middle East.

When leaders in Moscow and Washington made their decisions to airlift supplies, they were insensitive to the consequences of their choices, used different standards to evaluate their own and their adversary's behavior, and denied the contradictions between pursuit of their regional interests and crisis prevention. Through their mutual resupply of their local allies, both the Soviet Union and the United States made possible the quickening of the pace of battle, enhanced the political autonomy of their allies, and created the situation on the battlefield that they both wanted to avoid.

The Failure to Stop the Fighting

What could we do? We had to deal with an Egyptian leadership that played its own game. Israel played its own game.
It was a lesson for everyone.

—*Georgi Arbatov* [1]

"THOUGH EVENTS have gone too far," Brezhnev wrote to Nixon on 17 October, "they can still be managed."[2] The United States and the Soviet Union
were both shipping massive amounts of military supplies to their allies, but
they could still have prevented a serious crisis in their relationship if they had
ended the war before any of their allies risked serious defeat. Washington
and Moscow both wanted to prevent a humiliating Arab defeat, yet they
failed to stop the fighting before Egypt faced a catastrophic military defeat.
Their failure to stop the fighting before Egyptian armies were cut off and
encircled led directly to a serious confrontation. This chapter explores why
the Soviet Union and the United States were unable to end the fighting before
it created a serious crisis in their relationship.

The superpowers made three attempts to end the war. Moscow tried at
the beginning of the war, almost immediately after Egypt had completed its
dramatically successful crossing of the canal. The second attempt was made
by the Soviet Union and the United States, before both airlifts were fully in
place, and when the battlefield situation was relatively symmetrical. These
attempts failed. The Soviet Union tried a third time, when both airlifts were
in full swing and when Egypt was threatened with military catastrophe. The
superpowers agreed on a cease-fire, but within hours the fighting resumed
and very quickly the United States and the Soviet Union found themselves in
precisely the confrontation they had both hoped to avoid.

The repeated failure by the superpowers to end the fighting had multiple
causes. Although Soviet and American leaders shared the tactical objective
of ending the war without an Arab military defeat, their agreement masked
important differences. Soviet objectives were straightforward. Almost from
the beginning, Soviet leaders wanted to end the fighting before their Arab
allies suffered a military defeat. Given the past performance of Arab armies
in battle with Israel, Soviet leaders hoped to avoid serious Arab military
losses. Victor Israelian observed that "From the very beginning, we considered it a lost war. We tried to restrain them all the way. We sought a
cease-fire from the very first day."[3] Soviet leaders feared that serious Arab

setbacks, which they considered inevitable, could prompt a request for Soviet assistance.[4] From Moscow's perspective, the sooner the fighting stopped, the better.

American objectives were more complex. Nixon recalls that he wanted a military stalemate to create the conditions for a postwar settlement. "I believed that only a battlefield stalemate would provide the foundation on which fruitful negotiation might begin. Any equilibrium—even if only an equilibrium of mutual exhaustion—would make it easier to reach an enforceable settlement."[5] In fact, he and Kissinger did not want just "any equilibrium," but a limited Israeli military victory that confirmed the inability of Arab—and Soviet—leaders to extract concessions from Israel through the use of military force.[6] Only under these conditions could the pivotal postwar role of the United States be assured.

The tactical objectives of the superpowers had similar technical and political requirements. The United States and the Soviet Union needed accurate and timely battlefield intelligence if they were to stop the war at the appropriate moment. Both sets of leaders overestimated their capability to get the battlefield intelligence they needed. They were not alone. As we shall see, the Egyptian central command itself did not have reliable battlefield data when crucial decisions were being made. This created a double handicap for the Soviet Union. The United States was handicapped because Israel deliberately held back crucial intelligence about the position of its armies. The time lag in essential information complicated assessment and decision, slowed the pace of policy-making and wasted precious hours when Moscow and Washington were struggling to end the fighting.

The political independence of local allies also complicated attempts by Moscow and Washington to stop the war. When Soviet and American leaders attempted to end the fighting, they confronted stubbornly independent leaders in Egypt, Syria, and Israel. Just as the superpowers shared the constraint of avoiding a confrontation, so too they shared the problem of restraining obstreperous allies. At times, Moscow and Washington were more "managed" than "managers."[7]

Of the two superpowers, the United States faced the more difficult political and technical challenge. To achieve its broader political objectives, Washington needed to fine-tune the battlefield outcome. Kissinger gambled that he could use political pressure at the right moment to persuade Israel's leaders to accept a limited victory. He overestimated his capacity to monitor battlefield conditions accurately and to exercise political control.

THE VIEW FROM MOSCOW

The Soviet Union sponsored all three important initiatives to end the fighting in the Middle East. Soviet leaders were extraordinarily sensitive to the risks of escalation and confrontation inherent in an Arab military defeat. This was especially so for Brezhnev, Gromyko, and other members of the

Politburo committed to détente. They were pessimistic about Arab military prospects and worried that the fighting could complicate Soviet-American relations.[8] Andropov, Grechko, and some of the senior military did not share this concern.[9]

From the outset of the war, even as Brezhnev approved the resupply of Egypt and Syria, he, Kosygin, and Gromyko actively promoted an end to the fighting. The Politburo devoted much of its time in the first week of the war to a cease-fire. Two drafts of a cease-fire resolution were prepared. The "maximalist" version included a call for an immediate cease-fire and a withdrawal by Israel to the lines of 4 June 1967; it required Israel to return all the territories it had captured in the Six Day War. Gromyko stiffened the draft by adding the provision that Israel must withdraw within one month. The "minimalist" version, which made no territorial demands, simply appealed to interested governments "to take, without delay, all measures to stop all military operations in the area immediately."[10]

The first Soviet attempt at a cease-fire, thirty-six hours after the fighting started, came after Egypt and Syria had scored considerable military gains and before they had suffered major military losses. On 8 October, Ambassador Mukhitdinov went to ask President Hafiz al-Assad in Damascus for his assessment of the situation.[11] The ambassador relayed Moscow's belief that the sooner the war ended the better. Assad told Mukhitdinov that "I am ready for a cease-fire if Israel agrees to withdraw from occupied Arab territory." Mukhitdinov cabled back that "Assad is begging for a cease-fire." The ambassador mentioned Assad's political conditions, but emphasized the cease-fire. "Mukhitdinov," Ambassador Israelian observed ruefully, "was a complete fool."[12]

Gromyko told his assistants to instruct Ambassador Vinogradov to meet with Sadat, inform him of Assad's appeal, and secure his agreement for an introduction by the Soviet Union of a cease-fire resolution in the Security Council.[13] Expecting an Arab defeat, Gromyko exclaimed to his staff, "Comrades! Didn't I tell you that in two days they will want a cease-fire?"[14]

Conveying the message from Gromyko, Ambassador Vinogradov explained that President Assad of Syria, fearing that a prolonged conflict would not serve Arab interests, had asked the Soviet Union to propose formally a cease-fire within forty-eight hours.[15] A cease-fire in place would permit Egypt and Syria to retain the territorial gains they had made. The Egyptian president was appalled. Fresh from the success of his armed forces in crossing the canal with far fewer casualties than he had expected, this was not the reaction he expected from Soviet leaders. Sadat immediately telephoned President Assad in Damascus. The president of Syria denied having requested any such action from the Soviet Union. Sadat confronted Vinogradov with Assad's denial and rejected outright the Soviet request for a cease-fire.[16]

Brezhnev and Gromyko were angered both by Assad's denial and by Sadat's decision to believe his Syrian ally rather than Soviet leaders.[17] They had interpreted Assad's discussions with Ambassador Mukhitdinov as a "scream of despair" and as evidence that the Soviet government was right when it opposed the initiation of the war.[18] Ambassador Vinogradov was told again to discuss with Sadat a Soviet initiative for a cease-fire.

Brezhnev was shown the text of the telegram to Vinogradov before it was sent. He rewrote the text to emphasize the Soviet interest in a peaceful solution, reiterated again how "imprudent" Arab leaders had been to initiate war against Soviet advice, and objected to their "intention to interfere in the process of the development of political cooperation between the USSR and the USA."[19] Finally, he restated Soviet determination not to become involved in the fighting. Sadat again rejected Vinogradov's appeal.

This first attempt at a cease-fire reflected Brezhnev's overwhelming concern about an Arab military defeat and its consequences for Soviet-American relations. It was confounded by a failure of communication between Soviet and Arab leaders and wishful thinking by Ambassador Mukhitdinov. Even if there had been no errors of interpretation by the Soviet ambassador in Damascus, there was still little prospect that Syria and Egypt would have agreed to a cease-fire in place within the first forty-eight hours of fighting. Their armies had scored major advances, and they were anticipating military resupply from the Soviet Union. Sadat's primary objective was political: a commitment from Israel to withdraw from the territory it had captured in the 1967 war.[20] The proposed cease-fire in place provided no such assurance. Despite Brezhnev's judgment that an early cease-fire would consolidate Arab gains, he could neither persuade nor coerce Sadat and Assad. Although they depended on Soviet weapons and munitions, both Arab leaders felt sufficiently independent of Moscow that they could easily reject Soviet advice.

Even if the Soviet Union had been able to coerce its allies to accept a cease-fire, it is unlikely that the United States and Israel would have agreed to a cease-fire that left Egypt on the east bank of the Suez Canal and Syria in control of the Golan Heights. Kissinger supported a cease-fire *status quo ante*, partly in the expectation that once Israel mobilized its forces, it would reverse Arab military gains, and partly to commit Israel, before it made any military gains, to the principle of a return to prewar lines.[21] The symmetry of interest between the two superpowers that was necessary to terminate the fighting was absent.

The Soviet Union made a more serious attempt at a cease-fire between 10 and 13 October, when Egyptian and Israeli armies were locked in military stalemate, Israel had driven Syrian forces back behind the original cease-fire lines, the Soviet air- and sealift was in full swing, and the American airlift had not yet begun. Early in the morning of 10 October, acting on instructions from Gromyko, Anatoliy Dobrynin called Henry Kissinger with an important message. Consultations with Egypt and Syria had been "protracted" and "not easy." Nevertheless, the Soviet Union was prepared "not to block the adoption of a cease-fire resolution in the Security Council."[22] In an attempt to avoid open coercion of its allies, Moscow would abstain from a resolution favoring a simple cease-fire in place. The Soviet Union proposed the introduction of a resolution by a third party and joint abstention with the United States.

Soviet leaders took this initiative without prior agreement from Egypt or Syria. In a note sent to the United States on 10 October, Hafiz Isma'il, national security advisor to President Sadat, indicated that Egypt no longer insisted on the prior withdrawal of Israeli forces to the boundaries of 4 June 1967. It would consider a cease-fire if it were accompanied by a pledge from Israel to withdraw within a specified time limit.[23] Although Egypt had modified its earlier bargaining position and offered these terms as a proposal for consideration, President Sadat was not prepared to entertain a simple cease-fire in place.

The second Soviet attempt to end the war came before Israel launched its major offensive against Syria and before Soviet resupply of Egypt began in earnest. It reflected Moscow's judgment that Arab armies were unlikely to make any additional gains, and were probably likely to suffer reverses.[24] Soviet leaders were nevertheless not prepared to press Egypt and Syria hard to agree to an immediate cease-fire. As Israelian observed, "We wanted a cease-fire, but we were always looking over our shoulder at Egypt."[25] Nor was it obvious to Cairo and Damascus why they should agree to end the fighting just as the Soviet airlift of military supplies was getting into full swing. They expected that the resupply would permit Egypt to hold on to its military gains, Syria to go on the offensive against Israel's forces, and both to prolong the war until the costs to Israel became intolerably high.[26]

Torn between the value of their reputation in the Middle East and the imperatives of crisis prevention, Soviet leaders attempted to meet both objectives through a tentative initiative behind the scenes. Kissinger offered an astute analysis of Soviet motives in promoting a cease-fire. "The Soviets," he argued, "sought to combine the advantages of every course of action: détente with us, enough support for their Arab friends to establish their indispensability if things went well, but not so much as to tempt a confrontation with the United States."[27] Soviet leaders, Kissinger speculated, may have thought that their position in the Middle East would be stronger if they could stop the war when the Arab armies had made net gains of territory with the aid of Soviet weapons and before the Israeli counteroffensive had succeeded.[28]

Faced with Arab objections, however, Soviet leaders chose not to risk antagonizing their Arab allies. After the initiative was stillborn, Brezhnev had Dobrynin tell Kissinger that "the Arabs had changed their minds."[29] More accurately, Soviet leaders were unwilling and, in all likelihood, unable, to persuade their Arab allies to change their minds. They knew full well that without Arab agreement, China would veto any proposed cease-fire at the United Nations.[30] Their inability to control their allies compromised their strategy of crisis prevention.

THE VIEW FROM WASHINGTON

The United States did not face the same dilemma as the Soviet Union. It did not have to coerce its ally to agree to a cease-fire, with all the attendant costs. Israel was willing, indeed anxious, for a cease-fire. Israel was stalemated on the battlefield with Egypt and deeply alarmed about the slow pace of supplies from the United States. Despite repeated assurances from Washington, only a trickle of equipment had begun to arrive, and no system of delivery had yet been organized; seven El Al planes had been shuttling back and forth ferrying equipment.

When the Soviet Union floated its proposal for a cease-fire, Nixon was preoccupied with his vice president's resignation and the growing Watergate crisis. He left management of policy in the Middle East almost entirely to Henry Kissinger. The secretary of state considered that the Soviet proposal of a cease-fire in place had come at the worst possible moment: "Had we gone along with the Soviet plan and pressed Israel to agree," he explained in his memoirs, "the war would have ended in a clear-cut victory for the Soviet-supplied Arab forces. The United States' position in the postwar diplomacy would have been seriously impaired. The proposition that we alone among the superpowers could produce progress would have been exploded. Soviet arms would have achieved success. Soviet diplomacy would have protected it."[31] The administration's objective was to terminate the fighting *after* Israel had achieved a limited victory.

Kissinger therefore decided to delay action on the Soviet proposal for forty-eight hours to allow Israel to achieve a strategic victory on the Syrian front. The military outcome he hoped for would be achieved if Egypt remained in control of the east bank of the canal and Syrian forces were expelled from the Golan Heights and pushed back toward Damascus. Instead of pressing for an immediate end to the war, he encouraged Israel to take the offensive in the north. On 10 October, Kissinger pressed Ambassador Dinitz to move quickly. "There was no time for complicated moves. Everything depended on . . . pushing back to the prewar lines as quickly as possible, or beyond them on at least one front."[32]

At the same time as the United States pushed Israel to escalate the fighting, it sought to lull the Soviet Union in order to allow time for Israel to make gains against Syria.[33] Kissinger explicitly admits in his memoirs that he tried to manipulate détente. "There were increasing public complaints," he wrote, "led by Senator Henry Jackson and some columnists, that we were procrastinating in resupplying Israel and that détente was being exploited by the Soviets to lull us. The latter charge was especially ironic since, as we saw it, we were seeking to calm Moscow via détente to restore the [battlefield] situation."[34]

The next day, on 11 October, Israel swept across the cease-fire line with Syria while its aircraft struck deep behind the battle lines. By evening, forward Israeli positions were only twenty miles from Damascus. Kissinger was pleased. "This Israeli gain accorded with our preferred strategy," he acknowledged. "After all, we had been stalling the Soviets for over twenty-four hours on a cease-fire in place."[35]

The Soviet Union was extremely displeased. On 12 October, Ambassador Dobrynin advised Kissinger that the Soviet Union could not remain indifferent to threats to Damascus.[36] The warnings were repeated publicly by TASS, and Israel reacted to the Soviet threats with considerable concern. In response, the United States ordered an additional aircraft carrier into the Mediterranean, and Kissinger informed Israel's Ambassador Dinitz, that in his personal view—he had not yet checked with the president—the United States would intervene if "any Soviet personnel, planes or ground personnel, appear in the area."[37] Kissinger in effect promised Israel that it would deter Soviet intervention. In so doing, he tacitly encouraged further military action by Israel.

Israel nevertheless decided to halt its offensive in Syria. Worried about the Soviet response and concerned about their capacity to sustain a major advance with their depleted stocks, Israel informed the United States on 12 October that it would agree to a standstill cease-fire. Whether the delay in the transfer of military equipment to Israel was deliberate or the result of bureaucratic inefficiency, it had an obvious and immediate impact: it compelled America's ally to agree to end the fighting. Israel's ambassador to Washington acknowledged the causal connection. "I must tell you," Dinitz told Kissinger, "Our decision whether to start a new offensive [against Egypt] or not depends on our [military] power.[38] Without the transfer of armor, aircraft, and artillery from the United States, Israel was unable to launch a military offensive. And, if it was unable to initiate a major offensive, the best alternative was an immediate cease-fire.[39]

Once again Kissinger did not seize the opportunity to end the war. His explanation is disingenuous. "I could have acted on that assurance [by Israel that it would accept a standstill cease-fire]," he said, "but to make sure that nothing would get unstuck I . . . inquired whether there was any recommendation on timing."[40] Israel requested, and Kissinger agreed, that the resolution not be put to a vote for twenty-four hours. A few hours later, alarmed by a report from Kissinger of Soviet warnings of retaliation if Israel continued its attacks against Soviet merchant shipping, Prime Minister Meir authorized the United States to proceed immediately with the cease-fire.

Kissinger refused. He did so allegedly for the technical reason that none of the parties to the cease-fire would be ready to proceed on such short notice. Peter Rodman, assistant to the secretary of state, explained that the United States did not press ahead vigorously because "It [the Soviet proposal] wasn't serious. It was all phoney, positional maneuvering."[41] In practice, two other factors were decisive. Kissinger wanted to avoid the appearance of conceding to Soviet threats. "Any sudden show of American anxiety," he explained, "would invite new pressures. More important, I said, 'once you have been threatened it is better to stick to your course.' It was a rule I sought to follow whenever possible. A leader known to yield to intimidation invites it."[42]

Also relevant was Kissinger's desire to await the outcome of Israel's military offensive. In a frank conversation with Ambassador Dinitz, he acknowledged that he had deliberately delayed the introduction of a cease-fire resolution to allow time for Israel's army to advance. When he realized that Israel's forces had not advanced at all that day, he bemoaned the fact that he "had been stalling the diplomacy for nothing."[43] Kissinger sacrificed the first serious opportunity to end the war without a confrontation because of his overwhelming preoccupation with reputation and resolve and his determination to await the battlefield conditions that would position the United States as the pivot of postwar diplomacy.

It is of course debatable whether the cease-fire would have been accepted by Egypt and Syria had Kissinger pushed the diplomatic process ahead on 12 October. While Israel was not only willing but anxious for a cease-fire, there is little evidence to suggest that Egypt would have agreed. Military intelligence at the time suggested that Egypt was preparing to launch a large armored offensive in the Sinai. Britain's Sir Alec Home, who had been asked to put forward the resolution, thought that President Sadat would not accept anything less than an Israeli commitment to withdraw from all Arab territory captured during the war in 1967. Persuaded that Egypt would reject a cease-fire, and that it would ask China to use its veto if the Soviet Union and the United States abstained on the resolution, Britain refused to introduce the resolution in the Security Council.[44]

Skepticism of Egyptian willingness to agree to a cease-fire need not have aborted the attempt to stop the war. Dobrynin had informed Kissinger on 12 October that although he could not guarantee that Egypt would accept a cease-fire, he could promise that the United States would be taking a "good gamble" if the resolution were put forward on the assumption that Egypt might accept.[45] The next day, Dobrynin was even more explicit: the Soviet Union would abstain from vetoing a cease-fire resolution, irrespective of Sadat's preferences.[46]

If the United States had moved quickly, it could have put Egyptian intentions to the test. Washington had a potential opportunity to arrange for the introduction of a cease-fire resolution, with the approval of its ally and the assurance of abstention by the Soviet Union. Kissinger did not take that gamble, despite the expectation that the alternative, an airlift to Israel and an increase in the scope and intensity of the fighting, would probably increase the risk of confrontation with the Soviet Union. " 'Détente is not an end in itself,' I told him [Sir Alec Home]. 'I think developments now are going to drive us towards a confrontation.'. . . But we had no alternative anyway. If the Soviet-armed states won, the Soviets would control the postwar diplomacy."[47] Crisis prevention was clearly a lower priority for both superpowers than the preservation of their reputations and their search for unilateral advantage.

The Soviet and American failure on 13 October to terminate the fighting had immediate and predictable results. The next day, under intense pressure from its beleaguered Syrian ally, Egypt launched a major tank offensive in the Sinai. In the largest armored battle since World War II, Egypt suffered heavy losses. The United States began a massive airlift to Israel and assured of supplies, Israel began a large-scale counter attack in the Sinai. Within forty-eight hours, Israeli armor had penetrated a gap in Egyptian lines and a small number of tanks had crossed the Suez Canal. The battlefield changes Kissinger had been waiting for were in the making.

THE VIEW FROM MOSCOW

The Soviet Union began a new and far more serious attempt at war termination. On 15 October, the Politburo held a long meeting to evaluate the battlefield situation and the prospects for a cease-fire. Although there were no sharp exchanges, members expressed two quite different policy preferences.

Brezhnev reported to the Politburo that in the last few days, the United States, "in a state of frenzied activity," had sent eight large cargo planes, thirty-nine other planes, forty-two Phantoms, and twenty-nine helicopters to Israel. Egyptian pilots, he complained, were so incompetent that they were shooting down their own planes.[48] "We should tell Sadat absolutely frankly," Kosygin proposed, "that if he continues to lose a thousand tanks a week, we would not be able to make up the losses."[49] Brezhnev, Kosygin, and Gromyko thought it essential to negotiate a cease-fire in view of the scope of Arab military losses and the American airlift to Israel. Kosygin argued that the war must be stopped immediately, because its consequences were unpredictable and could jeopardize détente between the United States and the Soviet Union.[50] Brezhnev suggested that Kosygin be sent to Cairo to press Sadat to agree to stop the fighting.[51]

Grechko, Podgorny, and Andropov were more sensitive to the costs to the Soviet Union in the Arab world of a cease-fire. Grechko emphasized that Arab armies had successfully crossed the canal and exploited their surprise. In a prolonged war of attrition, a broad Arab coalition could inflict severe losses on Israel. He agreed that Kosygin go to Cairo, but only to listen to Sadat. The Politburo should make a decision about a cease-fire only after Kosygin returned. Podgorny did not oppose a cease-fire, but reminded his colleagues that it differed fundamentally from Sadat's position and from Soviet principles. Andropov urged flexibility and recommended that the cease-fire be explained to Sadat as a tactical pause which would allow Egypt to consolidate its political position.[52]

The majority at the meeting supported an attempt by Kosygin to secure Sadat's agreement to a cease-fire. In his lengthy summary of the discussion, Brezhnev fashioned a collective consensus in an attempt to avoid the difficult trade-offs. He emphasized the importance of securing a cease-fire, but referred to "our Arab friends" and spoke of the importance of reassuring

Sadat. He urged Kosygin not to quarrel with Sadat. "We can maneuver and retreat," Brezhnev insisted, "but we must not provoke Sadat to break our friendship. Tell Sadat that if a cease-fire is accepted and the Israelis do not withdraw from Arab territories, we shall help them build a powerful in-depth defense which would be a jumping-off place to finally expel the Israelis."[53]

Brezhnev asked Kosygin to inform Sadat that President Tito of Yugoslavia would consult with the nonpermanent members of the Security Council to secure their support for a resolution which called for an immediate cease-fire and a requirement for Israel to withdraw to the lines of 4 June 1967. The second clause fully met Arab and Soviet interests. Brezhnev recognized that it would be very difficult to secure the support of the United States for a complete withdrawal by Israel; it would require, in his words, "careful treading with the Americans."[54] Perhaps, he suggested, it might be necessary to reformulate the second clause to refer only to the necessity of a comprehensive and full adherence to Resolution 242, the resolution that was adopted by the United Nations after the war in 1967.[55]

At the same time, Brezhnev warned Kosygin against misleading Sadat. Although the Soviet government was willing to continue military support to Egypt on a large scale, it would not participate directly in the war. "It should be clear to everybody," he admonished at the end of the meeting, "that this would mean a world war."[56]

On the afternoon of 16 October, Kosygin flew to Cairo. Earlier that day, advance units of Israeli armor crossed to the west bank of the Suez Canal. The following day, Brezhnev sent a long letter to Nixon, reminding him of Soviet warnings in the past of an impending explosion in the Middle East, bemoaning American indifference to the Soviet warnings, and urging cooperation to find a solution to the conflict. That goal could be achieved, Brezhnev wrote, if Israel agreed unambiguously to withdraw from all Arab territories occupied in 1967. The letter ended with an emphasis on the importance of preventing damage to Soviet-American relations as a result of the war.[57]

Despite the deterioration in battlefield conditions, the discussions between Kosygin and Sadat were, in the words of a Soviet official, "long and difficult."[58] Israelian summarized the tone of their meetings:

> Kosygin's trip to Cairo was a complete failure. One has to know the characters. Kosygin was very cold, very dour, very difficult to get in touch with. This was a superpower talking to a client in the language of equality; it didn't work. Sadat was very angry about the military supplies we had sent and asked for more. Kosygin spoke about a political solution and a cease-fire. Sadat responded by asking for more equipment. They spoke different languages. It was a failure.[59]

Kosygin met with President Sadat and Hafiz Isma'il five times during his three-day visit in an effort to convince him to agree to a cease-fire. In an effort to persuade the president to accept a cease-fire, on 18 October Kosygin showed Sadat photographs flown in from Moscow that detailed the scope of the Israeli penetration of the west bank of the canal. Even then, Sadat was not fully convinced. "Even after the war began," Evgueny Pyrlin observed, "Sadat did not have adequate information about Israeli military action. As a rule he neglected the information provided by Egyptian military intelligence. He studied with sincere interest the information given to him by the experts from Soviet space intelligence, but it became even clearer after the breakthrough of Israeli tanks across the Suez Canal that Sadat did not appreciate the danger."[60] Kosygin left Cairo on 19 October with no specific agreement to a cease-fire.[61]

The acceleration of the Soviet airlift and the dramatic deterioration of Egypt's strategic position did not translate, as Soviet leaders expected, into Egyptian acceptance of the Soviet demand for an immediate cease-fire. The difficulty Kosygin experienced in convincing Sadat was in part a function of the poor military intelligence available to the Egyptian president and confusion among his senior military advisors. Mahmoud Riad, Secretary-General of the League of Arab States and a former foreign minister, testified that "The Egyptian Command announced . . . that the Israeli forces that had crossed the Canal amounted to a mere seven tanks; it was not made aware of the real size of the Israeli armored forces west of the Canal until their number surpassed that of the Egyptian forces remaining on the west bank."[62]

Sadat himself acknowledged the confusion in the Egyptian High Command. After Kosygin had left for Moscow, the president conferred with Hafiz Isma'il, his advisor on National Security. Isma'il reported that there had been negligence in relation to the gap between the Second and Third Armies; the initial reports had belittled its importance and danger and, on the basis of this inaccurate information, inappropriate orders were issued by the Command in Cairo. Ismail Fahmy paints a stark portrait of confusion in the Egyptian military after the Israeli crossing of the Canal. "This created a situation of near panic within both the military and political leadership of Egypt. There was confusion and fear in the military high command."[63]

Brezhnev was frustrated by the negotiations and by Kosygin's failure to secure Sadat's agreement to a cease-fire. "I gave such a clear and detailed account of our position at the meeting of the Politburo," Brezhnev remarked to Gromyko, "whereas Kosygin cannot explain that to Sadat."[64] He summoned a special meeting of the Politburo on 18 October, even before Kosygin's return to Moscow, to discuss the unsatisfactory progress of the negotiations in Cairo.

At the meeting, Suslov read aloud the transcripts of the telephone conversations between Brezhnev and Kosygin and extracts from Kosygin's telegrams. The Politburo was alarmed by the ambiguity in some of Kosygin's cables. Kosygin wrote that he had told Sadat that "the most important thing now is to come to an agreement on the problem of guarantees."[65] What "guarantees," Politburo members asked, were being discussed? The meeting ended inconclusively after a report from Grechko on the deteriorating military situation.

On 19 October, Kosygin returned to Moscow. His report was, Israelian recalled, "short and sweet": Sadat was obstinate and would not listen to Soviet advice. Yet, Egypt was totally dependent on Soviet supplies and military support.[66] This time, Brezhnev did not wait for approval from Egypt. The general secretary clearly was prepared to proceed over the objections of his allies; indeed, Syria was not even consulted about the cease-fire. The Soviet Union had COSMOS satellites making periodic passes over the battlefield area and therefore had some intelligence about the size of the Israeli force that had crossed the canal and of the forces that were waiting to cross.[67] An immediate cease-fire seemed the only way to prevent a catastrophic Egyptian defeat.

Even before Kosygin returned to Moscow, Brezhnev sent an urgent message to Washington on 18 October requesting a cease-fire. Dobrynin presented Brezhnev's draft proposal to Kissinger.[68] Kissinger made no immediate response. Within hours, acting on a suggestion from Dobrynin that Brezhnev thought had been prompted by Kissinger, the general secretary sent a second message requesting that Kissinger come immediately to Moscow to make appropriate arrangements for a cease-fire.[69] Brezhnev's message spoke of the increasing danger in the Middle East and the "harm" this might do to relations between the United States and the Soviet Union. "Time is essential," he warned, "and now not only every day but every hour counts."[70]

Dobrynin explained to Kissinger that Brezhnev wanted him to come to Moscow so that Brezhnev personally could participate in the negotiations.[71] Zamyatin elaborated on the reasons that led Brezhnev to invite Kissinger to Moscow: "Before Kissinger came to Moscow we heard that the U.S. fleet was sent to the Middle East. Brezhnev was deeply troubled by this and fearful that some kind of Soviet-American encounter would arise. He told the Politburo that we needed to talk with the Americans. Both sides wanted to avoid a clash."[72] Brezhnev also hoped that Kissinger's trip to Moscow would consolidate Moscow's reputation in the Middle East and reinforce détente.[73] At the same time as the invitation went to Kissinger, two Soviet destroyers went through the Dardanelles.

THE VIEW FROM WASHINGTON

The invitation to Kissinger to come to Moscow suited the administration's purposes. It would provide at least seventy-two hours of cover for further offensive action by Israel and would create the battlefield situation that was conducive to Washington's political goals. Kissinger insisted that Soviet leaders agree to limit the discussion to the cease-fire; the terms of any final settlement of the conflict were not to be discussed until after the war had ended.

Reflecting on the Soviet invitation, Kissinger saw the war in the Middle East largely through the prism of the Soviet-American competition. His primary objective was to make gains at Soviet expense. His strategy was to woo Egypt away from the Soviet Union by persuading Egypt that only the United States could help Egypt achieve its political goals.

> Three times they tried through the Soviet Union, and three times they failed. . . . We had created the conditions for a diplomatic breakthrough. We had vindicated the security of our friends. We had prevented a victory of Soviet arms. We had maintained a relationship with key Arab countries and laid the basis for a dominant role in postwar diplomacy. . . . We held the cards now. Our next challenge was to play our hand.[74]

The principal obstacles to the success of American strategy were likely objections from Israel to a cease-fire now that its forces were moving successfully against the Egyptian army, and the danger that events on the battlefield would develop their own momentum. To avoid both these contingencies, Kissinger briefed Ambassador Dinitz, warned him that Israel had only an additional forty-eight hours for military action, and requested that detailed military reports be sent to him while he was in Moscow.

While Kissinger was en route to Moscow, the Watergate crisis exploded in Washington. President Nixon fired the Watergate special prosecutor, Archibald Cox, rather than turn over the tapes as ordered by the Supreme Court. In protest against the president's action, Attorney General Elliot Richardson resigned, as did his deputy, William Ruckleshaus. Alexander Haig, Chief of Staff at the White House, admitted that the "Saturday night massacre," brought down a "fire storm" on the president. In the face of enormous public protest, Nixon handed over the tapes, but his authority at home was irreparably damaged and his future uncertain. Nixon faced one of the most acute domestic political crises in the history of the presidency. In the air on his way to Moscow, Kissinger was unaware of what had happened in Washington.

Discussions with Brezhnev and Gromyko began almost immediately after Kissinger's arrival in Moscow. In their unscheduled late-night meeting, Brezhnev referred again and again to the "special relationship" between the Soviet Union and President Nixon and its importance in preventing a superpower crisis. "To procrastinate," Kissinger said, "I fell in with the spirit of the occasion, discoursing on the principles of foreswearing unilateral advantage and avoiding exacerbation of tensions."[75]

As Kissinger and Sisco were preparing for substantive discussions with Brezhnev and Gromyko scheduled for 11 o'clock the next morning, an important difference in strategy developed between the secretary of state and the president. Nixon cabled Kissinger in Moscow instructing him to use the opportunity provided by the ending of the war to impose, jointly with the

Soviet Union, a comprehensive peace in the Middle East. Kissinger was to tell Brezhnev that President Nixon belatedly appreciated the correctness of the arguments the Soviet leader had made at their meeting in June. Persuaded that the Arabs and Israelis were incapable of approaching the problem "in a rational manner," Nixon was now prepared to work together with Brezhnev on the terms of a just settlement and then press their allies to accept these terms.[76] Nixon and Brezhnev were now in substantial agreement; at their late-night dinner, Brezhnev had again raised with Kissinger his proposal that the superpowers impose a comprehensive settlement of the Arab-Israel conflict.[77]

Kissinger disagreed strongly with the president's instructions. He explained that

American strategy so far had been to *separate* the cease-fire from a postwar political settlement and to reduce the Soviet role in the negotiations that would follow the cease-fire. What Nixon seemed to envisage now would involve us in an extensive negotiation whose results we would then have to impose on Israel as the last act of a war fought on the Arab side with Soviet weapons. Moscow would receive credit with the Arabs for having forced us into a course we had heretofore avoided. Our leverage on the Arab states would disappear. Their tendency would be to rely on the Soviet Union—unless the Soviets were willing to separate themselves from the hard-line Arab program, for which we have never seen one shred of evidence.[78]

In his objections, he concentrated yet again on the importance of making gains at the expense of the Soviet Union.

Kissinger sent an angry cable to Brent Scowcroft, Nixon's national security advisor, and called Alexander Haig on an open telephone line to protest. In his instructions, Nixon reportedly expressed his willingness "to pressure the Israelis to the extent required, regardless of the domestic consequences." Kissinger argued that it would be difficult enough to persuade Israel to accept a cease-fire, but impossible to convince them to agree to a comprehensive settlement.[79]

Kissinger's staff was bewildered by the president's new instructions. Sisco could not understand why Nixon sent such instructions to Kissinger without any prior consultation and in the middle of the cease-fire negotiations.[80] Rodman thought that "The president was winging it. This was not how policy was made. If they [Nixon and Kissinger] had been in the same room, they would have worked it out. Richard Nixon emoted a lot, but he was persuaded by strategic logic. Henry would have talked him out of it. In my view, Henry was correct to ignore these instructions."[81] Kissinger was confident that if he could talk directly to the president, he would be able to persuade him that his instructions were unrealistic. The secretary of state accordingly decided to ignore the president's directive.[82]

Brezhnev postponed his scheduled meeting with Kissinger the next morning for one hour to meet with the Politburo. He told his colleagues that

"Nixon feels deep respect for all Soviet leaders and for me personally," and that his negotiations with Kissinger were "quiet, business-like, and constructive."[83] He also reported to the Politburo that he had been awakened repeatedly that night by telephone calls from Ambassador Vinogradov, who was in constant communication with President Sadat in Cairo:

> I had hardly fallen asleep when at 4 o'clock I was awakened by Vinogradov's call. He said: "I have just now been called by Sadat who returned from the command post and after apologizing for calling at such a late hour, asked me to tell Leonid Ilyich that at the front he made a decision to ask his Soviet colleagues to take all possible measures to arrange for a ceasefire." "What are the conditions?" Vinogradov asked. Sadat answered that the troops should stay in the positions they occupied at the time even though Israel's forces were moving forward along the west bank of the Suez Canal.
>
> I finished my talk with Vinogradov, drank a cup of strong tea, and shaved. There was another phone call. Vinogradov had had another talk with Sadat. The President agrees to anything. "Of course," Sadat said, "the Arabs will continue the war, but the sooner an agreement to ceasefire is reached, the better."[84]

Sadat was now "begging" for a cease-fire on any terms and wanted the Soviet Union to make an effort to disengage the forces.[85]

Grechko and Kulikov provided a very "gloomy" battlefield assessment. They were particularly concerned about the breakthrough made by Israel's forces on the west bank of the Suez Canal. Dobrynin, who had flown to Moscow aboard Kissinger's plane, reported that American experts traveling with Kissinger did not consider the Arab military situation that desperate.

Kosygin, who was irritated that he had not been able to obtain Sadat's agreement to a cease-fire, asked that Vinogradov request a written appeal for a cease-fire from Sadat to Brezhnev.[86] A written request would eliminate any further misunderstandings between Cairo and Moscow, but Kosygin's demand was clearly designed to humiliate the Egyptian president.

Brezhnev insisted that it was essential that a cease-fire agreement be reached as quickly as possible. Warning that Sadat's desperate position was unknown to the Americans, he urged his colleagues not to reveal the information in any conversations that they might have with Kissinger and his staff. Podgorny and Andropov, as well as Gromyko, supported Brezhnev's call for an immediate cease-fire. Brezhnev suggested that, to make agreement on a cease-fire easier, the Soviet Union limit the proposed UN resolution to a single paragraph calling for an immediate cease-fire. Gromyko argued that Kissinger would accept an immediate cease-fire and a call for negotiations between the parties. The Soviet Union should try to salvage what it could of its broader political goals and include a reference to Resolution 242 in the draft cease-fire resolution. The meeting ended with an agreement to press for a cease-fire in the negotiations with Kissinger that were to follow.[87]

Brezhnev, Gromyko, Dobrynin, Kissinger, and Sisco and their staffs met in Brezhnev's office on 21 October. Agreement came swiftly. Gromyko had

had two different texts of a cease-fire resolution prepared: the maximalist draft included an immediate cease-fire, withdrawal to the 4 June 1967 borders within a specified time period, and recognition of all states in the area; the minimalist draft included only a cease-fire and a reference to Resolution 242 which had been passed by the Security Council after the war in 1967.[88] Unwilling to work from a Soviet draft, the American team drafted a resolution on the spot which conformed in essence to the minimalist text prepared by Soviet officials. It added a requirement of immediate negotiation between the parties concerned under "appropriate auspices."[89]

To clarify the meaning of the third clause of the draft resolution that referred to the negotiations that would follow the war, Gromyko and Kissinger prepared and initialed a private memorandum of understanding. The memorandum made clear that the phrase "under appropriate auspices" meant that negotiations between the parties concerned would take place with "the active participation" of the United States and the Soviet Union. Both superpowers undertook to "maintain the closest contact with each other and the negotiating parties" throughout the process.[90]

Brezhnev and Gromyko immediately accepted the American text. As Sisco noted, "We barely had time to draft a statement. We drafted Resolution 338 in the Kremlin itself. The Soviets were amazed. We sent instructions to our ambassador. This was a historic first. Our two ambassadors in New York were sent similar instructions."[91] The two sides agreed that the cease-fire would go into effect twelve hours after it was adopted by the United Nations' Security Council in New York.[92] Soviet officials cabled Ambassador Vinogradov in Cairo asking him to inform Sadat of the agreement.[93]

The first threat to the cease-fire grew out of the negotiations. Surprisingly, Gromyko and Kissinger made no provision for machinery to supervise and enforce the cease-fire. They did not even arrange for the return of United Nations' truce supervisory personnel to the field. For such seasoned and experienced diplomats, the omission is difficult to understand.

"There was a shortage of time," Kissinger explained. "There was too much to do. We had to get the cease-fire going. We were tired and pressed for time."[94] Sisco confirmed that "our preoccupation was the cease-fire and timing. Simplicity was the byword."[95] Rodman added that "Henry had his mind on bigger things. He was thinking about what would happen after the cease-fire. The trivia of how the cease-fire would be observed never came up."[96] Tired and distracted, experienced and able diplomats on both sides ignored an obvious problem.[97] The absence of adequate machinery to supervise the cease-fire and report on violations would prove to be one of the most serious technical obstacles to crisis prevention.

As soon as the meeting with Brezhnev and Gromyko ended, Kissinger and his staff returned to the state guest house to draft a report to President Nixon and a letter to be sent in his name to Prime Minister Meir. The letter assured Meir that the cease-fire would permit Israel's forces to remain where they were, that the resolution did not mention the word "withdrawal," and that the resolution gave Israel what it had long wanted, direct negotiations without conditions between the parties to the conflict.[98] Brent Scowcroft was instructed to give the letter to Ambassador Dinitz. Kissinger and his staff estimated that Meir would receive it at least nine hours before the Security Council began its scheduled meeting. Israel's Cabinet would therefore have ample time for deliberation.

Kissinger underestimated the technical, military, and political problems that could undermine the prospects of the cease-fire.[99] Technical problems began almost immediately. The American team experienced serious difficulties in communicating the necessary information to Washington. Several hours after the instructions were sent, Kissinger discovered, "to his horror," that none of the messages had been received in Washington. His staff had first tried to send the messages through the American embassy in Moscow, but its procedures for handling sensitive material were cumbersome and time-consuming. They then attempted to transmit directly from the presidential aircraft, parked at Moscow's Vnukovo II airport, via satellite hookup to the White House Situation Room. The messages arrived in Washington in nearly unreadable form. The letter to the prime minister of Israel was so garbled that it could not be transmitted to Ambassador Dinitz. In desperation, Lawrence Eagleburger called Brent Scowcroft on an open telephone line. The connection was so poor that all Scowcroft could decipher was that the United States and the Soviet Union had agreed to a cease-fire.[100] The American team had no choice but to revert to sending the messages through the cumbersome machinery of their embassy in Moscow.

Kissinger was apoplectic.[101] At least four hours had been lost in communicating with Israel. The time available for consultation with Israel was reduced by a third; consequently Israel's leaders read the message as an ultimatum rather than as the consultation they had been promised.[102] Kissinger speculated that the Soviet Union was responsible for the technical problems, that it had "pulled the plug on our communications in Moscow" to reduce the time available to Israel to conduct last-minute military operations before the cease-fire went into effect.[103]

If Kissinger is correct, Soviet interference was extraordinarily shortsighted.[104] By complicating the relationship between the United States and Israel, Moscow defeated its purpose of ensuring immediate compliance with the cease-fire by Israel. Joseph Sisco does not believe that the Soviet Union deliberately interfered with communications to Washington, even though a similar breakdown in the communications system of Kissinger's aircraft had occurred during his secret visit to Moscow in April 1972.[105] Soviet officials deny that the interference was deliberate.[106] It seems likely that the technical problems were accidental. Whatever the cause, the absence of adequate communications links seriously obstructed effective crisis prevention. When Kissinger arrived in Tel Aviv, he found an angry and distrustful leadership. Israel's officials felt cheated by the difference between the warning of a cease-fire that they had been promised and that they received.

Another serious problem was the poor quality of military intelligence available to Kissinger and his staff during their stay in Moscow. En route to the Soviet Union from Washington, Kissinger received two reports from Ambassador Dinitz. The first described the location of Israel's forces but did not discuss the time needed to achieve Israel's strategic objectives.[107] The second reported that the IDF had cut the road from Cairo to Suez but anticipated an Egyptian counterattack.

Kissinger acknowledged the reports and insisted on receiving a steady stream of up-to-date military intelligence. "I cannot overemphasize the urgent need to keep me fully informed of the military situation," he cabled Brent Scowcroft. "I need exact assessments, and I need them quickly and frequently. Dinitz must, repeat must, report to you at least three times a day, and I must then have these reports immediately. Tell him to get his communications set up now if he has not yet done so. These reports must be clearly identified. I cannot avoid mistakes if I am not kept fully up to date and know exactly what the situation on the ground is."[108] Kissinger received no military report from Israel while he was in Moscow and the information he received from Washington was contradictory.[109]

The CIA relayed to Kissinger the statement of an IDF spokesman that the army had cut all highways and railroads from Cairo to Ismailia and Suez. It reported heavy fighting in the vicinity of the Suez Canal and suggested that Egypt and Israel were both encountering serious military difficulties. The CIA reported that the IDF was concentrating its offensive activity between Great Bitter Lake and Ismailia as part of a northern thrust.[110] In fact, the Israeli army was advancing in both directions, and it was the attack toward the south that would eventually prove decisive.

The reports that Kissinger received from American intelligence "conveyed no particular sense of urgency."[111] While in Moscow, neither Kissinger nor his staff had any evidence that Egypt's military situation was rapidly becoming untenable. He received no warning that the IDF needed only a few days to encircle and cut off the Third Army. The encirclement and destruction of the Third Army was precisely the sort of humiliating Egyptian defeat that Kissinger had sought all along to avoid. With better intelligence, Kissinger might have conducted his negotiations in Tel Aviv differently and warned Israel's leaders explicitly against any further movement by its forces.

Once the superpowers had jointly agreed to a cease-fire, in sharp contrast to earlier attempts, Moscow faced no difficulty in obtaining the compliance of Egypt or Syria. Sadat had finally realized how grave the military situation had become and was desperately anxious for a cease-fire. Brezhnev did not bother to inform President Assad; he learned of the cease-fire resolution from news reports of the Security Council meeting.[112] The United States had a far more serious political problem in persuading Israel to agree to a cease-fire.

American and Israeli interests diverged sharply. Washington wanted an immediate cease-fire to avoid the defeat of Arab armies and the complications with the Soviet Union that might develop if the Egyptian army was humiliated. Israel's leaders wanted a clear-cut and decisive military victory. Israel's leaders wanted the victory primarily to improve their bargaining position in any negotiations that would follow the war, but also to avenge the surprise attack, restore the deterrent reputation of the IDF, and justify to the Israeli public the large number of military casualties suffered during the war. Predictably, Israel sought to stretch its battlefield opportunities to the outer limits.

Before departing for Moscow, Kissinger had promised Ambassador Dinitz that he would inform Israel immediately about any agreement.[113] When Prime Minister Meir belatedly and angrily received the news of the cease-fire agreement, she suggested that Kissinger stop in Tel Aviv on the way back from Moscow. He agreed, largely to reassure Israel's leaders.[114] Kissinger arrived in Tel Aviv on 22 October, about six hours before the cease-fire was scheduled to go into effect. He met privately with Prime Minister Golda Meir and then with a larger group of officials that included Defense Minister Moshe Dayan, Chief of Staff David Elazar, Foreign Minister Abba Eban, Deputy Prime Minister Yigal Allon, Minister without Portfolio Yisrael Galili, and former Chief of Staff and Ambassador to Washington, Yitzhak Rabin. Only on the eve of his departure, did he receive a military briefing from the IDF. What happened during his five hours of discussions with Israel's civilian and military leaders in Tel Aviv is the subject of intense controversy.

Some participants in the meetings allege that Kissinger quietly encouraged Israel to violate the cease-fire and continue its offensive, for at least several hours. Others insist that Kissinger was tough and emphasized the importance of the cease-fire.[115] Kissinger adamantly denies that he encouraged Israel to violate the cease-fire:

> I did not encourage the Israelis. I did not want to see the Third Army destroyed. I thought that they were emotionally exhausted and did not need a big sales pitch for a cease-fire. After all, they had gotten the direct negotiations that they had always wanted. I didn't press them hard because I didn't think that they needed to be pressed. I did not encourage the Israelis with more than minor adjustments. It is quite possible that the commanders in the field ran away with Golda.[116]

Joseph Sisco, who participated in the meetings, confirmed that "We took a tough line, a very tough line. The environment was very hostile. Golda Meir was furious. We took a very firm line."[117]

Kissinger did not feel it necessary to warn Israel explicitly against encircling the Egyptian Third Army and, consequently, inadvertently created false expectations in Tel Aviv. His behavior in Tel Aviv jeopardized his objective of a limited Israeli victory in order to detach Egypt from the Soviet Union in the postwar period. Several factors explain the ambivalence the secretary of state displayed. Kissinger did not explicitly warn Israel against encircling the Third Army in large part because the quality of military intelligence that he had at his disposal when the meetings began was poor. Until the very end of their stay in Tel Aviv, the Americans did not have accurate intelligence about the situation on the battlefield. Kissinger recalled that:

> Their [Israel's] major offensive was in the north. They told me that their armies were advancing in the north. I told them that they could horse around in the north for a few hours but that was it. I tried to stop them but I couldn't figure out where their armies were. We were looking toward the north. We were not looking in the south. Our satellites were fixed. We couldn't move them around. We were looking north. We didn't know where the Israeli army was.[118]

Rodman confirmed that "We didn't know where their armies were. We didn't know about the precariousness of the Third Army."[119] Kissinger was unaware at the outset of these critical meetings of the looming threat to the Egyptian Third Army to the south. He therefore underestimated the difficulty of persuading Israel to accept an immediate cease-fire and did not warn explicitly against a contingency that he thought was unlikely.

In Kissinger's summary of these meetings, he notes that the Third Army "did not loom large in the discussions." There were "grumbles" about how Egypt's Third Army "might have been fully encircled and destroyed in another *three* days of fighting. But," Kissinger insisted, "these were the same leaders whose repeated predictions—'we need three more days'—had consistently been proved overoptimistic."[120] Kissinger was confident that Israel's leaders recognized that they could not have been given an additional three days without risking a superpower crisis and the destruction of the American position in the Arab world.[121]

There is little evidence that Israel's military and civilian leaders had reached any such conclusion.[122] Only during the military briefing at the end of their meetings did Kissinger learn "for the first time what we had attempted to extract from the Israelis for a week: the exact location and objectives of their forces on the west bank of the Suez Canal. Maps showed all Egyptian routes of supply to the Third Army cut except one secondary road in the extreme south."[123] It was very likely that, with only one secondary road still open, Israel would attempt to complete its encirclement of the Third Army. Despite the information he now had, Kissinger failed to warn explicitly against such action.

Kissinger also paid little attention to the mechanics of the cease-fire. In an unwitting acknowledgment of the sloppiness of technical procedures, Kissinger reports that neither American nor Israeli officials were certain of the time at which the cease-fire was to go into effect.

> During the luncheon [between 2:30 and 4:00 P.M. on October 22] a message was brought in informing us that Egypt had accepted the ceasefire at 5:00 P.M. Cairo time. . . . A desultory discussion about ground rules ensued, soon submerged by a confusion that so often occurs at historic moments. There

was uncertainty about whether Cairo and Tel Aviv were in the same time zone. . . . I sent Eagleburger to a phone to check it out with Washington. While waiting for the official word, I suggested that Israel solve the issue by setting the time for 6:52 P.M. Israeli time . . . and let Cairo translate that into Egyptian time.[124]

In part because the technical details of the cease-fire got only desultory attention, some Israelis at the meeting concluded that Kissinger was not overly concerned with its implementation on schedule.[125]

Kissinger also hinted vaguely that he would look the other way at minor violations of the cease-fire. He subsequently admitted that "I also had a sinking feeling that I might have emboldened them; in Israel, to gain their support, I had indicated that I would understand if there was a few hours' 'slippage' in the cease-fire deadline while I was flying home to compensate for the four hours lost through the communications breakdown in Moscow."[126] Kissinger inadvertently created false expectations among Israel's leaders about how much time they would have for additional military action. These misunderstandings contributed to the breakdown of the cease-fire and the ensuing failure of crisis prevention.

Finally, Kissinger's failure to warn explicitly against further military action can be attributed in part to his personal conflict about the message he brought to Tel Aviv. Before he left for Moscow, he had promised Israel that he would consult and give them ample warning of any cease-fire agreement that was reached. Kissinger acknowledged that he felt guilty about the delay in communications from Moscow.[127] Rodman confirmed that "Henry felt very guilty about the communications failure because it seriously shortened the time we could give the Israelis to prepare for the cease-fire. Yet, Henry was stuck because Nixon undercut him by delegating authority to him and denying him the time to delay."[128] Uneasy and guilty about the shortened warning time he had provided, Kissinger misled Israel's leaders about the impact of "minor" violations of the cease-fire. In so doing, he compounded the already difficult issues of technical and political control which were so important if a crisis between the superpowers were to be prevented.[129]

Within a few hours of Kissinger's return to Washington, he learned from the CIA that heavy fighting had broken out between Egypt and Israel. Brezhnev, who had also learned of the renewed fighting, sent an urgent note to Kissinger personally, charging that Israel's forces were advancing southward along the west bank of the Suez Canal. The general secretary termed Israel's actions "unacceptable" and a "flagrant deceit."[130]

Only then did Kissinger recognize that a crisis between the superpowers was imminent. "We were now in a serious predicament," he wrote. "The urgency of Brezhnev's appeal suggested that the plight of the Egyptian Third Army was far more serious than our intelligence had yet discovered or the Israelis had told us. Now I understood. Israel had cut the last supply route to the city of Suez. The Egyptian Third Army on the east bank of the Canal was totally cut off. A crisis was upon us."[131] Within forty-eight hours, the Soviet Union and the United States found themselves in their most serious confrontation since the Cuban missile crisis in 1962. Crisis prevention had failed.

FAILURE TO TERMINATE THE WAR

The superpowers failed to prevent a crisis in their relationship in part because of the difficulty they experienced in ending the war. Termination of the war did not depend only on the United States and the Soviet Union but on their allies as well. Leaders in both capitals badly underestimated the difficulties they would experience in persuading their allies to agree to end the fighting. Despite Egypt's dependence on the Soviet Union for essential military supplies, President Sadat three times refused to agree to a cease-fire at Soviet request. Only when battlefield conditions became desperate, did he finally accept the Soviet recommendation of a cease-fire. Egyptian desperation on the battlefield was just what the Soviet Union and the United States had both sought to avoid.

By waiting until the Egyptian military position became dangerously precarious, Sadat dramatically shortened the time available to arrange and implement a cease-fire. The short time available compounded all the technical, operational, and political problems that we have already described.

Israel agreed to a cease-fire early on when the battlefield was stalemated and it was badly short of much needed military supplies. At that point neither Egypt nor the United States were anxious for a cease-fire. As soon as its military position improved, Israel resisted a cease-fire through every means at its disposal. It did so despite its political and military dependence on the United States.

In October 1973, war termination was a quadrilateral process. Battlefield conditions, not superpower pressures, determined the decisions of Egypt and Israel. But the battlefield inevitably produced asymmetrical preferences: when Israel considered its military position unfavorable, Egypt did not, and when Egypt recognized that its military situation was dangerously weak, Israel knew that it could destroy the Third Army and win a major military victory. The difficulties and the dangers are obvious: only when military action was conclusive, did Egypt agree to a cease-fire, but when military action became conclusive, the threat of a confrontation between the superpowers became real.

Kissinger compounded the structural difficulties of ending the war by overestimating the capacity of the United States to fine-tune the diplomacy of war termination with battlefield conditions. While the Soviet Union wanted to end the war without an Arab defeat, the United States wanted to end the war with a limited Israeli victory. As Kissinger put it, "the best outcome was an Israeli victory that pushed back the Arabs without producing an Arab debacle."[132] This kind of outcome was far more difficult—and dangerous—to accomplish. It led Kissinger to stall the diplomacy of war termination when battlefield positions were relatively symmetrical. Indeed, Ambassador Dinitz subsequently claimed that Kissinger privately discouraged Israel from accepting the cease-fire on 12 October.[133] Once Israel's armies went on the offensive, however, the conditions were created for a large-scale military victory that would rout Egyptian armies. Israel then had every incentive, other than American disapproval, to destroy the Third Army.

Kissinger's expectation that the United States could closely coordinate its diplomatic strategy with battlefield developments was also naive given the technical problems involved. Most serious was access to up-to-date battlefield intelligence. The United States got no accurate information on Israeli military dispositions in the four days that preceded the cease-fire on 22 October. Military intelligence supplied by Israel was deliberately or inadvertently vague; the accompanying analyses minimized the advances of Israel's army and the consequences for the Egyptian Third Army. The restricted flow of accurate intelligence compounded the difficulties already inherent in controlling an autonomous ally and in closely coordinating diplomatic strategy to battlefield conditions.

With more timely and accurate intelligence, Kissinger might have warned Israel more explicitly and vigorously against the encirclement of the Third Army instead of subtly encouraging "minor" violations of the cease-fire. We can only speculate on whether clear and vigorous warnings would have been more effective. Given the issues at stake for Israel and the incentives it had to defeat Egypt's army, it is doubtful. In seeking to terminate war among allies deeply engaged and intensely committed, there is no "technical fix" to deeply rooted political problems.

THE IRONY OF DÉTENTE

The failure to stop the war before the Egyptian Third Army was encircled was the last in a series of opportunities the United States and the Soviet Union had to prevent crisis between them. In tracing the origins of the crisis that followed, we have separated the failure of Moscow and Washington to impose a cease-fire before Egypt was on the verge of a humiliating defeat from their failure first to prevent and then to limit the war. These failures were interconnected: the failure to prevent and then to limit the war made termination of the fighting far more difficult. The failure of crisis prevention was the cumulative result of all the failures that went before.

A serious crisis should have been far less likely in 1973 than in 1962. The general context of the relationship between the two superpowers had improved dramatically in the eleven years since the Cuban missile crisis. In a context of strategic parity, both Moscow and Washington had acknowledged their shared fear of nuclear war and put in place channels of direct communication to avoid inadvertent escalation. Kissinger recognized that "Brezhnev was very eager for improved relations with the United States. He understood the big picture and was eager for nuclear arms reduction."[134] Détente was Brezhnev's proudest achievement.[135] Unlike 1962, both sides were persuaded that neither side wanted war. They were also sensitive to the possibility of escalation inherent in their competition in the Third World. Yet, even the mutually acknowledged fear of nuclear war, the recognition that local conflicts could escalate dangerously, some empathy with each other's interests, and good and frequent communication between the two sets of leaders were not enough.

Several factors account for the failure of crisis prevention. Misplaced confidence in deterrence blinded the United States to evidence of the impending war. Technical problems compounded the difficulties of crisis prevention, as did the far more serious problem of the political control of allies who were dependent militarily but independent politically. Even more fundamental were the political conceptions the United States and the Soviet Union brought to their joint task. Their pursuit of unilateral advantage in the Third World and their mutual denial of the difficult trade-offs between regional competition and global crisis prevention at each critical step along the way were the central factors in their failure to prevent a crisis neither wanted.

Even though the two superpowers had recognized their shared horror of nuclear war and agreed to collaborate to prevent its occurrence, their relationship was still intensely competitive on other issues. The Soviet leadership pursued "expansionist détente," and the United States attempted to persuade Egypt, directly and indirectly, to reverse alliances. Each sought to avoid losses or make gains at the expense of the other. Both the Soviet Union and the United States failed to face up to the difficult choices and painful trade-offs they would have to make if they were to avoid a crisis. Leaders in Moscow and Washington persuaded themselves that there was no conflict between their pursuit of relative advantage and crisis prevention.

Before the war broke out in the Middle East and even after the fighting started, Moscow chose to avoid immediate short-term losses in its relationship with its allies in the expectation that it would not confront longer-term costs in its relationship with Washington. The United States chose to pursue long-term gains in the Middle East at the expense of the Soviet Union in the expectation that it could avoid short-term costs in its relationship with Moscow. Neither Washington nor Moscow faced squarely the hard choices before them. On the contrary, they chose strategies that denied the contradictions and compounded the already difficult trade-offs they faced. When the Soviet leadership was confronted with the American request to restrain the resupply of its allies, it chose to treat the choice as routine and protect its regional interests at the expense of crisis prevention. Both the Soviet Union and the United States miscalculated badly and did serious damage to their relationship.

The superpowers were able to deny these contradictions in part, but only in part, because of their self-serving interpretations of détente. These selective understandings were perhaps a function of their need to deny the painful trade-offs they faced. Each expected that détente would limit the other's capacity to make gains. Soviet leaders anticipated that the favorable "correlation of forces" would limit the future capacity of the United States to exploit the kind of nuclear blackmail it had resorted to in the past. Nixon and Kissinger considered deterrence even more important in the context of strategic parity and added linkage within détente as an additional instrument to constrain a more powerful Soviet Union. Kissinger was explicit in his analysis of détente as a series of linked obligations. During the war, he told an international audience that "we will react if relaxation of tensions is used as a cover to exacerbate conflicts in international trouble spots. The Soviet Union cannot disregard these principles in any area of the world without imperiling its entire relationship with the United States. Our policy with regard to détente is clear . . . détente cannot survive irresponsibility in any area."[136]

In dealing with the contradictions between regional interests and global crisis prevention, leaders in Moscow and Washington used their selective interpretation of détente to deny the consequences of the painful choices they confronted. In the period before the outbreak of the war in the Middle East, Soviet leaders faced pressing demands from their allies which created painful policy dilemmas. Egypt, Moscow's ally, was deliberately trying to create the crisis that the Soviet Union was trying to avoid. Confronted with the possible loss of their most important ally in the Middle East, Soviet leaders finally responded to the military demands of Egypt. Brezhnev and his colleagues in the Politburo could not face the strategic and domestic consequences of sacrificing their relationship with Egypt and their reputation as a reliable and valuable ally. Instead, they persuaded themselves, despite strong evidence to the contrary, that the rearmament of Egypt would increase their leverage in Cairo. To hedge against adverse consequences in their relationship with Washington, they convinced themselves that by warning of impending war, they were meeting the technical requirements of détente. Ironically, they counted on their improved relationship with Washington to prevent a serious crisis.

Nixon and Kissinger saw the conflict in the Middle East largely through the prism of their competition with the Soviet Union. In the year preceding the outbreak of war, American leaders made no serious efforts to defuse the simmering conflict in the Middle East. Kissinger in particular deliberately encouraged a diplomatic deadlock because he hoped that it would induce Egypt to abandon its alliance with the Soviet Union and turn to the United States. Confident of the capacity of Israel's military superiority to prevent war, Washington did not see the coming explosion. Even after the fighting began, Washington ignored the contradiction between the imperatives of crisis prevention and military support of its ally which, Kissinger acknowledged, would lead to an expansion of the fighting. Kissinger was able to convince himself that a crisis could be prevented by matching and besting the Soviet Union in order to reinforce the reputation of the United States for resolve.

Leaders on both sides badly underestimated the risks of the strategies they chose. The explanation lies partly in well-documented psychological processes people use when they confront painful choices. Leaders denied the adverse consequences of their choices. They persuaded themselves that there was no contradiction between their pursuit of competitive advantage and crisis prevention. At times, Nixon and Kissinger also convinced themselves that there was no alternative to the strategy they preferred.

Ironically, détente was taken more seriously by their allies than by the superpowers themselves. President Sadat and his advisors expected the improved relationship between the United States and the Soviet Union to freeze an unacceptable status quo in the Middle East. This was one of the principal reasons that Sadat decided to go to war. Muhammad Hasanayn Haykal, one of his closest advisors, recalls a revealing exchange with the Egyptian president. "One day I said to President Sadat, 'I'm afraid it looks as though the détente is going to become a reality and impose itself on us before we can impose ourselves on it. The détente will set conditions for the Middle East problem instead of the Middle East problem setting conditions for the détente.' The President gave a very shrewd answer: 'Maybe we will just be able to catch the last part of the tail of détente.' "[137]

Contrary to expectations, détente and the accompanying norms of crisis prevention exacerbated rather than reduced the difficulties of crisis prevention. In Cairo, where détente was taken seriously, it contributed directly to Sadat's choice of war. In Moscow and Washington, where it was disaggregated and insulated as a distinct relationship or exploited as a cover to compete to avoid loss or make gain, it fueled rather then forestalled crisis. The mutually inconsistent and contradictory ways in which Soviet and American leaders interpreted détente made crisis prevention more rather than less difficult.

Deterrence also had a counterintuitive impact. In 1962, direct and extended deterrence provoked rather than prevented the crisis. Deterrence had a pernicious effect in 1973, but for different reasons. Nixon, Kissinger, and most of their advisors counted on Israel's military superiority and unquestioned willingness to use force in defense of its interests to deter Egypt and Syria from attacking.[138] Military support of Israel was a fundamental building block of the American strategy of crisis prevention.

Misplaced confidence in deterrence as a strategy of crisis prevention blinded American leaders to evidence and, indeed, explicit warnings, of the growing likelihood of war. Secretary of State Rogers had recognized the destabilizing impact of diplomatic deadlock and had tried, unsuccessfully, in the spring of 1973 to persuade President Nixon to authorize a new round of diplomacy in an effort to reach a partial settlement.[139] Confident of Israel's capacity to deter, Nixon and, to a far greater degree, Kissinger were insensitive to the growing desperation of Sadat. Deterrence became a substitute for an active strategy of conflict management. Their unwarranted confidence in deterrence also encouraged the attempt to shut the Soviet Union out of the Middle East and to seek a political monopoly of Arab-Israeli diplomacy. Reinforcement of Israel's deterrent capability would buy the time necessary to persuade the Arab world of the political irrelevance of the Soviet Union.[140] Deterrence in the Middle East made possible the pursuit of unilateral advantage under the cover of détente.

Finally, both superpowers underestimated the difficulties that they would confront in managing their allies and overestimated the control they could exert. Moscow and Washington were constrained by the military needs and the political strength of their allies in the Middle East. The needs of their allies were critical to their mutual failure to restrict the military supplies they sent to the Middle East, whereas the political independence of Egypt and Israel contributed directly to their failure to prevent the outbreak of war and then to terminate the fighting before the Egyptian Third Army was encircled.

It was not that the superpowers lost control of their allies as they struggled to prevent a crisis. At no point in the process before the crisis erupted between the superpowers—before the outbreak of the war and before their failure to stop the fighting after they had agreed on terms to end the war—did Moscow and Washington have political control. Georgi Arbatov noted ruefully in retrospect: "What could we do? We had to deal with an Egyptian leadership that played its own game. Israel played its own game. It was a lesson for everyone."[141]

Our analysis has identified a series of factors that contributed to the failure of crisis prevention. Leaders were unable to get the kind of information they badly needed, and they were unable to control their allies who were intensely committed participants in a bitter conflict. When confronted with painful choices, they discounted the evidence they did have and denied the risks of the strategies they chose. Most important, both superpowers believed that they could insulate and then exploit the bitter conflict in the Middle East to further their competitive interests. The fundamental cause of the failure of leaders in Moscow and Washington to prevent a crisis were the political conceptions and competitive goals they brought to the problem. In the face of these political conceptions, technical improvements in the process of crisis prevention would have done little to avoid failure.

When asked to reflect on the failure of the United States and the Soviet Union to prevent the crisis of October 1973, Aleksandr Kislov replied: "I worried then about Soviet-American engagement in the Middle East despite the intentions of leaders on both sides. There was insufficient appreciation of the inexorable logic of local events. Thank God, there were good relations in 1973. Imagine what would have happened during the height of the Cold War."[142] Georgi Arbatov, one of Brezhnev's advisors at the time, was equally explicit. "Our general relations," he said, "made all the difference in the world. It is terribly important to have good general relations if peripheral crises are to be contained."[143]

Soviet analysts are correct that the failure to prevent a crisis would have been far more dangerous at the height of the Cold War when tension ran high. But détente and an improved relationship were not enough to prevent a crisis. Even in retrospect, the confidence of Soviet experts in "good [political] relations" as the primary condition of effective crisis prevention between the United States and the Soviet Union seems naive. In 1973, the failure of crisis prevention was not technical but political. Only a fundamental rethinking of the political conceptions that governed their relationship and a willingness to face and make hard choices might have made a difference.

The Failure to Avoid Confrontation

Starving the Third Army out . . . was almost certain to bring
about a confrontation with the Soviets. They could not possibly hold still while a cease-fire they had cosponsored
was turned into a trap for a client state.

—Henry Kissinger [1]

We felt that Brezhnev was being pig-headed and we wanted to
teach him a lesson. We did not act on the basis of perceived
intent. We decided to end Brezhnev's bluffing.

—William Quandt [2]

Brezhnev saw what he wanted to see. He was very proud of
his relationship with Nixon and wanted joint action. It was
characteristic of Brezhnev to engage in wishful thinking
about joint Soviet-American action.

—Victor Israelian [3]

ON THE NIGHT OF 24 October 1973, the Soviet Union proposed joint military intervention with the United States to end the fighting. Moscow warned
that if joint action were impossible, it would consider taking unilateral action to halt Israel's military offensive. In response, the United States alerted
its nuclear and conventional forces worldwide in an attempt to deter Soviet
military intervention. The superpowers found themselves in their most dangerous confrontation since the Cuban missile crisis.

The crisis developed when it was least expected, after Brezhnev and
Kissinger had jointly negotiated the terms of a cease-fire. Both leaders
wanted to stop the fighting and to avoid a crisis between their two countries.
They shared the same tactical objectives. In the wake of Israel's battlefield
successes, the United States now fully shared the Soviet interest in ending the
war before the Egyptian Third Army was destroyed. Brezhnev and Kissinger

were also in constant communication with each other. Under these conditions, no crisis should have occurred. Yet, despite shared objectives and an agreement negotiated between Moscow and Washington, a serious crisis erupted that ended in confrontation. This chapter addresses this puzzle.

WHY WAS 1973 A CRISIS?

Cuba was a crisis because of mutual perception of acute threat, increased fear of war, and time pressure—the standard dimensions of an international crisis. In 1973, Soviet and American leaders felt that important interests were threatened. The superpowers also felt a sense of urgency as the pace of battlefield developments in the Middle East outstripped their capacity to cope.

In 1962, the crisis began for the United States with the discovery of Soviet missile sites in Cuba and, for the Soviet Union, a week later when President Kennedy announced the blockade. In contrast, the crisis in 1973 developed symmetrically in both capitals as leaders in Moscow and Washington responded to events on the battlefield. A few hours after Egypt and Israel accepted the cease-fire that Brezhnev and Kissinger had negotiated, fighting began again. Egypt and Israel each accused the other of violating the cease-fire first, but the IDF clearly took advantage of the violations to complete the encirclement of the Egyptian Third Army.

The crisis developed in Moscow in two phases. As the fighting continued on 23 and 24 October, Brezhnev anticipated a catastrophic military defeat of Egypt and a concomitant threat to the reputation of the Soviet Union as an ally and as an arms supplier to the Third World. The Soviet perception of threat in 1962 was greatly exaggerated; in 1973, it was accurate. The road to Cairo was undefended, and Egypt was on the verge of military disaster. Brezhnev also felt pressed for time. By 24 October, the Soviet Union had only hours to prevent an Egyptian defeat. Here too, his sense of urgency was grounded in reality.

For Soviet leaders, the second phase of the crisis began after the United States alerted its forces worldwide. Brezhnev and the Politburo were surprised and angered by the American alert. They met on 25 October for eight hours, in an angry and tense session. In this final phase of the confrontation, Politburo members did not worry about an intentional attack by the United States. Nevertheless, they were intensely angered and greatly disappointed by the American action and seriously concerned about the possibility of inadvertent escalation.

In Washington, the crisis also developed in two distinct but related phases that followed each other in rapid succession. In both phases, American officials perceived a threat, but the nature of the threat changed rapidly under the pressure of events during the course of thirty-six hours. Within hours after his return from Tel Aviv on the morning of 23 October, Kissinger learned of the cease-fire violations and received an urgent message from Brezhnev. He worried about the consequences of the destruction of the Egyptian Third Army for American relations with Egypt and with the Soviet Union. "The Egyptian Third Army on the east bank of the Canal was totally cut off," Kissinger explained. "A crisis was upon us."[4]

Nixon and Kissinger knew that the destruction of the Egyptian Third Army was unacceptable to Moscow. They also shared the Soviet objective of preventing an Egyptian defeat because it would seriously compromise their central objective of creating a postwar political monopoly. Kissinger not only understood Soviet constraints, he shared the estimate of the limited time available before the Egyptian Third Army would collapse. From early on 23 October until the evening of 24 October, Kissinger identified a threat to American objectives, empathized with Soviet concerns, and considered it urgent to halt Israel's offensive.

Once Brezhnev proposed joint intervention but then warned that he would consider acting alone if necessary to stop the fighting, the nature of the crisis changed dramatically. Kissinger defined the Soviet action as a threat not only to American interests in the Middle East but to the United States worldwide. If the United States backed down, he believed, its resolve in future encounters with the Soviet Union would be fundamentally compromised.[5] From Washington's perspective, the crisis was now primarily in the Soviet-American relationship. Kissinger, unlike his Soviet counterparts, did not worry about the risk of inadvertent escalation but focused on the threat to the American reputation for resolve.

Although they considered the risk of war low, Kissinger and his colleagues in the White House Situation Room nevertheless felt an acute sense of urgency. If the Soviet Union intended to send troops, it would do so in a matter of hours. The United States had very limited time to find an appropriate way to signal its determination to resist any deployment of Soviet forces in the Middle East. Although leaders in Moscow and Washington felt pressed for different reasons, as in 1962, the sense of urgency was real and shared, though not equally, in both capitals.

The crises in 1962 and 1973 are similar in some important respects. Both crises had an important emotional component. Like Kennedy in 1962, Brezhnev thought that he had been cheated by his adversary. His anger at Kissinger and sense of betrayal reduced his confidence that quiet diplomacy would succeed in saving the Egyptian Third Army. Unlike Khrushchev in 1962, who had secretly deployed the missiles deliberately to deceive Kennedy, Kissinger did not consciously attempt either to mislead or to deceive Brezhnev. Nevertheless, as it had in 1962, anger and intense emotion made crisis management more difficult in 1973.

Even though they felt threatened and pressed, Soviet leaders nevertheless recognized the difficulty of controlling allies and events in a rapidly changing battlefield. Again, like Kennedy in 1962, Brezhnev and his colleagues were sensitive to the dangers of inadvertent escalation. The unpleasantness of the available choices created additional stress for Soviet officials as it did for Kennedy and the Ex Comm.

The differences between the two crises are more striking than the similarities. The crisis in 1973 was far more concentrated in time than the missile crisis. It erupted almost simultaneously in both capitals, and leaders had very little time to make their decisions. They did not have a week, as Kennedy did, to cool their anger, consider their options, and think about the consequences of their choices.

The context in which the crisis erupted in 1973 was also much more benign than in 1962. Important interests were at stake, but both sides thought that the risk of war was low. Each superpower was convinced of the other's commitment to avoid war. Kissinger had no doubt about Brezhnev's intentions: "He was very eager for improved relations with the United States. He understood the big picture and was eager for nuclear arms reduction. Gromyko and I were friends. We liked each other and worked well together."[6] "The crisis underlined the importance of prior understandings and communication," observed Georgi Arbatov. "Kissinger could come to Moscow. . . . Our general relations made all the difference in the world."[7]

The Cuban missile crisis was one of misunderstanding: each side misjudged the basic intentions of the other. Both Kennedy and Khrushchev felt so gravely threatened because each misunderstood the other's goals and doubted the other's commitment to a peaceful resolution of the crisis. This was much less the case at the end of the October War. Unlike 1962, neither doubted the other's commitment to avoid war. In large part because neither questioned the other's commitment to avoid war, however, each felt free to seek advantage at the other's expense. In the final phase of the crisis, American and Soviet leaders badly misread each other's signals and provoked a confrontation. Ironically, this misreading of signals in a competitive context did lasting damage to the relationship between the United States and the Soviet Union.

The confrontation began when Brezhnev proposed joint intervention and then warned that the Soviet Union might consider acting alone to save the Third Army. He made his proposal and then issued his threat because Nixon and Kissinger had failed to compel Israel to stop its advance before it threatened the survival of the Third Army.

Our analysis begins with an examination of why the United States was unable to accomplish what was manifestly in its own as well as in the Soviet interest. We then look at why the Soviet Union urged joint intervention but also threatened that it might act alone to compel an end to the fighting. Then we explore the American response: a worldwide alert of its strategic as well as conventional forces to deter the deployment of Soviet forces in Egypt. Finally, we look at the Soviet reaction to the American alert. In answering these questions, we assess how effectively leaders used compellence, deterrence, and reassurance and examine why they failed to manage the crisis without a confrontation.

THE FAILURE OF AMERICAN COMPELLENCE

Back in Washington after his whirlwind trip to Moscow and Tel Aviv, Kissinger recognized that Israel's ongoing military offensive could lead to a serious confrontation with the Soviet Union. When he tried to enforce the cease-fire, Kissinger met serious obstacles. Events on the battlefield moved quickly and forced the pace of diplomacy. As the secretary of state observed, "Crises have their own momentum. A halt of military activities suited our diplomatic purposes, but it ran counter to military realities. Egypt's Third Army was bound to try to break out of its encirclement; cease-fire or not, Israel would be reluctant to give up the opportunity to end the war with a knockout blow."[8] Under these conditions, the secretary of state experienced far greater difficulty than he had anticipated in compelling Israel to observe the cease-fire.

There was still time, though not much, to avoid a confrontation. Thirty-six hours elapsed between reports of the first violations of the cease-fire and the receipt of Brezhnev's letter on the night of 24 October. During this critical period, the president was, in the words of his Chief of Staff Alexander Haig, "down, very down," over Watergate.[9] On 23 October, eight resolutions of impeachment were submitted to the Judiciary Committee of the House of Representatives. Again, the president was distracted, and Kissinger had primary responsibility for crisis management.

At first, Kissinger made a less-than-vigorous effort to compel Israel. By 24 October, however, *before* Brezhnev issued his threat, Washington tried vigorously to compel Israel to stop the fighting. American compellence succeeded, but by the time it did, it was too late. The threat to the Egyptian Third Army had provoked Brezhnev to warn that the Soviet Union would consider unilateral intervention.

There was also a fundamental ambiguity in American strategy. At the same time as the United States repeatedly warned Israel against the "destruction" of the Third Army and urged an immediate end to the fighting, it tacitly acquiesced in its encirclement. An encircled Third Army was a ticking time bomb.

On 23 October, Kissinger learned from Israel that all roads to the Egyptian Third Army had been cut. He immediately tried to arrange a second cease-fire through the United Nations in collaboration with Moscow. Prime Minister Meir, in a "blistering communication," informed Kissinger that Israel would not comply with or even discuss the proposed resolution.[10] Kissinger did not threaten Israel but persisted, over its objections, in negotiating a second cease-fire. He noted that it called for a return to a line which "we had carefully not specified."[11] In so doing, he tacitly signaled Jerusalem that the United States was willing to tolerate, at least for the moment, the encirclement of the Egyptian Third Army.[12]

When Kissinger learned of renewed fighting early on the morning of 24 October, he made a vigorous effort to compel Israel to observe the cease-fire. The secretary threatened to leave Israel alone if its actions provoked Soviet intervention:

> It was clear that if we let this go on, a confrontation with the Soviets was inevitable. . . . I told Dinitz [Israel's ambassador to Washington] that the art of foreign policy was to know when to clinch one's victories. There were limits beyond which we could not go, with all our friendship for Israel, and one of them was to make the leader of another superpower look like an idiot. I said to Dinitz that if Sadat asked the Soviets, as he had us, to enforce the cease-fire with their own troops, Israel would have out-smarted itself.[13]

In an effort to underline the seriousness of American intent, Kissinger asked Alexander Haig to call Ambassador Dinitz and demand, on behalf of the president, an immediate end to offensive military action by Israel.[14] Israel's response was positive but laced with ambiguity: the IDF was trying to absorb Egyptian fire without responding, it would not try to advance, and Israel would keep the American ambassador in Israel, Kenneth Keating, fully informed "in a further effort to calm the Secretary and demonstrate Israeli good intentions."[15]

American compellence worked, but it was too little and too late. Although Israel had promised not to advance any further, Kissinger observed that "This [their reply] left open the possibility of a war of attrition designed to use up Egyptian supplies and force the surrender of the Third Army."[16] The United States had not yet tried seriously to compel Jerusalem to permit food and medical supplies for the Third Army through their lines. Joseph Sisco explained why the United States concentrated so heavily on an end to the fighting:

> We put enormous pressure on Israel on October 23rd and 24th. We pressed first on the cease-fire, then on the siege of Suez City, and finally on the encirclement of the Third Army. We pressed hardest on the cease-fire, because that was the first priority: we wanted to stop the fighting. The distinction among the three issues was not that sharp in our minds. We concentrated on what we had to accomplish urgently. We succeeded in stopping the fighting by the afternoon of October 24th.[17]

Shortage of time and fast-moving events on the battlefield led Kissinger to concentrate on the urgent and difficult task at hand.

It is not surprising that it took the extraordinary threat from the United States to leave Israel to face Soviet intervention to compel Jerusalem to halt its military operations. Even then, the United States achieved only the first of several objectives. The secretary understood that he was asking Israel to exchange a tangible gain on the battlefield for a vague American promise about a peace process in the future and acknowledged how difficult it was for Israel's cabinet to see the logic of this kind of concession.[18] Nevertheless, the logic was overwhelming: "if Israel had been less shaken by the events of the previous weeks, it too would have understood that what it sought [the humiliation of Egypt] would end any hope for peace and doom it to perpetual struggle. . . . The peace process dominated by us would end before it even started."[19]

Kissinger's insight into Israel's national psychology was astute. Given his understanding of the forces propelling Israel's behavior, it is surprising that he expected that he would succeed in compelling Israel to observe the cease-fire before it had consolidated its military victory. Despite its dependence on the United States for military and diplomatic support, Israel's leaders looked at the conflict very differently than did Washington. They used every resource at their disposal to secure the military victory they and their population desperately wanted. Under these conditions, only an extraordinary effort permitted American compellence to succeed.

Even though American efforts to stop the fighting succeeded, the trapped Egyptian Third Army was still at risk because it had almost no food, water, and medical supplies. Kissinger's vigorous effort at compellence was also too late. By the time Ambassador Dinitz assured Kissinger that the fighting had stopped, a desperate President Sadat had already made his request for joint action by the United States and the Soviet Union. Within hours, Kissinger received a letter from Brezhnev proposing joint military action by the two superpowers. The Soviet leader also threatened that he would consider acting alone if the United States would not agree to join with the Soviet Union in enforcing the cease-fire.

THE FAILURE OF REASSURANCE

While the United States struggled to compel its ally, it simultaneously had an unparalleled opportunity to reassure Egypt. Cairo was receptive to an American initiative; indeed, it had gone to war in part to engage the United States. Shortly after the fighting began, Egypt took the unprecedented step of communicating directly with the United States in wartime. On the first day of the war, Foreign Minister el-Zayyat invited Kissinger to put forward a proposal for settlement of the conflict. "Now is your chance," he wrote the secretary of state, "to speak to . . . both [Egypt and Israel] without the great confidence that Israel had and the great lack of confidence which we had."[20]

Shortly thereafter, Hafiz Isma'il, President Sadat's national security advisor, sent Kissinger a message through intelligence channels, informing him of Egypt's terms for ending the war. Kissinger rightly observed that what was significant was the fact of the message, not its content. The Egyptian president was inviting American leadership in the postwar negotiations.[21] For the first time, as Kissinger acknowledges, he understood Sadat's objectives. His political strategy was to position the United States psychologically and politically to mediate between the belligerents.[22] Despite two decades of hostility and an ongoing war in which the United States was supplying Egypt's adversary, Cairo and Washington continued to communicate directly with one another on a daily basis throughout the fighting.

After the last road to the Third Army was cut, at 3:15 P.M. on 23 October President Sadat sent an urgent personal appeal directly to President Nixon. He proposed that the United States should "intervene effectively, even if that necessitates the use of forces, in order to guarantee the full implementation of the cease-fire resolution in accordance with the joint U.S.-USSR agreement."[23] Sadat alleged that the United States had offered a "guarantee" of the cease-fire and warned that its continuing violation by Israel "does not induce confidence in any other future guarantees."[24] Sadat's references to "forces" and "guarantees" should have alerted the United States to his desperation and to the corresponding need to reassure him.

Nixon's reply to Sadat, drafted by Kissinger, was measured in substance and tone. It first rejected Egypt's complaint that the United States had failed to honor its guarantee. "All we guaranteed—no matter what you may have been told from other sources—was to engage fully and constructively in promoting a political process designed to make possible a political settlement."[25] Nevertheless, the message continued, the United States had urged Israel to comply with the cease-fire resolution and it recommended that Egypt also make every effort to observe the cease-fire. Indeed, in a message sent a few hours earlier to Moscow, the United States claimed that "responsibility for the violation of the cease-fire belongs to the Egyptian side."[26] The emphasis on technicalities and the evenhandedness of the recommendations were hardly reassuring to the embattled Sadat. The failure to reassure him is especially surprising given the shared objective of the United States and Egypt in preventing the destruction of the Third Army.

A second cease-fire resolution, passed on the night of 23 October, also failed to stop the fighting. Although who renewed the fighting remains in doubt, Israel's forces seized the opportunity to attack Suez City.[27] The situation of the Third Army was growing increasingly desperate, and the road to Cairo was now open. Early on the morning of 24 October, Sadat again pleaded with the United States "to intervene, even on the ground, to force Israel to comply with the cease-fire. That much you have promised."[28]

Nixon's reply, while stronger in tone than his earlier message, did not reassure Sadat that his charges of continuing military action by Israel were being taken seriously. He told Egypt's president that

> The Israeli government has replied to the effect that the attacks are being initiated by the Third Egyptian Army; that Israeli forces are on the defensive and have been ordered to only shoot back on attack. *From here, the true facts are impossible to determine.* I want to assure you that the U.S. is unalterably opposed to offensive Israeli military action and is prepared to take effective

steps to end them. In the meantime, could you make sure that all military action is stopped also by your forces. Secretary Kissinger is getting in touch with Mr. Ismail later today about the possibility of direct conversations between our two sides about post-war diplomacy.[29]

Despite American assurances that it would end Israel's military offensive, Sadat was disturbed by Washington's claim that it could not determine what was happening on the battlefield. Egyptian officials simply did not believe that the United States was unaware of continuing military action by Israel. They regarded the disclaimer at best as an excuse for inaction and at worst as a pretext to allow Israel to inflict a crushing defeat on Egypt.[30]

Later that morning, acting "on the theory that so long as other countries are studying your communications, they cannot be thinking up initiatives of their own," Kissinger informed Sadat that Israel had instructed its forces to stay in defensive positions. Israel had also agreed to permit American military attachés in Tel Aviv to proceed immediately to the front.[31] Kissinger personally did not give this proposal great weight; he thought it an "essentially time-wasting device."[32] Kissinger's message concluded with another request to Sadat to instruct Egyptian forces to maintain strictly defensive positions.

American assurances clearly did not meet Egyptian concerns. Although the United States had promised to take effective measures to stop the fighting, the dispatch of military attachés to the front, as Kissinger himself acknowledged, did not constitute such action. Disturbed by Kissinger's claim that the United States could not determine what was happening on the battlefield and desperate about the plight of the Third Army, President Sadat took the action he did not want to take. He invited the Soviet Union and the United States to participate jointly in compelling observance of the cease-fire. In so doing, he provided the pretext for the Soviet threat that it would consider sending forces to Egypt unilaterally. His action was in large part a reaction to the failure by the United States to provide adequate reassurance.

THE SOVIET RESORT TO COMPELLENCE

On 24 October at 9:35 in the evening, Ambassador Dobrynin called Kissinger with an urgent letter from General Secretary Brezhnev. Dobrynin read Kissinger the most important passages:

> Let us together, the USSR and the United States, urgently dispatch to Egypt the Soviet and American military contingents, to insure the implementation of the decision of the Security Council of October 22 and 23 concerning the cessation of fire and of all military activities and also of our understanding with you on the guarantee of the implementation of the decisions of the Security Council. . . . It is necessary to adhere without delay. I will say it straight that if you find it impossible to act jointly with us in this matter, we should be faced

with the necessity urgently to consider the question of taking appropriate steps unilaterally. We cannot allow arbitrariness on the part of Israel.[33]

When Brezhnev sent his letter to Nixon, there was significant activity by Soviet paratroop and naval forces. On 23 October, Moscow sent two of its amphibious ships that had been anchored off the coast of Syria steaming toward Egypt.[34] Early the next morning, a Soviet helicopter carrier and two destroyers were moved from their positions off Crete to relieve the anticarrier group covering USS *Independence*.[35] Four airborne divisions were on ready-to-move status and an inflight command post was also established in southern Russia.[36] Preparations were made for the imminent departure of several airborne units, and transport aircraft were loaded. Communications nets surged with activity, and flight plans for the next day were changed.[37] The Soviet Union also halted its airlift to Egypt, thereby freeing significant numbers of transport aircraft.

The Politburo was not told of these military measures. When he was asked at the Politburo meeting on 25 October about Soviet military movements, Grechko responded that they were routine military maneuvers.[38] Andrei Alexandrov-Agentov, a senior aide to Brezhnev in 1973, explained that "Brezhnev liked and trusted Grechko. Very often, Grechko, confident of Brezhnev's trust, authorized measures of military preparedness without Brezhnev's knowledge or approval. He had a free hand."[39] Evgueny Pyrlin confirmed that "As a rule the Minister of Defense was authorized to order military actions short of the mobilization of reserves and the reinforcement of armored and air divisions. To be frank, Mr. Grechko as the Minister of Defense had wide liberty of action and sometimes didn't inform the political leadership of the details."[40]

Soviet intentions are controversial. Soviet officials all agree that Brezhnev made his proposal of joint military action with the United States in all seriousness. There is debate about what Brezhnev would have done if the United States rejected the proposal for joint action. There is good evidence that Brezhnev was bluffing; that he was not prepared to act unilaterally and send Soviet forces to Egypt.

Brezhnev's appeal for collective action with the United States was genuine. It was based on a serious misunderstanding that grew directly out of the drafting of the cease-fire agreement and an attached memorandum of understanding by Gromyko and Kissinger in Moscow. The third clause of the draft cease-fire resolution provided for negotiations "under appropriate auspices." To clarify the meaning of the phrase, Gromyko and Kissinger also prepared an additional document that was not made public. The document read:

> It is understood that the phrase "under appropriate auspices" in Point 3 of the resolution shall mean that the negotiations between the parties concerned will take place with the active participation of the United States and the Soviet Union at the beginning, and thereafter, in the course of negotiations when key

issues of a settlement are dealt with. Throughout the entire process of negotiation, the United States and the Soviet Union will in any case maintain the closest contact with each other and the negotiating parties.[41]

Brezhnev did not see either the private document, which was initialed by Gromyko and Kissinger, or the final text of the cease-fire resolution, which was drafted hurriedly by Kissinger, Sisco, and Gromyko and quickly cabled from Moscow to the United Nations and to Cairo and Damascus. President Sadat interpreted "appropriate auspices" as a Soviet-American guarantee to enforce the cease-fire if necessary.[42] Ambassador Vinogradov reported Sadat's understanding that the United States and the Soviet Union had "guaranteed" the cease-fire to Cairo.

Israelian explained how the confusion arose. The Politburo met on 23 October to discuss the appropriate response to the continued violations of the cease-fire. At the meeting, members of the Politburo argued that the agreement reached in Moscow "obligated" the United States and the Soviet Union to take the necessary steps to implement the resolution that had been adopted by the Security Council.

> The formula "under appropriate auspices" was interpreted as joint action by the USA and the USSR to guarantee the ceasefire in the Near East. For instance, Kosygin suggested at the Politburo meeting that a joint Soviet-American team of military officials should be sent to observe the ceasefire. His idea was that this group should include 200 or 250 observers from each of the two states. Kosygin was supported by Ustinov. They thought that this step should be agreed upon with the Americans and that the Americans should be reminded that, when Kissinger visited Moscow, an agreement was reached to "act as guarantors."[43]

Brezhnev's and Kosygin's interpretation of the critical clause did not go unchallenged at the Politburo meeting. Gromyko explained how the term "under appropriate auspices" had been interpreted in the document that he and Kissinger had initialed. He insisted that the dispatch of Soviet and American personnel would require approval by the Security Council; most likely, China would veto such a resolution. Besides, Gromyko added, there were already United Nations' personnel in Cairo.[44]

Kosygin irritably dismissed Gromyko's objections. "That's all formalities. They [the United Nations Truce Supervisory Organization personnel] are dead souls," he insisted. "The fact is that both we and the Americans committed ourselves to carrying out the Security Council decision and we should proceed from that assumption. Action is needed."[45] Brezhnev was adamant that the United States and the Soviet Union should cooperate in sending military personnel as "guarantors" of the cease-fire. At his urging, the Politburo agreed to make this suggestion to the United States.[46]

Kislov confirmed that Brezhnev meant his proposal of joint action: "The Soviet offer of joint intervention was serious."[47] Brezhnev hoped that the United States and the Soviet Union would act together to enforce the cease-fire as the capstone of détente. The first part of his letter to Nixon was not a threat, but an offer of collaboration based on what he thought was a joint understanding of their responsibilities.

The concept of joint military action had some precedent in the history of Soviet-American negotiations on the Middle East. In 1971, the State Department, at the initiative of Secretary of State William Rogers, held discussions with the Soviet Union about the principles of a settlement of the Arab-Israel conflict. Rogers had hinted at one point that as part of the guarantees of a settlement, the United States would consider the participation of Soviet soldiers in a Mideast peacekeeping force.[48] Although the context was entirely different, the concept of joint participation of American and Soviet military personnel had been legitimated in the eyes of the Soviet foreign ministry. Consequently, as bizarre as the proposal would sound in Washington, collective enforcement action was considered realistic in Moscow.[49]

The last sentence of Brezhnev's letter to Nixon is more controversial. Brezhnev warned that if the United States refused to act jointly with the Soviet Union, he would consider taking unilateral action.[50] Brezhnev did not explicitly threaten the use of military force, but his tone was menacing. This sentence was not in the original draft of the letter prepared for Brezhnev by Gromyko. Brezhnev added the warning at the last moment before the letter was sent.[51]

Some Soviet officials considered that the Soviet Union would actually have sent forces if the fighting had not stopped. Vadim Zagladin reports that Soviet leaders considered military intervention in the Cairo region.[52] Aleksandr Kislov described Soviet contingency plans. "Our most important objective was to stop the destruction of the Third Army. If the fighting had not stopped, we would have sent a minimum of two or three divisions. A battalion would have been insignificant. We needed to send enough troops to make an impression."[53]

Anatoliy Gromyko, who was in the Soviet Embassy in Washington on 24 October, was more cautious: "The Soviet Union seriously considered intervention. The plan was to send troops to the Cairo region. We would have put a cordon around Cairo. On the other hand, we were anxious not to get involved in the fighting. Some of my colleagues might say that this [Brezhnev's letter] was only a form of political pressure."[54] Gen. Yuri Yakovlevich Kirshin confirmed that military leaders were asked to prepare contingency plans for the optimal use of Soviet paratroopers.[55]

Soviet officials with more detailed knowledge of the Politburo meeting deny that the Soviet Union would have sent troops to Cairo. They insist that Brezhnev's threat was a bluff. Ambassador Dobrynin, who was in Washington on 24 October but in close contact with Soviet leaders, doubted that the Soviet Union would have sent troops.[56] Leonid Zamyatin was not with Brezhnev when his letter to Nixon was drafted, but also doubts that the Soviet Union would have sent forces to Egypt.[57] "This is dangerous. It would have been easy to get in but hard to get out."[58] Georgiy Kornienko, head of the American desk in the Foreign Ministry and one of the four members of the special working group drafted to work with the Politburo, was adamant: "I am absolutely certain that there were no plans to send Soviet forces to the Middle East. They were put on alert to put pressure on the Americans."[59]

Victor Israelian was present at Politburo meetings and took detailed notes. He insists that the warning was a bluff, that the Soviet Union had no intention whatsoever of sending troops to Egypt: "Kulikov [the Chief of Staff] opposed sending any officers there. He opposed sending even observers without a disengagement of Israeli and Egyptian forces. Members of the Politburo had not the slightest desire, on any level, to send forces. There might have been some contingency planning by the military, but there was no intention to send forces."[60]

At the Politburo meeting on 23 October, there was no discussion whatsoever of sending regular forces, only military observers. The Politburo did not meet on 24 October, before Brezhnev's letter was sent, nor did it discuss his message after the fact. Gromyko drafted the message for Brezhnev, and the two walked and talked with a few colleagues in the corridor.[61] "It was not a considered decision," Israelian explained. "No formal decision was ever made by the Politburo to threaten military intervention. Brezhnev added the threat to put pressure on Nixon to get the fighting stopped. He wanted to put pressure on the United States. He thought it was a clever thing to do."[62]

The threat to consider unilateral action to stabilize the cease-fire was the last in a series of steps with a common political purpose. In the first instance, Brezhnev hoped that joint action with the United States would end the fighting. The threat that the Soviet Union might act alone, like the blockade of Cuba, was added to signal to the United States the seriousness of Soviet interests at stake. Brezhnev hoped that if joint action were impossible, the threat that the Soviet Union would consider sending forces would be enough to compel the United States to stop Israel, that the visible preparation of Soviet troops and his warning would succeed in stabilizing the cease-fire and remove the danger to Cairo. After only limited consultation of his colleagues and staff, Brezhnev opted for a strategy of graduated compellence premised on a bluff.

BREZHNEV'S MOTIVES

Brezhnev acted in response to four reinforcing considerations: the failure of intensive negotiations with the United States to stop the fighting, the need to safeguard the political position of proponents of détente at home, the reputation of the Soviet Union as a reliable ally, and the multiplicative effect of anger fueled by a sharp sense of betrayal. Counteracting these pressures was a keen appreciation of the risks of any deployment of forces and the desire to avoid a confrontation with the United States.

The Failure of Diplomacy

Brezhnev threatened to send forces to stabilize the cease-fire only as a last resort. After he learned of the violations of the cease-fire on 22 October, he repeatedly asked the United States to ensure Israel's compliance. These requests were not couched as threats but as appeals to their joint undertaking agreed to in Moscow.

When Brezhnev first was informed of continuing forward movement of Israel's forces, he quickly summoned Gromyko, Andropov, and Grechko to his study to discuss appropriate measures. Gromyko suggested the immediate adoption of another resolution by the Security Council. Gromyko and his working group drafted a text of the resolution that was quickly approved by the participants at the meeting and prepared a draft letter to Kissinger. During the meeting, Brezhnev, Andropov, and Grechko referred repeatedly to the sense of Resolution 338; "it was the duty" of the two great powers to ensure that the cease-fire was honored.[63]

On 23 October, Brezhnev sent an urgent message addressed personally to Kissinger. Brezhnev labeled Israel's actions a "flagrant deceit" and suggested an immediate meeting of the Security Council to request the parties to withdraw to the lines they had held at the time the cease-fire resolution was passed by the Security Council.[64] Brezhnev's proposal was impractical because no one knew where the two armies had been when the cease-fire resolution was adopted by the United Nations. At the time the cease-fire was scheduled to go into effect, twelve hours after it was passed by the Security Council, there were no supervisory personnel in place. It was nevertheless clear that Israel had completed the encirclement of the Third Army after the cease-fire was scheduled to take effect.

A few hours later, in the first use of the hot line during the crisis, Brezhnev urged President Nixon to move decisively to stop the violations. Kissinger reports that "He [Brezhnev] curtly implied that we [the United States] even might have colluded in Israel's actions."[65] Brezhnev made no explicit threat. Rather, he urged the United States to cooperate quickly to end the fighting and arrange the withdrawal of the two armies to the lines they held when the resolution was passed in New York.

Kissinger replied quickly, in the president's name, assuring Brezhnev that the United States assumed "full responsibility to bring about a complete end of hostilities on the part of Israel."[66] He proposed that Moscow and Washington support a new cease-fire resolution that would call for a return to the positions occupied by the two sides, not when the cease-fire resolution was passed, but when it was scheduled to take effect. At the same time, Kissinger warned that it would be impossible to determine the exact location of the armies at the time and that a cease-fire line would have to be negotiated between Egypt and Israel. Within the hour, Brezhnev accepted the proposal.[67]

On 23 October, in the evening, the Security Council passed a second cease-fire resolution, but it too had little immediate effect. The fighting continued after the resolution was scheduled to go into effect early on 24 October. Egypt's military situation was grave. The Third Army was cut off, and Israel's forces were on the outskirts of Ismailia, threatening the rear of the Second Army.

Brezhnev sent yet another message to Nixon, charging Israel with "defiant" attacks and invoking their mutual agreement to end the war. "I wish to say it frankly," he wrote to Nixon, "that we are confident that you have the possibilities to influence Israel with the aim of putting an end to such provocative behavior of Tel Aviv. We would like to hope that we both will be true to our word and to the understanding we have reached."[68] Brezhnev fully expected the United States to restrain Israel.[69] He did not adequately appreciate the difficulty that Washington would have in controlling its ally, even though Moscow had difficulty in restraining Egypt and Syria.

That afternoon, Brezhnev received a reply from President Nixon, relaying assurances from Israel that it would observe the cease-fire and requesting that United Nations' observers be sent from Cairo to monitor the front. Soviet leaders were not reassured. Foreign Minister Andrei Gromyko complained to Kissinger that Israel was intensifying its military activity, despite its assurances to the contrary.[70]

Brezhnev and Gromyko had been in constant communication with Nixon and Kissinger for almost thirty-six hours, urging compliance with the cease-fire. Brezhnev had even used the hot line, for the first time during the Nixon administration, to emphasize the urgency of American action.[71] Late on 24 October, Brezhnev and his advisors reluctantly concluded that conventional diplomacy had failed. Brezhnev progressively eliminated one alternative after another. He resorted to the most dramatic option, the threat that the Soviet Union would consider unilateral action, only as a final alternative, and even then he proposed joint action first.

Domestic Politics

It was important for Brezhnev and those in the Politburo who supported détente to defend their policies against critics who charged them with weakness and betrayal of an ally. Four members of the Politburo spoke publicly about the war: two, Brezhnev and Kosygin, were proponents of détente but Grechko and Shelepin were critical.[72] Shelepin's speech was surprising in that he was not associated directly with Middle East policy, but he was a political opponent of Brezhnev. It might be taken as evidence that Brezhnev had become vulnerable on this issue.

Brezhnev faced no opposition from the military, who also opposed the dispatch of Soviet forces to Egypt. Marshal Grechko was very worried about the situation of the Egyptian army, but he was not anxious to help Sadat. "Grechko could not forgive Sadat," Israelian explained, "for his expulsion of Soviet personnel. He didn't believe in a political solution to the conflict, but Sadat undertook military action without consulting him. Therefore, he was very critical of Egypt."[73] Gen. Kulikov also opposed sending Soviet forces as long as the fighting continued.

Nonetheless, Brezhnev could not help but consider the charges his critics in the Politburo would level if the Soviet Union stood by and permitted the defeat of the Egyptian army. Détente would be jeopardized by the failure to honor the Soviet commitment to Egypt and the inability of the Soviet Union to get the United States to comply with an agreement they had negotiated together.[74] The strategy that Brezhnev had promoted publicly for a year would be at risk, and Brezhnev's authority in the Politburo would become less credible if Moscow were unable to prevent the defeat of the Egyptian army.[75]

Reputation

Brezhnev and his advisors felt that the reputation of the Soviet Union as a reliable ally was at stake. President Sadat wrote to Moscow describing the military situation as "dangerous." The threat to the Egyptian armies "was the result of Israeli treachery."[76] He urged that the Soviet Union and the United States take effective measures to guarantee the cease-fire. At the Politburo meeting on 23 October, Kulikov gave a very pessimistic briefing on the fate of the Egyptian military.[77] He estimated that in two days Cairo could fall.[78] Israelian observed: "There was fear about the situation of the Egyptian military. We dramatized the military situation on the battlefield as we wanted to see it. After all, we had warned the Egyptians again and again not to do it. The bad battlefield news met our need for wishful thinking. We had told them not to do it."[79] Politburo members considered the situation of the Egyptian army increasingly desperate as a result of the ongoing fighting.

Brezhnev had engineered a cease-fire with the United States and had assured Egypt that the cease-fire would be implemented. Sadat repeatedly referred to the "guarantees" he had received from the Soviet Union, and Brezhnev accepted this interpretation of Soviet obligations.[80] The encirclement of the Third Army after the cease-fire was scheduled to go into effect, Brezhnev believed, badly exposed the Soviet leadership abroad.[81]

Anatoliy Gromyko recalled that "Sadat was thought to be a good friend of ours. Brezhnev was committed to helping Sadat. Brezhnev was not eager to fight in the Middle East. But certain things got him very angry. He wanted to prove to the whole world and to Egypt that we were ready to adhere to our agreement. It was considered essential to come to the aid of Sadat, to aid a friendly state from being defeated. When the Third Army was cut off, we considered it possible that Israel would move against Cairo."[82]

Brezhnev only decided to threaten that he would consider sending forces after he received an explicit request from Egypt. That request came on the afternoon of 24 October, when President Sadat asked for Soviet and American "forces" to ensure the implementation of the cease-fire. The president of Egypt asked for an urgent meeting of the Security Council to authorize the dispatch of forces, including those of the permanent members.[83] The appeal was broadcast by Radio Cairo and increased the pressure on Moscow to take some action to prevent the destruction of the Third Army and preserve its own reputation.

The Egyptian request has become the subject of considerable controversy. Egyptian officials and commentators have suggested that President Sadat did not ask for Soviet and American "forces," but rather for "personnel" to observe the cease-fire. Muhammad Haykal, a close associate of President Sadat at the time, is unequivocal:

> On October 24, President Sadat sent identical messages to Brezhnev and Nixon. "You must," he [Sadat] said, "be in force on the ground to witness for yourself Israeli violations of the cease-fire.". . . [T]here was not on this day—nor on any other day for that matter—any suggestion by us or the Syrians that the Russians should move their forces into the area. The only demand ever made or contemplated was that Russians and Americans should come to observe.[84]

Senior Egyptian officials confirm that President Sadat wanted American not Soviet forces to enforce the cease-fire. The request for joint forces was designed as a cover to prevent a unilateral deployment of Soviet forces and to ensure that American as well as Soviet personnel would be deployed if the military situation deteriorated further.[85]

When Brezhnev decided at the last moment to threaten that the Soviet Union would consider military intervention, he did not consult Sadat before sending his letter to Nixon.[86] Soviet and Egyptian officials confirm that there was no coordination between senior Egyptian and Soviet military officers.[87] Officials in the Foreign Ministry who knew Sadat were shocked to discover that Brezhnev had threatened that the Soviet Union would consider unilateral military action. Israelian explained, "I was astounded, as was Sytenko [the head of the Middle East division]. We knew that Sadat would never have accepted unilateral Soviet intervention. He never would have agreed to a unilateral Soviet deployment. He was not consulted before the letter was sent, and he never would have accepted it. He wanted American forces, and would have accepted Soviet forces to get the Americans."[88] Officials from the Foreign Ministry were correct in their estimate of Sadat's likely reaction. Ismail Fahmy described the Egyptian response when the small contingent of 70 Soviet observers arrived in Cairo:

> While there was an unwelcome delay before the UN observers took up their posts, we were confronted with an influx of eager but unwanted Soviet observers. Moscow had suggested that both Soviet and American observers come to Cairo to monitor the cease-fire, but the Americans procrastinated, while the Soviet personnel arrived quickly. I greeted these observers in my office, but

informed the Soviet ambassador that they could not be deployed unless the Americans sent counterparts. The result was that they remained in Cairo for a few days and then went back home.[89]

It appears that, in those few critical hours, Brezhnev responded to a request President Sadat did not want to make and then proceeded to act independently of Cairo to threaten an action Egypt did not want.

Anger and Betrayal

Brezhnev's decision was also motivated by fury at what he considered to be Kissinger's duplicity. Brezhnev suspected, wrongly, that Kissinger had deliberately deceived him and encouraged Israel to violate the cease-fire.

Brezhnev was prone to intensely emotional reactions. Andrei Gromyko, then the foreign minister and a member of the Politburo, subsequently characterized Brezhnev as an "emotional man," who was "easily moved to tears." In 1979, when Brezhnev learned that Nur Mohammed Taraki, the general secretary of the Afghan Communist Party, had been brutally murdered in his study, "it was too much for Brezhnev to bear. He was simply beside himself."[90] Gromyko attributed the Soviet decision to send forces to Afghanistan in part to Brezhnev's highly emotional response to Taraki's murder. Gromyko's son, Anatoliy, concurred that Brezhnev was a very passionate man who "was easily possessed about things."[91] Kissinger, who had met Brezhnev several times, also described him as "hot tempered."[92]

Soviet officials, in interviews, referred again and again to Brezhnev's acute sense of betrayal and anger on 24 October. According to Georgi Arbatov, "Kissinger's policy antagonized Brezhnev and didn't increase trust between the two countries."[93] Vadim Zagladin emphasized the consternation of Soviet leaders as the cease-fire violations continued: "We had hoped to solve the crisis with the United States. But when we couldn't, it was a shock."[94] Yevgeny M. Primakov, one of Moscow's senior Middle Eastern experts, indicated that Soviet officials were angered by their suspicion that Kissinger deceived them; while agreeing to a cease-fire in Moscow, he gave Israel a free hand to continue its offensive.[95]

Ambassador Anatoliy Dobrynin described Brezhnev's reaction in vivid detail: "He was very emotional. He felt deceived by Nixon and Kissinger. I was worried about our relations with the United States and worried that Brezhnev's anger with Nixon and Kissinger would lead him to do something rash."[96] Additional evidence of Brezhnev's anger comes from Kissinger's report of his conversations with Ambassador Dobrynin on the afternoon and evening of 24 October. At four that afternoon, Dobrynin called Kissinger who told him that the United States would veto any resolution that called for the sending of troops by the permanent members of the Security Council. Dobrynin, Kissinger remembered, was "conciliatory."[97] Dobrynin called again at 7:00 P.M. He informed Kissinger that he had been "wrong" three hours earlier; the Soviet Union now wanted the United Nations to send troops—including Soviet troops—to the Middle East to enforce the cease-fire. In Moscow, he added, "they have become so angry that they want troops."[98]

Brezhnev was particularly angered by what he saw as Kissinger's deceit.[99] "Here in Moscow," Brezhnev said to some of his Politburo colleagues, "Kissinger fooled us and made a deal when he was in Tel Aviv."[100] Kosygin was also infuriated. At the Politburo meeting on 25 October, he charged that "Kissinger visited Moscow, lied to us, went to Tel Aviv, and fraternized with the Israeli people."[101] Victor Israelian recalled that "the fact that the United States refused to cooperate in regulating the Near-Eastern crisis irritated us and made us suspect that Kissinger was acting behind the back of the Soviet Union."[102] "Speaking honestly," Aleksandr Kislov added, "we were cheated by Kissinger. He went right to Israel from Moscow. It was an open secret that he told Israel to push ahead."[103] Soviet officials felt especially betrayed because they thought that Kissinger had violated the rules of the game that had been mutually agreed upon during the meeting in Moscow.

Brezhnev's angry reaction is directly analogous to Kennedy's response to the secret deployment of missiles in Cuba eleven years earlier. Kennedy also felt that Khrushchev had not played by the rules of the game, that he had violated his promise to the president that no missiles would be deployed. To Kennedy, Khrushchev's deceit was just as threatening as the missiles. So, too, it was for Brezhnev. He responded not only to the menace to the Egyptian armies but also to what he saw as American deceit.

Fear of Escalation

The pressures acting on Brezhnev could well have led him to decide to send forces to Egypt if Israel did not halt its military offensive and Cairo were directly threatened. The Soviet Union certainly had the capability to move forces quickly to Cairo West airfield. Gen. Aleksandr Ivanovich Vladimirov insists that had the Soviet Union wanted to send paratroop forces to Egypt, it would have taken very little time; four paratroop divisions were at full readiness and needed only twenty-four hours notice before they could board transport aircraft for deployment.[104] The Soviet Union did not have the airlift capability for four divisions, but some movement of troops could have begun quickly.[105]

Soviet leaders, however, were sensitive to the risks of escalation and confrontation that could grow out of a deployment of Soviet conventional forces in Egypt. "Of course, it was a situation of the utmost danger," explained Anatoliy Gromyko. "The possibility that the Soviet Union would be involved in military action was real. . . . There was a real possibility of escalation, the consequences of which I cannot envisage."[106]

Aleksandr Kislov was even more explicit about the likely consequences of the deployment of Soviet forces:

> We had a real concern about escalation. We imagined that if we sent troops to Egypt, they might see military action. It would have been difficult to control small units of Soviet and Israeli forces if they were in close proximity. Egyptian and Israeli forces were intermingled and if Soviet forces intervened, the chance of their coming under fire would have been great. Brezhnev was seriously worried about the consequences of Soviet military intervention. He feared that it would lead to a direct clash with the Israelis and possibly escalate beyond that to a very serious Soviet-American crisis.[107]

Victor Israelian confirmed that members of the Politburo were deeply concerned about escalation.[108]

Brezhnev worried about the escalation that could result from any deployment of Soviet troops. His fear of escalation led him to reject any Soviet military involvement in the fighting. As soon as the war began, he repeatedly made his opposition to the dispatch of Soviet troops clear to his colleagues in the Politburo and to President Sadat. It is very likely that when Brezhnev added that last threatening sentence to an otherwise temperate draft message, he was driven by anger and intense emotion. Anxious about the fate of Egypt, despairing of diplomacy, and angry at Kissinger's deceit, but fearful of the escalatory consequences of unilateral intervention, Brezhnev decided first to propose joint intervention but then to bluff. He saw no alternative.[109]

Brezhnev miscalculated badly in threatening that he would consider sending troops to Egypt to stabilize the cease-fire. His attempt at compellence did not accomplish his immediate or long-term political purposes. The United States misread the plea that was intended and put its forces on worldwide alert. As we demonstrate in the next chapter, the Soviet threat failed to elicit the desired response. It also had long-range adverse consequences for Soviet-American relations.

The threat that the Soviet Union might act unilaterally proved unnecessary and irrelevant to the outcome of the war. It was unnecessary because by the time Brezhnev wrote his letter to President Nixon, the fighting in the Middle East had stopped. Ambassador Dinitz reported to Kissinger at 3:45 P.M. in the afternoon Washington time, that the front with Egypt was now quiet. Kissinger reviewed the contradictory battlefield intelligence he received from Dinitz and Gromyko, who, ten minutes earlier, had charged that Israel was intensifying its military operations. He speculated that Dinitz and Gromyko were receiving information at different times and that word of the end of military operations might not have reached Moscow.[110]

Vadim Zagladin confirmed that communication between Cairo and Moscow was very poor: "We had little information. The line between Moscow and Cairo was down for several hours during the twenty-fourth of October."[111] Aleksandr Kislov tells much the same story: "Communication throughout the crisis was difficult. It took several hours to communicate between Cairo and Moscow."[112] The Soviet Union had supersonic MiG-25 Foxbats flying reconnaissance missions from Egyptian airfields, ships in the eastern Mediterranean that were intercepting the communications of the armies, navies, and air commands of Egypt, Syria, and Israel, and COSMOS satellites monitoring the battlefield.[113] The satellites beamed their photographs to the Yevpatoriya tracking station in the Crimea, but the transmissions were often of poor quality and apparently there was a delay of hours and, at times, days in their receipt.[114]

American intelligence confirmed that by the early evening of 24 October, before Brezhnev's letter was received in Washington, the fighting had stopped.[115] During the day, Israeli attacks against Suez and Ismailia had been beaten back, and United Nations' supervisory personnel had fanned out to observe the implementation of the cease-fire. By the time Brezhnev's letter reached the Soviet embassy in Washington and was read to Kissinger, it had been overtaken by events.

Brezhnev's attempt at compellence was also irrelevant because it did not deal with the central issue then at stake, the resupply of the trapped Third Army.[116] Before noon on 23 October, Kissinger learned from Prime Minister Meir that the last supply route to the Third Army had been cut.[117] From that time on, the issue was not only a cessation of the fighting, but also the passage of food and medical supplies through Israel's lines to prevent the destruction of the Third Army through slow but certain strangulation. "Starving the Third Army out," Kissinger acknowledged, "would be a slower process than destroying it militarily. But it would lead to the same result. . . . They [the Soviet Union] could not possibly hold still while a cease-fire they had cosponsored was turned into a trap for a client state."[118]

In their letters and hot-line telephone call to Nixon and Kissinger, Brezhnev and Gromyko never raised the predicament of the trapped Third Army.[119] Battlefield events moved so quickly that Soviet leaders, like their American counterparts, concentrated on stopping the fighting and dealt only with the cease-fire. By the time Brezhnev warned that the Soviet Union might act alone to enforce the cease-fire, the Third Army had been cut off for thirty-six hours. The condition of the Third Army became more desperate with every passing hour, even after the cease-fire went into effect.[120] Brezhnev's attempt at compellence lagged badly behind the battlefield. What he asked for had already been achieved, but what he asked for was not enough.

THE AMERICAN ALERT

The United States responded to the Soviet threat to consider unilateral military intervention with a worldwide alert of its forces. Secretary of Defense James Schlesinger and Secretary of State Kissinger made the decision to alert American forces, in consultation with CIA Director William Colby, Chairman of the Joint Chiefs of Staff Adm. Thomas Moorer, and the President's Chief of Staff, Alexander Haig, who was with the president in his personal quarters.[121]

President Nixon did not participate in the discussions, was not informed of the alert when it was ordered, and only approved the alert retroactively on the morning of 25 October.[122] Earlier that evening, Kissinger recalled, "Nixon was as agitated and emotional as I had ever heard him."[123] Confronting a growing prospect of impeachment, a troubled Nixon said to Kissinger: "They are doing it because of their desire to kill the President. And they may succeed. I may physically die. . . . They just don't realize they are throwing everything out the window. I don't know what in the name of God . . ."[124] Overwhelmed by the growing scandal of Watergate, the president was reportedly drunk and exhausted upstairs in his personal quarters in the White House.[125]

At 11:41 P.M., just over an hour after the meeting began in the White House Situation Room, Adm. Moorer issued orders to all military commands to increase readiness to Defense Condition III (DEFCON III). The alert made communications networks less vulnerable and better prepared to implement war plans. It included the Strategic Air Command (SAC) and the North American Air Defense Command (NORAD), in control of American strategic nuclear forces. SAC tested its systems, shortened the reaction time for command aircraft on ground alert, tightened security around bases and command centers and increased the readiness to deploy reconnaissance aircraft. B-52 bombers and aerial refueling tankers were dispersed to secondary airfields and ordered to begin nonroutine operations, marginal changes were made in the status of ICBMs, and European-based nuclear missile firing submarines were flushed from port.[126] All routine training missions were canceled, the command and control network was tested, and additional command and control aircraft were sent aloft. The airborne command post of the commander-in-chief of the Supreme Air Command was also placed on enhanced ground alert.

At 12:20 A.M. on 25 October, American intelligence reported that eight Soviet Antonov-22 transport planes were scheduled to fly from Budapest to Egypt within the next few hours and that elements of the East German armed forces had been alerted. In response, the Eighty-Second Airborne Division was ordered to be ready to deploy within four hours. At 12:25 A.M., the aircraft carrier *Franklin Delano Roosevelt* was sent to the eastern Mediterranean and *John F. Kennedy*, with its task force, was ordered to move at full speed from the Atlantic to the Mediterranean.[127]

Those who participated in the meeting in the White House Situation Room on the night of 24 October were divided in their estimate of Soviet intentions. Some thought the Soviet Union was bluffing, whereas others thought that Moscow would send a limited number of forces to Egypt. Brezhnev's letter and the intelligence data on Soviet military preparations were consistent with both a bluff and a serious intention to deploy forces in the Middle East. In the meeting that night, William Colby emphasized two important pieces of intelligence that suggested that the Soviet Union was preparing to intervene:

> The Soviet airborne divisions were suiting up, putting on packs and were ready to move. Second, we lost the Soviet air transport command for twelve hours. That scared the hell out of me. We couldn't find them anywhere on our screens. I was on the phone to our people at the NSA, asking "what have you got?" We were really worried about where they were. They were off our screens in an abnormal way. That was the key. We only found them the next day.
>
> These indicators were consistent with Brezhnev's letter. Therefore, my estimate was that it looks like they're preparing to move. We had to deal with that contingency. The indicators, and Brezhnev's letter, were certainly consistent with the preparation to move. It was the combination of the two.[128]

President Nixon, who did not participate in any of the discussions, charged after the fact that the intelligence indicated "that the Soviet Union was planning to send a very substantial force into the Middle East, a military force."[129]

Kissinger was more equivocal in his estimate of Soviet intentions, but he did think that Moscow would send limited forces to Egypt. After receiving Brezhnev's message from Dobrynin, Kissinger called Haig in the president's personal quarters.

> KISSINGER: I just had a letter from Brezhnev asking us to send forces in together or he will send them in alone.
> HAIG: I was afraid of that.
> KISSINGER: I think we have to go to the mat on this one . . .
> HAIG: Where are the Israelis at this point?
> KISSINGER: They've got the Third Army surrounded.
> HAIG: I think they [the Soviets] are playing chicken. They're not going to put forces in at the end of a war. I don't believe that.
> KISSINGER: I don't know. What's going to stop them from flying paratroops in?[130]

Later that night, Haig reportedly changed his mind and considered it likely that the Soviet Union would intervene.[131]

In his memoirs, Kissinger describes the discussion of Soviet motives that took place in the Situation Room that night:

> There were three possibilities: (1) The Soviets had intended this move all along and had invited me to Moscow to gain time for it; (2) they decided on it as the consequences of the Arab defeat began to sink in; or (3) they felt tricked by Israel and by us as the Israelis moved to strangle the Third Army after the cease-fire. I thought that the likely motivation was a combination of 2 and 3 . . . [T]he consensus emerged that the Kremlin was on the verge of a major decision. We expected the airlift to start at dawn in eastern Europe, about two hours away.[132]

The secretary was more explicit when asked directly about his estimate of Soviet intentions that night. "I attached a very high probability to Soviet intervention. Dobrynin's comment to me, 'I will report your message,' was very threatening. He didn't say, as he usually did, 'Come on, Henry, don't worry.' It was serious. I thought Soviet intervention was very likely."[133] Adm. Moorer pointed out that if the Soviet Union were going to deploy forces, it would do so within the next few hours.

Secretary of Defense James Schlesinger was far less certain that Moscow would send forces. He thought that the possibility of Soviet forces "being en route" was low.[134] Others speculated as well that the Soviet Union was bluffing. William Quandt, on the staff of the National Security Council, shared this estimate: "We did not believe that the Soviet Union intended to send troops. At most, we attached a five percent probability [to Soviet military intervention]. We felt that Brezhnev was being pig-headed and we wanted to teach him a lesson. We did not act on the basis of perceived intent. We decided to end Brezhnev's bluffing."[135]

Those in the Situation Room that night also considered that Washington had tried repeatedly since the war began to deter Moscow from any kind of military intervention. As early as 12 October, when Dobrynin emphasized that the Soviet Union could not remain indifferent to a threat to Damascus, Kissinger warned that "any Soviet military intervention would be resisted and wreck the entire fabric of U.S.-Soviet relations."[136] Later that same day, he warned Dobrynin again that any Soviet military intervention, regardless of pretext, would be met by American force.[137] "Kissinger had repeatedly explained to Dobrynin that we would not tolerate a joint Soviet-American intervention," William Quandt explained. "We did not want that kind of precedent. Brezhnev did not seem to understand."[138] The task was the education of Brezhnev. Only through a firm and resolute response could the United States teach Brezhnev a lesson.

No one at the meeting that night took Brezhnev's offer of joint intervention seriously. "We were not prepared to send American troops to Egypt, nor would we accept the dispatch of Soviet forces," Kissinger explained. "We had not worked for years to reduce the Soviet military presence in Egypt only to cooperate in reintroducing it as the result of a UN resolution. Nor would we participate in a joint force with the Soviets, which would legitimize their role in the area and strengthen radical elements. . . . Joint intervention was totally unacceptable to me."[139]

Although Kissinger had worked for years to expel Soviet forces from the Middle East, the expulsion of Soviet personnel from Egypt was as fortuitous as it was unexpected. President Sadat asked Soviet personnel to leave on his own initiative, for his own reasons, and to the great surprise of the Nixon administration.[140] Kissinger's determination to deny the Soviet Union the political influence associated with a military presence was consistent with his larger attempt to establish a political monopoly in the postwar diplomatic process. The United States, not the Soviet Union, was seeking diplomatic advantage.

There was considerable divergence of opinion on Soviet intentions on the night of 24 October. Some thought that Brezhnev was bluffing, whereas others thought that the Soviet Union might well send paratroopers to Egypt. These differences were not important to the choice of the appropriate response. Those who thought that the Soviet Union might deploy a limited number of forces were determined to deny the Soviet Union political and military opportunity in the Middle East. Those who thought that the Soviet Union was bluffing also accepted the necessity of an alert. James Schlesinger, Thomas Moorer, and Alexander Haig agreed with Kissinger that an alert was the appropriate response to Brezhnev's challenge. Schlesinger argued that even if the probability of Soviet military action were low, the United States must demonstrate that it could act firmly.[141]

Kissinger summarized the reasons for the choice of an alert: "I did not see it [the Soviet threat] as a bluff, *but it made no difference*. We could not run the risk that they were not [bluffing]. If we remained passive in the face of the threat, the Soviet leadership would see no obstacle to turning it into a reality. We had no choice except to call the bluff, if that was what it was, or face the reality if it was serious."[142] In Kissinger's words, "a leader known to yield to intimidation invites it."[143] Irrespective of their analysis of Soviet intent, American leaders concurred that the United States had been challenged and had no choice but to respond.

The alert had two purposes. If the Soviet Union had indeed decided to send forces to Egypt, its immediate objective was to deter the Soviet deployment. The Nixon administration was determined to deny Moscow the opportunity to introduce military forces into the Middle East. The alert was also designed to bank resolve and build reputation for the future. If Brezhnev was bluffing, the alert would "educate" the Soviet leadership. It was imperative to demonstrate resolve to convince Brezhnev that the United States could not to be coerced by Moscow. Washington wanted to demonstrate resolve firmly, visibly, and quickly. Everyone present agreed quickly on the necessity of an immediate, highly visible response that would be noticed rapidly by Soviet leaders and would either "shock" them into abandoning any intention to intervene with military force or would call their bluff.[144]

Several hours later, Kissinger, in Nixon's name, formally replied to Brezhnev. He deliberately delayed several hours in answering Brezhnev's letter to give Soviet leaders time to pick up signals of the alert. On 25 October at 5:40 A.M. Washington time, the reply to Brezhnev was delivered to Dobrynin. Kissinger first warned that "we must view your suggestion of unilateral action as a matter of gravest concern. . . . You must know that we could in no event accept unilateral action. . . . Such action would produce incalculable consequences which would be in the interest of neither of our countries and which would end all we have striven so hard to achieve."

Kissinger assured Brezhnev that, to the best of his knowledge, the ceasefire was holding and then invoked the agreements that the two countries had reached in the past. "I agree with you that our understanding to act jointly for peace is one of the highest value and that we should implement that understanding in this complex situation. . . . Mr. General Secretary, in the spirit of our agreements this is the time not for acting unilaterally, but in harmony and with cool heads."

The letter concluded with a face-saving proposal to the Soviet leader. "The United States approves and is willing to participate in an expanded United Nations truce supervisory force composed of noncombat personnel. It would be understood that this is an extraordinary and temporary action solely for the purpose of providing adequate information concerning compliance by both sides with the terms of the cease-fire."[145] With American forces on worldwide alert, Nixon and Kissinger then waited to see if the alert and the warning to Brezhnev had accomplished their purposes.

THE ILLOGIC OF THE ALERT

We evaluate the success of the alert as a deterrent in the next chapter when we look at the Soviet reaction. In the remainder of this chapter, we examine the logic of the choice of a worldwide alert given American objectives. Like the Soviet strategy of graduated compellence, it was equally ill-conceived.

The worldwide alert ordered the night of 24 October was a singularly inappropriate instrument of crisis management. It was ineffective, potentially dangerous, and ill-considered. The worldwide alert was inherently ineffective because, in the context of the Middle East, it did not signal a credible threat. It was potentially dangerous because it moved up the ladder of escalation and increased the risk of confrontation with the Soviet Union. Even more alarming, American leaders made their decision with little attention to its details, its risks, or its likely consequences. The leaders who made the decision did not understand the technical and operational requirements of the alert. It was chosen in haste, with little consideration either of its capacity to deter Soviet military intervention or of the alternative measures that might have constituted an effective signal with a reduced risk of escalation.

The obvious incredibility of a worldwide alert of American forces as a deterrent of Soviet intervention in the Middle East should have been apparent to American leaders. For it to work, Soviet leaders would have had to believe that the United States was prepared to risk a nuclear war to prevent a limited deployment of Soviet forces. The threat was so obviously out of proportion to the provocation that it was unlikely to be credible in Moscow. One strategic analyst pointedly observed: "In large part, a worldwide alert suffers from the same limitations that afflicted the strategic doctrine of massive retaliation. A universal alert offers the threat of an overwhelming retaliatory blow as a means of deterring an opponent. At best such an alert lacks credibility; at worst it is an irresponsible means of nuclear diplomacy."[146]

The credibility of the worldwide alert was further undermined by the fact that the United States and the Soviet Union were engaged in continuing negotiations to stabilize the cease-fire. As we shall see in the next chapter, Soviet leaders found the alert so incredible that it was incomprehensible to them. They considered it an irresponsible act in the nuclear age.

Even senior military personnel in the United States did not treat the alert as a serious prelude to possible military action. Because there was little expectation of combat, the strategic alert was ordered at a low level by the Joint Chiefs and executed in a perfunctory way by the military commanders.[147] After receiving orders for DEFCON III, the Joint Chiefs immediately began eliminating items from the standard checklist.[148] Adm. Moorer followed up the DEFCON III order with a secure telephone call to the unified and specified commanders to explain the purely political purpose of the alert.[149] At 3:37 A.M., he sent an second message that again emphasized the political context of the alert.[150]

Kissinger thought that the principal advantage of a DEFCON III alert was its visibility to the Soviet Union.[151] The alert would be recognized very quickly by Soviet intelligence because of the noticeable changes in the pattern and intensification of military communications. A worldwide alert would rise significantly above the existing noise level.[152] Almost within the hour, however, American officials decided that the alert would not be detected quickly enough and ordered some of their conventional forces to DEFCON II. Their reasoning defies understanding: if an alert of a restricted number of conventional forces would be detected more quickly in Moscow, then the alert of strategic forces was unnecessary and possibly provocative.

At their meeting that night in the White House, there was no discussion of an alert of conventional forces as an *alternative* to a combined alert of strategic and conventional forces.[153] William Quandt reports that officials did not make this kind of distinction. "We did not think in terms of a nuclear or a conventional alert. Standard operating procedures did not tailor the decision to distinguish between the alert of conventional and nuclear forces. We thought only in terms of increasing the readiness of our forces as a signal to the Soviet Union."[154]

An alert of specific conventional forces would have been more credible. If the Soviet Union had sent troops to Egypt, the United States would have responded with conventional forces. The United States could have ordered, as it ultimately did, the Eighty-Second Airborne Division to prepare for overseas deployment and could even have broadcast the orders *en clair*. It could also have brought several of its divisions in Europe to a higher state of readiness. Alternatively, Washington could have ordered a worldwide alert but exempted all strategic forces.[155] Any of these options would have been more credible to Soviet leaders while at the same time reducing the risk of provocation and possible escalation.

Some strategic analysts have argued that a conventional alert would not have been noticed quickly enough nor would it have been sufficiently credible.[156] As a result of the war in the Middle East, the Sixth Fleet was already at DEFCON II; when Vice Adm. Daniel Murphy received the orders for DEFCON III, he asked whether he should stand down the level of alert of his forces.[157] American aircraft were also actively involved in the airlift to Israel. In this context, it would have taken time for Moscow to notice the increased readiness of limited conventional forces. Soviet leaders also might not have considered the threat of a conventional deployment a credible deterrent.

These arguments are not persuasive. The same analysts who allege that a limited conventional alert would have been insufficient then conclude that it was the conventional component that lent credibility to the strategic alert.[158] Kissinger too admitted afterward that a selective alert of certain units might have been more effective than the worldwide DEFCON III that was chosen.[159]

Some analysts have speculated that the United States moved to a strategic alert because it worried about the conventional balance of forces, particularly at sea. Adm. Elmo Zumwalt reports that at the White House meeting at which the alert was ordered, Adm. Moorer argued that in naval combat between the United States and the Soviet Union in the eastern Mediterranean, "we would lose our ass."[160]

Kissinger denied that American officials felt that their naval strength in the Mediterranean was inferior to that of the Soviet Union. "I have seen statements that in 1973, the United States was affected in the conduct of the Middle East crisis by its fear of the Soviet navy. This may have been true of our Navy; it wasn't true of our government." At the time, he admitted, "We all suffered from the illusion that our navy was far superior to the Soviet navy, and we conducted ourselves accordingly."[161] For Kissinger at least, concern about naval inferiority played no role in the decision to order the DEFCON III alert.

The balance of naval forces in October 1973 in the eastern Mediterranean did not in fact strongly favor either the United States or the Soviet Union.[162] Late on 24 October, a Soviet helicopter carrier and two destroyers left their positions off Crete and relieved the anticarrier group covering *Independence*, the American naval forces nearest the war zone.[163] That same night, the Sixth Fleet quickly positioned itself to threaten the air routes a Soviet expeditionary force was likely to use.[164] The significant change in the deployment of the Soviet navy occurred after, not before, the alert.[165]

There is another possibility to consider. Even if the deliberate threat to escalate to nuclear war was inherently incredible, American leaders might still have expected that they could deter Soviet intervention as a consequence of the uncertainty created by the alert. Soviet leaders might have worried that the introduction of conventional forces in the Middle East in the context of a DEFCON III alert could have unanticipated escalatory consequences.

Thomas Schelling describes this kind of strategy as a "threat that leaves something to chance."[166] This is the strongest possible argument that can be made in favor of the alert. Strategic alerts designed to manipulate the risk of war trade off the political advantage they might bring against the risk of loss of control. For it to work, American leaders needed to convince Brezhnev that the nuclear alert made it more likely that the crisis might inadvertently spin out of control.[167]

There is no evidence that American leaders themselves thought about the alert as a deliberate manipulation of the risk of war. Kissinger and Schlesinger did not design the alert as a "threat that leaves something to chance." From the perspective of those who chose to go to DEFCON III, the alert was a straightforward attempt to deter and to bank resolve by a quick, clean, visible escalation up the nuclear ladder.

Finally, some of those who chose the alert did not fully understand its technical details. William Colby explained that "We considered the DEFCON III a minor signal. SAC was already on III, as was the navy. SAC did go up to DEFCON II, when everyone else went up a notch. The rest of the world went to III and SAC went to II."[168] In reality, SAC did not go up to DEFCON II. If it had, it would not have been, as Colby contends, "a minor signal."

Kissinger too did not completely understand the technical details of the alert. In his memoirs, Kissinger compared the DEFCON III alert to the selective alert of American forces during the Black September crisis of 1970 "when we had gone through similar alert measures."[169] The analogy is incorrect.[170] The alert of September 1970, ordered during a confrontation between Jordan and Syria, was not a worldwide alert but a selective and limited alert of airborne troops and naval forces in the Mediterranean.[171] No strategic forces whatsoever were involved in the alert.

Since Kissinger had been one of the principal architects of the alert in 1970, it is difficult to understand how he could draw an analogy between two alerts that differed so substantially in degree and in kind.[172] When asked directly about the comparison, he responded: "It was the same alert as in 1970. It was technically the same. It wasn't a nuclear alert because most forces were at Stage 3 anyway. The strategic forces didn't have to be alerted; they were already at Stage 3. In this alert too, it was principally our airborne forces and conventional forces that were alerted."[173]

Kissinger's understanding of the technical implications of the alert is not correct. Peter Rodman noted that at the meeting on 24 October, "The nuclear component of the alert was not the focus of the discussion."[174] In large part because the "nuclear component" was not discussed, William Quandt concluded, "Kissinger simply did not understand that DEFCON III would alert our forces on a worldwide basis, including our nuclear forces."[175]

Kissinger also did not expect the DEFCON III alert to become public. It was designed to be picked up quickly by Soviet intelligence, but not to increase the pressure on Soviet leaders by making the costs of retreat more painful and humiliating. Kissinger expected that it would become public knowledge only gradually. As he left the meeting in the Situation Room at the White House on 24 October, he warned Adm. Moorer, "You will keep this secret. Not a word of this is to leak." The Chairman of the Joint Chiefs responded, "Of course, Henry." Schlesinger, however, rolled his eyes.[176]

Kissinger discovered to his horror that the alert had become public within a matter of hours.

> At 6:30 A.M. Thursday morning, October 25—after three hours of sleep—I discovered that the American public had already learned of the worldwide alert of American forces. It was all over the morning news. I was shocked. This unexpected publicity would inevitably turn the event into an issue of prestige with Moscow, unleashing popular passions at home and seriously complicating the prospects of a Soviet retreat. It also showed the change in the discipline of our government in the three years since the Jordan crisis of September 1970. Then we had gone through similar alert measures; their extent had not become known until the crisis was already over, three days later. The current alert had leaked within three hours in the middle of the night; we would now have a *public* confrontation, and not with a Soviet surrogate as in 1970, but with the Kremlin itself.[177]

Although the orders for the alert requested "minimum public notice," it was obvious to some of the participants in the meeting in the Situation Room that an alert of that kind and magnitude simply could not be implemented in secrecy. "There is no way," Schlesinger said, "you can put more than two million soldiers and reservists suddenly on alert and make sure nobody else finds out about it."[178] When asked why he was not told by Schlesinger and Moorer at the meeting that the alert would quickly become public, Kissinger responded: "Schlesinger and Moorer knew that it would leak, because they leaked it. I knew that it would become public, but not that quickly."[179]

There is no evidence that the alert was deliberately made public by any senior official. William Colby doubted very seriously that Schlesinger and Moorer leaked the alert. "They are professionals. They would not play Machiavelli."[180] The alert was picked up by the press almost immediately when an airman was speeding to his base and was stopped by a traffic officer. When asked by the officer why he was speeding, he replied: "I'm going to a nuclear alert." "Now I've heard everything," responded the policeman. "Okay, call my base," answered the airman. The officer did, the base confirmed the alert, the airman sped off, and the policeman called the local radio station.[181]

None of the participants in the meeting that night who knew that a DEFCON III alert would quickly become public informed Kissinger. Their reticence seems to have been motivated by two concerns. Some senior military officials favored a DEFCON III alert because it would become known quickly and appear dramatic. Adm. Moorer felt that it was essential that Soviet leaders get the message quickly and publicly.[182] Some who favored the alert chose to keep quiet in the expectation that if Kissinger were told how quickly an alert would become public, it was less likely that he would choose to alert American forces worldwide.[183] Other Pentagon officials wanted to use the opportunity provided by a strategic alert to bring back the B-52 bombers based in Guam, a request long resisted by the State Department.[184] They too had no wish to raise any obstacles to the alert. Consequently, Kissinger chose an alert in the expectation that it would signal American resolve dramatically but privately to Soviet leaders on the verge of a critical decision.[185]

The decision demonstrated a troubling lack of understanding of the technical and operational requirements of the military procedures chosen to signal commitment and resolve. It is disturbing to consider that an alert of strategic forces can be ordered in the absence of a president who was incapacitated by the stress of a domestic crisis and by some of his most senior advisors who did not fully understand the technical and operational implications of what they were doing.

Most alarming of all, Kissinger and Schlesinger did not consider the potential escalatory consequences of a DEFCON III alert. Peter Rodman explained: "The Soviets had the fear of war in their bones. With them, there is no point in matching tit-for-tat. You deliberately overwhelm them to discourage escalation. We were sure that it would work. I never thought for a moment that things would get out of control."[186] In their one-hour discussion that night in the White House, American officials never considered what they would do if the Soviet Union were not deterred and Moscow sent troops to Egypt. Kissinger, Schlesinger, and their advisors did not consider what kind of military confrontation and at what level, might follow if the Soviet Union went ahead and deployed troops in Egypt.[187]

The decision to go to a DEFCON III alert left the United States with very few options to escalate up the nuclear ladder if deterrence failed and the Soviet Union went ahead and deployed troops. A move to DEFCON II, an alert designed for the contingency of a likely attack, would have been extraordinarily provocative.[188] It would also have been inappropriate because no American leader anticipated nuclear war with the Soviet Union over the Middle East. Escalation up the nuclear ladder would have served neither deterrent nor defensive purposes; it would have done nothing to deal with the challenge posed by Soviet troops en route to or already deployed in Egypt.

The most likely response to the failure of deterrence would have been a conventional military response. When the United States was faced with the possibility that the nuclear alert might not deter the deployment of Soviet troops, Kissinger searched desperately for an appropriate conventional option. A few hours after the decision to go to DEFCON III was made, the United States received unconfirmed intelligence that the first contingent of Soviet troops was on its way. In his memoirs, Kissinger says only that this report triggered discussion about whether the United States would be able to put its own troops in the area.[189] In fact, Kissinger began a frantic search for a conventional military option.

William Quandt provides a detailed—and vivid—description of the reaction in the White House:

> Later that night, we got a fragment of a message, the tail end of a message, suggesting the imminent arrival of Soviet forces at Cairo West airfield. Kissinger was frantic. He ordered Atherton and me to draft a plan to send American troops to the Middle East, immediately, but not to Israel. Atherton and I were bewildered. Where would the forces go? Kissinger replied that he did not know, but that the forces could not go to Israel, but that a plan was to be prepared immediately to deploy forces in the Middle East. This was the only time that Atherton and I were totally confused. We could not conceive of how to meet the request. As it turns out, the fragmented message referred to the Soviet observers who were being flown to Cairo West airfield.[190]

Early the next morning, after he briefed the president, Kissinger recalls, "Nixon was determined to match any Soviet troop buildup in the area."[191] When asked what kind of conventional military action he wanted, Kissinger replied: "We would have put down the 82nd Airborne if the Soviets had sent forces. We never got to that point. We never discussed it. It would have been very dangerous. That's why you get paid, for doing the dangerous jobs."[192] The possibility of deterrence failure received no serious attention, and no contingency plans were in place. There was no discussion of where American troops were to be deployed and the likelihood of combat with Soviet forces. "We had no plan for blocking [Soviet] intervention," Rodman confirmed. "We didn't think about it."[193] Instead of considering the consequences and their options should deterrence fail, American leaders hoped that deterrence would succeed.

If the Soviet Union had sent forces to Egypt and the United States had responded with a conventional deployment of its own, even limited encounters between the two forces in the context of a worldwide alert of American forces could easily have led to a broadening of the conflict. The Soviet Union might have mobilized additional forces in response. In this context, the worldwide alert could have worked against the localization and termination of the fighting in the Middle East, the principal objective of both Moscow and Washington.

Our evaluation of the American decision to alert its strategic as well as conventional forces worldwide is sobering. As we see in the next chapter, it was not effective in educating Soviet leaders in the way American leaders expected. It also did nothing to address the most likely contingency the United States confronted, a limited deployment of Soviet forces in Egypt. The strategic component of the alert as a deterrent was incredible on its own terms and was potentially dangerous. It met none of the central purposes of the United States. At best, it made logical sense only as a strategy to manipulate the risk of war, but leaders did not design their strategy that way at the time. Most alarming, some of those who met in the White House Situation Room did not completely understand the technical consequences of their choice and did not consider the political and military consequences if their strategy failed.

THE FAILURE TO AVOID CONFRONTATION

The United States and the Soviet Union entered the period of crisis with a jointly engineered agreement to end the fighting and a shared tactical objective. The prerequisites for effective crisis management were in place, but they were insufficient to avoid a confrontation. Some analysts have explained the confrontation that occurred at the end of the October War as entrapment of the superpowers by their allies. Like the great powers in 1914, Moscow and Washington were unwillingly dragged to the brink by the behavior of their allies who were fighting a bitter war. Certainly the war among their allies was a precipitating factor, but it was neither the only nor the primary cause of the crisis that occurred on the night of 24 October.

Our analysis demonstrates that the strategies of crisis management of both the United States and the Soviet Union were deeply flawed. They were ineffective, dangerous, and ill-considered. More fundamentally, these strategies were shaped by the competitive political goals of the United States and the Soviet Union. It was the exploitation of the Arab-Israel conflict as an arena to seek relative gain or avoid relative loss that contributed significantly to the failure to prevent a confrontation.

After the cease-fire agreement was negotiated in Moscow, the Soviet Union was the status quo power. Soviet leaders wanted primarily to avoid a loss and tried above all to make sure that the fighting stopped before Egypt suffered a military defeat and the reputation of the Soviet Union as a reliable ally was compromised. Brezhnev only threatened that the Soviet Union would consider sending military forces when a catastrophic Egyptian military defeat seemed imminent. Despite concern about escalation, Brezhnev saw no alternative once diplomacy had failed. As a status quo power trying to avoid relative loss, the Soviet Union resorted to compellence only after all the less threatening alternatives had been exhausted.

The Soviet dilemma was unenviable, and Moscow had very little room for maneuver. As Washington well understood, Soviet leaders could not stand by and watch as Egyptian armies were trapped. Yet, by the time Brezhnev resorted to a strategy of graduated compellence, his threat was unnecessary and irrelevant. The fighting had already stopped, and the threat to send troops to Egypt did nothing to address the urgent plight of the trapped Third Army. The Soviet strategy of crisis management lagged badly behind the pace of the battlefield.

Soviet strategy was driven not only by a sense of threat and urgency but also by anger at Kissinger's deceit and betrayal. Here Brezhnev overreacted.

Brezhnev was not correct in suspecting that Kissinger had purposely encouraged Israel to continue its offensive; his charge of deliberate deception does not stand up to the evidence.[194] Brezhnev badly underestimated the real difficulties the United States experienced in restraining its ally and interpreted Israel's actions as deliberately orchestrated with American acquiescence if not active cooperation. Just as Kennedy and his advisors saw Soviet actions on the last day of the Cuban missile crisis as intentional, so Brezhnev saw American action as deliberate and underestimated the difficulties of political control of an ally on the battlefield. It is surprising that he did so, given the acute difficulty Soviet leaders had experienced in controlling Egypt before, during, and at the end of the war.

If Brezhnev had been less angry and more accurate in his estimate of the difficulties inherent in controlling an ally, even under pressure he might have refrained from adding the last threatening sentence to his letter to Nixon. In part because Brezhnev was angry and under stress, he miscalculated the short- and long-term consequences of a strategy of bluff for the Soviet relationship with the United States.

The United States had far greater opportunities to manage the crisis effectively. It did not use them. Before and during the crisis, American leaders pursued a forward diplomatic strategy as they attempted to upset the status quo and detach Egypt from the Soviet Union. These political objectives led Kissinger to exaggerate American capacity to fine-tune diplomatic strategy to battlefield conditions. Although problems of technical and political control were serious, Kissinger's underestimation of their gravity led to misleading signals to Jerusalem and inadequate messages to Cairo and Moscow. In the thirty-six hours that elapsed between the violation of the first cease-fire and the receipt of Brezhnev's letter, the United States succeeded in compelling Israel to stop the fighting. The critical flaw in American management of the crisis was the failure to reassure Moscow and Cairo.

Finally, the decision in Washington to alert forces worldwide was made in the context of a deeply held belief in deterrence as a strategy of crisis management and the consequent importance of reputation and resolve. It is only understandable in this context. Yet the alert was incredible because it was so disproportionate to the action it was designed to prevent and anomalous in the context of ongoing negotiations with the Soviet Union, ineffective in its failure to address the problems that would be created by a limited deployment of Soviet troops in Egypt, ill-considered, and potentially dangerous in its potential for escalation.

Our analysis of crisis management by the Soviet Union and the United States demonstrates that both Moscow and Washington lost technical control of their strategies. The pace of the battlefield in the Middle East outstripped their capacity to design timely strategies of crisis management. In Washington, some leaders did not fully understand the technical and operational implications of the decisions they made. Although technical and operational problems contributed to the failure to prevent a confrontation, they were not, however, the critical factors. The difficulties inherent in controlling allies who exercised significant political autonomy were also real but not sufficient to explain the confrontation at the end of the war. Before the confrontation began on the night of 24 October, both Moscow and Washington had their allies under some semblance of control.

An important contributing factor was the anger and stress that shaped the context of crisis decisions. Critical decisions were made in anger in Moscow and under stress in Washington that contributed significantly to miscalculation in both capitals. We have already noted the impact of Brezhnev's intense anger. William Quandt recalls the atmosphere on the night of 24 October in the White House: "We were under considerable pressure. We felt there was some urgency, and we were tired, fatigued that night."[195] This was the context of the most serious Soviet-American confrontation since the Cuban missile crisis in 1962.

Beyond the immediate factors of technical complexities, serious problems in political control, and emotional stress, was the political competition that shaped the objectives of both sets of leaders. The failure of the superpowers to prevent the war, to limit its intensity, and to enforce the first cease-fire, was very much a function of their exploitation of the conflict in the Middle East to make gains or avoid losses at each other's expense. The United States and the Soviet Union were not entrapped by their allies but exploited the conflict between the Arabs and Israel as a theater to seek unilateral advantage.

After their meeting in Moscow, however, the United States and the Soviet Union were agreed on the terms to end the war. Ironically, Brezhnev and Nixon, though not Kissinger, were also agreed on the political necessity of an imposed peace. Whether or not a jointly sponsored settlement of the Arab-Israel conflict would have worked is a matter for speculation. Kissinger argued that this kind of strategy would have made control of Israel even more difficult, and he was in all likelihood correct. What is clear, however, is that, even as the cease-fire was being negotiated, Kissinger continued to seek unilateral gain at the expense of the Soviet Union.

After the cease-fire was jointly negotiated, Brezhnev attempted to preserve a shaky political investment in the Arab world and his personal investment in détente. Kissinger worked to upset the status quo not only before the crisis began but during the management of the crisis itself. Once an Egyptian military defeat became imminent, the principal responsibility for crisis management rested with the United States. The exploitation of the Arab-Israel conflict as an arena to seek American gains directly at Soviet expense contributed significantly to the failure to prevent a confrontation between the two superpowers. The failure of crisis management was not narrowly technical but broadly political.

The Crisis and Its Resolution

[T]he Soviets subsided as soon as we showed our teeth. We were thus able to use the crisis to shape events and reverse alliances in the Middle East in defiance of the pressures of our allies, the preferences of the Soviets, and the rhetoric of Arab radicals.

—Henry Kissinger [1]

The American alert was for home consumption. That doesn't mean that it wasn't dangerous, even if the alert was over a false issue. If you use it frivolously several times, nobody takes it seriously afterward. This is very typical of Americans.

—Georgi Arbatov [2]

THE CRISIS in 1973 had many of the classic hallmarks of an escalatory spiral. Israel had refused to stop the advance of its armies when they were on the verge of defeating Egypt. The Soviet Union threatened to consider unilateral action to enforce the cease-fire and, in response, the United States alerted its forces worldwide. These actions provoked a crisis between the superpowers. The crisis was resolved, however, without further escalation. The Soviet Union decided on the morning of 25 October not to respond with military measures to the American alert and thereby stopped the process of escalation. Officials of the Nixon administration insisted that the crisis did not escalate because the Soviet Union backed down in the face of the world-wide alert. We contend that American deterrence was irrelevant. We examine first why the crisis did not escalate further.

The crisis was resolved very quickly when Egypt and Israel observed the cease-fire and Egypt, the United States, and the Soviet Union agreed that a United Nations' peacekeeping force would police the cease-fire. The United States ended its alert at midnight on 25 October. One plausible explanation of why the crisis was resolved is Soviet compellence; the threat to consider unilateral action may have resolved the crisis by convincing the United States to restrain Israel. We argue that Soviet compellence was counterproductive. The crisis was resolved despite the threats and actions of both sides. In the second part of the chapter, we examine why the crisis was resolved.

Although the crisis ended without further escalation, the way it was resolved had damaging consequences for Soviet-American relations in the decade that followed. In many ways, it marked the beginning of the end of détente and the renewal of superpower tensions that reached a crescendo in the next decade. The conclusion to the chapter examines the lessons leaders did and did not learn from the crisis and their long-term impact on the relationship between the United States and the Soviet Union.

THE MILITARY CONTEXT

The worldwide alert of American forces in 1973 took place in a strategic environment that was very different from that of 1962. The force structures and military deployments of the United States and the Soviet Union in 1973 were far more evenly balanced. At the time of the Cuban missile crisis, the United States had overwhelming nuclear superiority. By 1973, the strategic balance was nearly symmetrical; Moscow had deployed its large and much more accurate third generation of ICBMs and its pronounced inferiority had disappeared. In all probability, enough Soviet nuclear submarines would have survived an American first strike to retaliate with a devastating attack.

During the Cuban missile crisis, strategic systems on both sides were also less tightly coupled and less potent. Strategic delivery systems, mostly bombers, were slow and recallable. Eleven years later, the nuclear missiles of both superpowers were capable of reaching their targets within minutes rather than hours. They were also less tolerant of error, because missiles, unlike bombers, could not be recalled. The command and control systems of both superpowers had become more complex, but they were vulnerable to quick decapitation by more sophisticated and accurate attacking forces.[3] In other ways, the strategic environment was safer than it had been in 1962. All American nuclear weapons, except those on submarines, were equipped with permissive action links to prevent unauthorized use and, most important, the second-strike capability of Soviet strategic forces significantly reduced the incentive for either side to preempt.

Escalation through technical loss of control of complex and tightly coupled strategic systems was more likely than in 1962. Military escalation could provoke counterescalation, and even minor steps up the ladder could trigger an escalatory spiral that could culminate in a war that neither side intended, wanted, or could win.[4] Escalation could also occur because leaders felt freer to make threats in the context of strategic parity. The relatively even strategic balance could encourage either government to believe that it was reasonably safe to use military alerts for political purposes because superpower war was unthinkable. Had the Soviet Union chosen to alert its strategic forces in response to the American alert, there was the possibility of further escalation up the nuclear ladder between tightly coupled forces.

The local military balance was also far more symmetrical in 1973 than it had been in 1962. During the Cuban missile crisis, the United States had overwhelming conventional superiority in the Caribbean. In 1973, both sides had impressive military capabilities in the Middle East. Moscow had developed its force projection capabilities in the aftermath of the Cuban missile crisis. In October 1973, using its air- and sealift capabilities, it could have sent at least five-thousand troops a day to Egypt. The Soviet Union also had impressive naval forces in the eastern Mediterranean that, although not the equal of the United States, could have inflicted substantial damage in any naval encounter.[5]

In October 1973, the United States was capable of extensive conventional operations in the Middle East. For the first time in almost a decade, its forces were no longer heavily committed in Vietnam. It could have transferred a substantial number of troops from Western Europe and the United States to the Middle East without stretching its forces too thin. A battalion of the Eighty-Second Airborne Division, placed on ready-to-move status on the night of 24 October, could have been airlifted to the Middle East within twenty-four hours, and the whole division could have been brought over within three weeks.

Confrontation among conventional forces on the ground was a possibility. If the Soviet Union had moved forces to Egypt, it is conceivable that Israel could have chosen to harass or interdict the transport aircraft, which would have had to fly beyond the range of fighter cover. An engagement was also possible between the Israel Defense Forces and Soviet troops; Brezhnev worried about precisely such a confrontation.[6] If Soviet troops had been deployed, Kissinger, despite his recognition of the danger of escalation, was prepared to order the deployment of units of the Eighty-Second Airborne Division.[7] Had American troops been introduced anywhere close to the theater of combat, Soviet-American incidents could have occurred and increased the pressure for further escalation.[8]

Particularly dangerous was the situation at sea, where the two navies were trailing each other closely in the Mediterranean. The possibility of an accidental or preemptive encounter at sea was real. In recognition of this danger, Moscow and Washington had signed the Incidents at Sea Agreement in 1972 to reduce the likelihood of confrontation between their naval forces.[9]

Until 24 October, the United States attempted to avoid provocative deployments that could be misread in Moscow. For this purpose, the positioning and movements of the Sixth Fleet were closely controlled from Washington. Throughout the war, Washington kept the Sixth Fleet clear of the war zones in the Mediterranean declared by Egypt and Syria.[10] The Soviet Union conducted significant naval operations in the war zones in conjunction with its air- and sealifts to Egypt and Syria.

During the course of the war, the navies of the two superpowers became very tightly coupled. Soviet "tattletales" closely shadowed American ships. They provided near real-time targeting information for Soviet ships, aircraft, and submarines equipped with conventional and nuclear antiship cruise missiles. American commanders knew that their ships were subject to a preemptive attack with virtually no warning time for self-defense.[11] In response, American destroyers and cruisers armed with antiship missiles were authorized to trail Soviet warships. Each navy maneuvered for tactical advantage and tried to be in position to strike first if necessary.

This tight coupling created strong incentives for preemption. Chief of Naval Operations Adm. Elmo R. Zumwalt, Jr. described the dangerous military environment in the Mediterranean:

> All this trailing is an effort to compensate for tactical asymmetries. A carrier outside the range of the cruise missiles on Soviet ships can clearly sink them easily with her aircraft. Therefore, the Russians trail us closely in order to be able to destroy most of a carrier's planes or disable the carrier herself before aircraft can take off. We adopted the retaliatory technique of trailing the trailer so as to prevent them from preventing us from launching our planes by knocking out most of their cruise missiles before many of them took off.[12]

When the United States went to DEFCON III, *Roosevelt* and *Kennedy* were ordered to join *Independence* in the eastern Mediterranean. The three U.S. carriers were positioned directly astride Soviet air- and sea-lanes to Egypt, in position to interdict a deployment of Soviet troops to Egypt. Navy support for the airlift to Israel was suspended, and all but two of the escorts were returned to *Independence* and *Roosevelt* groups.[13] To avoid provocative action, the U.S. carriers were placed in small, fixed operating areas and were consequently extraordinarily vulnerable to a preemptive attack by the Soviet fleet.[14] At the same time, U.S. warships and aircraft constantly targeted the Soviet fleet at point-blank range.[15] In response to the alert and the concentration of the Sixth Fleet in the Mediterranean, Soviet coverage of U.S. carrier and amphibious groups was increased, and on 26 October, the Soviet Navy began intensive anticarrier exercises which lasted through 3 November.[16]

The deployment of the two navies heightened tension among U.S. commanders. Adm. Zumwalt doubted "that major units of the U.S. Navy were ever in a tenser situation since World War II ended than the Sixth Fleet in the Mediterranean was for the week after the alert was declared."[17] The commander of the Sixth Fleet, Vice Adm. Daniel Murphy, echoed his concern. "The U.S. Sixth Fleet and the Soviet Mediterranean Fleet were, in effect, sitting in a pond in close proximity and the stage for the hitherto unlikely 'war at sea' scenario was set."[18]

Soviet commanders were also worried about the consequences of the tight coupling of the two navies and the consequent risk of an incident at sea.[19] Even before the alert, Brezhnev had been concerned about the prospect of an accidental encounter between the two navies and had worried about its esca-latory consequences.[20] Especially in the context of the alert of American forces, Soviet admirals feared that an inadvertent or accidental confronta-tion at sea could provoke a wider confrontation.[21]

High-value targets, powerful incentives to shoot first to avoid being de-stroyed, and tension at the command level are the conditions most condu-cive to preemption and loss of control. If a Soviet or American ship had fired a missile at the other in the mistaken belief that it was about to be attacked, there would have been no time for commanders to request permission to retaliate.[22] American rules of engagement did not require commanders to consult under these conditions. The Soviet rules of engagement are not known, but it is unlikely that Soviet captains would have required approval from above to retaliate when their ships were targeted at point-blank range by U.S. warships and aircraft.[23] The most authoritative analysis of the two navies in the crisis concludes that a single misjudgment could have produced a Soviet-American battle in the Mediterranean.[24]

There are inescapable trade-offs between increasing the credibility of threat-based strategies of crisis management and increasing the risk of war. To make their strategies credible, Minister of Defense Grechko increased the readiness of Soviet paratroopers and Washington alerted its forces world-wide. Yet neither compellence nor deterrence succeeded in accomplishing their objectives. We look first at the impact of these two strategies and then explain why further escalation was avoided and why the crisis was resolved.

THE IRRELEVANCE OF DETERRENCE

"The Soviets subsided," Kissinger claimed, "as soon as we showed our teeth."[25] His argument suggests that despite strategic and conventional par-ity and an acute domestic crisis in Washington, the alert persuaded Soviet leaders that President Nixon was willing to risk war to block unilateral in-tervention by Moscow.[26] Soviet leaders, according to this argument, reeval-uated the likely costs of intervention, changed their minds, and decided not to send troops to Egypt.

This explanation is similar in its essentials to the standard interpretation of the resolution of the Cuban missile crisis. The manipulation of the risk of war through a nuclear alert and preparations to invade Cuba allegedly con-vinced Soviet leaders that they had to withdraw their missiles from Cuba to avoid war. In 1973, there is no evidence to support the efficacy claimed for threat-based strategies.

If deterrence is to work, leaders who are considering military action must change their minds because they reconsider their estimate of its likely costs and consequences in the face of the threat from the deterrer. Even *before* the United States alerted its forces, Brezhnev had no intention of sending Soviet forces to Egypt. As early as 8 October, he instructed Ambassador

Vinogradov to emphasize Soviet determination not to become involved in the fighting.[27] Again on 15 October, during the Politburo meeting, Brezhnev warned Kosygin against misleading Sadat. Although the Soviet government was willing to continue military support to Egypt on a large scale, it would "under no circumstances participate directly in the war."[28] Brezhnev's threat to consider unilateral action was a bluff, issued in frustration at the failure of diplomacy to stop the fighting, and in anger at what Brezhnev considered Kissinger's duplicity. Since Brezhnev had no intention of sending forces, deterrence could not have changed his mind. At best, it was irrelevant.

The consequences of the American attempt to deter were not irrelevant. American leaders expected the alert to signal clearly and unequivocally their opposition to a unilateral Soviet deployment of forces in the Middle East and their willingness to risk war to prevent such a deployment. Soviet leaders were genuinely bewildered by the alert; to them, the American "signal" was not clear and unequivocal. They were also provoked and deeply angered by an action that they could not understand.

Shortly after Soviet intelligence picked up signs of the alert, Brezhnev convened the Politburo early on the morning of 25 October. The meeting was attended by almost all its members and discussion continued for more than eight hours. Gen. Kulikov began with a briefing on the alert of American forces, including strategic nuclear forces.

Members of the Politburo had a great deal of difficulty interpreting the political intent of the alert. "They could not understand it," Israelian explained. "They asked: 'Are they [the Americans] crazy? The Americans say we threaten them, but how did they get this idea?' "[29] Gromyko was advised by Kornienko, Sytenko, and Israelian that the American reaction was provoked by the last sentence of Brezhnev's letter to Nixon.[30] Brezhnev was incredulous when this explanation was suggested at the Politburo meeting. "Could this be the reason?" he asked. "Could Nixon choose an alert based on this one sentence? But this man Nixon knows that I stopped the airlift as a demonstration of my willingness to cooperate."[31]

Soviet officials were divided in their assessments of the causes and purposes of the alert. Brezhnev thought that Nixon had ordered the alert to demonstrate that he was Kennedy, the strong man in a domestic crisis.[32] This interpretation was widely shared by Politburo members. "It seemed to the Politburo," Ambassador Israelian recalled, "that Nixon's decision was determined mainly by domestic politics. In a situation of growing emotions surrounding Watergate, Nixon had to demonstrate that he was a 'strong president' and that the United States needed him. He wanted to imitate Kennedy's behavior in the Caribbean crisis."[33] Many Soviet officials saw the alert as so inconsistent with the ongoing negotiations and the frequent communication between the two capitals that they could find no explanation other than Watergate. The preeminent Soviet expert on American politics, Georgi Arbatov, put it bluntly. "The American alert was for home consumption."[34]

Not all senior officials agreed that the alert was largely a response to Watergate. Georgiy Kornienko, who was present as an aide to Gromyko at the Politburo meeting, thought that the alert was designed to intimidate the Soviet leadership: "The DEFCON III alert was taken seriously in Moscow. Some of us saw it as an attempt to intimidate us from sending forces to the Middle East. The alert was not dismissed as a response to Watergate. We took it seriously."[35] Anatoliy Dobrynin thought that the alert was intended both to intimidate the Soviet Union and to demonstrate resolve to American public opinion.[36]

Some Soviet officials also misunderstood the character of the alert and therefore downgraded its significance.[37] Like some of their civilian counterparts in Washington, they had little understanding of what a DEFCON III alert entailed.[38] Anatoliy Dobrynin, then the Soviet ambassador in Washington, insisted that it was only a partial alert, and rather low-level. He was surprised and not quite convinced when he was told years later that it was the highest-level alert since the Cuban missile crisis in 1962.[39]

Irrespective of their estimate of the purposes of the alert, Brezhnev and other members of the Politburo were "very emotional, very angry," remembered Israelian. "There was no feeling of fear, but of great disappointment and anger."[40] According to Dobrynin, Brezhnev was so emotional because he "felt deceived by Nixon and Kissinger." Dobrynin worried that Brezhnev's anger would lead him to do something irresponsible.[41]

Politburo members debated the appropriate response to the American alert in a highly charged emotional context. A significant minority supported a military response to the American "provocation." Marshal Grechko acknowledged that a large-scale mobilization of force would be very expensive but still recommended the mobilization of fifty- to seventy-five thousand troops in the Ukraine and the Northern Caucasus.[42] Ustinov, Kirilenko, Katushev, Andropov, and Kosygin all supported the mobilization of some Soviet forces in response to the alert. "We should respond to mobilization," Andropov argued, "by mobilization."[43] Ustinov thought that Soviet forces should be mobilized, but without public announcement.

Grechko also urged the Politburo to order the fifteen-hundred Soviet soldiers in Syria to occupy the Golan Heights. "In the past," he exclaimed, "we have never asked anybody if we could send our troops and we can do the same now."[44] His proposal clearly was not a response to the desperate plight of the Egyptian Third Army, but a reaction to what he considered an American attempt at intimidation.

Gromyko, Kirilenko, and Kosygin spoke vigorously against the proposal to involve Soviet troops in the fighting. "We shall send two divisions to the Near East," Kosygin argued, "and in response the Americans will send two divisions as well. If we send five divisions, the Americans will send their five. . . . Today nobody can be frightened by anybody. The United States will not start a war and we have no reason to start a war."[45] Kosygin dismissed the American threat as incredible. He did not oppose Soviet involvement in the Middle East because he was intimidated by the United States, but rather because of the futility of Soviet intervention.

The discussion grew more heated until the usually silent Brezhnev put the question: "Comrades, if we do not react at all, if we do not respond to the American mobilization, what will happen?"[46] Podgorny, Gromyko, Ponomarev, and Mazurov agreed that Soviet interests would not suffer from a decision not to respond to the American alert with military measures of their own. They agreed with the general secretary that the crisis in Soviet-American relations should be resolved by political rather than military measures.

The Politburo then discussed the possibility of sending Gromyko immediately to Washington to confer personally with Nixon. Kosygin recommended that Gromyko express Moscow's bewilderment at the American alert and discuss the possibility of sending Soviet and American observers to monitor observance of the cease-fire. Kosygin's proposal received no support in the Politburo. Brezhnev argued that to send a representative to Washington after the United States had alerted its forces would be interpreted as "weakness."[47] He rejected any attempt at reassurance in the face of the American attempt at deterrence.

In an emotional speech, Brezhnev summarized the appropriate response to the American alert. "The Americans say we threaten them," he said, "but they are lying to us."[48] He insisted again that the Soviet Union had given the United States no grounds to alert its forces and that a Soviet mobilization in response would accomplish nothing. "If we mobilize," he argued, "the people would start to worry and the Soviet Union would step aside from its policies of peace."[49] In strong language, Brezhnev emphasized again his opposition to any preparatory military measures.

WHY DETERRENCE WAS IRRELEVANT

Nixon and Kissinger are incorrect in their claim that the Soviet Union backed down because the United States bared its teeth. Deterrence was irrelevant because Brezhnev had no intention, before the alert, of sending forces. At the Politburo meeting on 15 October, Brezhnev had told his colleagues that "Soviet involvement in the fighting on behalf of Egypt would mean a world war."[50] "The alert," Aleksandr Kislov explained, "was important, of course it was noticed, but it did not change our policy."[51] Had Soviet leaders seriously considered a deployment to Egypt, the evidence suggests that the alert would not have deterred them. The implicit threat of the United States to go to war to prevent a Soviet deployment was not credible in Moscow. Politburo members considered the American alert irresponsible and worried only that Nixon, pressed by Watergate, might engage in further irrational action.

The American attempt at deterrence provoked anger, disappointment, and bitterness among Soviet leaders. What American officials regarded as deterrence, Soviet officials interpreted as intimidation or a response to domestic political weakness. Bewildered and angered, a significant group within the Politburo proposed the mobilization of Soviet forces *in response* to the alert. Although Brezhnev opposed a military response, he too could not understand the intent of the alert. Angered by the alert, he rejected a proposal that Gromyko attempt to reassure Nixon personally of Soviet intentions. He did so even though Soviet intentions were benign; deterrence only made the confrontation more difficult to resolve. Following the Politburo meeting, Brezhnev wrote to President Nixon that although the Soviet Union had chosen not to respond with military measures, the American action was unprovoked and not conducive to the relaxation of international tensions.[52] Under a different leader, the Politburo might well have chosen differently.

Deterrence did not prevent the escalation of the crisis. For reasons we will examine when we consider the resolution of the crisis, Brezhnev strongly preferred a political solution. He and others opposed a limited mobilization of Soviet forces, arguing that it was futile. It would not advance the Soviet interest in détente, and it would alarm the public at home. Once Brezhnev opted for a political solution to the crisis, the process of escalation stopped.

THE FAILURE OF SOVIET COMPELLENCE

The Soviet threat to intervene unilaterally if the fighting did not stop in the Middle East could have resolved the crisis. Brezhnev was attempting to compel the United States to press Israel to stop the fighting. Once the cease-fire was stabilized and the safety of the Egyptian Third Army assured, the crisis would end. We have already demonstrated that the Soviet threat provoked escalation; it led to the American alert. The evidence also suggests that the Soviet threat did not resolve the crisis. Like its American counterpart, it was both irrelevant and provocative.

By the time Brezhnev's letter arrived in Washington, the fighting had already stopped. Ironically, Brezhnev's threat interrupted the efforts of the United States to compel Israel to allow food and medical supplies to reach the trapped Third Army. Kissinger, who had been actively trying to prevent the destruction of the Third Army, stopped pressing Israel immediately after he received Brezhnev's letter on the evening of 24 October. He did not resume his attempt until after it was apparent the following morning that the crisis between the United States and the Soviet Union would be resolved. Then Kissinger pressed Israel to permit nonmilitary supplies to reach the

Third Army despite the fact that Brezhnev had made no such demand in his letter. By the time the United States finally extracted a commitment on 26 October from Israel to permit a one-time convoy to reach the Third Army, the crisis was over.

To assess the effectiveness of Soviet compellence, we look at reports by American and Israeli officials of their discussions during the critical hours immediately after the receipt of Brezhnev's letter. We also draw on memoirs and interviews of participants in the Cabinet meetings in Jerusalem. Although the evidence is not wholly consistent, the most directly relevant information about these discussions comes from Henry Kissinger, from Simcha Dinitz, Israel's ambassador in Washington, and from members of Israel's Cabinet. The Cabinet met three times, during the day on 24 October, throughout the night of 25 October, and again on the evening of 26 October.

The critical period was the thirteen hours from 7:00 P.M. on 24 October, when Dobrynin first informed Kissinger of Brezhnev's letter, until 8:00 A.M. the next morning when President Sadat withdrew his request for Soviet and American forces. It seemed unlikely to Kissinger that Moscow would send forces without Egyptian consent. During this period, Kissinger describes several conversations with Israel's ambassador to Washington. He first briefed Dinitz about the possibility of a Soviet deployment of troops at 7:35 P.M. on 24 October.[53] At 10:00 P.M., shortly after Brezhnev's message arrived, he met with Dinitz and assured him that the United States would reject "out of hand" the Soviet proposal for the joint dispatch of forces to the Middle East.[54] He also asked Dinitz for Israel's views on the appropriate response to the threat of Soviet action. At 11:00 P.M., Kissinger interrupted his meeting in the Situation Room at the White House to meet Dinitz in the deserted lobby of the West Wing. He repeated that the United States would reject the Soviet proposal and again requested Israel's view on the appropriate response.

At 11:25 P.M. Washington time, Dinitz presented Kissinger with Israel's plan for a proposed disengagement of forces.[55] Israel's leaders, who had been meeting throughout the night, had been discussing a plan to disengage forces between Egypt and Israel.[56] Kissinger immediately rejected the plan as far too complex given the short time available. When Golda Meir learned of Kissinger's rejection, she asked Dinitz to urge Kissinger not to press Israel to withdraw to the lines of 22 October. Dinitz met with Kissinger again at 1:35 A.M. on 25 October to relay the prime minister's request. For the third time, the secretary assured Dinitz that the United States "had no intention of coercing Israel in response to a Soviet threat."[57]

At their final meeting, at 2:09 A.M., Kissinger reassured Dinitz yet again that the United States would unequivocally reject joint military action. He went further and told him that Washington "would resist unilateral intervention by force, if necessary." By then, Kissinger was considering the deployment of the Eighty-Second Airborne if the Soviet Union sent forces. In a follow-up question which sent a strong signal to Israel, Kissinger asked Dinitz "for my information, how long it would take Israel to destroy the Third Army if a showdown became unavoidable."[58] Chief of Staff David Elazar subsequently testified that Kissinger had told Israel that it should prepare to attack the Third Army immediately if the Soviet Union intervened.[59] Kissinger was tacitly encouraging Israel to join the United States in action against any Soviet troop deployment.

Since Brezhnev's letter had been received in Washington seven hours earlier, Israel had as yet received no request to permit supplies to go through their lines to the Third Army. If Soviet compellence were effective, Kissinger should by then have asked Israel to lift the siege of the Third Army. Instead, Israel's leaders received a request for a contingency plan to destroy the Third Army. In the face of the Soviet threat, Kissinger subtly encouraged Israel to consider escalating military action.

Kissinger was strongly motivated to avoid the appearance of acquiescing to a Soviet threat. If the United States had tried to compel Israel to lift the siege of the Third Army, it is conceivable that he would omit any mention in his memoirs of such an attempt. When asked directly long after the crisis was over, however, Kissinger confirmed his refusal to be coerced: "The Soviet threat backfired. Only after the Russians caved in, did I turn on the Israelis. After the Soviets threatened, I asked the Israelis to develop an option to defeat the Third Army. Only after I knew that the Russians were caving in, did I press the Israelis really hard on Friday [25 October]."[60]

American officials who were in the White House that night uniformly confirm that the United States did not press Israel during this critical period. Peter Rodman, special assistant to Kissinger, was very specific. "We tried hard before Brezhnev's letter. We said 'enough.' When the crisis with the Soviets was over, then we got tough with the Israelis. The really tough negotiations took place after the crisis was over."[61] William Quandt, then on the staff of the National Security Council, is also explicit: "Kissinger did not try to compel Israel from the time he received Brezhnev's ultimatum until late the next morning. During that night, he met with Dinitz several times, but in none of these meetings did he try to coerce Israel to agree to the resupply of the Egyptian Third Army. Paradoxically, he did so intensively the day before and immediately after."[62] Joseph Sisco provides the most detailed summary of American attempts to compel Israel:

> We put enormous pressure on Israel on October twenty-third and twenty-fourth. We pressed first on the cease-fire, then on the siege of Suez City, and then on the encirclement of the Third Army. We pressed hardest on the cease-fire, because that was the first priority; we wanted to stop the fighting. But the distinction is not that sharp among the three issues.
>
> The letter from Brezhnev transformed the whole issue into a Soviet-American confrontation. We would not press Israel under those circumstances. We were *not* going to be blackmailed.[63]

Israel's leaders had every reason to publicize and even exaggerate whatever pressure the United States exerted to justify their enormously unpopular decision to permit the resupply of the Third Army. Yet Ambassador Dinitz confirmed that Kissinger made no effort during these thirteen hours to compel Israel to agree to withdraw or to lift their siege of the encircled Third Army.[64] It was only after the Soviet-American crisis was over that the pressure from the United States became "brutal."[65]

Moshe Dayan, then the minister of defense, who participated in the critical Cabinet meetings, was explicit in his published memoirs and in a private interview that Washington made no effort to coerce Israel to resupply the Third Army until after the crisis between Washington and Moscow was over:

> The Soviet-American friction had occurred when it appeared to the United States—so we were told—that the Soviet Union intended to send an expeditionary force to liberate the Third Army. I understood that the Russian troops planned to reach Cairo and move on from there to attack our forces west of the Canal. . . . (The episode cropped up again later [on 26 October], when we were asked angrily whether we wanted to precipitate a Soviet-American confrontation over the issue of food for the Third Army!) *The next day, October 26*, the ball was back in our court.[66]

Dayan was unequivocal that serious pressure came only late on 25 October, after the crisis between Moscow and Washington had "fizzled out."[67]

Kissinger slept from 3:30 to 6:30 A.M. on 25 October and returned to his office at 8:00 A.M. There he found a message waiting for him from President Sadat. The Egyptian president agreed to withdraw his request for a joint Soviet-American force and accept instead an international peacekeeping force without superpower participation. "We realized," Alexander Haig observed, "that the situation was coming under control."[68] Without Sadat's assent, it would be very difficult if not impossible for the Soviet Union to deploy forces unilaterally.[69] Kissinger was convinced that "We were on the verge of winning the diplomatic game."[70]

Additional evidence that Soviet compellence delayed rather than stimulated American attempts to restrain Israel is the strenuous effort Nixon and Kissinger made, *after* the threat of Soviet intervention had receded, to compel Israel to permit a convoy of food and medical supplies to reach the trapped Third Army. On Kissinger's instructions, U.S. Ambassador Kenneth Keating and Nicholas Veliotis, counselor at the American Embassy in Tel Aviv, met with Golda Meir and Yigal Allon on 25 October in Tel Aviv to impress upon them the urgency of the plight of the Third Army. Kissinger also spoke by telephone with Defense Minister Dayan and with Foreign Minister Eban and urged them to allow a convoy through their lines.[71] He pressed Israel to grant a one-time permit allowing an Egyptian convoy of nonmilitary supplies to reach the Third Army, after it became apparent to him that the crisis with Moscow was beginning to abate.

Early on the morning of 26 October, President Sadat sent an urgent message to President Nixon, charging that Israel was attempting to force the surrender of the Third Army. He threatened to break the cease-fire and start military action to reopen the supply lines to the Third Army. Kissinger recognized the seriousness of the situation: "We had dealt with the threat of Soviet intervention. But the problem that had given rise to it remained. The Egyptian Third army was still trapped; it was not under assault but was slowly being starved into submission."[72] For Kissinger, the problem in the Middle East had now taken a different shape: the issue was to forestall Egyptian military action and compel Israel to permit medical and food supplies through to the beleaguered Third Army. Kissinger's hopes for a dominant American role in the postwar Middle East depended on demonstrating to Sadat that the United States could protect Egyptian interests when the Soviet Union could not.

Kissinger now moved forcefully to press Israel to agree to permit water, food, and medical supplies to reach the increasingly desperate Third Army. He requested an immediate positive reply from Dinitz. He also threatened to allow the Soviet Union to resupply the Egyptians on their own, or if necessary, to have American forces resupply the trapped army.[73] Dayan remembered that "the Americans occasionally resorted to a tone that could not be described as the acme of civility."[74] Four hours later, by 2:00 P.M., an angry Kissinger had received no answer from Israel. He called Israel's ambassador and warned him explicitly that Israel would not be permitted to capture or destroy the Third Army. "I frankly think you will make a mistake," he added, "if you push into a total confrontation."[75] At the time, the Pentagon was proposing to resupply the Third Army using American C-130 aircraft and to terminate the airlift to Israel.[76]

At 4:15 that afternoon, after receiving another urgent message from Sadat, Kissinger again contacted Dinitz and warned that Israel would not be allowed to push the United States into another confrontation with the Soviet Union.[77] He proposed immediate discussions between Egypt and Israel and requested a reply before the next meeting of the Security Council. Called at Egypt's request, the meeting was scheduled for 9:00 P.M. on 26 October. At 7:10 that evening, Prime Minister Meir replied, agreeing to direct discussions with Egyptian representatives, but still offering no relief for the Third Army. In the interim, Kissinger learned that a message was on the way from Brezhnev. He called Dinitz at 8:45 P.M. and in blunt language told him that "I had the impression . . . that Israel preferred to be raped than to make a decision of its own accord." He informed Dinitz that "You will be forced [to permit supplies to reach the Third Army] if it reaches that point."[78]

Brezhnev's message arrived at 9:00 P.M. The Soviet leader warned that if within the next few hours the necessary measures were not taken to resolve the issues raised by President Sadat, "We will have the most serious doubts regarding the intentions of the American side."[79] The letter included no threat or ultimatum, only a request for a positive reply within hours. Kissinger considered the message "strange": it asked for an American response, but threatened no consequences; still, he argued, Soviet leaders could not tolerate forever their demonstrable "impotence."[80]

Kissinger moved forcefully. A few minutes before 11:00 P.M., he called Dinitz on behalf of Nixon. This time, Kissinger threatened Israel with serious consequences and imposed a deadline.

> Let me give you the President's reaction in separate parts. First, he wanted me to make it absolutely clear that we cannot permit the destruction of the Egyptian army under conditions achieved after a cease-fire was reached in part by negotiations in which we participated. Therefore it is an option that does not exist. . . . Secondly, he would like from you no later than 8:00 A.M. tomorrow an answer to the questions of nonmilitary supplies permitted to reach the army. If you cannot agree to that, we will have to support in the UN a resolution that will deal with the enforcement of [Resolutions] 338 and 339. We have been driven to this reluctantly by your inability to reach a decision. . . . I have to say again your course is suicidal. You will not be permitted to destroy this army. You are destroying the possibility for negotiation.[81]

Simultaneously, Kissinger tried to reassure Moscow on behalf of the president. He wrote to Brezhnev that Nixon would press Israel to permit nonmilitary supplies through to the Third Army. The president remained committed to the cease-fire.[82] Kissinger also transmitted to Hafiz Isma'il, Sadat's national security advisor, the proposal from Israel for direct talks to resolve the problem.

Golda Meir replied quickly to Kissinger's ultimatum. She railed against collaboration between Moscow and Washington to impose unacceptable terms on Israel.[83] Kissinger recognized that Meir's response was heavily influenced by domestic politics. It was easier for the prime minister to tell Israel's Cabinet and public that the United States had forced the government to permit supplies to reach the Third Army.[84]

The impasse was resolved by President Sadat. At 3:07 on the morning of 27 October, Isma'il informed Kissinger that Egypt would agree to direct talks between Egyptian and Israeli officers at the rank of major general to discuss implementation of the cease-fire resolutions. The talks could be held at Kilometer 101 on the Cairo-Suez road. The only conditions were complete observance of the cease-fire two hours before the meeting, and the passage of one convoy carrying nonmilitary supplies to the Third Army, under the supervision of the United Nations and the Red Cross.[85]

By 6:20 A.M., Kissinger learned that Israel had accepted the Egyptian proposal and immediately informed Sadat. Three hours later, Nixon wrote to Brezhnev, telling him of Israel's agreement to the convoy of supplies and of the agreement on talks at Kilometer 101. Early on 28 October, Egyptian and Israeli officers met, and the next day, hours after the United States began its efforts in earnest, the first convoy of supplies reached the Third Army.

WHY COMPELLENCE FAILED

The record of the discussions between the United States and Israel first shows a strong effort by Washington to compel Israel to observe the cease-fire in the hours before Brezhnev's letter arrived on the evening of 24 October. A sharp break then occurs from the time Kissinger first learned of the Soviet threat. A concerted and serious effort to force Israel to permit nonmilitary supplies to reach the Third Army began again only after President Sadat withdrew his request for Soviet and American forces. This pattern suggests several important conclusions.

Soviet compellence backfired. The United States responded to the Soviet threat by redefining the problem as a test of American resolve and ceased its attempts to compel its ally.[86] It might be argued nevertheless that Soviet compellence increased American incentives to coerce Israel once the crisis between Moscow and Washington passed. The evidence does not sustain this argument.

The United States had tried to compel Israel to observe the cease-fire *before* the Soviet Union issued its threat. As early as 19 October, Alexander Haig discussed the situation in the Middle East with Elliot Richardson, the attorney general:

> HAIG: The Soviets have sent us a desperate message. The Arabs are unraveling, there's a massive buildup of [the Soviet] fleet in the Med. Henry will be on his way to Moscow by midnight.
>
> RICHARDSON: Jesus!
>
> HAIG: Very serious. This puts Cuba to shame. If [the Soviets] intervene, that's all she wrote.
>
> RICHARDSON: Won't Israel hold back in light of that prospect [possible Soviet military action]?
>
> HAIG: Hard to say. We'll have to put . . . pressure on the Israelis or we are going to risk Soviet intervention.[87]

Nixon and Kissinger had also decided, again *before* the Soviet ultimatum, that they would not permit the destruction of the Egyptian Third Army.[88] Although Kissinger acquiesced in its encirclement, he was determined to prevent its surrender because of his desire to exclude the Soviet Union and monopolize the postwar peace process. Kissinger began his attempt to coerce Israel to permit the resupply of the Third Army *before* the Soviet Union raised the issue with the United States. Nixon and Kissinger also worried about a confrontation with Moscow *before* Brezhnev sent his letter. The evidence suggests strongly that the United States would have compelled Israel to accept a cease-fire and allow resupply of the Third Army in the absence of a Soviet threat.

The Soviet attempt at compellence was not only unnecessary but also irrelevant, poorly constructed, and counterproductive. Soviet leaders did not have real-time battlefield intelligence and did not know that the fighting had stopped by the time Brezhnev's letter arrived in Washington. Brezhnev's threat was poorly constructed, in that it did not raise the critical issue of the supply of the trapped Third Army. It was counterproductive because it interrupted the American attempt to coerce Israel.

Brezhnev and his advisors had no control over the time lag between events on the battlefield and the reports that reached the Politburo. However, when they issued their threat, they did know about the desperate plight of the Third Army. It is surprising and puzzling that they did not raise the issue of the destruction of the encircled army through attrition or starvation until 26 October, two days after Brezhnev's attempt at compellence. It seems that Soviet leaders were so preoccupied by their fear that Israel's forces would advance on Cairo that they concentrated their efforts on ending the fighting.[89]

It was also unrealistic of Moscow to expect that Washington could compel its ally to halt its offensive in a matter of hours. Brezhnev and Kosygin had repeatedly tried and failed to restrain Egypt and compel Sadat to agree to a cease-fire. When Washington tried seriously to force Israel to permit supplies to reach the Third Army, the process was time-consuming and difficult.

Kissinger empathized with the perspective of an ally that had just fought a difficult and costly war: "Maddened by the fact that they had been surprised, beside themselves with grief over the high casualties, deeply distrustful of Sadat, who had engineered their discomfiture, Israel's leaders wanted to end the war with his destruction. Their emotion was understandable."[90] Kissinger believed nevertheless that it was overwhelmingly in the interests of both the United States and Israel to create incentives for Arab leaders to enter into negotiation. Israel's leaders, in the throes of war, defined their interests differently. Nixon and Kissinger pushed Israel repeatedly and hard, yet the process was agonizingly slow. They threatened Israel with "brutal" consequences, but they did not succeed in convincing Israel to permit supplies to reach the trapped Third Army until Egypt offered a critical diplomatic concession.

Soviet compellence failed because it was based on faulty and unrealistic assumptions. Leaders in Moscow seriously underestimated the time, energy, and resources the United States needed to control its ally, just as they had consistently underestimated the difficulty of controlling their own allies. "What could we do?" Georgi Arbatov ruefully observed years later. "We had to deal with an Egyptian leadership that played its own game. Israel played its own game."[91] As a result of their miscalculation, Soviet leaders provoked precisely the responses they had wanted to prevent: a halt in American efforts to save the Egyptian Third Army and a worldwide alert of American forces that threatened the confrontation that Brezhnev wanted above all to avoid.

THE CRISIS RESOLVED

When the Soviet Union decided not to respond to the American alert with military measures, the process of escalation stopped. A halt in escalation was necessary but insufficient to resolve the crisis. To settle the crisis, the Soviet Union had to withdraw its threat to consider unilateral military intervention. Brezhnev did so implicitly on 25 October when he accepted Nixon's offer to send American and Soviet observers to monitor the cease-fire. Later that day, Ambassador Malik supported a resolution in the Security Council (Resolution 340) to dispatch a United Nations' Emergency Force which, by convention, excluded the forces of all permanent members of the Security Council, including those of the United States and the Soviet Union.

"It was not the military threat," Anatoliy Gromyko argued, "but diplomacy that finally found a solution."[92] As Brezhnev was concluding his emotional summary at the Politburo meeting on 25 October, Konstantin Chernenko, acting informally as secretary to the Politburo, passed him the text of Nixon's letter—drafted by Henry Kissinger. Brezhnev read the long letter aloud to the Politburo, emphasizing what he considered two particularly conciliatory phrases: "I agree with you that our understanding to act jointly for peace is one of the highest value and that we should implement that understanding in this complex situation," and "In the spirit of our agreements this is the time not for acting unilaterally, but in harmony and with cool heads."[93]

Brezhnev reported Nixon's assurance that the fighting had stopped in the Middle East.[94] He also read to his colleagues Nixon's offer to participate jointly with the Soviet Union in an expanded United Nations truce supervisory force composed of noncombat personnel.[95] Kosygin had made a virtually identical proposal a few hours earlier when he had suggested sending Gromyko to Washington. Nixon's proposal provided the Politburo with the opportunity to end the crisis without confrontation. It was accepted "with relief" and the Politburo ended its meeting.[96]

Nixon's offer provided the pretext to end the crisis. A face-saving offer was necessary to resolve the crisis, but it does not explain why the Soviet leadership was so anxious to find a political solution to the confrontation. Several competing explanations have been suggested for Brezhnev's decision. We have already argued that the American attempt at deterrence was irrelevant. We now examine and dismiss two other possibilities. Drawing on evidence from Soviet participants, we then explain why Soviet leaders quickly embraced a political solution to the crisis.

Kissinger speculated that Soviet leaders changed their minds because President Sadat withdrew his request for joint Soviet and American forces.[97] On the morning of 25 October, he agreed to the dispatch of a United Nations' peacekeeping force that would exclude the forces of the great powers.

Brezhnev would be very reluctant, Kissinger surmised, to send Soviet forces without Egyptian consent. The change in Sadat's position, the secretary felt, was the key to the diplomatic solution of the crisis.

Kissinger had compelled Sadat to withdraw his request for superpower forces. Before he received Brezhnev's letter on the evening of 24 October, but after Dobrynin had warned him of the Soviet threat, Kissinger sent an urgent message to Sadat on behalf of President Nixon. The message warned that the United States would veto any resolution in the Security Council that requested Moscow and Washington to send forces to the Middle East. If Egypt persisted in putting forward such a resolution, Kissinger would cancel his planned trip to Cairo. Kissinger made a stronger threat later that night. At 11:55 P.M., he sent a second message to Sadat in Nixon's name rejecting joint American-Soviet intervention. The operative paragraph, Kissinger notes, warned that if Soviet forces appeared, the United States would have to confront them on Egyptian territory. The message asked Sadat "to consider the consequences for your country if the two great nuclear countries were thus to confront each other on your soil."[98] Kissinger's objective was to close off Moscow's diplomatic options by compelling Cairo to withdraw its invitation to the Soviet Union to send troops.

Egyptian compliance came quickly. By 8:00 A.M. Washington time, on 25 October, Kissinger had two replies from Egypt. Hafiz Isma'il responded that he considered a combined American-Soviet force the best guarantee, but "since the U.S. refuses to take such a measure, Egypt is asking the Security Council to provide an *international* force."[99] The message from Sadat to Nixon subtly linked Egyptian compliance to American involvement in the postwar negotiations. The Egyptian president expressed the hope that his agreement to an international force would "pave the way" toward the implementation of a just peace in the area.[100]

Egyptian officials subsequently explained that the overriding consideration in their change of mind was not the threat of a confrontation between Soviet and American forces on Egyptian territory, although that was a risk, but rather President Sadat's strong incentive to assure American involvement in postwar diplomacy. It was the threat of the cancellation of Kissinger's scheduled visit to Cairo that was telling. Compliance was also made easier because Sadat had never really wanted Soviet forces.[101]

Politburo members, however, did not know of the change in the Egyptian position when they accepted Nixon's offer to send observers jointly with the United States. Victor Israelian summarized the very different information that the Politburo received from the Soviet ambassador in Cairo:

> On the morning of 25 October we received a telegram that Vinogradov sent from Cairo. He wrote of Sadat's "great and sincere gratitude" for everything that the Soviet Union did. He was greatly impressed by Brezhnev's letter to Nixon and the message that seventy Soviet observers would come to Cairo.

Though Nixon had informed Sadat that the United States would veto the resolution to send military observers, Sadat said that Egypt would continue to insist that the Security Council make its decision to send a military contingent.[102]

The Politburo therefore decided to accept a political solution even though they thought that Sadat would continue to press for a joint Soviet-American force. The announcement of the change in Egypt's request came after the Politburo meeting had ended. Egyptian compliance with the American request for an international force that excluded Soviet and American contingents cannot explain the Politburo decision.

A second possibility is that Soviet intelligence caught up with battlefield events and that Politburo members learned that the fighting had stopped in the Middle East. However, at their meeting on 25 October, no change in battlefield conditions was reported to the Politburo. On the contrary, Marshal Grechko asked his colleagues: "How can one save Egypt and Syria?"[103] The assessments of the military situation that were presented at the meeting were "far from favorable."[104] A change in estimates of battlefield conditions does not provide a convincing explanation of the Soviet decisions to agree to send observers jointly with the United States and to accept an international peacekeeping force.

Several important considerations help to explain Soviet acceptance of a political solution to the crisis. First and foremost, Soviet leaders did not consider the stakes in the Middle East worth the risk of confrontation and war. When Politburo members began their meeting after they learned of the American alert, the first issue that they discussed was whether the Soviet Union was prepared to confront the United States and fight a large-scale war. Despite the differences within the Politburo, the unanimous answer was "no." Kosygin put it bluntly: "It is not reasonable to become involved in a war with the United States because of Egypt and Syria."[105] Andropov, Kirilenko, Ponomarev, Gromyko, Kosygin, and Grechko all made essentially the same point.[106]

The belief that their relationship with Egypt and Syria was not worth a war was widespread. "Nobody shared Arab war aims," Israelian said. "Sadat was not Castro. Our relationship with him was not the same."[107] Castro was the first communist leader to come to power without the help of the Soviet army. Khrushchev and his colleagues were gratified and excited by the promise of the Cuban revolution. They regarded Castro both as a test case of the capacity of a communist leader to survive far from the borders of the Soviet Union and as an example to revolutionary forces throughout the Third World.

Brezhnev and his colleagues did not have the same kind of admiration and respect for Sadat. Although the reputation and the interests of the Soviet Union were heavily engaged in Egypt, the Soviet-Egyptian relationship had long been troubled. Leonid Zamyatin put the relationship in context:

Egyptian-Soviet relations began to deteriorate under Nasir, who was pro-Soviet in his foreign policy but repressive toward communists at home. We had even lower expectations of Sadat because of our dealings with him when he was in charge of the Aswan Dam project. He was a pain in the neck, always trying to renegotiate contracts. We became more cautious.[108]

Politburo members generally were conflicted in their attitudes toward Egypt and Syria. There was widespread anger in the Politburo that Sadat and Assad had ignored Soviet advice and had gone to war. In a protracted discussion of their relations with Egypt and Syria, Soviet leaders insisted that past Soviet policy toward their Arab allies was "correct." They agreed that their search for a political solution to the Arab-Israel conflict that would return Arab territories, as well as military aid to Egypt and Syria, should continue. "Our conscience is clear," Andropov exclaimed. "We tried to hold the Arabs back from going to war but they did not listen. Sadat expelled Soviet military advisors. Nevertheless, when the Arabs started the war, we supported them."[109]

The Politburo was angered by Egyptian military incompetence, by Sadat's expulsion of Soviet military advisors, and by his failure to heed its advice. Soviet stakes in the region were high but tempered by ideological, military, and personal differences between Arab and Soviet leaders. The Politburo was therefore not prepared to risk a Soviet-American confrontation to save Sadat. Even after he listened to a pessimistic evaluation of Egypt's military situation, Brezhnev said to his colleagues: "We must tell Sadat, 'We were right. We sympathize with you but we can't reverse the results of your military operations.' "[110]

A second consideration was the importance Brezhnev personally attached to good relations with the United States. Brezhnev considered détente the outstanding accomplishment of his foreign policy. Even before the alert, Brezhnev recognized that a deployment of Soviet forces in Egypt would seriously complicate the Soviet relationship with the United States. He therefore strongly preferred a diplomatic solution within the framework that he had negotiated with Kissinger when he came to Moscow. Arbatov speculated that Brezhnev thought that a political solution was possible because the superpowers had jointly agreed on a framework before the crisis.[111]

In large part because Brezhnev prided himself on his personal relationship with the American president, he was deeply angered by "Nixon's action." Anger can lead to ill-considered and risky action because people who are emotionally aroused are less likely to think through the consequences of their choice. In this case, it did not do so because of the impact of crosscutting emotions. Although Brezhnev was angered and disappointed by the American alert, he was also angry with Sadat for consistently ignoring Soviet advice. Anger pulled in opposite directions. These crosscutting emotions tempered Brezhnev's reaction and reduced the impact of his anger at the United States. He was therefore able to consider his response.

Even before he received Nixon's letter, Brezhnev told his colleagues at the Politburo meeting that "No matter how complicated the situation may be, our wish is to develop our relations with the United States."[112] Aleksandr Kislov explained that "We did not want to make a move that could be interpreted as provocative. We were searching for political not military solutions."[113] Brezhnev was not prepared to sacrifice his heavy personal investment in détente.

One other factor contributed significantly to the resolution of the crisis. During the Cuban missile crisis, Kennedy and Khrushchev both perceived a high risk of war. In 1973, there was an important asymmetry in the perception of the risks of war in Moscow and Washington. Leaders in Moscow worried about a confrontation between their military forces and those of Israel if Soviet troops were sent to Egypt. They feared that Soviet-Israeli combat could easily escalate into a wider engagement that could draw in the United States. Soviet leaders worried about runaway escalation before Washington alerted its forces.

No member of the Politburo thought that the worldwide alert of American forces meant that the United States was prepared to go to war over the Middle East. Israelian observed that "not a single member of the Politburo said, 'This is war.' Not even Grechko, the tough man. The feeling on October twenty-fifth was very different from 1962. Then there was a real threat, a real fear of war. Nobody at the top in 1973 had any real fear of war."[114] Politburo members nevertheless did worry that actions that *they* might take might lead inadvertently to war. "The steps we take," Kirilenko urged, "should not lead to war."[115]

Those analysts who argue that the crisis was resolved because the United States manipulated the risk of war miss the fundamental point.[116] Soviet leaders worried about the risk of war as a consequence of *their* military deployment, *before* the American alert. Their evaluation of the risks of war worked in favor of crisis resolution. It served as a powerful incentive to search actively for a political solution and as a brake on a military response to the American alert.

American leaders did not consider the risk of war and confrontation with Soviet forces significant even after their alert. Despite the public pronouncements to the contrary by Kissinger in his press conference on 25 October, nobody in Washington worried seriously about escalation and war.[117] In 1973, unlike 1962, the fear of war was not equitably shared.

Fortunately, the asymmetrical pattern of the fear of war worked in favor of crisis resolution. Soviet leaders, who worried seriously about escalation, had to make the critical decision about a response to the American alert. Their concern led them to search actively for a diplomatic solution to the crisis and to respond "with relief" to a face-saving offer from President Nixon.

We can only speculate about whether leaders in Washington or Moscow were right in their respective estimates of the risk of war. Certainly, the elements of a more serious crisis were present. The Politburo might well have decided to mobilize a significant number of Soviet forces in response to the American alert. The risk of an incident when the two large navies were tailing each other in the eastern Mediterranean was already high. If there had been a naval encounter when American forces were on worldwide alert and if some Soviet forces had been mobilized, further escalation would have been possible. On balance, it seems that Moscow was closer to the mark than Washington. If Soviet leaders had been as sanguine as their counterparts in Washington, the outcome of the crisis could well have been different. Fortunately, the Soviet fear of war was a self-denying prophecy.

THE LESSONS LEADERS DID AND DID NOT LEARN

Unlike the Cuban missile crisis, the crisis in 1973 was not resolved by a negotiated accommodation that permitted each side to learn about the other's interests and identify their own priorities. Only the Soviet leadership faced painful choices on 25 October and made some difficult trade-offs among competing interests. Even then, they denied the adverse consequences of the choice that they made. The quality of post-crisis learning was consequently very different in 1973 than it had been in 1962.

Kennedy and Khrushchev came away from the Cuban missile crisis with a new appreciation of the other's motives and interests. This new appreciation helped them to begin to build a more constructive relationship. In 1973, neither side learned about the other's interests. On the contrary, during the crisis they misread each other's intentions. The conclusions that leaders on both sides drew, therefore, tended to confirm some of the most deeply entrenched conventional wisdom of both sides. Where change did occur, leaders in Washington and Moscow abandoned some of the nuanced images of the other that they had begun to develop in the last several years and returned to more primitive, stereotypical images of their adversary.

The Failure to Learn

Failure is often an important stimulus to learning. After the Soviet Union and the United States had negotiated a joint agreement to end the fighting among their allies, they had a strong shared interest in the termination of the war. In the relatively benign context of their relationship at the time, the crisis should not have occurred at all. Leaders on both sides should and could have drawn important policy conclusions from their failure to prevent a crisis under these conditions. Yet they did not learn some of the obvious lessons from their failure, and the conclusions that they did draw were either incomplete or wrong.

One obvious lesson that leaders should have learned was the danger inherent in pursuing relative gain through the exploitation of conflict among smaller allies. As we have seen in the preceding four chapters, the attempt to achieve unilateral advantage was among the most important causes of the failure to prevent the crisis and to manage it before it escalated to a confrontation. The United States sought at all times to exclude the Soviet Union from the core of the Middle East. For many years before the crisis, Soviet leaders struggled to make gains in the Arab world at American expense. During the war and the crisis, Soviet leaders tried to avoid the loss of their Arab allies and to deny Washington relative gain.

During the crisis, the United States sought relative gain while the Soviet Union was struggling to avoid relative loss. Leaders attempting to avoid loss are generally more willing to run risks.[118] American officials were largely insensitive to the dangers of this kind of competition. At the height of the crisis on 24 October, when Kissinger thought that the Soviet Union was likely to intervene, he sent a message to Sadat warning that he was likely to cancel his planned trip to Cairo unless Sadat withdrew his request for joint Soviet and American forces. His purpose was to remove the political pretext for Soviet intervention, but even then he continued to seek gains at Soviet expense. "Obviously, both we and Cairo were trying to use my trip to maneuver for position," Kissinger observed, "to drive a wedge between the Soviet Union and Egypt."[119] Long after the crisis was over, Kissinger continued to try to exclude the Soviet Union from the Middle East. Years later, he considered that he had triumphed and that his strategy was correct.[120]

Soviet leaders also did not learn that competition in the Third World could jeopardize détente with the United States and provoke crisis. Before the war, Moscow armed Egypt and Syria, thereby making possible the war Moscow sought to avoid. When Egypt and Syria attacked, Soviet leaders repeatedly expressed anger at Arab refusal to listen to their advice, but they did not acknowledge the failure of their past strategy. Instead, Soviet leaders accused Egypt of obstinacy and stupidity.

At the critical meeting on 25 October, Politburo members were finally forced to face the difficult trade-off between military support of their Arab allies and good relations with the United States. Even though they chose not to jeopardize their relationship with the United States, all the participants nevertheless agreed that Soviet policy toward their Arab allies had been "correct." "Our conscience is clear," Andropov insisted, affirming past Soviet policy. Even when the failure of past policy should have been apparent, the Politburo agreed to do as they had done in the past and continue to supply military aid to Egypt and Syria. Only years later did Georgi Arbatov ruefully acknowledge that the Soviet experience with Egypt "was a lesson for everyone."[121]

Brezhnev also did not acknowledge that the threat to consider unilateral action could have provoked the crisis and jeopardized détente with the United States. When experts from the Foreign Ministry volunteered that perhaps the alert was a response to his threat, Brezhnev was incredulous and rejected the explanation out of hand. Rather, he and his colleagues accused

Nixon of irresponsibility and Kissinger of perfidy. Soviet leaders appeared to have learned little from their miscalculations.

American and Soviet leaders also learned little about the risks of war inherent in this kind of confrontation. The most serious risk of war was at sea where the two navies were tightly coupled. At the time, military leaders in the United States were sensitive to the risk of war in the Mediterranean through loss of control or preemption. Civilian leaders were not. Years later in his memoirs, Kissinger dismissively wrote that "the two fleets, signaling parallel intentions, later met off Crete and started milling around there."[122] The activity Kissinger described so casually as "milling around" was the targeting and countertargeting by the two navies that left only moments for response if an incident had occurred. Insofar as Kissinger paid attention at all to the risk of war at sea, he focused only on the "superiority" of the U.S. Navy at the time.[123] The critical issue, however, was not the relative balance of naval forces in the Mediterranean but their deployment, targeting practices, and rules of engagement. After the Soviet naval exercise began in response to the concentration of the Sixth Fleet in the eastern Mediterranean on 26 October, both navies had their fingers on the trigger.

No incidents at sea occurred. Both sides appeared to have observed the provisions of the Incidents at Sea agreement and no accidents or miscalculations occurred. That they did not, however, does not diminish the serious risk of an encounter between the two navies that existed after 24 October. Indeed, one prominent analyst has speculated that the outcome might have been very different if the Soviet naval exercise had begun on 24 October rather than two days later when the crisis had ended.[124] The timing of the Soviet exercise was not inadvertent, moreover, but a response to the changes in the U.S. naval deployments as a consequence of the DEFCON III alert. Civilian leaders in Washington, at the time and subsequently, dismissed the risk of war at sea and learned no lesson.

Unlike their counterparts in Washington, Soviet leaders were sensitive from the outset to the risk of escalation and war. Nevertheless, their estimates of the risk of war were narrowly focused; they paid attention primarily to the risk of war on the ground were they to send troops to Egypt. "It would have been difficult to control small units of Soviet and Israeli forces if they were in close proximity," Aleksandr Kislov observed. "Egyptian and Israeli forces were intermingled and if Soviet forces intervened, the chance of their coming under fire would have been great."[125]

Before the American alert, Brezhnev had been concerned about the escalatory consequences of a clash between the two navies. This was one of the considerations that led him to invite Kissinger to come to Moscow. After the alert, when two additional American carriers were positioned in the eastern Mediterranean and Soviet coverage of U.S. naval forces increased, the situation grew more dangerous. At its critical meeting on 25 October, however, the Politburo never discussed the risk of accidental escalation at sea. "Adm. Amelko may have worried about it," Israelian noted, "but the Politburo certainly didn't."[126] The next day, the Soviet navy began its intensive naval exercises. In analyses and commentaries published subsequently, there is no evidence to suggest that Soviet civilian leaders came away with a greater appreciation of the risk of a war at sea. In this, they resembled their counterparts in Washington.

Learning the Wrong Lessons

In the United States, the outcome of the crisis confirmed the lessons earlier leaders had mistakenly drawn from the Cuban missile crisis. It reinforced American confidence in deterrence and the political value of strategic alerts as an effective demonstration of resolve. Nixon and Kissinger were convinced that the Soviet Union backed away from the use of force because the United States "bared its teeth" and because its president had a reputation for using force.

Some scholars argued that it was the manipulation of the risk of war that deterred the Soviet Union and went so far as to claim that Israel's observance of the cease-fire was irrelevant to the consequences of the confrontation between the superpowers.[127] They considered the alert a model of successful crisis management. "Our traditional crisis management approach to the Soviets on the nuclear level," Lt. Gen. William Odom observed, "has been to escalate our threats very early to the highest level and then negotiate our way back down."[128] The resolution of the crisis at the end of the October War confirmed the correctness of that strategy in the minds of many in the policy-making community in Washington.

The Cuban missile crisis engendered a broad body of critical analysis and revisionist history. With a few important exceptions, there has been little critical evaluation of the crisis in 1973.[129] Only a few analysts considered the worldwide alert an overreaction and questioned the efficacy and appropriateness of a worldwide alert of forces as an instrument of crisis management.[130] One cogent critique argues that the restricted and low-key response of the American military apparatus was in part responsible for holding the seriousness of the crisis well below its potential.[131] It is possible that a more concerted organizational response would have been more likely to risk escalation. As we have seen, however, Soviet officials did not respond to these kind of nuances, but to broad political considerations.

The capacity of the alert to deter was irrelevant because Soviet leaders had no intention of sending forces. The political implications of the alert were not irrelevant, however, insofar as it disappointed and angered Brezhnev and his colleagues. From this perspective, deterrence was not part of the solution; it was part of the problem.

There was also some reassessment by American officials of the impact of the changing military balance on the use of strategic alerts in the future. Henry Kissinger, for example, subsequently asserted that he would not have dared to order a DEFCON III alert at the end of the decade, given the shift in the strategic balance in favor of the Soviet Union.[132] This reassessment by American officials is almost a complete reversal of the process of learning by participants in the Cuban missile crisis. Some members of the Ex Comm gave considerable weight to strategic superiority at the time but subsequently discounted its importance. In 1973, officials correctly gave little weight to the strategic balance, but years later inflated its importance.[133] In so doing, they learned the wrong lesson. Our evidence shows that Soviet leaders paid no attention whatsoever to relative strategic advantage in considering how to respond to the American alert.

In Moscow, officials and analysts emphasized two quite different lessons. They spoke of the importance of a more favorable "correlation of forces" that they believed restrained the United States. In private interviews, Soviet officials acknowledged that they had perhaps been overly optimistic in expecting that strategic parity would be sufficient to prevent Washington from engaging in what they termed "nuclear blackmail."[134] Most believed, however, that the United States would have acted even more irresponsibly if the United States had had the kind of strategic and local military advantage that it enjoyed in 1962. Soviet officials came away from the crisis convinced that the "correlation of forces" was a critical determinant of crisis behavior. In this too, they resembled their American counterparts.

At the same time, Soviet leaders referred again and again to the importance of "good relations" and communication in preventing a serious crisis between the United States and the Soviet Union. After the crisis was over, Brezhnev and Kosygin emphasized the importance that détente and superpower cooperation had played in preventing a world catastrophe. In a speech to the Indian parliament after the war, Brezhnev argued that:

> Matters would look quite different were it not for this factor of détente in the world, which emerged in the last two or three years. If the current conflict had flared up in a situation of universal, international tension and aggravation of relations, say between the United States and the Soviet Union, the clash in the Middle East might have become more dangerous, it might have assumed a scope endangering world peace.[135]

Kosygin made a similar argument.[136]

The speeches by Brezhnev and Kosygin might be dismissed as an attempt to defend and promote a policy that was by then under sustained attack. However, Soviet officials and analysts made the same basic point even more vigorously in private discussions of the crisis years later. They placed primary emphasis on the importance of the political context. In discussing the crisis in retrospect, Aleksandr Kislov drew an explicit link between the general context of relations and the capacity to prevent escalation and confrontation: "We had a real concern about escalation. Thank God, there were good relations in 1973: imagine what would have happened during the height of the Cold War."[137] Georgi Arbatov made the same point. "Fortunately the crisis was localized. The crisis underlines the importance of prior understandings and communication. Kissinger could come to Moscow. It was difficult to bluff. Everybody knew the limits. Our general relations make all the difference in the world. It is terribly important to have good general relations if peripheral crises are to be contained."[138]

A close look at the record reveals that from the time Brezhnev sent his letter until he made his decision not to respond to the American alert with a mobilization of forces, no negotiation took place between Moscow and Washington. There was no use of the hot line and no direct communication other than Nixon's formal reply to Brezhnev. Kissinger deliberately delayed the transmission of that reply for several hours so that Soviet intelligence could pick up signs of the alert before the message was received. In the context of that alert, Brezhnev was unwilling to send Gromyko to Washington to discuss the resolution of the crisis personally with Nixon because he feared that it would demonstrate weakness. The evidence suggests that just as American leaders overestimated the impact of deterrence, so Soviet leaders overestimated the importance of communication and the positive context of Soviet-American relations.

In 1962, Kennedy and Khrushchev provoked a crisis in large part because each misjudged the other's motives and intentions. During the crisis, each learned about the other's interests and modified his estimates of his adversary. In 1973, Brezhnev, Nixon, and Kissinger began with more complex images of their adversary but, during the crisis, misread signals and misjudged intentions. These misjudgments were not corrected but reinforced by the way the crisis was resolved. Kennedy and Khrushchev did face up to the difficult trade-offs they confronted, compromised through mutual concession, and learned some of the right lessons. Brezhnev, Nixon, and Kissinger did none of these in 1973. They did not confront the often painful trade-off between protection of their relationship and the search for unilateral advantage in indirect competition, and they did not compromise by establishing mutually acceptable limits to this kind of competition. Neither looked at their own objectives and behavior but only at the other's. If they had done so, they might have learned some of the right lessons. The crisis in October 1973 might then have served a useful educational purpose.

THE AFTERMATH OF THE OCTOBER CRISIS

Like the Cuban missile crisis, the confrontation in 1973 had important implications for future Soviet-American relations. Unlike the missile crisis, the crisis in 1973 had consequences that were almost uniformly negative. In Washington and Moscow, the confrontation strengthened the position of those opposed to détente. It triggered a self-reinforcing cycle of conflict that led to the progressive deterioration of the relationship between the superpowers for the rest of the decade. The crisis of October 1973 marked the beginning of the end of détente and the start of a second Cold War between the United States and the Soviet Union that would last for more than a decade.

Soviet actions before, during, and at the end of the war reverberated in the United States and badly damaged the fragile structure of détente that had begun to develop. Influential American political leaders and commentators argued that Soviet policy in the Middle East indicated that the Soviet Union was motivated by expansionist and offensive intentions. They insisted that the United States had been deceived by the Soviet Union as it prepared the Arabs for war and threatened military intervention on their behalf. American proponents of détente had to fight a rearguard action that they ultimately lost.

Soviet leaders badly miscalculated the consequences of their threat of military intervention. Brezhnev was motivated by what he considered a legitimate concern to defend a beleaguered ally, especially after he had reached an agreement with Washington, and he could not understand that others would see it differently. Brezhnev did not anticipate the worldwide alert of American forces, nor the strong political opposition to détente that would follow in Washington.[139] Soviet leaders miscalculated the Arab as well as the American reaction. By seeking to restrain Arab military action, they antagonized Arab leaders. At the end of the war, the Soviet position in the Arab world as well as in Washington had been irreparably damaged.

Mounting criticism of détente in the United States and the defection of Egypt encouraged the growth of the opposition to détente in the Soviet Union.[140] One prominent analyst of Soviet politics dates the beginning of the end of détente to October 1973.[141] Angered and disappointed by Nixon and Kissinger, Brezhnev made less effort to support détente at home and the "forces of moderation" in the United States.[142]

American leaders also misjudged the impact of their alert. Increasingly, the Soviet Union sought military strength and an improved "correlation of forces" to deter the United States in the Third World and to improve its relative bargaining position. The outcome of the crisis did not in itself create this reaction, but rather strengthened conservative tendencies within the Brezhnev Politburo that had long been present but had been less effective. Unlike the Soviet buildup in the 1960s, accelerated spending on strategic forces in the 1970s was not accompanied by a parallel attempt to moderate objectives, reduce the risk of war, and strengthen and institutionalize the relationship.

Reciprocal processes reinforced one another in Moscow and Washington. The Soviet military buildup prompted a vast increase in military spending in the latter years of Carter's presidency and throughout the Reagan administration that followed. The political influence of those who favored accommodation and restraint in both countries was weakened. The effects of inappropriate and limited learning in 1973 rippled through the Soviet-American relationship for the rest of the decade.

PART THREE

Deterrence, Compellence, and the Cold War

How Crises Are Resolved

With more farsighted and better informed governments, more
able to communicate with each other openly and honestly,
the Cuban missile crisis need never have happened.

—McGeorge Bundy [1]

FOR ALMOST a quarter-century, Kennedy's handling of the Cuban missile crisis has been hailed as a textbook case of compellence.[2] His success in getting the Soviet Union to withdraw its missiles from Cuba encouraged the belief that nuclear crises could be "won" by using military threats to convey resolve. Henry Kissinger and his colleagues shared this belief in 1973 when they ordered a worldwide alert of American forces. Our evidence suggests that threats are less effective than American leaders suppose. In 1962, they were only one component of crisis resolution. In 1973, threats failed to intimidate the leaders of either superpower or to resolve the crisis.

The misplaced American belief in the efficacy of threats has been encouraged by lack of information. Until recently, we had no direct evidence about the calculations that guided Soviet policy during the crises. Because the Soviet Union was generally regarded as an opportunistic aggressor, American leaders credited deterrence and compellence when Soviet leaders exercised restraint. In the absence of evidence, American analysts interpreted Soviet behavior in terms of their preconceptions. Incomplete information also misled analysts about American behavior and motives.

MILITARY CAPABILITY VERSUS FEAR OF WAR

The literature on crisis management contends that the military balance is an important determinant of the outcome of a crisis. Some analysts maintain that military superiority at every possible level of conflict, "escalation dominance" in the national security lexicon, confers a decisive bargaining advantage.[3] This approach to crisis management assumes that the effective demonstration of resolve is largely a function of military capability and that leaders on both sides recognize and respond appropriately to this elemental strategic truth.

For the Pentagon and many academic experts, the Cuban missile crisis confirmed the political value of military power. Khrushchev had backed down because he was outgunned.[4] For Henry Kissinger, the nuclear balance was decisive. "The crisis could not have ended so quickly and decisively," he wrote in November 1962, "but for the fact that the United States can win a general war if it strikes first and can inflict intolerable damage on the Soviet Union even if it is the victim of a surprise attack."[5] More recent analyses have emphasized the importance of conventional superiority. In his prize-winning book, *Danger and Survival*, McGeorge Bundy argued that the ability and readiness of American forces to invade Cuba was "a most compelling force on the Soviet chairman" and "determined the eventual outcome."[6]

Similar claims have been made for the role of the military balance in 1973. Henry Kissinger confessed that he would not have dared to order a DEFCON III alert in the late 1970s because of the unfavorable shift that had occurred in the strategic balance.[7] Lt. Gen. William Odom, former head of the National Security Agency, made a similar judgment.[8] Both men accept the conventional wisdom that the effective use of threats requires a favorable military balance.

No one questions the military superiority of the United States in 1962. Recently declassified documents indicate that the American nuclear advantage was even greater than imagined by the intelligence community at the time.[9] Soviet officials calculated that the Pentagon had something on the order of a 17-to-1 advantage in deliverable nuclear weapons.[10] According to Gen. Dimitri Volkogonov, the Soviet Union had only twenty operational ICBMs, not the hundred credited to it by American intelligence.[11] The Soviets worried about the imbalance. They need not have. The Kennedy administration could find no way to profit politically from its nuclear superiority. "Weapons that can never be used," Dean Rusk insisted, "don't translate into political influence."[12]

The standard interpretation holds that the Soviet Union capitulated because it had no prospect of successful military action. Had they attempted to run the blockade, Soviet merchantmen and submarines would have confronted a vastly superior naval force operating in its home waters and supported by an impressive aerial surveillance and attack capability. The alternative, horizontal escalation in Berlin or some other place where the Soviet Union had a conventional military advantage, would have provoked a wider war and could have led to a devastating American nuclear strike.

Soviet sources indicate that Khrushchev was impressed by American conventional superiority in the Caribbean. Marshal Rodion Malinovsky, the defense minister, had advised him that Cuba could be overrun in a few days.[13] Khrushchev was anxious to avoid giving Kennedy any pretext to attack the island. He was equally intent on avoiding horizontal escalation. Not long after he awoke on the morning of 23 October to learn of the blockade, Khrushchev received a telephone call from the East German leader, Walter Ulbricht. Ulbricht pleaded with him to insist on a Western retreat from Berlin as a condition for withdrawal of the Soviet missiles in Cuba.

Khrushchev was furious. In blunt language, he explained to Ulbricht that he faced a war-threatening crisis and the last thing he wanted to do was to make it more acute.[14]

To what extent was Khrushchev's caution a response to the unfavorable military balance? Soviet accounts indicate that it contributed to Khrushchev's restraint, but not in the way Western students of the crisis have surmised. Khrushchev worried that militants in the American government would exploit the crisis as an opportunity to attack Cuba and overthrow its communist government. His letters and memoirs bespeak this concern. To deprive Washington of any pretext for invasion, Khrushchev had Marshal Malinovsky give strict orders to Soviet forces in Cuba not to fire at American ships and planes unless they attacked Cuba.[15] From Moscow, Castro and Cuba looked very vulnerable; Cuban and Soviet forces were no match for the ground, air, and naval forces the Americans had assembled in the region and were steadily augmenting.

Khrushchev was concerned that American military superiority would make it very difficult for Kennedy, whose susceptibility to pressure by militants he exaggerated, to resist the clamor for an invasion. If Kennedy acquiesced, Khrushchev would be under enormous pressure to respond with military action of his own. If he ordered an attack against the American missiles in Turkey, Kennedy might strike directly at the Soviet Union. One reason Khrushchev withdrew his missiles was to prevent such tit-for-tat escalation. Khrushchev's fear of war was widely shared within the Presidium; by Sunday, all of its members agreed that the missiles had to be withdrawn to prevent war.

American conventional superiority in the Caribbean was instrumental in Kennedy's choice of the blockade. That superiority in the Caribbean also made an air strike against the missiles and an invasion of Cuba feasible. The forty-two thousand Soviet military personnel in Cuba were no more capable of protecting the island from an all-out American assault than the Western garrison in Berlin would have been able to defend that city from a determined Soviet attack. Soviet and Cuban forces were greatly outnumbered by the Americans, and possessed only a rudimentary air and naval capability. Their antiaircraft and surface-to-air missile (SAM) batteries could not have seriously impeded an air attack or an invasion.

For Kennedy, the decisive consideration was not military feasibility, but the political consequences of the use of force. He rejected an air strike and an invasion because of their risk of escalation. The joint chiefs insisted that an air strike would have to be followed within days by an invasion of Cuba. This would have almost certainly have led to engagements between American and Soviet forces as the latter had orders to resist any invasion and, Soviet officials insist, "were ready to fight to the death."[16]

Washington greatly underestimated the size and nature of the Soviet force in Cuba. There were forty-two thousand troops—not the ten-thousand "technicians" and military personnel estimated by American intelligence—

and they were organized in combat brigades.[17] Hundreds, perhaps thousands, of Soviet soldiers and technicians would have been killed in the course of an invasion. Misled by the CIA into believing that there were only eight-to ten thousand Soviet troops in Cuba, Kennedy was still concerned that an air strike or invasion could kill upward of a thousand Soviets and provoke military retaliation against the American presence in Berlin or Turkey. Robert McNamara thought there was "at least a fifty-fifty probability of a Soviet military response outside Cuba to a U.S. attack on Cuba."[18] The president was deterred from attacking Cuba for precisely the reason that the Americans expected their militarily insignificant garrison in Berlin to discourage any Soviet attempt to occupy the city.

For Kennedy and McNamara, the benefits of conventional superiority were counterbalanced and in part negated by their belief that even limited military action involved a significant risk of escalation. American nuclear superiority was meaningless because of the terrible consequences to the United States of any nuclear exchange. The air force would not rule out the possibility that some of the Soviet missiles in Cuba would survive an American air strike and be launched against targets in the southeastern United States.[19] The destruction of even one American city by a Soviet nuclear weapon would have been a horrendous loss, and could have compelled the president to order nuclear retaliation against the Soviet Union. This concern—reasonable given the intelligence available to the administration at the time—turns out to have been misplaced. On 22 October, the day Kennedy announced the blockade, none of the Soviet missiles capable of reaching the United States were combat ready. Gen. Anatoliy Gribkov revealed that they had not been fueled or supplied with oxidizing agents. Their warheads were some 250 or 300 kilometers from the launch sites and had not yet been released for use.[20]

There was greater danger of a direct nuclear confrontation in Cuba. Among the forty-two thousand Soviet military personnel on the island were four motorized rifle regiments, reinforced by three tactical nuclear missile batteries with six launchers for *Luna* missiles with a 60-kilometer range.[21] These weapons were tightly guarded by Soviet forces; they were not shared with the Cubans, who knew about their presence.[22] Gen. Gribkov insisted that the Soviet military was prepared to use the missiles against an American invasion force when "the American ships were 10 to 12 miles from Cuban shores, that is, when their concentration was high."[23]

Gen. Gribkov was ordered by Defense Minister Malinovsky to instruct Army Gen. Issa A. Pliyev, commander of the Soviet forces in Cuba that "'The missile forces will fire only if authorized by Nikita Sergeevich Khrushchev'—it was repeated—'only if instructed by the Supreme Commander-in-Chief himself.'" Gribkov was sent to Cuba with the express mission of assessing the circumstances in which the missiles should be used. He understood that Khrushchev would have given his authorization only in the case of a "direct invasion" by the United States.[24]

Control over the *Luna* missiles was not as secure as Gen. Gribkov's comments would indicate. The Soviet General Staff was not at all confident of their ability to maintain wartime communications between Havana and Moscow. They assumed that the Soviet communications ship off the Cuban coast would be attacked and sunk at the outset of an invasion. To guarantee that tactical nuclear weapons could be used against an invasion force, they gave advance authorization to the Soviet command in Cuba to use the *Lunas* "if there is no possibility to receive directives from the Ministry of Defense of the USSR." However, after the crisis began, Malinovsky, on Khrushchev's orders, rescinded that authorization. Khrushchev was more committed to preventing the unauthorized use of nuclear weapons than he was to guaranteeing the availability of these weapons for possible use.[25]

The administration seriously underestimated the number of Soviet conventional forces and did not discover the *Luna* launchers until 29 October.[26] Even then, the absolute, not the relative, cost of war was the decisive consideration for the president and his secretary of defense. To avoid this cost, Kennedy was willing to make concessions late in the crisis.

There was a significant division of opinion about the risks of war among Kennedy's advisors. Dean Acheson, Paul Nitze, John McCone, Douglas Dillon, and Maxwell Taylor were all convinced that Khrushchev would not dare respond militarily to an attack against the Soviet missiles in Cuba. The case for the air strike was repeatedly aired in the Ex Comm, and for much of the time it represented the majority position. Robert Kennedy reported that at least one high-ranking military official urged the president to order air strikes against Cuba *after* the Soviet Union had agreed to remove its missiles.[27]

Advocates of an air strike invoked the one-sided strategic balance to justify their confidence that the Soviets would not retaliate. Four months after the crisis, Curtis LeMay, then head of the Air Staff, explained to a group of officers that "The Soviets are rational people." American nuclear superiority and conventional superiority in the Caribbean meant that there had been "no real risk" of war during the crisis. "The problem," LeMay declared, "had been the flap at the White House. The thing to do next time was to head these people off."[28]

Such self-assurance was not limited to LeMay. Dean Acheson felt so strongly that the administration should have gone ahead with the air strike that he subsequently claimed that Kennedy had triumphed only because of "plain dumb luck."[29] Acheson's judgement was echoed in the official postmortem of the crisis prepared in February 1963 by Walt Rostow and Paul Nitze. The principal error of the president and his advisors, they concluded, had been to worry too much about the danger of nuclear war.[30]

The passage of more than a quarter-century has not altered the conviction of many former officials that the president and secretary of defense greatly exaggerated the likelihood of a Soviet military reaction to an air strike. Douglas Dillon still contends that American nuclear preponderance would have deterred Khrushchev. "That's what made the Russians back off, plus the fact of our total conventional superiority in the region." Why were Kennedy and McNamara so timid? Dillon thinks that "simple inexperience led to an inordinate fear of nuclear damage, the fear of what *might* happen."[31] Maxwell Taylor was much less charitable. In a 1983 interview, he voiced his opinion with frightening certainty.

> INTERVIEWER: Was [the final] outcome [of the crisis] unexpected to you?
>
> TAYLOR: I was so sure we had 'em over a barrel, I never worried much about the final outcome, but what things might happen in between.
>
> INTERVIEWER: The outcome to which I'm referring is Khrushchev's acceptance of our—
>
> TAYLOR: Well, at some time, he *had* to accept. I never expected it on that particular day.
>
> INTERVIEWER: Okay, you thought it was going to go a while longer—
>
> TAYLOR: Unless he was crazy and full of vodka. But I assumed his colleagues in Moscow would take care of him.
>
> INTERVIEWER: Now some of the civilians do recall worries about the time of that second Saturday; worries that really run to two or three steps up the ladder of escalation. The Soviets don't accept our demand; there follows an air strike; the Soviets then feel impelled to strike the missiles in Turkey; the Turks call on NATO for support; we feel we have to do something in Europe; the Soviets then launch a nuclear exchange—something like that was in some of their minds. I take it not in yours?
>
> TAYLOR: They never expressed it to a military ear, I'll say that.
>
> INTERVIEWER: That's interesting.
>
> TAYLOR: Not at all. It's the nature of some people [that] they can't have a legitimate worry, they create them. Apparently they had some of that in the group you're speaking of.
>
> INTERVIEWER: In your mind, there was no legitimacy in this worry?
>
> TAYLOR: Not the slightest.
>
> INTERVIEWER: Because Khrushchev could look up that ladder—
>
> TAYLOR: If he was rational. If he was *irrational*, I still expected his colleagues to look after him.
>
> INTERVIEWER: And at the top of the ladder, if I understand what you saw correctly, the imbalance between the damage we could do to the Soviets and they could do to us in a nuclear exchange was so—
>
> TAYLOR: Oh, of course.[32]

Taylor, Dillon, Acheson, and Nitze viewed the risks of escalation very differently than did Kennedy and McNamara. What mattered in Washington—and in Moscow—was not the military balance, about which there was little disagreement, but the *political meaning* of that balance. Taylor and the hawks believed that the air strike and invasion were realistic and compelling options because of the military balance. Kennedy and McNamara drew little comfort from American military superiority because they thought military action likely to provoke uncontrollable escalation.

Militants focused on relative cost and gain and assumed their adversaries did the same. The Soviet Union was outgunned and its leaders would back down. For Kennedy and Khrushchev, the determining consideration was absolute cost. That cost would be unacceptably high in a conventional war and unthinkable in nuclear war. The two leaders were sensitive to nonmilitary considerations that could push them toward war regardless of the balance. What distinguished Kennedy and Khrushchev from militants on both sides was not their understanding of the military balance, but their appreciation of the risks associated with the use of force.

The relationship between the military balance and crisis strategy has its ironies. In the United States, which had a wide margin of military advantage, the doves were probably right and the hawks wrong. Many Soviet officials believe that Khrushchev would have had no choice but to respond to an American attack against Cuba with military action of his own. Anastas Mikoyan told Castro after the crisis: "We would have been unable to refrain from responding to an aggression from the United States. That attack would have amounted to an attack on both you and us because we had Soviet troops and strategic missiles stationed in Cuba. A collision would inevitably have triggered a nuclear war."[33] Sergei Khrushchev was equally emphatic. "An American air strike would have compelled a Soviet response," not against Turkey, but against Berlin. "Berlin was an easier target because of its isolation. A strike against Turkey was more difficult, and we had no argument with the Turks."[34] Sergo Mikoyan thinks, "It would have been more dangerous to move against Berlin because it was more important to NATO than Turkey." In Turkey, "We had a pretext: the existence of the missiles. It would have been a direct pretext. Missiles for missiles would have been understandable."[35] Oleg Troyanovsky does not know what target Khrushchev would have selected but is convinced that he would have had to take some military action to save face. Even with the concessions he extracted from Kennedy, "Khrushchev was blamed, if not in public then behind the scenes, for his 'surrender to the imperialists.'"[36] Soviet military action would likely have provoked American counterretaliation, and possibly, further escalation.

In the militarily inferior Soviet Union, there were no hawks among the inner leadership. Even the most ideological recognized the need to withdraw the missiles if escalation were to be avoided. Some Soviet generals who reportedly opposed Khrushchev's cautious policy, were almost certainly right in their expectation that a hard line would have prompted American concessions. The testimony of Dean Rusk and other Americans makes it apparent that Kennedy probably would have agreed to a public exchange of Soviet and American missiles had Khrushchev stood fast for a few more days.

For the purposes of our argument, it is irrelevant whether the hawks or doves were right. What is important is their disagreement. It indicates that the military balance is a poor predictor of crisis behavior. Kennedy's choice of the blockade over the air strike, Khrushchev's decision to pull the missiles out, and Kennedy's seeming preference for a public missile exchange over an air strike, were dictated by their political values and instrumental under-standing of the meaning of the military balance. Leaders with different val-ues and different expectations might well have made different choices.

Some scholars have suggested that the military balance would be a better predictor of behavior if one could control for leaders' propensity to take risks.[37] The evidence from our cases does not support this proposition. Soviets and Americans have both described Khrushchev as a risk taker. His speech to the Twentieth Party Congress, commitment to the Virgin Lands program, and deployment of missiles in Cuba all lend substance to this characterization. However, during the crisis, Khrushchev was demonstrably risk-averse.

The military balance is no more useful in explaining the policies of any of the major participants in the crisis in 1973. The military asymmetries be-tween Egypt and Israel were striking. The Egyptian General Staff acknowl-edged that Israel had unquestioned superiority in the air that Cairo could not hope to equal. Egyptian generals worried about their capacity to move troops quickly across the Suez Canal and to storm the formidable defensive fortifications Israel had built along its east bank. President Sadat, although strongly committed to an attack, estimated that the Egyptian army would suffer massive casualties when it crossed the canal. Even after accelerated deliveries of Soviet equipment in the spring and summer of 1973, he still considered Egyptian military capability inferior to that of Israel.[38] If his pes-simistic reading of the military balance had weighed heavily, President Sadat should not have decided to go to war. Israel and the United States were convinced that Egypt would not attack because they shared Egypt's estimate of its military inferiority and gave it great weight.

President Sadat looked beyond the military balance to the trend in that balance, and to the intolerable political, economic, and international costs of Israel's continued occupation of the Sinai. He judged that Egypt had reached the zenith of its military capability and that it was unlikely to receive significant military aid in the future. Sadat concluded that although Egypt was still inferior to Israel, this was his best chance to break the diplomatic impasse and recover the Sinai for years to come. The military balance was a poor predictor of the far more complicated Egyptian decision to go to war.

Military capabilities were more instrumental in influencing wartime decisions, but not in ways anticipated by conventional analyses. On the brink of defeat and military catastrophe, Egypt requested joint Soviet-Amer-ican intervention. It was this request that precipitated the crisis between the superpowers. The Soviet Union was Egypt's exclusive supplier of sophisti-cated military equipment and was then engaged in a massive air and sealift to Egypt of matériel lost or expended in battle. However, at Kissinger's prompting, Sadat quickly withdrew his request for superpower forces. His behavior could not have been predicted by an analysis of his military needs.

The military balance between the United States and the Soviet Union in 1973 was far more symmetrical than it had been during the Cuban missile crisis eleven years earlier. Moscow's pronounced strategic inferiority had given way to a situation of rough strategic parity. The Soviet Union also had the capability to project military forces into the Middle East, and its naval forces in the eastern Mediterranean could have inflicted substantial damage on those of the United States.

From the symmetrical military balance, one could infer two quite contradictory consequences for crisis behavior. As neither superpower possessed "escalation dominance," steps up the military ladder by one government were likely to be reciprocated by the other and bring both closer to a war that neither could win. Fear of escalation could therefore prompt both superpowers to exercise restraint. Alternatively, military parity could also encourage escalation on the assumption that neither government wanted war and would not resort to force except in the face of the most extreme provocation. Escalation could then become the means both to signal commitment and to probe the other side's resolve.[39] Insofar as the effects of the military balance were indeterminate, it was a poor guide to behavior in 1973.[40]

The empirical evidence indicates that both Soviet and American leaders had acknowledged parity. There was no dispute about the strategic military balance. It was not the strategic balance, however, but once again its political meaning that was important. Several years after the crisis in 1973, Kissinger asserted that he would not dare to go to a DEFCON III alert in a future crisis, given the unfavorable shift in the strategic balance.[41] By implication, he suggests that he would have been constrained by strategic inferiority; if the Soviet Union had had the advantage, he would have hesitated to use an alert to signal American resolve. Kissinger's behavior is consistent with the interpretation of strategic parity as permissive of escalation. Brezhnev's behavior, on the other hand, is consistent with the interpretation of strategic parity as restraining through fear of escalation. From the moment the war began in the Middle East, he worried about any escalation in the context of strategic balance. The two men understood the political meaning of strategic parity very differently.

Kissinger also revealed that he and other top officials considered the balance of naval forces in the Mediterranean to be favorable to the United States in 1973. "We all suffered from the illusion that our navy was far superior to the Soviet navy, and we conducted ourselves accordingly."[42] Again, this was not the decisive criterion for senior naval officers who acknowledged that the Soviet navy could inflict substantial damage on American forces at sea. They considered the outcome of a contest between the two navies in the Mediterranean unpredictable; it would depend on the way the battle began.[43]

In October 1973, when the military balance was asymmetrical, as it was between Egypt and Israel, it was a misleading guide to the initiation of war. When it was symmetrical, as it was between the United States and the Soviet Union, leaders understood the political meaning of the balance differently. Moreover, our evidence suggests that Kissinger misread the meaning of the relative naval balance and behaved as if the United States were superior. In the Cuban missile crisis, and eleven years later in October 1973, the military balance was an unreliable guide to crisis resolution.

Soviet and American leaders in 1962 believed that war between them was unacceptable. By 1973, each was confident that the other shared the horror of war. However, the fear of war had somewhat different consequences in the two crises. In 1962, fear of war fueled the search for accommodation. Successful resolution of the crisis taught Kennedy and Khrushchev that their adversary was also committed to avoiding war. In 1973, the Soviet fear of war also halted the process of escalation. However, Kissinger and the other participants in the meeting in the White House on 24 October chose a DEFCON III alert to signal resolve because they did not take the risk of war seriously. The American expectation that Soviet leaders feared war complicated the resolution of the crisis.

THE MANIPULATION OF RISK

Deterrence and compellence are threat-based strategies that attempt to manipulate the risk of war by demonstrating resolve. Resolve can be signaled implicitly through the buildup and deployment of military forces, or explicitly through credible threats to use force or to court war through loss of control. The objective in all cases is to convince an adversary that force will be used unless its leaders accede to one's demands.[44]

In both crises, Soviet and American leaders sought to demonstrate resolve and, by doing so, to manipulate their adversary's estimate of the risk of war. In neither crisis were these efforts particularly successful. In Cuba, attempts by Kennedy and Khrushchev to ratchet up tension by threats and military preparations influenced the timing more than the substance of concessions. In 1973, the American nuclear alert was irrelevant, and Brezhnev's threat that he might send forces to Egypt was counterproductive. A closer look at how threat-based strategies played out in both crises indicates why they were much less successful than is generally supposed.

On Saturday morning, 27 October, Kennedy wrote to Khrushchev to express his willingness to issue a noninvasion pledge in return for the withdrawal of the Soviet missiles in Cuba. He made another important concession to the Soviets on the night of 27 October, when he authorized his brother to tell Ambassador Dobrynin that the United States was prepared to remove its Jupiter missiles in Turkey. That evening he considered a further concession, a public missile exchange, but it proved unnecessary.

Kennedy's concessions were prompted by several considerations. Most important was his recognition of the political costs to Khrushchev of retreating in response to American threats. From the outset of the crisis, the president expected that he would have to offer Khrushchev some kind of quid pro quo. He hoped that his offer on Saturday night to dismantle the Jupiters quietly after the crisis would make it easier for Khrushchev to remove the Soviet missiles in Cuba.

Kennedy's willingness to make a concession was independent of any Soviet attempt to manipulate the risk of war. *Before* announcing the blockade, he had confided to his brother that he would have to make a concession to Khrushchev.[45] The president felt strongly that a superpower crisis could not be resolved in a one-sided and humiliating way. Regardless of the relative interests at stake, the military balance, or any other asymmetry, there were clear limits to how unequal an agreement either superpower could expect to impose on the other.

The timing of Kennedy's offer to withdraw the Jupiters—as distinct from his general willingness to do so—was influenced by his perception of Khrushchev's resolve. The Soviet leader had publicly condemned the blockade as piracy and announced that Soviet sea captains had been ordered to use force to protect themselves. The pace of construction at the missile sites had also increased. Kennedy also had evidence of Khrushchev's caution. The navy had informed him that all Soviet ships en route to Cuba had stopped dead in the water before the blockade went into effect and that those vessels likely to be carrying military cargoes had changed course and were returning to the Soviet Union. On Wednesday, the first Soviet ship stopped by the navy had not offered any resistance. Kennedy reasoned that Khrushchev was unlikely to escalate the confrontation, but he was not likely to withdraw his missiles without further pressure. A concession might break this deadlock and obviate the need for additional threats or military action, both of which could lead to runaway escalation.

Thomas Schelling developed an influential theory of compellence largely on the basis of the missile crisis. He saw the crisis as a competition in risk taking, a nuclear variant of the teenage game of chicken. Kennedy "won" because he maneuvered Khrushchev into a position where he had to choose between unacceptable escalation and capitulation. Through threats and a massive military buildup, Schelling argued, Kennedy manipulated Khrushchev's estimate of risk. The Soviet leader agreed to remove the missiles from Cuba because he believed that failure to do so would result in a humiliating military defeat.[46]

Schelling's analysis needs to be turned on its head to capture Kennedy's behavior on Friday. It was Khrushchev who tried and largely succeeded in manipulating Kennedy's estimate of risk. By condemning the blockade, he forced the president to choose between concession and escalation. Kennedy chose to offer a concession because he viewed escalation as too risky. At this stage of the crisis, risk manipulation was largely independent of the military balance and the perceived balance of interests. Kennedy regarded both as extremely favorable to the United States. This did not prevent Khrushchev from successfully exploiting the risk of war.

Kennedy's consideration of a further concession on Saturday night, 27 October, was based on a different calculus. That morning, the Ex Comm received one piece of disturbing news after another. First came a report from the Federal Bureau of Investigation that, the previous evening, Soviet diplomats in New York had prepared to destroy sensitive documents in the expectation that war was imminent.[47] The latest CIA and military intelligence indicated that a Soviet ship was approaching the blockade line and that Soviet construction crews were still working round-the-clock at the missile sites in Cuba.[48] At 10:17 A.M., the news ticker began to print out a message from Khrushchev demanding withdrawal of the American missiles in Turkey as a precondition for the removal of the Soviet missiles in Cuba.[49] A few minutes later, the Ex Comm learned that an American U-2 had been shot down over Cuba, probably by a Soviet SAM. The Soviet air-defense network in Cuba was apparently operational, and Moscow seemed to have no compunction about shooting down unarmed American aircraft.[50]

These developments led to speculation that the Soviet Union and Cuba were preparing for battle. Robert Kennedy had "the feeling that the noose was tightening on all of us, on Americans, on mankind, and that the bridges to escape were crumbling."[51] Theodore Sorensen offered a similar account.

> Our little group seated around the Cabinet table in continuous session that Saturday felt nuclear war to be closer on that day than at any other time in the nuclear age. If the Soviet ship continued coming, if the SAMs continued firing, if the missile crews continued working and if Khrushchev continued insisting on concessions with a gun at our head, then—we all believed—the Soviets must want a war and war would be unavoidable.[52]

Most Ex Comm participants thought that if war broke out it would be the result of a high-level decision in Moscow. "By the second Saturday," McGeorge Bundy recalled, "we were worrying more and more about the possibility of an intense confrontation at a non-nuclear level as a result of a deliberate Soviet decision."[53] Dean Rusk remembered a rising concern about nuclear war. "We wondered about Khrushchev's situation, even whether some Soviet general or member of the Politburo would put a pistol to Khrushchev's head and say, 'Mr. Chairman, launch those missiles or we'll blow your head off!'"[54]

Kennedy and McNamara worried most about war arising from tit-for-tat escalation. Khrushchev had warned of this danger in his letter on Friday. "We and you ought not now to pull on the ends of the rope in which you have tied the knots of war," he wrote, "because the more the two of us pull, the tighter the knot will be tied."[55] McNamara maintains that this was the threat that he took seriously. "I never feared that nuclear war was imminent in the sense that someone would start it as opposed to momentum which could lead to a conventional and even possibly a nuclear war." "I didn't know," he confessed, "how we would stop the chain of military escalation once it began."[56]

Kennedy's and McNamara's fear of escalation was well-placed and all the more remarkable because it was based on a false understanding of the events that they found so troubling. By Saturday, Khrushchev was as anxious as they were to forestall escalation and had done what he could to prevent military incidents. Aside from the confusion about his morning message, he was not responsible for any of the day's incidents that alarmed the president and the Ex Comm. He was either unaware of them or equally misinformed about their causes.

The FBI report that Soviet diplomats had prepared to destroy sensitive documents evoked memories of Pearl Harbor. Japanese diplomats in Washington had burned documents the night before the attack.[57] "Some of us wondered," Dean Rusk recalled, "if history was about to repeat itself."[58] Ambassador Dobrynin insists that no papers were burned.[59] It is possible that the FBI was misinformed, or that the "precautionary measures" that Dobrynin admits were taken by Soviet diplomats included readying vital documents for destruction. Whatever the explanation, nobody in the Kremlin had ordered or likely even knew about any preparations to burn documents.[60]

The second disturbing piece of news was that *Grozny*, a *Kazbeck*-class oil tanker, was preparing to challenge the blockade. The ship's intentions remain a mystery. On Friday, it had set a course toward Cuba. On Saturday morning, as it entered the quarantine zone, it was buzzed by an RB 47-K reconnaissance aircraft and approached by an American destroyer. *Grozny*'s captain radioed Moscow for instructions and afterwards reversed his ship's course and came to a halt outside the quarantine zone. A confrontation was narrowly averted.[61] By all accounts, Khrushchev was ignorant of this incident.[62]

The most serious incident of the day—and of the crisis—was the destruction of Major Anderson's U-2 by a Soviet SAM. Khrushchev at first assumed that the Cubans had shot down the plane because the Soviet rules of engagement prohibited firing at any American aircraft unless Cuba was attacked.[63]

Khrushchev subsequently gave two different accounts of how the U-2 had been destroyed. In his 1970 memoir, he contends that it was brought down by Cuban artillery. His cable to Castro on 28 October also blames Cuban forces.[64] In *The Glasnost Tapes*, he acknowledges that Soviet forces shot down the plane but claims they did so on Castro's orders. Khrushchev says that the incident prompted him to command Gen. Pliyev "to obey only orders from Moscow."[65]

Aleksandr Alekseev also thought that Cuban forces had shot down the plane; he was told this by Soviet generals in Havana. "Only fifteen years later did I learn [the truth]—the ambassador of the USSR in Cuba!"[66] It appears that Soviet radar operators detected the plane at an altitude of twenty-two thousand meters and reported up the chain of command that in two minutes it would be in range of a SAM-2 battery. The information was relayed to Lt. Gen. Stepan N. Grechko, who tried and failed to reach air-defense commander, Col. Gen. Pavel B. Davidkov and Gen. Issa Pliyev, the overall commander of Soviet forces in Cuba. At 10:21 A.M. Grechko and

Gen. Leonid S. Garbuz, acting on their own authority, gave the order to fire. Two missiles brought the plane down.[67]

Marshal Malinovsky's standing orders specifically prohibited Soviet forces from using their weapons unless Cuba was attacked. The Soviet generals in Cuba, Fidel Castro explained, had a strong sense of "solidarity" with their Cuban comrades and regarded the United States as their "common enemy."[68] Gen. Pliyev had received requests from his commanders to fire on American reconnaissance aircraft and had asked and been denied permission by the Ministry of Defense to do so. Pliyev and Grechko subsequently argued that aerial reconnaissance was a form of attack. Malinovsky was furious when he heard about the incident.[69]

The events of Saturday morning, especially the downing of Major Anderson's U-2, led the president and many members of the Ex Comm to worry that Khrushchev—or whoever was in charge in the Kremlin—had decided to fight. Destruction of the U-2 put great pressure on Kennedy to order a retaliatory air strike against one or more Soviet SAM batteries in Cuba. He refused because he feared that military escalation would become increasingly difficult to contain. McGeorge Bundy remembers that there "was the feeling on Saturday that the situation was becoming so tense, so full of unpredictable encounters, so near to spinning out of control, that only an immediate conclusion could protect us from unacceptable risk of escalation even to nuclear exchange."[70]

The president and his advisors assumed incorrectly that all of these actions were part of a coherent strategy formulated in Moscow and reflected the emergence of a harder line. "We worried," Dean Rusk remembered, "about the possibility that Khrushchev might respond with a full nuclear strike; that he might be in such a situation the he could not control his own Politburo [sic], whatever his own personal views were, because he had a major problem on his hands in dealing with his Politburo [sic]."[71]

These erroneous attributions promoted a greatly exaggerated estimate of Soviet resolve. Khrushchev was firmly in control in the Kremlin and at least as anxious as Kennedy to end the confrontation. He intended his signals—continued Soviet restraint in the face of the blockade, and his messages of Friday and Saturday—to be conciliatory and to provide a mutually acceptable basis for resolution of the crisis. Khrushchev made no attempt on Saturday to frighten the United States into believing that war was imminent or more likely.

Khrushchev's concessions were influenced by his estimate of risk. However, his estimate bore only an indirect relationship to attempts by Kennedy to manipulate risk. Khrushchev's major concession, his offer to withdraw the missiles from Cuba in return for a noninvasion pledge, was communicated in his letter on Friday to Kennedy. That letter was written in response to intelligence that an American invasion of Cuba was imminent. Soviet and Cuban intelligence agencies had monitored the American military buildup in the Caribbean and southeastern United States and had warned

Khrushchev that these forces were ready to go into action and were likely to do so very soon.

Kennedy had not tried to foster an expectation of invasion. Well before the crisis, he had ordered McNamara to develop plans for an invasion of Cuba that could be executed at short notice; his objective was to assist an indigenous rebellion against Castro. Some force deployments had taken place before 16 October. When the missile sites were discovered, McNamara instructed the joint chiefs to accelerate their preparations for a possible invasion. Kennedy thought it very likely that he would have to use force to get the missiles out of Cuba. His thinking changed during the first week of the crisis. For reasons we have made clear, he became increasingly concerned about the escalatory consequences of an air strike or an invasion and chose instead to impose a naval blockade. During the second week, he became even more wary of military action, and all but ruled it out unless Soviet provocations left him no choice. Preparations for an invasion nevertheless continued and were expected to reach fruition on Tuesday the thirtieth.[72] McNamara says that Kennedy allowed the buildup to continue largely because he recognized that any countermanding order would incur the wrath of the military and the militants in the Ex Comm.[73]

Khrushchev's haste to settle the crisis on Sunday was motivated by his fear that the United States was about to attack Cuba and possibly the Soviet Union. Western students of the crisis generally attributed Khrushchev's "capitulation" to Robert Kennedy's warning to Ambassador Dobrynin that his brother would have no choice but to attack Cuba if the Soviet Union did not immediately agree to withdraw its missiles. This is not entirely correct.

When Robert Kennedy met Anatoliy Dobrynin on Saturday night, he warned him of the heightened risk of escalation caused by the destruction of an American U-2. Kennedy told Dobrynin that the pressures for an invasion were mounting. This was an undeniable attempt to manipulate Soviet perceptions of the risk of war. But Khrushchev had already decided to withdraw the Soviet missiles from Cuba. Dobrynin's cable reporting his conversation with Kennedy influenced primarily the timing of Khrushchev's decision.

By Saturday night-Sunday morning, all the elements of a settlement were in place. Khrushchev had learned (or so he thought) from Walter Lippmann that Kennedy would dismantle the Jupiters, and Kennedy knew from Khrushchev's messages that he was prepared to pull the missiles out of Cuba. There was very little last-minute bargaining. The official and back-channel communications between the two leaders on Saturday were used by Kennedy to clear up the confusion created by Khrushchev's two different messages, and by Khrushchev to try to get written confirmation of Kennedy's apparent willingness to dismantle the Jupiters. The threat of invasion did not determine the terms of the settlement, although it created a great sense of urgency in Moscow and prompted Khrushchev's extraordinary radio message on Sunday. The substance of that message would have been the same in any case. Perhaps the most important consequence of Kennedy's warning was to provide Khrushchev with a strong argument to justify his concessions to the Presidium. Kennedy's warning was used by Khrushchev to influence other Soviet officials' estimate of the risk of war.

Khrushchev's fear of invasion derived from the visible and impressive military preparations made by the United States. He did not believe that Kennedy could prevent American military and civilian militants from carrying out an invasion once all the preparations were in place. Khrushchev did not fear Kennedy's intentions but his inability to restrain his hawks. His concern was as misplaced as was Kennedy's suspicion on Saturday that Khrushchev had become the captive of Kremlin militants.

The faulty estimates of both leaders can be traced in part to their stereotyped understanding of each other's political system. Khrushchev and his colleagues used Marxist-Leninist concepts to analyze the workings of the American government. They viewed the president and other public officials as agents of capitalism, and greatly underestimated their autonomy from Wall Street.[74] The capitalist class seemed implacably hostile to Castro because of the threat he posed to American hegemony in Latin America; their most influential organs of opinion like *Time* and the *Wall Street Journal* repeatedly called for his overthrow. Khrushchev doubted that Kennedy could prevent the CIA and the military from using the opportunity provided by the crisis to invade Cuba and eliminate Castro.[75]

The American understanding of the Soviet political system was equally flawed. Although scholars and policymakers alike recognized that Khrushchev did not exercise as much dictatorial power as his ruthless predecessor, they nevertheless exaggerated his ability to control Soviet foreign policy at every level. The president and his advisors were correspondingly insensitive to the possibility that any Soviet action could be unauthorized or reflect poor coordination and inadequate guidance from above. In a "totalitarian" dictatorship, all political and military actions were carefully orchestrated components of a policy formulated and directed by the central leadership. Undersecretary of State U. Alexis Johnson expressed the consensus of the Ex Comm when he exclaimed: "You could have an undisciplined . . . Cuban anti-aircraft fire, but to have a SAM-site and a Russian crew fire is not any accident."[76] In Washington as well as Moscow, leaders made estimates of risk that were largely wrong and quite independent of attempts by the other side to manipulate their perception of risk.

There are interesting similarities and important differences between risk assessment in the two crises. Threats were misunderstood in both. In 1962, the misunderstanding facilitated crisis resolution by encouraging compromise. In 1973, faulty threat assessment had a pernicious effect; it was irrelevant to the resolution of the crisis, but damaged the long-term relationship between the superpowers.

As in the missile crisis, leaders tried to signal resolve through threats, military alerts, and increased military preparedness. Once again, leaders estimated the risk of confrontation and war independently of the attempts by their adversary to manipulate their assessment. The crisis in 1973 was also different in that risk assessment was asymmetrical and one-sided. Moscow worried seriously about the risk of escalation; the United States did not.

Kissinger, unlike some other senior officials, took Brezhnev's threat that he might send forces to Egypt seriously, but the threat did not significantly alter his estimate of the likelihood of a serious confrontation with the Soviet Union. Once Israel's forces crossed the Suez Canal, Nixon and Kissinger worried about a crisis with Moscow. They actively tried to restrain Israel because of their interest in developing a relationship with Egypt in the post-war period, but also because they recognized the overwhelming Soviet interest in preventing a humiliating Egyptian military defeat. Alexander Haig worried about the risk of Soviet intervention even before Kissinger went to Moscow to negotiate the cease-fire and urged that Israel be pressed to stop its armies.[77] When Kissinger learned of renewed fighting in the Middle East early on the morning of 24 October, he protested in strong language. "It was clear that if we let this go on," Kissinger told Israel's ambassador in Washington, "a confrontation with the Soviets was inevitable. . . . There were limits beyond which we could not go."[78] Kissinger complained to Israel about the consequences of its military action *before* Brezhnev issued his threat. His assessment of the risk of war was formed independently of the subsequent Soviet attempt to manipulate his estimate.

The Soviet attempt to compel the United States to restrain Israel had precisely the opposite impact. Instead of convincing Kissinger to intensify American pressure on Israel, it prompted him to halt his attempts to compel Israel to stop the fighting and to order a worldwide alert. Kissinger interpreted the Soviet threat as a direct challenge to the United States, not as a desperate attempt to end the war in the Middle East before Egypt was overwhelmed. The Soviet threat intensified the crisis.

Even after Brezhnev issued his threat and American forces were put on DEFCON III, most officials in Washington did not worry very much about escalation. Their estimates of the risk of war were not high. Peter Rodman, Kissinger's assistant, was confident that "The Soviets had the fear of war in their bones. We were sure that it [the alert] would work."[79] Kissinger shared this low estimate of the risk of war. He was nevertheless concerned about the risk if the United States sent troops to the Middle East in response to a Soviet deployment. Kissinger discussed his plan and its attendant risks only with Nixon. Although Kissinger recognized that Soviet and American troops in close proximity had considerable potential for escalation, he nevertheless insisted that the president would have gone ahead with the deployment if necessary.[80] The Soviet attempt to manipulate the risk of war did not compel Washington to take the action Brezhnev wanted, nor did it raise the risk of war sufficiently to constrain American responses.

American threats were no more successful. Many senior American officials believed that the worldwide alert of American forces persuaded Soviet leaders that unilateral military intervention on their part would provoke a serious confrontation with the United States.[81] Soviet leaders did not consider the alert a credible threat. They did not believe that the United States would go to war to prevent a limited deployment of Soviet troops in Egypt. "Not a single member of the Politburo said, 'This is war,'" Victor Israelian observed. "The feeling on October twenty-fifth was very different from 1962. Then there was a real threat, a real fear of war. Nobody at the top in 1973 had any real fear of war."[82] The alert did not directly raise Soviet estimates of the risk.

Brezhnev could not understand why American leaders had ordered a worldwide alert, in large part because he underestimated the impact of the last threatening sentence in his letter to Nixon. It made no sense, he told his colleagues. Groping for an explanation, Soviet leaders interpreted the alert as primarily a response to the Watergate crisis.[83] They saw it as evidence of political weakness and irresponsibility, not as testimony to American resolve. Their interpretation of the alert raised their estimate of risk, but not in the way American leaders intended. Some Soviet leaders worried that Nixon would act irresponsibly in the Middle East to save his presidency.[84] A beleaguered president, in the midst of a grave domestic crisis, was unpredictable.

Unlike their American counterparts, Soviet officials worried about the escalatory potential of their own actions. As soon as the war began, Brezhnev expressed concern that Soviet forces would be drawn into the fighting if they were sent to Egypt and that any local engagement could rapidly escalate into a wider conflict. Other Politburo members also opposed any action that would risk escalation. "The steps we take," Kirilenko insisted, "should not lead to war."[85] The Politburo worried about the risk of war as a consequence of military action that they might take, quite independently of the American alert.

Fortunately, the skewed pattern of risk assessment worked in favor of crisis resolution. It was Soviet leaders who had to make the critical decisions in response to the failure of the cease-fire and to the subsequent American alert. They acknowledge that their estimate of the risks of a deployment, formed long before the American demonstration of resolve, led them to search actively for a diplomatic solution. The demonstration of resolve did not increase their estimates of the risk of war, but it angered and disappointed them.

Resolve is widely considered a critical determinant of the outcome of international crises. The conventional wisdom holds that outcomes are generally one-sided compromises by the party that was weaker in "bargaining power." Bargaining power is a function of resolve, which in turn is established by relative military strength and the balance of interests.[86] In these two cases, the causal links among demonstrations of resolve through threats and military action, adversarial perceptions of resolve and the risk of war, and the outcomes of the crises are neither as strong nor as straightforward as commonly supposed.

Leaders in both crises exaggerated and underestimated the gravity of adversarial threats. In 1962, they saw themselves as the targets of threats that were never made or intended. At critical junctures of the missile crisis, Kennedy and Khrushchev judged each other's resolve largely on the basis of misleading evidence. Khrushchev's assessment of the probability of an American attack against Cuba was inversely proportional to the real threat. The risk of an air strike or invasion was greatest in the week before Kennedy announced the quarantine. For much of that week, the air strike was the preferred option of most of the Ex Comm. The president was also initially attracted to a surgical strike. While the debate raged between advocates of an air strike and a blockade, Khrushchev lived in a world of illusion; he was sublimely confident that American intelligence would not discover the missiles before he revealed their presence to the world in the middle of November.

After the announcement of the quarantine, Khrushchev became increasingly fearful that the United States would attack Cuba. To prevent an attack, he sent a conciliatory message to Kennedy on Friday and, on Sunday afternoon, broadcast his acceptance of Kennedy's Saturday proposal. Khrushchev did not realize that Kennedy had become increasingly opposed to either an air strike or invasion during the course of the week because of his concern that they would provoke further, perhaps unstoppable, escalation. One of the ironies of the crisis is that Khrushchev rushed to make an agreement at the same time that Kennedy contemplated a further concession.

In 1973, Kissinger inferred Brezhnev's resolve largely from the interests he believed the Soviet Union had at stake in the crisis. Brezhnev and his colleagues ruled out Soviet military intervention from the moment the war began in the Middle East and paid more attention to Nixon's domestic political crisis than they did to the American strategic alert.

In both cases, there was at best a weak relationship between demonstrations of resolve and adversarial estimates of resolve and risk. These estimates were significantly shaped by unintended "signals," perceptions of interests, and stereotyped views of the other's political system. These factors, as well as other strategies, were more important than demonstrations of resolve in promoting concessions and determining the outcome of the two crises.

THE BALANCE OF INTERESTS AND LEARNING ABOUT INTERESTS

Some students of international conflict maintain that interest is at least as important as the military balance in determining a state's resolve.[87] The "balance of interests" has also been invoked to explain the outcome of crises.[88] Robert Jervis, a highly regarded specialist in international security, maintains that the United States prevailed in the Cuban missile crisis because it had vital interests at stake and the Soviet Union did not.[89]

For the concept of balance of interests to be a useful analytical tool, two conditions must be met: leaders and scholars must be able to calculate the interests that both sides have at stake, *and* the resulting balance must be interpreted roughly the same way by the protagonists. Evidence from the two crises indicates that interests are subjective and were understood very differently by the protagonists. It also suggests that calculations of interest, even when asymmetrical, can play a critical role in crisis resolution.

Neither Soviet nor American leaders calculated their relative interests in a political vacuum. Their assessments were significantly influenced by their estimates of the intentions of their adversary. Each set of leaders regarded the other as inherently aggressive and committed to making gains at its expense. Each saw itself as the champion of a superior social system that had to be defended against subversion, intimidation, or direct challenge. Each discounted the other's protestations of good will—"peaceful coexistence" in the jargon of the day—as mendacious propaganda.

American and Soviet leaders alike saw themselves as the defender and their adversary as the challenger. Their conceptions of their defensive role made it very difficult for them to consider the possibility that the other superpower could feel threatened and act for similar defensive reasons. Each recognized that they shared an overriding interest in the avoidance of nuclear war. In 1962, neither was sure that the other recognized this shared interest. But even this imperative was insufficient to break through the cognitive barrier of mistrust that forty years of ideological division and fifteen years of cold war had erected.

Khrushchev had tried and failed to make the mutual interest in avoiding war the basis for détente. Soviet critics had ridiculed the "spirit of Camp David" and Khrushchev as naive. They treated Eisenhower's acceptance of responsibility for the U-2 incident as convincing evidence that capitalism had not changed. Khrushchev's fiery denunciation of the United States at the abortive Paris summit and his subsequent challenge to the Western position in Berlin strengthened the hands of those in the United States and Europe who insisted that Khrushchev was no different from Stalin.

Neither Washington nor Moscow could see any legitimate need for the other to strengthen its military arsenal, deploy forces beyond its borders, or use force to aid regional allies. Critics who saw parallels in the behavior of the superpowers were accused of ignoring the all-important moral distinction between them. In May 1961, during an in camera session of the Senate Foreign Relations Committee, Senator J. William Fulbright (D-Ark), tried to get Secretary of State Dean Rusk to admit the essential similarity between American and Soviet military bases in Europe. Rusk rejected the comparison. "There is a difference in what the Sino-Soviet bloc is up to and what the United States and its allies are up to," he told the Committee. "This is a fundamental difference for the future of the human race. I think the notion that a NATO base is the equivalent of a Sino-Soviet base will not stand up in terms of the purposes of the powers that are involved . . . [W]e are right on our side in this battle."[90] Such a Manichaean view of the Cold War, by no means unique to the secretary of state, made it all but impossible for the Kennedy administration to empathize with Khrushchev and understand the likely impact of their threats. Soviet leaders suffered from the same myopia.

The self-righteous role conceptions of the superpowers were reinforced by self-serving conceptions of the status quo. In opposing the deployment of missiles in Cuba, the Kennedy administration never doubted that it was defending the status quo, a Western hemisphere free of foreign military bases and subversion. Soviet leaders defined the status quo as the successful revolution in Cuba. Ambassador Alekseev explained that the Soviet military buildup in Cuba was intended to protect Castro against an attack by the United States.[91] Beyond the protection of Cuba, Khrushchev told his colleagues, the missiles would repay the Americans in kind, for the deployment of missiles in Cuba would restore the strategic status quo that the American deployment of Jupiter missiles in Turkey had altered.[92]

These very different conceptions of the context of the missile deployment encouraged different estimates of the balance of interests,[93] Khrushchev and his advisors never doubted that the Soviet Union had more at stake because it was defending itself from American intimidation and Cuba from American aggression. Many Soviet officials still adhere to this assessment. "It is undeniable," Sergo Mikoyan insists, "that the Soviet Union and the entire socialist camp would have lost much more from the overthrow of Castro than the United States could possibly have gained."[94]

For Kennedy and his advisors, the balance of interests was just the reverse. The missiles in Cuba were a gratuitous and grave challenge to vital domestic and foreign-policy interests. In the indignant words of Theodore Sorensen, they "represented a sudden, immediate and more dangerous and secretive change in the balance of power, in clear contradiction of all U.S. commitments and Soviet pledges. It was a move which required a response from the United States, not for reasons of prestige or image but for reasons of national security in the broadest sense."[95]

These differing conceptions of the status quo and the relative balance of interests had important consequences at every stage of the confrontation. They were an underlying cause of the crisis insofar as they made members of the Kennedy administration insensitive to the ways in which Moscow would feel threatened by their deployment of missiles in Turkey, claims of strategic superiority, and efforts to isolate and topple Castro. Subjective judgments of relative interest also blinded the CIA and the administration to the possibility that Khrushchev would seek to deploy missiles in Cuba. "We knew," McGeorge Bundy explained, "that we were not about to invade Cuba and we saw no reason for the Russians to take a clearly risky step because of a fear that we ourselves understood to be baseless."[96] With no compelling Soviet interests perceived to be at stake, American leaders all but discounted the possibility, as Arthur Schlesinger, Jr. put it, "that Khrushchev would be so stupid as to do something which as much as invited an invasion."[97]

Khrushchev in turn did not understand how threatening a secret deployment of missiles would be to Washington. Because he did not consider any vital American interests to be at stake, he expected Kennedy to do nothing more than complain. An attack against Cuba or the missile sites could trigger a Soviet-American war, and this, Khrushchev insisted, would be "irrational" and completely out of proportion to the level of provocation represented by the missiles. He regarded the American missiles in Turkey and Italy as more threatening to the Soviet Union, but he had refrained from taking any military action against them because of the likely consequences. "The sober-minded politicians in America," he told Ambassador Alekseev, "should reason just as we do today."[98]

The final misunderstanding was the Soviet assessment of the American naval "quarantine" of Cuba. Moscow saw the blockade as yet another offensive American move.[99] Khrushchev worried about the cost to the Soviet Union of withdrawing its missiles; Cuba would be open to invasion, and the Soviet Union more vulnerable to intimidation. Senior Soviet officials and military officers also worried that the Chinese and Albanians would accuse them of appeasement or weakness.[100] Khrushchev's estimate of the costs of retreat was very much greater than the Americans supposed.

Such diametrically opposed assessments of the balance of interests did not bode well for crisis resolution. They encouraged each side to expect that the other could be coerced into backing down because of its relatively lower costs of retreat. From the American perspective, the only significant cost to Khrushchev appeared to be the loss of face that he would suffer by withdrawing his missiles in the face of public American pressure. In Moscow, Khrushchev had no inkling of the domestic and foreign costs the Kennedy administration thought it would pay if the missiles were not removed from Cuba.

The balance of interests did not determine the resolution of the crisis. Interests were important but not in the way the conventional wisdom expects. Khrushchev's decision to withdraw the missiles from Cuba was a quid pro quo for Kennedy's pledge not to invade Cuba and to withdraw the Jupiter missiles from Turkey. Fear of war was a major catalyst for these concessions. Equally important was the intensive diplomacy that led to a clarification of the interests of both sides. Clarification of interests provided the basis for mutual attempts at reassurance that reshaped the context of the confrontation for both leaders and significantly reduced their perceived costs of concession.

The blockade is almost always characterized as compellence. It also served to communicate American interests to Moscow. Once Kennedy overcame his initial anger about the deployment, he speculated that when Khrushchev made his decision to send missiles to Cuba, he might have been unaware of the domestic and foreign-policy interests that made the deployment so unacceptable to the administration. If Khrushchev did not want to bring the superpowers to the brink of war, he might be persuaded to withdraw the missiles once he appreciated American interests and understood the extent of his miscalculation.

Kennedy chose the blockade because it combined many of the advantages of the air strike and secret diplomacy without their drawbacks. It conveyed resolve without precluding diplomacy and gave Kennedy the opportunity to explain American interests to Khrushchev without appearing to plead for his assistance. Ex Comm critics objected, and the president agreed, that the blockade did nothing to remove the missiles or stop construction at the missile sites. However, this drawback was not critical if an important purpose of the blockade was to create a context in which Khrushchev could learn that his own interests as well as those of the United States required removal of the missiles.

Kennedy was right to try to educate Khrushchev about American interests and intentions. In the process, Kennedy also learned about Soviet interests. The blockade dramatized American interests and convinced Khrushchev that the missiles would have to be withdrawn. The Kennedy-Dobrynin meetings and the Kennedy-Khrushchev exchange of letters helped to make each side aware of what the other thought was at stake. They allowed the two leaders to work out an accommodation that safeguarded the interests of both and permitted Khrushchev to retreat with minimal loss of face.

The first of these meetings took place at the Soviet embassy on Tuesday night, 23 October, the day after the president announced the blockade. Dobrynin reports that this encounter with Robert Kennedy was very emotional, with both men heatedly expressing their views about Castro's Cuba, American military bases overseas, and the legitimacy and motives behind the Soviet missile deployment.[101]

As Robert Kennedy sought out Dobrynin at his brother's request, it can safely be assumed that he reported the substance of their meetings to him in detail. The exchanges with Dobrynin were an education for the attorney general who, like most of the other members of the Ex Comm, had viewed the missile deployment as gratuitously aggressive. Dobrynin seems to have convinced him, and through him, the president, that Khrushchev took seriously the threat of an American invasion and conceived of the missiles as an appropriate and justified response to the American military bases ringing the Soviet Union.

Dobrynin provided the Kennedy brothers with a different perspective on the crisis. To the extent that they gave any credence to Dobrynin's defensive explanation of the deployment of the missiles, and there is reason to believe that they did, the missiles became less threatening although no more acceptable. In his letters, Khrushchev also wrote about his reasons for the deployment and his anger with the United States for threatening Cuba with invasion and the Soviet Union with nuclear destruction. Without the personal exchanges that occurred during the Kennedy-Dobrynin talks, it is possible that the president would have dismissed Khrushchev's explanation of his motives as an ex post facto rationalization for a deployment that was carried out for basically offensive reasons.

Kennedy's expectation that withdrawal of the Jupiter missiles would have beneficial consequences for Soviet-American relations may have been the result of his new understanding, through Dobrynin, of the linkage Khrushchev made between the missiles in Cuba and Turkey. Dobrynin had assured Robert Kennedy that a commitment to remove the Jupiters would be regarded in Moscow as a very important gesture. The meetings with Dobrynin lent the same salience to Khrushchev's plea for a pledge not to invade Cuba.

Learning was a two-way process. Robert Kennedy explained to Dobrynin just why the administration found the deployment of missiles in Cuba intolerable. We do not know if he talked about the terrible domestic dilemma the missiles had created for the administration. He did convincingly portray the president's anger at having been betrayed by Khrushchev, who had repeatedly assured him that he would not put missiles into Cuba and would take no action in Cuba that would embarrass Kennedy before the congressional elections in November. The attorney general explained the administration's concern that allowing the missiles to remain in Cuba would only encourage further Soviet challenges and seriously weaken the confidence of European allies in the United States.

Dobrynin says that he "conveyed all of Robert Kennedy's statements to Moscow word for word, including those that were not particularly flattering to Khrushchev and Gromyko, to give Moscow a real idea of the state of agitation close to the president's own."[102] Dobrynin's cables reporting on his conversations with the attorney general appear to have influenced Khrushchev's thinking about the United States. Like the president, the chairman had a one-sided understanding of the interests at stake and had been grossly insensitive to the administration's domestic and foreign-policy interests. Kennedy's letters to Khrushchev read against the background of Dobrynin's cables led him to understand the blockade and Kennedy's objectives differently. Long after the crisis, Khrushchev confirmed that Robert Kennedy had played a critical role in explaining the American position. "I have to say that he showed a great deal of fortitude and he sincerely helped to prevent a conflict."[103]

In 1973, overlapping role conceptions and misunderstanding of the interests at stake were not an important cause of the crisis. Soviet leaders saw their role as largely defensive. American officials at times saw their role as defensive but also openly acknowledged important offensive goals as they used détente to try to make gains at Soviet expense.

The Soviet Union did not regard Israel's occupation of the Sinai as legitimate or acceptable. Soviet leaders considered the relevant status quo to be the armistice line that existed before the war in 1967. Although they opposed military action by Egypt to recapture the Sinai, they did so because they thought Egypt would be defeated once again. Soviet leaders understood Egyptian and Syrian military action as a legitimate but foolhardy response to the occupation of their territory. By extension, they considered their support of their Arab allies, both before the war and after the fighting began, as defensive rather than offensive. Late in the war, Brezhnev resorted to compellence to prevent a total military defeat of Egypt. Once again, Soviet leaders viewed their behavior as defensive and legitimate; it was a response to Israel's violation of the cease-fire negotiated jointly by both superpowers.

As the prospect of a catastrophic Egyptian defeat grew, Brezhnev tried actively to signal Soviet interests to Washington. Just as Kennedy used the blockade to signal interest as well as to communicate resolve, so too did Brezhnev's threat to consider unilateral military action have this double purpose. There are striking parallels between the two leaders' strategies. Almost as soon as the first cease-fire resolution was passed, Brezhnev appealed to Washington to stop the fighting. As early as 23 October, he resorted to the hot line to signal the Soviet sense of urgency that Israel's offensive be halted. The next day, the general secretary again appealed to President Nixon to honor the terms of their joint agreement: "We would like to hope that we both will be true to our word and to the understanding we have reached."[104]

Only after these appeals failed did Brezhnev resort to compellence to educate American leaders about the urgency of Soviet interests. The letter from Brezhnev that provoked the American alert was an attempt to signal the intensity of Soviet interests as much as it was an attempt to compel an end to the fighting. It openly acknowledged the threat to Soviet interests, then seriously proposed joint Soviet-American action, and, only as a last resort, threatened possible unilateral action.[105] As incredible as it may have seemed in Washington, Soviet officials insist that their offer of joint action was genuine.[106]

The United States also viewed its role as partly defensive. The Nixon administration did not support Israel's retention of the Sinai or the Golan Heights, but it did not regard the status quo before the war in 1967 as acceptable. It insisted strongly on negotiation and recognition of Israel by Arab states as a necessary condition for the return of these territories. In extensive discussions in the early years of the Nixon administration, Secretary of State William P. Rogers had repeatedly explained Washington's position to Moscow. After the surprise attack by Egypt and Syria, the United States viewed its airlift to Israel as a defensive response to the Soviet air- and sealift. "Our commitment was to help Israel," William Colby explained. "They were in a tough situation. The balance of forces was overwhelmingly against them."[107] The Americans also saw the alert of their forces as a defensive response to an aggressive Soviet challenge.

At the same time, Kissinger openly acknowledged offensive goals in the Middle East. Again and again he expressed his determination to separate Cairo from Moscow. "Our policy," he later admitted, was "to reduce and where possible to eliminate Soviet influence in the Middle East."[108] For this reason, he was determined to prevent the deployment of Soviet forces in Egypt. "If Soviet forces appeared dramatically in Cairo, . . . Egypt would be drawn back into the Soviet orbit [and] the Soviet Union and its radical allies would emerge as the dominant factor in the Middle East."[109] Soviet influence in the region could not be eliminated if Moscow were permitted to rescue Egypt from a military defeat.

In Cuba, competing notions of the status quo blinded each side to the interests the other believed it had at stake. This was less true in 1973. During the crisis, there was considerable American empathy with the symbolic interests of the Soviet Union. Kissinger acknowledged Brezhnev's interest in preventing an Egyptian military defeat, all the more so after he and Brezhnev had jointly agreed to a cease-fire. He repeatedly warned Israel about the dangers of humiliating the Soviet Union and, until Brezhnev threatened that he might send forces to Egypt, struggled to compel Israel to observe the cease-fire.

Only after the Soviet Union threatened possible military action did the United States attempt to educate Soviet leaders about American interests. William Quandt explained that even those who thought that the probability of Soviet intervention was low supported the alert: "Kissinger had repeatedly explained to Dobrynin that we would not tolerate a joint Soviet-American intervention. We did not want that kind of precedent. Brezhnev did not seem to understand. We felt that Brezhnev was being pig-headed and we wanted to teach him a lesson."[110] The educational instrument was the worldwide alert of American forces.

In the final phase of the crisis, leaders on both sides badly misread each other's signals. The crisis was not resolved because the two sides learned about each other's interests and reconsidered the balance of interests, as Kennedy and Khrushchev had. American and Soviet misreading of the signals momentarily made the crisis more difficult to resolve. Far more serious was the long-lasting damage it did to their relationship.

Although role conceptions and the balance of interests were more accurately perceived by the two sets of leaders in 1973 than they were in 1962, even then they were not a good predictor of the outcome of the crisis. Brezhnev saw the Soviet Union exclusively as the "defender" and the United States as the "challenger," whereas Kissinger saw both the Soviet Union and the United States as simultaneously challenger and defender. Other things being equal, analysts of bargaining expect that this configuration of role conceptions should confer an advantage on the defender, who is more strongly motivated to defend its interests than is the challenger.[111] As we have seen, the other important determinant of resolve, the balance of military capability, was relatively symmetrical. The outcome of the crisis does not reflect this alleged advantage of the Soviet Union.

The way Brezhnev ordered Soviet interests provides a far better explanation of the outcome of the crisis. Long before the climactic meeting of the Politburo on 25 October, Brezhnev had set limits on what the Soviet Union would do to preserve its relationship with Egypt and Syria. Brezhnev gave priority to the Soviet relationship with the United States. When he finally had to make a choice on 25 October between preserving the Soviet relationship with the United States and promoting Moscow's reputation as a reliable ally in the Middle East, Brezhnev did not compare the Soviet-American balance of interests. He focused on the Soviet interest and investment in good relations with the United States and decided not to respond to what he considered the provocative American alert. Even then, he and his colleagues denied the contradictions in the strategies they had followed in the past and reaffirmed the correctness of their policy toward their Arab allies.

In the Cuban missile crisis, mutual learning about the other's interests contributed to the resolution of the crisis. Both sides reconsidered their assessments of the costs of concessions as they developed a better understanding of the other's definitions of their interests. In 1973, neither side changed its estimate of the other's interests. The misjudgments both sides made of the other's interests and intentions in the final phase were reinforced by the way the crisis was resolved.

REASSURANCE

Like deterrence, reassurance presumes ongoing hostility but roots the source of that hostility in adversarial vulnerabilities. Whereas deterrence attempts to discourage resorts to force by persuading the leaders contemplating such action that it would be too costly, reassurance seeks to reduce the incentives leaders have to use force. In the broadest sense, strategies of reassurance try to ameliorate adversarial hostility by reducing the fear, misunderstanding, and insecurity that are so often responsible for crises and wars.

The "hidden" history of the missile crisis indicates that reassurance played an important role in facilitating the mutual concessions that resolved the crisis. It did so by changing each leader's estimate of the other's intentions. As a result, Kennedy and Khrushchev came to believe that concessions might be more effective in achieving their goals than continued confrontation.

Khrushchev's most immediate concern was to prevent an invasion of Cuba. It was also the concern that Kennedy found the easiest to assuage. He had no intention of invading Cuba, unless it became necessary to remove the Soviet missiles and SAM sites. In his Saturday letter, Kennedy expressed his readiness to issue the pledge not to invade that Khrushchev had requested on Friday. Khrushchev also hoped to compel the Americans to recognize that the Soviet Union had the same right to security that the United States claimed for itself. Kennedy's willingness to remove the Jupiters was greeted by Khrushchev as an important concession. It provided a strong incentive for him to reciprocate.

From Khrushchev's perspective, the most significant form of reassurance that Kennedy practiced was self-restraint. Khrushchev was surprised that Kennedy did not exploit the early American discovery of the missiles in Cuba to overthrow Castro and humiliate the Soviet Union. Kennedy's forbearance reduced Khrushchev's fear that the president would use his country's nuclear superiority to try to extract political concessions.[112] "Kennedy was a clever and flexible man," Khrushchev observed. "America's enormous power could have gone to his head, particularly if you take into account how close Cuba is to the United States and the advantage the United States had in the number of nuclear weapons by comparison to the Soviet Union."[113]

The president's unexpected ability to restrain the American military encouraged Khrushchev to hope that American militants would not succeed in sabotaging détente with Kennedy the way they had with Eisenhower. Kennedy's behavior altered Khrushchev's estimate of the future possibilities for Soviet-American relations. From Khrushchev's new perspective, the expected costs of withdrawing Soviet missiles were greatly reduced and the possible rewards enhanced.

The crisis also redefined the context of Soviet-American relations for Kennedy. Khrushchev's restraint along the blockade line, his revealing messages, and the Kennedy-Dobrynin meetings convinced the president that the Soviet leader had bungled his way into a crisis he had not wanted and was desperately searching for a face-saving way to retreat. By Saturday night, when Kennedy considered a public missile exchange, he was less fearful that Khrushchev would interpret American concessions as a sign of weakness and respond by becoming more aggressive. He thought that there was a good chance that the Soviet leader would see concessions as evidence of his commitment to avoid war and to reciprocate with tension-reducing measures of his own.[114]

It is possible, even likely, that Khrushchev would have withdrawn the missiles in the absence of clarification of interests and reassurance. He was desperately anxious to avoid war and convinced that the Americans would use force against the missile sites and Cuba if they were not withdrawn. Clarification of interests and reassurance made it that much easier for Khrushchev to back down. However, their most important consequence was for postcrisis relations. If Khrushchev had been compelled to withdraw the missiles solely by American threats, he and other Soviet leaders would have been qualitatively more resentful in the aftermath of the crisis. Mutual clarification of interests and reassurance provided the basis for the superpowers to move away from confrontation and toward détente.

The conventional wisdom holds that the missile crisis was worth the risk because it taught Khrushchev and the Soviet Union that aggression did not pay because the United States would resist. Today, this most enduring lesson of the crisis seems questionable. Khrushchev did not send missiles to Cuba because he doubted American resolve, and he did not remove them because of newfound respect for that resolve. They were deployed to overcome vulnerabilities and fears and were removed in part because American reassurance reduced those vulnerabilities and fears. Kennedy and Khrushchev came away from the crisis convinced that war could be avoided and their security enhanced by mutual cooperation. The crisis, in the words of McGeorge

Bundy, "was a tremendously sobering event with a largely constructive long-term result."[115]

The crisis in 1973 did not have the same benign consequences. Neither the United States nor the Soviet Union seriously attempted to reassure the other about their intentions. During the Politburo meeting on 25 October, when Kosygin suggested that Gromyko go to Washington to discuss the crisis with Nixon, Brezhnev rejected the proposal out of hand. In the context of the American alert, he felt that an attempt at reassurance would be interpreted as "a sign of weakness."[116] Nixon's offer in his letter to Brezhnev on 25 October, of joint participation in a truce supervisory force, was intended to allow Moscow to save face. Drafted by Kissinger, the letter referred to the need to act together to preserve the peace, but offered no reassurance about American intentions in the Middle East.[117]

Soviet and American leaders did not attempt to reassure because their interests were competitive and their intentions were not benign. Unlike Kennedy and Khrushchev, neither Brezhnev nor Nixon and Kissinger changed their estimate of the others' intentions; on the contrary, negative images were reinforced by behavior during the crisis. Nor did they redefine their competitive goals. Brezhnev and his colleagues in the Politburo reaffirmed the correctness of their past support of Arab allies and Kissinger remained committed to the elimination of Soviet influence from the Middle East. Insofar as no learning took place, Brezhnev, Nixon, and their advisors saw no need to reassure. Unlike the Cuban missile crisis, which led to an improvement in Soviet-American relations, the crisis in October 1973 marked the beginning of the end of the nascent détente between Moscow and Washington.

DETERRENCE, COMPELLENCE, AND CRISIS RESOLUTION

Our analysis suggests a set of lessons strikingly at odds with the accepted wisdom. We find that the conventional faith in the efficacy of threat-based strategies is misplaced. In Cuba, compellence was important, but only one of the factors that contributed to Khrushchev's decision to remove the missiles. In 1973, Soviet compellence and American deterrence were irrelevant and counterproductive.

Strategies of deterrence and compellence depend in part on credible threats. It is very difficult to make threats credible, especially nuclear threats, when the cost of using force to the threatener is so high. Analyses of deterrence and compellence accordingly focus on the tactics leaders can use to try to make their threats believable. We think these efforts misplaced: in both crises, judgments of adversarial resolve bore little relationship to the deliberate attempts by leaders to make their threats credible. In 1962, Kennedy and Khrushchev exaggerated the likelihood that their adversary would resort to force because of their faulty understanding of its political system. In 1973,

Soviet leaders did not consider the American nuclear alert a credible threat and worried about American irresponsibility. Kissinger overestimated Soviet resolve and attached a high probability to Soviet intervention.

The credibility of threats also depends on the balance of interests. Theorists of deterrence, like other bargaining theorists, assume that the side with more at stake can make more believable threats to use force. It is generally assumed that interests are obvious and easily communicated. At the outset of the missile crisis, however, neither superpower understood what the other side thought it had at stake and had very different estimates of the balance of interests. Discussions before the crisis involving the American president, attorney general, and secretary of state, and the Soviet foreign minister, ambassador, and the chairman's special emissary did little to break down the cognitive barriers that made each side's interests and fears opaque to the other.

The relationship between credibility and interests was the reverse of what is generally expected by theorists of deterrence. The credibility of threats was not established because of leaders' recognition of their adversary's interests. Rather, threats succeeded in communicating interests. It took the missile deployment and the blockade, and the increased threat of war that these reciprocal escalations raised, to create an environment in which learning became possible. Even then, leaders on both sides at first interpreted the other's behavior as opportunity-driven and offensively motivated. Frank and blunt written exchanges between Kennedy and Khrushchev and heated personal encounters between Robert Kennedy and Anatoliy Dobrynin were necessary to clarify national interests and objectives.

In the crisis in 1973, the superpowers began with a far better understanding of each other's interests but chose to ignore these interests to avoid relative losses or make relative gains. Brezhnev, like Kennedy, resorted to a threat not only to compel but also to communicate Soviet interests. The threat backfired in part because Nixon and Kissinger were already aware of Soviet interests. The crisis could not be resolved by clarifying interests and objectives, because they were fundamentally incompatible. When Brezhnev tried to signal Soviet interests through a veiled threat, Kissinger reacted to what he considered a Soviet challenge. In 1973, deterrence and compellence were part of the problem rather than the solution.

The missile crisis was resolved because of mutual concessions. These concessions came after interests were clarified and Kennedy and Khrushchev attempted to reassure each other that interests could best be satisfied by accommodation. Interest was also critical in 1973 in the Middle East, but in a different way. The United States urged restraint on Israel before any Soviet threat was made because Nixon and Kissinger wanted to establish a new relationship with Egypt. To do this, they had to restrain Israel and prevent a humiliating defeat of the Egyptian army. The Soviet Union wanted to prevent an Egyptian defeat and to protect its reputation as a reliable ally, but ruled out the deployment of forces in Egypt because it wanted to protect and promote its relationship with Washington. Although their fundamental objectives remained incompatible, the superpowers found themselves in temporary agreement on tactical objectives. Despite the misunderstandings that arose as a result of the way the crisis was managed, this convergence of tactical objectives allowed the crisis to be resolved without further escalation. The crisis was resolved because tactical interests converged, not because leaders learned and compromised.

The crises of 1962 and 1973 were fundamentally different. The missile crisis grew out of mutual misunderstanding about interests, motives, and intentions. The crisis of 1973 arose because the superpowers pursued incompatible objectives and failed to make painful trade-offs in their respective foreign policies. The critical first step in resolving the missile crisis was the elimination of some of the most serious misunderstandings. Leaders of both sides then had to be persuaded that their respective interests could be better served through accommodation. Mutual reassurance was very helpful; it gave Kennedy and Khrushchev confidence that the concessions they made would not be exploited by their adversary but instead would help to structure a more secure and promising international environment. Soviet and American leaders in 1973 emerged from the crisis with no such confident and optimistic expectations. On the contrary, they recommitted themselves to the pursuit of relative advantage.

Analysis of these cases suggests that the type of crisis should dictate the strategy of crisis management. Clarification of interests and reassurance were critical in the missile crisis, but inappropriate in 1973 because each superpower was consciously seeking advantage at the other's expense. Had their tactical interests not converged, the crisis could have escalated and become much more difficult to resolve. We can only speculate that the overriding mutual interest in avoiding war would eventually have created a sufficiently compelling incentive for Soviet and American leaders to moderate their objectives and reach an accommodation before the crisis escalated to the flash point.

Crises arise when leaders pursue competing objectives. Clashing objectives may be largely the result of misunderstanding, as they were in the missile crisis, or of genuine incompatibility of goals, as they were in 1973. Crises of misunderstanding arise because leaders misinterpret their adversary's intentions and misjudge their interests. This is especially likely to occur when strategic vulnerabilities and domestic political pressures generate compelling incentives to challenge adversaries through threatening rhetoric, force deployments, or direct military action. When leaders become desperate, they behave aggressively even though the military balance is unfavorable and they have no grounds to doubt their adversary's resolve.[118] When leaders are motivated by need, deterrence and compellence can exacerbate rather than resolve crises. These strategies can intensify the pressures on leaders to act, make the costs of inaction unbearable, and inadvertently provoke the kind of behavior they are designed to prevent.

In crises of misunderstanding, especially where one or both leaders are driven by need, the incompatibility of interests is more apparent than real. Leaders must explain to their adversary why they feel threatened, discover why their adversary feels threatened, and, to the extent possible, reduce these fears through reassurance. Better crisis management can do much to prevent war and safeguard important interests.

Crises also occur when leaders understand each other's interests but pursue incompatible goals and relative advantage. In these kinds of crises, deterrence and compellence may be appropriate. They are most likely to work against an opportunity-driven opponent whose motivation to challenge is not great because the value of the interests at stake is not high. The opposing leader should also be relatively free of domestic political constraints. Deterrence and compellence are more likely to succeed when they are attempted early, before an adversary becomes fully committed to action. Once leaders are committed, the political and psychological costs of backing down increase significantly.

Even in crises of incompatibility between politically secure opponents, threat-based strategies can fail for two quite different reasons. Preferences may make deterrence or compellence impossible. Leaders may prefer war to concession when the interests at stake are central. Threat-based strategies obviously cannot succeed against an adversary who strongly prefers war to compromise. Despite the firm demonstration of resolve to use the overwhelming force assembled in the Gulf in 1990, compellence did not succeed against Saddam Hussein. He preferred war to withdrawal of his forces from Kuwait.[119] The great historical example is Adolf Hitler. Western leaders and scholars have made the counterfactual argument that had deterrence been tried against Hitler, it would have succeeded. There are good grounds to believe that here, too, deterrence would have failed, given Hitler's preference for war rather than compromise.[120] The mistake was to make a dubious counterfactual speculation into the universal truth of the nuclear age. Evidence from the missile crisis suggests, moreover, that for nuclear powers, the fear of war dominates even when the most basic interests are at stake.

Threat-based strategies may fail for a second reason. It is difficult, as deterrence theorists have long acknowledged, to make credible threats to use force when nuclear war is a possible outcome of confrontation. In 1962, threats were credible largely because of the stereotyped images Kennedy and Khrushchev had of the other's political system; each worried that the other might be driven to use force by militants at home. By 1973, Soviet and American leaders had developed a more nuanced understanding of the other's political system as their relationship improved. The shared horror of nuclear war had encouraged both sides to try to reduce the risk of inadvertent war and to manage their incompatibilities among their interests through diplomacy. The improvement in their relationship in turn limited the credibility of nuclear threats. The reality of nuclear deterrence compromised the strategies of deterrence and compellence.

Crises that grow out of the pursuit of incompatible objectives by nuclear powers are difficult to resolve. The outcome of the crisis will depend in large part on the importance of the issues at stake to the parties and how incompatible their objectives are. If the value of the interests at stake is not great, one side may prefer to concede rather than risk escalation, or tactical interests may converge, as they did in 1973.

There is a cost to this kind of crisis resolution. The resolution of a crisis through temporary convergence of tactical interests or capitulation is likely to damage the relationship between the parties long after the crisis is over. The fundamental problem of nuclear crisis management is not strategies and tactics but goals. Leaders can try to educate each other about the consequences of their continuing pursuit of incompatible goals, so that one or both sides reconsider their interests and moderate their goals. Crisis resolution is most effective when leaders "learn" about other's interests as well as their own, when they reorder or modify their objectives in light of the risk of war, and then engage in fundamental trade-offs. In large part because learning was so limited, the crisis in 1973 was the beginning of the end of the second détente between the United States and the Soviet Union.

Deterrence and Crisis Management

What is of concern is the fact that both governments were so far out of contact really. I don't think that we expected that he [Khrushchev] would put missiles in Cuba. . . . Now, he obviously must have thought that he could do it in secret and that the United States would accept it. So that he did not judge our intentions. . . .

When you look at all those misjudgments which brought on war [in 1914 and 1939], and then you see the Soviet Union and the United States, so far separated in their beliefs . . . and you put the nuclear equation into that struggle, that is what makes this . . . such a dangerous time. . . . One mistake can make this whole thing blow up.

—John F. Kennedy [1]

THE CUBAN missile crisis spawned a large literature on crisis management.[2] Much of it stressed the importance of deterrence and compellence and analyzed the tactics that could give credibility to the threats that are at the core of those strategies.[3] More recent studies have identified technical, organizational, and political constraints that make it very difficult, and sometimes impossible, for leaders to manipulate the risk of war with precision. Critics of deterrence and compellence also maintain that political leaders have been insufficiently sensitive to the risk of inadvertent war inherent in these strategies.[4]

The evidence from our cases supports these criticisms of deterrence. The previous chapter demonstrated how perceptions of the risk of war were largely independent of adversarial attempts to manipulate those risks. The unpredictable relationship between threats and their consequences made it difficult to derive bargaining advantages from putative asymmetries in the balance of interests or military capability. This chapter develops a different critique of deterrence. It hypothesizes a strong relationship between precrisis reliance on deterrence to prevent challenges and difficulty in coping with those challenges when deterrence fails. Deterrence can impede early warning, lead to exaggerated threat assessments, contribute to stress, increase the domestic and allied pressures on leaders to stand firm, and exacerbate the problem of loss of control.

DETERRENCE AND INTELLIGENCE

Deterrence conceives of aggression as opportunity-driven. Challenges occur when defenders lack the military capability or political will to defend their commitments. Deterrence further assumes that adversaries assess the risks and likely consequences of their challenge before proceeding. Leaders who put their faith in deterrence are likely to rely on the military balance as a good predictor of challenges; they will expect their adversary to behave cautiously when the military balance is unfavorable. They are also likely to be insensitive to challenges driven by need and to the possibility of serious miscalculations by their adversary.

In the missile crisis, Kennedy and his principal advisors, operating within the assumptions of deterrence, did not consider that the missile deployment might have been driven by defensive concerns. Their confidence in deterrence also led them to discount the likelihood of a deployment, given the overwhelming military advantage the United States possessed in the Caribbean. Almost nobody in the upper levels of the government believed that Khrushchev would violate his private assurances about the missiles.[5] The only important exception was CIA Director John A. McCone, who did not assume that Khrushchev would behave prudently or rationally.[6]

During the summer and early fall of 1962, the CIA actively monitored the Soviet military buildup in Cuba but missed its significance because analysts put too much credence in the efficacy of deterrence and the rationality of their adversary.[7] Two Special National Intelligence Estimates considered and rejected the possibility of a Soviet missile deployment on the grounds that it would be too risky.[8] In discounting a serious Soviet challenge in Cuba, the CIA was further misled by its high regard for Soviet intelligence. The Soviet embassy was known to have extraordinarily competent intelligence officers who "were constantly plumbing both White House and congressional feelings" and presumably transmitting their findings back to Moscow. Sherman Kent, director of the Office of National Estimates, assumed that Ambassador Dobrynin, who "was no dummy to the West" would "certainly . . . have been warning Khrushchev on the dangers of a U.S. riposte if the Soviets placed offensive missiles in Cuba."[9] It never occurred to CIA analysts that Ambassador Dobrynin could be as uninformed about Khrushchev's intentions as they were and reluctant to offer assessments at odds with the expectations of the foreign ministry or the Kremlin.

The administration's discovery of the missiles was facilitated by its belief that they were not there. There were no U-2 flights over the western part of Cuba between 5 September and the flight that discovered the missile sites on 14 October. Aerial surveillance was restricted after the loss of a U-2 over China on 9 September and the suspected operational readiness of SAM-2 antiaircraft batteries in western Cuba. The decision to authorize the fateful 14 October U-2 mission was made on 4 October by the Committee on Overhead Reconnaissance in response to disturbing but confusing reports from anti-Castro Cubans that Soviet missiles were being deployed in the San Cristóbal area. The flight was delayed almost ten days because of State Department resistance and bickering between the air force and the CIA over who would fly the mission.[10]

The 14 October U-2 mission was also a response to charges by Senator Kenneth Keating of New York and other Republicans that the Soviet Union was secretly deploying missiles in Cuba. The administration was angered by Keating's charges, given great prominence by the press, and by his rejection of the president's request to share with him whatever information he might have about Soviet missiles in Cuba. National Security Advisor McGeorge Bundy ordered stepped-up intelligence operations because of disturbing information from Cuba, but the president also wanted to make a more convincing case to the American public that Keating's allegations were baseless.[11] It is one of the ironies of the crisis that the U-2 overflight that discovered the San Cristóbal missile base was ordered at least in part by Bundy to refute Republican charges that there were Soviet missiles in Cuba.

In 1973, belief in deterrence prevented Tel Aviv and Washington from receiving timely warning of war. Once again, the problem was not the lack of information but the misleading set of assumptions that guided intelligence assessment in both capitals. Israeli military intelligence assumed that military superiority would be sufficient to deter an attack. Egypt would remain resentful but quiescent until its air force could strike at Israel's airfields, and Syria would only attack in conjunction with Egypt. The Egyptian General Staff had made the same argument throughout much of 1972 and their opposition to war was known to Israeli intelligence. Using the Egyptian estimate of Israeli air superiority, and fully confident themselves of their advantage in the air, Israel's military analysts were persuaded that President Sadat would not be so irrational as to start a war.[12]

The United States was warned by Leonid Brezhnev and Andrei Gromyko in April 1973, by Brezhnev again in May, and by King Hussein of Jordan in June, that war was likely. A staff report of the National Security Council prepared at Henry Kissinger's request nevertheless concluded that "There is a low probability that Sadat will renew fighting to break the deadlock, not because Sadat would not want to go to war, but because he is conscious of the severe results of such a step in view of the balance of power in the area, the relative weakness of Egypt and the current international circumstances."[13] The CIA and a mid-May interagency report concurred with this estimate. The only dissenting voice was the State Department's Bureau of Intelligence and Research (INR). On 31 May, INR submitted a memorandum to Secretary of State William Rogers warning that if the diplomatic stalemate were not broken, "the resumption of hostilities by autumn will become a better than even bet."[14]

American intelligence erred because it operated with the same assumptions as Israel: every estimate that considered war unlikely argued that Egypt and Syria would not attack because they lacked the military capability to regain the territory captured by Israel in 1967. After the fact, Henry Kissinger ruefully observed that "The premises were correct. The conclusions were not."[15]

On September 30, after receiving reports that Syrian armor was massing on the Golan Heights, Kissinger asked for another interagency estimate. Large-scale Egyptian military movements in the vicinity of the Suez Canal, described as an exercise by Cairo, were also under way. Even the State Department's intelligence unit did not think these deployments signified war. "In our view," INR advised, "the political climate in the Arab states argues against a major Syrian military move against Israel at this time. The possibility of a more limited Syrian strike, perhaps one designed to retaliate for the pounding the Syrian Air Force took from the Israelis on September 13, cannot of course be excluded."[16] On 3 October, only three days before the attack, the Defense Intelligence Agency (DIA) concluded that "The movement of Syrian troops and Egyptian military readiness are considered to be coincidental and not designed to lead to major hostilities."[17] On 4–5 October, the CIA informed the White House that "the military preparations that have occurred do not indicate that any party intends to initiate hostilities."[18]

Washington was also reassured by Israel's confidence that there would be no war. Israeli officials had been sharing their estimates of Egyptian intentions with CIA analysts and administration officials. In a meeting with Kissinger in New York on 4 October, Foreign Minister Abba Eban advised that Egyptian military movements were routine and that "the voice of reason" would prevail in Damascus.[19] Kissinger noted that "Our own reporting was a mirror image of Israel's."[20] In retrospect, he acknowledged the failure to anticipate the Egyptian attack as "one of our biggest intelligence failures."[21]

The partial failure of American intelligence in 1962 and the complete American and Israeli intelligence failure in 1973 can be traced largely to exaggerated confidence in deterrence. The assumption that deterrence, based on superior military capability, would prevent an attack drove intelligence collection and evaluation. It blinded intelligence analysts to Khrushchev's and Sadat's objectives and made them insensitive to the pressures both leaders faced. Israel's analysts were so much the prisoners of their assumption that they discounted the tactical intelligence that indicated attack was imminent on two fronts.

The intended victim of surprise rarely gets the kind of warning that Kennedy had. Policymakers and intelligence analysts governed by the logic of deterrence are generally sensitive only to threats they consider rational. Those informed by its logic assume their adversaries are capable of making reasonably accurate assessments of the relative military balance and that they will refrain from challenges that are extraordinarily risky or have little chance of success. Neither Khrushchev's decision to send missiles to Cuba nor Sadat's choice to go to war conformed to these expectations. Khrushchev believed that the missiles could be deployed secretly and that Kennedy would tolerate them after their presence was announced. Khrushchev's estimates of risk were superficially derived and seriously flawed, and his reasons for expecting Kennedy to limit his response to verbal protests, like his motives for deploying the missiles, were opaque to American intelligence. There are many other well-documented cases of threatening military deployments and resorts to force based on unrealistic estimates of adversarial responses.[22] Most of these challenges, like Khrushchev's, were motivated by a combination of strategic and domestic pressures, and the leaders who initiated them were strongly motivated to believe that they would succeed. Intelligence interpreted through the prism of deterrence is therefore likely to fail when it is needed the most.

DETERRENCE AND THREAT ASSESSMENT

When defenders believe that deterrence has failed, they rarely question the appropriateness of the strategy. Instead, they use its assumptions to explain their adversary's behavior. Analyses informed by the logic of deterrence frequently result in exaggerated estimates of threat.

Working within the framework of deterrence, one explanation of failure posits adversarial goals commensurate with the risk or cost of war. Because leaders know that they are unprepared to tolerate a provocation, they assume their adversary also knew this and acted in full knowledge of the likely consequences of its behavior. A challenge under these conditions reveals the willingness of adversarial leaders to risk war in pursuit of far-reaching aggressive designs. Only the prospect of large gain could justify the risk or cost of war.

Deterrence sometimes fails for this reason. Hitler invaded Poland in September 1939 in full recognition that Poland would resist and France and Britain would declare war, but that war was the only way of achieving the goals he sought.[23] However, when challengers miscalculate their adversary's response to their actions, this kind of explanation encourages an exaggerated estimate of threat. The missile crisis is a case in point.

The president and the Ex Comm were shocked by the missile deployment because it appeared to indicate Khrushchev's willingness to risk war with the United States. Americans knew that they could not accept Soviet missiles in Cuba for domestic and foreign-policy reasons and assumed that these reasons were apparent to Khrushchev. To take such a risk, the president and the Ex Comm reasoned, Khrushchev must have expected to reap great gains. They accordingly attributed aggressive objectives to Khrushchev: he had sent missiles to Cuba to weaken NATO, spread communism in Latin America, and provide the security umbrella he needed to take decisive action against the Western presence in Berlin.[24]

An alternative explanation for Khrushchev's risk taking would have invoked pressing domestic or foreign needs. The president and Ex Comm considered and rejected defensive motives for the deployment. They rejected a defensive interpretation of Khrushchev's action in part because they could not empathize; they did not understand the perception of threat their strategic and Caribbean policies engendered in Moscow. With no understanding of the magnitude of the threat Khrushchev perceived, nor of the domestic problems the missile deployment was intended to address, they also rejected the defensive explanation because the risks of confrontation inherent in a secret missile deployment appeared wholly disproportionate to any threat it might be intended to address.

In this explanation of deterrence failure, the assumptions of deterrence are reinforced by two common cognitive biases: the fundamental attribution error and the proportionality bias. The fundamental attribution error not only leads people to exaggerate the importance of dispositional over situational factors in explaining the undesirable behavior of others but also to expect that others will understand their undesirable behavior in terms of situational constraints.[25]

As the fundamental attribution error would predict, Kennedy and the Ex Comm explained their behavior in terms of their situational constraints. They considered the president's warnings before the crisis and the imposition of the quarantine once the missiles were discovered as policies dictated by domestic and foreign-policy needs. They interpreted the Soviet military buildup in Cuba and the attempt to deploy the missiles secretly as reflective of the aggressive disposition of Soviet communism. Khrushchev made similar kinds of attributions; he considered the missile deployment as a response to pressing domestic and foreign needs and attributed Kennedy's hostility to Castro, and later the quarantine, as consistent with the aggressive nature of capitalism.[26]

The proportionality bias assumes that people will make an effort proportional to the ends they seek.[27] We make inferences about the nature and importance of others' goals from the costs they are willing to pay to attain their objectives.[28] The Soviet Union's seeming willingness to court war in Cuba accordingly reflected its leaders' expectation of the possibility of enormous rewards. A similar logic dictated the assessment by the Carter administration of Soviet motives for invading Afghanistan.[29]

A second explanation for deterrence failure, consistent with the strategy's assumptions, is that the defender did not implement the strategy properly. Deterrence predicts that challenges will occur when defenders have failed to develop adequate military capability or demonstrate resolve. Because leaders estimate the costs of confrontation to be extremely high and consider their adversary to be instrumentally rational, they reason that they have failed to convince their adversary of their military capability or resolve. When leaders believe that their adversary has underestimated their resolve, they will see any retreat as fraught with symbolic as well as substantive costs.

Kennedy and his advisors made this assessment in 1962. They were convinced, falsely we now know, that Khrushchev had gone ahead with the missile deployment because he did not believe that Kennedy had the courage to provoke a confrontation. There was a consensus, Robert McNamara reported, that "if we did not respond forcefully in Cuba, the Soviets would continue to poke and prod us elsewhere."[30] The president worried particularly about Berlin, where he expected the costs of confrontation to be much higher and his ability to resist Soviet action to be correspondingly less, given the unfavorable military balance. The need to prevent a confrontation in Berlin was probably the principal foreign-policy concern driving the blockade decision.

In 1973, Kissinger and his colleagues also worried that Soviet leaders would underestimate American resolve if they did not respond to Breznev's threat that he might act unilaterally. Unlike Kennedy and the Ex Comm, they did empathize with the objectives of Soviet leaders and did consider a defensive interpretation of Soviet objectives. They nevertheless considered Brezhnev's letter a challenge to the United States. Kissinger speculated that the Soviet Union had threatened that it might intervene because Nixon was crippled by Watergate. Echoing the lessons of Munich, Kissinger observed that "A leader known to yield to intimidation invites it."[31] The alert would bank resolve and build the deterrent reputation of the United States for the future.

These two explanations of deterrence failure are based on contrasting premises. The first assumes reasonably accurate assessment of the defender's resolve by a challenger, whereas the second assumes miscalculation of the defender's resolve. Logically, the two explanations are mutually exclusive. Empirical evidence indicates that they can be reinforcing. In Cuba, the same Ex Comm officials made both arguments; they interpreted the missile deployment as evidence of the Kremlin's willingness to risk war *and* the result of the administration's failure to develop an adequate reputation for resolve. The two interpretations together created an enormous sense of threat. Kennedy was convinced that he not only had to get the missiles out of Cuba but he had to do so in a public confrontation that would teach Khrushchev respect for American resolve. In 1973, the sense of threat was less because American leaders argued only that Brezhnev could not be allowed to miscalculate American resolve. Even then, the threat was exaggerated.

The strategy of deterrence makes unrealistic assumptions about the way people reason. Evidence from these as well as many other cases indicates that human beings are not always instrumentally rational and are even less likely to be so in acute crises when they are emotionally aroused and confront intense conflict among their objectives. Yet this is precisely the situation in which defenders most rely on deterrence. The policy-making environment is also far from transparent. Cultural, political and personal barriers to assessment frequently combine to make it opaque to outsiders.

The missile crisis was resolved in part because Kennedy revised his initially high estimate of threat. The Soviet leader's caution during the crisis, his letters to Kennedy, and the information that reached the White House through the Dobrynin-Robert Kennedy back channel led the president to take seriously the possibility that Khrushchev's decision to send missiles to Cuba may have been prompted by at least some defensive objectives. He also recognized that Khrushchev had seriously miscalculated the consequences of his own action.

Policymakers who have relied on deterrence are reluctant to reconsider its validity once it fails. They more often use its assumptions to explain its failure. As we have seen in the cases of 1962 and 1973, this leads to exaggerated estimates of threat and responses that can provoke crises and make them more acute. Only after Kennedy reconsidered his initial interpretation of Khrushchev's goals that had been informed by the logic of deterrence, did the crisis become easier to resolve.

DETERRENCE AND STRESS

When deterrence fails, it can create stress by denying leaders early warning and the time they need to consider their options. It can also trigger shock and anger because commitments that leaders have made have been challenged. Stress can seriously degrade performance in the crisis that follows the failure of deterrence.[32]

In his analysis of the impact of stress on crisis decision making, Alexander George contends that no aspect of the policy-making process is immune to its effects. Stress can impair attention and perception: important aspects of the crisis situation may escape scrutiny, conflicting values and interests at stake may be ignored, the range of perceived alternatives is likely to narrow but not necessarily to the best option, and the search for relevant options tends to be dominated by past experience. There is a tendency to fall back on familiar solutions that have worked in the past whether or not they are appropriate to the present situation.

Acute stress can also increase cognitive rigidity. It can impair the ability to improvise and reduce creativity, diminish receptivity to information that challenges existing beliefs, increase stereotyped thinking, and reduce tolerance for ambiguity leading to a premature termination of the search for information. Stress can also shorten and narrow leaders' perspectives. They will pay less attention to longer-range consequences of their options and to the side effects of the alternatives they are considering. Finally, stress can encourage leaders to shift the burden of decision to their opponent. Under stress, leaders tend to believe that their options are quite limited and that their opponent can prevent an impending disaster.[33]

These stress-induced decisional pathologies have been well-documented in analyses of important crises in this century.[34] Critics contend that these cases are atypical and deny that stress poses a serious problem for crisis management.[35] The disagreement is in part a function of the failure to distinguish among different kinds of stress.

We identify three different kinds of stress. Stress can be induced by the recognition that there is insufficient time to perform allotted tasks and by insufficient rest from the demands of the task. Stress can also be triggered when a threat of loss provokes internal conflict. Severe stress can be created when situational threats exacerbate already existing internal conflict.[36] There is evidence of the first two kinds of stress in the crises of 1962 and 1973.

In the Cuban missile crisis, leaders were exhausted by their increased work load. Dean Rusk reports that President Kennedy and his advisors got very little sleep for two weeks:

> I averaged about four hours of sleep per night during the crisis, and John Kennedy could not have slept much either. In his memoirs even Nikita Khrushchev admitted that he slept on his office couch during the crisis. Sleeplessness, suspicion, ignorance about what the other fellow is going to do all take their toll. In a future crisis how long can human beings hold up? Would there be a point at which exhaustion might affect judgment and some leader might say, 'the hell with it,' and push the button?[37]

In 1973, American officials also testified to the numbing effect of fatigue-induced stress. Joseph Sisco, then assistant secretary for Near Eastern and South Asian affairs, believes that it accounts for the otherwise inexplicable failure of Gromyko and Kissinger at their meeting in Moscow on 20 October to make provision for personnel to supervise the cease-fire in the field:

> Before we left for Moscow, I hadn't slept for twenty-four hours and Henry was very tired. I said to him: "Henry, you must insist that when we get to Moscow, we have no meetings. We need the sleep." Henry answered: "I promise, I promise." Of course, when we got to Moscow, Brezhnev wanted to see us right away. We had one of those huge Russian dinners that lasted until three in the morning. We tried to stay away from substance, but inevitably the talk turned that way. I couldn't stay awake. Candidly, it was too much. The meeting was scheduled for 11 A.M. the next morning. We barely had time to draft a document.[38]

Exhausted and preoccupied with larger issues, very experienced and able officials simply forgot to build in machinery to supervise the cease-fire.

The effects of fatigue and time pressure were also evident on the night of 24 October. Kissinger and his colleagues met in the White House Situation Room to consider their response to Brezhnev's letter. They estimated that if the Soviet Union were going to send forces to Egypt, it would do so in a matter of hours. In little more than an hour they had decided to alert American forces worldwide.

There was very little discussion of the likelihood that the Soviet Union would deploy troops. The issue was quickly transformed into the search for an immediate response to a Soviet challenge, irrespective of whether Moscow intended to implement its threat. The worldwide alert of strategic forces was chosen with little consideration of its capacity to deter Soviet military intervention. There was virtually no discussion of alternative measures that might have constituted an effective signal to Moscow with a reduced risk of escalation. The failure to understand the operational and technical requirements of the alert decision was in part the result of inadequate time to think it through, to familiarize participants in the meeting with its consequences, and to consider alternatives that would have minimized the risks.

Stress induced by information overload, time constraints, and fatigue was not crippling. However, it did degrade performance. In 1973, Brezhnev, acutely conscious of the urgency of the plight of the trapped Egyptian army, added the last threatening sentence to his letter to Nixon, and American leaders quickly chose a DEFCON III alert without adequate consideration of its consequences. In the missile crisis, the evidence indicates that Kennedy and Khrushchev actually performed *better* at the end of the crisis than they did at the beginning, even though they were tired and operating under greater time constraints. Their thinking was less stereotyped, their diplomacy more imaginative, and they demonstrated increased rather than diminished ability to concentrate and think through problems.

A second kind of stress occurs when a threat of severe loss provokes internal conflict. Motivational psychologists portray policymakers as emotional beings, not rational calculators, who are beset by doubts and uncertainties and are reluctant to make irrevocable choices. Important decisions generate conflict, defined as simultaneous opposing tendencies to accept and reject given courses of action. This conflict and the stress it generates become acute when policymakers realize that any available course of action entails a risk of serious loss.[39]

Policymakers who confront this kind of dilemma are likely to practice defensive avoidance: they procrastinate, shift responsibility for the decision, and bolster. Bolstering allows people to convince themselves that their policy will succeed. It is most likely to happen when policymakers have lost hope of finding a satisfactory option and are unable to postpone a decision or transfer responsibility to someone else. Instead, they commit themselves to the least objectionable option and proceed to exaggerate its positive consequences and minimize its costs. They continue to think about the problem but ward off anxiety by selective attention and other forms of distorted information processing designed to insulate themselves from information that points to the risks of their policy. If confronted with such information, they alter its implications through a process of wishful thinking and rationalization that argues against the prospect of serious loss if the current policy is unchanged.[40]

Late on the night of 24 October, when a piece of misleading tactical intelligence suggested that the Soviet Union might send troops to Egypt despite the nuclear alert, Kissinger searched desperately for an appropriate conventional response. A "frantic" Kissinger ordered Roy Atherton and William Quandt to draft a plan to deploy American troops immediately to the Middle East, although not to Israel. Quandt subsequently admitted to his confusion about where American forces would be sent.[41] Kissinger could find no good option, but felt pressed to respond to what he thought was an imminent Soviet deployment. If Brezhnev sent forces to the Middle East, so would the United States, even if no country would receive them. Early the next morning, Kissinger advised the president, and Nixon agreed, to send American forces to the Middle East if the Soviet Union deployed forces in Egypt.[42] Fortunately, the threat dissipated before Nixon and Kissinger had to implement their decision.

The American discovery of Soviet missiles in Cuba created a personal and political crisis for President Kennedy because he had believed Khrushchev's assurances that he would exercise restraint and had declared publicly that the introduction of offensive weapons into Cuba would be unacceptable. At the first Ex Comm meeting on the morning of 16 October, President Kennedy gave evidence of acute stress. Normally an exceedingly articulate man, he found it difficult to complete a simple declarative sentence; he repeatedly interrupted himself and spoke in poorly linked phrases, many of them seeming non sequiturs. The excerpt below indicates how difficult he found it to focus his thoughts.

> I don't think we got much time on these missiles. They may be. . . . So it may be that we just have to, we can't wait two weeks while we're getting ready to, to roll. Maybe just have to just take *them out*, and continue our other preparations if we decide to do that. That may be where we end up. I think we ought to, beginning right now, be preparing to. . . . Because that's what we're going to do *anyway*. We're certainly going to do number one; we're going to take out these, uh, missiles.[43]

Kennedy's manner and bearing also betrayed stress. "He was very clipped, very tense," remembers Deputy Secretary of Defense Roswell Gilpatric. "I don't recall a time when I saw him more preoccupied and less given to any light touch at all."[44] The White House tapes reveal that Kennedy was an uncompromising hawk on 16 October. He appeared committed to an air strike against the missiles followed by an invasion, and devoted much of the Ex Comm's first meeting to a discussion of the military preparations these operations would require.[45]

Kennedy's stress on 16 October was attributable in the first instance to shock and anger. Throughout the summer he had been under increasing pressure to take a more militant stance against Castro but had wisely recognized that an invasion would be costly and had the potential of escalating into a wider conflict with the Soviet Union. He had tried to finesse his political problem by publicly committing the United States to oppose something he did not expect the Soviet Union to do. He was now forced to recognize that he had made a serious miscalculation. By practicing deterrence, he had exacerbated his political and international difficulties.[46]

Kennedy was particularly vulnerable after he warned Khrushchev not to send missiles to Cuba. If Khrushchev chose to ignore his warnings and deploy the missiles, the costs would be far greater once Kennedy had publicly warned the Soviet leader. Leaders who have been challenged after they had made commitments have been known to engage in denial. Kaiser Wilhelm in 1914, Joseph Stalin in 1941, and Jawaharlal Nehru in 1962 manipulated their country's intelligence networks so that they reported only positive information and assessments. When confronted with discrepant and threatening information, they did their best to deny, discredit, or distort the information to make it consistent with their needs. They then all suffered dissociative reactions or crippling disabilities when the threatening events occurred.[47]

Pushed by domestic political pressure and John McCone's persistence, Kennedy ordered increased intelligence coverage of Cuba. Because he was reasonably confident that no missiles would be discovered, intensive surveillance of Cuba aroused little anxiety. The president was open-minded in his search for and evaluation of new information. Ironically, the president's confidence in deterrence freed him to search actively for information he did not expect to find.

Kennedy was reluctant to give credit to unsubstantiated refugee reports of missiles, as was the CIA for legitimate professional reasons. However, throughout the summer and fall, he periodically summoned Ray Cline of the CIA to the White House to brief him on the latest intelligence about Cuba. According to Cline, the president was anxious to hear the facts about the Soviet buildup; he never encouraged the CIA to shade their reports to suit his political needs.[48]

Kennedy's open-mindedness and his insistence on a major intelligence effort had important, positive consequences for his ability to cope with the discovery of Soviet missile bases in Cuba. It facilitated the American discovery of the missile bases before Khrushchev announced their presence. This significantly reduced the psychological shock of discovery. The discovery provoked extreme anger—directed at himself as well as at Khrushchev—and great stress but did not incapacitate the president or stampede him into an emotional and poorly thought out response.

Of equal importance, the discovery of the missiles provided the administration with a week to gather additional information and consider an appropriate response. When the missiles were first discovered, Kennedy's stress was also a function of the decisions he faced. Decisional conflict and its associated stress become acute when people realize that any course of action open to them entails a risk of serious loss. The choice, as Kennedy conceived it on 16 October, was between accepting the Soviet missiles—out of the question because of domestic politics and reputational costs—and military action, with all its attendant risks of a wider and possibly nuclear war. During the week they had to consider their options, the president and his advisors were able to control their anger and frame the problem they faced in a broader and more appropriate perspective. The Ex Comm summaries and tapes, and the memoirs of its participants, attest to the thoughtful way in which they weighed the relative merits and drawbacks of the blockade, air strike, and invasion, and then planned the implementation of the blockade once the president had made his decision. Kennedy's choice of the blockade can be regarded not only as an astute political strategy but also as a clever psychological one. It was an attempt by the president to buy time and escape, at least temporarily, the frightening and anxiety-ridden choice between negotiation (capitulation) and force (war). The John Kennedy who chose the blockade on 21 October had come a long way, emotionally and intellectually, from the frightened and stressed leader who had presided over the 16 October Ex Comm meeting.

Kennedy subsequently recognized that his judgment had been affected by anger and stress. Looking back on the crisis, he confessed that if it had been necessary to act in the first two days, "I don't think probably we would have chosen as prudently as we finally did."[49] Former Ex Comm members have the same impression. Robert McNamara is convinced that if the president had been forced to make a decision early in the crisis, he would have launched an air strike against Cuba as a prelude to an invasion.[50]

Unlike Kennedy, Khrushchev tried to insulate himself from threatening information. His precrisis behavior was characterized by bolstering and denial. He dismissed Kennedy's September warnings out of hand and never questioned his belief that the Soviet missile bases in Cuba would be fully operational before they were discovered. Irrefutable evidence may be necessary to overcome such defenses.[51] However, for people who need to protect themselves against a threatening reality, almost any evidence is refutable. For at least twenty-four hours, Stalin refused to believe that the German invasion of the Soviet Union was anything more than an unauthorized large-scale border incursion. He would not allow Soviet forces to counterattack for fear that it would trigger a real invasion.[52] Khrushchev at first also sought refuge in delusion: shortly after the quarantine was announced, he tried to convince himself and his colleagues in the Presidium that the blockade was evidence that Kennedy was prepared to accept the missile bases.[53]

Khrushchev's precrisis behavior outwardly resembled that of other leaders who subsequently resorted to extreme defense mechanisms. But Khrushchev's response to the reality he had sought to deny was not as severe. His initial attempt at denial, apparent in the Presidium meeting, gave way to outbursts of anger and threats of war. Although severely stressed, Khrushchev refrained from taking any immediate action. Within a few days, he had mustered the inner resources to confront and cope creatively with his political and personal dilemma.

Khrushchev's adaptive response may have been a reflection of his greater mental stability. For Kaiser Wilhelm, Stalin, and Nehru, evidence of their miscalculations represented an acute threat to their political goals and personality structures. For Khrushchev, such evidence appears to have threatened only his political goals. He had bolstered his difficult and risky decision to send missiles to Cuba but was secure enough to be able to acknowledge his miscalculation.

Khrushchev's adaptive response was also facilitated by Kennedy's choice of the blockade. It gave the Soviet leader more time to react and consider his response. Kennedy also gave Khrushchev additional time by deciding to allow a Soviet oil tanker and an East German passenger ship to pass unchallenged through the blockade line. Soviet officials report that Khrushchev needed at least a few days to marshall his inner resources, confront the unpleasant reality of his miscalculation, and work out the outlines of the Soviet response. Khrushchev's agitated emotional state during the first forty-eight hours of the crisis provides additional evidence for the supposition that an unannounced American air strike against the missile bases might have had catastrophic consequences. It would have significantly sharpened the dilemma that Khrushchev confronted at precisely the moment that he was least capable of responding rationally.

Our analysis suggests that different kinds of stress can contribute to crisis and seriously impair the quality of policy making. In 1962, stress triggered by the threat of loss helped to create the crisis because the coping mechanisms Khrushchev adopted blinded him to the likely adverse consequences of his policies and encouraged him to brush aside Kennedy's warnings. Kennedy and Khrushchev were severely stressed when the crisis began for them but had time to recover from its effects before having to make critical decisions. Discovery of the missile sites by American intelligence and the administration's ability to keep that discovery a secret provided Kennedy and his advisors with almost a week to formulate their response. Kennedy's experience with stress sensitized him to its dangers and led him to try to give Khrushchev enough time to overcome his shock and consider his predicament rationally. Kennedy later told the National Security Council that he was convinced that if Soviet leaders had to react to the blockade in only "an hour or two, their actions would have been spasmodic and might have resulted in nuclear war."[54] Without time, crisis management would have been seriously impaired. In 1973, stress was triggered principally by shortage of time and fatigue. Although this kind of stress is less severe than the stress triggered by the threat of loss, it had significant consequences for crisis management.[55]

Our analysis suggests a paradoxical relationship between deterrence and stress. The best antidote to stress engendered either by situational factors that provoke internal conflict or by external conditions is time. Time is often a function of early warning. Early warning, however, is less likely when leaders' analysis of information is shaped by the logic of deterrence. Crises that grow out of the failure of deterrence are least likely to provide the time leaders need to cope with the stress generated by the challenge to their deterrent commitments.

DETERRENCE AND THE POLITICAL ROOM TO MANEUVER

Deterrence and compellence depend in part on imparting credibility to commitments. To make their threats credible, leaders often "burn their bridges" by making their commitments public. A public commitment enhances credibility by increasing the political price of backing down. Deterrence and domestic politics accordingly stand in a complex relationship to one another. Leaders must secure the support of important domestic groups if their threats are to be credible, but they must avoid becoming prisoners of the public expectations and passions they help to create. The crises in 1962 and 1973 illustrate two different facets of the complex relationship between domestic politics and threat-based strategies.

In 1962, even before President Kennedy warned the Soviet Union that deployment of Soviet missiles in Cuba would be unacceptable, he faced strong public and congressional pressure. Anti-Castro passions ran high and were stoked by Republicans who hoped to embarrass and weaken the administration. Kennedy exacerbated his domestic political problem by declaring publicly that deployment of Soviet missiles in Cuba would be unacceptable to the United States. Reasonably confident that Khrushchev would not be so "irrational" as to send missiles to Cuba, Kennedy drew the line. When the Soviet missile sites were discovered, Kennedy was caught between a duplicitous adversary and an aroused public opinion.

Faced with this choice, Kennedy desperately searched for a way out of the crisis. His solution, a public-private exchange of missiles, resolved the crisis and largely circumvented the political constraints created by deterrence. By withholding information about the Jupiters, Kennedy created the political space he needed to manage the crisis, keep the support of the public and Congress, preserve the fragile consensus of the Ex Comm, and gain the political freedom to make the concessions necessary to resolve the crisis. His public pledge not to invade Cuba and the secret concession on the Jupiters convinced Khrushchev to withdraw the Soviet missiles. The president calculated that a pledge not to invade Cuba would offend the strongly anti-Castro forces but would not significantly erode his public standing. He judged correctly. In the eyes of most Americans, Kennedy won a great victory by demonstrating resolve and forcing the Soviet Union to withdraw its missiles.

In 1973, domestic political pressures pushed in the other direction and complicated the administration's attempt at deterrence. Nixon was in the midst of the acute domestic political crisis of Watergate. Suspicion of the president's motives and actions was widespread in the Congress, the media, and the public at large. Public confidence in Nixon was low. At the meeting in the White House on the night of 24 October, Kissinger and his staff speculated about whether the Soviet Union would have challenged a "functioning" president. "There was some discussion," Kissinger wrote in his memoirs, "about whether the United States—in response to the Soviet dispatch of troops to Egypt—would be [politically] able to make a countervailing move by putting its own troops in the area. There was concern whether our domestic political situation would permit such a military move. But I was adamant that we would have to act in the national interest regardless of media skepticism or political opposition."[56] Kissinger told his staff that night: "If we can't do what is right because we might get killed, then we should do what is right. We will have to contend with the charge in the domestic media that we provoked this. The real charge is that we provoked this by being soft."[57]

At a press conference at noon the next day, reporters peppered the secretary with provocative questions. They asked if the Soviet Union had exploited the domestic crisis in Washington and if Nixon had created a crisis with the Soviet Union to distract attention from the domestic political crisis at home. "The queries as to our motives . . ." Kissinger observed, "showed how narrow was our margin for policy. If we courted confrontation, following the advice of the anti-détente zealots, we would almost surely be undermined by the Watergate bloodhounds who would treat every challenge to the Soviet Union as a maneuver by which their hated quarry, Nixon, was trying to escape them. . . . I tremble at the thought of what fate would have been in store for us in such an environment if we had had to sustain a crisis for very many days."[58]

Kissinger was correct in believing that the margin for deterrence as a strategy of crisis management was narrow. Open public skepticism undercut whatever credibility the strategic alert had and would have made it difficult for Nixon and Kissinger to have deployed American troops to the Middle East had the Soviet Union sent forces to the region. In 1973, unlike in 1962, domestic political pressures simultaneously undermined the credibility of threats and worked against the escalation of the crisis.

Brezhnev and his advisors interpreted the alert as a response to Watergate. Their assessment contributed to the resolution of the crisis in two quite unexpected ways. Insofar as Soviet leaders understood the alert as an attempt to distract the American people from Nixon's domestic problems, they saw no need to match the American action. Soviet leaders were also concerned about what else a politically pressed Nixon might be tempted to do to deflect the intense criticism he faced at home. In 1962, Khrushchev and Kennedy worried that the other would be captured by militants opposed to concessions and committed to military confrontation. In 1973, Brezhnev and his advisors worried that Nixon would choose to deal with Watergate by engaging in "irresponsible" action. In both 1962 and 1973, the concern to forestall escalation pushed Soviet leaders to find a quick political solution to the crisis.

In the United States, public opinion enhanced the credibility of threats in 1962 and undermined their credibility in 1973. Greater recognition of the costs of nuclear war, memories of Vietnam, and distrust of Richard Nixon all contributed to this shift. Although any future crisis will obviously have its idiosyncratic characteristics, the general trend of public opinion, at least until Operation Desert Storm, has been increasing concern about war. The trend line suggests that future domestic political pressures are more likely to resemble the demands for restraint on Nixon in 1973 than the calls to action that Kennedy confronted in 1962. Presidents may find themselves constrained in their capacity to manipulate the risk of war to achieve their objectives in a crisis.

To the extent that American public opinion is willing to run the risk of war only when it is convinced that vital national interests are at stake, presidents will have much less leeway to manipulate public opinion at home to signal resolve abroad. If leaders cannot persuade their own people that vital national interests are at stake, they will find it difficult, if not impossible, to convince adversaries of their interests and resolve.[59] The limited evidence currently available suggests that Saddam Hussein decided to stand firm in part because he doubted the credibility of the American threat to compel. He did not believe that the American people would support war or permit the president to continue the fighting once the casualties mounted.[60] Under these conditions, the use of threat-based strategies to deter or compel the other side to back down by raising the risk of war can prove especially dangerous. A president may draw the line, but find that an adversary, paying attention to a president's domestic political constraints, nevertheless decides to cross that line. Leaders could find themselves engaged in a war that they did not expect and that domestic public opinion did not support. More so than in the past, successful deterrence and compellence will depend on the capacity to communicate interests to domestic constituencies as well as to adversaries abroad.

DETERRENCE AND LOSS OF CONTROL

Strategies of crisis management can be victimized by unintentional errors in their execution. Loss of control is likely to be more acute when leaders practice deterrence and compellence to manage the crisis. Leaders are frequently insensitive to these risks when they use military alerts and deployments to signal resolve and make their threats more credible.

Analyses of crises in this century suggest that leaders sometimes worry that their adversaries will present serious threats to their control of policy, but almost invariably minimize the problems they are likely to face from disaffected subordinates, unwieldy bureaucracies, and independent allies.[61]

Evidence from the crises of 1962 and 1973 indicate that such optimism is misplaced. When American and Soviet leaders alerted or deployed forces to deter or compel, they encountered insubordination, institutional planning, and politically autonomous allies that interfered with their ability to control strategy and made both crises more difficult to manage.

In both countries, but especially in the Soviet Union, disgruntled military officers attempted to take matters into their own hands during the Cuban missile crisis. Soviet generals willfully misinterpreted their orders not to fire at American airplanes or ships unless Cuba was attacked. Outraged at having to tolerate American intelligence overflights of Cuba, they gave a Soviet SAM commander permission to shoot down a U-2. The downing of this aircraft and the death of its pilot was arguably the most serious moment of the crisis. When word of the incident reached the Ex Comm, there was "almost unanimous agreement" that the president should authorize a retaliatory air-strike.[62] Further attacks on American aircraft would have left him little choice but to do so.

In the United States, Gen. Thomas S. Power, commander of the Strategic Air Command, without the knowledge or authorization of the joint chiefs or secretary of defense, ordered the DEFCON II alert broadcast *en clair*, not in the encrypted form required by regulations.[63] If the Soviet Union had alerted its forces in response, Power might well have gone to the president to plead for a preemptive nuclear strike, arguing that the Soviet alert was the precursor of an attack and that preemption was necessary to save millions of American lives.[64]

Soviet and American military insubordination in the missile crisis was motivated by dissatisfaction with national policy. Serious civilian-military conflict can also arise for institutional reasons. In crisis, political leaders often try to minimize the risks of war associated with military alerts, deployments, or limited operations. Even when they fully support national policy, military leaders naturally attempt to maintain their institutional authority and are reluctant to expose their forces to what they consider unnecessary risks. Generals and admirals may oppose, resist, or disobey directives that threaten these traditional military concerns.[65]

Robert McNamara met an extremely hostile reception from the chief of naval operations, Adm. George Anderson, when he visited the "flagplot," the navy's command center. Anderson was outraged by what he regarded as McNamara's unwarranted interference with the navy's plans and procedures for implementing the blockade. McNamara was angered by Anderson's opposition to his attempt to review these procedures in the hope of preventing unnecessary or provocative use of force against Soviet vessels. However, contrary to many of the allegations that have been made, the navy was scrupulous in carrying out McNamara's instructions, and kept him fully informed of its activities in the Atlantic and along the blockade line.[66]

The time and energy that went into managing the blockade were time and energy that Kennedy and McNamara could not devote to overseeing other military operations. Unknown to anyone in the White House, the first of the fifteen Jupiters became operational on 22 October, the day Kennedy announced the quarantine of Cuba. The Turkish military was given control over the missiles in an elaborate and well-attended public ceremony. Nobody told the president, before or after. Dean Rusk also did not know; he assumed that the missiles were already operational.[67]

Soviet military intelligence had been carefully monitoring the progress of the Jupiters and knew about the transfer of authority to Turkey. The information was passed on to Khrushchev, who may have assumed that Kennedy knew about the ceremony and allowed it to proceed in spite of the crisis.[68] The Jupiter ceremony, and its infelicitous timing, could have provided the incentive, or at least a justification, for the Soviet Union to continue and increase the pace of construction at its missile sites in Cuba.[69] That decision, made by Khrushchev the following morning, appeared ominous to the United States.[70]

By far the most serious American mishap occurred on Saturday morning, at about 10:30 A.M. Washington time. A U-2 operated by SAC's Strategic Reconnaissance Wing at Eielson Air Force Base in Alaska strayed into Soviet air space over the Chukotski Peninsula in eastern Siberia. The pilot radioed for assistance, and fighter aircraft armed with low-yield nuclear air-to-air missiles were sent to escort him home.[71] Soviet MiGs were also scrambled from a base near Wrangel Island. The U-2 left Soviet airspace without any shots being fired.[72] When he heard the news, Roger Hilsman ran upstairs and found Kennedy, Bundy, and several other officials in the office of Evelyn Lincoln, the president's secretary. "The President knew at a glance that something was terribly wrong. Out of breath and shaky from over thirty hours without sleep, I told my story . . . The President gave a short ironic laugh that broke the tension. 'There is always some [son of a bitch] who doesn't get the word.'"[73]

The intrusion provoked a sharp Soviet response. In his letter on 28 October, Khrushchev warned that this kind of overflight could have disastrous consequences:

> The question is, Mr. President: How should we regard this? What is this, a provocation? One of your planes violates our frontier during this anxious time we are both experiencing, when everything has been put into combat readiness. Is it not a fact that an intruding American plane could be easily taken for a nuclear bomber, which might push us to a fateful step; and all the more so since the U.S. Government and Pentagon long ago declared that you are maintaining a continuous nuclear bomber patrol?[74]

The missile crisis was a watershed in American crisis management. It was the Pentagon's first experience with civilian "micromanagement," and many senior officers were predictably outraged. During the following decade, generals and admirals became more sensitive to the political implications of all levels of military operations and more accustomed to civilian oversight. Unfortunately, political leaders did not become correspondingly more aware of the military implications of the political use of force.

In 1973, senior naval officers were deeply concerned about the tactical implications of the orders issued by the White House to the Sixth Fleet in the Mediterranean. Following the DEFCON III alert, three American aircraft carriers were ordered through the appropriate military chain of command to position themselves directly astride Soviet air- and sea-lanes to Egypt. Their possible mission was to interdict the deployment of Soviet troops to Egypt.[75] To reduce the risk of an unintended military encounter, the White House ordered the carriers to remain in narrowly confined operating areas.[76] The commander of the Sixth Fleet had to get permission from the Joint Chiefs of Staff to modify the fleet's operating orders.[77] The decreased room for tactical maneuvers made American ships more vulnerable to a preemptive strike by the Soviet navy and sharply increased tension among naval commanders. To protect themselves, commanders on the scene, acting on their own authority, countertargeted threatening Soviet naval units. Tight political control of the Sixth Fleet by the White House resulted in a more rather than less tactically dangerous situation at sea.[78]

Senior naval officers were deeply worried about the military risks in the Mediterranean. Adm. Thomas Moorer voiced his concern at a White House meeting on the night of 24 October and spoke in support of Vice Adm. Murphy's request for greater freedom of action.[79] His request was turned down by the White House. Despite the concern of senior naval officers, there was no significant loss of control by the political leadership. Naval commanders grumbled but obeyed their orders.

The problem was not the navy but the failure of civilian leaders to understand the risks of the tight coupling of the Soviet and American navies in the Mediterranean. In his desire to use the navy to signal resolve, Kissinger remained insensitive to the dangers created at sea even when they were brought to his attention by senior naval commanders. Fortunately, the crisis was not as acute as the Cuban missile crisis, and neither American nor Soviet commanders thought there was a serious risk of war. They were accordingly willing to exercise much more restraint than they might have in a war-threatening crisis. In such a confrontation, the mutual loading, arming, and "locking on" of nuclear-tipped missiles and cruise missiles, most at exceedingly short range, could have provoked a catastrophic incident.[80]

In 1973, senior military commanders were fully aware of the dangers of inadvertent nuclear war. Unlike their counterparts in 1962, they were more cautious than the civilian leadership. Adm. Moorer followed up the DEFCON III alert order with a secure telephone call to the unified and special commanders to explain the purpose of the alert in greater detail.[81] At 3:37 A.M., he sent them an additional message to explain the political context of the alert.[82] The purpose of the telephone call and follow-up message was to emphasize the political nature of the alert and to ensure its more relaxed and restrained implementation.

In 1962, American officials were on the whole overconfident about their ability to control and coordinate the alerting and deployment of forces. McGeorge Bundy remembered that "At no time did any consideration of nuclear alerts affect us in *any* way. That just wasn't part of our sense of danger."[83] Robert McNamara admits that neither he nor the president gave much thought to the dangers of a strategic alert or conventional military preparations. "Perhaps we should have been more concerned, but we never discussed it."[84] They did not realize the ways in which insubordination, bureaucratic rigidity, and human error could interfere with strategies of compellence and threaten its objectives.

Subsequent administrations appear to have learned little of value from the missile crisis. In discussing the worldwide strategic alert of October 1973, one of Kissinger's special assistants remarked:

> We did not worry about the alert. The whole point was to face them [the Soviet Union] down. We were sure it would work. There is a certain margin for error. I was never afraid that anything would get out of control.[85]

Although civilian officials continued to overestimate their ability to control alerts and deployments, the American military in 1973 was far better attuned to the political objectives of the use of force than their predecessors had been in 1962, and far more concerned about controlling escalation.[86] Fortunately, the Cold War has ended and strategic systems are no longer tightly coupled.[87] The Soviet Union is no longer a unified state, and the future of its remaining nuclear weapons is uncertain. The problem has largely disappeared, but leaders did not learn the right lessons.

A more serious threat to crisis management is the independent actions of allies. The crises in 1962 and 1973 offer dramatic evidence of how third parties interfered with superpower efforts to control escalation and avoid war when forces were alerted and deployed. In the missile crisis, Fidel Castro was the major offender. At the outset of the crisis, Havana had mobilized its reserve of fifty antiaircraft batteries in expectation of an attack.[88] On Friday, 26 October, Castro decided that he would no longer tolerate low-level reconnaissance flights because they were a precursor to a surprise attack. He informed Gen. Pliyev of his decision, and Cuban batteries opened fired the next day.[89]

Havana's belligerence stood in sharp contrast to Moscow's caution. Castro justified his decision to shoot at reconnaissance aircraft as necessary to deny Washington critical intelligence it needed to launch a surprise attack. His intervention with Soviet generals led to the downing of the U-2. Khrushchev was "absolutely shocked" to learn that a U-2 had been downed and sent a cable to Castro pleading with him not to shoot at any more American planes.[90] Castro conceded that another incident could "seriously harm" Soviet-American efforts to resolve the crisis and promised to instruct Cuban batteries to withhold their fire as long as negotiations were under way. He nevertheless warned that under current conditions there was still a danger of "accidental incidents."[91]

In the immediate aftermath of the crisis, Castro was bitterly angry at Khrushchev for having agreed to withdraw the Soviet missiles in return for what he considered a worthless pledge by the United States not to invade Cuba.[92] On 28 October, the day Castro learned of the Soviet-American agreement, he ordered Cuban forces to keep shooting at American planes and went to visit an antiaircraft battery at San Antonio. No incident occurred because Kennedy suspended all low-level flights at that morning's Ex Comm meeting.[93] According to Sergo Mikoyan, Ambassador Alekseev pleaded unsuccessfully with Castro to stop shooting at the planes. "Fidel is a very independent man. And he said: 'No! I shall not permit it [continued American overflights]! We are an independent country and we cannot permit any violation of our airspace!'"[94]

Soviet officials report that Cuban forces surrounded four Soviet missile bases on 28 October to prevent the withdrawal of any missiles. They remained at three of the sites for three days, and at the fourth until 3 November.[95] Castro subsequently gave several reasons for his admittedly "defiant and almost intransigent attitude in the wake of the crisis." The Cubans had accepted the missiles, at great risk to themselves, to assist the socialist camp, or so they believed. Yet, the missiles were withdrawn without consulting them. At the very least, Castro explained, the Soviets "could have informed us of the messages of the twenty-sixth and twenty-seventh. We heard over the radio that there had been an agreement. So we were humiliated." The Cubans also felt sorely used when they found out that the Soviet Union exchanged the missiles in Cuba for missiles in Turkey. The country's security, Castro insisted, had been endangered by Khrushchev who used Cuba as a "bargaining chip."[96]

Anastas Mikoyan was sent to Havana to persuade Castro to let the Soviet Union withdraw its missiles and IL-28 bombers. It took Mikoyan sixteen days of intensive diplomacy to secure Castro's approval.[97] On his way home, Mikoyan stopped off in Washington and confided to the Americans that "Castro is crazy."[98] Castro remained adamant in his refusal to cooperate in any of the external inspection and verification measures that the United States had demanded and that the Soviet Union had accepted. As a result, the Kennedy administration withheld its quid pro quo and refused to issue the promised formal assurances that the United States would not invade Cuba.[99]

The crisis in 1973 was a multilateral confrontation with five principal actors: the United States, the Soviet Union, Israel, Egypt, and Syria. The independent policies of Egypt and Israel imperiled crisis management at every stage of the crisis. The interests of Cairo and Jerusalem were not the same as those of Moscow and Washington: the conflict between Egypt and Israel was fundamental and basic to their respective national survival. They gave far lower priority to preventing and resolving a crisis between the superpowers than did the Soviet Union and the United States.

The Soviet Union tried and failed to prevent Egypt from going to war.[100] Soviet leaders tried and failed to get Egypt to agree to a cease-fire before it suffered a military defeat. The United States tried and succeeded only belatedly in persuading Israel to halt its military offensive against Egypt after a cease-fire had been negotiated. Both Brezhnev and Nixon underestimated the difficulty they would face at every step in controlling militarily dependent but politically independent allies.

The evidence from these cases suggests that although technical obstacles to control were real, political threats constituted a far more serious danger to national leaders trying to manage an acute international crisis. The technical threat has received considerable attention, whereas political threats to loss of control tend to be all but ignored in crisis planning. They are ignored in part because of the continued reliance on deterrence and compellence as strategies of crisis prevention and management.

Deterrence and compellence require leaders to make commitments credible, to demonstrate resolve, and to raise the risk of war. They encourage leaders to rely on military alerts and deployments and to court possible loss of control to demonstrate resolve where it would otherwise be difficult to threaten war credibly. Leaders have accordingly been reluctant to consider the risks and dangers inherent in these kinds of actions. As evidence from these two cases also demonstrates, allies whose interests differ from those of their patrons will try to exploit the opportunities these commitments provide to advance their own agendas. Shortly after the missile crisis, Robert McNamara is reported to have exclaimed: "There is no longer any such thing as strategy, only crisis management."[101] In response to some of the new evidence that has since become available, McNamara confessed that "'Managing' crises is the wrong term; you don't 'manage' them because you *can't* 'manage' them." Crisis management, he now insists, "is a dangerous metaphor, because it's misleading."[102] Deterrence and compellence, with their currency of threats and commitments that court loss of control, combined with allied willingness to exploit these commitments for their own ends, make them dangerous strategies in crisis.

DETERRENCE, COMPELLENCE, AND CRISIS

Deterrence and compellence were not terribly successful in preventing or managing crises in these two cases. In 1962, deterrence as practiced by both sides provoked the crisis. Compellence by the United States did help to resolve the crisis, not only by raising the risk of war but also by communicating American interests effectively to the Soviet leadership. In 1973, Israeli deterrence helped to provoke an Egyptian and Syrian challenge and blinded Israel's and American leaders to the likelihood of an attack. Soviet compellence and American deterrence were both irrelevant in the resolution of the crisis. Soviet compellence backfired by provoking the American alert and the alert in turn angered the Soviet leadership.

This chapter explored the dangers of deterrence and compellence and the consequences of their failure for crisis prevention and management. Confidence in deterrence can blind leaders to the likelihood of a challenge, generate exaggerated threat assessments that then provoke crises and make them more difficult to manage, exacerbate stress when leaders' commitments are challenged, run the risk of loss of control when military alerts and deployments are used to raise the risk of war and signal resolve, and provide allies with the opportunity to exploit deterrent commitments.

The dangers of deterrence and compellence do not imply their wholesale rejection as strategies of crisis prevention and management. There is a class of cases, as we noted in the last chapter, in which deterrence and compellence are appropriate. When adversaries are opportunity-driven expansionists and relatively free of domestic constraints, threat-based strategies can be appropriate in crisis prevention and management. Even then, they may not work, for reasons not directly related to the strategies.[103] Leaders need to recognize the limitations and dangers of the strategies of deterrence and compellence and balance their costs against their possible rewards. A careful cost calculus of this kind will encourage leaders to put more emphasis on alternative strategies of conflict prevention and management.

Nuclear Threats and Nuclear Weapons

THE ROLE of nuclear weapons in Soviet-American relations has been hotly debated. Politicians, generals, and most academic strategists believe that America's nuclear arsenal restrained the Soviet Union throughout the Cold War. Critics maintain that nuclear weapons were a root cause of superpower conflict and a threat to peace. Controversy also surrounds the number and kinds of weapons necessary to deter, the political implications of the strategic balance, and the role of nuclear deterrence in hastening the collapse of the Soviet imperium.

These debates have had a distinctly theological quality. Partisans frequently defended their positions without recourse to relevant evidence. Some advocated strategic doctrines that were consistent with military postures that they supported. "War-fighting" doctrines were invoked by the air force to justify silo-busting weapons like the MX missile.[1] Mutual Assured Destruction (MAD) was espoused by arms controllers to oppose the deployment of particular weapons systems.

More careful analysts have been alert to the difficulty of making definitive judgments about deterrence in the absence of valid and reliable information about Soviet and Chinese objectives and calculations. McGeorge Bundy, in his masterful *Danger and Survival*, tells a cautionary tale of the impatience of leaders to acquire nuclear weapons, their largely futile attempts to exploit these weapons for political purposes and, finally, their efforts through arms control, to limit the dangers nuclear weapons pose to their owners as well as their targets. Bundy emphasizes the uncertainty of leaders about the dynamics of deterrence and their concerns about the risks of escalation in crisis.[2]

Richard K. Betts, in another exemplary study, illustrates how difficult it is to assess the efficacy of nuclear threats.[3] He found great disparity between the memories of American leaders and the historical record. Some of the nuclear threats American presidents claim were successful were never made.[4] Other threats were so oblique that it is difficult to classify them as threats. Betts was understandably reluctant to credit any nuclear threat with success in the absence of information about the internal deliberations of the target states. When these states behaved in ways that were consistent with their adversary's demands, it was often unclear if the threat was successful or irrelevant. Leaders could have complied because they had been deterred or compelled, they could have been influenced by considerations unrelated to the threat, or they could have intended originally to behave as they did.

Newly declassified documents and extensive interviews with Soviet and American officials permitted us to reconstruct the deliberations of leaders of both superpowers before, during, and after the two most serious nuclear crises of the last thirty years. This evidence sheds new light on some of the controversies at the center of the nuclear debate. Needless to say, definitive judgments must await the opening of archives and more complete information about the calculations of Soviet and American leaders in other crises, as well as those of other nuclear powers.

THE FOUR QUESTIONS

Our analysis is organized around four questions. Each question addresses a major controversy about nuclear deterrence and its consequences. The first and most critical question is the contribution nuclear deterrence made to the prevention of World War III. The conventional wisdom regards deterrence as the principal pillar of the postwar peace between the superpowers. Critics charge that deterrence was beside the point or a threat to the peace. John Mueller, who makes the strongest argument for the irrelevance of nuclear weapons, maintains that the superpowers were restrained by their memories of World War II and their knowledge that even a conventional war would be many times more destructive.[5]

More outspoken critics of deterrence charge that it greatly exacerbated superpower tensions. The deployment of ever more sophisticated weapons of destruction convinced each superpower of the other's hostile intentions and sometimes provoked the kind of aggressive behavior deterrence was intended to prevent. The postwar peace endured despite deterrence.[6]

The second question, of interest to those who believe that deterrence worked, is why and how it works. Some advocates insist that it forestalled Soviet aggression; in its absence Moscow would have attacked Western Europe and possibly have sent forces to the Middle East.[7] More reserved supporters credit the reality of nuclear deterrence with moderating the foreign policies of both superpowers. They maintain that the destructiveness of nuclear weapons encouraged caution and restraint and provided a strong incentive for Moscow and Washington to make the concessions necessary to resolve their periodic crises.[8]

The third question concerns the military requirements of deterrence. In the 1960s, Defense Secretary Robert S. McNamara adopted MAD as the official American strategic doctrine. McNamara contended that the Soviet Union could be deterred by the American capability to destroy 50 percent of its population and industry in a retaliatory strike. He welcomed the effort by the Soviet Union to develop a similar capability in the expectation that secure retaliatory capabilities on both sides would foster stability.[9]

Many military officers and civilian strategists rejected MAD on the grounds that it was not credible to Moscow. To deter the Soviet Union, the United States needed to be able to prevail at any level of conflict. This required a much larger nuclear arsenal and highly accurate missiles necessary to dig out and destroy Soviet missiles in their silos and the underground bunkers where the political and military elite would take refuge in any conflict. "War-fighting" supplanted MAD as the official strategic doctrine during the presidency of Jimmy Carter. The Reagan administration spent vast sums of money to augment conventional forces and to buy the strategic weapons and command and control networks that Pentagon planners considered essential to war-fighting.[10]

An alternative approach to nuclear weapons, "finite deterrence," maintained that Soviet leaders were as cautious as their Western counterparts and just as frightened by the prospects of nuclear war. Nuclear deterrence was far more robust than proponents of either MAD or war-fighting acknowledged and required only limited capabilities—several-hundred nuclear weapons would probably suffice. The doctrine of finite deterrence never had visible support within the American government.[11]

Differences about the requirements of deterrence reflected deeper disagreements about the intentions of Soviet leaders. For war-fighters, the Soviet Union was an implacable foe. Its ruthless leaders would willingly sacrifice their people and industry in pursuit of world domination. They could only be restrained by superior capabilities and demonstrable resolve to use force in defense of vital interests. Partisans of MAD thought the Soviet Union aggressive but cautious. Soviet leaders sought to make gains but were even more anxious to preserve what they already had. The capability to destroy the Soviet Union as a modern industrial power was therefore sufficient to deter attack, but not necessarily to make its leaders behave in a restrained manner. Proponents of war-fighting and MAD stressed the overriding importance of resolve; Soviet leaders had to be convinced that the United States would retaliate if it or its allies were attacked and come to their assistance if they were challenged in other ways.

Finite deterrence was based on the premise that both superpowers had an overriding fear of nuclear war. Small and relatively unsophisticated nuclear arsenals were sufficient to reinforce this fear and the caution it engendered. Larger forces, especially those targeted against the other side's retaliatory capability, were counterproductive; they exacerbated the insecurity of its leaders, confirmed their belief in their adversary's hostility, and encouraged them to deploy similar weapons. Supporters of finite deterrence put much less emphasis on the need to demonstrate resolve. The possibility of retaliation, they believed, was enough to deter attack.

The fourth question concerns the broader political value of nuclear weapons. War fighters maintained that strategic superiority was politically useful and conferred bargaining leverage on a wide range of issues.[12] Most supporters of MAD contended that strategic advantages could only be translated into political influence in confrontations like the missile crisis, in which vital interests were at stake.[13] Other supporters of MAD, and all advocates of finite deterrence, denied that nuclear weapons could serve any purpose beyond deterrence.

Restraining, Provocative, or Irrelevant?

Students of deterrence distinguish between general and immediate deterrence. General deterrence relies on the existing power balance to prevent an adversary from seriously considering a military challenge because of its expected adverse consequences.[14] It is often a country's first line of defense against attack. Leaders resort to the strategy of immediate deterrence only after general deterrence has failed, or when they believe that a more explicit expression of their intent to defend their interests is necessary to buttress general deterrence. If immediate deterrence fails, leaders will find themselves in a crisis, as Kennedy did when American intelligence discovered Soviet missiles in Cuba, or at war, as Israel's leaders did in 1973. General and immediate deterrence represent a progression from a diffuse if real concern about an adversary's intentions to the expectation that a specific interest or commitment is about to be challenged.

Both forms of deterrence assume that adversaries are most likely to resort to force or threatening military deployments when they judge the military balance favorable and question the defender's resolve. General deterrence pays particular importance to the military dimension; it tries to discourage challenges by developing the capability to defend national commitments or inflict unacceptable punishment on an adversary. General deterrence is a long-term strategy. Five-year lead times and longer are common between a decision to develop a weapon and its deployment.

Immediate deterrence is a short-term strategy. Its purpose is to discourage an imminent attack or challenge of a specific commitment. The military component of immediate deterrence must rely on forces in being. To buttress their defensive capability and display resolve, leaders may deploy forces when they anticipate an attack or challenge, as Kennedy did in the aftermath of the summit in June 1961. In response to Khrushchev's ultimatum on Berlin, he sent additional ground and air forces to Germany and strengthened the American garrison in Berlin. These reinforcements were designed to communicate the administration's will to resist any encroachment against West Berlin or Western access routes to the city.

General Deterrence

The origins of the missile crisis indicate that general deterrence, as practiced by both superpowers, was provocative rather than preventive. Soviet officials testified that the American strategic buildup, deployment of missiles in Turkey, and assertions of nuclear superiority, made them increasingly insecure. The president viewed all of these measures as prudent, defensive precautions. American actions had the unanticipated consequence of convincing Khrushchev of the need to protect the Soviet Union and Cuba from American military and political challenges.

Khrushchev was hardly the innocent victim of American paranoia. His nuclear threats and unfounded claims of nuclear superiority were the catalyst for Kennedy's decision to increase the scope and pace of the American strategic buildup. The new American programs and the Strategic Air Command's higher state of strategic readiness exacerbated Soviet perceptions of threat and contributed to Khrushchev's decision to send missiles to Cuba. In attempting to intimidate their adversaries, both leaders helped to bring about the kind of confrontation they were trying to avoid.

Kennedy later speculated, and Soviet officials have since confirmed, that his efforts to reinforce deterrence also encouraged Khrushchev to stiffen his position on Berlin.[15] The action and reaction that linked Berlin and Cuba were part of a larger cycle of insecurity and escalation that reached well back into the 1950s, if not to the beginning of the Cold War. The Soviet challenge to the Western position in Berlin in 1959–61 was motivated by Soviet concern about the viability of East Germany and secondarily by Soviet vulnerability to American nuclear-tipped missiles stationed in Western Europe. The American missiles had been deployed to assuage NATO fears about the conventional military balance on the central front, made more acute by the creation of the Warsaw Pact in 1955. The Warsaw Pact, many Western authorities now believe, represented an attempt by Moscow to consolidate its control over an increasingly restive Eastern Europe.[16]

Once the crisis erupted, general deterrence played an important moderating role. Kennedy and Khrushchev moved away from confrontation and toward compromise because they both feared war. Kennedy worried that escalation would set in motion a chain of events that could lead to nuclear war. Khrushchev's decision to withdraw the missiles indicated that he too was prepared to make sacrifices to avoid war. His capitulation in the face of American military pressure was a humiliating defeat for the Soviet Union and its leader. Soviet officials confirm that it was one factor in his removal from power a year later.[17] For many years, Americans portrayed the crisis as an unalloyed American triumph. Kennedy's concession on the Jupiters and his willingness on Saturday night to consider making that concession public indicate that, when the superpower leaders were "eyeball to eyeball," both sides blinked. One reason they did so was their fear of nuclear war and its consequences.

General deterrence also failed to prevent an Egyptian decision to use force in 1973. President Sadat and his military staff openly acknowledged Egyptian military inferiority. They had no doubt about Israel's resolve to defend itself if attacked. Sadat still chose to fight a limited war. He decided to attack Israel because of intense domestic political pressures to regain the Sinai. He had lost all hope in diplomacy after the failure of the Rogers missions, and although he recognized that the military balance was unfavorable, he expected it to get even worse in the future.

Israel's practice of general deterrence—it acquired a new generation of fighters and bombers—convinced Sadat to initiate military action sooner rather than later. Egyptian military planners devised a strategy intended to compensate for their military inferiority. Egyptian officers sought to capitalize on surprise, occupy the east bank of the Suez Canal, defend against Israeli counterattacks with a mobile missile screen, and press for an internationally imposed cease-fire before their limited gains could be reversed by a fully mobilized Israel. The parallels between 1962 and 1973 are striking. In both cases, attempts to reinforce general deterrence against vulnerable and hard-pressed opponents provoked rather than prevented unwanted challenges.

General deterrence had contradictory implications in the crisis that erupted between the United States and the Soviet Union at the end of the October War. Leaders of both superpowers were confident that the other feared war; general deterrence was robust. This confidence allowed the United States to alert its forces worldwide without fear of escalation. Brezhnev and some of his colleagues, on the other hand, worried about escalation if Soviet forces were deployed in positions in Egypt where they were likely to encounter advancing Israelis. The Politburo agreed that they did not want to be drawn into a military conflict that could escalate. Fear of war restrained the Soviet Union and contributed to the resolution of the crisis.

Immediate deterrence is intended to forestall a specific military deployment or use of force. For immediate deterrence to succeed, the defender's threats must convince adversaries that the likely costs of a challenge will more than offset any possible gains.[18] Immediate deterrence did not prevent the missile crisis. After Khrushchev had decided to send missiles to Cuba, Kennedy warned that he would not tolerate the introduction of Soviet missiles in Cuba. The president issued his threat in the belief that Khrushchev had no intention of establishing missile bases in Cuba. In the face of the president's warnings, Khrushchev proceeded with the secret deployment.

Students of the crisis disagree about why deterrence failed. Some contend that the strategy could not have worked, whereas others insist that Kennedy attempted deterrence too late.[19] Whatever the cause, the failure of deterrence exacerbated the most acute crisis of the Cold War. By making a public commitment to keep Soviet missiles out of Cuba, Kennedy dramatically increased the domestic political and foreign-policy costs of allowing the missiles to remain after they were discovered. A threat originally intended to deflect pressures on the administration to invade Cuba would have made that invasion very difficult to avoid if Soviet leaders had not agreed to withdraw their missiles.

Israel chose not to practice immediate deterrence in 1973. Its leaders were convinced that Egypt would only attack when it could neutralize Israel's air force. Confidence in general deterrence blinded Israel's leaders to the growing desperation of Sadat and his imperative to find a limited military strategy that would achieve his political objective. Israel's leaders worried instead that limited deterrent or defensive measures on their part might provoke Egypt to launch a miscalculated attack.

Even if Israel had practiced immediate deterrence, the evidence suggests that it would have made no difference. It is unlikely that public warnings and mobilization of the Israel Defense Forces would have deterred Egypt; Sadat had expected Israel to mobilize its reserves and reinforce the Bar-Lev Line in response to Egyptian military preparations. He was surprised and pleased that Israel did not take defensive measures and that Egyptian forces did not sustain the high casualties that he had anticipated and was prepared to accept.[20]

When the cease-fire negotiated jointly by Moscow and Washington failed to stop the fighting, Brezhnev threatened to consider unilateral intervention. The United States resorted to immediate deterrence to prevent a Soviet deployment. This was not the first time since the war began that Kissinger had attempted to deter Soviet military intervention. As early as 12 October, he told Dobrynin that any attempt by the Soviet Union to intervene with force would "wreck the entire fabric of U.S.-Soviet relations."[21] Later that day, he warned the Soviet ambassador that any Soviet intervention, regardless of pretext, would be met by American force.[22] On the evening of 24 October, when Brezhnev asked for joint intervention and threatened that he might act alone if necessary, the United States went to a DEFCON III alert.

Immediate deterrence was irrelevant since Brezhnev had no intention of sending Soviet forces to Egypt. Soviet leaders had difficulty understanding why President Nixon alerted American forces. Brezhnev and some of his colleagues were angered, dismayed, and humiliated. Immediate deterrence was at best irrelevant in resolving the crisis and, at worst, it damaged the long-term relationship between the superpowers.

Deterrence had diverse and contradictory consequences for superpower behavior. General and immediate deterrence were principal causes of the missile crisis, but general deterrence also facilitated its resolution. In 1973, general deterrence contributed to the outbreak of war between Egypt and Israel and provided an umbrella for competition between the United States and the Soviet Union in the Middle East. Immediate deterrence failed to prevent the superpower crisis that followed, but general deterrence constrained the Soviet leadership and helped to resolve the crisis. These differences can best be understood by distinguishing between the strategy and reality of nuclear deterrence.

The strategy of deterrence attempts to manipulate the risk of war for political ends. For much of the Cold War, Soviet and American policymakers doubted that their opposites were deterred by the prospect of nuclear war. They expended valuable resources trying to perfect the mix of strategic forces, nuclear doctrine, and targeting policy that would succeed in restraining their adversary. They also used military buildups, force deployments, and threats of war to try to coerce one another into making political concessions. In Berlin and Cuba, these attempts were unsuccessful but succeeded in greatly aggravating tensions.

The reality of deterrence derived from the inescapable fact that a superpower nuclear conflict would have been an unprecedented catastrophe for both sides. Superpower leaders understood this; by the late 1960s, if not earlier, they had come to believe that their countries could not survive a nuclear war. Fear of war, independent of the disparity in the strategic capabilities of the two sides, helped to keep both American and Soviet leaders from going over the brink and provided an important incentive for the mutual concessions that resolved the Cuban missile crisis. The moderation induced by the reality of deterrence helped to curtail the recklessness encouraged by the strategy of deterrence.

The contradictory consequences of deterrence are not fully captured by any of the competing interpretations. Proponents of deterrence have emphasized the positive contribution of the reality of deterrence but ignored the baneful consequences of the strategy. The critics of deterrence have identified some of the political and psychological mechanisms that made the strategy of deterrence provocative and dangerous. But many ignored the ways in which the reality of deterrence was an important source of restraint.

WHEN AND WHY DOES DETERRENCE WORK?

Proponents of deterrence have advanced two contrasting reasons for its putative success. The conventional wisdom holds that deterrence restrained the Soviet Union by convincing its leaders that any military action against the United States or its allies would meet certain and effective opposition. Those who credit deterrence with preserving the peace assume that, in its absence, the Soviet Union would have been tempted to use force against its Western adversaries or their allies in the Middle East.

Throughout the years of Soviet-American rivalry, American leaders regarded their adversary as fundamentally aggressive and intent on expanding its influence by subversion, intimidation, or the use of force. Soviet leaders were frequently described as cold, rational calculators who were constantly probing for opportunities. They carefully weighed the costs and benefits and abstained from aggressive action only if its costs were expected to outweigh the gains. In this context, the peace always looked precarious to American leaders and the remarkable success in avoiding war needed an extraordinary explanation. The strategy of nuclear deterrence provided the explanation.

The strategy of deterrence seemed ideal for coping with a fundamentally aggressive and opportunity-driven adversary. It sought to prevent Soviet aggression by denying its leaders opportunities to exploit. The United States consequently developed impressive military capabilities—general deterrence—and publicly committed itself to the defense of specific interests—immediate deterrence—when it appeared that these interests might be challenged. The conventional wisdom, eloquently expressed in many of the scholarly writings on deterrence, assumed that Soviet aggression would wax and wane as a function of Soviet perceptions of American military capability and resolve. Soviet leaders would be most restrained when they regarded the military balance as unfavorable and American resolve as unquestionable.[23]

Our analyses of the crises in 1962 and 1973 do not support this assessment of deterrence. In 1962, the strategy of deterrence provoked a war-threatening crisis, and, in 1973, nuclear deterrence provided the umbrella under which each sought to make or protect gains at the expense of the other until they found themselves in a tense confrontation.

The alternative interpretation holds that fear of nuclear war made both superpowers more cautious than they otherwise would have been in their competition for global influence and thereby kept the peace. Although far more convincing than the argument that credits the strategy of nuclear deterrence with preserving the peace, this explanation also is not fully persuasive. The reality of nuclear deterrence had a restraining effect on both Kennedy and Khrushchev in 1962 and on Brezhnev in 1973. When superpower leaders believed that they were approaching the brink of war, fear of war pulled them back.[24]

It is difficult to judge how much of the fear of war can be attributed to nuclear weapons. At the time of the Korean War, the United States had only a limited nuclear arsenal, but Stalin may have exaggerated American ability to launch extensive nuclear strikes against the Soviet Union.[25] Robert McNamara subsequently testified that President Kennedy worried primarily that the missile crisis would lead to a conventional war with the Soviet Union.[26] Other members of the Ex Comm disagree; they say it was the threat of nuclear war that was in the back of their minds and, probably, the president's.[27] McNamara also admits that he had little expectation that a conventional conflict could be contained. "I didn't know how we would stop the chain of military escalation once it began."[28]

Soviet leaders also worried about war in the missile crisis, but neither the written record nor the testimony of Soviet officials offers any evidence of the kind of war Khrushchev thought most likely. There is no evidence that Khrushchev or Kennedy speculated about war scenarios; they were desperately trying to resolve the crisis. They had no political or psychological incentive to investigate the consequences of failure—quite the reverse. Their fear of war remained strong but diffuse.

In 1973, the United States did not see war as a likely possibility, but Soviet leaders worried actively about war. They feared the consequences of a conventional Soviet-Israeli engagement somewhere between the canal and Cairo, or an accidental encounter at sea. However, there is no evidence that Soviet speculation progressed to more detailed consideration of how either could escalate to nuclear war. Again, the fear of war was strong but diffuse. Soviet leaders feared not only nuclear war but any kind of Soviet-American war. Their fear translated into self-deterrence; Brezhnev ruled out the commitment of Soviet forces on Egypt's behalf before the United States practiced deterrence.

The absence of superpower war is puzzling only if at least one of the superpowers was expansionist and aggressive. On the basis of the evidence now available, the image that each superpower held of the other as opportunity-driven aggressors can be discredited as crude stereotypes. Khrushchev and Brezhnev felt threatened by what they considered the predatory policies of their adversary, as did American leaders by Soviet expansionist policies. For much of the Cold War, Soviet leaders were primarily concerned with preserving what they had, although like their American counterparts, they were not averse to making gains that appeared to entail little risk or cost. Serious confrontations between the superpowers arose only when one of them believed that its vital interests were threatened by the other.

With the benefit of hindsight, it is apparent that although both superpowers hoped to remake the world in their image, neither Moscow nor Washington was ever so dissatisfied with the status quo that it was tempted to go to war to force a change. It was not only the absence of *opportunity* that kept the peace, but also the absence of a strong *motive* for war. Without a compelling motive, leaders were unwilling to assume the burden and responsibility for war, even if they thought its outcome would be favorable. In the late 1950s and early 1960s, when the United States might have destroyed the Soviet Union in a first strike with relatively little damage to itself, American leaders never considered a preventive war. The Soviet Union never possessed such a strategic advantage, but there is no reason to suspect that Khrushchev or Brezhnev had any greater interest than Eisenhower and Kennedy in going to war. The reality of deterrence helped to restrain leaders on both sides, but their relative satisfaction with the status quo was an important cause of the long peace.

How Much is Enough?

There was never a consensus in Washington about what was necessary to deter the Soviet Union. Proponents of MAD maintained that Soviet leaders would be deterred by the prospect of their country's destruction. Robert McNamara's "whiz kids" at Defense calculated that MAD required the capability to destroy 50 percent of the Soviet Union's population and industry in a retaliatory strike.[29] McNamara recommended to Premier Aleksei Kosygin in 1967 that the Soviet Union acquire roughly the same kind of second-strike capability so that deterrence would become more stable. Many military officers and conservative civilian strategists rejected MAD on the grounds that it was not a credible strategy. No American president, they argued, could ever convince his Soviet counterpart that he would accept certain destruction of the United States to punish the Soviet Union for invading Western Europe. To deter Soviet aggression, the United States needed clear-cut, across-the-board strategic superiority to decapitate the Soviet political and military leadership, destroy their command, control, and communications network, penetrate hardened targets, and outfight Soviet forces at every level.[30] Proponents of finite deterrence, the smallest of the three communities, argued that nuclear deterrence was robust and required only limited capabilities. Strategic thinkers in France and Israel have, of necessity, voiced this kind of argument.

The outcome of the missile crisis supports the argument of finite deterrence. The American advantage was overwhelming. The CIA estimated that the Soviet Union, which had only a hundred missiles and a small fleet of obsolescent bombers, could attack the United States with at most three-hundred-fifty nuclear weapons. The United States had a strategic nuclear strike force of thirty-five-hundred weapons and far more accurate and reliable delivery systems. Because Soviet missiles were unreliable and Soviet bombers vulnerable to air defenses, it was possible that very few Soviet weapons would have reached their American targets. Had the missiles in Cuba been fully operational and armed with nuclear weapons, they would have augmented the Soviet arsenal by fewer than sixty warheads.[31]

Military superiority offered little comfort to the administration. It was not "usable superiority," McGeorge Bundy explained, because "if even one Soviet weapon landed on an American target, we would all be losers."[32] Robert McNamara insists that "The assumption that the strategic nuclear balance (or 'imbalance') mattered was absolutely wrong."[33] He recalled a CIA estimate that the Soviets might be able to deliver thirty warheads against the United States in a retaliatory attack. "Does anyone believe that a president or a secretary of defense would be willing to permit thirty warheads to fall on the United States? No way! And for that reason, neither we nor the Soviets would have acted any differently before or after the Cuban deployment."[34] In McNamara's judgment, no president would be willing "to consciously sacrifice an important part of our population or our land and place it in great jeopardy to a strike by Soviet strategic forces, whether it be one city, or two cities, or three cities." The Soviet Union had the capability to do this even before deploying any missiles in Cuba. "And therefore, we felt deterred from using our nuclear superiority and that was not changed by the introduction of nuclear weapons into Cuba."[35]

Proponents of war-fighting, MAD, and finite deterrence would all expect Khrushchev to be deterred by the one-sided American strategic advantage. Only proponents of finite deterrence would anticipate that Kennedy would be deterred by the small Soviet arsenal.

Ironically, Kennedy was not fully confident before or during the crisis that even overwhelming American strategic superiority would restrain the Soviet Union. Khrushchev, by contrast, was confident—before the crisis—that the small and inferior Soviet arsenal would deter Kennedy. He worried rather that the United States would exploit its strategic superiority for political purposes. His confidence in finite deterrence permitted him to deploy missiles in Cuba with the expectation that Kennedy would not go to war.

During the crisis, Khrushchev's confidence in deterrence wavered. He worried both that Kennedy would be unable to control the militants in the military and the CIA who did not share his sober recognition of the futility of war and that the crisis might spin out of control. These fears were partly responsible for the concessions that he made. Kennedy, too, worried that Khrushchev would be ousted by militants determined to go to war. Even when the United States had the overwhelming superiority that proponents of war-fighting recommend, Kennedy's confidence in deterrence was limited. He, too, then made the concessions necessary to resolve the crisis.

In making critical judgments about the robustness of deterrence during the crisis, Kennedy and Khrushchev paid little attention to the military balance. They concentrated instead on the political pressures that might push either side into using force. Their success in resolving the crisis increased their confidence that the other shared their horror of war.

Although deterrence was robust in 1962, not everybody drew the same positive lessons from the missile crisis as did Khrushchev and Kennedy. Influential members of the Soviet elite believed that the Kennedy administration had acted aggressively in Cuba because of its strategic advantage. Many Americans concluded that Khrushchev had retreated because of Soviet inferiority. The lesson of the missile crisis was clear: the United States needed to maintain its strategic advantage, or failing that, strategic parity. In Moscow, too, there was a renewed commitment to ending the strategic imbalance. The missile crisis did not trigger the Soviet strategic buildup of the 1960s—it had been authorized by Khrushchev before the missile crisis—but it mobilized additional support for that program and made it easier for Brezhnev to justify when resources grew scarce in the 1970s.[36]

The crisis in 1973, the most serious superpower confrontation since the missile crisis, occurred when the strategic balance was roughly equal and both sides had a secure second-strike capability. Proponents of finite deterrence would expect the reality of nuclear deterrence to be robust and the strategy of nuclear deterrence to fail unless the security of the homeland was threatened. Given the reality of nuclear deterrence when both sides had an assured capacity to retaliate, advocates of MAD would also expect the strategy of deterrence to fail unless vital interests were at stake. War-fighters would reason differently. Since neither side possessed "escalation dominance," the side that estimated a lower risk of war would have the advantage.

The predictions of the three schools with respect to the American alert cannot be tested directly, since deterrence was irrelevant. The Soviet Union had no intention of sending forces to Egypt before the United States alerted its forces. We can nevertheless assess the Soviet interpretation of the American attempt at deterrence and examine its fit with the expectations of the three schools. Soviet leaders dismissed the American nuclear alert as incredible. They could do so in a context in which nuclear weapons were regarded as so unusable that nuclear threats to defend anything but the homeland or vital interests were incredible. There is no evidence, moreover, that political leaders in Moscow made any attempt to assess the relative strategic balance. The Soviet interpretation is consistent with the expectations of finite deterrence and MAD and inconsistent with those of war-fighters.

Analysis of these two crises reveals that it was not the balance or even perceptions of the balance but rather the judgments leaders made about its meaning that were critical. The understanding leaders had of their adversary's intentions was much more important than their estimates of its relative capabilities. Deterrence was as robust in 1962 as proponents of finite deterrence expected, and at least as robust in 1973 as proponents of MAD anticipated. Yet, worst-case analyses remained the conventional wisdom for many years among militants in both the United States and the Soviet Union. Many on both sides continued to assume that the strategic balance was and would continue to be the critical determinant of superpower behavior.

War-fighters drew a direct relationship between the strategic balance and Soviet behavior. The Soviet Union would be most restrained when the United States had a strategic advantage and would behave more aggressively when the military balance tilted in their favor.[37] Proponents of finite deterrence denied that any relationship existed between the strategic balance and aggression, whereas adherents of MAD could be found on both sides of the debate. The proposition that the aggressiveness of Soviet leaders intensified or diminished in accordance with their perception of the strategic balance became the fundamental assumption of strategic analysis and force planning in the United States. Deterrence was considered primarily a military problem, and many American officials and strategists worked on the assumption that Washington could never have too powerful a military or too great a strategic advantage.[38]

The link between Soviet foreign policy and the military balance is an empirical question. To test this relationship, we examined Soviet-American relations from the beginning of the Cold War in 1947 to 1985, when Mikhail Gorbachev came to power. Drawing on formerly classified estimates of the strategic balance and public studies of the balance prepared by prominent strategic institutes, we developed a composite measure of the relative strategic potency of the two superpowers. Our analysis suggests that the nuclear balance went through three distinct phases. The first, 1948 to 1960, was a period of mounting American advantage. The second, 1961 to 1968, was characterized by a pronounced but declining American advantage. The third, 1968 to 1985, was an era of strategic parity.[39]

There is no positive correlation between shifts in Soviet assertiveness and shifts in the strategic balance. Soviet challenges are most pronounced in the late 1940s and early 1950s in central Europe and Korea and again in the late 1950s and early 1960s in Berlin and Cuba. A third, lesser period of assertiveness occurred from 1979 to 1982 in Africa and Afghanistan.[40] The first and second peaks occurred at a time when the United States had unquestioned nuclear superiority. The third peak coincides with the period of strategic parity, before the years of the putative American "window of vulnerability." During this period of alleged Soviet advantage, roughly 1982 to 1985, Soviet behavior was restrained. The relationship between the military balance and Soviet assertiveness is largely the reverse of that predicted by proponents of war-fighting. The United States had unquestioned supremacy from 1948 to 1952 and again from 1959 to 1962, the principal years of Soviet assertiveness. Soviet challenges were most pronounced when the Soviet Union was weak and the United States was strong.

This pattern challenges the proposition that aggression is motivated primarily by adversaries who seek continuously to exploit opportunities. When leaders became desperate, they behaved aggressively even though the military balance was unfavorable and they had no grounds to doubt their adversary's resolve. In the absence of compelling need, leaders often did not challenge even when opportunities for an assertive foreign policy were present.[41] A definitive answer to the question, "How much is enough?" must await detailed analyses of other nuclear crises with other leaders. Drawing on the analysis of leaders' thinking in these two cases and the broad pattern in their relationship during the Cold War, we can suggest a tentative answer: finite nuclear capabilities in the context of a shared fear of war. In this circumstance, a little deterrence goes a long way.

The Political Value of Nuclear Weapons

Just as there was no consensus during the Cold War on how much deterrence was enough, so there was no agreement on the political value of nuclear weapons. War-fighters contended that nuclear power was fungible; they insisted that strategic advantages could be successfully exploited for political purposes. Most proponents of MAD argued that nuclear threats were likely to be effective only in defense of a state's most vital interests. Proponents of finite deterrence took the most restrictive view of the political value of nuclear weapons. They argued that nuclear weapons could only deter attacks against one's own state and perhaps against one's closest allies.

War-fighters, who were dubious about the efficacy of deterrence and set the most demanding conditions, nevertheless expressed the greatest confidence in compellence. Advocates of finite deterrence, who maintained that nuclear deterrence was relatively easy to achieve, doubted that nuclear threats would succeed in compelling nuclear adversaries. Proponents of MAD thought deterrence was somewhat easier to achieve than compellence.

These seeming contradictions between the schools of war-fighting and finite deterrence can be reconciled by examining why each argued that deterrence and compellence would succeed or fail. For war-fighters, the critical factor was the military balance. When a state possessed a decisive strategic advantage, it could more convincingly demonstrate resolve and more readily deter and compel an adversary. Parity made deterrence possible but compellence extraordinarily difficult.

Advocates of finite deterrence reasoned that leaders had a pronounced fear of the consequences of nuclear war. This fear had a low threshold and was independent of the level of destruction leaders could inflict on their adversaries. The strategic balance was therefore irrelevant to deterrence, and strategic advantage did not make compellence any easier. So long as the target state had some nuclear retaliatory capability, nuclear threats for any purpose other than retaliation lacked credibility.

Proponents of MAD also denied the utility of strategic superiority. They placed the threshold of deterrence higher than did advocates of finite deterrence and argued that a state needed an unquestioned capability, after sustaining a first strike, to retaliate in sufficient force to destroy approximately 50 percent of its adversary's population and industry. Additional nuclear capabilities did not make deterrence any more secure. Some advocates of MAD believed that strategic advantages were critical for compellence but only in limited, well-specified circumstances. Like the advocates of finite deterrence, they argued that the unprecedented destructiveness of nuclear weapons made it very difficult to make credible nuclear threats against nuclear adversaries. Such threats would carry weight only when a state's most vital interests were unambiguously threatened.[42]

Proponents of war-fighting and MAD argued that the Cuban missile crisis was consistent with their expectations. They both maintained that Khrushchev sent missiles to Cuba because he doubted American resolve and withdrew them because he respected American military capability.[43] The crisis illustrated a general truth to war-fighters: strategic superiority confers important bargaining advantages in crisis. Advocates of MAD maintained that the missile crisis was a special case. Compellence succeeded not only because of the American military advantage, but because of the asymmetry of interests. The United States was defending a vital interest, the Soviet Union was not.[44]

Both arguments took as their starting point the apparently one-sided outcome of the crisis in favor of the United States. Khrushchev withdrew the Soviet missiles in return for a face-saving pledge from Kennedy not to invade Cuba. Proponents of war-fighting and MAD treated this pledge as largely symbolic because the administration had no intention of invading the island other than to remove the missiles. Both believed that the missiles would have significantly affected the military or political balance and therefore treated their withdrawal as a major concession.

These interpretations that congealed in the 1960s are contradicted by newly available evidence. Although the administration had ruled out an invasion of Cuba, Khrushchev considered Kennedy's pledge not to invade an extremely important concession. With other Soviet leaders, he was convinced that the United States was preparing to overthrow the Castro government and was only prevented from doing so by the missile deployment. In the eyes of the president and his secretary of defense, the missiles in Cuba had much less military value than many students of the crisis have alleged. Their withdrawal was important for domestic and foreign political reasons.

We now know that Kennedy made a second, important concession to Khrushchev: he agreed to remove the American Jupiter missiles from Turkey at a decent interval after the crisis. The decision to withdraw the missiles was not made before the crisis, as some administration officials contended, but was offered to Khrushchev as a concession. However, Kennedy insisted that the Kremlin keep it secret. The removal of the Jupiters had little military value but was of enormous symbolic importance to Khrushchev.

The outcome of the missile crisis is best explained by finite deterrence. The terms of the settlement did not reflect the strategic balance, but mutual fears of war. Despite pronounced Soviet strategic inferiority, the crisis ended in a compromise, not in a one-sided American victory. American leaders judged it too risky to rely on their strategic advantage to compel withdrawal of the Soviet missiles without making compensating concessions.

The advocates of finite deterrence, MAD, and war-fighting would all expect compellence to be very difficult in the strategic context of 1973. War-fighters would predict that neither the Soviet Union nor the United States could compel the other side to achieve political benefit since neither had a decisive strategic advantage. Under conditions of parity and a secure capability to retaliate, proponents of MAD and finite deterrence would predict that compellence would be very difficult unless vital interests were demonstrably at stake.

The failure of Soviet compellence in 1973 is consistent with the shared expectation of all three schools. Brezhnev did not succeed in compelling the United States to restrain Israel, even though it was very much in Washington's interest to stop the fighting. On the contrary, Brezhnev's attempt to compel backfired and escalated the crisis. Although Kissinger recognized Soviet interests, particularly the heavy cost of its humiliating failure to stop the fighting, he nevertheless interpreted Brezhnev's threat that he might consider unilateral action as a direct challenge to the reputation and resolve of the United States.

All three approaches expect, although for quite different reasons, strategic parity to confer no political advantage. To distinguish among the three schools, we need detailed evidence of the calculations of American leaders about the strategic balance. Yet, when Kissinger and his colleagues chose to respond to Brezhnev's threat that he might consider unilateral military action, they made no reference at all to the strategic balance.[45] When they chose not to comply with Brezhnev's threat, the strategic balance was not salient in their minds.

Our analysis of these two cases is most consistent with the arguments of finite deterrence. The overwhelming strategic advantage of the United States in the missile crisis was negated by the fear of war. When the strategic balance was roughly equal, the Soviet Union could not compel even when the United States recognized the strong Soviet interest in protecting an endangered ally and their own interest in saving the Egyptian Third Army. Our evidence suggests that nuclear weapons are unusable for any political purpose but the defense of vital interests.

NUCLEAR THREATS AND NUCLEAR WEAPONS

The role of nuclear threats and nuclear weapons in Soviet-American relations during the Cold War runs counter to much of the conventional wisdom. Throughout the Cold War, superpower leaders expected their adversary to exploit any strategic advantage for political or military gain. Consequently, they devoted scarce resources to military spending to keep from being disadvantaged. For four decades Soviet and American leaders worried about the political and military consequences of strategic inferiority. These fears, coupled with the worst-case analysis each side used to estimate the other's strategic capabilities, fueled an increasingly expensive arms race. In the late 1940s, the Soviet Union made an intensive effort to develop its own nuclear arsenal in the aftermath of Hiroshima and Nagasaki. In the early 1950s, both sides developed thermonuclear weapons. Following the success of Sputnik in 1957, the United States accelerated its commitment to develop and deploy ICBMs. President Kennedy's decision to expand the scope of the American strategic buildup in the spring of 1961 triggered a reciprocal Soviet decision. The Reagan buildup of the 1980s was a response to Brezhnev's intensive spending of the previous decade and widespread concern that it had bought the Soviet Union a strategic advantage.

This pervasive fear of strategic inferiority was greatly exaggerated. We offer a set of general observations about the impact of nuclear threats and nuclear weapons that summarize our arguments based on the new evidence. These observations must remain tentative until additional evidence becomes available about other critical confrontations during the Cold War and about the role of nuclear weapons in Sino-American and Sino-Soviet relations.

1. *Leaders who try to exploit real or imagined nuclear advantages for political gain are not likely to succeed.* Khrushchev and Kennedy tried and failed to intimidate one another with claims of strategic superiority in the late 1950s and early 1960s. Khrushchev's threats and boasts strengthened Western resolve not to yield in Berlin and provoked Kennedy to order a major strategic buildup. Kennedy's threats against Cuba, his administration's assertion of strategic superiority, and the deployment of Jupiter missiles in Turkey—all intended to dissuade Khrushchev from challenging the West in Berlin—led directly to the Soviet decision to send missiles to Cuba. Both leaders were willing to assume the risks of a serious confrontation to avoid creating the impression of weakness or irresolution.

2. *Credible nuclear threats are very difficult to make.* The destructiveness of nuclear weapons makes nuclear threats more frightening but less credible. It is especially difficult to make nuclear threats credible when they are directed against nuclear adversaries who have the capability to retaliate in kind. Many Soviets worried about nuclear war during the missile crisis, but Khrushchev judged correctly that Kennedy would not initiate a nuclear war in response to the deployment of Soviet missiles. Khrushchev's principal concern was that the president would be pushed into attacking Cuba and that armed clashes between the invading Americans and the Soviet forces on the island committed to Cuba's defense would escalate into a wider and perhaps uncontrollable war.

In 1973, the American alert had even less influence on the Soviet leadership. It was inconceivable to Brezhnev and his colleagues that the United States would attack the Soviet Union with nuclear weapons. They did not believe that the interests at stake for either the United States or the Soviet Union justified war. The American nuclear threat was therefore incomprehensible and incredible.

3. *Nuclear threats are fraught with risk.* In both 1962 and 1973, American leaders were uninformed about the consequences and implications of strategic alerts. In 1973, they did not fully understand the technical meaning or the operational consequences of the DEFCON III alert and chose the alert in full confidence that it entailed no risks. During the missile crisis, when conventional and nuclear forces were moved to an even higher level of alert, it was very difficult to control alerted forces. Military routines and insubordination posed a serious threat to the resolution of the crisis.

Evidence from these two cases suggests that there are stark trade-offs between the political leverage that military preparations are expected to confer and the risks of inadvertent escalation they entail. American leaders had a poor understanding of these trade-offs: they significantly overvalued the political value of nuclear alerts and were relatively insensitive to their risks.[46]

4. *Strategic buildups are more likely to provoke than to restrain adversaries because of their impact on the domestic balance of political power in the target state.* Stalin, Khrushchev, and Brezhnev all believed that strategic advantage would restrain adversaries. Khrushchev believed that the West behaved cautiously in the 1950s because of a growing respect for the economic as well as the military power of the socialist camp. He was convinced that the visible demonstration of Soviet power, through nuclear threats and the deployment of missiles in Cuba, would strengthen the hands of the "sober realists" in Washington who favored accommodation with the Soviet Union. Khrushchev's actions had the reverse impact: they strengthened anti-Soviet militants by intensifying American fears of Soviet intentions and capabilities. Kennedy's warnings to Khrushchev not to deploy missiles in Cuba and his subsequent blockade were in large part a response to the growing domestic political pressures to act decisively against the Soviet Union and its Cuban ally.

Brezhnev's strategic buildup was a continuation of Khrushchev's program. American officials believed that the Soviet buildup continued after parity had been achieved. Soviet strategic spending appeared to confirm the predictions of militants in Washington that Moscow's goal was strategic superiority, even a first-strike capability. Brezhnev, on the other hand, expected Soviet nuclear capabilities to prevent the United States from engaging in "nuclear blackmail." Instead, it gave Republicans the ammunition to defeat President Carter and the SALT II agreement. The Soviet arms buildup and invasion of Afghanistan contributed to Ronald Reagan's landslide victory in 1980 and provided the justification for his administration's massive arms spending. American attempts to put pressure on the Soviet Union through arms buildups were equally counterproductive.

5. *Nuclear deterrence is robust when leaders on both sides fear war and are aware of each other's fears.* War-fighting, MAD, and finite deterrence all mistakenly equate stability with specific arms configurations. More important than the distribution of nuclear capabilities, or leaders' estimates of relative nuclear advantage, is their judgment of an adversary's intentions. The Cuban missile crisis was a critical turning point in Soviet-American relations because it convinced Kennedy and Khrushchev, and some of their most important advisors as well, that their adversary was as committed as they were to avoiding nuclear war. This mutually acknowledged fear of war made the other side's nuclear capabilities less threatening and paved the way for the first arms-control agreements.

By no means did all American and Soviet leaders share this interpretation. Large segments of the national security elites of both superpowers continued to regard their adversary as implacably hostile and willing to use nuclear weapons. Even when Brezhnev and Nixon acknowledged the other's fear of war, they used the umbrella of nuclear deterrence to compete vigorously for unilateral gain. Western militants did not begin to change their estimate of Soviet intentions until Gorbachev made clear his commitment to ending the arms race and the Cold War.

DETERRENCE IN HINDSIGHT

The Cold War began as a result of Soviet-American competition in Central Europe in the aftermath of Germany's defeat. Once recognized spheres of influence were established, confrontations between the superpowers in the heart of Europe diminished. Only Berlin continued to be a flash point until the superpowers reached an understanding about the two Germanies. The conventional and nuclear arms buildup that followed in the wake of the crises of the early Cold War was a reaction to the mutual insecurities they generated. By the 1970s, the growing arsenal and increasingly accurate weapons of mass destruction that each superpower aimed at the other had become the primary source of mutual insecurity and tension. Moscow and

Washington no longer argued about the status quo in Europe but about the new weapons systems each deployed to threaten the other. Each thought that deterrence was far less robust than it was. Their search for deterrence reversed cause and effect and prolonged the Cold War.

The history of the Cold War provides compelling evidence of the pernicious effects of the open-ended quest for nuclear deterrence. But nuclear weapons also moderated superpower behavior, once leaders in Moscow and Washington recognized and acknowledged to the other that a nuclear war between them would almost certainly lead to their mutual destruction.

Since the late 1960s, when the Soviet Union developed an effective retaliatory capability, both superpowers had to live with nuclear vulnerability. There were always advocates of preemption, ballistic missile defense, or other illusory visions of security in a nuclear world. But nuclear vulnerability could not be eliminated. MAD was a reality from which there was no escape short of the most far-reaching arms control. Even after the dissolution of the Soviet Union and the proposed deep cuts in nuclear weapons, Russia and the United States will still possess enough nuclear weapons to destroy each other many times over.[47]

Nuclear vulnerability distinguished the Soviet-American conflict from conventional conflicts of the past or present. In conventional conflicts, leaders could believe that war might benefit their country. Leaders have often gone to war with this expectation, although more often than not they have been proven wrong. The consequences of war turned out very differently than expected by leaders in Iraq in 1980, Argentina in 1982, and Israel in 1982.

Fear of the consequences of nuclear war not only made it exceedingly improbable that either superpower would deliberately seek a military confrontation with the other; it made their leaders extremely reluctant to take any action that they considered would seriously raise the risk of war. Over the years they developed a much better appreciation of each other's interests. In the last years of the Soviet-American conflict, leaders on both sides acknowledged and refrained from any challenge of the other's vital interests.

The ultimate irony of nuclear deterrence may be the way in which the strategy of deterrence undercut much of the political stability the reality of deterrence should have created. The arms buildups, threatening military deployments, and the confrontational rhetoric that characterized the strategy of deterrence effectively obscured deep-seated, mutual fears of war. Fear of nuclear war made leaders inwardly cautious, but their public posturing convinced their adversaries that they were aggressive, risk-prone, and even irrational.

This kind of behavior was consistent with the strategy of deterrence. Leaders on both sides recognized that only a madman would use nuclear weapons against a nuclear adversary. To reinforce deterrence, they therefore tried, and to a disturbing degree, succeeded in convincing the other that they might be irrational enough or sufficiently out of control to implement their threats. Each consequently became less secure, more threatened, and less confident of the robust reality of deterrence. The strategy of deterrence was self-defeating; it provoked the kind of behavior it was designed to prevent.

The history of the Cold War suggests that nuclear deterrence should be viewed as a powerful but very dangerous medicine. Arsenic, formerly used to treat syphilis and schistosomiasis, and chemotherapy, routinely used to treat cancer, can kill or cure a patient. The outcome depends on the virulence of the disease, how early the disease is detected, the amount of drugs administered, and the resistance of the patient to both the disease and the cure. So it is with nuclear deterrence. Finite deterrence is stabilizing because it prompts mutual caution. Too much deterrence, or deterrence applied inappropriately to a frightened and vulnerable adversary, can fuel an arms race that makes both sides less rather than more secure and provoke the aggression that it is designed to prevent. As with any medicine, the key to successful deterrence is to administer correctly the proper dosage.

The superpowers "overdosed" on deterrence. It poisoned their relationship, but their leaders remained blind to its consequences. Instead, they interpreted the tension and crises that followed as evidence of the need for even more deterrence. Despite the changed political climate that makes it almost inconceivable that either Russia or the United States would initiate nuclear war, there are still influential people in Washington, and possibly in Moscow, who believe that new weapons are necessary to reinforce deterrence. Deeply embedded beliefs are extraordinarily resistant to change.

Deterrence and the End of the Cold War

I like many others knew that the USSR needed radical change. Khrushchev tried it, Kosygin tried it. . . . If I had not understood this, I would never have accepted the position of General Secretary. At the end of 1986, we feared that the process of reform was slowing down and that the same fate could befall our reforms as befell Khrushchev's.

—*Mikhail S. Gorbachev* [1]

THE FINAL CLAIM made for nuclear deterrence is that it helped to end the Cold War. As impeccable a liberal as *New York Times* columnist Tom Wicker reluctantly conceded that Star Wars and the massive military buildup in the Reagan administration had forced the Soviet Union to reorient its foreign and domestic policies.[2] The conventional wisdom has two components. American military capability and resolve allegedly convinced Soviet leaders that aggression anywhere would meet unyielding opposition. Forty years of arms competition also brought the Soviet economy to the edge of collapse. The Reagan buildup and Star Wars, the argument goes, were the straws that broke the Soviet camel's back. Moscow could not match the increased level of American defense spending and accordingly chose to end the Cold War.

We cannot examine these propositions about the impact of deterrence on the end of the Cold War with the same quality of evidence we used to assess the role of deterrence in superpower relations during the Cold War. Nevertheless, the absence of a large body of documents, interviews, and memoirs has not discouraged columnists and scholars from rendering judgments about the end of the Cold War. Nor will it prevent policymakers from using these interpretations as guides to action in the future. It is therefore essential that the conventional wisdom does not go unexamined. The limited evidence that is now available is not consistent with these two propositions about the role of deterrence in ending the Cold War. Within the confines of the available evidence, we sketch the outlines of a very different interpretation.

THE END OF THE COLD WAR

Soviet officials insist that Gorbachev's withdrawal of Soviet forces from Afghanistan, proposals for arms control, and domestic reforms took place *despite* the Reagan buildup. Mikhail Sergeevich Gorbachev came to power in March 1985 committed to liberalizing the domestic political process at home and improving relations with the West so that the Soviet Union could modernize its rigid economy. Within a month of assuming office, he announced his first unilateral initiative—a temporary freeze on the deployment of Soviet intermediate-range missiles in Europe—and in a series of subsequent proposals tried to signal his interest in arms control. President Reagan continued to speak of the Soviet Union as an "evil empire" and remained committed to his quest for a near-perfect ballistic-missile defense.

Gorbachev came to office imbued with a sense of the urgency of domestic reform and with a fundamentally different attitude toward the West. He was confident that the United States would not deliberately attack the Soviet Union and that the serious risk was an accidental or miscalculated exchange.[3] In conversations with his military advisors, he rejected any plans that were premised on a war with the United States. "During the period of stagnation," he observed, "we had assumed that such a war was possible, but when I became general secretary, I refused to consider any such plans."[4] Since he saw no threat of attack from the United States, Gorbachev was not "afraid" of any military programs put forward by the Reagan administration and did not feel forced to match them. Rather, he saw arms spending as an unnecessary and wasteful expenditure of scarce resources. Deep arms reductions were not only important to the reform and development of the Soviet economy, but also an imperative of the nuclear age.[5]

Rather than facilitating a change in Soviet foreign policy, Reagan's commitment to the Strategic Defense Initiative (SDI) complicated Gorbachev's task of persuading his own officials that arms control was in the Soviet interest. Conservatives, much of the military leadership, and captains of defense-related industries took SDI as further evidence of the hostile intentions of the United States and insisted on increased spending on offensive countermeasures. Gorbachev, Eduard Shevardnadze, Aleksandr Yakovlev, and many foreign-ministry officials did not feel threatened by Star Wars but were constrained and frustrated by the political impact of Reagan's policies at home.[6]

To break the impasse, Gorbachev used a two-pronged strategy. In successive summits he tried and finally convinced Reagan of his genuine interest in ending the arms race and restructuring East-West relations on a collaborative basis. When Reagan changed his estimate of Gorbachev, he also modified his assessment of the Soviet Union and became the leading dove of his administration. Gorbachev also worked hard to convince Western publics that he intended a radical departure from past Soviet policies. The withdrawal from Afghanistan, freeing of Soviet political prisoners, and liberalization of the Soviet political system evoked widespread sympathy and support in the West and generated strong public pressures on NATO governments to respond positively to his initiatives.

The first breakthrough—an agreement on intermediate nuclear forces (INF)—was the unintended result of the Reagan administration's need to placate American and European public opinion. American officials were deeply divided on the question of theater arms control and settled on the "double zero" proposal only because they thought that Moscow would reject the offer. The proposal required the Soviet Union, which had already deployed a new generation of nuclear delivery systems in Europe, to make deeper cuts in its arsenal than the United States, which had only just begun to field new weapons in Europe. Washington expected Gorbachev to reject the proposal and hoped thereby to make him appear responsible for the failure of arms control. They were astonished when he agreed in principle.[7] Soviet officials contend that Gorbachev accepted "double zero," not because of Soviet weakness, but in the expectation that it would trigger a reciprocal process of accommodation. President Gorbachev subsequently described the INF agreement as a watershed in Soviet-American relations. "Working on the treaty and the treaty itself," he said, "created trust and a network of personal links."[8] To Gorbachev, the absolute gain of accommodation was far more important than the relative distribution of military advantage in any particular arms-control agreement.[9]

Gorbachev's political persistence broke through Reagan's wall of mistrust. At their Reykjavik summit in October 1986, the two leaders talked seriously about eliminating all their ballistic missiles within ten years and significantly reducing their arsenals of nuclear weapons. No agreement was reached because Reagan was unwilling to limit SDI. The Reykjavik summit, as Gorbachev had hoped, nevertheless began a process of mutual reassurance and accommodation.[10] That process continued after an initially hesitant George Bush became a full-fledged partner. In hindsight, it is apparent that Gorbachev's initiatives began the process that brought the Cold War to an end.

DEFENSE AND THE ECONOMY

The conventional wisdom assumes that the Soviet Union was forced to match American defense spending and to end the Cold War when it could no longer compete. There is no evidence that Soviet defense spending rose or fell in response to American defense spending. Revised estimates by the CIA indicate that Soviet defense expenditures remained more or less constant throughout the 1980s. Neither the Carter-Reagan buildup nor Star Wars had any impact on gross spending levels. Their only demonstrable impact was to shift in marginal ways the allocation of defense rubles. After SDI, more funds were earmarked to developing countermeasures to ballistic defense.[11]

If American defense spending bankrupted the Soviet economy and led Gorbachev to end the Cold War, a sharp decline in defense spending should have occurred under Gorbachev. Despite his rejection of military competition with the United States, CIA statistics show that Soviet defense spending remained relatively constant as a proportion of Soviet gross national product during the first four years of Gorbachev's tenure. The Soviet gross national product declined precipitously in the late 1980s and early 1990s; Gorbachev's domestic reforms had a profoundly negative impact on the Soviet economy. Soviet defense spending was reduced only in 1989 and did not shrink as rapidly as the overall economy. In the current decade, Soviet, and then Russian defense spending has consumed a higher percentage of disposable national income than it did in the Brezhnev years.[12]

From Stalin through Gorbachev, annual Soviet defense spending consumed about 25% of Soviet disposable income. This was an extraordinary burden on the economy. Not all Soviet leaders were blind to its likely consequences. In the early 1970s, some officials recognized that the economy would ultimately stagnate if the military continued to consume such a disproportionate share of resources.[13] Brezhnev, however, was even more heavily dependent than Khrushchev on the support of a coalition in which defense and heavy industry were well represented. In defense, as in other budgetary outlays, allocations reflected the relative political power of different sectors of the economy. Within the different sectors, spending and investment were controlled by bureaucracies with strong vested interests. As a result, not only military but also civilian spending was frequently wasteful and inefficient. Logrolling among competing groups compounded the problem by increasing the aggregate level of spending.[14] Because Soviet defense spending under Brezhnev and Gorbachev was primarily a response to internal imperatives, it is not correlated with American defense spending. Nor is there any observable relationship between defense spending and changes in the political relationship between the superpowers, until the cuts in the American defense budget in 1991.

The proposition that American defense spending bankrupted the Soviet economy and forced an end to the Cold War is not sustained by the available evidence. The critical factor in the Soviet economic decline was the rigid "command economy" imposed by Stalin in the early 1930s. It offered little or no reward for individual or collective initiative, freed productive units from the competition normally imposed by the market, and centralized production and investment decisions in the hands of an unwieldy bureaucracy immune from market forces and consumer demands. The command economy predates the Cold War and was not a response to American deterrence.[15]

WHY SOVIET FOREIGN POLICY CHANGED

To explain the dramatic reorientation of Soviet foreign policy, we need to look first at the domestic agendas of Soviet leaders. Khrushchev's and Gorbachev's efforts to transform East-West relations and Brezhnev's more limited attempt at détente were motivated in large part by their economic objectives.

Khrushchev sought an accommodation with the West to free manpower and resources for economic development. He hoped that success in reducing East-West tensions would enhance his domestic authority and make it more difficult for conservative forces to block his economic and political reforms. Gorbachev had a similar agenda and pursued a similar strategy. *Perestroika* required peaceful relations abroad to succeed at home. Accommodation with the West would permit a shift in resources from the military to productive investment; attract credits, investment, and technology from the West; and weaken the power of the conservatives opposed to Gorbachev and his reforms. Accommodation with the West was especially critical for Gorbachev because the Soviet economy had deteriorated sharply since the early 1970s and the brief détente between the United States and the Soviet Union. The impetus for domestic reform was structural; economic decline, or the threat of serious decline, motivated Gorbachev, like Khrushchev and Brezhnev, to implement domestic reforms and seek accommodation with the West.

The need to arrest economic decline and improve economic performance cannot by itself explain the scope of reforms or the kind of relationship Gorbachev tried to establish with the West. Only a few central Soviet leaders responded to economic imperatives by promoting a radical restructuring of the Soviet relationship with the West.[16] Almost all the fundamental components of Gorbachev's "new thinking" about security were politically contested.[17] Traditional thinkers powerfully placed within the defense ministry and the Soviet General Staff vigorously challenged the new concepts of security. Indeed, Gorbachev had to go outside the establishment to civilian and academic specialists on defense in the policy institutes in Moscow for new ideas about Soviet security.[18] Insofar as senior Soviet leaders and officials in the Gorbachev era disagreed fundamentally about the direction of Soviet foreign and defense policy, structural imperatives alone cannot adequately explain the change in Soviet thinking about security under Gorbachev.

Gorbachev differed significantly from Khrushchev and Brezhnev in his conception of security. Previous Soviet leaders had regarded the capitalist West as the enemy and had feared military aggression against the Soviet Union or its allies. Like their Western counterparts, they measured security in terms of military and economic power; Soviet military prowess and socialist solidarity were necessary to deter attack and restrain the capitalist powers. Khrushchev and Brezhnev wanted to improve relations with the West, but they remained committed to their ideological view of a world divided into two hostile camps. Unlike Stalin, they recognized that nuclear weapons had made war between the superpowers irrational and unlikely, but they believed in the fundamental antagonism between the incompatible systems of capitalism and socialism.

Gorbachev and his closest advisors rejected the traditional Soviet approach to security. In their view, it had helped to create and sustain the Cold War and had placed a heavy burden on the Soviet economy. *Perestroichiks* were especially critical of the domestic consequences of postwar Soviet foreign policy; conflict with the West had been exploited by the Communist Party to justify its monopoly on power and suppression of dissent.[19]

Gorbachev's vision of Soviet security was cooperative rather than competitive. He and Eduard A. Shevardnadze repudiated the class basis of international relations that had dominated Soviet thinking about security since the Soviet state was created. They explicitly condemned as mistaken the thesis developed in the Khrushchev and Brezhnev years that peaceful coexistence was a specific form of the class struggle.[20] "New thinking" about security was based on five related propositions: the primacy of universal, "all-human" values over class conflict; the interdependence of all nations; the impossibility of achieving victory in nuclear or large-scale conventional war; the need to seek security in political and economic rather than military terms; and the belief that neither Soviet nor Western security could be achieved unilaterally.[21] Gorbachev called for the development of "a new security model" based on "a policy of compromise" among former adversaries.[22] National security was to be replaced by a "common, indivisible security, the same for all." The goal of the Soviet Union was to join a "common European house" that would foster security and prosperity through "a policy of cooperation based on mutual trust."[23]

Gorbachev, Shevardnadze, and other committed democrats believed in a complex, two-way relationship between domestic reform and foreign policy. Accommodation with the West would facilitate *perestroika*, but it was more than an instrument of reform and economic rejuvenation.[24] For the Soviet Union to join the family of nations, it had to become a democratic society with a demonstrable respect for the individual and collective rights of its citizens and allies. Granting independence to the countries of Eastern Europe was the international analogue to emptying the gulags, ending censorship in the media, and choosing members of the Supreme Soviet through free elections.

Gorbachev was able to pursue a more far-reaching and dramatic strategy of accommodation than his predecessors because of the evolution in the superpower relationship since the acute confrontations of the 1960s. He was much less fearful of Western intentions than Khrushchev and less concerned that the United States and its allies would exploit concessions as a sign of weakness. Khrushchev's fear of the West severely constrained his search for accommodation. He never considered, as did Gorbachev, that soft words and unilateral initiatives would evoke enough public sympathy and support so that Western governments would be pushed by their own domestic publics to reciprocate. Khrushchev did make some unilateral concessions; he reduced the size of the armed forces and proclaimed a short-lived moratorium on nuclear testing. When his actions were not reciprocated, the militant opposition at home forced him to revert to a confrontational policy. His inflammatory rhetoric in turn strengthened the forces in the West who opposed accommodation with the Soviet Union.

Gorbachev could not have succeeded in transforming East-West relations and ending the Cold War if the West had not become his willing partner. Unlike Khrushchev, whose quest for a German peace treaty frightened France and West Germany, Gorbachev met a receptive audience when he attempted to end the division of Europe. Disenchantment with the Cold War, opposition to the deployment of new weapons systems, and a widespread desire to end the division of Europe, given voice by well-organized peace movements, created a groundswell of support for exploring the possibilities of accommodation with the Soviet Union.

THE IMPACT OF AMERICAN POLICY

Throughout the Cold War, many leaders in the West argued that the internal structure and foreign-policy goals of the Soviet Union were ideologically determined and largely unaffected by the policies of other states. The West could only restrain Soviet aggression through a policy of strength. Many academic analysts rejected the argument that Soviet domestic and foreign policies were immutable. They maintained that Western policies made a difference, but disagreed among themselves about the nature of the interaction between Soviet and American foreign and domestic policies.

Some scholars contended that the links were reciprocal. Soviet "orthodoxy", which favored heavy industry, restricted individual freedoms, and a strong military, was strengthened by an international environment that appeared to confirm the enemy image of the capitalist West. Conciliatory Western policies could weaken the influence of Soviet militants and strengthen the hand of those officials who favored reform and accommodation with the West.[25] Other scholars subscribed only to the first of these propositions. Citing the Khrushchev experience, they agreed that a threatening international environment undermined reform and accommodation, but, drawing on the Brezhnev years, they denied the corollary that détente encouraged domestic liberalization.[26] The contrast between Gorbachev and Brezhnev led some specialists to argue that reform only came when the leadership confronted the prospect of domestic and foreign-policy disaster.[27]

The available evidence suggests a different proposition about the relationship between American and Soviet foreign policy. The critical factor was the agenda of Soviet leaders. American influence was limited when Soviet leaders were not seriously committed to internal reform. Confrontation then exacerbated Soviet-American tensions, but conciliation did not necessarily improve the relationship, nor did it encourage internal reforms. Jimmy Carter's efforts to transform Soviet-American relations had little effect because they came after Brezhnev had lost interest in domestic reform at home.

When the principal objective of Soviet leaders was economic reform and development, they were anxious to reach some kind of accommodation with the West. Gorbachev, like Khrushchev, was committed to domestic economic reform. Under these conditions, American policy, whether confrontational or conciliatory, had its greatest impact. Confrontation was most likely to provoke an aggressive response because it exacerbated the foreign-policy problems of Soviet leaders, undercut their domestic authority, and threatened their domestic economic goals. Conciliation was most likely to be reciprocated because Soviet leaders expected an improved relationship to enhance their authority at home, free scarce resources for development, and provide access to Western credits and technology.

If American policy did have an impact when Soviet leaders were committed to reform, then the strategy of deterrence likely prolonged the Cold War. The Cold War ended when Soviet leaders became committed to domestic reform and to a concept of common security that built on the reality of nuclear deterrence, and when Western leaders reassured and reciprocated. We cannot support these propositions with the kind of evidence we marshaled in support of our contention that the strategy of deterrence had complex but largely negative consequences for superpower relations during the Cold War. The same kind of detailed reconstruction of Soviet and American policy during the Gorbachev era will only be possible when documents, memoirs, and interviews of key participants become available. Until then, this alternative interpretation of the impact of the strategy of nuclear deterrence on the end of the Cold War may help to stimulate an important debate about the enduring lessons of the Cold War and its demise.

• N O T E S •

PREFACE

1. Interview, Georgiy Shaknazarov, Cambridge, Mass., 11 October 1987.

CHAPTER ONE
Introduction

1. *Budget of the U.S. Government, Fiscal Year 1992* (Washington, D.C.: Government Printing Office, 1991), pt. 7, table 8.1, p. 78; Department of Defense, Office of the Comptroller, "National Defense Estimates for FY 1992," March 1991, mimeograph, p. 151.

2. National Science Foundation, *Patterns of R&D Resources: 1990*, NSF 90–316 (Washington, D.C.: Government Printing Office, 1990), p. 9. These figures are for 1990, when the National Science Foundation (NSF) estimated that 28 percent of the total national research and development (R&D) was defense-related and another 5 percent was space-related. Some of the latter is defense-oriented. See also "Clinton to Promote High Technology with Gore In Charge," *New York Times*, 10 November 1992, pp. B5–6.

3. See the articles by Ulrich Albrecht, Antony Clemson, Judith Reppy, David Edgerton, Alexander H. Flax, N. H. Hughes, and Bernd W. Kubbig, in Philip Gummett and Judith Reppy, eds., *The Relationships between Defence and Civil Technologies* (Boston: Kluwer, 1988).

4. Deterrence seeks to prevent undesired behavior by convincing those who might contemplate such action that its likely cost will exceed its anticipated gain. Compellence attempts to stop a target from doing something it is already doing or coerce it to do something it would not otherwise have done. In contrast to deterrence, which requires the target merely to refrain from some action—often an invisible concession—compellence requires the target to act in ways that are highly visible.

5. George F. Kennan, "The G.O.P. Won the Cold War? Ridiculous," *New York Times*, 28 October 1992, p. A15.

6. Theodore C. Sorensen, *Kennedy* (New York: Harper & Row, 1965), p. 705.

7. Central Intelligence Agency, *The Soviet Bloc Armed Forces and the Cuban Crisis. A Chronology: July–November 1962*, National Indications Center, 18 June 1963, p. 94.

8. The absence of Soviet source material did not prevent Western analysts from writing about these crises. They tried to reconstruct Soviet motives and calculations from Soviet behavior. The conclusions of many of these studies were determined by their starting assumptions. Analysts who viewed the Soviet Union as aggressive—as most did—confirmed this premise in their examination of the foreign policies of Khrushchev and Brezhnev. So, too, did the minority who believed that Soviet policy had been largely defensive and reactive. For many Cold Warriors and revisionist critics, the Soviet Union was a political Rorschach test onto which they could project their own political agendas.

9. See the White House Tapes, "Transcript of 27 October 1962," transcribed by McGeorge Bundy, John F. Kennedy Library, mimeograph, 22 July 1987. All documents, unless otherwise noted, are found in the National Security Archives.

10. "Retrospective on the Cuban Missile Crisis," Atlanta, Ga., 22 January 1983. Participants: Dean Rusk, McGeorge Bundy, Edwin Martin, Donald Wilson, and Richard E. Neustadt (hereafter referred to as Retrospective); "Transcript of a Discussion About the Cuban Missile Crisis," Washington, D.C., June 1983. Participants: Robert McNamara, George Ball, U. Alexis Johnson, McGeorge Bundy, and Richard E. Neustadt (hereafter referred to as Discussion).

11. David A. Welch, ed., *Proceedings of the Hawk's Cay Conference on the Cuban Missile Crisis, 5–8 March 1987* (Cambridge, Mass.: Harvard University, Center for Science and International Affairs, Working Paper 89–1, 1989), hereafter cited as *Hawk's Cay Conference*.

12. *Hawk's Cay Conference*; David A. Welch, ed., *Proceedings of the Cambridge Conference on the Cuban Missile Crisis, 11–12 October 1987*, (Cambridge, Mass.: Harvard University, Center for Science and International Affairs, April 1988), final version mimeograph, hereafter cited as *Cambridge Conference*; Bruce J. Allyn, James G. Blight, and David A. Welch, eds., *Back to the Brink: Proceedings of the Moscow Conference on The Cuban Missile Crisis, January 27–28, 1989*, CSIA Occasional Paper no. 9 (Lanham, Md.: University Press of America, 1992), hereafter cited as *Moscow Conference*; Transcript of "Cuba Between the Superpowers," Antigua, 3–7 January 1991, mimeograph, forthcoming as James G. Blight, David Lewis, and David A. Welch, eds., *Cuba Between the Superpowers: The Antigua Conference on the Cuban Missile Crisis* (Savage, Md.: Rowman and Littlefield, in press), hereafter cited as *Antigua Conference*.

13. We gratefully acknowledge the assistance provided to us in this connection by Ambassador Raymond L. Garthoff and Professor David A. Welch.

14. Ray S. Cline, "Commentary: The Cuban Missile Crisis," *Foreign Affairs* 68 (Fall 1989), pp. 190–96. Cline has subsequently come to regard much of the Soviet testimony as sincere. Interview, Ray S. Cline, Washington, D.C., 2 June 1992.

15. In retrospect, it seems apparent that these kinds of disclosures helped to delegitimate the Communist Party and the Soviet government in the eyes of its citizens. During the same period, Soviet officials revealed that Stalin had Trotsky murdered because of his opposition. The texts of the now openly acknowledged secret protocols of the Stalin-Hitler Pact that gave advance German approval for Soviet conquest of the Baltic States and Bessarabia were also released.

16. *Moscow Conference*, pp. 78–85, 142–44.

17. Ibid., pp. 92–93.

18. N. Khrushchev, *Khrushchev Remembers: The Glasnost Tapes*, trans. and ed. Jerrold L. Schecter with Vyacheslav V. Luchkov (Boston: Little, Brown, 1990).

19. Sergei Khrushchev, *Khrushchev on Khrushchev: An Inside Account of the Man and His Era*, trans. and ed. William Taubman (Boston: Little, Brown, 1990), pp. 233–321, on the memoirs and their subsequent history.

20. Khrushchev, *Khrushchev Remembers: The Glasnost Tapes*, pp. 177–78.

21. "With the Historical Truth and Morale of Baraguá," *Granma*, 2 December 1990, pp. 2–5. Cuban officials were angry that *The Glasnost Tapes* did not make it clear that Castro had asked Khrushchev to attack the United States with nuclear weapons only if the United States invaded Cuba.

22. This point is also made by Raymond L. Garthoff, "Evaluating and Using Historical Hearsay," *Diplomatic History* 14 (Spring 1990), p. 229.

23. Interview, Fedor Burlatsky, Cambridge, Mass., 12 October 1987.

24. E. J. Dionne, Jr., "Scholars Fault Stalin," *Washington Post*, 26 July 1990, p. A3. The *United States Institute of Peace Journal*, 3 (October 1990), is devoted to the

June and July conferences in Moscow and Washington at which Soviet and American historians discussed the nature and origins of the Cold War.

25. Mark Kramer, "Remembering the Cuban Missile Crisis: Should We Swallow Oral History?" *International Security* 15 (Summer 1990), pp. 212–16.

26. Former Soviet officials report that this was a deliberate policy initiated after the death of Stalin to encourage free expression of opinion.

27. See chapter 4.

28. Elie Abel, *The Missile Crisis* (Philadelphia: Lippincott, 1966).

29. Arthur M. Schlesinger, Jr., *A Thousand Days: John F. Kennedy in the White House* (Boston: Houghton, Mifflin, 1965); Sorensen, *Kennedy*; Roger Hilsman, *To Move A Nation: The Politics of Foreign Policy in the Administration of John F. Kennedy* (Garden City, N.Y.: Doubleday, 1967); Robert F. Kennedy, *Thirteen Days: A Memoir of the Cuban Crisis* (New York: Norton, 1969).

30. Graham T. Allison, *Essence of Decision: Explaining the Cuban Missile Crisis* (Boston: Little, Brown, 1971).

31. David L. Larson, *The "Cuban Crisis" of 1962: Selected Documents, Chronology and Bibliography*, 2d ed. (Lanham, Md.: University Press of America, 1986), is a compilation of documents available up through the mid-1980s. Other than the Kennedy-Khrushchev messages, it consists entirely of public statements. The Kennedy-Khrushchev correspondence includes only messages sent during the crisis; the pre-crisis correspondence has not yet been declassified. Under the auspices of the Freedom of Information Act, thousands of relevant documents have now been declassified. This process began in the 1970s.

32. Raymond L. Garthoff to Malcolm DeBevoise, 22 May 1991.

33. Dean Rusk as told to Richard Rusk, *As I Saw It*, Daniel S. Papp, ed. (New York: Norton, 1990), p. 214.

34. Cited by Walter Isaacson, *Kissinger: A Biography* (New York: Simon & Schuster, 1992), p. 827.

35. Interview, Georgiy Shakhnazarov, 11 October 1987, Cambridge, Mass.

36. Interviews with officials of the Bush administration, on a not-for-attribution basis, indicate that the president and at least some of his advisors saw many parallels between the two confrontations and that the president hoped to replicate Kennedy's success.

37. Henry Kissinger, *Years of Upheaval* (Boston: Little, Brown, 1982), p. 980.

38. Kennedy, *Thirteen Days*.

39. Authors' record of luncheon conversation, Hawk's Cay, Fla., 6 March 1987.

40. Comments of Robert McNamara, *Hawk's Cay Conference*, pp. 53–54, passim.

41. Georgiy Shakhnazarov, *Cambridge Conference*, pp. 46–47; but especially his comments at dinner on 12 October. The same point was made to the authors in the Kremlin on 18 May 1989 by Gorbachev's foreign-policy advisor, Vadim Zagladin.

CHAPTER TWO
Missiles to Cuba: Foreign-Policy Motives

1. "President John F. Kennedy's Message of 22 October 1962 to General Secretary, Nikita S. Khrushchev," *Department of State Bulletin* 169, 19 November 1973, pp. 635–36. Reprinted in David L. Larson, *The "Cuban Crisis" of 1962: Selected Documents, Chronology and Bibliography*, 2d ed. (Lanham, Md.: University Press of America, 1986), pp. 57–58.

2. American expectations and intelligence estimates are discussed in chapter 13.

3. Some of the most prominent examples are Arnold L. Horelick, "The Cuban Missile Crisis: An Analysis of Soviet Calculations and Behavior," *World Politics* 16 (April 1964), pp. 363–89; Albert and Roberta Wohlstetter, "Controlling the Risks in Cuba," *Adelphi Paper* no. 17 (London: Institute for Strategic Studies, 1965); Roger Hilsman, *To Move A Nation: The Politics of Foreign Policy in the Administration of John F. Kennedy* (Garden City, N.Y.: Doubleday, 1967), pp. 159–229; Adam Ulam, *Expansion and Coexistence: The History of Soviet Foreign Policy, 1917–67* (New York: Praeger, 1968), pp. 661–77; Michel Tatu, *Power in the Kremlin: From Khrushchev to Kosygin*, trans. Helen Katel (New York: Viking, 1970), pp. 229–360; Graham T. Allison, *Essence of Decision: Explaining the Cuban Missile Crisis* (Boston: Little, Brown, 1971); Jerome H. Kahan and Anne K. Long, "The Cuban Missile Crisis: A Study of its Strategic Context," *Political Science Quarterly* 87 (December 1972), pp. 564–90; Alexander L. George and Richard Smoke, *Deterrence in American Foreign Policy: Theory and Practice* (New York: Columbia University Press, 1974), pp. 447–99. A more recent study, incorporating much of the new Soviet evidence, is Raymond L. Garthoff, *Reflections on the Cuban Missile Crisis*, rev. ed. (Washington, D.C.: The Brookings Institution, 1989).

4. "Transcript of the Proceedings of the Havana Conference on the Cuban Missile Crisis, January 9–12, 1992," mimeograph, p. 210, forthcoming as James G. Blight, Bruce J. Allyn, and David A. Welch, eds., *Cuba on the Brink: Castro, the Missile Crisis, and the Soviet Collapse* (New York: Pantheon Books, in press), hereafter referred to as *Havana Conference*. "I asked many questions of all the Politburo members: Kosygin, Gromyko. . . . I asked all of them, one by one, 'How was this decision made? Which were the arguments used?' And I wasn't able to get a single word. They often simply didn't reply to my questions. And of course, you can't be impertinent and say, 'Hey, answer my question.'"

5. The decision-making process associated with the missile deployment is analyzed in chapter 4.

6. On the American side, neo-revisionist historian, Thomas G. Paterson, "Fixation with Cuba: The Bay of Pigs, Missile Crisis, and Covert War Against Castro," in Thomas G. Paterson, ed., *Kennedy's Quest for Victory: American Foreign Policy, 1961–1963* (New York: Oxford University Press, 1989), pp. 121–55, makes the argument that Cuban-American tensions were the fundamental cause of the missile crisis.

7. Karl E. Meyer and Tad Szulc, *The Cuban Invasion: The Chronicle of a Disaster* (New York: Praeger, 1962); Haynes Johnson, *The Bay of Pigs: The Leaders' Story of Brigade 2506* (New York: Norton, 1964); Arthur M. Schlesinger, Jr., *A Thousand Days: John F. Kennedy in the White House* (Boston: Houghton, Mifflin, 1965), pp. 219–78; E. Howard Hunt, *Give Us This Day* (New Rochelle, N.Y.: Arlington House, 1973); Peter Wyden, *Bay of Pigs: The Untold Story* (New York: Simon & Schuster, 1979); Lucien S. Vandenbroucke, "Anatomy of a Failure: The Decision to Land at the Bay of Pigs," *Political Science Quarterly* 99 (Fall 1984), pp. 471–91.

8. Robert McNamara, *Havana Conference*, pp. 315–17.

9. In a Gallup poll in early May, 65 percent of the respondents expressed support for Kennedy's decision not to commit American troops to the faltering invasion. Only 24 percent thought he should have sent the Marines. Schlesinger, *A Thousand Days*, p. 277. Kennedy's popularity also rose to a record high of 85 percent. Lloyd Jensen, *Explaining Foreign Policy* (Englewood Cliffs, N.J.: Prentice-Hall, 1982), p. 141.

10. Theodore C. Sorensen, *Kennedy* (New York: Harper & Row, 1965), p. 670.

11. Ibid.; George Gallup, "U.S. Not 'Invasion Minded' on Cuba, Poll Shows," *St. Louis Post Dispatch*, 14 October 1962, p. 17; Department of State, *American Opinion Survey*, no. 101, 18 October 1962. United Nations Archives, Office of Public Opinion Studies, indicate that up to the missile crisis in mid-October, public opinion was no more "invasion minded," as Gallup put it, than they were immediately after the Bay of Pigs. Fully 63 percent of those interviewed were opposed to U.S. military action against Castro at that time.

12. "The Ugly Choice," *Time*, 14 September 1962, pp. 25–26; William Leo-Grande, "Uneasy Allies: The Press and the Government During the Cuban Missile Crisis," New York University Center for War, Peace, and the Media, Occasional Paper no. 3, 1987, pp. 3–9, for an analysis of press treatment of Cuba in the summer and fall of 1962.

13. "The Monroe Doctrine and Communist Cuba," *Time*, 21 September 1962, pp. 17–21.

14. U.S. Congress. U.S. Senate Select Committee to Study Governmental Operations with respect to Intelligence Activities, *Interim Report: Alleged Assassination Plots Involving Foreign Leaders*, 94th Cong., 1st sess. (Washington, D.C.: Government Printing Office, 1975), p. 157–58. Hereafter cited as Church Committee.

15. "Record of Actions by the National Security Council at its Four Hundred and Seventy-Eighth Meeting held on April 22, 1961," John F. Kennedy Library; Chester Bowles, *Promises to Keep: My Years in Public Life, 1941–1969* (New York: Harper & Row, 1971), pp. 329–31.

16. "Record of Actions by the National Security Council at its Four Hundred and Eighty-Third Meeting held on May 5, 1961," John F. Kennedy Library; Interview with Chester Bowles by R. R. Brooks, 2 February 1965, 33, John F. Kennedy Library. Cited in Arthur M. Schlesinger, Jr., *Robert Kennedy and His Times* (Boston: Houghton, Mifflin, 1978), p. 472; Walt W. Rostow, cited in Wyden, *Bay of Pigs*, p. 289.

17. Bowles, *Promises to Keep*, p. 332.

18. Taylor Branch and George Crile III, "The Kennedy Vendetta: An Account of the CIA's Entanglement in the Secret War Against Castro," *Harper's* 251 (August 1975), pp. 49–63, quotation on p. 50.

19. Schlesinger, *Robert Kennedy and His Times*, pp. 459, 444–46, 465.

20. Quoted in Branch and Crile, "The Kennedy Vendetta," pp. 49–63, quotation on p. 52; see also Walt W. Rostow, cited in Wyden, *Bay of Pigs*, p. 289.

21. *Operation ZAPATA: The "Ultrasensitive" Report and Testimony of the Board of Inquiry on the Bay of Pigs* (Frederick, Md.: Aletheia Books, 1981), p. 52; Gary Wills, *The Kennedy Imprisonment: A Meditation on Power* (Boston: Little, Brown, 1982), chap. 20.

22. "Record of Actions by the National Security Council at its Four Hundred and Seventy-Eighth Meeting held on April 22, 1961," John F. Kennedy Library; Taylor Commission report and commentary, see Maxwell D. Taylor to John F. Kennedy, 13 June 1961, and the four attached memorandums, *Operation ZAPATA*, pp. 1–53; Schlesinger, *A Thousand Days*, pp. 273–74, and *Robert Kennedy and His Times*, pp. 459–60; Maxwell D. Taylor, *Swords and Ploughshares* (New York: Norton, 1972), pp. 184–94; Lloyd S. Etheredge, *Can Governments Learn? American Foreign Policy and Central American Revolutions* (New York: Pergamon, 1985), pp. 62–71; Church Committee, p. 135.

23. Schlesinger, *Robert Kennedy and His Times*, pp. 473–75.

24. On 7 September, Congress prohibited assistance to any country that aided Cuba unless the president determined that the national interest warranted an exception. Three weeks later, Congress adopted a joint resolution calling on the administration to take direct measures against Cuba. The administration was quick to respond. On 6 December, the State Department submitted a document to the Inter-American Peace Committee describing Cuba's ties to the Soviet Union and arguing that the Castro regime constituted a threat to the hemisphere. During the last week in January, the Punta del Este Conference of the Organization of American States (OAS) met in Uruguay. At the request of the United States, Cuba was barred from participation and several anti-Cuban resolutions were passed calling on member states to cooperate to combat the menace of a communist Cuba. On 3 February 1962, President Kennedy announced an embargo on all trade with Cuba excepting necessary medical supplies. On 24 March, the United States imposed a ban on the importation of merchandise originating in whole or in part from Cuba.

25. Nikita S. Khrushchev, "For New Victories of the World Communist Movement," delivered at the meeting of party organizations of the Higher Party School, the Academy of Social Sciences and the Institute of Marxism-Leninism, Moscow, 6 January 1961, published in *Pravda*, 15 January 1961. Reprinted in Nikita S. Khrushchev, *Kommunizm-mir i schast's narodov* [Communism—Peace and Happiness of the Peoples] 2 vols. (Moscow: Gospolitizdat, 1962), I, pp. 9–68, p. 36 for quotation.

26. Schlesinger, *A Thousand Days*, p. 302, and Transcript of "Cuba between the Superpowers," Antigua, 3–7 January 1991, mimeograph, pp. 34–35, forthcoming as James G. Blight, David Lewis, and David A. Welch, eds., *Cuba Between the Superpowers: The Antigua Conference on the Cuban Missile Crisis* (Savage, Md.: Rowman and Littlefield, in press), hereafter referred to as *Antigua Conference*; Chester Bowles, *Promises to Keep*, p. 335; Schlesinger, *Robert Kennedy and His Times*, pp. 422–25; Dean Rusk as told to Richard Rusk, *As I Saw It*, ed. Daniel S. Papp (New York: Norton, 1990), p. 219; Stewart Alsop, "Kennedy's Grand Strategy," *Saturday Evening Post*, 31 March 1962, pp. 11–17. The quotation is on p. 12 of Alsop, and is based on interviews with the president and his advisors.

27. Television and radio interview; "After Two Years: A Conversation with the President," 17 December 1962; Sorensen, *Kennedy*, pp. 543–50; Schlesinger, *A Thousand Days*, pp. 358–74.

28. Charles A. Stevenson, *The End of Nowhere: American Policy toward Laos Since 1954* (Boston: Beacon Press, 1972); David Hall, "The Laotian War of 1961 and the Indo-Pakistan War of 1971," in Barry Blechman and Stephen S. Kaplan, ed., *Force without War: U.S. Armed Forces as a Political Instrument* (Washington, D.C.: Brookings, 1978), pp. 135–221; Hilsman, *To Move A Nation*, pp. 91–155; Schlesinger, *A Thousand Days*, pp. 302–6; Sorensen, *Kennedy*, pp. 639–48.

29. Hilsman, *To Move A Nation*, pp. 142–51; Ball, *Promises to Keep*, p. 340; Sorensen, *Kennedy*, p. 643; Schlesinger, *A Thousand Days*, pp. 310, 316–17; Stevenson, *The End of Nowhere*, pp. 129–54.

30. Schlesinger, *A Thousand Days*, pp. 515–16; Stevenson, *The End of Nowhere*, p. 140.

31. Stevenson, *The End of Nowhere*, pp. 155–79; Hilsman, *To Move A Nation*, pp. 151–55; Schlesinger, *A Thousand Days*, pp. 517–18.

32. "Soviet Aide-Memoire handed to President Kennedy at Vienna, 4 June 1961," United States Senate, Committee on Foreign Relations, *Documents on Ger-*

many, 1944–1961, reprinted version (New York: Greenwood Press, 1968), p. 645; Alexander Akalovsky's "Record of Vienna Summit Meeting, 3 June 1961, 3 P.M., at residence of U.S. ambassador." In attendance: Nikita S. Khrushchev, V. M. Sukhodrev (Soviet translator), John F. Kennedy, Alexander Akalovsky (American translator). Sorensen, *Kennedy*, pp. 543–50, and Schlesinger, *A Thousand Days*, pp. 366–74, provide detailed secondary accounts of the summit.

33. Rusk, *As I Saw It*, pp. 220–21.

34. Sorensen, *Kennedy*, p. 549.

35. Quoted in William Manchester, "John F. Kennedy: Portrait of a President," *Holiday* 31 (April 1962), p. 167.

36. *Time*, 5 January 1962, p. 12.

37. Sorensen, *Kennedy*, pp. 586–91; Schlesinger, *A Thousand Days*, pp. 375–78; Rusk, *As I Saw It*, pp. 221–23; Jack Schick, *The Berlin Crisis: 1958–1962* (Philadelphia: University of Pennsylvania Press, 1971), pp. 149–52; Richard K. Betts, *Nuclear Blackmail and Nuclear Balance* (Washington, D.C.: The Brookings Institution, 1987), pp. 96–100.

38. Sorensen, *Kennedy*, pp. 550, 586–91; Schlesinger, *A Thousand Days*, pp. 390–93; Bowles, *Promises to Keep*, p. 342.

39. On the Berlin crisis, see Schlesinger, *A Thousand Days*, pp. 379–405; Sorensen, *Kennedy*, pp. 583–601; Marc Trachtenberg, "The Berlin Crisis," in Marc Trachtenberg, *History and Strategy* (Princeton, N.J.: Princeton University Press, 1991), pp. 169–234; George and Smoke, *Deterrence in American Foreign Policy*, pp. 414–44; Walther Stützle, *Kennedy und Adenauer in der Berlin-Krise, 1961–1962* (Bonn: Neue Gesellschaft, 1973); Robert M. Slusser, *The Berlin Crisis of 1961* (Baltimore: Johns Hopkins University Press, 1973); Schick, *Berlin Crisis*, passim; Jean Edward Smith, *The Defense of Berlin* (Baltimore: Johns Hopkins University Press, 1963).

40. Schlesinger, *A Thousand Days*, p. 395.

41. Bowles, *Promises to Keep*, p. 342.

42. Schlesinger, *Robert Kennedy and His Times*, pp. 444–46, quoting a 1 June 1961 memorandum of Robert Kennedy, and *A Thousand Days*, p. 289.

43. "The Cuba matter is being allowed to slide," he complained to his brother in a memorandum of 1 June 1961. Quoted in Schlesinger, *Robert Kennedy and His Times*, p. 473.

44. Church Committee, p. 148.

45. Church Committee, pp. 135–42, 163; Schlesinger, *Robert Kennedy and His Times*, p. 475.

46. National Security Council, Special Group (Augmented) [SG(A)], Untitled summary of meeting on developing a long-range program against the Castro regime under the direction of Edward Lansdale, 1 December 1961; John F. Kennedy to the Secretary of State et al., 30 November 1961, Church Committee, p. 139.

47. Church Committee, pp. 139–42; Schlesinger, *Robert Kennedy and His Times*, pp. 476–77. In addition to Maxwell Taylor, the SG(A) comprised Robert Kennedy, CIA director John McCone, Chairman of the JCS Gen. Lyman Lemnitzer, National Security Advisor McGeorge Bundy, and Under Secretary of State U. Alexis Johnson, Deputy Secretary of Defense Roswell Gilpatric. Secretary of State Dean Rusk and Defense Secretary McNamara were not formal members but attended some of the meetings.

48. In February, in the hope of securing formal approval for his actions, Lansdale submitted a revised schedule for overthrowing Castro to Mongoose's overseers,

the SG(A). This ambitious six-phase operation, to culminate in an "open revolt and the overthrow of the Communist regime" was turned down by the SG(A), which instructed Lansdale to keep his covert operations at a level that would not inspire insurrection or "require U.S. armed intervention." Edward W. Lansdale, "The Cuba Project," 20 February 1962; "Guidelines for Operation Mongoose," 14 March 1962.

49. Church Committee, p. 141; Schlesinger, *Havana Conference*, p. 140. For Lansdale's plans for Operation Mongoose, see his letter of 2 March 1962 to Robert Kennedy et al. John McCone, "Memorandum of MONGOOSE Meeting Held on Thursday, October 4, 1962," and Richard Helms, "Memorandum for the Record, MONGOOSE Meeting with the Attorney General, 16 October 1962," Mary S. McAuliffe, ed., *CIA Documents on the Cuban Missile Crisis 1962* (Washington, D.C.: History Staff, Central Intelligence Agency, October 1992), pp. 111–13, 153–54. They indicate Robert Kennedy's continuing dissatisfaction with the relative lack of action and success in sabotage.

50. Church Committee, pp. 146–47; Branch and Crile, "The Kennedy Vendetta," pp. 51–59; Schlesinger, *Robert Kennedy and His Times*, pp. 477–80; Thomas Powers, *The Man Who Kept the Secrets: Richard Helms and the CIA* (New York: Alfred A. Knopf, 1979), pp. 135–43. John McCone, "Memorandum of MON-GOOSE Meeting Held on Thursday, October 4, 1962," and Richard Helms, "Memorandum for the Record, MONGOOSE Meeting with the Attorney General, 16 October 1962," *CIA Documents on the Cuban Missile Crisis*, pp. 111–13, 153–54.

51. On Robert Kennedy's possible involvement in various assassination attempts, see Church Committee, pp. 131–35, 150–51; Howard J. Osborn, "Memorandum on Robert A. Maheu, 24 June 1966"; Branch and Crile, "The Kennedy Vendetta," p. 60; Schlesinger, *Robert Kennedy and His Times*, pp. 496–98, maintains that Robert Kennedy did not authorize Castro's assassination. Powers, *The Man Who Kept the Secrets*, pp. 144–45, 153–56, argues that Kennedy probably knew about and supported the attempts on Castro's life.

52. Church Committee, pp. 71–86, 91, 97, 125–26, 181–88; George Crile III, "The Mafia, the CIA and Castro," *Washington Post*, 16 May 1976; Schlesinger, *Robert Kennedy and His Times*, pp. 481–85.

53. James G. Hershberg, "Before 'The Missiles of October': Did Kennedy Plan a Military Strike Against Cuba?" Occasional Paper 89–1, Tufts University Nuclear Age History and Humanities Center, October 1989, p. 76, citing a 5 November telephone conversation with Robert McNamara. A revised version of this paper has appeared under the same title in *Diplomatic History* 14, 2 (Spring 1990), pp. 163–98.

54. *Antigua Conference*, p. 37. George Ball, a critic from the start, observed that "The amount of effort and theology with which that whole business was invested was totally incommensurate with anything we ever got out of it." Interview with Jean Stein, 1968, cited in Schlesinger, *Robert Kennedy and His Times*, p. 972.

55. Quoted in Branch and Crile, "The Kennedy Vendetta," p. 52.

56. Church Committee, pp. 136–37; David C. Martin, *Wilderness of Mirrors* (New York: Harper & Row, 1980), pp. 140–41; Edward Lansdale, "Memorandum for the Special Group (Augmented), 12 March 1962," on CIA involvement and requests for military assistance in carrying out operations against Cuba.

57. Bundy advised McCone that "we should either make a judgment that we

would have to go in militarily (which seemed to him intolerable) or alternatively we would have to learn to live with Castro, and his Cuba and adjust our policies accordingly." John McCone, "Memorandum of Discussion with Mr. McGeorge Bundy, Friday, October 5, 1962, 5:15 P.M.," *CIA Documents on the Cuban Missile Crisis*, pp. 115–17.

58. Robert McNamara in David A. Welch, ed., *Proceedings of the Cambridge Conference on the Cuban Missile Crisis, 11–12 October 1987*, (Cambridge, Mass.: Harvard University Center for Science and International Affairs, April 1988), final version, mimeograph, p. 63, hereafter referred to as *Cambridge Conference*. John McCone, Memorandum for the File, "Discussion in Secretary Rusk's Office at 12 o'clock, 21 August 1962," *CIA Documents on the Cuban Missile Crisis*, pp. 21–23, makes it apparent that the principals at CIA, State, Defense, and the Joint Chiefs recognized the president's "reluctance, as previously, to the commitment of military forces because of the task involved and also because of retaliatory actions of the Soviets elsewhere throughout the world."

59. John McCone, "Memorandum of MONGOOSE Meeting Held on Thursday, October 4, 1962," *CIA Documents on the Cuban Missile Crisis*, pp. 111–13, reveals that an earlier meeting had "clarified General Lansdale's authority over the entire MONGOOSE operation and that the CIA organization was responsive to his policy and operational guidance, and this was thoroughly understood."

60. *Cambridge Conference*, p. 63.

61. Special National Intelligence Estimate 85–61, "The Situation and Prospects in Cuba," pp. 4–5; Church Committee, pp. 136–37.

62. Schlesinger, *Robert Kennedy and His Times*, pp. 485–94.

63. Church Committee, Testimony of Robert McNamara, 11 July 1975, p. 158.

64. Church Committee, passim.

65. "Outline of Significant Exercise: LANTPHIBEX I–62," 9 April 1962; "Command History—CINCLANTFLT, 1962," OPNAV Report 5750–5, 21 May 1963, p. 14. *New York Times*, 10, 14–16, 25 April 1962.

66. Gen. W. F. Hausman to Gen. David Shoup, Commanding General, Fleet Marine Force Atlantic, "Report of Exercise 'QUICK KICK'," 20 September 1962; "Command History—CINCLANTFLT, 1962," p. 14; *New York Times*, 29 April 1962.

67. *New York Times*, 6, 9, 12, 19 August 1962.

68. Robert F. Kennedy Memorandum, dictated 1 June 1961, Robert Kennedy Papers, cited in Schlesinger, *Robert Kennedy and His Times*, p. 472. Ambassador Charles "Chip" Bohlen is reported to have been the principal partisan of military action but Charles E. Bohlen, *Witness to History, 1929–1969* (New York: Norton, 1973), pp. 473, 476–79, says that he opposed the initial invasion on the grounds that Castro had more popular support than the CIA estimated. He urged CIA Director Allen Dulles instead to send in small groups of guerilla fighters to create the basis for an ultimate insurrection.

69. Transcript of comments to the Institute of Politics, John F. Kennedy School of Government, Harvard University, 13 October 1987.

70. Robert McNamara in Bruce J. Allyn, James G. Blight, and David A. Welch, eds., *Back to the Brink: Proceedings of the Moscow Conference on The Cuban Missile Crisis, January 27–28, 1989*, CSIA Occasional Paper no. 9 (Lanham, Md.: University Press of America, 1992), pp. 6–9, hereafter referred to as *Moscow Conference*; *Antigua Conference*, p. 46; *Havana Conference*, p. 141.

71. Interview with Robert McNamara, Cambridge, Mass., 12 October 1987; Transcript of comments to the Institute of Politics, John F. Kennedy School of Government, Harvard University, 13 October 1987. McNamara's distinction between contingency plans and intentions is cogent. But then why did the military go to such lengths to perfect its operational plans if the president and secretary of defense were adamantly opposed to an invasion of Cuba? The Pentagon had plans for a wide range of contingencies, but none was so actively rehearsed in the spring and summer of 1962. Part of the answer is to be found in Gen. Lansdale's management of Operation Mongoose. Although directed by the president to conduct a low-key operation, Lansdale hoped to foment an uprising in Cuba and asked the Pentagon to draw up plans for intervention in support of the rebels. Edward G. Lansdale to John F. Kennedy et al., "The Cuba Project," 18 January 1962. Responding to his request—and perhaps to pressure from Robert Kennedy as well—the joint chiefs in February 1962 made the completion of all Cuban contingency plans a "first priority." Jean R. Moenk, *USCONARC Participation in the Cuban Crisis 1962* (Fort Monroe, Va.: Headquarters, U.S. Continental Army Command, October 1963), p. 17, John F. Kennedy Library.

72. McGeorge Bundy to Secretary of State et al., National Security Action Memorandum no. 181, 23 August 1962; Church Committee, p. 147. On the buildup, see Adam Yarmolinsky, "Memorandum: Department of Defense Operations During the Cuban Crisis, 12 February 1963."

73. "Memorandum of Mongoose Meeting Held on Thursday, October 4, 1962"; *CINCLANT Report*, pp. 3, 19–22, 39–40, 58, 162–63; Moenk, *USCONARC Participation in the Cuban Crisis 1962*, pp. 7–8.

74. For a different argument, see Hershberg, "Before 'The Missiles of October'."

75. Military requirements were offered as justification. See, for example, Marine Corps Emergency Actions Center, Headquarters, U.S. Marine Corps, "Summary of Items of Significant Interest, Period 110701–120700 October 1962," United States Marine Corps Archives, that makes the argument that landing-force readiness will deteriorate after four to six weeks and that a failure to use those forces to invade will "have a chain effect" estimated as at least two months on the scheduled rotation of key Marine units.

76. United States Marine Corps, "*Phibriglex-62* Exercise Controller (TG 147.3)," 12 October 1962; Dan Caldwell, ed., "Department of Defense Operations During the Cuban Crisis, A Report by Adam Yarmolinsky, special assistant to the secretary of defense, 12 February 1963," *Naval War College Review* 31 (July-August 1979), pp. 83–89; Elie Abel, *The Missile Crisis* (Philadelphia: Lippincott, 1966), p. 86; *New York Times*, 19, 21, 22 October 1962.

77. N. Khrushchev, *Khrushchev Remembers*, trans. Strobe Talbott (Boston: Little, Brown, 1970), p. 488; Sergo Mikoyan, *Antigua Conference*, p. 39.

78. Interview, Sergo Mikoyan, 12 October 1987; Interview, Aleksei Adzhubei, Moscow, 15 May 1989; Georgiy Kornienko, *Antigua Conference*, pp. 28–29, and Oleg Darusenkov, p. 32, who reports that Castro's class background—his family were large landowners—at first aroused suspicion; Aleksandr A. Alekseev, "Karibskii krizis: kak eto bylo," [The Caribbean Crisis: As It Really Was], *Ekho Planety*, no. 33 (November 1988), pp. 27–37, cite on p. 27.

79. Khrushchev, *Khrushchev Remembers*, pp. 488–90; Maurice Halperin, *The Rise and Decline of Fidel Castro: An Essay in Contemporary History* (Berkeley:

University of California Press, 1972), chaps. 5–20, and Jacques Lévesque, *The USSR and the Cuban Revolution: Soviet Ideological and Strategical Perspectives, 1959–77*, trans. D. D. Leboeuf (New York: Praeger, 1978), pp. 8–47, on Soviet-Cuban relations from the Cuban revolution through the missile crisis.

80. For an American perspective on this conflict, see Philip W. Bonsal, *Cuba, Castro, and the United States* (Pittsburgh: University of Pittsburgh Press, 1971), the former ambassador to Cuba, and for a more sympathetic account, Halperin, *The Rise and Decline of Fidel Castro*, chaps. 5–11.

81. Gen. Sergio del Valle, *Antigua Conference*, p. 20, confirms that beginning in 1961, Cuba pressed the Soviet Union to accelerate the delivery of military supplies. This led to the signing of an agreement on 30 September 1961 that provided for the transfer of MiG 15 fighters, Il-28 bombers, Mi-4 helicopters, radar and radio stations, artillery, tanks, armored cars, transport vehicles, airfield equipment, workshops, and ammunition for all the weapons systems.

82. Khrushchev, *Khrushchev Remembers*, p. 491.

83. Interview with Aleksei Adzhubei, Moscow, 15 May 1989.

84. *Moscow Conference*, pp. 11–12.

85. Khrushchev, *Khrushchev Remembers*, p. 505.

86. Rusk, *As I Saw It*, p. 245.

87. Khrushchev, *Khrushchev Remembers*, p. 505; Oleg Darusenkov, *Antigua Conference*, p. 152, reporting a conversation with Khrushchev following his visit to Bulgaria in May 1961.

88. See chapter 4.

89. Khrushchev, *Khrushchev Remembers*, p. 493.

90. N. Khrushchev, *Khrushchev Remembers: The Glasnost Tapes*, trans. and ed. Jerrold L. Schechter with Vyacheslav V. Luchkov (Boston: Little, Brown, 1990), p. 170.

91. "Record of Vienna Summit Meeting, 3 June 1961, 3 P.M."; Sorensen, *Kennedy*, p. 546, also provides a synopsis of this conversation.

92. Newspapers published a spate of articles and official statements accusing the United States of "preparing for aggression against Cuba." TASS release from Havana, 1 September 1962. Cited in *The Soviet Bloc Armed Forces and the Cuban Crisis. A Chronology: July–November 1962* (Washington, D.C.: National Indications Center, 18 June 1963), p. 13. On 11 September, TASS described the president's request for authority to call up 150,000 reservists as "a screen for aggressive plans and intentions." The United States, TASS insisted, "wants to repeat against little heroic Cuba what it tried to do against the Soviet Union in 1917." TASS release of 11 September, *The Soviet Bloc Armed Forces*, p. 14. A *Pravda* editorial took up the same theme on 13 September, acknowledging that "a certain quantity of armament" had been supplied to Castro because of "aggressive U.S. designs against Cuba." *Pravda*, 11 September 1962, *The Soviet Bloc Armed Forces*, pp. 14–15. In his address to the United Nations General Assembly on 21 September, Soviet Foreign Minister Andrei A. Gromyko accused the Kennedy administration of whipping up war hysteria. *The Soviet Bloc Armed Forces*, p. 16. Subsequent Soviet accounts of the crisis continued to depict the United States as having been on the verge of invading Cuba and portrayed the missile deployment as an appropriate and effective response to this threat. Anatoliy A. Gromyko, "The Caribbean Crisis, Part I," *Voprosy Histori* [Questions of History], no. 7 (1971). Reprinted in English translation by William Mandel in Ronald R. Pope, *Soviet Views on the Cuban Missile*

Crisis: Myth and Reality in Foreign Policy Analysis (Washington, D.C.: University Press, 1982), pp. 161–94.

93. Khrushchev, *Khrushchev Remembers*, pp. 494–95.

94. "Letter from Chairman Khrushchev to President Kennedy, 26 October 1962," and "Letter from Chairman Khrushchev to President Kennedy, 28 October 1962," in Larson, *The "Cuban Crisis" of 1962*, pp. 179, 189–93; Khrushchev, *Khrushchev Remembers*, p. 494, and *Khrushchev Remembers: The Glasnost Tapes*, p. 171.

95. *The Soviet Bloc Armed Forces*, p. 42; Khrushchev had previously confided to Kekkonen his fear that Berlin would be the cause of a world war. Schlesinger, *A Thousand Days*, p. 353.

96. Central Intelligence Agency, Office of Current Intelligence, "Evidence of a Soviet Military Commitment to Defend Cuba," 19 October 1962, p. 3.

97. Sorensen, *Kennedy*, p. 677.

98. Oleg Troyanovsky, *Havana Conference*, p. 39.

99. Mikoyan insisted that Khrushchev spoke the truth; "the immediate motive" for the missile deployment, "was the defense of Fidel's regime." *Cambridge Conference*, pp. 42–43; Fedor Burlatsky subsequently reaffirmed his opinion that "The immediate motive for the missile deployment was . . . our desire to give assistance to the Cuban leaders in defending the island against direct or indirect intervention originating in the United States. "The Caribbean Crisis and its Lessons," *Literaturnaya Gazeta*, 11 November 1987, 4, English translation in FBIS-SOV-87–221, 17 November 1987.

100. *Moscow Conference*, pp. 147–48.

101. Andrei A. Gromyko, "The Caribbean Crisis: On Glasnost Now and Secrecy Then," *Izvestiya*, 15 April 1989, p. 5. Abridged English translation in *Current Digest of the Soviet Press*, 41, no. 16 (1989), pp. 15–18. Gromyko made a similar statement at the *Moscow Conference*, pp. 6–7.

102. Georgiy N. Bol'shakov, "A Hot Line—How the Secret Channel of Communication Between John Kennedy and Nikita Khrushchev Worked," *New Times*, no. 4, 27 January 1989, p. 41.

103. Sergei Khrushchev, *Moscow Conference*, pp. 37–40, and *Antigua Conference*, pp. 16–17.

104. Interview, Sergei Khrushchev, Moscow, 17 May 1989.

105. Ibid.

106. *Moscow Conference*, pp. 37–38; Sergo Mikoyan, "The Crisis of Misperceptions: One More Retrospective Appraisal of the Missile Crisis," in James A. Nathan, ed., *The Cuban Missile Crisis Revisited* (New York: St. Martin's Press, 1992), p. 60, citing Malinovsky; General Anatoliy Gribkov, "Ander Schwelle zum Atomkrieg," *Der Spiegel*, no. 16, 1992, pp. 152–54, reports that Malinovsky told Khrushchev that it would take "three or four days, not longer than a week" to overrun Cuba. *Khrushchev Remembers: The Glasnost Tapes*, pp. 181–82. Khrushchev adds: "When I told this to Fidel he was bitter and tried to prove to me that Malinovsky was mistaken, that it was a faulty evaluation. 'We wouldn't let that happen,' said Fidel."

107. Khrushchev, *Khrushchev Remembers: The Glasnost Tapes*, p. 176, reports that Alekseev told Castro of his KGB affiliation. Former Soviet foreign ministry officials report that the previous ambassador to Cuba had been very proper and always dressed in suits. Alekseev was more relaxed and became a drinking partner of Fidel who trusted him and very much wanted him as ambassador.

108. Alekseev, "Karibskii krizis," pp. 29–31. Alekseev also commented on Khrushchev's fear of invasion at the *Moscow Conference*, pp. 11–13. Chapter 4 describes this Kremlin meeting and its context.

109. This question is discussed in chapter 5.

110. *Antigua Conference*, pp. 1–30; Interview, Georgiy Shakhnazarov, Cambridge, 12 October 1987.

111. Gen. Escalante, *Antigua Conference*, pp. 1–12, provided a more detailed list of anti-Cuban activities and invasion preparations which were passed on to Moscow. Risquet, *Moscow Conference*, pp. 14–16, detailed the sequence of events that led the Cuban leadership to brace itself for another attack. This included the expulsion of Cuba in January 1962 from the OAS, the imposition of economic sanctions, the military buildup and exercises in the Caribbean, and the incitement of sabotage and counterrevolutionary activity within Cuba. "The Soviet government and intelligence drew the same conclusion from this as we did."

112. *Cambridge Conference*, pp. 63–64; Interview, Georgiy Shakhnazarov, Cambridge, 12 October 1987.

113. This kind of false inference is what psychologists call the "fundamental attribution error." It refers to the tendency of people to exaggerate the importance of dispositional over situational factors in explaining the undesirable behavior of others. We describe its implications for crisis management in chapter 13.

114. *Cambridge Conference*, pp. 62–64. There was a similar encounter at the *Moscow Conference*, pp. 6–9, at which McNamara assured Gromyko that he and Kennedy had rejected all thought of an invasion. With hindsight, McNamara admitted, "if I had been a Cuban leader, I think I might have expected a U.S. invasion." In his view, "the Soviet action to install missiles with that as its objective was, I think, based on a misconception—a clearly understandable one, and one that we, in part, were responsible for." Sergo Mikoyan, "The Crisis of Misperceptions" in *The Cuban Missile Crisis Revisited*, pp. 55–76, who was present at several of the missile crisis conferences still maintains that Kennedy intended to invade Cuba.

115. The standard analysis of Soviet statements and doctrinal changes concerning Soviet strategic power and the "correlation of forces" from 1958 to 1965 is Arnold L. Horelick and Myron Rush, *Strategic Power and Soviet Foreign Policy* (Chicago: University of Chicago Press, 1966), pp. 35–102. Other studies include Herbert Dinerstein, *War and the Soviet Union* (New York: Praeger, 1959); David Holloway, *The Soviet Union and the Arms Race* (New Haven: Yale University Press, 1982), pp. 34–42. Horelick and Rush maintain that Khrushchev's exaggerated claims were designed to influence the West. James Gerard Richter, *Action and Reaction in Khrushchev's Foreign Policy: How Leadership Politics Affect Soviet Responses to the International Environment*, Ph.D. diss., University of California, Berkeley, 1989, pp. 496–97, argues that Khrushchev's statements were also directed at domestic audiences and the Chinese.

116. Interview with *Le Figaro*, excerpted in *Pravda*, 27 March 1958.

117. In June, Khrushchev claimed that "the balance of power is not in favor of the imperialist countries, and with every passing year this balance will shift still further," *Pravda*, 9 May 1959.

118. Khrushchev's 6 January speech, *Pravda*, 15 January 1961.

119. On Khrushchev's strategic deception, see Horelick and Rush, *Strategic Power and Soviet Foreign Policy*, pp. 42–70; Betts, *Nuclear Blackmail and Nuclear Balance*, pp. 90, 91, 93.

120. *Pravda*, 11 October 1957.

121. Ibid., 28 January 1959.

122. Ibid., 18 November 1959, 15 January 1961. Sergei Khrushchev, *Havana Conference*, p. 179, questioned his father's claim that Soviet factories were turning missiles out like sausages. "I said then, 'How can you say that, since we only have two or three?' He said, 'The important thing is to make the Americans believe that. And that way we prevent an attack.' And on these grounds our entire policy was based. We threatened with missiles we didn't have. That happened in the case of [the] Suez crisis, and the Iraqi crisis."

123. Published in *Pravda* on 15 January 1961.

124. For secondary accounts of Khrushchev's use of nuclear bluffs, see Horelick and Rush, *Strategic Power and Soviet Foreign Policy*, pp. 105–30; Thomas W. Wolfe, *Soviet Power and Europe, 1945–1970* (Baltimore: Johns Hopkins University Press, 1970), p. 93; Hannes Adomeit, *Soviet Risk-Taking and Crisis Behavior: A Theoretical and Empirical Analysis* (London: Allen & Unwin, 1982), p. 225.

125. Quoted in Wolfe, *Soviet Power and Europe*, p. 93, and Adomeit, *Soviet Risk-Taking and Crisis Behavior*, p. 255. The original cite is Averell Harriman, "My Alarming Interview with Khrushchev," *Life*, 13 July 1959, p. 33. Harriman apparently omitted from his account the dialogue that ensued. "I [Harriman] laughed. He [Khrushchev] asked, 'What are you laughing about?' I said, 'What you're talking about would lead to war, and I know you're too sensible a man to want to have war.' He stopped a minute and looked at me and said, 'You're right'." Glenn T. Seaborg with Benjamin S. Loeb, *Kennedy, Khrushchev, and the Test Ban* (Berkeley: University of California Press, 1981), p. 252. Harriman's contemporary account to the State Department also omits the story, leading Robert Jervis, *The Meaning of the Nuclear Revolution* (Ithaca, N.Y.: Cornell University Press, 1989), p. 32, to question its validity.

126. Dean Rusk, Robert S. McNamara, John A. McCone, and Lyman L. Lemnitzer, Memorandum for the President, "Report on Implications for U.S. Foreign and Defense Policy of Recent Intelligence Estimates," and attachment: "Report of the Special Inter-Departmental Committee on Implications of NIE 11–8-62 and Related Intelligence," 23 August 1962. Both documents are reprinted with an incisive commentary in Raymond L. Garthoff, *Intelligence Assessment and Policymaking: A Decision Point in the Kennedy Administration* (Washington, D.C.: The Brookings Institution, 1984), pp. 37–39, 40–53. A similar argument was made by Maxwell Taylor to McGeorge Bundy, "Comments on 'Report on Implications for U.S. Foreign Policy of Recent Soviet Intelligence'," 23 August 1962, John F. Kennedy Library.

127. Robert L. Perry, *The Ballistic Missile Decisions* P-3686 (Santa Monica, Calif.: RAND, 1967), p. 14; Richard A. Aliano, *American Defense Policy from Eisenhower to Kennedy: The Politics of Changing Military Requirements, 1957–61* (Athens: Ohio University Press, 1975), pp. 204–22; For an excellent review of the public debate, see Paul H. Nitze to McGeorge Bundy, 17 June 1963, enclosing a "Memorandum for the Record: The Missile Gap, 1958–1960—the Public Record," John F. Kennedy Library.

128. In August 1958, Kennedy warned that "Soviet missile power will be the shield from behind which they will slowly, but surely advance—through sputnik diplomacy, limited brushfire wars, indirect non-overt aggression, intimidation and subversion, internal revolution, increased prestige or influence, and the vicious

blackmail of our allies. The periphery of the free world will slowly be nibbled away. The balance of power will gradually shift against us," 88th Cong., 2d sess., Senate Document no. 79, *John Fitzgerald Kennedy: A Compilation of Statements and Speeches Made During His Service in the United States Senate and House of Representatives* (Washington, D.C.: Government Printing Office, 1964), 14 August 1958, pp. 705–15.

129. *Congressional Record, House of Representatives*, 11 April 1962, p. 6392.

130. *Aviation Week & Space Technology*, 5 September 1960, p. 29.

131. *New York Times*, 15 September 1961, reporting Kennedy's speech of 14 September. See, *Congressional Quarterly Weekly Report*, 13 January 1961, p. 32; Aliano, *American Defense Policy from Eisenhower to Kennedy*, pp. 230–37, and Desmond Ball, *Politics and Force Levels: The Strategic Missile Program of the Kennedy Administration* (Berkeley: University of California Press, 1980), pp. 15–25, on Kennedy speeches and policy preferences during the campaign and interregnum.

132. "No man entering office," the president declared, "could fail to be staggered upon learning—even in this brief ten day period—the harsh enormity of the trials through which we must pass in the next four years. Each day, the crises multiply. Each day the solution grows more difficult. Each day we draw nearer the hour of maximum danger, as weapons spread and hostile forces grow stronger. I feel I must inform the Congress that our analyses over the last ten days make it clear that—in each of the principal areas of crisis—the tide of events has been running out and time has not been our friend." *Department of State Bulletin* 44 (13 February 1961), 207–14; Schlesinger, *Robert Kennedy and His Times*, p. 424.

133. Sorensen, *Kennedy*, pp. 608–10, 613–17; Ball, *Politics and Force Levels*, pp. 107–26.

134. Office of the Historian, Strategic Air Command, *Development of the Strategic Air Command 1946–1976* (Omaha: Strategic Air Command, 1976), pp. 79, 81, 88, 97; U.S. Navy, Strategic Systems Project Office, *Polaris and Poseidon Chronology* (Washington, D.C.: Department of the Navy, 1973), p. 6, and *Polaris and Poseidon FBM Facts* (Washington, D.C.: Department of the Navy, 1973), p. 11; Ball, *Politics and Force Levels*, pp. 43–53.

135. Estimates of Gen. Dimitri Volkogonov, *Moscow Conference*, pp. 52–53, and interview Leonid M. Zamyatin, Moscow, 16 December 1991.

136. Robert McNamara, "Memorandum for the President, The Missile Gap Controversy, 4 March 1963," John F. Kennedy Library; *New York Times*, 11 December 1960, 1 March 1961; Schlesinger, *A Thousand Days*, pp. 498–500; Edgar M. Bottome, *The Missile Gap: A Study of the Formulation of Military and Political Policy* (Cranbury, N.J.: Farleigh Dickenson University Press, 1971), pp. 229–31; Ball, *Politics and Force Levels*, pp. 88–90; Lawrence D. Freedman, *U.S. Intelligence and the Soviet Strategic Threat* (London: Macmillan, 1977), pp. 62–80; John Prados, *The Soviet Estimate: U.S. Intelligence Analysis and Russian Military Strength* (New York: Dial Press, 1982), pp. 111–26. Ray S. Cline, deputy director of intelligence at the time, reports widespread disbelief when satellite pictures revealed that the Soviet Union had many fewer missiles than expected: "That was very hard for us to believe, because many of the military people were confident that Khrushchev had created a superior missile system. In fact, it turned out, since we started up our missile production very efficiently and very promptly, we ended up with four times the number of Soviet missiles." *Havana Conference*, p. 116.

137. *Washington Post*, 7 February 1961; *New York Times*, 8 February 1961; *Wall Street Journal*, 9 February 1961; Ball, *Politics and Force Levels*, pp. 90–91. McNamara in *Havana Conference*, pp. 186–87, provides an amusing description of the briefing and its consequences.

138. McNamara, "The Missile Gap Controversy," p. 5; Hilsman, *To Move A Nation*, p. 163; Schlesinger, *A Thousand Days*, pp. 288, 498; Ball, *Politics and Force Levels*, pp. 91–95; Prados, *The Soviet Estimate*, pp. 111–26.

139. *National Intelligence Estimate 11–8/1–61*, as described in a memorandum from Lawrence McQuade to Paul Nitze, "But Where Did the Missile Gap Go?" 31 May 1963, p. 15. Appended to Paul H. Nitze to McGeorge Bundy, 30 May [sic] 1963, John F. Kennedy Library; *Washington Post*, 25 September 1961; *New York Times*, 19, 20 November 1961; Ball, *Politics and Force Levels*, p. 96.

140. Briefing by Dean Rusk, Marshall Carter, and Robert McNamara before Executive Session of the Foreign Relations and Armed Services Committee, 5 September 1962.

141. Additional intelligence was collected by SAMOS II, launched on 31 January 1961 and its successor, SAMOS IV, launched in December of that year. General Electric, Summary, "U.S. Air Force Discoverer Satellite Recovery Vehicle Program," I Through XIV, Philadelphia, no date, p. 7; Philip J. Klass, *Secret Sentries in Space* (Stanford, Calif.: Hoover Institution Press, 1972), pp. 98–105; Ball, *Politics and Force Levels*, pp. 100–102; Prados, *The Soviet Estimate*, pp. 114–26.

142. From the spring of 1960 until his arrest in October 1962, Penkovskiy provided British and American intelligence with extensive intelligence about Soviet strategic developments. In May 1961, he is supposed to have delivered microfilm of top secret reports indicating the number of SS-6 ICBMs deployed by the Soviets as well as details about the problems the military was experiencing with this missile. Even if Penkovskiy did provide the West with this kind of intelligence, it would not have been considered conclusive in the absence of independent confirmation. The role of satellite intelligence was critical in this connection. Oleg Penkovskiy, *The Penkovskiy Papers* (Garden City, N.Y.: Doubleday, 1965); Victor Marchetti and John D. Marks, *The CIA and the Cult of Intelligence* (New York: Dell, 1975), pp. 184–85; *Herald Tribune*, 15 April 1971, and *Washington Post*, 16 April 1971, quoting Richard Helms, the CIA director at the time, to the effect that the pictures of medium-range ballistic missiles (MRBMs) provided by Penkovskiy had been critical in identifying the Soviet missiles in Cuba; Ball, *Politics and Force Levels*, p. 103, citing an interview with a former CIA official; Garthoff, *Reflections on the Cuban Missile Crisis*, p. 63n.

143. Sorensen, *Kennedy*, pp. 617–19.

144. Ibid., p. 619.

145. Ibid., pp. 619–20; Schlesinger, *A Thousand Days*, p. 398.

146. Robert Kennedy's notes, dictated 1 September 1961, quoted in Schlesinger, *Robert Kennedy and His Times*, p. 429.

147. Schlesinger, *A Thousand Days*, p. 461.

148. Ibid., p. 460.

149. *Current Soviet Policies IV: The Documentary Record of the Twenty-Second Congress of the Communist Party of the Soviet Union* (New York: Columbia University Press, 1962), p. 54. Hereafter cited as *Current Soviet Policies*. For an analysis of this part of Khrushchev's speech, see Slusser, *The Berlin Crisis of 1961*, pp. 312–13.

150. Slusser, *The Berlin Crisis of 1961*, pp. 387–88.

151. General Assembly Resolution 1632 (XVI), U.S. Arms Control and Disarmament Agency, *Documents on Disarmament, 1961* (Washington, D.C.: Government Printing Office, 1962), p. 552; Slusser, *The Berlin Crisis of 1961*, pp. 389–91, for an evaluation of Khrushchev's nuclear testing policy.

152. *Current Soviet Policies*, p. 54.

153. Ibid., p. 51.

154. Roger Hilsman, chief of State's intelligence division, described the logic behind the administration's decision: "Khrushchev's several ultimatums on Berlin indicated that, if he were allowed to continue to assume that we still believed in the missile gap, he would probably bring the world dangerously close to war. Thus the decision was reached to go ahead with telling the Soviets that we now knew." *To Move A Nation*, p. 163.

155. Gilpatric's speech was cleared by Dean Rusk and McGeorge Bundy. Abel, *The Missile Crisis*, p. 38; interview with McGeorge Bundy, 16 March 1988.

156. *Documents on Disarmament, 1961*, pp. 542–50.

157. Ibid.

158. David Lawrence, *New York Herald Tribune*, 24 October 1961, cited in Slusser, *The Berlin Crisis of 1961*, p. 374.

159. *Department of State Bulletin* 45, 13 November 1961, pp. 801–2.

160. Walter Isaacson and Evan Thomas, *The Wisemen: Six Friends and the World They Made* (New York: Simon & Schuster, 1986), p. 614. Ball, *Politics and Force Levels*, p. 98, citing an interview with Paul Nitze, reports that this lunch took place before Gilpatric's speech. Nitze also gave a well-publicized speech to the Association of the United States Army on 7 September in which he rattled the American nuclear saber and warned of the ability of the United States to strike at Soviet weak points, and at the Soviet Union directly with nuclear weapons. Paul H. Nitze, "The World Situation: Strengthening of the United States Armed Forces," Address to the annual meeting of the Association of the United States Army, Washington, D.C. 7 September 1961, Reprinted in the *New York Times*, 8 September 1961.

161. News Conference of 8 November 1961, reproduced in Harold W. Chase and Allen H. Lerman, *Kennedy and the Press: The News Conferences* (New York: Crowell, 1965), p. 125.

162. "Was There Ever a 'Missile Gap?'—or Just an Intelligence Gap?", *Newsweek*, 13 November 1961, p. 23.

163. The meeting between the two men is alleged to have occurred in Kennedy's office on 6 October. Klass, *Secret Sentries in Space*, pp. 107–8; Ball, *Politics and Force Levels*, p. 98, and Betts, *Nuclear Blackmail and Nuclear Balance*, pp. 105–6, citing Klass.

164. Schlesinger, *A Thousand Days*, p. 391.

165. McGeorge Bundy sent a handwritten note to the president on 22 October 1962 warning him that "if the Soviet nuclear build-up in Cuba continues, it would be a threat to the whole strategic balance of power because really large numbers of missiles from this launch could create a first-strike temptation." John F. Kennedy Library.

166. Garthoff, *Reflections on the Cuban Missile Crisis*, pp. 202–11, reprints and offers commentary on a report he wrote in October 1962 for the Ex Comm on the military significance of the missiles.

167. Horelick and Rush, *Strategic Power and Soviet Foreign Policy*, pp. 93, 137; Garthoff, *Reflections on the Cuban Missile Crisis*, pp. 202–3, citing a memorandum he wrote for the Ex Comm on 27 October 1962.

168. Khrushchev, *Khrushchev Remembers: The Glasnost Tapes*, p. 170, writes: "We looked at a map and selected the launch sites. Then we picked targets to inflict the maximum damage."

169. Horelick and Rush, *Strategic Power and Soviet Foreign Policy*, p. 15.

170. *Pravda*, 24 October 1961. See Slusser, *The Berlin Crisis of 1961*, pp. 377, 380–87 for a discussion of the speech and its background.

171. Over the next few months, Soviet statements about the strategic balance were modified to bring them in line with reality. Horelick and Rush, *Strategic Power and Soviet Foreign Policy*, p. 85; William Zimmerman, *Soviet Perspectives on International Relations* (Princeton, N.J.: Princeton University Press, 1967), pp. 194–99.

172. Horelick and Rush, *Strategic Power and Soviet Foreign Policy*, p. 86.

173. *Pravda*, 11 July 1962.

174. The characterization of the interview is McGeorge Bundy's, *Danger and Survival: Choices About the Bomb in the First Fifty Years* (New York: Random House, 1988), p. 418.

175. Stewart Alsop, "Kennedy's Grand Strategy," *Saturday Evening Post*, 31 March 1962, pp. 11–17. Quotation on p. 14.

176. *Pravda*, 20 May 1962, reprinted in *Current Digest of the Soviet Press*, 14 June 1961, p. 7. On 9 May, *Pravda* reprinted a Khrushchev speech that also criticized Kennedy's statements to Alsop and offered them as justification for more strenuous Soviet defense measures.

177. Horelick and Rush, *Strategic Power and Soviet Foreign Policy*, pp. 86–87.

178. *Pravda*, 11 July 1962.

179. The source is János Radványi, at the time Hungarian chargé d'affaires in Washington. In *Hungary and the Superpowers: The 1956 Revolution and Realpolitik* (Stanford, Calif.: Hoover Institution Press, 1972), p. 137, Radványi described the encounter.

180. Claude Julien in *Le Monde*, 22 March 1963, citing an interview with Castro.

181. Castro, *Havana Conference*, pp. 208–9.

182. *Moscow Conference*, pp. 50–51. Jorge Risquet, a member of the Politburo and longtime associate of Fidel Castro, also insists, *Moscow Conference*, p. 26, that "We agreed on the installation of the missiles, noting, first of all, that this assured an improvement in the socialist camp's defense capabilities, and that if the socialist camp was prepared to run a risk on Cuba's behalf, then Cuba should also assume its share of the risk." This argument is repeated in an official Cuban commentary on the crisis, "With the Historical Truth and Morale of Baraguá," *Granma*, 2 December 1990, p. 2.

183. Khrushchev, *Khrushchev Remembers*, p. 494.

184. Interview, Sergo Mikoyan, Cambridge, 12 October 1987.

185. *Cambridge Conference*, pp. 25–26, 44, 49–50.

186. Ibid., pp. 17–18, 58, 75–76.

187. According to Volkogonov, until recently employed by the Institute of Military History, the missile deployment was intended to equalize the strategic balance. According to St. John the Divine, he explained, "God has seven cups of anger which he could pour out onto the earth. So applying this analogy to us, we could

say that the Soviet side had at that time only half-a-cup. The Americans had seven cups. . . . Therefore if we placed our missiles in Cuba, then we would have a full cup," *Moscow Conference*, pp. 52–53. The September 1961 NIE estimated that the Soviets had fifty ICBMs. See references 139–41 for citations. By October 1962, American intelligence estimated seventy-five operational ICBMs. Garthoff, *Reflections on the Missile Crisis*, p. 202, citing a memorandum he wrote for the Ex Comm on 27 October 1962. Later analyses led to a retroactive estimate of forty-four ICBM launchers in October 1962. Raymond L. Garthoff to Richard Ned Lebow, 9 July 1992.

188. *Moscow Conference*, pp. 38–39.

189. Interview, Leonid M. Zamyatin, Moscow, 16 December 1991.

190. Interview, Oleg Grinevsky, Stockholm, 23 October 1992. From 1957 to 1964, Novikov was first deputy head of the foreign ministry's Department for International Organizations, where he was in charge of disarmament and security policy in the foreign ministry. He was the Soviet Union's first ambassador to India.

191. *Moscow Conference*, pp. 44–45.

192. Quoted in Robert Scheer, *With Enough Shovels: Reagan, Bush and Nuclear War* (New York: Random House, 1982), p. 217.

193. Schlesinger, *Robert Kennedy and His Times*, p. 425.

194. Bundy, *Danger and Survival*, pp. 416–17.

195. Testimony of Gen. Lauris Norstad in 87th Cong., 1st sess., U.S. Senate, Committee on Government Operations, *Hearings, Organizing for National Security* (Washington, D.C.: Government Printing Office, 1961), I, p. 34; Timothy Stanley, *NATO in Transition* (New York: Praeger, 1965), pp. 162–63; Michael H. Armacost, *The Politics of Weapons Innovation: The Thor-Jupiter Controversy* (New York: Columbia University Press, 1969), pp. 181–87.

196. Armacost, *The Politics of Weapons Innovation*, p. 186; Jerome H. Kahan, *Security in the Nuclear Age: Developing U.S. Strategic Arms Policy* (Washington, D.C.: The Brookings Institution, 1975), p. 44. Eisenhower later declared that he had opposed the Italian Jupiter deployment from the outset. "Memorandum of Conference with the President by John Eisenhower, 13 January 1961—11:30 A.M."

197. Armacost, *The Politics of Weapons Innovation*, p. 185; Testimony of Nathan Twining before House Committee on Appropriations, *Hearings, Department of Defense Appropriations 1960* (Washington, D.C.: Government Printing Office, 1959), p. 45. The opposite argument, that the Jupiters were a strategic liability, was forcefully put by Albert Wohlstetter, "The Delicate Balance of Terror," *Foreign Affairs* 37, 2 (January 1959), pp. 211–34.

198. Raymond Hare to Secretary of State, 26 October 1962, National Security Files, Kennedy Library; 88th Cong., 1st sess., U.S. House of Representatives, Committee on Armed Services, *Hearings on the Military Posture* (Washington, D.C.: Government Printing Office, 1963), pp. 277–85; Armacost, *The Politics of Weapons Innovation*, pp. 187–204; David N. Schwartz, *NATO's Nuclear Dilemmas* (Washington, D.C.: The Brookings Institution, 1983), pp. 66–74.

199. Christian A. Herter to Dwight D. Eisenhower, "Memorandum for the President, on Completion and Announcement of IRBM Agreement with Turkey During Khrushchev Visit, 16 September 1959," Dwight D. Eisenhower Library; *Records of U.S. Air Forces in Europe*, U.S. Army Missile Command Historical Office, pp. 103–4; William H. Brubeck, "Memorandum for Mr. McGeorge Bundy, Jupiters in Italy and Turkey, 22 October 1962," John F. Kennedy Library.

200. United States Air Force, Air Training Command, "Jupiter (SM-78) Missile Weapon System Training Plan 1 May 1961 (Revised 15 February 1962)"; Brubeck, "Jupiters in Italy and Turkey"; W. W. Rostow to McGeorge Bundy, "Turkish IRBMs," 30 October 1962, Kennedy Library.

201. "Memorandum of Conference With The President, 16 June 1959," 19 June 1959, p. 1, in DDEL/WHO, Office of the Staff Secretary, Subject Series, State Department Subseries, Box 3. On 17 June, Eisenhower made the same point to Neil McElroy, Douglas Dillon, and Gordon Gray. Andrew J. Goodpaster, "Memorandum of Conference with the President, 17 June 1959," Dwight D. Eisenhower Library. Goodpaster's notes of the 17 June meeting indicate that this was not the first occasion on which Eisenhower drew an analogy between Turkey on the one hand, and Cuba and Mexico on the other.

202. Testimony of Robert McNamara, in 88th Cong., 1st sess., House of Representatives, *Military Procurement Authorization, Fiscal Year 1964* (Washington, D.C.: Government Printing Office, 1963), p. 7.

203. Joint Committee on Atomic Energy Ad Hoc Subcommittee Study of U.S. and NATO Nuclear Weapons Arrangements, 11 February 1961; *Hearings on the Military Posture*, pp. 248–50, 283.

204. 87th Cong., 1st sess., Senate Foreign Relations Committee, "Hearings on United States Foreign Policy," in *Executive Sessions of the Senate Foreign Relations Committee*, Historical Series, (Washington, D.C.: Government Printing Office, 1984), vol. 8, Part I, p. 220.

205. National Security Action Memorandum no. 35, "Deployment of IRBMs to Turkey, 6 April 1961," signed by McGeorge Bundy, John F. Kennedy Library. Gen. Lauris Norstad, commander of NATO, strongly dissented from this judgment, arguing that the Jupiters were militarily important for the defense of Turkey. George C. McGhee, "Memorandum for Mr. McGeorge Bundy, 22 June 1961," John F. Kennedy Library.

206. John Eisenhower, "Memorandum of a Conference with the President, January 13, 1961—11:30 AM," Dwight D. Eisenhower Library. At this meeting Defense Secretary Thomas Gates pointed out the political difficulties that a cancellation of the deployment was likely to cause with Turkey. He agreed that the missiles "were actually more symbolic than useful." John A. McCone, then Chairman of the Atomic Energy Commission, thought the missiles "more symbolic than useful." Years later, he told an interviewer: "Nobody ever thought the missiles in Turkey were worth anything anyway—or those in Italy either. They never should have been put there in the first place. I opposed them. I wanted them taken out a couple of years before [the Cuban missile crisis]." "Interview with John A. McCone by Joe B. Frantzo, 19 August 1970," p. 13, John F. Kennedy Library.

207. McGeorge Bundy, *Danger and Survival*, p. 435.

208. James G. Blight Interview with Dean Rusk, Athens, Ga., 18 May 1987.

209. Interview, Dean Rusk, Athens, Ga., 21 September 1987; Rusk, *As I Saw It*, p. 239, for a similar statement. John McCone had voiced the same objection to Eisenhower, advising him that a Jupiter missile is "so vulnerable that a high-powered rifle can knock it out." John Eisenhower, "Memorandum of a Conference with the President, January 13, 1961—11:30 A.M."

210. Averell A. Harriman, "Memorandum on Kremlin Reactions, 22 October 1962," John F. Kennedy Library.

211. Interview, Dean Rusk, Athens, Ga., 21 September 1987; Rusk, *As I Saw It*, p. 239; Bundy, *Danger and Survival*, p. 433. The conversation occurred in April 1961 at a meeting of the Central Treaty Organization in Ankara.

212. Statements by Khrushchev and articles critical of the deployment appeared in *Pravda*, 22 December 1957, 31 May and 7 June 1959, *New Times*, no. 27, 1960, pp. 22–23, and *International Affairs* (Moscow), 37, no. 4, 1961, pp. 108–10.

213. "Record of Vienna Summit Meeting, 3 June 1961, 3 P.M., at residence of U.S. ambassador." Sorensen, *Kennedy*, pp. 543–50, summarizes these conversations.

214. 87th Cong., 2d sess., 1962, United States Senate, Committee on Foreign Relations, *Executive Sessions of the Senate Foreign Relations Committee* (Historical Series), (Washington, D.C.: Government Printing Office, 1988), "Appendix C: Soviet Public Statements With Respect to Cuban Security," 10 September 1962, pp. 821–24.

215. George C. McGhee, "Memorandum for Mr. McGeorge Bundy, 22 June 1961"; John McCone, "Interview with John A. McCone," p. 13, thought that institutional momentum was another reason why the deployment went ahead. "Sometimes, you know, when you spend a few billion dollars developing something, you've got to do something with it."

216. Interview, Dean Rusk, Athens, Ga., 21 September 1987.

217. Ibid.

218. National Security Action Memorandum, no. 181, 23 August 1962, signed by McGeorge Bundy.

219. Bundy, *Danger and Survival*, pp. 428–29; John McCone, "Memorandum of Meeting with the President, 23 August 1962," in *CIA Documents on the Cuban Missile Crisis*, pp. 27–29, contains an exchange in the presence of the president in which McCone questions the value of the Jupiters in Turkey only to be told by a sympathetic McNamara how difficult politically it is to remove them.

220. Khrushchev, *Khrushchev Remembers*, p. 458, and *Khrushchev Remembers: The Last Testament*, trans. Strobe Talbott (New York: Bantam, 1974), pp. 555–58. The ill will was mutual. Nixon, quoted in *Time*, 13 August 1984, described Khrushchev as "a man of great warmth and totally belligerent."

221. Khrushchev, *Khrushchev Remembers: The Last Testament*, pp. 564–67.

222. "Record of Vienna Summit Meeting, 3 June 1961, 3 P.M., at residence of U.S. ambassador."

223. Khrushchev, *Khrushchev Remembers*, p. 567.

224. Statements by Khrushchev and articles critical of the deployment appeared in *Pravda*, 22 December 1957, 31 May and 7 June 1959, *New Times*, no. 27, 1960, pp. 22–23, and *International Affairs* (Moscow), 37, no. 4, 1961, pp. 108–10; Letter from Frederick Dutton to J.W. Fulbright, "Soviet Public Statements with Respect to Cuban Security," 10 September 1962. On 16 October 1962, on the eve of the crisis, Khrushchev had a long conversation with Foy D. Kohler, the new American ambassador in Moscow. He used the opportunity to lodge another sharp protest about the Jupiter deployments in Italy and Turkey. Cited in Raymond L. Garthoff, *Reflections on the Cuban Missile Crisis*, p. 28.

225. He told Knox that "the U.S. would have to learn to live with Soviet missiles in Cuba, just as the Soviet Union had learned to live with American missiles in Turkey and elsewhere." Roger Hilsman, "Khrushchev's Conversation with Mr. W. E. Knox, President Westinghouse Electrical International," Moscow, 24, 26 October 1962, pp. 1–2.

226. Letter from Chairman Khrushchev to President Kennedy, 27 October 1962, in Larson, *The 'Cuban Crisis' of 1962*, p. 184.

227. Interview, Sergei Khrushchev, Moscow, 17 May 1989.

228. "Compendium of Soviet Remarks on Missiles, March 2, 1961." The conversation took place on 26 July 1959.

229. Khrushchev, *Khrushchev Remembers*, pp. 423, 568.

230. *Moscow Conference*, pp. 28–29.

231. Khrushchev, *Khrushchev Remembers: The Last Testament*, p. 568.

232. Ibid., pp. 417–18, 422–24; Fedor Burlatsky, *Chruschtschow: Ein politisches Porträt* (Düsseldorf, Claassen, 1990), pp. 244–45, 261.

233. Alekseev, "Karibskii krizis," p. 29, quoting Nikita Khrushchev; Interview, Anatoliy Dobrynin, Moscow, 17 December 1991. According to Sergei Khrushchev, his father "felt the pinch of a great state around which were placed military bases where the aviation of a possible adversary could reach any vital center of the Soviet Union." "Somewhere," his son believes, he had "the desire to make the United States feel what it was like—that they, a great state, could be in the same situation." *Moscow Conference*, pp. 38–39. Khrushchev does not believe that this was his father's principal motive.

234. Georgiy Kornienko, "Something New About the Caribbean Crisis," typescript, p. 10. Interviews, Leonid M. Zamyatin, Moscow, 16 December 1991, and Anatoliy A. Dobrynin, Moscow, 17 December 1991, also stressed Khrushchev's concern for convincing the Americans of Soviet military equality. Burlatsky, *Chruschtschow*, pp. 245, 259, 261; "Burlatsky Memoir," p. 3, Interview, Cambridge, Mass., 12 October 1987; *Cambridge Conference*, pp. 23, 35–36, 117; and "The Caribbean Crisis and Its Lessons," *Literaturnaya Gazeta*, 11 November 1987, p. 22 (English translation in FBIS-SOV-87-221, 17 November 1987, pp. 21–24), argue that this was Khrushchev's principal motive.

235. Interview, Leonid M. Zamyatin, Moscow, 16 December 1991.

236. On Khrushchev's plans for a new peace offensive on Berlin, see Tatu, *Power in the Kremlin*, pp. 232–34, 238–39; Horelick and Rush, *Strategic Power and Soviet Foreign Policy*, pp. 126–27, 136–40; Jack M. Schick, *The Berlin Crisis: 1958–1962* (Philadelphia: University of Pennsylvania Press, 1971), pp. 208–41; Richter, *Action and Reaction*, pp. 580–81.

237. American estimates of Khrushchev's motives are discussed in chapter 5.

238. Averell W. Harriman, "Memorandum on Kremlin Reactions, 22 October 1962," John F. Kennedy Library.

239. Interviews, Dean Rusk, Athens, Ga., 21 September 1987; Robert McNamara, McGeorge Bundy, and Theodore Sorensen, Cambridge, Mass., 12 October 1987.

240. This distinction is made by Patrick M. Morgan, *Deterrence: A Conceptual Analysis* (Beverly Hills, Calif.: Sage Library of Social Science, 1977).

241. Schlesinger, *A Thousand Days*, pp. 347–48. This point is also made by George and Smoke, *Deterrence in American Foreign Policy*, pp. 429, 579.

242. On Berlin, see Trachtenberg, *History and Strategy*, pp. 169–234. On the Warsaw Pact, see Robin Allison Remington, "The Changing Soviet Perception of the Warsaw Pact," (Cambridge, Mass.: MIT Center for International Studies, 1967); Christopher D. Jones, *Soviet Influence in Eastern Europe* (New York: Praeger, 1981); David Holloway, "The Warsaw Pact in Transition," in David Holloway and Jane M. O. Sharp, eds., *The Warsaw Pact: Alliance in Transition?* (Ithaca, N.Y.: Cornell University Press, 1984), pp. 19–38.

CHAPTER THREE
Missiles to Cuba: Domestic Politics

1. Khrushchev told this to Yevtushenko a month before he died in 1971. Quoted in Stephen F. Cohen and Katrina vanden Heuvel, *Voices of Glasnost: Interviews with Gorbachev's Reformers* (New York: Norton, 1989), p. 264.

2. Milovan Djilas, *Conversations with Stalin* (New York: Harcourt, Brace, & World, 1962), p. 122.

3. Khrushchev also used agriculture as "an offensive weapon" against Malenkov. On his rise to power, see Robert Conquest, *Power and Policy in the USSR: The Study of Soviet Dynastics* (London: Macmillan, 1961), pp. 234–35; Edward Crankshaw, *Khrushchev: A Career* (New York: Viking, 1966), p. 176; Myron Rush, *Khrushchev and the Stalin Succession: A Study of Political Communication in the USSR*, Rand RM-1883 (Santa Monica, Calif.: RAND, 20 March 1987).

4. Useful secondary sources on the Khrushchev period include, George W. Breslauer, *Khrushchev and Brezhnev as Leaders: Building Authority in Soviet Politics* (London: Allen & Unwin, 1982); Carl A. Linden, *Khrushchev and the Soviet Leadership: 1957–1964* (Baltimore: Johns Hopkins University Press, 1966); Lincoln P. Bloomfield, Walter C. Clemens, and Franklyn Griffiths, *Khrushchev and the Arms Race: Soviet Interests in Arms Control and Disarmament, 1954–1964* (Cambridge, Mass.: M.I.T. Press, 1966); Timothy Colton, *Commissars, Commanders, and Civilian Authority* (Cambridge, Mass.: Harvard University Press, 1979); Roy A. Medvedev and Zhores A. Medvedev, *Khrushchev: The Years in Power* (New York: Columbia University Press, 1976); Alexander Yanov, *The Drama of the Soviet 1960s: A Lost Reform* (Berkeley: University of California Press, 1984); Robert O. Crummey, ed., *Reform in Russia and the U.S.S.R* (Urbana: University of Illinois Press, 1989), especially the debate between William Taubman and Alexander Yanov; James Gerard Richter, *Action and Reaction in Khrushchev's Foreign Policy: How Leadership Responses Affect Soviet Responses to the International Environment*, Ph.D. diss., University of California, Berkeley, 1989.

5. On agricultural statistics and problems of Soviet agriculture, see Medvedev and Medvedev, *Khrushchev: The Years in Power*, for a Soviet perspective; and for Western accounts, Erich Strauss, *Soviet Agriculture in Perspective: A Study of its Successes and Failures* (London: Allen & Unwin, 1969). Lazar Volin, *A Century of Russian Agriculture: From Alexander II to Khrushchev* (Cambridge, Mass.: Harvard University Press, 1970), p. 344 has statistics on grain yields. On Khrushchev's agricultural policies, see Sidney I. Ploss, *Conflict and Decision-Making in Soviet Russia: A Case Study of Agricultural Policy, 1953–1963* (Princeton, N.J.: Princeton University Press, 1965).

6. *Pravda*, 15 September 1953; Nikita S. Khrushchev, *Stroitel'stvo kommunizma v SSSR i razvitie sel'skogo khoziaistva* [The building of communism in the USSR and the development of agriculture], 8 vols. (Moscow: Gospolitizdat, 1962–64), vol. I, p. 180, vol. II, p. 91; Breslauer, *Khrushchev and Brezhnev as Leaders*, pp. 12, 55–56.

7. *Stroitel'stvo kommunizma*, vol. I, pp. 126, 142, 178–79, 182–83, 279, 394–95, 489–92; *Pravda*, 5 September 1952, and 21 March 1954.

8. Linden, *Khrushchev and the Soviet Leadership*, pp. 84–85, 209.

9. Fedor Burlatsky, "Brushstrokes in a Political Portrait," *Literaturnaya Gazeta*, 24 February 1988, p. 14. Reprinted in *The Current Digest of the Soviet Press* 40, 30 (March 1988), p. 4. See also Sergei Khrushchev, *Khrushchev on Khrushchev: An*

Inside Account of the Man and His Era, trans. William Taubman (Boston: Little, Brown, 1990), pp. 23–27.

10. See especially, N. Khrushchev, *Khrushchev Remembers: The Glasnost Tapes*, trans. Jerrold Schecter with Vyacheslav V. Luchkov (Boston: Little, Brown, 1990), pp. 202–3, and Muhammad Haykal, *The Sphinx and the Commissar: The Rise and Fall of Soviet Influence in the Middle East* (New York: Harper & Row, 1978), p. 132.

11. This point is also made by Linden, *Khrushchev and the Soviet Leadership*, pp. 34–35, and Breslauer, *Khrushchev and Brezhnev as Leaders*, p. 43.

12. According to Interview, Oleg Grinevsky, Vienna, 11 October 1991, Khrushchev was vulnerable to criticism from hardliners in the army, party, and KGB. This opposition was particularly pronounced in the spring of 1959 in response to Khrushchev's pursuit of détente with the United States and his invitation to Eisenhower to visit the Soviet Union.

13. Speech of 14 January 1960. N. S. Khrushchev, *O vneshnei politike sovetskogo soiuza, 1960 god* [On the Foreign Policy of the Soviet Union] 2 vols. (Moscow: Gospolitizdat, 1961), I, p. 57.

14. S. Khrushchev, *Khrushchev on Khrushchev*, p. 22; Richter, *Action and Reaction*, pp. 581–82.

15. On Sino-Soviet relations in this period, see Donald S. Zagoria, *The Sino-Soviet Conflict, 1956–1961* (Princeton, N.J.: Princeton University Press, 1962); William E. Griffith, *The Sino-Soviet Rift* (Cambridge, Mass.: M.I.T. Press, 1964); Robert C. North, *Moscow and the Chinese Communists*, 2d ed. (Stanford, Calif.: Stanford University Press, 1965).

16. Charles Bohlen, *Witness to History, 1929–1969* (New York: Norton, 1973), p. 462.

17. N. Khrushchev, *Khrushchev Remembers*, trans. Strobe Talbott (Boston: Little, Brown, 1970), pp. 220–21. Stalin's remarks were made in connection with Berlin and Eisenhower's refusal to accept a German surrender on the eve of the Soviet offensive against Berlin and thus forgo the opportunity to occupy the city first.

18. N. Khrushchev, *Khrushchev Remembers: The Last Testament*, trans. Strobe Talbott (New York: Bantam, 1975), p. 420.

19. Khrushchev sometimes brought up his peasant background with pride, although in circumstances that suggest he really felt uncomfortable about it. Haykal, *The Sphinx and the Commissar*, p. 137, tells a revealing story in this connection. On the last day of Khrushchev's visit to Egypt, Alexei Adzhubei reported to Haykal that his father-in-law was very angry with him for his newspaper account of the Soviet leader. When Haykal confronted the angry Khrushchev, he was told that " 'It's something you wrote—about me being a peasant.' " Haykal protested: " 'But, Mr. Chairman, you've always spoken with such pride of being a peasant!' " To which Khrushchev replied: " 'But you wrote I was like a peasant from a story by Dostoevsky—why didn't you say a peasant from Tolstoy?' "

20. *Khrushchev Remembers: The Last Testament*, p. 438. Haykal, *The Sphinx and the Commissar*, p. 135, reveals that Khrushchev had the same concern on his visit to Egypt in 1964.

21. Haykal, *The Sphinx and the Commissar*, p. 135.

22. Khrushchev, *Khrushchev Remembers: The Last Testament*, p. 423.

23. Ibid., p. 471.

24. Sergei Khrushchev, *Khrushchev on Khrushchev*, p. 356.

25. Khrushchev, *Khrushchev Remembers: The Last Testament*, p. 471.

26. *New York Times*, 30 September 1959.

27. *Newsweek*, 5 October 1959.

28. Interviews, Leonid M. Zamyatin, Moscow, 16 December 1991, and Oleg Grinevsky, Stockholm, 24 October 1992, citing his discussions with Andrei Gromyko.

29. Ibid.

30. Oleg Grinevsky to authors, 16 December 1992; Michael R. Beschloss, *Mayday: Eisenhower, Khruschev and the U-2 Affair* (New York: Harper & Row, 1986), pp. 238–39, citing interviews with Richard Bissell and Arthur Lundahl.

31. David Wise and Thomas B. Ross, *The U-2 Affair* (New York: Random House, 1962), and the more recent Beschloss, *Mayday: Eisenhower, Khrushchev and the U-2 Affair*; Khrushchev, *Khrushchev Remembers: The Last Testament*, pp. 504–7; Oleg Grinevsky to authors, 16 December 1992; Interviews with anonymous Soviet military officials.

32. Interview, Oleg Grinevsky, Stockholm, 24 October 1992; Alexander Werth, *The Khrushchev Phase: The Soviet Union Enters the "Decisive" Sixties* (London: R. Hale, 1961), pp. 246–54.

33. In a prescient analysis, Michel Tatu, *Power in the Kremlin: From Khrushchev to Kosygin*, trans. Helen Katel (New York: Viking Press, 1968), p. 51, correctly infers from Khrushchev's unreported absence, the sparse mention of Mikoyan in the press, and Molotov's sudden attempt at a comeback, that Khrushchev's political fortunes had seriously ebbed.

34. *Pravda*, 26 April 1960; *New York Times*, 26 April 1960. For Khrushchev's most provocative speeches of this period, see 86th Cong., 2d sess., Committee on Foreign Relations, *Events Incident to the Summit Conference: Hearings Before the Committee on Foreign Relations: May 27, 31, June 1, 2, 1960* (Washington, D.C.: Government Printing Office, 1960).

35. Interview, Oleg Grinevsky, Vienna, 11 October 1991.

36. *Events Incident to the Summit Conference*, pp. 57–58; 86th Cong., 2d sess., *Executive Sessions of the Senate Foreign Relations Committee* (Historical Series), (Washington, D.C.: Government Printing Office, 1982), 12, p. 335. Khrushchev had never complained directly to Eisenhower about the U-2 overflights, before or during the Camp David talks. He rejected this course of action because he thought he would appear weak. His reticence encouraged Eisenhower to believe that he had come to accept the flights as an inevitable part of the Cold War.

37. Stephen E. Ambrose, "Secrets of the Cold War," *New York Times*, 27 December 1990, p. A15; Lt.-Gen. of Justice N. F. Christyakov, *Po zakonu i sovesti* [By law and conscience] (Moscow: Voyenizdat [Military Publishing House], 1979), p. 144.

38. Interview, Aleksei Adzhubei, Moscow, 15 May 1989; *Boston Globe*, 10 May 1960, for the Associated Press bulletin.

39. Interview, Aleksei Adzhubei, Moscow, 15 May 1989.

40. News Conference on 11 May 1960. Quoted in Tatu, *Power in the Kremlin*, p. 63.

41. Tatu, *Power in the Kremlin*, p. 48.

42. Harrison E. Salisbury, *A Journey for Our Times: A Memoir* (New York: Harper & Row, 1983), pp. 489–90. In retirement, Khrushchev told A. McGhee Harvey, "A 1969 Conversation with Khrushchev: The Beginning of His Fall from

Power," *Life*, 18 December 1970, p. 488, that "From the time Gary Powers was shot down in a U-2 . . . I was no longer in full control." This seems an exaggeration, but nevertheless indicative of the political cost to Khrushchev of the U-2.

43. Interviews, Leonid M. Zamyatin, Moscow, 16 December 1991, and Oleg Grinevsky, Vienna, 11 October 1991, and Stockholm, 23 October 1992; Georgi Arbatov, *The System: An Insider's Life in Soviet Politics* (New York: Random House, 1992), p. 96. There has always been speculation in the West that the incident was a pretext, not a cause, of Khrushchev's reversion to a harder line. Tatu, *Power in the Kremlin*, pp. 44–52, 79–84; Linden, *Khrushchev and the Soviet Leadership*, pp. 93–94; Richter, *Action and Reaction*, pp. 465–77, all detect a more confrontational stance in Khrushchev's speeches in the month or two before the U-2 was shot down. Tatu, *Power in the Kremlin*, pp. 41–68, comes closest to making this argument. On p. 44, he suggests that "the U-2 affair may have . . . played a decisive role in the reversal of Soviet policy," and on p. 57, that "the incident itself was only the last touch that enabled the advocates of a hard foreign policy to achieve what they had been seeking for several months." Beschloss, *Mayday*, adheres to the more traditional interpretation that credits the May Day U-2 as the catalyst for the change in Khrushchev's foreign policy.

44. Tatu, *Power in the Kremlin*, pp. 114–21; Linden, *Khrushchev and the Soviet Leadership*, pp. 105–6; Breslauer, *Khrushchev and Brezhnev as Leaders*, pp. 81–82; Richter, *Action and Reaction*, pp. 465–77. Breslauer argues that Khrushchev denied the country's economic problems until the summer-fall of 1960 and then became seriously troubled by them.

45. Volin, *A Century of Russian Agriculture*, pp. 327–535; Strauss, *Soviet Agriculture in Perspective*, pp. 166–227; Alec Nove, *An Economic History of the USSR* (London: Allen Lane, 1969), pp. 363–68; Tatu, *Power in the Kremlin*, pp. 114–15, 166–70; Breslauer, *Khrushchev and Brezhnev as Leaders*, pp. 80–114.

46. By early 1961, nearly half of the announced reduction had taken place. The program then slowed in response to the growing crisis in Berlin and was officially terminated on 8 July 1961. For a recent Western analysis of Soviet conventional force levels, see Raymond L. Garthoff, "Estimating Soviet Military Force Levels: Some Light from the Past," *International Security* 14 (Spring 1990), pp. 93–116.

47. Herbert S. Dinerstein, *War and the Soviet Union*, (New York: Praeger, 1959), pp. 144, 215–16, on Marshal Zhukov's earlier defense of the need for a large army in a nuclear war. George F. Minde II and Michael Hennessey, "Reform of the Soviet Military under Khrushchev and the Role of America's Strategic Modernization," in Crummey, ed., *Reform in Russia*, pp. 182–206, argue that Khrushchev believed in minimum deterrence and would have imposed this strategy on the military if the deterioration in Soviet-American relations and his own fortunes had not compelled him to compromise with the military.

48. The Western literature recognizes Khrushchev's swings between collaboration and confrontation and regards it as one of the key puzzles of the period. Arnold L. Horelick and Myron Rush, *Strategic Power and Soviet Foreign Policy* (Chicago: University of Chicago Press, 1966), pp. 105–40, and William Taubman, "Khrushchev and Détente: Reform in the International Context," pp. 144–55, see Khrushchev's attempts at collaboration as largely tactical. Another view explains his shifts in foreign policy as a response to the changing power balance in the policymaking elite between hard and soft-liners. Robert M. Slusser, *The Berlin Crisis: Soviet-Amer-*

ican Relations and the Struggle for Power in the Kremlin (Baltimore: Johns Hopkins University Press, 1973); Tatu, *Power in the Kremlin*; Linden, *Khrushchev and the Soviet Leadership*; and Christer Jonsson, *Soviet Bargaining Behavior: The Nuclear Test Ban Case* (New York: Columbia University Press, 1979), subscribe to this position to varying degrees. A third interpretation, associated with Breslauer, *Khrushchev and Brezhnev as Leaders*, explains Khrushchev's post-1960 foreign policies by his need to salvage his domestic program. Yanov, *The Drama of the Soviet 1960s*, also links Khrushchev's foreign policy to his domestic program but goes further than Breslauer in portraying him as a committed reformer who resorted to increasingly extreme action to control and remold the bureaucracy. Richter, *Action and Reaction in Khrushchev's Foreign Policy*, argues that Khrushchev's foreign policy was a response to contradictory domestic and international pressures, and that he sought to reconcile these pressures through a series of dramatic actions.

49. "Transcript of the Proceedings of the Havana Conference on the Cuban Missile Crisis, January 9–12, 1992," mimeograph, p. 240, forthcoming as James G. Blight, Bruce J. Allyn, and David A. Welch, eds., *Cuba on the Brink: Castro, the Missile Crisis, and the Soviet Collapse* (New York: Pantheon Books, in press), hereafter referred to as *Havana Conference*.

50. Breslauer, *Khrushchev and Brezhnev as Leaders*, p. 83.

51. S. Khrushchev, *Khrushchev on Khrushchev*, p. 21.

52. According to Oleg A. Troyanovsky, "The Caribbean Crisis: A View from the Kremlin," *International Affairs* (Moscow) 4–5 (April-May 1992), p. 149, the deployment and subsequent withdrawal of the missiles was "one of the most serious accusations" made against Khrushchev.

53. Strauss, *Soviet Agriculture in Perspective*, pp. 168–80; Volin, *A Century of Russian Agriculture*, pp. 484–96; Medvedev and Medvedev, *Khrushchev: The Years in Power*, pp. 60, 74, 117–20, 165; Martin McCauley, *Khrushchev and the Development of Soviet Agriculture: The Virgin Lands Programme 1953–1964* (New York: Holmes & Meier, 1976), pp. 79–106, 147–89.

54. Nikita S. Khrushchev, *Stroitel'stvo kommunizma v SSSR*, vol. 3 (1963), p. 207.

55. Strauss, *Soviet Agriculture in Perspective*, pp. 168–80; Volin, *A Century of Russian Agriculture*, pp. 484–96; Medvedev and Medvedev, *Khrushchev: The Years in Power*, pp. 60, 74, 117–20, 165; McCauley, *Khrushchev and the Development of Soviet Agriculture*, pp. 79–106, 147–89.

56. This analogy is also drawn by Troyanovsky, "The Caribbean Crisis," p. 149.

57. Breslauer, *Khrushchev and Brezhnev as Leaders*, p. 108, argues that Khrushchev gambled on the Virgin Lands because he needed to shore up his slipping authority with a "quick win." William Taubman, in David A. Welch, ed. *Proceedings of the Hawk's Cay Conference on the Cuban Missile Crisis, 5–8 March 1987* (Cambridge, Mass.: Harvard University, Center for Science and International Affairs, Working Paper 89-1, 1989), mimeograph, pp. 23–24, hereafter cited as *Hawk's Cay Conference*, and "Khrushchev and Detente," in Crummey, ed., *Reform in Russia*, p. 149, argues that a similar calculation underlay his decision to send missiles to Cuba; a dramatic foreign-policy success would have enhanced his domestic standing at an opportune moment.

We think it a mistake to understand the missile decision as a tactical maneuver to maintain and consolidate power. Khrushchev was driven by concern for the future of his domestic policies, not by worry about his authority. In a broader sense, of course, authority and policy were related. More than anyone else, Khrushchev recognized that his authority depended in the long term on the success of his policies. But in the short term, he was not concerned with threats to his authority, only to his programs. Sergei Khrushchev reveals, *Khrushchev on Khrushchev*, pp. 83–162, that as late as October 1964, his father was relatively blind to his political vulnerability and did not give credence to reports that other Presidium members were conspiring against him. Soviet officials testify that Khrushchev was at the height of his power in 1962 and, as we shall see in the next chapter, was able to ignore the objections of his colleagues to the missile deployment. Paradoxically, it was Khrushchev's authority, not its absence, that enabled him to dismiss objections to his plans and to proceed with risky and poorly considered actions.

58. Fidel Castro, *Havana Conference*, p. 208.

59. Mikoyan's views are discussed in chapter 4.

60. When the missile deployment failed, Khrushchev tried to exploit their withdrawal to move toward accommodation. See his message of 28 October 1962 to President Kennedy, *Problems of Communism* 41 (Spring 1992), pp. 52–58, which contains a strong expression of interest in détente between NATO and Warsaw Pact. "We should like to continue the exchange of views on the prohibition of atomic and thermonuclear weapons, general disarmament, and other problems relating to the relaxation of international tension."

61. Important exceptions are Roger Hilsman, *To Move A Nation: The Politics of Foreign Policy in the Administration of John F. Kennedy* (Garden City, N.Y.: Doubleday, 1967), and Jerome H. Kahan and Anne K. Long, "The Cuban Missile Crisis: A Study of Its Strategic Context," *Political Science Quarterly* 87 (December 1972), pp. 564–90.

62. Interview, Aleksei Adzhubei, Moscow, 15 May 1989.

63. Ibid., p. 94.

64. Interview, Sergo Mikoyan, 12 October 1987.

65. Oleg A. Troyanovsky, *Havana Conference*, p. 42, and "The Caribbean Crisis," p. 152. Kuznetsov was representing the foreign ministry because Gromyko had not yet returned from the United States.

66. Some Western scholars also argue that Khrushchev's most aggressive policies were designed to bring about accommodation. Linden, *Khrushchev and the Soviet Leadership*, p. 82; William Taubman, "Khrushchev and Détente: Reform in the International Context," in Crummey, ed., *Reform in Russia*, p. 149; Richter, *Action and Reaction*, pp. 581–82.

67. *New York Times*, 2 September 1961.

68. Fedor Burlatsky, *Chruschtschow: Ein politisches Porträt* (Düsseldorf: Claassen, 1990), p. 244; Interviews, Leonid M. Zamyatin, Moscow, 16 December 1991, and Georgiy M. Kornienko, Moscow, 17 December 1991.

69. Sergei Khrushchev in Bruce J. Allyn, James G. Blight, and David A. Welch, eds., *Back to the Brink: Proceedings of the Moscow Conference on The Cuban Missile Crisis, January 27–28, 1989*, CSIA Occasional Paper no. 9 (Lanham, Md.: University Press of America, 1992), pp. 37–38, hereafter referred to as *Moscow Conference*.

70. Gen. Dimitri Volkogonov, *Moscow Conference*, pp. 27–29, says that there were "about 40,000 men" in Cuba and that their purpose was deterrence. The Cubans, "With the Historical Truth and Morale of Baraguá," *Granma*, 2 December

1990, p. 3, give a figure of 43,000 Soviet forces, in addition to 270,000 Cubans in regular units, and 150,000 additional troops in the people's defense force.

71. Khrushchev, *Khrushchev Remembers: The Glasnost Tapes*, p. 171.

72. Central Intelligence Agency, Office of Current Intelligence, "Evidence of a Soviet Military Commitment to Defend Cuba," 19 October 1962, p. 3.

73. *The Soviet Bloc Armed Forces and the Cuban Crisis. A Chronology: July-November 1962* (Washington, D.C.: National Indications Center, 18 June 1963), p. 42; Khrushchev had previously confided to Kekkonen his fear that Berlin would be the cause of a world war. Arthur M. Schlesinger, Jr., *A Thousand Days: John F. Kennedy in the White House* (Boston: Houghton, Mifflin, 1965), p. 379.

74. David A. Welch to the authors, 5 August 1991, points out that the intelligence reports indicating a September-October invasion may have come *after* Khrushchev made his May-June decision to send missiles to Cuba. In this circumstance, the deployment was irrational and dangerous for the reasons given in the next paragraph of the narrative.

75. Aleksandr A. Alekseev, "Karibskii krizis: kak eto bylo," [The Caribbean Crisis: As It Really Was], *Ekho Planety*, no. 33 (November 1988), p. 29, reports that he and the Cubans believed that all the missiles and their warheads were in place at the time of the blockade. However, American intelligence, which monitored the buildup and withdrawal of Soviet equipment, found no evidence of nuclear weapons in Cuba. Intelligence officials suspected that warheads were en route to Cuba, aboard the Soviet cargo ship *Poltava*, when the blockade was announced. *Poltava* returned to the Soviet Union. At the *Moscow Conference*, pp. 27–30, and in subsequent conversations, Gen. Dimitri Volkogonov confirmed that there were warheads on *Poltava* but insisted that twenty warheads had already reached Cuba. They were later removed on *Aleksandrovsk*. Garthoff, *Reflections on the Cuban Missile Crisis*, pp. 37–42, reviews the conflicting evidence about the warheads and finds Volkogonov's report consistent with the information collected by American intelligence at the time. Gen. Anatoliy Gribkov, *Havana Conference*, p. 29, also insists that there were warheads in Cuba and that one ship bringing additional warheads was not unloaded. After spending a few days in port, it returned to the Soviet Union.

76. For a discussion of this literature and its relevance to international relations, see Robert Jervis, *Perception and Misperception in International Politics* (Princeton, N.J.: Princeton University Press, 1976), pp. 128–42; Richard Ned Lebow, *Between Peace and War: The Nature of International Crisis* (Baltimore: Johns Hopkins University Press, 1981), pp. 101–19.

77. Khrushchev's decision and his consultations with other Soviet officials are analyzed in chapter 4.

78. Irving L. Janis and Leon Mann, *Decision Making: A Psychological Analysis of Conflict, Choice, and Commitment* (New York: Free Press, 1977); Lebow, *Between Peace and War*, pp. 107–20, and passim, for a discussion of this literature.

79. Sergei Khrushchev, *Khrushchev on Khrushchev*, p. 408, made this remark in connection with his father's economic reforms. "No matter how much his reforms incorporated the concept of material incentives he always carried them out within the framework of the administrative-command system." He was increasingly aware, however, of the contradiction between his goals and the system. "By the end of his years in power, Father had already begun to understand that the existing system of economic management would never be able to function efficiently," p. 409. Khru-

shchev, *Khrushchev: The Glasnost Tapes*, pp. 111–12, 202–3, comes close to recognizing the systemic failings of a police state and command economy. These paragraphs were dictated after his fall from power. Breslauer, *Khrushchev and Brezhnev as Leaders*, p. 43, and Yanov, "In the Grip of an Adversarial Paradigm," in Crummey, ed., *Reform in Russia*, pp. 167–68, argue that Khrushchev also backed away from recognizing the way the system impeded his political reforms. He never faulted the system, only those who served it.

CHAPTER FOUR
Why Did Khrushchev Miscalculate?

1. Aleksandr Alekseev, "Transcript of the Proceedings of the Havana Conference on the Cuban Missile Crisis, January 9–12, 1992," mimeograph, p.50, forthcoming as James G. Blight, Bruce J. Allyn, and David A. Welch, eds., *Cuba on the Brink: Castro, the Missile Crisis, and the Soviet Collapse* (New York: Pantheon Books, in press), hereafter cited as *Havana Conference*.

2. Oleg Troyanovsky, "The Caribbean Crisis: A View from the Kremlin," *International Affairs* (Moscow) 4–5 (April-May 1992), pp. 147–57, quotation on p. 148.

3. *Department of State Bulletin* 47, 24 September 1962, p. 450.

4. *New York Times*, 8 September 1962.

5. *Department of State Bulletin* 47, 1 October 1962, pp. 481–82.

6. Elie Abel, *The Missile Crisis* (Philadelphia: Lippincott, 1966), pp. 9–10; Robert F. Kennedy, *Thirteen Days: A Memoir of the Cuban Crisis* (New York: Norton, 1969), pp. 24–26.

7. Theodore C. Sorensen, *Kennedy* (New York: Harper & Row, 1965), pp. 667–68.

8. Abel, *Missile Crisis*, p. 50; Chester A. Bowles, *Promises to Keep: My Years in Public Life 1941–1969* (New York: Harper & Row, 1971), p. 418.

9. Nikita S. Khrushchev to John F. Kennedy, 18 April 1962, Cable 2550 from U.S. Embassy in Moscow, John F. Kennedy Library; Nikita S. Khrushchev to John F. Kennedy, 22 April 1961, *Department of State Bulletin* 46, 8 May 1961, pp. 664–67. Abel, p. 16, refers to two letters the president received from Khrushchev in late April expressing no interest in establishing missile bases in Cuba. Only the second letter does this.

10. Kennedy, *Thirteen Days*, pp. 24–26; Sorensen, *Kennedy*, pp. 667–68. Dobrynin read the text of Khrushchev's message to Sorensen two days later. To Sorensen's rejoinder that the Soviet buildup in Cuba had already aggravated world and domestic tensions, Dobrynin replied that the Soviet Union "had done nothing new or extraordinary in Cuba—that the events causing all the excitement had been taking place somewhat gradually and quietly over a long period of time—and that he stood by his assurances that all these steps were defensive in nature and did not represent any threat to the security of the United States."

11. *New York Times*, 12 September 1962.

12. Abel, *Missile Crisis*, p. 50.

13. Sorensen, *Kennedy*, p. 668; Arthur M. Schlesinger, Jr., *A Thousand Days: John F. Kennedy in the White House* (Boston: Houghton, Mifflin, 1965), p. 820. Sorensen reports that this message did not reach President Kennedy until after he became aware of the missiles in Cuba on 16 October.

14. On Bol'shakov and his role as an intermediary, see Arthur M. Schlesinger, Jr., *Robert Kennedy and His Times* (Boston: Houghton, Mifflin, 1978), pp. 499–502;

Pierre Salinger, *With Kennedy* (Garden City, N.Y.: Doubleday, 1966); Georgiy Bol'shakov in Bruce J. Allyn, James G. Blight, and David A. Welch, eds., *Back to the Brink: Proceedings of the Moscow Conference on The Cuban Missile Crisis, January 27–28, 1989*, CSIA Occasional Paper no.9 (Lanham, Md.: University Press of America, 1992), pp. 136–37, hereafter cited as *Moscow Conference*; Georgiy Bol'shakov, "Goriachaia linii: kak diestvoval sekretnyi kanal svizi Dzhon Kennedi-Nikita Khrushchev," [The Hot-Line: the secret communication channel between John Kennedy and Nikita Khrushchev], *New Times*, nos. 4–6, 1989, and "Karibskii krizis: kak eto bylo," [The Caribbean crisis: as it really was], *Komsomolskaya pravda*, 4 February 1989, p. 3.

15. See, for example, Abel, *Missile Crisis*; Arnold L. Horelick, "The Cuban Missile Crisis: An Analysis of Soviet Calculations and Behavior," *World Politics* 16 (April 1964), pp. 363–89; Graham T. Allison, *Essence of Decision: Explaining the Cuban Missile Crisis* (Boston: Little, Brown, 1971), pp. 231–35; Alexander L. George and Richard Smoke, *Deterrence in American Foreign Policy: Theory and Practice* (New York: Columbia University Press, 1974), pp. 459–65; Dino A. Brugioni, *Eyeball to Eyeball: The Inside Story of the Cuban Missile Crisis* (New York: Random House, 1991), p. viii; David A. Welch, ed., *Proceedings of the Hawk's Cay Conference on the Cuban Missile Crisis, 5–8 March 1987* (Cambridge, Mass.: Harvard University, Center for Science and International Affairs, Working Paper 89–1, 1989), mimeograph, pp. 21–22, hereafter cited as *Hawk's Cay Conference*. For the statement of George Ball and the dissent of Arthur Schlesinger, Jr., see also "Transcript of Conference on Cuba Between the Superpowers," Antigua, 3–7 January 1991, mimeograph, p. 35, forthcoming as James G. Blight, David Lewis, and David A. Welch, eds., *Cuba Between the Superpowers: The Antigua Conference on the Cuban Missile Crisis* (Savage, Md.: Rowman and Littlefield, in press), hereafter cited as *Antigua Conference*.

16. Abel, *Missile Crisis*, pp. 35–36; James Reston, "What Was Killed Was Not Only the President But the Promise," *New York Times Magazine*, 15 November 1964, p. 126; Schlesinger, *A Thousand Days*, pp. 391, 796; Sorensen, *Kennedy*, pp. 676, 724; Arnold Horelick and Myron Rush, *Strategic Power and Soviet Foreign Policy* (Chicago: University of Chicago Press, 1966), pp. 142–43; Graham T. Allison, *Essence of Decision*, pp. 231–35; George and Smoke, *Deterrence in American Foreign Policy*, p. 465.

17. Allison, *Essence of Decision*, pp. 235–37.

18. *New York Herald-Tribune*, 16 March 1966; I. F. Stone, "The Brink," *New York Review of Books*, 14 April 1966.

19. Schlesinger, *A Thousand Days*, p. 391.

20. Sorensen, *Kennedy*, p. 676.

21. *Department of State Bulletin* 47, 12 November 1962, pp. 715–20.

22. Richard Ned Lebow, "The Cuban Missile Crisis: Reading the Lessons Correctly," *Political Science Quarterly* 98 (Fall 1983), pp. 431–58; Raymond L. Garthoff, *Reflections on the Cuban Missile Crisis*, rev. ed. (Washington, D.C.: The Brookings Institution, 1989).

23. Lebow, "The Cuban Missile Crisis," and "Deterrence Failure Revisited," *International Security* 12 (Summer 1987), pp. 197–213.

24. Abel, *Missile Crisis*, p. 37. James Reston, *New York Times Magazine*, 15 November 1964, also speculated that Khrushchev might have been influenced by Kennedy's age. George and Smoke, *Deterrence in American Foreign Policy*, p. 464, repeat Reston's charge.

25. Mikhail Menshikov to the Foreign Ministry, 11 July 1961; Robert Herman interview with Yuri Shvedkov, Moscow, 6 August 1992. Boris Poklad, "From the Memoirs of Boris Poklad," *Pravda*, 22 October 1992, reports that Andrei Gromyko also encouraged the view of the American president as "the kid in shorts."

26. Schlesinger, *A Thousand Days*, pp. 358–59, 362. Dean Rusk as told to Richard Rusk, *As I Saw It*, Daniel S. Papp, ed. (New York: Norton, 1990), p. 220, thinks that the Soviet leader was jealous of Kennedy's youth. Schlesinger, *A Thousand Days*, p. 362, reported that Charles de Gaulle drew the opposite inference about the president's age; he thought his youth and inexperience made him unnecessarily rash and risk-prone.

27. Roger Hilsman to Dean Rusk, Memorandum on Khrushchev's Conversation with W. E. Knox, 26 October 1962.

28. Reston, *New York Times Magazine*, 15 November 1964, p. 126.

29. Abel, *Missile Crisis*, p. 37; George and Smoke, *Deterrence in American Foreign Policy*, p. 465.

30. This point is also made by Robin Edmonds, *Soviet Foreign Policy, 1962–1973: The Paradox of Soviet Power* (London: Oxford University Press, 1975), pp. 24–25; Henry M. Pachter, *Collision Course: The Cuban Missile Crisis and Coexistence* (New York: Praeger, 1963), p. 64, argues that Khrushchev would not have conducted his subsequent Berlin offensive so cautiously if he had underestimated Kennedy in this way at Vienna. Roger Hilsman, *To Move A Nation: The Politics of Foreign Policy in the Administration of John F. Kennedy* (Garden City, N.Y.: Doubleday, 1967), pp. 191–92, also dismisses the importance of Vienna as a determinant of Khrushchev's judgment of American resolve. For firsthand accounts of the meeting, see Schlesinger, *A Thousand Days*, pp. 543–50; Pierre Salinger, *With Kennedy* (Garden City, N.Y.: Doubleday, 1966), pp. 175–88; Khrushchev, *Khrushchev Remembers: The Last Testament*, trans. and ed. Strobe Talbott (New York: Bantam, 1976), pp. 562–72.

31. Schlesinger, *A Thousand Days*, p. 361, and *Robert Kennedy and His Times* (Boston: Houghton, Mifflin, 1978), p. 427n, and *Antigua Conference*, p. 36.

32. Kenneth P. O'Donnell and David F. Powers with Joe McCarthy, *"Johnny, We Hardly Knew Ye": Memories of John Fitzgerald Kennedy* (Boston: Little, Brown, 1970), p. 295.

33. Interview, Dean Rusk, Athens, Ga., 21 September 1987; Georgiy Kornienko, "Something New About the Caribbean Crisis," typescript, p. 12. Fedor Burlatsky and Sergo Mikoyan insist that the summit meeting in Vienna influenced Khrushchev's decision to send missiles to Cuba. Soviet defector Arkady Shevchenko, *Washington Post*, 25 July 1985, claims that "After the Vienna meeting, I heard Khrushchev himself telling that Kennedy is a weak president. He is not a strong man. . . . He will not dare to do something . . . to stop what the Soviets are doing."

Interview, Fedor Burlatsky, Cambridge, Mass., 12 October 1987; Burlatsky, *Chruschtschow: Ein Politisches Porträt*, (Düsseldorf: Claassen, 1990), p. 243, insists that Kennedy made a bad impression on Khrushchev at the summit. Sergo Mikoyan says that Khrushchev had a stereotyped image of intellectuals; he thought them "weak, indecisive, and unable to stand up under pressure." Interview with Sergo Mikoyan, Cambridge, Mass., 12 October 1987. He speculates that, by emphasizing ideology and trying to engage Khrushchev in a debate about the relative merits of capitalism and socialism, Kennedy may have unwittingly undercut the impression of resolve he was trying so hard to convey. Burlatsky thinks that Khrushchev came away from Vienna convinced that Kennedy was "too intellectual" and therefore "not well-prepared for decision making in crisis situations."

Neither Burlatsky nor Shevchenko are reliable sources. Western scholars and intelligence officials reject many of Shevchenko's "revelations" as his memoirs are filled with factual errors and demonstrably fictional episodes. In 1962, it was very unlikely that Shevchenko, quite a junior official at the time, heard Khrushchev say anything directly. For a devastating critique of Shevchenko, see Edward J. Epstein, "The Spy Who Came In To Be Sold," *New Republic* 193, 15 and 22 July 1985, pp. 35–42.

Our earlier review of Burlatsky's account of how and where Khrushchev decided on the missile deployment demonstrated his tendency to change and embroider evidence to make his stories more dramatic and interesting to Western audiences. At the time of the missile crisis, Burlatsky was a young man working for Yuri Andropov in the Central Committee department for relations with other socialist countries. Sergei Khrushchev, *Khrushchev on Khrushchev: An Inside Account of the Man and His Era*, trans. William Taubman (Boston: Little, Brown, 1990), p. 404, insists that "he had hardly known father," and that his information is all secondhand. Knowledgeable Soviet officials also dismiss Burlatsky. Interview, Ambassador Georgiy Kornienko, Moscow, 17 December 1991, and "Something New About the Caribbean Crisis," pp. 2 and 7, contends that Burlatsky "does not possess any factual information concerning the issues under discussion, but indulges in rich fantasy." Nobody questions Mikoyan's integrity, but by his own admission, his views concerning Khrushchev's appraisal of Kennedy are speculation.

The translator's record and the secondary accounts of the summit by administration officials challenge Burlatsky's and Mikoyan's depiction of the summit. It was Khrushchev, not Kennedy, who wanted to debate ideology and began his remarks with a long discourse on the meaning of freedom and the ultimate victory of communism over capitalism. Kennedy tried to steer the conversation to more practical matters. "You're not going to make a Communist out of me and I'm not going to make a capitalist out of you," he told Khrushchev after the latter's speech, "so let's get down to business." Some of the administration's Soviet experts, most notably George Kennan, thought that Kennedy had made a mistake by not offering an ideological defense of capitalism and the West. Alexander Akalovsky's "Record of Vienna Summit Meeting, 3 June 1961, 3 P.M., at residence of U.S. ambassador." In attendance: Nikita S. Khrushchev, V. M. Sukhodrev (Soviet translator), John F. Kennedy, Alexander Akalovsky (American translator); Schlesinger, *A Thousand Days*, pp. 358–74; Sorensen, *Kennedy*, pp. 543–50; Rusk, *As I Saw It*, pp. 220–21.

Even if, for the sake of argument, we accept Burlatsky's characterization of the summit, it indicates that Kennedy damaged his credibility for very different reasons than Western students of the crisis have supposed. It was not his putative failure to stand up to Khrushchev that caused a problem, but his verve and skill in defending U.S. policy. The speculations of Burlatsky and Mikoyan are contradicted by Khrushchev's recollections of the summit. His memoirs and comments at the time to Soviet and American officials are full of praise for Kennedy's performance in Vienna; he was impressed by his confidence and "grasp of international issues." Khrushchev, *Khrushchev Remembers: The Last Testament*, pp. 562–72.

There is a logical problem with inferring Khrushchev's confidence from his judgment of Kennedy's performance in Vienna. Burlatsky thinks that Khrushchev might have regarded Kennedy as irresolute and likely to give ground against a determined adversary. Mikoyan suggests that Khrushchev "thought [that] Kennedy was not a strong politician and would submit to CIA preference[s], led by Allen Dulles." David A. Welch, ed., *Proceedings of the Cambridge Conference on the Cuban Missile Cri-*

sis, 11–12 October 1987 (Cambridge, Mass.: Harvard University, Center for Science and International Affairs, April 1988), final version, mimeograph, p. 42, hereafter cited as *Cambridge Conference*. However, Burlatsky and Mikoyan argue, and other Soviets agree, that Khrushchev and all of his advisors saw the CIA as uncompromisingly anti-Soviet and unreconciled to Castro. The CIA's expected ability to manipulate a weak president should have made Khrushchev *more*, not less, concerned about the possibility of a violent American response to his missile deployment. The missiles could have provided the pretext the CIA was so anxiously seeking to compel the president to invade Cuba.

34. Sorensen, *Kennedy*, p. 549; Hugh Sidey, "What the K's Really Told Each Other," *Life*, 16 June 1961, pp. 48–49, reports that the White House told him that "Khrushchev was even tougher than they had imagined, but they are sure that Khrushchev was impressed by Kennedy's own knowledge and toughness. Khrushchev even said so to the Austrians after Kennedy left for London."

35. Georgiy Kornienko, "Something New About the Caribbean Crisis," pp. 12–13.

36. Sergei Khrushchev, *Khrushchev on Khrushchev*, pp. 50–51.

37. Khrushchev, *Khrushchev Remembers: The Last Testament*, pp. 566–67; in May 1962, Khrushchev told Pierre Salinger, Kennedy's press secretary, that "he believed John Kennedy was not only intelligent, but also well-equipped to handle important international affairs. And he compared him to Dwight Eisenhower; he said, 'you know, when I met with Eisenhower, I would ask Eisenhower a question, and one of Eisenhower's aides would have to answer the question. But when I asked a question to Kennedy, he would answer it himself; he knew the subject, he was able to discuss it.' " *Moscow Conference*, pp. 126–27.

38. See, Pachter, *Collision Course*, pp. 83–84; Abel, *Missile Crisis*, p. 36; Horelick, "The Missile Crisis," p. 383; Allison, *Essence of Decision*, p. 231; George and Smoke, *Deterrence in American Foreign Policy*, pp. 465–67; and Rusk, *As I Saw It*, p. 242.

39. Alexander Akalovsky's "Record of Vienna Summit Meeting, 3 June 1961, 3 P.M., at residence of U.S. ambassador"; Sorensen, p. 546; Schlesinger, *A Thousand Days*, p. 362; Interview, Sergei Khrushchev, Moscow, 17 May 1989; "Letter from Premier Khrushchev to President Kennedy, 26 October 1962," in David L. Larson, *The "Cuban Crisis" of 1962: Selected Documents, Chronology and Bibliography*, 2d ed. (Lanham, Md.: University Press of America, 1986), p. 178. Andrei Gromyko, *Memories*, trans. Harold Shukman (London: Hutchinson, 1989), p. 177, reports that Kennedy told him during their discussion on 18 October that the Bay of Pigs had been a mistake.

40. Sorensen, *Kennedy*, p. 675; See also Hilsman, *To Move A Nation*, p. 196. For the domestic political pressures on the president and their influence on his Cuban policy, see chapter 5.

41. Mikhail Menshikov to the Foreign Ministry, 11 July 1961; Robert Herman interview with Yuri Shvedkov, Moscow, 6 August 1992. Boris Poklad, "From the Memoirs of Boris Poklad," *Pravda*, 22 October 1992. The relevant part of the cable reads: "On July 11, 1961, there was a conversation between Robert Kennedy and Menshikov. Kennedy said that the Americans will defend their right of access to West Berlin by force. If this happens, World War III will become inevitable. The USA is prepared for such a risk. . . . I think that these new American 'leaders' get on their high horse while there is still time, but when things approach the moment of decision, then they will be the first to shit in their pants."

42. Hilsman, *To Move A Nation*, pp. 91–155; Schlesinger, *A Thousand Days*, pp. 320–54; Charles A. Stevenson, *The End of Nowhere: American Policy Toward Laos Since 1954* (Boston: Beacon Press, 1972); David Hall, "The Laotian War of 1961 and the Indo-Pakistan War of 1971," in Barry Blechman and Stephen S. Kaplan, eds., *Force Without War: U.S. Armed Forces as a Political Instrument* (Washington, D.C.: The Brookings Institution, 1978), pp. 135–221; Arthur J. Dommen, *Conflict in Laos: The Politics of Neutralization* (New York: Praeger, 1965).

43. Interview, Oleg Grinevsky, Vienna, 11 October 1991.

44. Interview, Georgi Arbatov, Ithaca, N.Y., 15 November 1991; Stephen E. Ambrose, "Secrets of the Cold War," *New York Times*, 27 December 1990, p. A15. Raymond L. Garthoff to authors, 9 July 1992, thinks that Arbatov may have intended his comment to refer to Khrushchev's challenge to the West on Berlin in 1958.

45. Interviews, Leonid Zamyatin and Georgiy Kornienko, Moscow, 16 and 17 December 1991; Georgiy Shakhnazarov, *Antigua Conference*, p. 79; Georgi Arbatov, *Moscow Conference*, p. 40. Zamyatin thinks that Khrushchev had toyed with the idea since the beginning of the year.

46. Oleg Grinevsky to authors, 21 July 1992. Khrushchev, *Khrushchev Remembers: The Last Testament*, pp. 393–95, describes the interview but not this exchange.

47. Khrushchev, *Khrushchev Remembers*, p. 493. Khrushchev returned from Bulgaria on 20 May, and according to Anatoliy Dobrynin, "The Caribbean Crisis: An Eyewitness Account," *International Affairs* (Moscow), no. 8 (August 1992), pp. 47–48, told the president that the idea of stationing missiles in Cuba had occurred to him in Varna.

48. Ibid., pp. 493–94. In Bulgaria, Khrushchev had spoken out against the American missiles in Turkey. Speech in Varna, Bulgaria, "Celebration of Fraternal Friendship on Bulgarian Soil," *Pravda*, 17 May 1962. English translation in *Current Digest of the Soviet Press* 14, 20 (1962), pp. 3–7. In Sofia, he lashed out at Kennedy for suggesting that there were certain circumstances in which the United States would strike first with nuclear weapons. "Rally of 250,000 Working People in Sofia in Honor of Soviet Party-Government Delegation," *Pravda*, 17 May 1962.

49. Interview, Fedor Burlatsky, Cambridge, Mass., 12 October 1987, reporting on a conversation with Yuri Andropov. Khrushchev must have known about the Jupiters before this because the Soviets had mounted a major political campaign against the deployment. For details, see Michael Armacost, *The Politics of Weapons Innovation: The Thor-Jupiter Controversy* (New York: Columbia University Press, 1969), pp. 203–4.

Burlatsky gave a slightly different version of the story. He recalled how he had received instructions from Yuri V. Andropov—then head of the Central Committee's Department of Socialist Countries—to edit a letter from Khrushchev to the Cuban leadership. In the letter, Khrushchev described how he had hit upon the idea of a missile deployment in the Crimea. "He began a bit lyrically, about how he was strolling along the shore of the Black Sea with Marshal Malinovsky. And Malinovsky said that on the other side there were Turkish bases which could in a short time destroy all our southern cities. Why, he asks, do the Americans have such a possibility—they have surrounded us with bases on all sides, and we have no such possibility and right to do the same." *Moscow Conference*, p. 46. Gen. Anatoliy Gribkov, "Operation 'Anadyr,'" *Der Spiegel*, no. 16, 1992, p. 152, tells a similar story.

Burlatsky subsequently claimed that the letter was given personally to him by Andropov in Berlin in January 1963, during Khrushchev's visit to the Seventh Congress of the Socialist Unity Party in East Berlin. Burlatsky tells a third version of the story in an unpublished memoir of the crisis, in *Chruschtschow*, p. 255, and "The Lessons of Personal Diplomacy," *Problems of Communism* Special Issue 41 (Spring 1992), pp. 8–13. Another variant appears in *New York Times*, 23 October 1992.

Interview, Aleksei Adzhubei, Moscow, 15 May 1989. Adzhubei dismisses Burlatsky's Crimea story as "a canard." Interview, Sergei Khrushchev, Moscow, 17 May 1989. Khrushchev gives no credence to either version of the story but agrees that his father's Crimean holiday may have heightened his concern over the Jupiter deployment. The letter that Burlatsky supposedly helped to draft in January 1963 was acquired from the Cubans and makes no reference to the conversation. It is, of course, possible that the reference was deleted before the letter was sent.

50. *Cambridge Conference*, p. 42.

51. Ibid., p. 38; Sergo Mikoyan, "The Caribbean Crisis Seen from a Distance," *Latinskaya Amerika*, no. 1 (January 1988), pp. 70–71; Interview, Sergei Khrushchev, Moscow, 18 May 1989.

52. There is complete agreement among all the Soviet officials we interviewed about the identity of the participants in these discussions. Sergo Mikoyan, *Cambridge Conference*, p. 43; Sergei Khrushchev, *Moscow Conference*, pp. 128–31; Interview, Sergei Khrushchev, Moscow, 17 May 1989; Aleksandr I. Alekseev, "The Caribbean Crisis: As It Really Was," *Ekho Planety*, no. 33 (November 1988), pp. 27–37. Interview, Leonid M. Zamyatin, Moscow, 16 December 1991, reports that Khrushchev had a female stenographer who kept notes of all official meetings and of many informal conversations. According to Alekseev, *Havana Conference*, pp. 47–48, Kozlov, Gromyko, Malinovsky, Rashidov, Mikoyan, and Biryuzov all attended the first Presidium meeting. Khrushchev, *Khrushchev Remembers*, pp. 494–95, and N. Khrushchev, *Khrushchev Remembers: The Glasnost Tapes*, trans. and ed. Jerrold L. Schechter with Vyacheslav V. Luchkov (Boston: Little, Brown, 1990), p. 170; Andrei A. Gromyko, "Karibskii Krizis: o Glasnosti Teper' i Skrytnosti Togda," [The Caribbean Crisis: On Glasnost Now and Secrecy Then] *Izvestiya* 106 (15 April 1989), English translation in *The Current Digest of the Soviet Press*, XLI, no. 16 (1989), pp. 15–18; Donald Trelford, "A Walk in the Woods with Gromyko," *The Observer* (London), 2 April 1989.

53. Sergei Khrushchev, *Moscow Conference*, pp. 128–29.

54. Interview, Sergei Khrushchev, Moscow, 18 May 1989.

55. Khrushchev, *Khrushchev Remembers: The Glasnost Tapes*, p. 170; Gen. Anatoliy Gribkov, *Havana Conference*, p. 17, reported that the High Command received instructions in the middle of May to prepare a draft operational plan and force structure for securing the defense of Cuba.

56. Georgiy Kornienko, "Something New About the Caribbean Crisis," p. 7. Malinovsky was not a member of the Presidium and generally functioned as a transmission belt for orders from the leadership to the military. In this instance, he was used by Khrushchev to lend legitimacy to his scheme.

57. Interview, Anatoliy A. Gromyko, Moscow, 18 May 1989; Sergo A. Mikoyan, "The Caribbean Crisis Seen from a Distance," *Latinskaya Amerika*, no. 1 (January 1988), pp. 70–71; Sergei Khrushchev, *Moscow Conference*, pp. 128–30; Kornienko, "Something New About the Caribbean Crisis," p. 7.

58. Sergo Mikoyan, *Cambridge Conference*, pp. 42–43; Mikoyan, "The Caribbean Crisis Seen from a Distance," pp. 70–71; Interviews, Sergei Khrushchev and Sergo Mikoyan, Moscow, 17–18 May 1989.

59. Gromyko, "Karibskii Krizis"; Trelford, "A Walk in the Woods with Gromyko." Alekseev, "Lessons of the Caribbean Crisis," and interview with A. I. Alekseev by Yu. Sigov, *Argumenty i fakty*, no. 10 (11–17 March 1989), p. 5, reports that in May 1962 Gromyko told him about his conversation with Khrushchev and of his own misgivings. Troyanovsky, "The Caribbean Crisis," p. 149, also accepts Gromyko's claim to have expressed reservations. Other Soviet diplomats doubt that Gromyko would have risked Khrushchev's displeasure by speaking out so directly, even in private, against a plan the general secretary appeared to favor. By all accounts, Gromyko kept quiet during the Presidium discussions. Interviews, Oleg Grinevsky, Vienna, 11 October 1991; Leonid Zamyatin, Moscow, 16 December 1991; Georgiy Kornienko, 17 December 1991. Kornienko could not imagine Gromyko objecting to any initiative Khrushchev appeared to favor. At most, "he would have raised questions and pointed out difficulties, telling Khrushchev he should be prepared for trouble. He would never insist on his own position." It is possible that, after the fact, Gromyko presented his objections as more forceful than they had been.

60. Alekseev, "The Caribbean Crisis," pp. 28–29, *Moscow Conference*, pp. 150–51. At the *Havana Conference*, pp. 48–49, Alekseev reported that he told Khrushchev that Castro would not accept the missiles because they would provoke "a rejection of the Cuban Revolution from the rest of the hemisphere."

61. Alekseev, "The Caribbean Crisis," pp. 28–29.

62. Dobrynin, "The Caribbean Crisis," p. 47; Alekseev, "The Caribbean Crisis," p. 28, and *Havana Conference*, pp. 48–49. At this meeting, Khrushchev described to the Presidium Alekseev's doubts about Castro's willingness to accept the missiles and urged the delegation about to depart for Cuba to convince Castro that "there was no other alternative for the effective defense of Cuba, and see how Fidel Castro reacted to that."

63. Alekseev, "The Caribbean Crisis," p. 34, says he arrived in Havana in early May, but corrected himself at the *Moscow Conference*, pp. 150–51, and reported it was early June. Garthoff, *Reflections on the Cuban Missile Crisis*, p. 15, sets the date as 30 May.

64. Interview, Leonid Zamyatin, Moscow, 16 December 1991; Interview, Sergei Khrushchev, Moscow, 17 May 1989. Khrushchev believes that Army Gen. Issa A. Pliyev, later commander of the Soviet expeditionary forces in Cuba, was also added to the delegation.

65. Alekseev, "The Caribbean Crisis," pp. 29–30, and his comments, *Moscow Conference*, pp. 150–51.

66. Ibid.; Jorge Risquet, *Antigua Conference*, p. 70; Alekseev, *Havana Conference*, pp. 49–50; Garthoff, *Reflections on the Cuban Missile Crisis*, p. 16, citing interviews in Moscow with Alekseev, Jorge Risquet, and Emilio Aragonés. Fidel Castro, *Havana Conference*, pp. 200–201, maintains that it was Rashidov who maintained that the missiles would contribute to our defense and "the defensive power of the entire socialist camp."

67. Alekseev, *Moscow Conference*, pp. 151–52; Interview, Sergo Mikoyan, 12 October 1988; Sergo Mikoyan, *Moscow Conference*, pp. 54–55; Jorge Risquet, *Antigua Conference*, p. 71.

68. Emilio Aragonés, Secretary of the Central Committee of the Cuban Commu-

nist Party at the time, *Moscow Conference*, p. 32; Jorge Risquet, *Antigua Conference*, pp. 71–72; Fidel Castro, *Havana Conference*, pp. 201–2; Claude Julien in *Le Monde*, 21 and 23 March 1963. The Central Committee was composed of Fidel and Raúl Castro, Osvaldo Dorticós Torrado, Che Guevara, Blas Roca, and Aragonés. Khrushchev, *Khrushchev Remembers: The Glasnost Tapes*, p. 182, recalls that he could not convince Castro that the missiles were intended to defend Cuba. Even after the crisis "He still believed that we had installed the missiles not so much in the interests of Cuba, but primarily in the military interests of the Soviet Union and the whole socialist camp." Anastas Mikoyan also failed to persuade Castro, who insisted that the missiles were for "the protection of the interests of the entire Socialist camp." Felix N. Kovaliev, *Antigua Conference*, pp. 56–57, citing Mikoyan's cables of 6 and 8 November 1962 from Havana to the Foreign Ministry.

69. Castro, *Havana Conference*, pp. 56–57, 62.

70. Mikoyan, "The Caribbean Crisis Seen from a Distance"; *Cambridge Conference*, pp. 42–43; Interview, Sergo Mikoyan, Moscow, 12 October 1988. According to Mikoyan, *Antigua Conference*, p. 80, when his father arrived in Cuba in November, he asked Castro why he had agreed to accept the missiles. "Fidel said with some bewilderment, 'But we thought that *you* needed it.' . . . There was a misunderstanding: we thought that we were doing it for them; they thought that we were doing it for ourselves."

71. Interview, Sergei Khrushchev, Moscow, 17 May 1989; Gribkov, "Ander Schwelle zum Atomkrieg," *Der Spiegel*, no. 16, 1982, p. 147; Khrushchev, *Khrushchev Remembers: The Glasnost Tapes*, p. 171. According to Oleg Darusenkov, *Antigua Conference*, p. 152, "The security people assured us that it was possible. They said the palm trees there would keep our missiles from being seen in the air." Fidel Castro, *Havana Conference*, pp. 61–62, dismisses this as nonsense. The missiles were visible to American intelligence because of their command facilities and foundations for launching platforms. He is convinced today that the missiles could have been kept secret if the American U-2s had been shot down from the outset. "So, in my judgment, there were political mistakes, there was excessive caution."

72. Alekseev, *Moscow Conference*, p. 98, *Havana Conference*, pp. 50–51. "The only thing he advised was, 'Do not rush. Do everything in such a way that U.S. public opinion will not be aware of this until November 4th or after November 4th. After that there won't be any great difficulties.'" Sergo Mikoyan, "The Crisis of Misperceptions: One More Retrospective Appraisal of the Missile Crisis," in James A. Nathan, ed., *The Cuban Missile Crisis Revisited* (New York: St. Martin's Press, 1992), p. 62, contends that Kennedy was to be informed confidentially about the missiles. His father told him aboard a plane to Cuba on 1 November 1962 that "Khrushchev had intended to let Kennedy handle the issue of whether and how to reveal that Soviet missiles had been placed in Cuba."

73. Gen. Dimitri Volkogonov, Director of the Soviet Ministry of Defense Institute of Military History, *Moscow Conference*, p. 29; Burlatsky, *Chruschtschow*, p. 255.

74. Interview, Gen. Dimitri A. Volkogonov by Raymond L. Garthoff, Moscow, 1 February 1989; Anatoliy Gribkov, *Havana Conference*, pp. 18–21, 28–29, and "Operation 'Anadyr,'" p. 154; Lt. Col. Anatoliy Dokuchaev, "Operatsiia Anadyr," [Operation Anadyr] *Krasnaya Zvezda* [Red Star], 21 October 1992, p. 3.

75. Roy Medvedev, *Khrushchev*, trans. Brian Pearce (New York: Doubleday, 1982), p. 184; Interview, Sergo Mikoyan, Moscow, 18 May 1989; Gen. Sergio del Valle, *Antigua Conference*, pp. 119–20; Alekseev, *Havana Conference*, p. 51.

76. Alekseev, "The Caribbean Crisis," p. 30, *Havana Conference*, p. 50; Emilio Aragonés, *Moscow Conference*, pp. 123–24; Interview, Sergo Mikoyan, Moscow, 18 May 1989; Jorge Risquet, *Antigua Conference*, pp. 22–23; Anatoliy Gribkov, *Havana Conference*, p. 46; Fidel Castro, *Havana Conference*, pp. 58–59, 202; "With the Historical Truth and Morale of Baraguá," *Granma*, 2 December 1990, p. 2; Khrushchev, *Khrushchev Remembers: The Glasnost Tapes*, p. 172, insists that "After installing the missiles we, together with the Cuban government, intended to announce their presence in a loud voice. There was no sense in keeping the missiles secret, because they were not means for attack. The missiles were the means for deterring those who would attack Cuba."

77. Emilio Aragonés, *Moscow Conference*, pp. 51–52, 123–24; Jorge Risquet, *Moscow Conference*, pp. 70–71; Jorge Risquet and Gen. Sergio del Valle, *Antigua Conference*, pp. 22–23, 120, 127; Alekseev, "The Caribbean Crisis," pp. 30–31; Alekseev, *Havana Conference*, p. 50, who had prepared the Spanish draft of the proposed agreement, admitted that "There were a great many technical provisions; the political aspects were rather thin, and Fidel introduced the necessary corrections, and some time later, in August, Che Guevara was sent to Moscow where he met with Khrushchev. At that moment, the agreement was initialed by Malinovsky and Raúl Castro." Fidel Castro, *Havana Conference*, pp. 58–59, confirmed that the final draft, which he wrote by hand, filled in many of the "gaps and loopholes" in the first draft's treatment of the political context. A copy of the August 1962 Draft Agreement is in the National Security Archive, and an English-language translation is to be found in Laurence Chang and Peter Kornbluh, eds., *The Cuban Missile Crisis, 1962* (New York: New Press, 1992), pp. 54–56.

78. Arthur Schlesinger, Jr., "Four Days with Fidel: A Havana Diary," *New York Review of Books*, 26 March 1992, pp. 22–29.

79. Jorge Risquet, *Moscow Conference*, p. 71; Fidel Castro, *Havana Conference*, pp. 59–60, 213–15. In retrospect, Castro argued that secrecy "was very damaging because Kennedy had a lot at stake. He already had the Bay of Pigs setback. He was going into his second year. There were going to be elections." Alekseev, *Havana Conference*, p. 55, notes Raúl Castro also favored a public deployment. In September, Emilio Aragonés and Che Guevara suggested that the operation be brought out into the open, and that the agreement be made public.

80. Emilio Aragonés and Jorge Risquet, *Moscow Conference*, pp. 51–52, 71–72; Bruce J. Allyn et al., "Essence of Revision: Moscow, Havana, and the Cuban Missile Crisis," *International Security* 14 (Winter 1989–90), p. 151n., citing an interview in Moscow with Emilio Aragonés; "With the Historical Truth and Morale of Baraguá," p. 2; According to Castro, *Havana Conference*, pp. 60–61, Khrushchev was not so concerned about the consequences of discovery because of the legality of the missile deployment. He told Aragonés and Guevara: "Maybe a couple goes to the beach and rents a room in a hotel; they are not betraying anyone, they are not committing any crime. What we were doing was something completely legal."

81. He declared that "when our Revolution can say that it is in a position to repulse a direct attack, the last danger hanging over it will have disappeared." "Fidel en el noveno anniversario del 26–27," [Fidel and the Ninth Anniversary of the 26–27th] *Hoy* 27 July 1962. Che Guevara and Raúl Castro also dropped oblique hints about Soviet military guarantees to Cuba. In a speech to Cuban officers in training, Raúl Castro boasted that "if they touch Cuba a third world war could begin and rockets could drop on their territory." Agence France Presse, "Guevara

Remarks," [remarks by Che Guevara in conversation with Agence France Presse correspondent], 9 September 1962; "Raúl Castro Remarks," TASS in English to Europe, 13 September 1962, Foreign Broadcast Information Service, USSR International Affairs, 14 September 1962, National Security Archive. Such hints seem irrational given Fidel's concern that the greatest risk of invasion was a situation in which the missiles were discovered before they became operational and had deterrent value.

82. Interview, Sergo Mikoyan, Moscow, 18 May 1989; Jorge Risquet, *Antigua Conference*, pp. 22–23.

83. Interview, Vadim Bogdanov, Moscow, 15 May 1989, reporting on his discussion with Khrushchev's translator at his meeting with Gomułka. Interview, Aleksei Adzhubei, Moscow, 15 May 1989, confirmed the story. Roger Hilsman to Secretary of State, 26 October 1962, reveals that during the crisis Khrushchev told the same story to visiting American businessman, William Knox.

84. Interviews, Sergei Khrushchev, Moscow, 17 May 1989, and Anatoliy Dobrynin, Moscow, 17 December 1991; Georgiy Kornienko, "Something New About the Caribbean Crisis," p. 14.

85. Discussion with Theodore Sorensen and McGeorge Bundy, Cambridge, Mass., 12 October 1987. Sorensen, *Cambridge Conference*, p. 54 and *Moscow Conference*, p. 20; Sorensen, *Moscow Conference*, p. 19–20.

86. Dobrynin, "The Caribbean Crisis," p. 47.

87. Khrushchev, *Khrushchev Remembers*, pp. 493–94.

88. Hawk's Cay Conference on the Cuban Missile Crisis, 6–8 March 1987, Lebow record, p. 4; McNamara explained that an additional reason for caution was that "we put little trust in those CIA estimates," *Hawk's Cay Conference*, p. 43.

89. Interview, Aleksei Adzhubei, Moscow, 15 May 1989.

90. In his account of the Vienna summit, Khrushchev, *Khrushchev Remembers: The Last Testament*, pp. 561, 568, 570, praised Kennedy for his commitment to peace. He attributed it to the president's recognition of "the shift in the balance of power." "Kennedy was a capitalist," Khrushchev explained, and "was faithful to the capitalist class right up to the last day of his life. But he understood that the socialist camp had gained such economic and cultural might—and was in possession of so much scientific and technical knowledge, including the means of war—that the United States and its allies could no longer seriously consider going to war against us. I'll always respect him for that."

91. Interview, Aleksei Adzhubei, Moscow, 15 May 1989. The incident is described in Khrushchev, *Khrushchev Remembers*, pp. 459–60, and *Khrushchev Remembers: The Last Testament*, pp. 578–79; Burlatsky, *Chruschtschow*, p. 248; Schlesinger, *Robert Kennedy and His Times*, p. 500; Jean Edward Smith, *The Defense of Berlin* (Baltimore: Johns Hopkins University Press, 1963), pp. 322–24. The most accurate portrayal, drawing on Soviet as well as Western sources, is Raymond L. Garthoff, "Berlin 1961: The Record Corrected," *Foreign Policy* no. 84 (Fall 1991), pp. 142–56.

92. Schlesinger, *Robert Kennedy and His Times*, p. 500, and Smith, *The Defense of Berlin*, pp. 322–24, report a back-channel message from Kennedy to Khrushchev, via Georgiy Bol'shakov, on 27 October, requesting the Soviet Union to withdraw its tanks. Garthoff, p. 152, reveals that Kennedy promised to withdraw the American tanks as part of a mutual disengagement. From the Soviet perspective, Garthoff argues, this was welcome news and was interpreted as successful deterrence; the

Soviet show of force had convinced the Americans to give up their plans for breaching the Berlin Wall.

93. Interview, Aleksei Adzhubei, Moscow, 15 May 1989.

94. Alekseev, "The Caribbean Crisis," p. 29.

95. This linkage was salient for the administration even before the crisis. Speaking for the White House, McGeorge Bundy spoke of "the very definite relationship between Cuba and other trouble spots, such as Berlin." John McCone, Memorandum for the File, "Discussion in Secretary Rusk's Office at 12 o'clock, 21 August 1962," in Mary S. McAuliffe, ed., *CIA Documents on the Cuban Missile Crisis 1962* (Washington, D.C.: History Staff, Central Intelligence Agency, October 1962), pp. 21–23.

96. Khrushchev, *Khrushchev Remembers: The Glasnost Tapes*, p. 174, denies that there was a difference between the two deployments. The Americans, he writes, did not inform us beforehand about the Jupiters. "We were just copying" their methods. The comparison is fatuous; the American missiles were deployed openly and the Soviets knew about them beforehand. Khrushchev's argument is an unconvincing attempt to justify, ex post facto, his initiative to himself and sympathetic Soviet readers. Ambassador Georgiy Kornienko, *Antigua Conference*, pp. 65–66, rejects Khrushchev's argument. He conceded that "the greatest mistake—perhaps next to the decision to deploy the missiles in the first place—was the decision to do this secretly." It was not feasible technically and a disaster politically.

97. Theodore Sorensen, *Cambridge Conference*, pp. 60–61.

98. Transcript of a Discussion About the Cuban Missile Crisis, p. 5; Sorensen, *Kennedy*, p. 684, also notes the provocative implications of Khrushchev's secrecy. Paul Nitze had a similar reaction. Interview, Paul Nitze, by James Blight, Washington, D.C., 6 May 1987; James G. Blight and David A. Welch, *On the Brink: Americans and Soviets Reexamine the Cuban Missile Crisis* (New York: Hill and Wang, 1989), p. 141.

99. *Moscow Conference*, p. 20.

100. Chapter 5 examines the American response to the discovery of the missiles.

101. Interview, Sergei Khrushchev, Moscow, 17 May 1989; Sergei Khrushchev and Sergo Mikoyan, *Antigua Conference*, pp. 76–77, 80; "With the Historical Truth and Morale of Baraguá," p. 2. To this day, many Soviet officials are convinced that an open deployment, as Andrei Gromyko put it, "would just not have worked." *Moscow Conference*, pp. 19–20. "I am absolutely convinced," Georgiy Shakhnazarov declared, "that the government of the United States would not have tolerated it." It would also have played into their hands by providing the administration with a propaganda tool "to win public opinion over to their side" for an invasion. *Moscow Conference*, pp. 22–23.

102. Chapter 5 reviews the CIA reports on the status of the missiles.

103. The intelligence problem is discussed in chapter 13. For the standard literature, see Klaus Knorr, "Failures in National Intelligence Estimates: The Case of the Cuban Missiles," *World Politics* 16 (April 1964), pp. 455–67; Roberta Wohlstetter, "Cuba and Pearl Harbor: Hindsight and Foresight," *Foreign Affairs* 43 (July 1965), pp. 691–707; Hilsman, *To Move A Nation*, pp. 159–92; Allison, *Essence of Decision*, pp. 117–23, 187–92; John Prados, *The Soviet Estimate: U.S. Intelligence and Russian Military Strength* (New York: Dial Press, 1982), pp. 127–50; McGeorge Bundy, *Danger and Survival: Choices About the Bomb in the First Fifty Years* (New York: Random House, 1988), pp. 413–20.

104. Khrushchev, *Khrushchev Remembers: The Last Testament*, pp. 487–90. The fliers subsequently released were from an unrelated RB-47 mission; Powers remained in prison.

105. Ibid., p. 491. Schlesinger, *A Thousand Days*, pp. 301–2, reports that Khrushchev had also told American Ambassador Llewellyn Thompson that he had deliberately refrained from releasing Powers to aid the Democrats.

106. Khrushchev, *Khrushchev Remembers: The Last Testament*, pp. 489–90.

107. Ibid., pp. 488–89.

108. Sorensen, *Kennedy*, p. 668, reporting on a talk with Dobrynin at the Soviet embassy on 6 September 1962.

109. Aleksandr Alekseev, *Moscow Conference*, pp. 151–52.

110. Anatoliy Gribkov, *Havana Conference*, pp. 21–22; in "Operation 'Anadyr,'" p. 161, he says that 85 ships made 150 trips.

111. Sergo Mikoyan, *Cambridge Conference*, p. 45.

112. Interview, Sergei Khrushchev, Moscow, 17 May 1989.

113. Khrushchev, *Khrushchev Remembers: The Glasnost Tapes*, p. 171; Gribkov, "Operation 'Anadyr,'" p. 158, maintains that Pliyev was chosen because he was an army general and had nothing to do with missiles; his presence would mask the missile deployment and emphasize the defensive nature of the Soviet buildup.

114. Interview, Sergo Mikoyan, Cambridge, Mass., 12 October 1987; Interview, Sergei Khrushchev, 17 May 1989; Sergei Khrushchev and Oleg Darusenkov, *Antigua Conference*, pp. 77, 153; Defense Intelligence Agency, "Biographical Data: Army General Issa Aleksandrovich Pliyev," April 1969.

115. Georgiy Kornienko, *Antigua Conference*, p. 65; Interview, Adm. Nikolai N. Amelko, Moscow, 18 December 1991, who was certain that Khrushchev had never asked for expert advice from the military or military intelligence. Any query would have gone to the chief of the general staff, and Amelko was his deputy. They would have passed it on to the commander of the chemical troops because they were responsible for camouflage (*maskirovka*) for all Soviet forces.

116. Alekseev, *Havana Conference*, pp. 50–52; Troyanovsky, "The Caribbean Crisis," p. 150.

117. Sergo Mikoyan, *Cambridge Conference*, p. 45; Khrushchev, *Khrushchev Remembers*, p. 495, incorrectly asserts that the Americans did not become suspicious until *after* the Soviets began shipping missiles. Khrushchev contradicts himself by admitting that the Americans had learned about the earlier delivery of IL-28 bombers from their aerial reconnaissance.

118. *No Return for U-2* (Moscow: Foreign Languages Publishing House, 1960); *The Trial of the U-2* (Chicago: Translation World Publishers, 1960), pp. 84–87; On the basis of what the Soviets knew, one Western expert, Amron Katz, *The Soviets and the U-2 Photos—An Heuristic Argument* RM-3584 PR (Santa Monica, Calif.: Rand Corporation, March 1963), p. v, has testified, they "could not have expected that their missile sites in Cuba would escape detection, given the likelihood of closely spaced surveillance." This is also the opinion of Dino A. Brugioni, a former CIA photo-intelligence analyst, *Eyeball to Eyeball*, pp. 204–5.

119. Georgiy Kornienko and Jorge Risquet, *Antigua Conference*, pp. 65, 72.

120. Interview, Adm. Nikolai Amelko, Moscow, 18 December 1991.

121. Troyanovsky, "The Caribbean Crisis," p. 150, was surprised that American intelligence only discovered the missile deployment belatedly in mid-October.

122. Interview, Fedor Burlatsky, Cambridge, Mass., 12 October 1987, reported that "Khrushchev once joked that it was very strange that Voice of America informed us of our Presidium meetings after one-half hour. It would have been impossible to discuss it [the missile deployment] openly and maintain secrecy."

123. Sergo Mikoyan, *Cambridge Conference*, pp. 40–41; Oleg Darusenkov, *Antigua Conference*, p. 128, reports that when the military agreement with Cuba was translated, a number of translators were used and none of them saw the entire document, only individual phrases.

124. Ibid., p. 44.

125. Interview, Adm. Nikolai Amelko, Moscow, 18 December 1991.

126. Medvedev, *Khrushchev*, p. 184.

127. Dimitri Volkogonov, *Moscow Conference*, pp. 27–29; Burlatsky, *Chruschtschow*, p. 260; Raymond Garthoff, "The Military Significance of the Soviet Missile Bases in Cuba," Memorandum prepared for the Executive Committee of the National Security Council, 27 October 1962, reprinted in Garthoff, *Reflections*, pp. 302–3; Gribkov, *Havana Conference*," pp. 18–20, 28, reports that six of the missiles were for training purposes; the other thirty-six medium-range R-12 missiles were to become operational.

128. Fidel Castro, *Havana Conference*, p. 212.

129. U.S. Congress, House of Representatives, Committee on Appropriations, Subcommittee on Department of Defense Appropriations, *Hearings*. 88th Cong., 1st sess. (Washington, D.C.: Government Printing Office, 1963), p. 10. Allison, *Essence of Decision*, pp. 102–9, discusses this and other anomalies associated with the deployment.

130. Brugioni, *Eyeball to Eyeball*, pp. 196–200; *Hearings*, p. 9, and Hilsman, *To Move A Nation*, p. 185, incorrectly assert that the trapezoidal placement of the SAM sites and the "four-slash" signature of excavations for MRBM revetments first attracted the attention of American photo-intelligence analysts and alerted them to the deployment. This was the pattern they associated with MRBM base construction within the Soviet Union.

131. U-2s could still have been used to fly up and down the coast of Cuba outside of Cuban airspace. Much of the island could have been covered in this manner. Low-level aerial surveillance could also have been conducted by fighter planes. Missions of this kind were flown during the crisis and proved effective once the speed at which film advanced through the camera was increased. Interview, Gen. Lloyd R. Leavitt, USAF ret., 18 July 1988.

132. Hilsman, *To Move A Nation*, p. 183.

133. Sorensen, *Kennedy*, p. 673.

134. Raymond L. Garthoff discussion with Gen. Dimitri Volkogonov, Moscow, 27 January 1989; Gen. Dimitri Yazov, "I Have My Uniform, Ready to Fight," *Granma Weekly Review*, 23 April 1989. Yazov, who later became Minister of Defense under Mikhail Gorbachev, was commander of a Soviet motorized infantry regiment in Cuba.

135. Allison, *Essence of Decision*, pp. 109–12; Sergo Mikoyan, *Cambridge Conference*, pp. 48–49.

136. Sergei Khrushchev, *Antigua Conference*, p. 116, argued that the deployment showed "the slovenliness so characteristic of the Soviet Army." Sergo Mikoyan, *Cambridge Conference*, p. 45, does not believe this subterfuge would have worked. "The only thing . . . that delayed American discovery was very bad weather."

137. Anatoliy Dobrynin, *Moscow Conference*, p. 145.

138. Kennedy, *Thirteen Days*, pp. 26–27.

139. Gromyko, "Karibskii Krizis"; Interview, Anatoliy Gromyko, Moscow, 18 May 1989; Sergo Mikoyan, *Cambridge Conference*, p. 45, believed it possible that Gromyko was restrained because he was not yet a full Presidium member and extraordinarily calculating by nature.

140. Interviews, Oleg Grinevsky, Vienna, 11 October 1991; Leonid Zamyatin, Moscow, 16 December 1991; Georgiy Kornienko, 17 December 1991. Gromyko's cables back from Washington are discussed in chapter 6.

141. Oleg Troyanovsky, *Havana Conference*, pp. 40–41, and "The Caribbean Crisis," pp. 147, 149–50. Troyanovsky learned about the deployment from Vladimir Lebedev, Khrushchev's advisor on ideological issues, who was himself shocked by the missile deployment. His conversation with Khrushchev took place sometime at the beginning of June. According to Troyanovsky, "The Caribbean Crisis," p. 149, Khrushchev hardly ever expressed anger at his immediate subordinates; instead, he vented his spleen against third parties. This made it easier for Troyanovsky, who, in addition, had a good working relationship with his boss, to voice his doubts.

142. Khrushchev, *Khrushchev Remembers: The Glasnost Tapes*, pp. 103, 123, indicates that Mikoyan and Khrushchev had been foreign-policy allies as far back as 1953 when Mikoyan supported Khrushchev's effort, after the death of Stalin, to heal the breech with Yugoslavia. According to Sergo Mikoyan, *Cambridge Conference*, p. 42, the two men "had a curious relationship. They were friends, but Khrushchev was envious of my father's background and education. Khrushchev did not think of himself as my father's superior."

143. Khrushchev, *Khrushchev Remembers: The Glasnost Tapes*, p. 122; Oleg Penkovskiy, *The Penkovskiy Papers* (Garden City, N.Y.: Doubleday, 1965), p. 207; James Gerard Richter, "Action and Reaction in Khrushchev's Foreign Policy: How Leadership Responses Affect Soviet Responses to the International Environment," dissertation, University of California at Berkeley, 1989, pp. 517–18, argues that a close reading of *Pravda* during and after the Berlin crisis indicates that Mikoyan argued for the primacy of national over ideological interests and espoused a more cautious foreign policy.

144. Anatoliy Gribkov, *Havana Conference*, p. 53.

145. *Moscow Conference*, pp. 83–84.

146. *Cambridge Conference*, p. 34.

147. Coit D. Blacker, "The Kremlin and Détente: Soviet Conceptions, Hopes, and Expectations," in Alexander L. George, ed., *Managing U.S.-Soviet Rivalry: Problems of Crisis Prevention* (Boulder, Colo.: Westview, 1983), pp. 119–38; Franklyn Griffiths, "The Sources of American Conduct: Soviet Perspectives and Their Policy Implications," *International Security* 9 (Fall 1984), pp. 3–50; Raymond L. Garthoff, *Détente and Confrontation: American-Soviet Relations From Nixon to Reagan* (Washington, D.C.: The Brookings Institution, 1985), pp. 36–68; Interview, Aleksei Adzhubei, Moscow, 15 May 1989.

148. Richard Ned Lebow, *Between Peace and War: The Nature of International Crisis* (Baltimore: Johns Hopkins University Press, 1981); Robert Jervis, Richard Ned Lebow, and Janice Gross Stein, *Psychology and Deterrence* (Baltimore: Johns Hopkins University Press, 1985).

149. For a discussion of bolstering and its role in decision making, see Irving L. Janis and Leon Mann, *Decision Making: A Psychological Analysis of Conflict, Choice, and Commitment* (New York: Free Press, 1977), pp. 55–58, 74, 107–33.

150. Janis and Mann, *Decision Making*, pp. 57–58, 74–95, 107–33.

151. Gromyko, "Karibskii Krizis," p. 32. Interview, Anatoliy Gromyko, Moscow, 18 May 1989, says his father told him that "Khrushchev did not consult, but informed him of his decision."

152. Interview, Sergo Mikoyan, Cambridge, Mass., 12 October 1987.

153. S. Khrushchev, *Khrushchev on Khrushchev*, p. 152.

154. Interview, Vadim Zagladin, Moscow, 18 May 1989.

155. Leon Festinger, *A Theory of Cognitive Dissonance* (Stanford: Stanford University Press, 1957); Leon Festinger, ed., *Conflict, Decision, and Dissonance* (Stanford: Stanford University Press, 1962); Jack W. Brehm and Arthur Cohen, *Explorations in Cognitive Dissonance* (New York: Wiley, 1962); Janis and Mann, *Decision Making*, pp. 309–38, 437–40. Janis and Mann, whose formulation we follow, disagree with Festinger. They describe spreading of the alternatives as a form of bolstering, which they see as motivated by the need to ward off the stress of decisional conflict and only secondarily by a need to maintain cognitive consistency. They accordingly make the case for pre- and post-decisional bolstering.

156. Joseph de Rivera, *The Psychological Dimension of Foreign Policy* (Columbus: Charles E. Merrill, 1968), p. 146; Janis and Mann, *Decision Making*, pp. 56, 74–79; Lebow, *Between Peace and War*, pp. 110, 114, and passim for cases in which this phenomenon is documented.

157. Khrushchev, *Khrushchev Remembers: The Glasnost Tapes*, p. 175.

158. *Moscow Conference*, pp. 49–50.

159. Interview, Aleksei Adzhubei, Moscow, 15 May 1989; Interview, Georgiy Shakhnazarov, Cambridge, Mass., 12 October 1987.

160. Interview, Aleksei Adzhubei, Moscow, 15 May 1989; *Boston Globe*, 10 May 1960, for the Associated Press bulletin.

161. Khrushchev, *Khrushchev Remembers*, p. 508; Burlatsky, *Chruschtschow*, p. 234.

162. Harold Macmillan, *Memoirs*, vol. III, *Pointing the Way: 1959–1961* (New York: Harper & Row, 1972), p. 202.

163. Khrushchev, *Khrushchev Remembers*, p. 515.

164. Interview, Leonid M. Zamyatin, Moscow, 16 December 1991; Interview, Georgiy Kornienko, Moscow, 17 December 1991.

165. Interview, Aleksei Adzhubei, Moscow, 15 May 1989.

166. Khrushchev, *Khrushchev Remembers*, p. 494, gives two other reasons: protecting Cuba from U.S. attack and equalizing the strategic balance of power.

167. Khrushchev, *Khrushchev Remembers: The Glasnost Tapes*, p. 175.

168. Allison, *Essence of Decision*, p. 234; George and Smoke, *Deterrence in American Foreign Policy*, pp. 463–64.

169. Bundy, *Danger and Survival*, p. 415.

170. The one exception was CIA director John McCone who was convinced that Khrushchev might be tempted to send missiles to Cuba. McCone's views and the more general intelligence problems raised by the missile deployment are discussed in chapter 13.

CHAPTER FIVE
Why Did the Missiles Provoke a Crisis?

1. Interview, William E. Knox, 24 October 1962. William E. Knox, "Close Up of Khrushchev During a Crisis," *New York Times Magazine*, 18 November 1962; Elie Abel, *The Missile Crisis* (Philadelphia: Lippincott, 1966), pp. 132–33.

2. David A. Welch, ed., *Proceedings of the Cambridge Conference on the Cuban Missile Crisis, 11–12 October 1987* (Cambridge, Mass.: Harvard Univ., Center for Science and International Affairs, April 1988), final version, mimeograph, pp. 59–60.

3. The photographic mission that discovered the construction of missile bases in Cuba was flown on 14 October and it took approximately twenty-four hours for the film to be returned, processed, delivered to the National Photographic Interpretation Center and scanned by its analysts. Technical analysis did not turn up anything until late afternoon on the fifteenth, and key members of the government were informed that evening. Ray S. Cline, Memorandum for the Record, "Notification of NSC Officials of Intelligence on Missiles Bases in Cuba, 27 October 1962," in Mary S. McAuliffe, ed., *CIA Documents on the Cuban Missile Crisis 1962* (Washington, D.C.: History Staff, Central Intelligence Agency, October 1962), pp. 149–51.

4. Theodore C. Sorensen, *Kennedy* (New York: Harper & Row, 1965); Arthur M. Schlesinger, Jr., *A Thousand Days: John F. Kennedy in the White House* (Boston: Houghton, Mifflin, 1965); Elie Abel, *The Missile Crisis* (Philadelphia: Lippincott, 1966).

5. The best revisionist critiques are: I. F. Stone, "The Brink," *New York Review of Books*, 14 April 1966; Ronald Steel, "End Game," *New York Review of Books*, 13 March 1969; James A. Nathan, "The Missile Crisis: His Finest Hour Now," *World Politics* 27 (October 1974), pp. 265–81; Barton J. Bernstein, "The Week We Almost Went to War," *Bulletin of Atomic Scientists* 32 (1976), pp. 13–21, and "The Cuban Missile Crisis: Trading the Jupiters in Turkey?" *Political Science Quarterly* 95 (Spring 1980), pp. 97–125; see Gary Wills, *The Kennedy Imprisonment: A Meditation on Power* (Boston: Little, Brown, 1982), pp. 235–74, for a more recent revisionist critique.

6. Stone, "The Brink," pp. 12–16. Ronald Steel, "End Game," pp. 15–22, made essentially the same argument. He stressed Kennedy's political vulnerability on Cuba and corresponding need to get the missiles out before election day. Steel also emphasized the importance of Kennedy's obsession with his image and fear that Khrushchev would never again take him seriously if he backed down on Cuba. For both of these reasons, Kennedy decided against making any kind of private overture to Khrushchev before he proclaimed the blockade. Steel believes that such an overture would have led to resolution of the conflict and avoided the crisis.

7. For a recent argument of this kind, see David A. Welch and James G. Blight, "The Eleventh Hour of the Cuban Missile Crisis: An Introduction to the Ex Comm Transcript," *International Security* 12 (Winter 1987–88), p. 25. Welch, letter to Richard Ned Lebow, 5 August 1991, differentiates between Kennedy's political fortunes and other domestic considerations (e.g., protecting the stock market, avoiding panic, controlling the military). He believes the president was particularly concerned with the latter, and would have been willing to suffer a "political bloodbath" if it was necessary to trade to get the missiles out.

8. David A. Welch, ed., *Proceedings of the Hawk's Cay Conference on the Cuban Missile Crisis, 5–8 March 1987* (Cambridge, Mass.: Harvard University, Center for Science and International Affairs, Working Paper 89–1, 1989), mimeograph, p. 63,

hereafter cited as *Hawk's Cay Conference*. In McGeorge Bundy *Danger and Survival: Choices About the Bomb in the First Fifty Years* (New York: Random House, 1988), pp. 394, 411–12, Bundy acknowledges the importance of domestic political factors in Kennedy's thinking.

9. Theodore C. Sorensen, *The Kennedy Legacy* (New York: Harper & Row, 1969), p. 190; Bundy, *Danger and Survival*, p. 412.

10. Welch and Blight, "An Introduction to the Ex Comm Transcripts," p. 25.

11. Quoted in Steel, "End Game," p. 119.

12. Dean Rusk as told to Richard Rusk, *As I Saw It*, ed. Daniel S. Papp (New York: Norton, 1990), p. 230.

13. Roger Hilsman, *To Move A Nation: The Politics of Foreign Policy in the Administration of John F. Kennedy* (Garden City, N.Y.: Doubleday, 1967), p. 196.

14. Rusk, *As I Saw It*, p. 230; Roger Hilsman, "An Exchange on the Missile Crisis," *New York Review of Books*, 16 March 1969, p. 37.

15. *Hawk's Cay Conference*, p. 115.

16. John McCone, Memorandum for the File, "Leadership Meeting on October 22nd at 5:00 P.M., 24 October 1962," *CIA Documents on the Cuban Missile Crisis 1962*, pp. 275–79; *New York Times*, 23 October 1962; Sorensen, *Kennedy*, pp. 702–3; Rusk, *As I Saw It*, pp. 234–35; Kenneth P. O'Donnell and David F. Powers with Joe McCarthy, *"Johnny We Hardly Knew Ye": Memories of John Fitzgerald Kennedy* (Boston: Little, Brown, 1970), p. 327, for Kennedy's reaction; *Congressional Record*, 87th Cong., 2d sess., 20 and 26 September 1962, vol. 108, nos. 170 and 174, pp. 18892–951, 19702–53.

17. The resolution was adopted on 20 September. Laurence Chang and Donna Rich, eds., *Chronology of the Cuban Missile Crisis* (Washington, D.C.: National Security Archive, September 1988), p. 80.

18. O'Donnell et al., *"Johnny We Hardly Knew Ye,"* p. 310.

19. Robert Kennedy, *Thirteen Days: A Memoir of the Cuban Missile Crisis* (New York: Norton, 1969), p. 67.

20. Irving L. Janis and Leon Mann, *Decision Making: A Psychological Analysis of Conflict, Choice, and Commitment* (New York: Free Press, 1977), pp. 74–95. For its application to foreign policy, see Richard Ned Lebow, *Between Peace and War*, (Baltimore: Johns Hopkins University Press, 1981), passim, and Robert Jervis, Richard Ned Lebow, and Janice Gross Stein, *Psychology and Deterrence* (Baltimore: Johns Hopkins University Press, 1985), chapters 3–4, 9.

21. Bundy, *Danger and Survival*, pp. 394, 411–12.

22. James Blight interview with Robert S. McNamara, Washington, D.C., 21 May 1987, in James G. Blight and David A. Welch, *On the Brink: Americans and Soviets Reexamine the Cuban Missile Crisis* (New York: Hill & Wang, 1989), p. 190; "Transcript of Cuba Between the Superpowers," Antigua, 3–7 January 1991, mimeograph, pp. 163–64, forthcoming as James G. Blight, David Lewis, and David A. Welch, eds., *Cuba Between the Superpowers: The Antigua Conference on the Cuban Missile Crisis* (Savage, Md.: Rowman and Littlefield, in press), hereafter cited as *Antigua Conference*. Much the same point is made by Bundy, *Danger and Survival*, pp. 392–93, who argues that "In the light of these public commitments it was clear to the president throughout the crisis that every course of action must be measured by its effectiveness in removing the missiles."

23. "Transcript of Ex Comm meeting, 6:30–7:55 P.M., 16 October 1962," pp. 45–48, John F. Kennedy Library.

24. Ibid., p. 12, for the views of Gen. Maxwell Taylor.

25. "Let me say that the line between offensive and defensive weapons was drawn in September, and it was not drawn in a way which was intended to leave the Soviets any ambiguity to play with. I believe the President drew the line precisely where he thought the Soviets were not and would not be. . . . I am suggesting that one reason the line was drawn at zero was because we simply thought the Soviets weren't going to deploy any there anyway." Theodore Sorenson, *Hawk's Cay Conference*, p. 51; *Cambridge Conference*, pp. 60–61.

26. Theodore C. Sorensen, "Memorandum for the President, 17 October 1962," advised the president that it was "generally agreed that these missiles, even when fully operational, do not significantly alter the balance of power—i.e., they do not significantly increase the potential megatonnage capable of being unleashed on American soil, even after a surprise American nuclear strike." The previous evening, Chairman of the Joint Chiefs of Staff Maxwell Taylor had warned the Ex Comm that the missiles "*can* become a very, a rather important adjunct and reinforcement to . . . the strike capability of the Soviet Union." The ensuing discussion made it apparent that neither the president nor his advisors were at all certain about the military importance of the missiles. Transcript of "Off-the-Record Meeting on Cuba, October 16, 1962, 6:30–7:55 P.M." John McCone, Memorandum for the File, "Memorandum of Meeting, Wednesday, October 17th, at 8:30 A.M., and again at 4:00 P.M.," *CIA Documents on the Cuban Missile Crisis*, pp. 169–73, indicates that much the same points were made on Wednesday about how the missiles would affect the military balance.

During the first week of the crisis, two additional memoranda on the missiles were submitted to the president and secretary of state. Theodore C. Sorensen, "Memorandum, October 19, 1962," Sorensen Files, box 49, pp. 1–4, and W. W. Rostow, "Memorandum to the Secretary of State, October 22, 1962," National Security Files, box 36A-37, p. 3, John F. Kennedy Library. The first professional evaluation of their military implications did not become available to the Ex Comm until 27 October. It was prepared by Raymond L. Garthoff, special assistant for Soviet bloc, politico-military affairs in the State Department. Garthoff argued that twenty-four MRBM launchers and twelve to sixteen IRBM launchers in Cuba would increase Soviet first-strike capability against targets in the continental United States by over 40 percent. This advantage would be offset in part by the missiles' vulnerability to an American first strike. Raymond L. Garthoff, *Reflections on the Cuban Missile Crisis*, rev. ed. (Washington, D.C.: The Brookings Institution, 1989), pp. 202–3, reprints his report. Garthoff's evaluation is of academic interest only because the decision for the blockade had been made and implemented before it reached the White House.

27. Transcript of "Off-the-Record Meeting, October 16, 6:30–7:55 P.M.," pp. 12–13, 36; Hilsman, *To Move A Nation*, p. 195. After the crisis, Deputy Secretary of Defense Roswell Gilpatric told the *New York Times*, 12 November 1962, that "the military equation was not altered" by the missiles in Cuba. "It was simply an element of flexibility introduced into the power equation that the Soviets had not heretofore possessed." O'Donnell et al., *"Johnny We Hardly Knew Ye,"* p. 309, report that "President Kennedy never felt that the installation of the missiles really changed the balance of military power."

28. Sorensen, *Kennedy*, p. 683.

29. Rusk, *As I Saw It*, p. 230.

30. *Hawk's Cay Conference*, p. 22.

31. The Central Intelligence Agency was alert to this possibility. Its Special National Intelligence Estimate Number 85-3-61, "The Military Build-up in Cuba," 19 September 1962, had hypothesized that "the main purpose of the present military build-up in Cuba is to strengthen the Communist regime there against what the Cubans and Soviets conceive to be a danger that the U.S. may attempt by one means or another to overthrow it."

32. Sorensen, *Kennedy*, pp. 676–78.

33. "Off-the-Record Meeting on Cuba, October 16, 1962, 11:50 A.M.–12:57 P.M.," pp. 14–15.

34. Transcript of "Off-the-Record Meeting on Cuba, 11:50 A.M.–12:57 P.M.," p. 15. Special National Intelligence Estimate 11–18–62, "Soviet Reactions to Certain U.S. Courses of Action on Cuba," 19 October 1962 (Excerpt), *CIA Documents on the Cuban Missile Crisis*, pp. 197–202, indicates that this was also the view of the intelligence community.

35. Ibid., "6:30–7:55 P.M. meeting," pp. 25–26.

36. Schlesinger, *A Thousand Days*, p. 742.

37. Sorensen, *Kennedy*, pp. 677–78. George Ball, "6:30–7:55 P.M. Ex Comm Meeting of 16 October," pp. 25–26, also speculated about this possibility.

38. According to the first Central Intelligence Agency estimate of Khrushchev's goals, Special National Intelligence Estimate 11–18–62, "Soviet Reactions to Certain U.S. Courses of Action on Cuba, 19 October 1962," "A major Soviet objective in their military buildup is to demonstrate that the world balance of forces has shifted so far in their favor that the U.S. can no longer prevent the advance of Soviet offensive power even into its own hemisphere." The CIA went on to argue that acquiescence to the deployment would lead to "a loss of confidence in U.S. power and determination and a serious decline of U.S. influence generally." Agency analysts downplayed the prospect of Soviet military retaliation in response to a U.S. air strike or invasion of Cuba. "Soviet leaders," in their view, "would not deliberately initiate general war or take military measures, which in their calculation, would run the gravest risks of general war." Rather, they were expected to limit themselves to pressure against Berlin.

39. Sorensen, *Kennedy*, p. 677.

40. Schlesinger, *A Thousand Days*, p. 796.

41. Bundy, *Danger and Survival*, p. 411; for a similar statement by Dean Rusk, see "The Cuban Missile Crisis," transcript of a discussion conducted by the Alfred P. Sloan Foundation, New York, 1983, Reel no. 5, p. 33.

42. James Blight interview with Robert S. McNamara, Washington, D.C., 21 May 1987, in Blight and Welch, *On the Brink*, p. 193.

43. "Off-the-Record Meeting on Cuba, 16 October 1962, 6:30–7:55 P.M.," p. 13. A few minutes later he rued the day he had declared missiles in Cuba unacceptable. "Last month I should have said . . . we don't care. But when we said we're *not* going to and then they go ahead and do it, and then we do nothing, then . . . I think that our risks increase," p. 15.

44. O'Donnell et al., *"Johnny, We Hardly Knew Ye,"* p. 306.

45. Stone, "The Brink," p. 12.

46. Steel, "End Game," pp. 15–22.

47. See chapter 2.

48. Ernest R. May, *"Lessons" of the Past: The Use and Misuse of History in American Foreign Policy* (New York: Oxford University Press, 1973), for the relevance of the 1930s to American intervention in Vietnam; and Richard Ned Lebow,

"Generational Learning and Conflict Management," *International Journal* 40 (Autumn 1985), pp. 556–85, for a broader treatment of the lessons of the 1930s and their relevance to post-war American foreign policy.

49. John F. Kennedy, *Why England Slept* (New York: W. Funk, 1940).

50. *New York Herald-Tribune*, 16 March 1966; Stone, "The Brink"; Schlesinger, *A Thousand Days*, p. 391; Reston, *New York Times Magazine*, 15 November 1964, p. 126.

51. Sorensen, *Kennedy*, p. 549; Hugh Sidey, "What the K's Really Told Each Other," *Life*, 16 June 1961, pp. 48–49; N. Khrushchev, *Khrushchev Remembers: The Last Testament*, trans. Strobe Talbott (Boston: Little, Brown, 1974), pp. 491–98.

52. Abel, *The Missile Crisis*, p. 70; Frank A. Sieverts, "The Cuban Crisis, 1962," [internal State Department memorandum] p. 49, reproduces a very similar quote and attributes it to the 16 October Ex Comm meetings. The quotation is not in the edited transcripts of that day's meetings.

53. "Final Draft Scenario for Air strike against offensive missiles bases and bombers in Cuba," undated.

54. John McCone, Memorandum for the File, "Memorandum of Meeting, Wednesday, October 17th, at 8:30 A.M., and again at 4:00 P.M," *CIA Documents on the Cuban Missile Crisis*, p. 171.

55. White House Tapes, "Transcripts of Ex Comm Meeting of 16 October 1962, 11:50 A.M.–12:57 P.M.," John F. Kennedy Library, mimeo, p. 10.

56. John McCone, "Memorandum of Meeting with the President, Attorney General, Secretary McNamara, Gen. Taylor, and Mr. McCone, 10:00 A.M.-10/21/62," *CIA Documents on the Cuban Missile Crisis*, pp. 241–42; Kennedy, *Thirteen Days*, pp. 31, 34, 38–39; Schlesinger, *A Thousand Days*, pp. 738–39; Sorensen, *Kennedy*, p. 684.

57. Charles E. Bohlen, *Witness to History, 1929–69* (New York: Norton, 1973), pp. 491–92; John McCone, Memorandum for the File, "Memorandum of Meeting, Wednesday, October 17th, at 8:30 A.M., and again at 4:00 P.M.," 19 October 1962, *CIA Documents on the Cuban Missile Crisis*, pp. 169–73; Sorensen's notes of the 18 October 1962 Ex Comm meeting, p. 1, and "Memorandum," 17 October 1962, pp. 1–4; Sorensen, *Kennedy*, p. 683; Arthur M. Schlesinger, Jr., *Robert Kennedy and His Times* (Boston: Houghton, Mifflin, 1978), p. 513; Comments of McGeorge Bundy and Theodore Sorensen, *Cambridge Conference*, pp. 54–57, and of Sorensen, in Bruce J. Allyn, James G. Blight, and David A. Welch, eds., *Back to the Brink: Proceedings of the Moscow Conference on The Cuban Missile Crisis, January 27–28, 1989*, CSIA Occasional Paper no.9 (Lanham, Md.: University Press of America, 1992), pp. 47–48, hereafter cited as *Moscow Conference*.

58. Ibid.

59. *Cambridge Conference*, p. 57.

60. Comments of McGeorge Bundy, *Cambridge Conference*, pp. 54–55.

61. Steel, "End Game," pp. 18–19.

62. *Washington Post*, 25 October 1962.

63. Bundy, *Danger and Survival*, pp. 408–10, makes a similar argument.

64. Fedor Burlatsky, "The Caribbean Crisis and Its Lessons," *Literaturnaya Gazeta* [Literary Gazette], 11 November 1987. For a bad English translation see Foreign Broadcasting Information Service, *Soviet Union* 1987, no. 221, pp. 21–24. Earlier, Burlatsky told the *Cambridge Conference*, pp. 56–57, that Khrushchev

would have realized "that he would need now to negotiate about a *new* situation." Interview, Fedor Burlatsky, Cambridge, Mass., 12 October 1987.

65. See chapter 3.

66. See chapter 6.

67. Fidel Castro to Nikita Khrushchev, 31 October 1962; Interview with Fidel Castro by Maria Schriver, broadcast on NBC "Sunday Today," 28 February 1988. See also the testimony of Sergo Mikoyan and Georgiy Shakhnazarov, *Cambridge Conference*, pp. 73, 80–83, 99–100; Aleksandr A. Alekseev, *Moscow Conference*; Aleksandr A. Alekseev, "The Caribbean Crisis: As It Really Was," *Ekho Planety* no. 33 (November 1988), pp. 27–37; Fidel Castro, "Transcript of the Proceedings of the Havana Conference on the Cuban Missile Crisis, January 9–12, 1992," mimeograph, p. 206, forthcoming as James G. Blight, Bruce J. Allyn, and David A. Welch, eds., *Cuba on the Brink: Castro, the Missile Crisis, and the Soviet Collapse* (New York: Pantheon Books, in press), hereafter cited as *Havana Conference*.

68. For example, James A. Robinson, "Crises," *International Encyclopedia of the Social Sciences* (New York: Macmillan and the Free Press, 1968), III, pp. 510–13; Oran Young, *The Politics of Force: Bargaining During International Crises* (Princeton, N.J.: Princeton University Press, 1968), pp. 6–24; Charles F. Hermann, *Crises in Foreign Policy: A Simulation Analysis* (Indianapolis: Bobbs-Merrill, 1960), pp. 21–36; Herman Kahn and Anthony J. Weiner, eds., *Crises and Arms Control* (Hastings-on-Hudson, N.Y.: Hudson Institute, 1962), pp. 7–11; Glenn H. Snyder and Paul Diesing, *Conflict Among Nations: Bargaining, Decision Making, and System Structure in International Crisis* (Princeton, N.J.: Princeton University Press, 1977), pp. 6–20; Phil Williams, *Crisis Management: Confrontation and Diplomacy in the Nuclear Age* (New York: Wiley, 1972), pp. 10–31; Lebow, *Between Peace and War*, pp. 7–12.

69. Schlesinger, *A Thousand Days*, pp. 734–35.

70. "Off-the-Record Meeting On Cuba, October 16, 1962, 11:50 A.M.–12:57 P.M.," p. 27.

71. *Hawk's Cay Conference*, pp. 72–73, 77.

72. Interview, McGeorge Bundy, Cambridge, Mass., 22 July 1987; Maxwell D. Taylor, "General Taylor Reflects on Lessons from the Cuban Missile Crisis," *International Herald Tribune*, 13 October 1982, also worried that once operational the missiles would be mobile and much more difficult to destroy; Raymond L. Garthoff, letter to authors, 22 May 1991, maintains that Ex Comm opposition to allowing the missiles to become operational reflected concern that a new status quo legitimating the deployment would emerge.

73. On 16 October, at the first Ex Comm meeting, McNamara argued "that if we are going to conduct an air strike against these [missile] installations, or against any part of Cuba, we must agree now that we will schedule that prior to the time these missiles sites become operational . . . Because, if they become operational before the air strike, I do not believe we can state we can knock them out before they can be launched." "Excerpts from Off-the-Record Meeting on Cuba, October 16, 1962, 11:50 A.M.–12:57 P.M.", p. 11. Questioned about this statement at Hawk's Cay, *Hawk's Cay Conference*, pp. 77–78, McNamara explained "That this was the first day. . . . We were forming our initial reactions to the news. But after we began to think about it, that restriction began to look irrelevant." McNamara might also have added that it was before the Ex Comm had received the first CIA briefing indicating that some missile sites probably already had some operational capability. Bundy, *Danger and Survival*, pp. 424–25, makes a similar point. "As I look back on it," he writes, "I do

not think that any such position was required by the continuing Soviet efforts at the missile sites. I now believe that by that time the advantage had shifted in our direction in ways we could have understood better than we did—and would have come to recognize if the warnings given by John Scali and Robert Kennedy had been rejected."

74. Interview, McGeorge Bundy, New York, 22 July 1987.

75. *Hawk's Cay Conference*, pp. 71–74.

76. Hawk's Cay Conference, author's record, p. 4; McNamara explained that an additional reason for caution was that "we put little trust in those CIA estimates," *Hawk's Cay Conference*, p. 73.

77. Central Intelligence Agency, "Report on the Construction of Missile Sites in Cuba," 19 October 1962, p. 2 [the word "now" is penned in after the printed phrase "2 sites operational"]; *Chronology of JCS Decisions Concerning the Cuban Crisis*, prepared by the Historical Division, Joint Secretariat, Joint Chiefs of Staff, 21 December 1962, p. 19, reporting on intelligence available on 19 October. The same evaluation appeared in Special National Intelligence Estimate 11–19–62, "Major Consequences of Certain U.S. Courses of Action on Cuba," 20 October 1962, *CIA Documents on the Cuban Missile Crisis*, pp. 211–20. Supplement 1 to Joint Evaluation of Soviet Missile Threat in Cuba, 20 October 1962 (Excerpt), *CIA Documents on the Cuban Missile Crisis*, pp. 227–34, reduced the lead time to launch to eight hours.

78. "Robert S. McNamara's Notes on October 21, 1962 Meeting With the President," p. 2. Also present at this meeting were Robert Kennedy, Gen. Maxwell Taylor, and Gen. Walter C. Sweeney. Central Intelligence Agency, "Report on Readiness Status of Soviet Missiles in Cuba," 21 October 1962, presumably given to the president at this time, noted that some of the other missile sites probably had an emergency capability.

79. Ray S. Cline, "DDI notes for DCI for NSC Briefing at 3 P.M. in Cabinet Room," 22 October 1962, *CIA Documents on the Cuban Missile Crisis*, pp. 271–73; Central Intelligence Agency, "Readiness Status of Soviet Missiles in Cuba," 23 October 1962, p. 1.

80. "Supplement 7 to Joint Evaluation of Soviet Missile Threat in Cuba," 27 October 1962 (Excerpt), *CIA Documents on the Cuban Missile Crisis*, pp. 323–25; Central Intelligence Agency, Memorandum, *The Crisis: USSR/Cuba*, 27 October 1962, Summary and I-1; *Chronology of JCS Decisions*, p. 48, reporting intelligence available on 27 October.

81. *Hawk's Cay Conference*, p. 43.

82. Ibid.; Douglas Dillon disagreed with McNamara. He insists that the joint chiefs and some members of the Ex Comm were legitimately concerned with the military consequences of the missiles becoming operational. "It may not have influenced McNamara," he insisted, "but it sure as hell concerned me." Hawk's Cay Conference, author's record, p. 6. Dean Rusk also insists that the operational status of the missiles mattered to him because it put a number of SAC bases at risk to attack with little or no warning. Interview, Dean Rusk, Athens, Ga., 21 September 1987. McGeorge Bundy, "Retrospective," p. 22, took a position between these two. "Logically," he insisted, "it wouldn't have made any difference" if the missiles were operational, "but psychologically it would have made a very big one."

83. Hawk's Cay Conference, author's record, p. 6.

84. Interview with George Ball, 6 March 1987, Marathon, Fla.

85. Rusk, *As I Saw It*, p. 231.

86. Bundy, *Danger and Survival*, pp. 395–97; Rusk, *As I Saw It*, p. 231; Robert

McNamara, "Presentation to the Crisis Stability Project," Cornell University Peace Studies Program, 21 August 1985, pp. 12–13, insisted, that "Without a question," the administration would have had to have acted if the story had broken in the newspapers.

87. The U-2 that photographed missile sites under construction in Cuba did so on the morning of 14 October. By the following evening, CIA analysts were certain of their findings and notified top CIA officials who in turn telephoned the news to McGeorge Bundy. Bundy did not break the news to the president until the following morning, 16 October. Sorensen, *Kennedy*, pp. 672–73.

88. Lunchtime conversation, 7 March 1987, Hawk's Cay Conference.

89. "Minutes of the 507th Meeting of the National Security Council on Monday, 22 October 1962, 3:00 P.M."

90. *Hawk's Cay Conference*, pp. 43, 46; Interview, McGeorge Bundy, New York, 22 July 1987; Interview, Dean Rusk, Atlanta, Ga., 18 May 1987.

91. Dean Acheson, also an air-strike advocate, had withdrawn from the Ex Comm after Kennedy's decision in favor of the blockade.

92. Interview, Dean Rusk by James Blight, Athens, Ga., 18 May 1987, p. 15; According to McGeorge Bundy, all reference to this recommendation has been censored out of the declassified version of the Ex Comm record. *Hawk's Cay Conference*, pp. 55, 63.

93. *Hawk's Cay Conference*, p. 39.

94. Ibid.

95. Hilsman, *To Move A Nation*, p. 197, also notes the analogy to Korea.

96. Lebow, *Between Peace and War*, pp. 169–84.

97. John Spanier, *The Truman-MacArthur Controversy and the Korean War*, rev. ed. (New York: Norton, 1965); Ronald J. Caridi, *The Korean War and American Politics: The Republican Party As a Case Study* (Philadelphia: University of Pennsylvania Press, 1969).

CHAPTER SIX
The Crisis and Its Resolution

1. Nikita Khrushchev's informal talk to the navy chiefs after the missile crisis. Interview, Adm. Nikolai N. Amelko, Moscow, 18 December 1991.

2. Interview, Sergo Mikoyan, Cambridge, Mass., 12 October 1987.

3. The most recent study to assert this is Alexander L. George, ed., *Avoiding War: Problems of Crisis Management* (Boulder, Colo.: Westview, 1991). Unlike authors of many earlier studies, George also argues that mutual fear of war also played an important role in resolving the crisis.

4. Ray S. Cline, Memorandum for the Record, "Notification of NSC Officials of Intelligence on Missile Bases in Cuba, 27 October 1962," in Mary S. McAuliffe, ed., *CIA Documents on the Cuban Missile Crisis 1962* (Washington, D.C.: History Staff, Central Intelligence Agency, October 1992), pp. 149–52; Theodore C. Sorensen, *Kennedy* (New York: Harper & Row, 1965), p. 673; McGeorge Bundy, *Danger and Survival: Choices About the Bomb in the First Fifty Years* (New York: Random House, 1988), pp. 395–96; Dean Rusk as told to Richard Rusk, *As I Saw It*, Daniel S. Papp, ed. (New York: Norton, 1990), p. 230; Roger Hilsman, *To Move A Nation: The Politics of Foreign Policy in the Administration of John F. Kennedy* (Garden City, N.Y.: Doubleday, 1967), pp. 193–94; Elie Abel, *The Missile Crisis* (Philadelphia: Lippincott, 1966), pp. 28–34.

5. Georgiy Kornienko, "Cuba Between the Superpowers, Antigua, 3–7 January 1991," mimeograph, p. 90, forthcoming as James G. Blight, David Lewis, and David A. Welch, eds., *Cuba Between the Superpowers: The Antigua Conference on the Cuban Missile Crisis* (Savage, Md.: Rowman and Littlefield, in press), hereafter cited as *Antigua Conference*, and interview, Moscow, 17 December 1991, remembers that by 21 October there was alarm in the Washington embassy that "something was up" because of the "increased agitation" within the executive branch. No mention of these suspicions was made to Moscow. Fidel Castro, "Transcript of the Proceedings of the Havana Conference on the Cuban Missile Crisis, January 9–12, 1992," mimeograph, p. 217 in James G. Blight, Bruce J. Allyn, and David A. Welch, eds., *Cuba on the Brink: Castro, the Missile Crisis, and the Soviet Collapse* (New York: Pantheon Books, in press), hereafter cited as *Havana Conference*, reported that the Cubans had alerted their forces on 22 October in response to intelligence reports of troop movements and extraordinary meetings in Washington. According to Jorge Risquet, *Antigua Conference*, p. 88, the Cuban leadership expected that Kennedy's nationally televised address would announce the discovery of Soviet missiles in Cuba.

6. Gromyko had dinner the night before with Dean Rusk at the State Department. Rusk, *As I Saw It*, p. 233; Abel, *The Missile Crisis*, pp. 74–77; Sorensen, *Kennedy*, pp. 689–91; Arthur M. Schlesinger, Jr., *A Thousand Days: John F. Kennedy in the White House* (Boston: Houghton, Mifflin, 1965), p. 805; Andrei Gromyko, *Memories*, trans. Harold Shukman (London: Hutchinson, 1989), p. 177; Anatoliy Dobrynin, "The Caribbean Crisis: An Eyewitness Account," *International Affairs* (Moscow) no. 8 (August 1992), pp. 47–60, quote on pp. 50–51.

7. Ibid.

8. Abel, *Missile Crisis*, p. 77; Sorensen, *Kennedy*, pp. 689–90, reports that Ex Comm sentiment was unanimously against telling Gromyko about the missiles.

9. Gromyko, *Memories*, p. 179. Gromyko, in Bruce J. Allyn, James G. Blight, and David A. Welch, eds., *Back to the Brink: Proceedings of the Moscow Conference on The Cuban Missile Crisis, January 27– 28, 1989*, CSIA Occasional Paper no.9 (Lanham, Md.: University Press of America, 1992), p. 54, hereafter cited as *Moscow Conference*, says that President Kennedy never asked him directly if the Soviet Union was sending "nuclear missiles" to Cuba. "If he had, I would have answered. The answer would have been, I hope, the appropriate one." It seems unlikely that Gromyko, who had been exceedingly careful not to express opinions at variance with Khrushchev's, would have exposed the Soviet deception. There is no evidence that Khrushchev had authorized him to do this; all the Soviet testimony and Khrushchev's memoirs indicate that Khrushchev was intent on keeping the deployment secret until the missiles were fully operational.

10. N. Khrushchev, *Khrushchev Remembers: The Glasnost Tapes*, trans. and ed. Jerrold L. Schecter with Vyacheslav V. Luchkov (Boston: Little, Brown, 1990), p. 175. Khrushchev remembers that at their dinner, Rusk showed Gromyko the photographs of the missiles, photographs that had already been published in the papers. Gromyko is said to have denied all knowledge of them. Gromyko left the United States on Monday afternoon, 22 October; Kennedy did not make his television speech announcing the discovery of the missiles to the world until that evening. In his memoirs, Khrushchev probably ran together Gromyko's dinner with Kennedy with Dobrynin's meeting with Rusk on the eve of the president's television address. Rusk did show photographs to the incredulous Dobrynin.

11. "From the Memoirs of Boris Poklad," *Pravda*, 22 October 1992, and Dobrynin, "The Caribbean Crisis," pp. 50–51, describing Gromyko's cable. Interviews, Leonid M. Zamyatin, Anatoliy F. Dobrynin, and Georgiy Kornienko, Moscow, 16–17 December 1991, and Oleg Grinevsky, Vienna, 11 October 1991. Gromyko, of course, told nobody in the embassy that missiles were going into Cuba and could not deal with the issue directly in his cable to Moscow lest he reveal the secret.

12. Interview, Anatoliy Dobrynin, Moscow, 17 December 1991.

13. Interviews, Leonid M. Zamyatin, Anatoliy F. Dobrynin, and Georgiy Kornienko, Moscow, 16–17 December 1991, and Oleg Grinevsky, Vienna, 11 October 1991, and New York, 10 November 1991.

14. *New York Times*, 22 October 1962. Jorge Risquet, *Antigua Conference*, p. 88, reports that the Cubans suspected that Kennedy's speech would be about the missiles and put their forces on alert. According to Gen. Anatoliy Gribkov, "Operation 'Anadyr,'" *Der Spiegel*, Part II, no. 17, 1992, p. 202, Soviet forces in Cuba monitored the 14 October U-2 flight that photographed the missiles in San Cristóbal but there is no evidence of any warning being passed on to Moscow.

15. Interview, Dean Rusk, Athens, Ga., 21 September 1987; Rusk, *As I Saw It*, p. 235; Anatoliy F. Dobrynin, *Moscow Conference*, pp. 144–45; According to Georgiy Shakhnazarov, in David A. Welch, ed., *Proceedings of the Cambridge Conference on the Cuban Missile Crisis, 11–12 October 1987* (Cambridge, Mass.: Harvard University, Center for Science and International Affairs, April 1988), final version, mimeograph, p. 78, hereafter cited as *Cambridge Conference*, Dobrynin exclaimed " 'It cannot be!' He was very surprised."

16. Oleg Troyanovsky, *Havana Conference*, p. 41–43, and "The Caribbean Crisis: A View from the Kremlin," *International Affairs* (Moscow) 4–5 (April–May 1992), pp. 149–50.

17. Troyanovsky, "The Caribbean Crisis," pp. 150–51.

18. Ibid. Kuznetsov was the senior foreign ministry official at the meeting because Foreign Minister Andrei Gromyko was in New York for the opening of the United Nations General Assembly.

19. Ibid.

20. Kohler attributed this to both the unexpected nature of the crisis and its war-threatening severity. Central Intelligence Agency, *The Soviet Bloc Armed Forces and the Cuban Crisis. A Chronology: July-November 1962* (Washington, D.C.: National Indications Center, 18 June 1963), p. 94. Troyanovsky, "The Caribbean Crisis," p. 151, says that Khrushchev's suggestion was also impractical as more than half of the participants did not have Kremlin suites in which to spend the night.

21. N. Khrushchev, *Khrushchev Remembers*, trans. Strobe Talbot (Boston: Little, Brown, 1970), p. 497.

22. Interviews, Aleksei Adzhubei, Oleg Grinevsky, and Leonid Zamyatin, Moscow, Vienna, and Moscow, 15 May 1989, 11 October 1991, and 16 December 1991.

23. Georgiy Kornienko, "Something New About the Caribbean Crisis," typescript, p. 20, reporting a discussion with Kuznetsov who flew to New York on 28 October; Dobrynin, "The Caribbean Crisis," p. 53, and interview, Moscow, 17 December 1991. The ambassador, who had met Robert Kennedy on the evening of 23 October, reported Kennedy's remarks to Moscow as evidence of the seriousness of the crisis, as he felt constrained from offering his own opinion. Robert Kennedy, "Memorandum for the President from the Attorney General, 24 October 1962,"

describing his 23 October meeting with Ambassador Dobrynin. János Radványi, *Hungary and the Superpowers: The 1956 Revolution and Realpolitik* (Stanford, Calif.: Stanford University Press, 1972), p. 130, Hungarian chargé d'affaires in Washington during the crisis, reports that at a meeting of Soviet-bloc diplomats on 26 October, Dobrynin announced that he still had received no instructions on how Moscow would respond to the blockade.

24. Khrushchev, *Khrushchev Remembers*, p. 497; Interviews, Sergei Khrushchev, Moscow, 17 May 1989; Oleg Grinevsky, Vienna and New York, 11 October and 10 November 1991; and Leonid Zamyatin, Georgiy Kornienko, and Anatoliy Dobrynin, Moscow, 16–17 December 1991.

25. Interview, Sergei Khrushchev, Moscow, 17 May 1989; Alekseev, "The Caribbean Crisis," p. 31; Fidel Castro, *Havana Conference*, pp. 217–18; *Granma*, 2 December 1990, reprints the Khrushchev-Castro correspondence between 26 and 31 October.

26. Alekseev, *Havana Conference*, p. 94. Interviews, Leonid M. Zamyatin, Anatoliy F. Dobrynin, and Georgiy Kornienko, Moscow, 16–17 December 1991; and Oleg Grinevsky, Vienna, 11 October 1991. Troyanovsky, "The Caribbean Crisis," p. 152, reports that sometimes Presidium members received the texts of messages rather than meeting. If any corrections were suggested, they were invariably minor.

27. Interviews, Oleg Grinevsky, Vienna, 11 October, and New York, 10 November 1991; Leonid Zamyatin, Moscow, 16 December 1991; and Felix N. Kovaliev, Moscow, 18 December 1991. There was tension between the two groups because of the long-standing rivalry between the foreign ministry and Central Committee staff. The primary responsibility of the Department of Relations with Communist and Workers' Parties of the Socialist Parties of the CPSU Central Committee (known as the Central Committee Department) was to coordinate relations with other communist parties. Foreign-ministry officials maintain that their world view was shaped by these parties and was extraordinarily unrealistic and ill-informed.

28. The quotation is from an interview with Oleg Grinevsky, Vienna, 11 October, 1992. Additional documentation was provided by interviews with Oleg Grinevsky, New York, 10 November 1991; Leonid Zamyatin, Moscow, 16 December 1991; and Felix N. Kovaliev, Moscow, 18 December 1991. According to Troyanovsky, "The Caribbean Crisis," p. 151, the officials who prepared letters on the basis of Khrushchev's unpolished dictation were so adept at their job that he cannot recall an instance when Khrushchev was dissatisfied with the drafts they submitted.

29. Ibid.

30. Ibid.

31. In chapter 4 we documented Malinovsky's judgment, which Khrushchev accepted, that Cuba could be overrun in a matter of days by American forces. With regard to the missiles, Nikita Khrushchev wrote to Fidel Castro on 30 October 1962, *Granma*, 2 December 1990, p. 4: "And it must be said that they could have knocked them all out."

32. Interview, Sergei Khrushchev, Moscow, 17 May 1989.

33. Fidel Castro to Nikita Khrushchev, 28 October 1962; Nikita Khrushchev to Fidel Castro, 30 October 1962, *Granma*, 2 December 1990, pp. 4–5; Khrushchev, *Khrushchev Remembers: The Glasnost Tapes*, p. 178.

34. Sergo Mikoyan, *Cambridge Conference*, pp. 99–100.

35. Interview, Aleksei Adzhubei, Moscow, 15 May 1989.

36. Ibid.

37. *The Soviet Bloc Armed Forces and the Cuban Crisis*, p. 64, reporting on photographic intelligence acquired on 24 October; Hilsman, *To Move A Nation*, pp. 214–16. We are assuming that Khrushchev gave, or at least acquiesced to the orders to do this. It is, of course, conceivable, that the Soviet military or local commanders acted on their own authority.

38. Department of Defense, "Chronology of the Cuban Crisis, October 15–28, 1962," 14 November 1962, p. 4, indicates that the alert entailed largely symbolic measures such as canceling leaves. The Strategic Rocket Forces and military combat forces maintained their regular state of readiness.

39. Lester A. Sobel, ed., *Cuba, the U.S., and Russia 1960–1963* (New York: Facts on File, 1964), p. 68.

40. *The Soviet Bloc Armed Forces and the Cuban Crisis*, p. 50.

41. "Chairman Khrushchev's Message of 23 October 1962," *Department of State Bulletin* 69, no. 1795, 19 November 1973, pp. 637–38; Letter from Chairman Khrushchev to Lord Bertrand Russell, 25 October 1962, *New York Times*, 25 October 1962; Both letters are reprinted in David L. Larson, *The "Cuban Crisis" of 1962: Selected Documents, Chronology and Bibliography*, 2d ed. (Lanham, Md.: University Press of America, 1986), pp. 67–68, 148–50, and *Problems of Communism* Special Edition 41 (Spring 1992), pp. 31–32, 36–37, which contains Russian-and English-language versions of the messages.

42. Robert F. Kennedy, *Thirteen Days: A Memoir of the Cuban Missile Crisis* (New York: Norton, 1969), pp. 68–69.

43. *The Soviet Bloc Armed Forces and the Cuban Crisis*, p. 57; William E. Knox, "Close Up of Khrushchev During a Crisis," *New York Times Magazine*, 18 November 1962.

44. *Moscow Conference*, pp. 79, 80.

45. Interview, Anatoliy F. Dobrynin, Moscow, 17 December 1991.

46. Interview, Adm. Nikolai N. Amelko, Moscow, 18 December 1991. Troyanovsky, "The Caribbean Crisis," reports that another reason for caution was that Khrushchev and the military were very concerned about keeping Soviet military hardware from falling into American hands.

47. Dissident Soviet historian Roy Medvedev, *All Stalin's Men*, trans. Harold Shukman (New York: Doubleday, 1982), p. 52, alleges that Khrushchev was so infuriated by the blockade that he ordered Soviet captains to ignore the American navy and continue on course to Cuba. Just as the first Soviet ships were approaching the blockade line, Mikoyan allegedly overrode Khrushchev's order and instructed their captains to stop just short of the line. James G. Blight and David A. Welch, *On the Brink: Americans and Soviets Reexamine the Cuban Missile Crisis* (New York: Hill and Wang, 1989), p. 306, report that Sergo Mikoyan confirmed the story in a conversation with them after the Cambridge conference.

Joseph F. Bouchard, *Command in Crisis: Four Case Studies* (New York: Columbia University Press, 1991), pp. 253–54, n. 117, points out the inconsistency between Medvedev's claim and Soviet ship movements. Raymond L. Garthoff, *Reflections on the Cuban Missile Crisis*, 2d ed. rev. (Washington, D.C.: The Brookings Institution, 1989), p. 66, n. 106, also doubts the Medvedev story. He speculates that Khrushchev's initial impulse may have been to challenge the blockade and that he may have been persuaded not to by Mikoyan and others. CIA, "Crisis USSR/Cuba," 25 October 1962, p. II-1; "Chronology of JCS Decisions," p. 42, indicates that on Monday evening, when the blockade was announced, there were nine Soviet merchant ships close enough to the blockade line to warrant stopping and boarding. The president instructed the navy to wait. Moscow had high frequency (HF) radio links with its merchant fleet and used this channel on Tuesday morning to order all Soviet ships en route to Cuba, including tankers and freighters carrying nonmilitary cargo, to stop or turn back. These course changes were executed at around noon eastern standard time on Tuesday. According to Alekseev, "The Caribbean Crisis," p. 31, this order was given "so as not to exacerbate the conflict."

48. *Cuba History*, "Memorandum for McGeorge Bundy, January 9, 1963," prepared by Gordon Chase, p. 6a; "Personal History or Diary of Vice Admiral Alfred G. Ward, U.S. Navy, While Serving as Commander Second Fleet," October–November 1962, pp. 6–11; Garthoff, *Reflections on the Cuban Missile Crisis*, pp. 68–69; Richard Ned Lebow, "Was Khrushchev Bluffing in Cuba?" *Bulletin of Atomic Scientists* 44 (April 1988), pp. 38–43.

49. Interview, Oleg Grinevsky, Vienna, 11 October 1991.

50. Office of the Secretary of Defense, "Department of Defense Operations During the Cuban Crisis," 12 February 1963, pp. 6, 12–14; Atlantic Command, Headquarters of the Commander-in-Chief, "CINCLANT Historical Account of Cuban Crisis—1963," 29 April 1963, pp. 56, 58–85, 133–39, 165; USAF Historical Division Liaison Office, Headquarters USAF, "The Air Force Response to the Cuban Crisis," December 1962; Historical Division, Joint Secretariat, Joint Chiefs of Staff, "Chronology of JCS Decisions Concerning the Cuban Crisis," 21 December 1962.

51. Interview, Pierre Salinger, Ithaca, N.Y., 13 November 1987; Pierre Salinger, *Moscow Conference*, pp. 75–76; Kenneth P. O'Donnell and David F. Powers with Joe McCarthy, *"Johnny, We Hardly Knew Ye": Memories of John Fitzgerald Kennedy* (Boston: Little, Brown, 1970), pp. 324–25, report that top officials were given pink identification cards that indicated that, if the need arose, they were to accompany the President and Mrs. Kennedy to an underground shelter. There were complaints from staff and cabinet members about what would happen to their wives and children. Rusk, *As I Saw It*, p. 244, received instructions that he and his family would be evacuated to shelters in West Virginia.

52. Sorensen, *Kennedy*, p. 705.

53. *Cambridge Conference*, p. 89.

54. Schlesinger, *A Thousand Days*, pp. 736–38; Sorensen, *Kennedy*, pp. 687–88.

55. "Department of Defense Operations During the Cuban Crisis," p. 1; "CINCLANT Historical Account of Cuban Crisis—1963," pp. 39–48; Robert McNamara, "Off-the-Record Meeting on Cuba, 16 October 1962, 11:50 A.M.–12:57 P.M.," pp. 11–12, and *Moscow Conference*, pp. 97–99; Gen. William Y. Smith, *Antigua Conference*, pp. 110–11.

56. White House Tapes, "Transcript of 27 October 1962," John F. Kennedy Library, mimeograph, pp. 39, 96, 98.

57. David A. Welch, ed., *Proceedings of the Hawk's Cay Conference on the Cuban Missile Crisis, 5–8 March 1987* (Cambridge, Mass.: Harvard University, Center for Science and International Affairs, Working Paper 89–1, 1989), mimeograph, pp. 81–82, hereafter cited as *Hawk's Cay Conference*.

58. Interview, Dean Rusk, Atlanta, Ga., 21 September 1987.

59. Oral History Interview With Llewellyn E. Thompson by Elizabeth Donahue, 25 March 1964, p. 11.

60. "Transcript of Ex Comm Meeting, 27 October," pp. 39, 94, 96–98.

61. Ibid., pp. 17, 49.

62. Schlesinger, *A Thousand Days*, pp. 758–59; Sorensen, *Kennedy*, pp. 197–200; O'Donnell et al., *"Johnny, We Hardly Knew Ye,"* p. 340; Graham T. Allison, *Essence of Decision: Explaining the Cuban Missile Crisis* (Boston: Little, Brown, 1971), pp. 195, 219–20.

63. O'Donnell et al., *"Johnny, We Hardly Knew Ye,"* p. 341.

64. "Letter from Chairman Khrushchev to President Kennedy, 27 October," *Department of State Bulletin* 47, no. 1220, 12 November 1962, pp. 741–43, reprinted in Larson, *The "Cuban Crisis" of 1962*, pp. 183–86, and *Problems of Communism*, pp. 45–50.

65. Kennedy, *Thirteen Days*, pp. 108–9. Robert Kennedy's personal notes, cited in Arthur Schlesinger, Jr., *Robert Kennedy and His Times* (Boston: Houghton, Mifflin, 1978), p. 523, indicate that he told Dobrynin that the missiles would be out within five months.

66. Ibid., p. 108.

67. Interview, Dean Rusk, Athens, Ga., 21 September 1987; Secretary of State to Raymond Hare and Thomas Finletter, 24 October 1962. The cable was drafted by George Ball. "Thomas Finletter to Secretary of State, 25 October 1962," and "Raymond Hare to Secretary of State, 26 October 1962."

68. "Raymond Hare to Secretary of State, 26 October 1962."

69. Schlesinger, *A Thousand Days*, p. 811, reports that on Sunday evening, 20 October, Robert Kennedy drew him aside and explained that "We will have to make a deal in the end, but we must stand absolutely firm now. Concessions must come at the end of negotiations not at the beginning."

70. "Memorandum of Conversation between President John F. Kennedy and Prime Minister Harold Macmillan, 25 October 1962"; Harold Macmillan, *At the End of the Day: 1961–1963* (New York: Harper & Row, 1973), pp. 210–11. Kennedy is reported to have raised the prospect of Soviet withdrawal of their missiles in Cuba in return for an American pledge not to invade Cuba.

71. John McCone, "Memorandum for the File, 19 October 1962," *CIA Documents on the Cuban Missile Crisis*, pp. 183–86.

72. Leonard Meeker's "Minutes of the 19 October 1962 Ex Comm meeting, 11:00 A.M.;" George W. Ball, *The Past Has Another Pattern* (New York: Norton, 1982), p. 295; Rusk, *As I Saw It*, p. 240, notes that John J. McCloy also favored a trade.

73. Adlai Stevenson to John F. Kennedy, 17 October 1962; Schlesinger, *A Thousand Days*, pp. 807–8; Kennedy, *Thirteen Days*, p. 49; Abel, *Missile Crisis*, p. 49.

74. Averell Harriman, "Memorandum on Kremlin Reactions, 22 October 1962"; Harriman to Under Secretary, 26 October 1962.

75. White House Tapes, "Transcript of 22 October 1962," pp. 4, 6. In the previous day's Ex Comm meeting, the president had said "we will get the Soviet strategic missiles out only by invading Cuba or by trading." Bromley Smith, "Summary Record of NSC Executive Committee Meeting, October 26, 1962, 10:00 A.M."

76. "Transcript of Ex Comm Meeting, 27 October 1963," p. 120.

77. Ibid., pp. 34, 47–48, 120; Interview, McGeorge Bundy, New York, 22 July 1987.

78. "Transcript of Ex Comm Meeting, 23 October, 1963," p. 48.

79. White House Tapes, "Transcript of 27 October," passim; Theodore C. Sorensen, "Possible World Consequences of Military Action," undated, emphasized the negative consequences for European relations of an air strike. Among other

things, he noted the irony that it might sow discord in Europe rather than strengthen NATO, and thereby tempt Khrushchev to put pressure on Berlin.

80. Interview, McGeorge Bundy, New York, 22 July 1987; Interview, Dean Rusk, Athens, Ga., 21 September 1987. McGeorge Bundy, telephone conversation, 11 May 1992, believes that Rusk's change of mind on the Jupiters was brought about by his perception of the president's needs and the Hare telegram from Ankara.

81. Dean Rusk reports that this initiative was predicated on Khrushchev's hint in his first communication to the president that the crisis might be resolved on the basis of an American assurance not to invade Cuba. According to Rusk, the "Trollope ploy"—responding to Khrushchev's first communication and ignoring his second— was not suggested by Robert Kennedy, but by Llewellyn Thompson. Interview, Dean Rusk, 21 September 1987.

82. "Letter from Chairman Khrushchev to President Kennedy," 26 October 1962, *Department of State Bulletin* 69, no. 1795, 19 November 1973, pp. 640–43. Reprinted in Larson, *The "Cuban Crisis" of 1962*, pp. 175–80, and *Problems of Communism*, pp. 37–45.

83. "Letter from President Kennedy to Chairman Khrushchev," 27 October 1962, *Department of State Bulletin* 47, no. 1220, 12 November 1962, p. 743. Reprinted in Larson, *The "Cuban Crisis" of 1962*, pp. 187–88, and *Problems of Communism*, pp. 50–52.

84. James Blight interview with Dean Rusk, Athens, Ga., 18 May 1987; Rusk, *As I Saw It*, p. 240.

85. Bundy, *Danger and Survival*, pp. 432–33; Theodore Sorensen, *Moscow Conference*, pp. 92–93; Robert McNamara and Theodore Sorensen, *Cambridge Conference*, pp. 88–89. At the Hawk's Cay and Cambridge conferences there was disagreement among the participants as to whether Robert Kennedy's message could properly be characterized as an ultimatum.

86. James Blight, interview with Dean Rusk, Athens, Ga., 18 May 1987, pp. 23, 25; McGeorge Bundy, telephone conversation, 11 May 1992.

87. Bundy, *Danger and Survival*, p. 433; Interview, Dean Rusk, Athens, Ga., 21 September 1987.

88. Interview, Dean Rusk, Athens, Ga., 21 September 1987; Interview, Dean Rusk by James Blight, Athens, Ga., 18 May 1987, p. 10.

89. "Briefing on Cuban Developments," 25 January 1963, *Executive Sessions of the Senate Foreign Relations Committee* (Historical Series), 15, pp. 105–6, 111.

90. McNamara testified that "without any qualifications whatsoever there was absolutely no deal . . . between the Soviet Union and the United States regarding the removal of the Jupiter weapons from either Italy or Turkey." U.S. Congress, House of Representatives, House Appropriations Committee, *Department of Defense Appropriations for 1964*, Part I, p. 57. 88th Cong., 1st sess.

91. Bundy, *Danger and Survival*, p. 434; Interview, 22 July 1987.

92. Dean Rusk, Robert McNamara, George Ball, Roswell Gilpatric, Theodore Sorensen, McGeorge Bundy, "The Lessons of the Cuban Missile Crisis," *Time*, 27 September 1982, p. 35.

93. Interview, Robert S. McNamara by James Blight, Washington, D.C., 21 May 1987, in Blight and Welch, *On the Brink*, p. 191.

94. Abel, *Missile Crisis*, pp. 190–92; Hilsman, *To Move A Nation*, pp. 202–3; Schlesinger, *Robert Kennedy and His Times*, p. 519; Kennedy, *Thirteen Days*, pp.

94–95; O'Donnell et al., *"Johnny, We Hardly Knew Ye,"* pp. 323–24, 337; Allison, *Essence of Decision*, p. 226, all give credence to the story.

95. Hilsman, *To Move A Nation*, p. 203; Dean Rusk to James G. Blight, 25 February 1987, describes this initiative in detail.

96. Abel, *Missile Crisis*, pp. 192–93.

97. Ibid., p. 191. Llewellyn E. Thompson, "Oral History Interview with Llewellyn E. Thompson by Elizabeth Donahue," 25 March 1964, John F. Kennedy Library, p. 12, also reported that the Jupiter missiles in Turkey "were very much on the President's mind and he several times expressed annoyance that the [State] Department had not yet carried out the decision which had been taken long before the Cuban crisis to remove them." He hastened to add that "He [Kennedy] seemed to forget that he had agreed in the plans for their removal which required careful preparation with the Turks and others."

98. Kennedy, *Thirteen Days*, pp. 94–95.

99. Kennedy, *Thirteen Days*, pp. 94–95; Schlesinger, *Robert Kennedy and His Times*, p. 519, wrote that "The president had ordered the forever dilatory State Department to get them out of Turkey months before and was incensed to find them still there."

100. Kennedy's role in the deployment was first surmised by Donald L. Hafner, "Bureaucratic Politics and 'Those Frigging Missiles': JFK, Cuba and U.S. Missiles in Turkey," *Orbis*, 21 (Summer 1977), pp. 307–34. Further documentation was brought to light by Barton Bernstein, "The Cuban Missile Crisis: Trading the Jupiters in Turkey?" *Political Science Quarterly*, 95 (Spring 1980), pp. 97–125. See especially pp. 98–102.

101. National Security Action Memorandum 181 of 23 August 1962. Bernstein, "The Cuban Missile Crisis," 102–5, and Marc Trachtenberg, "The Influence of Nuclear Weapons in the Cuban Missile Crisis," *International Security* 10 (Summer 1985), pp. 145–46n, make the same point.

102. National Security Action Memorandum, no. 181, 23 August 1962, signed by McGeorge Bundy. John McCone, "Memorandum of Meeting with the President, 23 August 1962," in *CIA Documents on the Cuban Missile Crisis*, pp. 27–29.

103. Dean Rusk to James G. Blight, 25 February 1987; Interview, Dean Rusk by James Blight, 18 May 1987, p. 7; Rusk, *As I Saw It*, p. 239; Ball, *The Past Has Another Pattern*, p. 501. "Transcript of the Off-the-Record Meeting on Cuba, 16 October, 1962, 6:30–7:55 P.M.," p. 26, seems to indicate that Kennedy was unaware of the missiles in Turkey, but this was most probably a sign of stress. In that morning's meeting, "Transcript of the Off-the-Record Meeting on Cuba, 16 October, 1962, 11:50 A.M.–12:57 P.M.," p. 14, he had asked how many nuclear weapons the United States had in Turkey, and had been reminded about the Jupiters by Gen. Taylor.

104. Bundy, *Danger and Survival*, pp. 428–29.

105. McNamara recalled that "I went to the Pentagon and ordered them withdrawn, cut up, and photographed, so that I could personally see that those missiles had been destroyed." On 25 April 1963, McNamara sent the president a handwritten note informing him that "The last Jupiter missile in Turkey came out yesterday." "Memorandum from Robert McNamara to John F. Kennedy, 25 April 1963." Press reports that the Jupiters were being dismantled were confirmed by the State Department on 25 March 1963. State Department News Briefing, 25 March 1963.

106. Kennedy, *Thirteen Days*, pp. 106–9.

107. Khrushchev, *Khrushchev Remembers: The Glasnost Tapes*, p. 179.

108. "Khrushchev Confidential Message of 28 October 1962," [delivered on 29 October by Anatoliy Dobrynin to Robert Kennedy], *Problems of Communism* Special Issue 41 (Spring 1992), pp. 60–62; *Moscow Conference*, pp. 78–84, 142–45, interview, Moscow, 17 December 1991, and "The Caribbean Crisis," p. 59, for Dobrynin's version of his meetings with Robert Kennedy. His account is confirmed by Georgiy Kornienko, interview, Moscow, 17 December 1991, and "Something New About the Caribbean Crisis," pp. 29–30. At the Moscow Conference, Dobrynin described the meeting as having taken place on Sunday, but American records indicate that it occurred on Monday. Dobrynin had received Khrushchev's cable on Sunday but could not have discussed it in person with Robert Kennedy who was in New York and did not return until the next day. In "The Caribbean Crisis," Dobrynin agrees that the meeting was on Monday, but also states that he met with Robert Kennedy at 5 P.M. on Sunday to convey Khrushchev's willingness to dismantle the missiles in Cuba.

109. *Moscow Conference*, pp. 92–93.

110. *Moscow Conference*, pp. 92–93. Dean Rusk confirms Sorensen's account, as do Robert Kennedy's papers. Interview, Dean Rusk, Athens, Ga., 21 September 1987; Rusk, *As I Saw It*, p. 240. Schlesinger, *Robert Kennedy*, p. 523, reports that two days later, on 29 October, Dobrynin returned to Robert Kennedy with an unsigned draft letter from Khrushchev in which he sought to commit the United States to withdrawal of its missiles in Turkey as a quid pro quo for Soviet withdrawal of its missiles from Cuba. Kennedy called Dobrynin the following day to inform him that the president would not sign such a letter. He also warned him that the administration would deny any Soviet assertions about such a deal and that any claims of this kind would damage Soviet-American relations and cause the administration to rethink its position about the Jupiters. Dean Rusk, James Blight interview, p. 10, reports that Dobrynin returned shortly thereafter "with a piece of paper in his hand which seemed to register this business of the Turkish missiles as some kind of agreement, and we returned that piece of paper to Dobrynin, and told him that that was inappropriate under the circumstances."

111. Anatoliy Dobrynin, *Moscow Conference*, pp. 79–81, 142–43, and interview, Moscow, 17 December 1991, remembered meeting with Robert Kennedy on 23, 24, 26–28 October. Interviews, Oleg Grinevsky, New York, 10 November 1991, and Georgiy Kornienko, Moscow, 17 December 1991, and Washington, D.C., 4 June 1992, indicate meetings on 23, 24 or 25, and 27, 29–30 October. Dobrynin, "The Caribbean Crisis," pp. 53, 57–59, speaks of meetings on 23, 27–30 October, and 1 November. Kennedy, *Thirteen Days*, pp. 65–66, 106–09, "Memorandum for the President from the Attorney General, 14 October 1962," and "Memorandum for the Secretary of State from the Attorney General, 30 October 1962," describe 23 and 27 October meetings with Dobrynin. Theodore Sorensen and McGeorge Bundy confirm the meetings of 29–30 October. Dobrynin's revised estimates, contained in his article, are based on a search of the foreign-ministry archives and match more closely with American recollections.

112. Dobrynin's comments at the *Moscow Conference*, pp. 78–84, 142–45 and "The Caribbean Crisis," pp. 56–58; Interviews, Oleg Grinevsky, New York, 10 November 1991, and Anatoliy Dobrynin and Georgiy Kornienko, Moscow, 17 December 1991. At the Moscow Conference, Dobrynin told a less elaborate and somewhat different version of the meeting. In response to his raising the missiles, Robert Kennedy replied: " 'You are interested in the missiles in Turkey?' He thought pensively

and said: 'One minute, I will go and talk to the President.' He went out of the room. I do not know what he did, I assume he spoke with the President, and when he appeared he said: 'The President said that we are ready to consider the question about Turkey. To examine favorably the question of Turkey.'"

113. Interview, Dean Rusk, Athens, Ga., 21 September 1987; Dean Rusk to James G. Blight, 25 February 1987.

114. Interview, Dean Rusk, Athens, Ga., 21 September 1987; Dean Rusk to James G. Blight, 25 February 1987; Rusk, *As I Saw It*, pp. 240–41; McGeorge Bundy's comments at Hawk's Cay Conference on the Cuban Missile Crisis, author's record.

115. "Transcript of the Ex Comm meetings of 27 October 1962," p. 96; Kennedy, *Thirteen Days*, p. 98. John McCone, "Memorandum of Meeting of Executive Committee of the NSC, 10:00 A.M., October 23, 1962," *CIA Documents on the Cuban Missile Crisis*, pp. 283–85, indicated that if a U-2 were fired on, "a prompt decision for retaliation would then be made by the President."

116. *Hawk's Cay Conference*, p. 58; McNamara, *Cambridge Conference*, pp. 88–92, insisted that "Invasion was not inevitable, though it was a possibility. To my mind, it was very unlikely." Contrary to McNamara's claim, the military prepared to conduct an air strike.

117. Testimony of C. Douglas Dillon, Robert McNamara, and McGeorge Bundy, *Hawk's Cay Conference*, pp. 58, 81–82, Theodore Sorensen, *Cambridge Conference*, pp. 95–96, and Robert McNamara and Theodore Sorensen, *Moscow Conference*, pp. 99–105; Bundy, *Danger and Survival*, p. 427. Arthur Schlesinger, Jr., *Antigua Conference*, p. 63, also believes that Kennedy would have tried some other diplomatic overture in lieu of an invasion.

118. Interview, Dean Rusk, 21 September 1987; Rusk, *As I Saw It*, pp. 238, 240–41.

119. Sorensen, *Kennedy*, p. 696. McGeorge Bundy also made this argument at the 27 October meeting. "Transcript of the Ex Comm meeting of 27 October 1962," pp. 8, 33.

120. Robert McNamara, Hawk's Cay Conference, author's record.

121. Interview, Paul Nitze by James Blight, 6 May 1987, Washington., D.C., in Blight and Welch, *On the Brink*, p. 150.

122. Dean Acheson, "Homage to Plain Dumb Luck," *Esquire*, February 1969, pp. 76–77, 44–46. Dillon and Taylor ultimately came to believe that Kennedy had been right to eschew force.

123. Interview, C. Douglas Dillon by James Blight, 15 May 1987, New York, in Blight and Welch, *On the Brink*, p. 162.

124. Ibid., p. 171.

125. Kennedy, *Thirteen Days*, p. 98.

126. Interview, Robert S. McNamara by James Blight, Washington, D.C., 21 May 1987, in Blight and Welch, *On the Brink*, p. 191.

127. This point is also made by Bundy, *Danger and Survival*, p. 436.

128. Interview, Dean Rusk, Athens, Ga., 21 September 1987.

129. Garthoff, *Reflections of the Cuban Missile Crisis*, p. 79.

130. John Scali, "I Was the Secret Go-Between in the Cuban Crisis," *Family Weekly*, 25 October 1964, pp. 4–5, 12–14; Hilsman, *To Move A Nation*, pp. 217–19; Aleksandr Fomin, *Moscow Conference*, pp. 112–14.

131. Sorensen, *Kennedy*, p. 712; Kennedy, *Thirteen Days*, pp. 86, 90–91. For the

text of the message, see "Letter from Chairman Khrushchev to President Kennedy, 26 October 1962," *Department of State Bulletin* 69, no. 1795, 19 November 1973, pp. 640–43. Reprinted in Larson, *The "Cuban Crisis" of 1962*, pp. 175–80, and *Problems of Communism*, pp. 37–45.

132. Schlesinger, *A Thousand Days*, p. 755.

133. Sorensen, *Kennedy*, p. 712.

134. Abel, *Missile Crisis*, p. 180, giving his impression of the paraphrased version.

135. Rusk, *As I Saw It*, p. 239.

136. Schlesinger, *A Thousand Days*, p. 755, also reads the message this way. It was not "hysterical," he writes, "though it pulsated with a passion to avoid nuclear war and gave the impression of having been written in deep emotion, why not?" Hilsman, *To Move A Nation*, p. 219, criticizes the portrayal of Khrushchev as hysterical, as does McGeorge Bundy, *Danger and Survival*, pp. 441–43, who writes: "To read this full text in retrospect is to have renewed respect for the man who wrote it." Bundy observes that it represents a significant shift in tone. Khrushchev informs Kennedy that none of the missiles in Cuba would be fired and that the blockade will not be challenged. He goes on to justify his previous actions and warns Kennedy against doing anything that would make war unavoidable.

137. "Chairman Khrushchev's Message of 24 October 1962," *Department of State Bulletin* 69, 19 November 1973, pp. 637–38, reprinted in Larson, *The "Cuban Crisis" of 1962*, pp. 127–29, and *Problems of Communism*, pp. 33–36.

138. "President Kennedy's Message of 25 October 1962," *Department of State Bulletin* 69, 19 November 1973, p. 639, reprinted in Larson, *The "Cuban Crisis" of 1962*, p. 145, and *Problems of Communism*, pp. 36–37.

139. Kornienko, "Something New About the Caribbean Crisis," pp. 23–24, Kornienko and Sergei Khrushchev, *Antigua Conference*, pp. 66–67, 117, and interview, Kornienko, Moscow, 17 December 1991. Kornienko thinks this letter might also have demanded withdrawal of the Jupiter missiles in Italy.

140. Kornienko, "Something New About the Caribbean Crisis," pp. 23–24, and interview, Moscow, 17 December 1991; Kornienko and Sergei Khrushchev, *Antigua Conference*, pp. 66–67, 117–18; Interview, Oleg Grinevsky, Vienna, 11 October 1991.

141. Kornienko, "Something New About the Caribbean Crisis," pp. 23–25, *Antigua Conference*, pp. 66–67, and interview, Moscow, 17 December 1991. A Soviet intelligence officer picked up this story at the National Press Club from a friend of Russian origin who had heard it from two well-known American journalists. Cuba was to be attacked "today (October 25), or tomorrow night." The intelligence officer alleged that he had been able to contact one of the journalists who confirmed the information. Radványi, *Hungary and the Superpowers*, p. 131, told Dobrynin sometime on the twenty-sixth that his information indicated that invasion preparations were nearly completed and American missiles were targeted on Cuba. "Only a go-ahead signal from the president was needed." Dobrynin concurred with his analysis.

142. Sergei Khrushchev, *Antigua Conference*, pp. 117–18; Interview, Oleg Grinevsky, Vienna, 11 October 1991. Kornienko, interview, Moscow, 17 December 1991, reported that the intelligence warning of an impending assault arrived in "bits and pieces" from different places. The raw intelligence was passed directly on to Moscow and to Khrushchev, although officials at the embassy tried to put it in context.

143. Kornienko, "Something New About the Caribbean Crisis," p. 25, *Antigua Conference*, p. 67, and interview, Moscow, 17 December 1991; Interview, Oleg Grinevsky, Vienna, 11 October 1991.

144. "Letter from Chairman Khrushchev to President Kennedy, 26 October 1962," *Department of State Bulletin*, pp. 640–43; Larson, The *"Cuban Crisis" of 1962*, pp. 175–80, and *Problems of Communism*, pp. 37–45.

145. "Letter from Chairman Khrushchev to President Kennedy, 27 October 1962," *Department of State Bulletin*, pp. 741–43; Larson, The *"Cuban Crisis" of 1962*, pp. 183–86.

146. White House Tapes, "Transcript of 27 October," pp. 12–13; Abel, *The Missile Crisis*, pp. 188–89; Kennedy, *Thirteen Days*, p. 96.

147. Aleksandr Fomin, *Moscow Conference*, pp. 112–14; Sergo Mikoyan and Georgiy Kornienko, *Antigua Conference*, pp. 58, 67–68; Troyanovsky, "The Caribbean Crisis," p. 156. According to Hilsman, *To Move A Nation*, p. 219, the Ex Comm viewed Fomin's remarks and Khrushchev's message as "really a single package."

148. Foy Kohler [United States ambassador in Moscow] to Secretary of State, 6 November 1962, reports on a conversation with the French ambassador who claims to have learned from a reliable Soviet source that Khrushchev had personally written and dispatched the message of 26 October. When other leaders learned of his action that night, a long and heated discussion ensued, leading to the dispatch of the Saturday letter.

149. Interviews, Aleksei Adzhubei, Moscow, 15 May 1989, Oleg Grinevsky, New York, 10 November 1991, Leonid Zamyatin and Georgiy Kornienko, Moscow, 17 December 1991.

150. Troyanovsky, "The Caribbean Crisis," pp. 152–53.

151. *Washington Post*, 25 October 1962.

152. Allison, *Essence of Decision*, p. 43.

153. Max Frankel, "U.S. Sees Moscow Caught Off Guard," *New York Times*, 24 October 1962, and "Blockade Starts: Moscow is Believed to be Undecided on Next Step," *New York Times*, 25 October 1962.

154. Cambridge Conference, author's record, contains observations by Shakhnazarov about the appeal of a trade that are omitted from the *Cambridge Conference* proceedings. Oleg Troyanovsky, "The Caribbean Crisis," p. 153, makes the same point.

155. Sergo Mikoyan, Fedor Burlatsky, and Georgiy Shakhnazarov, *Cambridge Conference*, pp. 69–74, [in the preliminary version only] and in conversation on 12 October 1987; Interview, Georgiy Kornienko, Moscow, 17 December 1991; Oleg Troyanovsky, "The Caribbean Crisis," p. 152; Radványi, *Hungary and the Superpowers*, pp. 130–31. In his Saturday conversation with John Scali, Aleksandr Fomin cited Lippmann's column as the source of the missile-swap proposal. Hilsman, *To Move A Nation*, p. 222. So did Soviet Deputy Premier Anastas I. Mikoyan in his post-crisis discussions with Fidel Castro in Havana. "Extracts from the record of a conversation between Anastas Mikoyan and Fidel Castro . . . on November 3, 1962 at Fidel Castro's residence," in *International Affairs* (Moscow), no. 10 (October 1992), pp. 108–44, citation on p. 117.

156. According to Oleg Troyanovsky, "The Caribbean Crisis," p. 153, "Nobody foresaw that by making public the Turkish angle of the deal we created additional difficulties to the White House." For Khrushchev and his advisors there was no

contradiction between the perceived need to reach a quick settlement and the Jupiter demand.

157. *Cambridge Conference*, p. 69 [preliminary version].

158. The misinterpretation of the Lippmann column is a striking illustration of how difficult it is for officials from radically different political systems to understand and communicate with one other. It never occurred to American leaders, accustomed to an independent press, that Khrushchev or his colleagues could have given such weight to the Lippmann column. Only "Tommy" Thompson, one of the Ex Comm's two Soviet experts, speculated about this possibility. White House Tapes, "Transcript of 27 October 1962," p. 112. Nobody in the Ex Comm appears to have taken his suggestion seriously.

159. Radványi, *Hungary and the Superpowers*, pp. 130–31.

160. Kornienko, "Something New About the Caribbean Crisis," pp. 26–29, *Antigua Conference*, pp. 68–69; Garthoff, *Reflections on the Cuban Missile Crisis*, p. 82, relying on an earlier interview with Kornienko.

161. Anatoliy Gribkov, "Operation 'Anadyr,'" *Der Spiegel*, no. 17, 1992, p. 205.

162. Interview, Oleg Grinevsky, Vienna, 11 October 1991.

163. Troyanovsky, "The Caribbean Crisis," p. 152.

164. Dobrynin, *Moscow Conference*, pp. 85–86; Interviews, Aleksandr Kislov, Moscow, 18 May 1989; Anatoliy Dobrynin and Georgiy Kornienko, Moscow, 17 December 1991; Kornienko, "Something New About the Caribbean Crisis," p. 27, and *Antigua Conference*, pp. 70, 99.

165. Dobrynin, *Moscow Conference*, pp. 85–86; Interviews, Anatoliy Dobrynin and Georgiy Kornienko, Moscow, 17 December 1991; Kornienko, "Something New About the Caribbean Crisis," p. 27, and *Antigua Conference*, pp. 70, 99.

166. According to Michel Tatu, *Power in the Kremlin: From Khrushchev to Kosygin* (New York: Viking Press, 1968), p. 265, n. 1, and Bundy, *Danger and Survival*, pp. 443–44, Khrushchev's message of 26 October was delivered to the American embassy at 4:43 P.M. Moscow time. The State Department in Washington received it in four sections, between 6 P.M. and 9 P.M. local time. There was a twelve-hour delay altogether, including a six to nine hour delay in transmission, between the time the cable was received in Moscow and delivered to the White House.

167. Bundy, *Danger and Survival*, p. 444.

168. Interviews, Leonid Zamyatin and Georgiy Kornienko, Moscow, 16–17 December 1991; Troyanovsky, "The Caribbean Crisis," p. 153.

169. Ibid.

170. Interviews, Oleg Grinevsky, New York, 10 November 1991, and Leonid Zamyatin and Georgiy Kornienko, Moscow, 16–17 December 1991.

171. Interviews, Leonid Zamyatin and Georgiy Kornienko, Moscow, 16–17 December 1991.

172. Interview, Oleg Grinevsky, Vienna, 11 October 1991, and New York, 10 November 1991; Georgiy Shakhnazarov, *Cambridge Conference*, p. 76.

173. Khrushchev later told the Supreme Soviet and the Cubans that he had received very precise warnings that the Americans would carry out an air strike within forty-eight hours. "The Present International Situation and the Foreign Policy of the Soviet Union," Report by Comrade N. S. Khrushchev at Session of USSR Supreme Soviet, 12 December 1962, *Pravda* and *Izvestiya*, 13 December 1962. English translation in Ronald R. Pope, ed., *Soviet Views on the Cuban Crisis: Myth and Reality*

in Foreign Policy Analysis (Washington, D.C.: University Press of America, 1982), pp. 71–107. Khrushchev, *Khrushchev Remembers*, p. 87, refers to warnings from Cuban and other sources, including an intercepted cable, that an American attack was imminent. American intelligence heard the same story from a Soviet ambassador in Western Europe. *Soviet Bloc Armed Forces and the Cuban Crisis*, p. 84. Sergo Mikoyan, *Cambridge Conference*, p. 89, wondered if this cable had not been a special leak engineered by the Americans "to impress us with an imminent invasion." When Fidel Castro visited the Soviet Union in April–May 1963, Khrushchev apologized that there had been no time to consult him before agreeing to remove the missiles. He explained that "trustworthy information was received from the United States about the decision taken by the American military command to begin bombing on 29 or 30 October the Soviet military installations and Cuban military targets with a subsequent invasion of the island." Alekseev, "The Caribbean Crisis," p. 32.

174. Kennedy, *Thirteen Days*, pp. 106–10, and "Memorandum for the Secretary of State from the Attorney General," 30 October 1962; Dobrynin, *Moscow Conference*, p. 144, "The Caribbean Crisis," pp. 56–58, and interview, Moscow, 17 December 1991.

Khrushchev, *Khrushchev Remembers*, pp. 497–98; "The Present International Situation and the Foreign Policy of the Soviet Union," Report by Comrade N. S. Khrushchev at Session of USSR Supreme Soviet, 12 December 1962, Pope, *Soviet Views on the Cuban Crisis*, pp. 71–107, portrayed the Kennedy-Dobrynin meeting very differently. He claimed that Dobrynin's cable described near panic in Washington, with the president worrying that the military was about to overthrow him and seize power. Khrushchev alleged that he quickly agreed to withdraw the missiles to avert a coup.

Interview, Georgiy Kornienko, 17 December 1991. Kornienko, who helped Dobrynin compose his cable to Moscow reporting the Kennedy meeting, insists that there was no mention of a coup. "That could only have been Khrushchev's doing." Sergei Khrushchev, *Cambridge Conference* [preliminary version], p. 91, also believes that Kennedy's alleged appeal for help to avoid a military coup was his father's invention. Kornienko thinks that Khrushchev's purpose was to demonstrate to militants at home the need to withdraw the missiles from Cuba. After the crisis, Khrushchev used the story to buttress his authority among his colleagues. In his speech to the Supreme Soviet and in his memoirs he portrayed himself as a sober leader who had agreed to the American terms in the interests of world peace. Khrushchev, *Khrushchev Remembers*, p. 498.

175. Kennedy, *Thirteen Days*, pp. 106–10; Dobrynin, *Moscow Conference*, pp. 85–86, and "The Caribbean Crisis," pp. 56–57. Interviews, Anatoliy Dobrynin and Georgiy Kornienko, Moscow, 17 December 1991; Kornienko, "Something New About the Caribbean Crisis," p. 30. Robert Kennedy's (or Theodore Sorensen's) account in *Thirteen Days*, pp. 106–9, is slightly more emphatic. Dobrynin was warned that "Time was running out." "We had only a few more hours—we needed an answer immediately from the Soviet Union. I said we must have it the next day."

176. Dobrynin, *Moscow Conference*, pp. 142–45, "The Caribbean Crisis," pp. 56–58, and interview, Anatoliy Dobrynin, Moscow, 17 December 1991.

177. Interviews, Anatoliy Dobrynin and Georgiy Kornienko, Moscow, 17 December 1991; Kornienko, *Antigua Conference*, pp. 69–70.

178. Oleg Troyanovsky, *Havana Conference*, pp. 43–44, and "The Caribbean Crisis," p. 154, paraphrasing Dobrynin's cable as understood by Soviet officials.

Interviews, Leonid Zamyatin and Georgiy Kornienko, Moscow, 16–17 December 1991, indicate that nobody at the meeting read the actual cable until after the crisis, and there is no record that it was ever read by Khrushchev.

179. Fidel Castro to Nikita S. Khrushchev, 27 October 1962, *Granma*, 2 December 1990, p. 3; Aleksandr Alekseev, *Moscow Conference*, pp. 158–59; Felix N. Kovaliev and Georgiy Kornienko, *Antigua Conference*, pp. 97–99. Soviet and Cuban officials downplay the importance of Castro's cable because by the time Khrushchev was informed of its contents—sometime early Sunday morning—he had already made his decision to withdraw the missiles. Mikoyan-Castro Conversation, p. 115; Interview, Georgiy Kornienko, Moscow, 17 December 1991; Jorge Risquet and Sergei Khrushchev, *Antigua Conference*, pp. 74–75, 85, 118; Oleg Troyanovsky, *Havana Conference*, p. 90, and "The Caribbean Crisis," p. 153, maintain that the Alekseev and Castro cables nevertheless had an important influence on Khrushchev's state of mind on Sunday.

180. Aleksandr Alekseev, *Moscow Conference*, pp. 158–59, *Havana Conference*, pp. 94–95. "We spoke and thought for a long time." Alekseev remembers. "There were two of us there—[Konstantin] Monakhov and I were there, and [Oleg] Darusenkov was around somewhere—as Fidel was dictating and we were . . . translating and writing." "The letter was two or three pages long, and I must say that I recall that Fidel was choosing his words very precisely, because this was an immense responsibility."

181. Fidel Castro to Nikita S. Khrushchev, 27 October 1962, *Granma*, 2 December 1990, p. 3. Castro did not refer directly to the missiles, but to air attacks "against certain targets." Jorge Risquet, *Antigua Conference*, pp. 125–26. Risquet, pp. 100–102, points out that Alekseev's and Castro's warnings were sent in ignorance of the 26–27 October exchanges between Khrushchev and Kennedy. Their estimates of the likelihood of an attack would have been much less if they had known that the basis for an agreement was already taking shape.

182. Castro's cable, delivered to the telegraph office at 6:40 A.M. on 27 October, was delayed in transmission, and was not received in Moscow until 1:10 A.M. local time on the twenty-eighth. A preliminary cable from Alekseev, advising that "Fidel believes that a strike is imminent and will take place within 24 to 72 hours," arrived in Moscow at 2:20 P.M. on the twenty-seventh. Felix N. Kovaliev, Georgiy Kornienko, and Jorge Risquet, *Antigua Conference*, pp. 97–100, and Oleg Troyanovsky and Aleksandr Alekseev, *Havana Conference*, pp. 90–94, give slightly different arrival times for the cables. Troyanovsky, "The Caribbean Crisis," p. 153, recalls telephoning the contents of the cable to Khrushchev at his dacha.

183. Dobrynin, "The Caribbean Crisis," p. 58; Mikoyan-Castro Conversation, p. 123; Gribkov, "Operation 'Anadyr,' " p. 205; Aleksandr Alekseev, *Moscow Conference*, pp. 158–59; Khrushchev, *Khrushchev Remembers: The Glasnost Tapes*, pp. 176–77; Oleg Troyanovsky, *Havana Conference*, p. 90. Sergei Khrushchev, *Moscow Conference*, pp. 89–90, and *Antigua Conference*, pp. 117–19, argues that the Castro letter reinforced Khrushchev's belief that the missiles had to be withdrawn. On 30 October, Khrushchev wrote to Castro to explain why he had agreed to remove the Soviet missiles from Cuba without further consultations with the Cuban government. He defended his decision as necessary to avoid war and beneficial to Castro because of the promise he had extracted from the Americans not to invade Cuba. Khrushchev told Castro that his cable of 26 October had been "a very well-founded alarm." Together with information he

had received from other reports, it had convinced him that "if we had continued our consultations, we would have wasted time and this attack would have been carried out." Nikita Khrushchev to Fidel Castro, 30 October 1962, *Granma*, 2 December 1990, p. 4. Castro was "offended" by Khrushchev's failure to consult with him, but his assessment of the situation had undeniably contributed to Khrushchev's growing sense of desperation on Sunday. Alekseev, "The Caribbean Crisis," p. 32.

184. Oleg Troyanovsky, *Havana Conference*, p. 90.

185. Bundy, *Danger and Survival*, pp. 438–39, believes that the Fomin report must have been particularly persuasive to Khrushchev.

186. Scali, "I Was the Secret Go-Between in the Cuban Crisis," pp. 12–14; Hilsman, *To Move A Nation*, pp. 217–19, 222–24; Bundy, *Danger and Survival*, p. 690, n. 81, citing a conversation with Dean Rusk confirming that Scali's "strong language" was his own idea. Troyanovsky, "The Caribbean Crisis," p. 156, has no recollection of Fomin's cable having any effect on Khrushchev's decisions.

187. Oleg Troyanovsky, *Havana Conference*, p. 43, and "The Caribbean Crisis," p. 154. What had been announced was a rerun of Kennedy's earlier speech.

188. Oleg Troyanovsky, *Havana Conference*, p. 42, described the U-2 incident as the tensest moment of the crisis for Khrushchev and his advisors. Defense Department Chronology, p. 14; Interview of Col. John A. Des Portes, Major C. B. Stratton, Gen. David Power, Lt. Col. A. Leatherwood, and Col. J. R. King by Ron Caywood, Headquarters, Strategic Air Command, 25 May 1965, p. 56; Hilsman, *To Move A Nation*, p. 221; and "The Cuban Crisis: How Close We Were to War," *Look* 28, 25 August 1964.

189. "Letter from Chairman Khrushchev to President Kennedy, 28 October 1962," *Department of State Bulletin* 47, 12 November 1962, pp. 743–45. Reprinted in Larson, *The "Cuban Crisis" of 1962*, pp. 189–93, and *Problems of Communism*, pp. 52–58; Interview, Leonid Zamyatin, Moscow, 16 December 1991; Kornienko, "Something New About the Caribbean Crisis," pp. 30–31, and *Havana Conference*, p. 70.

190. Nikita Khrushchev to Fidel Castro, 28 October 1962, *Granma*, 2 December 1962, p. 3, urges Castro not to shoot at any more American aircraft. Khrushchev, *Khrushchev Remembers*, p. 499. *Khrushchev Remembers: The Glasnost Tapes*, p. 178, indicates that some years after the crisis Khrushchev came to believe that Castro had convinced the Soviet military to shoot the U-2 down. The downing of the U-2 is discussed in chapter 13.

191. Alekseev, "The Caribbean Crisis," p. 32, *Havana Conference*, pp. 94–95; Sergei Khrushchev, *Moscow Conference*, pp. 89–90; Oleg Troyanovsky, "The Caribbean Crisis," p. 155; Interviews, Oleg Grinevsky, Vienna, 11 October 1991, and Leonid Zamyatin, Moscow, 16 December 1991.

192. Interview, Oleg Grinevsky, Vienna, 11 October 1991, who had accompanied Kuznetsov and Mendelevich to the airport. Afterward, he returned to the Khrushchev dacha.

193. Alekseev, "The Caribbean Crisis," p. 32.

194. Interviews, Oleg Grinevsky, Vienna, 11 October 1991, and Leonid Zamyatin and Georgiy Kornienko, Moscow, 16–17 December 1991; Kornienko, "Something New About the Caribbean Crisis," p. 31; Troyanovsky, "The Caribbean Crisis," p. 154.

195. See chapter 2.

196. Interviews, Oleg Grinevsky, Vienna, 11 October 1991, and Leonid Zamyatin, Moscow, 16 December 1991.

197. Soviet press coverage of the crisis hints at differences among the leadership, and dissatisfaction within the military. *Izvestiya*, edited by Aleksei Adzhubei, was more ready than *Pravda* to seek an accommodation with the United States. *Red Star*, the military newspaper, was more uncompromising than either *Pravda* or *Izvestiya*. Detailed analyses of the Soviet press during the crisis are provided by Herbert S. Dinerstein, *The Making of a Missile Crisis: October 1962* (Baltimore: Johns Hopkins University Press, 1976), pp. 150–229, 239–62. Rumors circulated that thirty-five to forty high-ranking officers boycotted Khrushchev's speech to the Supreme Soviet in December to demonstrate their opposition to his handling of the crisis. *The Soviet Bloc Armed Forces and the Cuban Crisis*, p. 115. Interview, Adm. Nikolai Amelko, Moscow, 18 December 1991, confirmed that there was a lot of dissatisfaction in the navy. After the crisis, Khrushchev felt it necessary to explain his policy to high-ranking naval officers. "I'm not a czarist officer who has to kill myself if I fart at a masked ball," he told them. "It's better to back down than to go to war."

198. "The Cuban Missile Crisis: An Anniversary," editorial by Norman Cousins, *Saturday Review*, 15 October 1977, p. 4.

199. Khrushchev, *Khrushchev Remembers: The Glasnost Tapes*, p. 175.

200. Kornienko, *Antigua Conference*, p. 70; Troyanovsky, "The Caribbean Crisis," p. 155; Interviews, Leonid Zamyatin and Georgiy Kornienko, Moscow, 16–17 December 1991, and Oleg Grinevsky, Vienna, 11 October 1991.

201. Interviews, Leonid Zamyatin, Moscow, 16 December 1991, and Oleg Grinevsky, Vienna, 11 October 1991; Oleg Troyanovsky, *Havana Conference*, p. 44, and "The Caribbean Crisis," p. 155.

202. Interview, Leonid Zamyatin, Moscow, 16 December 1991; Georgiy Kornienko, *Antigua Conference*, p. 70; Melor Sturua, *Moscow Conference*, pp. 109–10, and "Dialectics of the Caribbean Crisis," *Izvestiya*, 6 February 1989, reports that he was sent from the dacha to *Izvestiya*. Another junior official, Mikhail Kharlamov, was part of the group that went to Radio Moscow. "Our cars were given 'green light' on every street, from the Kremlin to Pushkin Square."

203. Interviews, Oleg Grinevsky, Vienna, 11 October 1991, and New York, 10 November 1991, and Leonid Zamyatin, Moscow, 16 December 1991.

204. Ibid.

205. A few minutes before 9:00 A.M. Washington time, Radio Moscow announced that a message of special importance would be broadcast on the hourly news. American networks monitoring Radio Moscow broadcast live or rebroadcast the message to their audiences.

206. At 9:09 A.M., the Foreign Broadcast Information Service flashed a short bulletin by Teletype, followed two minutes later by a longer report. At 9:40, an extended paraphrase of the entire message came across the wires. This was presumably the text that Bundy handed to the president. Sorensen, *Kennedy*, p. 716; Bundy, *Danger and Survival*, p. 406, and interview, New York, 10 November 1991.

207. Interview, Oleg Grinevsky, New York, 10 November 1991.

208. "Khrushchev Confidential Message of 28 October 1962"; Interview, Georgiy Kornienko, Moscow, 17 December 1991; "Something New About the Caribbean Crisis," p. 30, and *Antigua Conference*, p. 70; Troyanovsky, "The Caribbean Crisis," p. 155.

209. Ibid.

210. See Adam B. Ulam, *Expansion and Coexistence: The History of Soviet Foreign Policy, 1917–67* (New York: Praeger, 1968), p. 630; Edward Crankshaw, *Khrushchev: A Career* (New York: Viking, 1966), p. 279; William Hyland and Richard W. Shyrock, *The Fall of Khrushchev* (New York: Funk & Wagnalls, 1968), p. 48; Garthoff, *Reflections on the Cuban Missile Crisis*, p. 132.

211. Stewart Alsop and Charles Bartlett, "In Time of Crisis," *Saturday Evening Post*, 235, 8 December 1962, pp. 16–20. Kennedy, *Thirteen Days*, p. 18, quotes Rusk as having said: "We looked into the mouth of the canon; the Russians flinched." Interview, Dean Rusk, Athens, Ga., 21 September 1987, was "furious" that his comment leaked because it threatened the president's objective of letting Khrushchev save face.

212. Quoted in Abel, *Missile Crisis*, p. 153.

213. Fedor Burlatsky, *Cambridge Conference*, p. 101.

214. *Cambridge Conference*, p. 36 in preliminary version.

215. Interview, Sergei Khrushchev, Moscow, 17 May 1989.

216. Interview, Aleksei Adzhubei, Moscow, 15 May 1989.

217. Troyanovsky, "The Caribbean Crisis," p. 157; Interview, Georgiy Shaknazarov, Cambridge, Mass., 12 October 1987.

218. Abel, *Missile Crisis*, p. 203; *Cambridge Conference*, pp. 89–90.

CHAPTER SEVEN
The Failure to Prevent War, October 1973

1. Interview, Henry Kissinger, New York, 19 June 1991.

2. Interview, Victor Israelian, State College, Pa., 8 January 1992.

3. Interview, Henry Kissinger, New York, 19 June 1991.

4. Anwar el-Sadat, *In Search of Identity: An Autobiography* (New York: Harper & Row, 1977); Hassan el-Badri, Taha el Magdoub, and Mohammed Dia el-Din Zhody, *The Ramadan War* (Dunn Loring, Va.: T.N. Dupuy Assoc., 1978); and Janice Gross Stein, "Calculation, Miscalculation, and Conventional Deterrence I: The View from Cairo," in Robert Jervis, Richard Ned Lebow, and Janice Gross Stein, *Psychology and Deterrence* (Baltimore: Johns Hopkins University Press, 1985), pp. 34–59.

5. Anwar el-Sadat, Speech to the People's Assembly, 4 February 1971, *Al-Ahram*, 5 February 1971. See also Sadat, *In Search of Identity: An Autobiography*, pp. 279–80.

6. One exception was Ezer Weizman, a former commander of the Israel Air Force and a member of the Cabinet during the War of Attrition, who argued that Israel had lost the war. See *On Eagles' Wings* (London: Weidenfeld and Nicolson, 1976).

7. Janice Gross Stein, "Calculation, Miscalculation, and Conventional Deterrence II: The View from Jerusalem," *Psychology and Deterrence*, pp. 60–88.

8. See *The Agranat Report: A Partial Report by the Commission of Inquiry to the Government of Israel* (Jerusalem: Government Press Office, Press Bulletin, 2 April 1974). This is the authoritative report of an independent commission of inquiry appointed by the government to investigate the causes of the intelligence failure in 1973.

9. Anwar el-Sadat, Speech, Cairo, 1 May 1973, *Al-Ahram*, 2 May 1973.

10. The original military objective was to cross the Suez Canal and dig in on its

east bank under the cover of the antiaircraft missiles. There was some discussion of advancing as far as the strategic passes in the Sinai, but this issue was not resolved before the war. Interview, senior military commander, Cairo, May 1977.

11. George W. Breslauer, "Soviet Policy Toward the Arab-Israeli Conflict," in George W. Breslauer and Philip E. Tetlock, eds., *Learning in U.S. and Soviet Foreign Policy* (Boulder, Colo.: Westview Press, 1991), pp. 551–85.

12. Oles Smolansky, *The Soviet Union and the Arab East Under Khrushchev* (Lewisburg, Pa., Bucknell University Press, 1974); George W. Breslauer, "Ideology and Learning in Soviet Third World Policy," *World Politics* 39, 3 (April 1987), pp. 429–48; Yaacov Ro'i, *From Encroachment to Involvement: A Documentary Study of Soviet Policy in the Middle East, 1945–1973* (New York: John Wiley & Sons, 1974).

13. Cited by Erwin Weit, *At the Red Summit: Interpreter Behind the Iron Curtain* (New York: Macmillan, 1973), pp. 139–40. Weit was Gomułka's interpreter and this description is drawn from his notes of the meeting between Brezhnev, Ulbricht, and Gomułka.

14. Brezhnev used the term "perestroika" in November 1972. See *Leninskim kursom: Rechi i stat'i*, vol. IV (13 November 1972), p. 26. The concept of the "channeling" of international conflict was first put forward by Georgi Arbatov in August 1963, during the brief period of détente under Khrushchev, at about the same time as Burlatsky advanced the concept of "imperialist adaptation." See *Pravda*, 13 May 1963. We are indebted to Franklyn Griffiths for Russian-language citations in this chapter.

15. For Kissinger's description of the negotiations that began at Soviet initiative, see Henry Kissinger, *Years of Upheaval* (Boston: Little, Brown, 1972), pp. 274–86. Raymond L. Garthoff provides a detailed analysis of the negotiations culminating in the two agreements. See *Détente and Confrontation: American-Soviet Relations from Nixon to Reagan* (Washington, D.C.: The Brookings Institution, 1985), pp. 330–59. See also Alexander L. George, *Towards a Soviet-American Crisis Prevention Regime: History and Prospects* (Los Angeles: UCLA, ACIS Working Paper 28, 1980) and *Managing U.S.-Soviet Rivalry: Problems of Crisis Prevention* (Boulder, Colo.: Westview Press, 1983).

16. U.S. Department of State, *The Washington Summit: General Secretary Brezhnev's Visit to the United States, June 18–25, 1973* (Washington, D.C.: Government Printing Office, 1973, Publication 8733), pp. 30–31.

17. *Leninskim kursom: Rechi i stat'i*, vol. IV (11 July 1973), p. 197.

18. Georgi Arbatov, "Soviet-American Relations at a New Stage," *Pravda*, 22 July 1973, cited by Garthoff, *Détente and Confrontation*, p. 333.

19. *The Washington Summit*, broadcast by Leonid Brezhnev in the United States, 24 June 1973, pp. 43–48.

20. *Department of State Bulletin*, 26 June 1972, pp. 898–99.

21. Quoted by Murrey Marder, "Brezhnev Extols A-Pact," *Washington Post*, 24 June 1973, cited by Garthoff, *Détente and Confrontation*, p. 344. The official TASS release two days later went on to describe the agreement as "one of the most significant agreements in contemporary international relations." TASS, Radio Moscow, 25 June 1973, in *Foreign Broadcast Information Service* (FBIS), Daily Report: Soviet Union, 25 June 1973, p. AA4, cited by Garthoff, pp. 344–45.

22. In the first year after the agreement, there were numerous favorable references by Soviet leaders and in the academic, military, and popular press. As Garthoff ob-

serves, in the Soviet Union, the Prevention of Nuclear War Agreement was generally ranked, together with the Basic Principles Agreement of 1972 and the SALT I agreement, as the most important of the Soviet-American accords. *Détente and Confrontation*, p. 345.

23. Spartak Beglov, "Mr. Brezhnev's Visit," *New York Times*, 29 June 1973.

24. Georgi Arbatov, *Pravda*, 22 July 1973, cited by Garthoff, *Détente and Confrontation*, p. 352.

25. "Soviet-American Relations at a New Stage," *Pravda*, 22 July 1973, pp. 4–5.

26. M. Kudrin, *Mezhdunarodnaya zhizn'* 9 (1973), p. 14, cited by Garthoff, *Détente and Confrontation*, p. 349. See also Coit D. Blacker, "The Kremlin and Détente: Soviet Conceptions, Hopes, and Expectations," in George, *Managing U.S.-Soviet Rivalry*, pp. 121–29.

27. Henry Trofimenko, *Changing Attitudes Toward Deterrence* (Los Angeles: University of California at Los Angeles, Center for International and Strategic Affairs, ACIS Working Paper 25, 1980), pp. 4–11.

28. D. Volsky, "Peaceful Coexistence and the Third World," *Soviet Military Review* (Moscow) 1 (January 1973), pp. 52–54; O. Mikhailov, "A Turn Toward Cooperation," *Soviet Military Review* 8 (August 1973), pp. 44–46; A. Kiva, "Détente and the National Liberation Movement," *Soviet Military Review* 7 (July 1974), pp. 49–51, cited by Garthoff, *Détente and Confrontation*, p. 348.

29. Brezhnev argued that in view of the irreconcilable differences and the class aims of the two social systems, the international class struggle would continue in economics, politics, and ideology. At the same time, the Soviet Union was ready to cooperate with all governments and peoples prepared to uphold the peace. *Leninskim kursom: Rechi i stat'i*, vol. IV (21 December 1972), p. 81.

30. Khrushchev's successors often linked strategies of political and economic reform at home to the Soviet relationship with the Western capitalist countries abroad. Partly in reaction to the humiliation of the Cuban missile crisis, Khrushchev's successors were determined to avoid the "appeasement" of the United States that followed in its wake. At home, they sought to provide less "erratic," more predictable, and more stable leadership. They rejected Khrushchev's commitment to radical political and social transformation from below. Within that broad consensus, the most senior members of the Politburo disagreed sharply about domestic priorities and strategies toward the United States and Europe in the early years after Khrushchev's ouster. The important domestic issues were the relative importance of agriculture and light industry, the priority of the rural and urban consumer, appropriate administrative reform, and the role of material incentives and party incentives in stimulating labor productivity. George Breslauer, *Khrushchev and Brezhnev as Leaders: Building Authority in Soviet Politics* (London: Allen & Unwin, 1982), p. 140.

Kosygin's domestic and foreign preferences were closely connected. Reacting in part to the failed experiments under Khrushchev, Kosygin advocated an emphasis on industrial and consumer goods and administrative reform to decentralize decisions into the hands of factory and plant managers. Abroad, he was a strong supporter of international economic exchange with capitalist countries which he expected to improve economic efficiency in the Soviet Union. *Pravda*, 5 April 1965. Alone among the four, Kosygin urged economic cooperation with all the capitalist countries, including the United States, and a stable political relationship that would facilitate economic cooperation.

Nikolai Podgorny's domestic and international preferences were less "radical" than those of Kosygin. He, too, supported administrative decentralization to transfer authority to factory managers, not, as Kosygin proposed, to make socialism more efficient but to improve delivery of public goods, the housing and social services available to the Soviet worker. He also supported restraint in defense spending to free resources for social consumption. Abroad, he urged the formation of a broad international coalition of capitalist and Third World governments to resist American imperialism. *Pravda*, 1 April 1966. He advocated trade with capitalist countries other than the United States to further his objectives of reform at home and a worldwide coalition against the United States abroad.

Brezhnev also linked his domestic and foreign preferences, but these preferences were dramatically different from those of Kosygin and Podgorny. The General Secretary gave priority to agriculture and opposed decentralization. He emphasized the leading role of the party in the economy but nevertheless encouraged an expanded role for experts, specialists, and scientists to improve technological innovation. Abroad, Brezhnev supported international cooperation only with other socialist powers and urged support of armed revolutionaries battling capitalism in the Third World. "Peace . . . depends . . . on strengthening the cohesion of all anti-imperialist forces and in the first place on the unity of socialist countries and the world communist movement." *Pravda*, 20 October 1964. He argued that it was "necessary to force the imperialists to refrain from interference in internal affairs of other peoples, from loosing local wars." *Pravda*, 11 September 1965, 24 October 1965. Brezhnev was the strongest advocate among the four of military spending on both conventional and nuclear arms.

Mikhail Suslov, like Brezhnev, gave priority to defense, but emphasized investment in Soviet industry, not agriculture. He too favored continuing centralized administration to manage the economy. His strategy abroad and that of his protégé Boris Ponomarev, who headed the International Department of the Central Committee, were consistent with their vision of the progress of socialism at home. They supported a broad ideological alliance with communist parties and progressive governments in the Third World to bring about socialist transformation. *Pravda*, 28 April 1965. For an excellent summary of the preferences of the senior leadership during this period, see Richard Anderson, *Competitive Politics and Soviet Foreign Policy: Authority-Building and Bargaining in the Brezhnev Politburo*, Ph.D. diss., University of California, Berkeley, 1989.

31. Harry Gelman, *The Brezhnev Politburo and the Decline of Detente* (Ithaca, N.Y.: Cornell University Press, 1984), p. 84.

32. Leonid I. Brezhnev, *Leninskim kursom: Rechi i stat'i* vols. I–V (Moscow: Politizdat, 1970–76), II (13 April 1970), p. 520. Brezhnev modified his earlier concentration on agriculture and defense and began to emphasize the importance of the scientific and technological revolution in production, the need to increase labor productivity through a mixture of incentives and mobilization, and the importance of improving planning by raising the level of technical expertise among party cadres. Peter Volten, *Brezhnev's Peace Program: A Study of Soviet Domestic Political Process and Power* (Boulder, Colo.: Westview Press, 1982), p. 67. For the first time, despite falling growth rates, the Ninth Five-Year Plan (1971–1975) called for an increase in investment in light industry that would exceed the increase in investment in heavy industry.

33. For an analysis of Soviet thinking on comparative economic performance, see Bruce Parrott, *Politics and Technology in the Soviet Union* (Cambridge, Mass.: MIT Press, 1983), chap. 6.

34. The concept of imperialist "adaptation" was first advanced in 1963 by Fedor M. Burlatsky, one of Khrushchev's principal speechwriters. *Pravda*, 25 July 1963. It was later endorsed by Suslov in 1965 and by Brezhnev in November 1967. For an analysis of Soviet "reformist" and "expansionist" thinking, see Franklyn Griffiths, "Attempted Learning: Soviet Policy Toward the United States in the Brezhnev Era," in George Breslauer and Philip Tetlock, eds., *Learning in U.S. and Soviet Foreign Policy*, pp. 630–83.

35. Georgi Arbatov, *The War of Ideas in Contemporary International Relations* (Moscow: Progress Publishers, 1973), pp. 103, 121–22.

36. This position was long advocated by Aleksei Kosygin. As early as 1966, Kosygin argued that the expansion of trade could overcome the chronic technological sluggishness of the Soviet economy. He expected a synergistic linkage between trade and security: trade would create a friendlier attitude to the Soviet Union in the West while Soviet diplomacy would simultaneously increase the scope for trade. *Pravda*, 5 April 1966. For an analysis of the opposition of Politburo members to increasing trade with the United States, see Garthoff, *Détente and Confrontation*, pp. 88–89. For a discussion of selective détente, see Garthoff, *Détente and Confrontation*, p. 14.

37. Breslauer, "Ideology and Learning in Soviet Third World Policy," pp. 566–67, makes a similar argument that Soviet leaders responded to heightened perceptions of both opportunity and risk.

38. Breslauer, *Khrushchev and Brezhnev as Leaders*, and Anderson, *Competitive Politics and Soviet Foreign Policy*, develop the concepts of authority-building and political consolidation.

39. For an analysis of the Politburo under Brezhnev, see Gelman, *The Brezhnev Politburo and the Decline of Detente*; Breslauer, *Khrushchev and Brezhnev as Leaders*; and John Lenczowski, *Soviet Perceptions of U.S. Foreign Policy: A Study of Ideology, Power, and Consensus* (Ithaca, N.Y.: Cornell University Press, 1982).

40. Analysts of Soviet politics distinguish between several types of domestic politics that condition foreign policy. Some view the Politburo as an oligarchy, responsible to no constituency, and treat foreign policy as a compromise among oligarchs. See, for example, Gelman, *The Brezhnev Politburo and the Decline of Detente*. Breslauer emphasizes not the compromise among interests but the imperatives of authority-building in a Politburo that functioned by consensus, *Khrushchev and Brezhnev as Leaders*. Anderson sees political competition among Politburo members for the support of domestic constituencies outside the Politburo, which leads members to differentiate their positions sharply, to advance contradictory proposals, and then to compromise, Richard D. Anderson, *Visions of Socialism: Competitive Politics and the Dynamics of Soviet Global Policy*, unpublished manuscript, 1990. Franklyn Griffiths sees broad tendencies at work among the Soviet political elite, "Attempted Learning: Soviet Policy Toward the United States in the Brezhnev Era."

41. Interview, Georgiy Kornienko, Moscow, 16 December 1991.

42. Interview, Victor Israelian, State College, Pa., 8 January 1992.

43. Henry Kissinger, *White House Years* (Boston: Little, Brown, 1979), pp. 1139–40.

44. Interview, Leonid Zamyatin, Moscow, 16 December 1991.

45. Georgi Arbatov, *The System: An Insider's Life in Soviet Politics* (New York: Random House, 1992), p. 183. Andropov subsequently told Arbatov confidentially that great pressure had been put on Brezhnev to cancel the meeting.

46. Arbatov, *The System*, p. 184.

47. Arbatov, *The System*, pp. 186, 172.

48. He challenged Brezhnev's contention that trade was important in its own right; in front of Nixon, he insisted that SALT was more important than commercial ties because it dealt with national security.

Kissinger, *White House Years*, pp. 1214–16, provides a vivid portrait of Brezhnev, Kosygin, and Podgorny at the summit sessions.

These meetings with the top Soviet leadership, though inconclusive, provided interesting insights into the Soviet power structure. Brezhnev held no governmental position but was clearly the top man; yet he appeared to need the support of Kosygin and Podgorny to carry the Politburo with him. At any rate, he made a great show of involving them in all decisions, going so far as to insist that the invitation for a Soviet return visit to the United States—which was included in the communiqué—mention the names of his associates.

Of Brezhnev's colleagues, Kosygin was by far the most impressive. Though subordinate to Brezhnev in power and authority and not charged with conducting definitive talks on sensitive issues, he spoke on them with assurance and always with great precision. . . . But outside the economic area, on foreign policy questions, for example, Kosygin struck me as orthodox if not rigid. It seemed almost as if he compensated for managerial pragmatism by the strictest piety on ideological matters.

As for Podgorny, he was the hardest to fathom, perhaps because there was no depth there to penetrate. He clearly was third in influence among our hosts. . . . He had neither the elemental force of Brezhnev nor the sharp intellect of Kosygin. He spoke his piece; he sometimes intervened in eccentric ways; but he never gave the impression of someone who was expected to prevail, dominate, or exercise a decisive influence.

49. At one of the sessions, Brezhnev said: "It was certainly difficult for us to agree to hold this meeting under present circumstances. And yet we did agree to hold it. I want to explain why. We felt that preliminary work prior to the meeting warranted the hope that two powers with such economic might and such a high level of civilization and all the other necessary prerequisites could come together to promote better relations between our two nations." Cited by Kissinger, *White House Years*, p. 1226.

50. Gelman, *The Brezhnev Politburo and the Decline of Detente*, p. 157.

51. Kornienko remembers that "Before Nixon came to Moscow for the summit there was harsh discussion. Podgorny opposed the visit. He favored better relations with the United States but was against the visit then because of the timing." Interview, Georgiy Kornienko, Moscow, 16 December 1991.

52. Interview, Leonid Zamyatin, Moscow, 16 December 1991.

53. Interview, Victor Israelian, State College, Pa., 6 January 1992.

54. Analysts of Soviet politics, drawing on indirect evidence, suggest that Brezhnev, the general secretary and preeminent member of the Politburo, was strongly in favor of the summit, as were Prime Minister Aleksei Kosygin, Andrei

Kirilenko, a loyal Brezhnev supporter, and A. Y. Pelshe. Brezhnev could also count on the support of Shcherbitsky, Kunayev, and Kulakov. Chairman of the Supreme Soviet Nikolai V. Podgorny favored restriction of military spending but was skeptical of a détente with the United States that would constrain the Soviet Union and favored postponement of the summit. Mikhail Suslov, responsible for policies in the international communist movement, and two other Politburo members, K. T. Mazurov and Petr Shelest, were evidently opposed. Outside the Politburo, Marshal Andrei Grechko, responsible for defense, K. F. Katushev, responsible for liaison with ruling communist parties, and Boris Ponomarev, head of the International Department of the Central Committee, apparently were deeply skeptical of a détente that would constrain in any way the Soviet capacity to compete actively in the Third World. This reconstruction of the preferences of members of the Politburo draws on the analyses of Anderson, *Visions of Socialism*, Volten, *Brezhnev's Peace Program*, and Grey Hodnett, "Succession Contingencies in the Soviet Union," *Problems of Communism* 24, 1 (January–February 1975), pp. 21–37.

55. Victor Israelian noted that, during this period, Brezhnev was able to remove those who opposed him or appoint them to positions to get them out of his way. For example, during the October War, he appointed Suslov as chairman of the Commission of the Politburo on the Middle East, where he was able to neutralize his influence. Interview, State College, Pa., 8 January 1992.

56. Interview, Leonid Zamyatin, Moscow, 16 December 1991.

57. Interviews, Victor Israelian, State College, Pa., 8 January 1992 and Leonid Zamyatin, Moscow, 16 December 1991.

58. For testimony to the importance of Andropov in sponsoring and protecting the careers of younger reformers during the Brezhnev years, see Stephen F. Cohen and Katrina vanden Heuvel, *Voices of Glasnost: Interviews with Gorbachev's Reformers* (New York: Norton, 1989).

59. Interview, Victor Israelian, State College, Pa., 8 January 1992.

60. Interviews, Victor Israelian, State College, Pa., 8 January 1992 and Leonid Zamyatin, Moscow, 16 December 1991.

61. Arbatov, *The System*, p.172.

62. Interview, Victor Israelian, State College, Pa., 8 January 1992.

63. Ibid.

64. Gelman, *The Brezhnev Politburo and the Decline of Detente*, p. 60.

65. Interview, Vadim Zagladin, Moscow, 18 May 1989.

66. See Griffiths, "Attempted Learning," p. 54. On military matters, Brezhnev also had access to the advice of the Defense Council. The existence of the Defense Council was only made public by Brezhnev in 1976. *Pravda*, 9 May 1976. Chaired by Brezhnev, it apparently included ex officio Premier Kosygin, Nikolai Podgorny, Defense Minister Grechko, Dimitri Ustinov, then secretary of the Central Committee in charge of defense production, Gen. Kulakov, the chief of the General Staff, and L. V. Smirnov, the chairman of the Military-Industrial Commission. See Raymond Garthoff, "SALT and the Soviet Military," *Problems of Communism*, 24, 1 (January–February 1975), p. 29. The Council, a body that excluded most of the Politburo, provided an independent body of advice to the General Secretary on military matters.

Kissinger provides somewhat contradictory evidence on the role of the Defense Council. In describing the sessions at the summit, he first observes: "On military matters Brezhnev as Chairman of the Council of National Defense seemed to have exclusive authority; hence he met Nixon alone to discuss SALT." *White House*

Years, p. 1214. In a subsequent meeting with Gromyko during the summit, Kissinger notes that the foreign minister "was accompanied by a personality new to all Americans present. He was introduced as Deputy Premier L. V. Smirnov . . . he held the position of chairman of the Soviet Military-Industrial Commission, a Party-state organization in charge of all defense industries. Smirnov turned out to be bullet-headed, heavyset, and brilliant." *White House Years*, pp. 1233–34.

67. In the domestic political arena, Breslauer notes: "He [Brezhnev] was able to have his way on agricultural investment priorities, the role of party intervention in public administration, the role of party mobilization in incentive policy, aggrandizement of the budgetary claims of the military-industrial complex, the relative status of party officials versus executives and specialists, and the relationship of foreign trade and détente to Soviet domestic policy. All of these were contentious issues within the leadership, and while we may assume that Brezhnev felt constrained to forge compromises, it is also clear that his basic biases prevailed. Moreover, Brezhnev was able to seize the initiative from Kosygin, co-opt, preempt, and redefine issues, and force through changes in direction. It remains an open question whether these successes resulted largely from Brezhnev's alliance with the more conservative political forces, or from his control over the levers of power through the office he occupied." *Khrushchev and Brezhnev as Leaders*, pp. 264–65. Whatever the source, Brezhnev had by now accumulated sufficient authority to avoid issue-trading.

68. Kissinger, *White House Years*, p. 230.

69. Interview, Georgi Arbatov, Moscow, 19 May 1989.

70. Jack Snyder, "The Gorbachev Revolution: A Waning of Soviet Expansionism?" *International Security* 12, 3(Winter 1987/88), pp. 93–131.

71. *New York Times*, June 15, 1973. Archie Brown argues that "though Brezhnev is more than a first among equals within the Politburo, he is much less than a Khrushchev. There is no doubt that the Politburo collectively is now more powerful than the general secretary individually." "Political Developments: Some Conclusions and an Interpretation," in Archie Brown and Michael Kaser, eds., *The Soviet Union Since the Fall of Khrushchev* (London: Macmillan, 1978), pp. 218–75, quotation on p. 234. Peter Volten is even more conservative in his estimate of Brezhnev's power during this period: "Brezhnev was part of a collective leadership with basically shared responsibilities." *Brezhnev's Peace Program*, p. 75. Breslauer, by contrast, considers Brezhnev's power in this period significant: "Brezhnev was far more than a broker among interests. It is difficult to find many instances where Brezhnev was rebuffed or defeated on questions of priority and the direction of policy. Conflict on these matters was real and frequent, but Brezhnev almost always won." *Khrushchev and Brezhnev as Leaders*, p. 245.

72. Arbatov, *The System*, p. 201.

73. Interview, Victor Israelian, State College, Pa., 8 January 1992.

74. Fedor Burlatsky, "Brezhnev and the Collapse of the Thaw: Thoughts on the Nature of Political Leadership," *Literaturnaya Gazeta* 14 September 1988, no. 37, pp. 13–14.

75. Fedor Burlatsky, "Democratization is a Long March," in Cohen and Heuvel, *Voices of Glasnost: Interviews with Gorbachev's Reformers*, pp. 174–96, quotation on p. 182.

76. Donald Trelford, "A Walk in the Woods with Gromyko," *The Observer* (London), 2 April 1989; interview, Victor Israelian, State College, Pa., 8 January 1992.

77. Interview, Georgiy Kornienko, Moscow, 16 December 1991.

78. Interview, Henry Kissinger, New York, 19 June 1991.

79. Alvin Z. Rubinstein, *Red Star on the Nile: The Soviet-Egyptian Influence Relationship since the June War* (Princeton, N.J.: Princeton University Press, 1977), p. 139, n. 22, disputes the contention that Sadat had no success in securing Soviet arms. He reports that in March and April of 1971, after a secret visit by Sadat to Moscow, the Soviets sent 150 MiG-21s and 20 Sukhoi-7 fighter-bombers, and thickened the air-defense system in the interior of Egypt. This would not have met Sadat's requests for sophisticated long-range attack aircraft and missiles that his generals considered a critical prerequisite for an attack against Israel. During his trip to Moscow in October 1971, Sadat's request for additional military assistance was not met.

80. *Pravda*, 27 May 1971.

81. Mahmoud Riad, *The Struggle for Peace in the Middle East* (London: Quartet Books, 1981), p. 180.

82. *Pravda*, 30 April 1972, emphasis added.

83. As late as 1 May 1973, Sadat noted: "There are no differences between us and the Soviet Union, except over one thing. . . . Continuation of the cease-fire serves Israel and serves U.S. aims in the end. . . . Our friends in the Soviet Union continue to believe in the forthcoming process of the peaceful solution. . . . We appreciate the attitude of our friends. We may differ from them, but we do so honestly." Radio Cairo, 1 May 1973.

84. Lt. Gen. Saad el-Shazly, *The Crossing of the Suez* (San Francisco: American Mideast Research, 1980), p. 143.

85. Evgueny Pyrlin, *Some Observations (Memoirs) About the Arab-Israeli War (1973)*, unpublished memorandum commissioned for this project, Moscow, August 1992.

86. Yevgeny Primakov, a leading Middle Eastern specialist, subsequently acknowledged that the economic and political difficulties of Arab governments were increasing visibly. "Egypt," he noted, "was compelled to keep a mass army and spend about 1,000 million Egyptian pounds per year on defense. Syria's defense spending claimed 60 percent of its budget appropriations." Yevgeny Primakov, "The Fourth Arab-Israeli War," *World Marxist Review* 16, 12(December 1973), pp. 52–60, quotation on p. 56.

87. Interview, senior official in President Sadat's office, Cairo, May 1977. Saudi Arabia and Kuwait agreed to provide the hard currency at a special meeting of the Arab Defense Council in Cairo in January 1973. They gave Egypt $300–$500 million in hard currency for weapons and $500 million in balance-of-payments support. Rubinstein, *Red Star on the Nile*, p. 241. Egyptian officials maintain that although the lack of hard currency was a problem, this was not the major stumbling block in securing arms deliveries from the Soviet Union. Interview, Ambassador Tahseen Bashir, Los Angeles, 27 August 1990.

88. Pyrlin, *Some Observations (Memoirs) About the Arab-Israeli October War (1973)*, p. 6.

89. Apart from his meeting with Brezhnev and Gromyko, Isma'il met with Gromyko and his deputy Kuznetsov from the Foreign Ministry, Army Chief-of-Staff Kulikov, and Deputy Economics Minister Arkhipov. Galia Golan, "Soviet Decisionmaking in the Yom Kippur War, 1973," in Jiri Valenta and William Potter, eds., *Soviet Decisionmaking for National Security* (London: Allen & Unwin, 1984), pp. 185–217, at p. 194.

90. *Izvestiya*, 11 February 1973.

91. Kissinger, *White House Years*, pp. 296–98.

92. Cited by Richard M. Nixon, *RN: The Memoirs of Richard Nixon* (New York: Grosset and Dunlap, 1978), pp. 879, 884–86.

93. Interview, Aleksandr Kislov, Moscow, 18 May 1989, emphasis added.

94. Brezhnev's surprising request for an unscheduled meeting late at night with President Nixon and his emotional tone may seem inconsistent with an intentional warning. An interesting parallel occurred at the Moscow summit in 1972. At an unplanned meeting in Brezhnev's dacha, Brezhnev, pounding the table, engaged in an emotional diatribe against American policy in Vietnam. Kissinger subsequently observed that "Suddenly the thought struck me that for all the bombast and rudeness, we were participants in a charade. . . . The Soviet leaders were not pressing us except with words. They were speaking for the record, and when they had said enough to have a transcript to send to Hanoi, they would stop." *White House Years*, p. 1227. Emotional attacks by Brezhnev were consistent with deliberate, planned interventions.

95. President Sadat informed the Soviet Ambassador to Egypt, Vladimir Vinogradov, that a coordinated military attack by Egypt and Syria was imminent. President Assad of Syria also informed the Soviet Ambassador to Syria, Nuritidin Mukhitdinov. V. Vinogradov, "October War Counter Claims," *al-Safir* (Beirut), 16 April 1974, reprinted in *Journal of Palestine Studies* 3, 4 (Summer 1974), pp. 161–64. At the same time as Soviet dependents were evacuated, a COSMOS satellite was launched over the area, ships were moved out of Alexandria and other Egyptian and Syrian ports, and the Soviet fleet took up positions off Crete.

96. Drawing on his notes taken at the time, Victor Israelian writes that he was called to the office of Foreign Minister Andrei Gromyko, along with Vasiliy V. Kuznetsov, the first deputy to the foreign minister, Georgiy U. Kornienko, the head of the Department of the U.S., and Mikhail Sytenko, the head of the Department of the Near East, on 4 October at 7:00 P.M. Gromyko informed them that Egypt and Syria had made their final decision to attack on Saturday, 6 October, at 2:00 P.M. Gromyko informed them that measures were being taken to evacuate Soviet citizens from Egypt and Syria and ordered the group to prepare telegrams to Ambassador Vinogradov in Cairo and Ambassador Mukhitdinov in Damascus. Victor Israelian, *The Kremlin: October 1973*, unpublished manuscript, p. 1.

97. Interview, Aleksandr Kislov, Moscow, 18 May 1989.

98. Interview, Victor Israelian, State College, Pa., 8 January 1992.

99. Interview of senior Egyptian official, May 1988. Podgorny made this argument repeatedly in his discussions with Egyptian officials. See Anderson, *Visions of Socialism*.

100. Anderson, *Visions of Socialism*, offers this explanation of Podgorny's unusual preeminence in policy toward the Arabs in 1971.

101. Interview, Aleksandr Kislov, Moscow, 16 December 1991.

102. Interview, Leonid Zamyatin, Moscow, 16 December 1991.

103. The Politburo included the eleven members from 1966 who were reelected: L. I. Brezhnev, A. P. Kirilenko, A. N. Kosygin, K. T. Mazurov, A. Ya. Pel'she, N. V. Podgorny, D. S. Polyansky, M. A. Suslov, A. N. Shelepin, P. E. Shelest, and G. I. Voronov. In 1971, Brezhnev expanded the membership of the Politburo to include V. V. Shcherbitsky, premier of the Ukraine, D. A. Kunayev, first secretary of the Kazakhstan party, F. D. Kulakov, the secretary of the Central Committee responsible

for agriculture, and V. V. Grishin, first secretary of the Moscow party. The first three were strong Brezhnev supporters. The four additions brought the total membership to fifteen.

104. For a discussion of "political competition" and authority building in Soviet politics, see Anderson, *Visions of Socialism*. Anderson argues that in addition to separating the Middle East and Vietnam from global strategy, Brezhnev's authorization of a crackdown on separatist activity in the Ukraine was a partial concession to Suslov and his protégé Ponomarev and induced them to approve Brezhnev's foreign policy. At the same meeting, as a direct individual payment, Ponomarev was promoted to alternate membership in the Politburo.

105. For analysis of changes within the Politburo and their impact on foreign and domestic policy, see Gelman, *The Brezhnev Politburo and the Decline of Detente*. Breslauer, *Khrushchev and Brezhnev as Leaders*, examines changes in the Politburo as a function of political competition and the building of authority. For an analysis that argues that Politburo members are accountable to their peers rather than to constituencies, see Lenczowski, *Soviet Perceptions of U.S. Foreign Policy*.

106. This argument is made by Gelman, *The Brezhnev Politburo and the Decline of Detente*, p. 155; Robert O. Freedman, *Soviet Policy Toward the Middle East Since 1970* (New York: Praeger, 1978), pp. 88, 132–34; and Bruce Porter, *The USSR in Third World Conflicts: Soviet Arms and Diplomacy in Local Wars, 1945–1980* (Cambridge: Cambridge University Press, 1984), pp. 121–22.

107. Ismail Fahmy, *Negotiating for Peace in the Middle East* (Baltimore: The Johns Hopkins University Press, 1983), p. 9.

108. Interview, Victor Israelian, State College, Pa., 8 January 1992.

109. Pyrlin, *Some Observations (Memoirs) About the Arab-Israeli October War (1973)*, pp. 3–4.

110. Interview, senior Egyptian officer in military planning, April 1988.

111. Interview, Aleksandr Kislov, Moscow, 18 May 1989.

112. Primakov, "The Fourth Arab-Israeli War," p. 57.

113. Pyrlin, *Some Observations (Memoirs) About the Arab-Israeli War (1973)*, p. 2.

114. Interview, Georgiy Kornienko, Moscow, 16 December 1991. See also Golan, "Soviet Decisionmaking in the Yom Kippur War, 1973," pp. 189–93.

115. Interview, Aleksandr Kislov, Moscow, 18 May 1989.

116. See Dina Rome Spechler, *Domestic Influences on Soviet Foreign Policy* (New York: University Press of America, 1978), for indirect evidence of the views of the military based on an analysis of the military press.

117. Interview, Gen. Yuri Yakovlevich Kirshin, Moscow, 17 December 1991.

118. Interview, Vadim Zagladin, Moscow, 18 May 1989.

119. George Breslauer makes a related if distinct argument in his analysis of the imperatives of "collaboration-competition." See his *Soviet Strategy in the Middle East* (London: Unwin Hyman, 1989).

120. Pyrlin, *Some Observations (Memoirs) About the Arab-Israeli October War (1973)*, pp. 6–7.

121. Interview, Victor Israelian, State College, Pa., 8 January 1992.

122. Interview, Vadim Zagladin, Moscow, 18 May 1989.

123. Cairo Radio, 3 April 1974. President Sadat was even more explicit on 1 May 1973: "Our friends in the Soviet Union must know that the peaceful solution, which the United States has been talking about, is fictitious." *Radio Cairo*, 1 May 1973. See

also Muhammad Hasanayn Haykal, *The Sphinx and the Commissar* (London: Collins, 1978).

124. From February to June 1973, Egypt received more arms from the Soviet Union than it had in the previous two years.

125. Cited in Haykal, *The Sphinx and the Commissar*, p. 254.

126. See Stein, "Calculation, Miscalculation, and Conventional Deterrence I: The View from Cairo," in *Psychology and Deterrence*, pp. 34–59.

127. Janice Gross Stein, "Proxy wars—how superpowers end them: the diplomacy of war termination in the Middle East," *International Journal* 35, 3 (Summer 1980), pp. 478–519, at pp. 514–15.

128. The text of the Soviet-American communiqué that dealt with the Middle East read as follows: "The two Sides set out their positions on this question. They reaffirm their support for a peaceful settlement in the Middle East in accordance with Security Council Resolution 242. Noting the significance of the constructive cooperation of the parties concerned with the Special Representative of the UN Secretary General, Ambassador Jarring, the US and the USSR confirm their desire to contribute to his mission's success and also declare their readiness to play their part in bringing about a peaceful settlement in the Middle East. In the view of the US and the USSR, the achievement of such a settlement would open prospects for normalization of the Middle East situation and would permit, in particular, consideration of further steps to bring about a military relaxation in that area." Cited in Kissinger, *White House Years*, p. 1493, n. 3. It was the last sentence that particularly angered Sadat.

129. Sadat, *In Search of Identity*, p. 229; Interview, Tahseen Bashir, Ottawa, 17 February 1981.

130. Fahmy, *Negotiating for Peace in the Middle East*, p. 6.

131. Interview, Victor Israelian, State College, Pa., 8 January 1992.

132. *Newsweek*, 9 April 1973.

133. Interview, Victor Israelian, State College, Pa., 8 January 1992.

134. For a discussion of the impact of "loss aversion" on strategic choices, see Janice Gross Stein and Louis Pauly, eds., *Choosing to Cooperate: How States Avoid Loss* (Baltimore: Johns Hopkins University Press, 1993).

135. "Expansionist internationalism" argued that the Soviet Union must support anti-imperialist forces in the struggle of opposed systems to compel the United States to cooperate on terms favorable to the Soviet Union. "Reformative internationalism" insisted that the struggle between opposed social systems must be "channeled" by cooperating at the interstate level to demilitarize the struggle and advance socialism through peaceful competition in areas of disputed interest. For an analysis of "tendencies" in Soviet thinking about the United States, see Franklyn Griffiths, "The Sources of American Conduct: Soviet Perspectives and Their Policy Implications," *International Security* 9, 2 (Fall 1984), pp. 3–50. Griffiths' analysis does not focus on constituencies and political competition, but rather on broad strains of thinking that persisted in Soviet discourse and combined differently when domestic and international conditions varied.

136. Interview, Gen. Yuri Yakovlevich Kirshin, Moscow, 17 December 1991.

137. This combination of tendencies was dominant throughout the 1970s in Soviet thinking about the Third World. See S. Neil MacFarlane, *Superpower Rivalry and Third World Radicalism: The Idea of National Liberation* (Baltimore: Johns Hopkins University Press, 1985); Elizabeth K. Valkenier, *The Soviet Union and the*

Third World: An Economic Bind (New York: Praeger, 1983); Mark N. Katz, *The Third World in Soviet Military Thought* (London: Croom Helm, 1982); and Breslauer, "Ideology and Learning in Soviet Third World Policy," pp. 429–48.

138. Gelman, *The Brezhnev Politburo and the Decline of Detente*, pp. 20, 46, 52–58, 83. Jack Snyder develops a similar concept of "offensive détente" in *Myths of Empire: Domestic Politics and International Ambition* (Ithaca, N.Y.: Cornell University Press, 1991), pp. 246–50.

139. Interview, Victor Israelian, State College, Pa., 8 January 1992.

140. Text of President Nixon's news conference on 27 January 1969, *New York Times*, 28 January 1969, p. 12.

141. For a detailed analysis of the beliefs of Nixon and Kissinger, see Deborah Welch Larson, "Learning in U.S.-Soviet Relations: The Nixon-Kissinger Structure of Peace," in George W. Breslauer and Philip E. Tetlock, eds., *Learning in U.S. and Soviet Foreign Policy*, pp. 350–99.

142. Text of President Nixon's news conference on 27 January 1969, *New York Times*, 28 January 1969, p. 12.

143. Richard M. Nixon, *U.S. Foreign Policy for the 1970s: Building for Peace* (Washington, D.C.: Government Printing Office, 25 February 1971) and Kissinger, *Years of Upheaval*, pp. 235–46.

144. Nixon privately promised the Soviet Union a grain agreement and revoked an executive order requiring that 50 percent of grain be carried on U.S. ships. See Garthoff, *Détente and Confrontation*, p. 183 and Larson, "Learning in U.S.-Soviet Relations: The Nixon-Kissinger Structure of Peace," pp. 383–84.

145. U.S. Senate, *Détente*, Hearings Before the Committee on Foreign Relations, 93d Cong., 2d sess. (Washington: U.S. Government Printing Office, 1975), p. 249.

146. Alexander L. George, "The Basic Principles Agreement of 1972: Origins and Expectations," in *Managing U.S.-Soviet Rivalry*, pp. 107–19, at p. 109; and "The Arab-Israeli War of October 1973: Origins and Impact," in *Managing U.S.-Soviet Rivalry*, pp. 139–54, at p. 139.

147. Interview, Henry Kissinger, New York, 19 June 1991.

148. Kissinger, *Years of Upheaval*, p. 482.

149. Ibid., p. 594.

150. Interview, Vadim Zagladin, Moscow, 18 May 1989.

151. *White House Years*, p. 1141.

152. Interview, senior official in President Sadat's Bureau, Cairo, April 1987.

153. Stein, "Calculation, Miscalculation, and Conventional Deterrence I," p. 64; *Agranat Report*, p. 7.

154. Stein, "Calculation, Miscalculation, and Conventional Deterrence I," pp. 45–46.

155. *White House Years*, p. 1296.

156. Kissinger, *Years of Upheaval*, pp. 296–98.

157. Garthoff, *Détente and Confrontation*, p. 365, n. 17, citing an interview with a senior member of the staff of the National Security Council involved in the contingency study.

158. Kissinger, *Years of Upheaval*, pp. 298.

159. Kissinger, *Years of Upheaval*, p. 461.

160. Interview, Henry Kissinger, New York, 19 June 1991.

161. Nixon, *RN: Memoirs of Richard Nixon*, pp. 339, 433.

162. Interview, Henry Kissinger, New York, 19 June 1991.

163. Kissinger, *White House Years*, pp. 1285–92 and *Years of Upheaval*, pp. 196, 204.

164. Kissinger, *Years of Upheaval*, p. 1248. Kissinger continued: "Peter Rodman, who was keeping the record for our side, obviously considered this an aspersion on his reliability, and kept interrupting me to hand me the precise text of Gromyko's proposal, which he had written down verbatim the first time it had been put forward. My repeated elbows in his side would not deter Peter each time we came to a new 'principle' on Gromyko's list."

165. Kissinger, *White House Years*, p. 1248. Drawing on interviews with a senior official in the Nixon administration, Alexander George confirms the deceptive quality of Kissinger's strategy toward the Soviet Union. See "The Arab-Israeli War of October 1973," pp. 143–44.

166. Kissinger, *White House Years*, p. 1247.

167. Kissinger, *Years of Upheaval*, p. 225.

168. Interview, former senior official of the State Department, Washington, April 1991.

169. Cited by Kissinger, *Years of Upheaval*, p. 211.

170. Nixon, *RN: Memoirs of Richard Nixon*, p. 786.

171. Kissinger, *Years of Upheaval*, pp. 205–6.

172. William B. Quandt, *Decade of Decisions: American Policy Toward the Arab-Israeli Conflict* (Berkeley: University of California Press, 1977), pp. 158–59.

173. Kissinger, *Years of Upheaval*, p. 296.

174. Interview, Aleksandr Kislov, Moscow, 18 May 1989.

175. Stein, "Calculation, Miscalculation, and Conventional Deterrence II: The View from Jerusalem," in *Psychology and Deterrence*, pp. 60–88.

176. See Griffiths, "The Sources of American Conduct," and "Attempted Learning."

177. Interview, Henry Kissinger, New York, 19 June 1991.

178. Garthoff, *Détente and Confrontation*, p. 338; George, *Managing U.S.-Soviet Rivalry*.

179. For a related but distinct argument, see George Breslauer, "Why Détente Failed: An Interpretation," in George, ed., *Managing U.S.-Soviet Rivalry*, pp. 319–39. Breslauer argues that détente was originally defined as a mixed collaborative-competitive relationship. It failed because each side tried to define the terms of the competition and collaboration in ways geared more toward maximizing unilateral advantage than toward expanding the mutual interest in institutionalizing the relationship.

CHAPTER EIGHT
The Failure to Limit the War: The Soviet and American Airlifts

1. Interview, Ambassador Victor Israelian, State College, Pa., 8 January 1992.

2. Henry Kissinger, *Years of Upheaval* (Boston: Little, Brown, 1982), pp. 515, 518.

3. Discussion at the Politburo meeting on 15 October, cited by Victor Israelian, *The Kremlin: October 1973*, unpublished monograph, pp. 13–14. Israelian was in a unique position to observe and record the discussion at Politburo meetings of 6–25 October. He explained that

I was with Brezhnev for almost a month, sitting and listening in the Kremlin. A working group of four people from the Foreign Ministry was constituted—Kuznetzov, who is now dead, Kornienko, Sytenko, and me—to attend all the meetings of the Politburo and take notes on the political action that would be required. I took personal notes throughout these meetings. It is because I have these notes that I remember so well. For the others, it was one of many crises. For me, it was the only Politburo meetings that I ever attended. Perhaps that is why I remember so well.

Interview, State College, Pa., 8 January 1992. Israelian drew on these notes to write *The Kremlin: October 1973*.

4. *Krasnaia zvezda*, *Komsomol'skaia Pravda*, *Trud*, and *Sovetskaia Rosiia*, all emphasized the importance of assuring the credibility of the Soviet Union as a reliable ally and supplier. See Galia Golan, "Soviet Decisionmaking in the Yom Kippur War, 1973," in Jiri Valenta and William Potter, eds., *Soviet Decisionmaking for National Security* (London: Allen & Unwin, 1984), pp. 185–217.

5. Henry Kissinger, Press Conference, 12 October 1973, *Department of State Bulletin*, 29 October 1973.

6. Interview, Victor Israelian, State College, Pa., 8 January 1992.

7. Chernenko drafted the decisions of the group. "This was always done by a grey-haired man who was sitting at a separate little table close to Brezhnev. He wrote everything down very painstakingly; from time to time he would pass documents and written messages to Brezhnev. He watched very carefully what was going on among the people who came. He was not just a secretary present at the meetings but their organizer. It was Chernenko who in a decade would occupy the place of the chairman at meetings of that kind." Israelian, *The Kremlin: October 1973*, p. 7.

8. Israelian, *The Kremlin: October 1973*, p. 7.

9. Ibid., pp. 7–8.

10. Interview, Gen. Yuri Yakovlevich Kirshin, Moscow, 17 December 1991.

11. Evgueny Pyrlin, *Some Observations (Memoirs) About the Arab-Israeli October War (1973)*, unpublished memorandum commissioned for this project, Moscow, August 1992, p. 2.

12. *The Kremlin: October 1973*, pp. 8–9, and interview, Victor Israelian, State College, Pa., 8 January 1992.

13. Interview, Victor Israelian, State College, Pa., 8 January 1992.

14. William B. Quandt, *Soviet Policy in the October War*, Rand R-1864-ISA (Santa Monica, Calif.: Rand, 1976), p. 33.

15. The general alert of the seven airborne divisions was at the level the Soviet Union refers to as "increased combat readiness." Douglas M. Hart, "Soviet Approaches to Crisis Management: The Military Dimension," *Survival* 26, 5 (September/October 1984), pp. 214–23.

16. Joseph F. Bouchard, *Command in Crisis: Four Case Studies* (New York: Columbia University Press, 1991), p. 170.

17. Jon Glassman, *Arms for the Arabs: The Soviet Union and the War in the Middle East* (Baltimore: The Johns Hopkins University Press, 1975), pp. 130–31.

18. Golan, "Soviet Decisionmaking in the Yom Kippur War," pp. 201–2.

19. Interview, Aleksandr Kislov, Moscow, 18 May 1989.

20. Interview, senior Egyptian official who was in the Crisis Operations Center during the war, April 1988.

21. Interview, Victor Israelian, State College, Pa., 8 January 1992.

22. Interview, Aleksandr Kislov, Moscow, 18 May 1989.

23. Interview, Leonid Zamyatin, Moscow, 16 December 1991.

24. Interview, Victor Israelian, State College, Pa., 8 January 1992. Israelian considers Kulikov's briefings biased against the Arab military leadership.

25. Interview, Aleksandr Kislov, Moscow, 18 May 1989.

26. Ibid.

27. Interviews, Aleksandr Kislov, Moscow, 18 May 1989 and Victor Israelian, State College, Pa., 8 January 1992.

28. Marshal Grechko, Minister of Defense and a member of the Politburo, spoke in Warsaw on 11 October and referred to the Middle East war as "proof" of the continued power of reactionary and aggressive forces in the world. *Pravda* did not report the speech but *Krasnaia zvedza* did. See Golan, "Soviet Decisionmaking in the Yom Kippur War," p. 203.

29. Pyrlin, *Some Observations (Memoirs) About the Arab-Israeli October War (1973)*, p. 5.

30. One of the most authoritative—and sympathetic—analyses of Soviet policy during the October War suggests that the alert of airborne divisions and the airlift of supplies were both motivated largely by defensive concerns; the alert was precautionary against an advance by Israel into Syria once the Golan Heights had been recaptured and deterrent against interference by Israel in the air and sea operation that was under way. Golan, "Soviet Decisionmaking in the Yom Kippur War," p. 202. William Quandt, then deputy to Harold Saunders in the Middle East office of the National Security Council staff, concurs. See William B. Quandt, *Decade of Decisions: American Policy Toward the Arab-Israeli Conflict, 1967–76* (Berkeley: University of California Press, 1977), p. 179. See also Dina Rome Spechler, *Domestic Influences on Soviet Foreign Policy* (New York: University Press of America, 1978).

31. Kissinger, *Years of Upheaval*, p. 499; Interview, Victor Israelian, State College, Pa., 8 January 1992.

32. Kissinger, *Years of Upheaval*, p. 499.

33. Unknown to the Politburo, Israel had sustained heavy losses and was running seriously low in stocks of consumable war material.

34. Interview, Aleksandr Kislov, Moscow, 16 December 1991.

35. Golan, "Soviet Decisionmaking in the Yom Kippur War," p. 204, suggests that Soviet leaders "must have calculated that their airlift to the Arabs would spark a US resupply of Israel (the discussion of which in Washington may well have been known to the Russians)." Soviet Embassy personnel in Washington were aware of the pressures on Washington to begin an airlift to Israel. Interview, Anatoliy Gromyko, Moscow, 18 May 1989.

36. Kissinger, *Years of Upheaval*, p. 499.

37. Interview, Victor Israelian, State College, Pa., 8 January 1992.

38. Brezhnev informed his colleagues at the meeting of the Politburo on 25 October that "Yesterday I gave instructions even to break the air bridge for some time." Israelian, *The Kremlin: October 1973*, p. 29.

39. The WSAG was established in 1969 and generally included the deputy secretaries of state and defense, the director of the CIA, and the chairman of the Joint Chiefs of Staff, together with whatever other experts were required. Kissinger, *Years of Upheaval*, p. 316; Quandt, *Decade of Decisions*, p. 170, n. 11.

40. Kissinger, *Years of Upheaval*, p. 459.

41. Ibid., p. 497.

42. Walter Isaacson, *Kissinger: A Biography* (New York: Simon & Schuster, 1992), p. 514. In his reconstruction of decision making on the airlift, Isaacson draws on transcripts of telephone conversations; memos of conversations taken by staff members; meeting notes; and interviews, Henry Kissinger, 21 January and 8 May 1990; James Schlesinger, 16 October and 17 November 1989; Simcha Dinitz, 16 March 1990; Joseph Sisco, 5 March and 26 March 1990; Richard Nixon, 11 October 1990; Kenneth Rush, 9 January 1991. Some of the records of meetings and telephone transcripts were shown to Isaacson on the condition that quotations not be directly attributed.

43. Transcript of Kissinger-Haig telephone conversation, 6 October 1973, cited by Isaacson, *Kissinger: A Biography*, p. 513.

44. Alan Dowty, *Middle East Crisis: U.S. Decision-Making in 1958, 1970, and 1973* (Berkeley: University of California Press, 1984), p. 227.

45. Steven L. Spiegel, *The Other Arab-Israeli Conflict: Making America's Middle East Policy from Truman to Reagan* (Chicago: University of Chicago Press, 1985), p. 250; Kissinger, *Years of Upheaval*, pp. 485–86.

46. Isaacson, *Kissinger: A Biography*, p. 515.

47. Israel has never acknowledged officially that it has a nuclear capability. Seymour M. Hersh, *The Samson Option: Israel's Nuclear Arsenal and American Foreign Policy* (New York: Random House, 1991), pp. 225–27, reports that Prime Minister Meir's "kitchen cabinet" ordered the arming and targeting of Jericho missiles capable of carrying nuclear warheads on 8 October. Shimon Peres, the director-general of the Ministry of Defense when Israel began its nuclear program and primarily responsible for the development of the Jericho missile, categorically denied that Jericho missiles were made ready, much less armed. At most, he insisted, there was an operational check. The cabinet never approved any alert of Jericho missiles. Interview, Shimon Peres, Toronto, 31 March 1993.

48. Interview, William Quandt, 9 January 1992.

49. Kissinger, *Years of Upheaval*, p. 493; Golda Meir, *My Life* (New York: Dell, 1975), p. 415.

50. Kissinger, *Years of Upheaval*, p. 493.

51. Richard M. Nixon, *RN: Memoirs of Richard Nixon* (New York: Grosset and Dunlap, 1978), p. 922. On 9 October, Kissinger, *Years of Upheaval*, p. 496, told Dinitz that

> On your special requests, the President has approved the entire list of consumables, that is, ordnance, electronic equipment—everything on the list except laser bombs. The President has agreed—and let me repeat this formally—that *all* your aircraft and tank losses will be replaced. Of the tanks you will be getting, a substantial number will be M-60s, our newest. As for the planes, for immediate delivery, you will be getting 5 F-4s, 2 plus 3. For the rest, you will work out a schedule. . . . On the anti-tank ammunition and anti-tank weapons, Schlesinger is all set. This is everything on the list, except the laser bombs and aircraft. On tanks, you will have to work out a schedule. . . . The problem of tanks isn't what you need in this battle, but the situation after this battle. You have assurances that you will have replacements. You have the additional assurance that if it should go very badly and there is an emergency, we will get the tanks in even if we have to do it with American planes.

52. Dowty, *Middle East Crisis*, p. 232.

53. Transcript of Kissinger-Schlesinger telephone conversation, 9 October 1973, cited by Isaacson, *Kissinger: A Biography*, p. 518.

54. Kissinger, *Years of Upheaval*, p. 480; Spiegel, *The Other Arab-Israeli Conflict*, p. 253.

55. Interview, Joseph Sisco, 17 April 1991.

56. Nixon, *RN: Memoirs of Richard Nixon*, p. 924.

57. There has been heated discussion about whether the delays in organizing the airlift to Israel were inadvertent or deliberate, and, if deliberate, who was responsible. See Kissinger, *Years of Upheaval*, pp. 512–15; Dowty, *Middle East Crisis*, pp. 233–39; Spiegel, *The Other Arab-Israeli Conflict*, pp. 250–56.

58. Interview, Peter Rodman, Washington, D.C., 24 April 1991. Kissinger telephoned Schlesinger in the early hours of 13 October at home, and complained that the lack of ammunition had caused Israel to halt its advance against Syria. This, he said was "near disaster" for America's diplomatic strategy and it was due to "massive sabotage" within the Pentagon. Nevertheless, when Schlesinger suggested using military transports, Kissinger rejected the suggestion. "One thing we cannot have now," he insisted, "given our relationship with the Soviets, is American planes flying in there." Telephone conversation between James Schlesinger and Henry Kissinger, 13 October 1973, cited by Isaacson, *Kissinger: A Biography*, pp. 521–22.

59. Interview, Peter Rodman, Washington, D.C., 24 April 1991.

60. Interview, Joseph Sisco, Washington, D.C., 17 April 1991.

61. Charter companies were unwilling to enter a war zone unless legal steps, such as a declaration of emergency, were taken. Dowty, *Middle East Crisis*, pp. 235, 236, n. 139.

62. Interview, Henry Kissinger, New York, 19 June 1991.

63. "Statement to a press conference on 26 October 1973", *Department of State Bulletin*, 69, 19 November 1973, p. 624.

64. *Department of State Bulletin*, 12 November 1973.

65. Kissinger, *Years of Upheaval*, pp. 471–72.

66. Cited by Kissinger, *Years of Upheaval*, p. 513.

67. Interview, Adm. Moorer, cited by Dowty, *Middle East Crisis*, p. 235, n. 134.

68. Kissinger, *Years of Upheaval*, pp. 493–95.

69. Transcript of telephone conversation between Alexander Haig and Henry Kissinger, 12:45 A.M., 13 October 1973, summarized by Isaacson, *Kissinger: A Biography*, p. 521.

70. Kissinger, *Years of Upheaval*, p. 513. For a comprehensive discussion of Israel's response, see Michael Brecher with Benjamin Geist, *Decisions in Crisis: Israel, 1967 and 1973* (Berkeley: University of California Press, 1980), pp. 206–17.

71. Interview, James Schlesinger, cited in Spiegel, *The Other Arab-Israeli Conflict*, p. 255. A senior official at the State Department commented: "There was not a good relationship between Kissinger and Schlesinger. They didn't like each other." Interview, Washington, D.C., April 1991. See also Kissinger, *Years of Upheaval*, p. 514 and Isaacson, *Kissinger: A Biography*, p. 522.

72. Spiegel, *The Other Arab-Israeli Conflict*, p. 255; Kissinger, *Years of Upheaval*, pp. 512–15; Nixon, *RN: Memoirs of Richard Nixon*, p. 921. There are some differences in detail between Nixon's and Kissinger's account of the final decision to

order a full-scale airlift. Nixon maintains that he overruled Kissinger's objections and ordered a full-scale airlift on 13 October. Kissinger writes that a decision was made by WSAG at a meeting on 13 October to accelerate deliveries of F-4 Phantoms, that C-5A transport planes would fly directly to Israel until the charters were arranged, and that supplies already in the Azores and beyond El Al's capacity would be moved to Israel in American C-141s. He alleges that on Sunday, 14 October, the recommendation of a full-scale airlift went to the president.

73. *RN: Memoirs of Richard Nixon*, p. 921.

74. Interview of Richard Nixon by David Frost, *New York Times*, 13 May 1977, p. A8.

75. Nixon, *RN: Memoirs of Richard Nixon*, p. 921.

76. Interview, Peter Rodman, Washington, D.C., 24 April 1991.

77. William Quandt subsequently acknowledged that the United States may have exaggerated the tonnage and quality of the Soviet airlift: "We monitored the number of planes but not their contents. Egyptian officials have informed us that many of the earlier planes arrived half empty." Interview, William Quandt, Washington, D.C., 7 December 1988.

78. Interview, Peter Rodman, Washington, D.C., 24 April 1991.

79. Dowty, *Middle East Crisis*, pp. 245–46.

80. Kissinger, *Years of Upheaval*, pp. 518, 515, 520.

81. *Aviation Week and Space Technology*, 99 (10 December 1973), pp. 16–19; William B. Quandt, *Peace Process: American Diplomacy and the Arab-Israeli Conflict since 1967* (Washington, D.C.: Brookings, 1993), p. 547, n.49.

82. Quandt, *Peace Process*, p. 166.

83. By the time it concluded in November, the American airlift transferred a larger volume of matériel—22,500 tons—more quickly than did the Soviet airlift that moved 15,000 tons of supplies. The slower Soviet sealift moved the largest quantity, 85,000 tons, on thirty ships.

84. In his conversations with Kissinger on 12 October, when military resupply of Israel was stalled, Ambassador Dinitz stressed that Israel was running out of ammunition and that it would exhaust its supply in two or three days. Yet earlier that same day, Dinitz had been urging a cease-fire without any reference to shortages of ammunition. A Defense Intelligence Agency (DIA) estimate given to Kissinger the next morning estimated that Israel could continue military operations at the existing rate of expenditure for another ten days. Kissinger, *Years of Upheaval*, p. 513.

85. Dowty makes this argument. See *Middle East Crisis*, p. 231.

86. Interview, Victor Israelian, State College, Pa., 8 January 1992.

87. Hersh, *The Samson Option*, pp. 226–27. Hersh alleges as well that the arming of nuclear weapons compelled the Soviet Union to urge Egypt and Syria to limit their offensive. Soviet officials subsequently asserted that they knew nothing of any Israeli nuclear alert. Interview, Adm. Amelko, deputy chief of the USSR Navy in 1973, Moscow, 17 December 1991 and Victor Israelian, State College, Pa., 8 January 1992. Evgueny Pyrlin confirms that "The Soviet leadership had no information about a nuclear alert in Israel and about the order—which became known after the fact—of Prime Minister Meir and Defense Minister Dayan to prepare nuclear weapons for their possible use in the case of unhappy developments on the Egyptian and Syrian fronts." *Some Observations (Memoirs) About the Arab-Israeli October War (1973)*, p. 3.

88. Cited in Dowty, *Middle East Crisis*, p. 245.

89. Interviews, Henry Kissinger, New York, 19 June 1991, and Simcha Dinitz, Jerusalem, 7 January 1989. See also Isaacson, *Kissinger: A Biography*, p. 518.

90. Interview, William Colby, 11 January 1992.

91. Interview, member of the staff of the National Security Council in 1973, February 1988.

92. Interview, Victor Israelian, State College, Pa., 8 January 1992.

93. William Quandt recalls these complaints in conversations with Egyptian officials. Interview, Washington, D.C., 7 December 1988. Henry Kissinger writes that: "After the war, all Arab leaders complained to me that the Soviet airlift was grudging and that the sealift was slow, as if to rub in the Arabs' dependency." *Years of Upheaval*, p. 507.

94. Israelian, *The Kremlin: October 1973*, p. 11.

95. Richard Ned Lebow, *Between Peace and War: The Nature of International Crisis* (Baltimore: Johns Hopkins University Press, 1981); Robert Jervis, Richard Ned Lebow, and Janice Gross Stein, *Psychology and Deterrence* (Baltimore: Johns Hopkins University Press, 1985); Irving Janis and Leon Mann, *Decision Making: A Psychological Analysis of Conflict, Choice, and Commitment* (New York: The Free Press, 1977).

96. Robert Jervis, *Perception and Misperception in International Politics* (Princeton, N.J.: Princeton University Press, 1976).

97. Kissinger, *Years of Upheaval*, p. 518. It is possible that this is post-decisional bolstering.

98. See Spiegel, *The Other Arab-Israeli Conflict*, pp. 223–36, for an analysis of the central beliefs of the Nixon administration officials responsible for policy in the Middle East.

99. Georgi Arbatov suggests that this fear shaped Soviet foreign policy in the Brezhnev years and accounts for many of its contradictions. See *The System: An Insider's Life in Soviet Politics* (New York: Random House, 1992), pp. 164–89.

CHAPTER NINE
The Failure to Stop the Fighting

1. Interview, Georgi Arbatov, Moscow, 19 May 1989.

2. Victor Israelian, *The Kremlin: October 1973*, unpublished monograph, p. 18.

3. Interview, Victor Israelian, State College, Pa., 8 January 1992.

4. Interview, Vadim Zagladin, Moscow, 18 May 1989.

5. Richard M. Nixon, *RN: Memoirs of Richard Nixon* (New York: Grosset and Dunlap, 1978), p. 921.

6. William B. Quandt, *Decade of Decisions: American Policy Toward the Arab-Israeli Conflict* (Berkeley: University of California Press, 1977), p. 184.

7. For a more detailed discussion of the difficulties the United States and the Soviet Union have encountered in preventing crises, see Janice Gross Stein, "The Managed and the Managers: Crisis Prevention in the Middle East," in Gilbert R. Winham, ed., *New Issues in International Crisis Management* (Boulder, Colo.: Westview Press, 1988), pp. 171–98.

8. Israelian, *The Kremlin: October 1973*, p. 3.

9. Ibid., pp. 11–12. *Krasnaia zvezda* speculated on 13 October that the war would be long and that Israel would be at a disadvantage in a war of attrition.

See Dina Rome Spechler, *Domestic Influences on Soviet Foreign Policy* (New York: University Press of America, 1978); Galia Golan, "Soviet Decisionmaking in the Yom Kippur War, 1973," in Jiri Valenta and William Potter, eds., *Soviet Decisionmaking for National Security* (London: Allen & Unwin, 1984), pp. 184–217, at p. 204.

10. Israelian, *The Kremlin: October 1973*, p. 9.

11. Anwar el-Sadat is incorrect in his report that the visit took place only six hours after the fighting began. Interview, Victor Israelian, State College, Pa., 8 January 1992. For Sadat's version, see *Al-Hawadith*, 19 March 1975 and *Al-Jumhurriyah*, 24 October 1975.

12. Interview, Victor Israelian, State College, Pa., 8 January 1992; *The Kremlin: October 1973*, p. 5.

13. Israelian, *The Kremlin: October 1973*, p. 5.

14. Ibid.

15. *The Journal of Palestine Studies* ("October War Counter Claims,") 3, 4(Summer 1974), pp. 161–64, published an account of these conversations attributed to Ambassador Vinogradov. On October 7, "I received another message from Moscow to the effect that Syria had repeated her request, that she believed that the military situation and the liberation of the Bar-Lev line were favorable to the Arabs' objectives. She wanted a cease-fire, and I was asked by the Soviet command about President Sadat's views on the new request." Sadat responded that "the goal was the accomplishment of a specific action to change the balance of military and political power in the Arabs' favor, to destroy the theory of Israeli security, and to unblock the crisis. I informed the President of the Soviet command's view that this goal had already been achieved, and that it was logical to ask for a cease-fire at this stage, before Israel recovered from the shock of the surprise defeat—unless other and wider objectives were intended."

16. Israelian, *The Kremlin: October 1973*, p. 5.

17. Interview, Ismail Fahmy, Cairo, April 1988. The incident is also reported in detail by Ismail Fahmy in *Negotiating for Peace in the Middle East* (London: Croom Helm, 1983), p. 26. Fahmy writes that "Sadat's refusal to believe that Assad had requested a cease-fire angered the Soviet Union greatly. Both Gromyko and Brezhnev were later to bring up this issue with me, declaring that they were appalled by Assad's denial that he had requested a cease-fire and by Sadat's decision to believe Damascus rather than Moscow. Both pointed out that the Soviet Union had documents proving that Assad had requested a cease-fire, not once but three times."

18. Israelian, *The Kremlin: October, 1973*, p. 5.

19. Ibid., pp. 5–6.

20. Vinogradov suggests that Sadat gave independent weight to military objectives in rejecting a cease-fire. When the ambassador argued that an early cease-fire was logical, before Israel recovered from the shock of the surprise attack, Sadat replied that he wanted "to exploit the immense military success achieved on the Egyptian front to develop the attack and to advance to recover the passes." "October War Counter Claims," p. 162. A senior official in President Sadat's office was unequivocal, however, in his insistence that Sadat's overriding purpose was to extract a commitment from Israel to withdraw from the occupied territories. The president anticipated that, after the initial attack, the risk of confrontation would move the superpowers to impose these terms. Interview, Cairo, April 1988.

21. "There was no hope for a cease-fire *status quo ante*," Kissinger recalled, "but I wanted to get the Israelis to sign on to the principle so we could use it against them if they turned the war around." Interview, Henry Kissinger, 20 November 1991, cited by Walter Isaacson, *Kissinger: A Biography* (New York: Simon & Schuster, 1992), p. 515.

22. Cited by Henry Kissinger, *Years of Upheaval* (Boston: Little, Brown, 1982), p. 498.

23. Ibid., p. 500.

24. Interview, Victor Israelian, State College, Pa., 8 January 1992.

25. Ibid.

26. Interview, senior officer in the Crisis Operations Center, Cairo, April 1988.

27. Kissinger, *Years of Upheaval*, p. 519.

28. Ibid.

29. Ibid., p. 521.

30. Interview, Victor Israelian, State College, Pa., 8 January 1992. Soviet leaders considered it "inexpedient" for its delegation in New York to introduce a cease-fire resolution without a guarantee that it would be adopted by the Security Council. *The Kremlin: October 1973*, p. 10.

31. Kissinger, *Years of Upheaval*, p. 498.

32. Ibid., p. 499. Later that same day, Brent Scowcroft met again with Ambassador Dinitz and urged that Israel make the maximum effort in the next forty-eight hours.

33. Ibid., p. 504.

34. Ibid.

35. Ibid.

36. Ibid., p. 508.

37. Ibid., p. 511.

38. Ibid., p. 512. See Michael Brecher with Benjamin Geist, *Decisions In Crisis: Israel, 1967 and 1973* (Berkeley: University of California Press, 1980), p. 214.

39. *Years of Upheaval*, p. 513.

40. Ibid., p. 509.

41. Interview, Peter Rodman, Washington, D.C., 24 April 1991.

42. Kissinger, *Years of Upheaval*, p. 509.

43. Kissinger's version of the conversation is reported in *Years of Upheaval*, p. 512.

44. Kissinger, *Years of Upheaval*, pp. 517–20; Israelian, *The Kremlin: October 1973*, p. 10.

45. Kissinger, *Years of Upheaval*, p. 511.

46. Ibid., p. 517.

47. Ibid., p. 518.

48. Israelian, *The Kremlin: October 1973*, p. 11.

49. Ibid.

50. Evgueny Pyrlin, *Some Observations (Memoirs) About the Arab-Israeli October War (1973)*, unpublished memorandum commissioned for this project, Moscow, August 1992, p. 5.

51. Ibid.

52. Ibid., p. 12.

53. Ibid., p. 13.

54. Ibid.

55. Resolution 242 was adopted by the United Nations Security Council on 22 November 1967. The resolution is a delicately balanced compromise between Arab demands for return of the captured territories and Israel's insistence on full peace and security. It called for "withdrawal of Israeli armed forces from territories occupied in the recent conflict" and "termination of all claims of belligerency and respect for and acknowledgement of the sovereignty, territorial integrity, and political independence of every State in the area and their right to live in peace within secure and recognized boundaries free from threats or acts of force." It did not call on Israel to withdraw from *all* territories and on Arab governments to make *full* peace with Israel. The resolution also called for freedom of navigation through international waterways in the area, a just solution to the refugee question, a guarantee of the territorial inviolability and political independence of every state in the area, and for the appointment of a representative of the United Nations to work with the parties to the conflict. See *Resolutions and Decisions of the Security Council, 1967* (New York: United Nations, 1968), pp. 8–9.

56. Israelian, *The Kremlin: October 1973*, pp. 13–14. Brezhnev ordered that there be no formal summary at the end of the meeting and that his summary serve as the directive to Kosygin. As Israelian notes, "Brezhnev's summing up demonstrated his indubitable skill to smooth over critical situations and to make statements that everybody could accept." Ibid., p. 14.

57. Israelian, *The Kremlin: October 1973*, pp. 14–15.

58. Interview, Aleksandr Kislov, Moscow, 18 May 1989.

59. Interview, Victor Israelian, State College, Pa., 8 January 1991.

60. Pyrlin, *Some Observations (Memoirs) About the Arab-Israeli October War (1973)*, p. 3.

61. Interview, Aleksandr Kislov, 18 May 1989, Moscow. Only after Kosygin had left for Moscow did President Sadat summon Ambassador Vinogradov and tell him that Egypt would agree to a cease-fire. Speech by President Sadat, *Cairo Radio*, 15 September 1975. Sadat confirmed that he agreed to a cease-fire only after Kosygin left Cairo and that, indeed, Kosygin left because of his continued refusal to agree. Soviet officials confirm that Kosygin returned to Moscow without specific Egyptian approval of a cease-fire. Interviews, Aleksandr Kislov, Moscow, 18 May 1989, and Victor Israelian, State College, Pa., 8 January 1992.

62. Mahmoud Riad, *The Struggle for Peace in the Middle East* (London: Quartet Books, 1981), pp. 251–52.

63. Fahmy, *Negotiating for Peace in the Middle East*, p. 27.

64. Israelian, *The Kremlin: October 1973*, p. 15.

65. Ibid.

66. Ibid., p. 16.

67. The information was not available to the Egyptian military at the time. Interview, senior officer, Crisis Operations Center, Cairo, April 1988.

68. The draft called for a cease-fire in place, an immediate phased withdrawal by Israel from occupied Arab territories, and appropriate consultations to establish a just peace. The demand for an immediate withdrawal of Israeli forces would clearly not be acceptable to Israel. Kissinger, *Years of Upheaval*, pp. 539–40; Israelian, *The Kremlin: October 1973*, p. 15.

69. In one of his telegrams to Moscow, Dobrynin referred to his warm relationship with Kissinger and suggested that it would be reasonable to invite Kissinger to Moscow. Dobrynin wrote that he was convinced Kissinger would accept the invita-

tion. Brezhnev thought that it was Kissinger who had prompted the invitation. Israelian, *The Kremlin: October 1973*, p. 16.

70. Cited in Kissinger, *Years of Upheaval*, p. 542.

71. When Kissinger received the message through Dobrynin from Brezhnev, he inquired from Dobrynin why Gromyko could not come to Washington. Dobrynin replied that Soviet decisions would require the participation of Brezhnev. *Years of Upheaval*, p. 542.

72. Interview, Leonid Zamyatin, Moscow, 16 December 1991.

73. Pyrlin, *Some Observations (Memoirs) About the Arab-Israeli October War (1973)*, pp. 4–5.

74. Kissinger, *Years of Upheaval*, p. 544.

75. Ibid., p. 549.

76. Ibid., p. 551.

77. Ibid., p. 550.

78. Ibid., p. 551.

79. Cited in Kissinger, *Years of Upheaval*, pp. 550–51. It is impossible to establish whether Nixon or Kissinger was more accurate in his estimate of the difficulty of persuading Israel to accept an imposed settlement. The strategy had not been seriously tried. The evidence suggests that Kissinger's judgment was the more prescient. When he arrived in Tel Aviv, Prime Minister Meir questioned him intensely about the terms of the agreement he had reached with the Soviet Union.

80. Interview, Joseph Sisco, Washington, D.C., 17 April 1991.

81. Interview, Peter Rodman, Washington, D.C., 24 April 1991.

82. This was not the first time that Kissinger had ignored instructions from the president. When Nixon was extremely agitated, he would bark orders in rapid succession. "In these circumstances," Kissinger observed, "it was usually prudent not to argue and to wait twenty-four hours to see on which of these orders Nixon would insist after he calmed down." Henry Kissinger, *White House Years* (Boston: Little, Brown, 1979), p. 495.

83. Israelian, *The Kremlin: October 1973*, p. 17.

84. Ibid., pp. 17–18.

85. Interview, Victor Israelian, State College, Pa., 8 January 1992; *The Kremlin: October 1973*, p. 18.

86. Israelian, *The Kremlin: October 1973*, p. 18.

87. Ibid., pp. 18–19.

88. Interview, Victor Israelian, State College, Pa., 8 January 1992.

89. Kissinger, *Years of Upheaval*, p. 554.

90. Personal communication from Victor Israelian, 9 March 1992.

91. Interview, Joseph Sisco, Washington, D.C., 17 April 1991.

92. The first part of the agreement called for an immediate cease-fire in place. The second called on the parties to begin the implementation of Security Council Resolution 242 "in all its parts." The third provided for immediate negotiations between the parties concerned under appropriate auspices. The text of the agreement became United Nations Security Council Resolution 338. Dusan J. Djonovich, ed. *United Nations Resolutions*, Series II, Resolutions and Decisions adopted by the Security Council, vol. IX, 1972–1975 (New York: Oceana Publications, 1990), p. 44. Kissinger, *Years of Upheaval*, p. 554; Interview, Joseph Sisco, Washington, D.C., 17 April 1991, for details of the drafting of the resolution.

93. Israelian and his colleagues were told to prepare a telegram to Vinogradov, informing him that "Soviet leaders had considered Sadat's appeal very seriously," and, "in difficult negotiations with Kissinger," had succeeded in working out an agreement. Israelian, *The Kremlin: October 1973*, p. 20.

94. Interview, Henry Kissinger, New York, 19 June 1991.

95. Interview, Joseph Sisco, Washington, 17 April 1991.

96. Interview, Peter Rodman, Washington, D.C., 24 April 1991.

97. Isaacson, *Kissinger: A Biography*, pp. 525–26, reports that Kissinger deliberately stalled for time by delaying discussion of the technical details of implementing the cease-fire. According to Isaacson, when Kissinger was asked by Foreign Minister Gromyko if he had any suggestions, Kissinger replied that he had left the relevant documents at the guesthouse in the Lenin Hills. Rodman interrupted to volunteer that he had the papers with him, but Kissinger glared in response. Isaacson seems to be conflating two quite different meetings. When Kissinger was in Moscow for the summit in 1972, he met with Gromyko to discuss the principles for a settlement of the Arab-Israel conflict. To delay, he asked Gromyko to repeat some of his formulations again and again, even though Rodman was taking notes. Rodman interrupted Kissinger repeatedly to hand him the text of Gromyko's proposals, despite "repeated elbows in his side" from the secretary. "I raised so much cain with him afterward over his excess of zeal," Kissinger observed, "that never again would either he or Winston Lord hand over a document to me in front of another delegation during a negotiation—even when I asked for it." *White House Years* (Boston: Little, Brown, 1979), p. 1248. Peter Rodman and Joseph Sisco, who were with Kissinger in the negotiations in Moscow about the cease-fire, both maintain that in the press of work, the technicalities of implementing the cease-fire were ignored. Interviews, Peter Rodman, Washington, D.C., 24 April 1991 and Joseph Sisco, Washington, D.C., 17 April 1991.

98. The full text of the letter from Nixon to Meir, cited in Kissinger, *Years of Upheaval*, pp. 555–56, is as follows:

> Madame Prime Minister, we believe that this is a major achievement for you and for us and supportive of the brave fighting of your forces. [First:] It would leave your forces right where they are. [Second:] There is absolutely no mention of the word "withdrawal" in the resolution; third, for the first time, we have achieved the agreement of the Soviet Union to a resolution that calls for direct negotiation without conditions or qualifications between the parties under appropriate auspices. At the same time we and the Soviets have agreed privately to make our joint auspices available to you and to the Arabs to facilitate this process, if this is agreeable to the parties.

99. For a similar argument, see Alan Dowty, *Middle East Crisis: U.S. Decision-Making in 1958, 1970, and 1973* (Berkeley: University of California Press, 1984), p. 253. Dowty attributes Kissinger's underestimation of the problem of loss of control to his emphasis on global considerations and the superpower relationship.

100. Kissinger, *Years of Upheaval*, p. 556.

101. Kissinger cites a reconstruction of the episode by Lawrence Eagleburger in a letter to him: "I looked up, to find you standing in the middle of the room with smoke issuing from nose, eyes, and ears, and no one else (with an exception I'll mention in a minute) in sight. All twenty or thirty people—no doubt led by [Joseph]

Sisco—had exited with a speed and facility that would have put Houdini to shame. The single exception was Winston Lord, who was sort of huddled in a corner, but— God bless him—prepared to hang around for the pyrotechnics and to clean up the blood (mine) when it was all over." *Years of Upheaval*, p. 557.

102. Kissinger, *Years of Upheaval*, p. 558. For an analysis of Israel's decision making, see Brecher with Geist, *Decisions in Crisis*, pp. 219–21.

103. Interview, Henry Kissinger, New York, 19 June 1991; Kissinger, *Years of Upheaval*, p. 557.

104. The inability to transmit was unusual enough to prompt an investigation after the fact. The aircraft radio operator routinely reserved a wide range of frequencies across the radio spectrum to protect against atmospheric interference that would make some frequencies unusable. The majority of experts concluded that atmospheric interference was responsible: the aircraft radio operator, Kissinger reports, remained convinced that such prolonged and extensive interference could only have been man-made. See Kissinger, *Years of Upheaval*, p. 557.

105. Interview, Joseph Sisco, Washington, D.C., 17 April 1991.

106. In an unconvincing explanation, Leonid Zamyatin speculated that the technical difficulties might have occurred because no radio communications were permitted in the vicinity of the airport in order not to interfere with air-traffic control. Interview, Moscow, 16 December 1991.

107. The report read in part: "All our actions have to be guided by considerations related to the possibility of a rapidly approaching cease-fire/standstill. When the cease-fire comes into force it should find us holding a line that makes sense from a politico-military point of view. The further drive that we still have to develop will be made possible by the magnificent fighting spirit of our forces. However, we must bear in mind that they have been engaged in heavy combat almost incessantly since October sixth." Cited by Kissinger, *Years of Upheaval*, p. 546. Kissinger chose to emphasize that part of the message which referred to the approaching cease-fire and the war-weariness of Israel's forces. Kissinger, *Years of Upheaval*, p. 545.

108. Kissinger, *Years of Upheaval*, p. 546.

109. Kissinger speculated that Israel's leaders themselves may have been uncertain about the location of their rapidly moving forces, or about which prong of a multipronged attack would become the most rapid line of advance. Kissinger, *Years of Upheaval*, p. 546. More likely, Israel was not anxious to communicate to Kissinger the precise movements of their armed forces as they moved to encircle and cut off the Egyptian Third Army. Interview, senior officer in Israel's Military Intelligence, June 1989.

110. Kissinger, *Years of Upheaval*, pp. 552–53.

111. Ibid., p. 553.

112. Statement by President Assad, *Radio Damascus*, 29 October 1973.

113. Kissinger, *Years of Upheaval*, p. 543.

114. Ibid., p. 559. See also Brecher with Geist, *Decisions in Crisis*, pp. 220–23.

115. See Steven L. Spiegel, *The Other Arab-Israeli Conflict: Making America's Middle East Policy from Truman to Reagan* (Chicago: University of Chicago Press, 1985), pp. 261–62.

116. Interview, Henry Kissinger, New York, 19 June 1991.

117. Interview, Joseph Sisco, Washington, D.C., 17 April 1991.

118. Interview, Henry Kissinger, New York, 19 June 1991. American satellites, the SK 71, covered the whole battlefield. It is likely that the intelligence Kissinger received was the result of an error by analysts who were focusing their attention on the north.

119. Interview, Peter Rodman, Washington, D.C., 24 April 1991.

120. Kissinger, *Years of Upheaval*, p. 561.

121. Ibid.

122. Kissinger recalls that when he asked Prime Minister Meir what Israel's next objective would have been had the cease-fire not intervened, she mentioned Port Fuad, at the northern end of the canal, in the area of the Second rather than the Third Army. *Years of Upheaval*, p. 561. Whether her answer was the result of ongoing confusion in the General Staff or an attempt at deliberate deception, the military briefing Kissinger received a few hours later should have alerted him to the obvious next step. See also Brecher with Geist, *Decisions in Crisis*, pp. 220–23.

123. Kissinger, *Years of Upheaval*, p. 565.

124. Ibid.

125. Interview, senior officer of the Israel Defense Forces, April 1988. See also Dowty, *Middle East Crisis*, p. 254, for a similar argument.

126. Kissinger, *Years of Upheaval*, p. 569. In addition, an Israeli officer present at the meeting observed that the cease-fire in Vietnam had not gone into effect on schedule. The comment went unchallenged at the meeting. Dowty, *Middle East Crisis*, p. 254.

127. Interview, Henry Kissinger, New York, 19 June 1991.

128. Interview, Peter Rodman, Washington, D.C., 24 April 1991.

129. In the words of one analyst, the most charitable interpretation of American behavior was that "it represented a misjudgment regarding superpower control of a volatile local conflict." Dowty, *Middle East Crisis*, p. 254.

130. Cited by Kissinger, *Years of Upheaval*, p. 570.

131. Kissinger, *Years of Upheaval*, pp. 570–71.

132. Ibid., p. 494.

133. Dowty, *Middle East Crisis*, p. 239.

134. Interview, Henry Kissinger, New York, 19 June 1991.

135. Interview, Victor Israelian, State College, Pa., 8 January 1992.

136. "The Nature of the National Dialogue," address delivered to the Pacem in Terris III Conference, Washington, D.C., 8 October 1973.

137. Muhammad Hasanayn Haykal, *Road to Ramadan* (New York: Quadrangle, 1975), pp. 205–6.

138. Richard M. Nixon, Statement, 1 July 1970, *Public Papers of the President* (Washington, D.C.: U.S. Government Printing Office), 1970, p. 558.

139. There was also strong opposition in the Department of State and among some senior officials in the Pentagon to this strategy. Interview, Joseph Sisco, Washington, D.C., 17 April 1991; Spiegel, *The Other Arab-Israeli Conflict*, pp. 174–81.

140. At one point, Nixon wrote to Kissinger: "We are for Israel because Israel in our view is the only state in the Mideast which is pro-freedom and an effective opponent to Soviet expansion." Nixon, *RN: Memoirs of Richard Nixon*, p. 481.

141. Interview, Georgi Arbatov, Moscow, 19 May 1989.

142. Interview, Aleksandr Kislov, Moscow, 18 May 1989.

143. Interview, Georgi Arbatov, Moscow, 19 May 1989.

CHAPTER TEN
The Failure to Avoid Confrontation

1. Henry Kissinger, *Years of Upheaval* (Boston: Little, Brown, 1982), p. 575.
2. Interview, William Quandt, Washington, D.C., 7 December 1988.
3. Interview, Victor Israelian, State College, Pa., 8 January 1992.
4. Kissinger, *Years of Upheaval*, p. 571.
5. Interview, Henry Kissinger, New York, 19 June 1991.
6. Ibid.
7. Interview, Georgi Arbatov, Moscow, 19 May 1989.
8. Kissinger, *Years of Upheaval*, p. 575.
9. Cited by Kissinger, *Years of Upheaval*, p. 575.
10. Ibid., p. 573.
11. Ibid.
12. Interview, former member of Prime Minister Meir's staff, April 1988.
13. Kissinger, *Years of Upheaval*, p. 576.
14. Hanoch Bartov, *Dado—Arbaim Ve'Shmoneh Shanim V'Esraim Yom* (Dado—48 Years and Twenty Days), 2 vols. (Tel Aviv: Ma'ariv Book Guild, 1978), vol. I, p. 592, reports that every five minutes that morning, calls were coming in from the White House warning Israel to stop its offensive. Israel was informed that Kissinger was boiling with rage. This biography of Gen. David Elazar, the chief of staff of the IDF during the war, is based on the private papers of the chief of staff that are not yet publicly available.
15. Cited by Kissinger, *Years of Upheaval*, p. 579. See also Michael Brecher with Benjamin Geist, *Decisions in Crisis: Israel, 1967 and 1973* (Berkeley: University of California Press, 1980), pp. 224–28.
16. Kissinger, *Years of Upheaval*, p. 579.
17. Interview, Joseph Sisco, Washington, D.C., 17 April 1991.
18. Kissinger, *Years of Upheaval*, p. 573.
19. Ibid.
20. Cited by Kissinger, *Years of Upheaval*, p. 476.
21. Ibid., p. 481.
22. Ibid., p. 482.
23. Ibid., p. 574.
24. Ibid.
25. Ibid.
26. Ibid., p. 572. Richard M. Nixon, *RN: Memoirs of Richard Nixon* (New York: Grosset and Dunlap, 1978), pp. 936–37, writes: "I sent a reply that according to our information, Egypt was the first party to violate the cease-fire."
27. It has been alleged that local Egyptian forces renewed the fighting by attempting to break through the siege of the Third Army. These efforts were undertaken by local commanders and were not ordered by the Egyptian Command. Interview, senior military officer, Cairo, April 1988.
28. Cited by Kissinger, *Years of Upheaval*, p. 576.
29. Ibid., p. 577, emphasis added.
30. Interview, senior officer of Egyptian military intelligence, Cairo, April 1988, and member of President Anwar el-Sadat's office, Cairo, April 1988.
31. Kissinger, *Years of Upheaval*, pp. 577–78.
32. Ibid., p. 576.

33. Cited by Kissinger, *Years of Upheaval*, p. 583.

34. Galia Golan, "Soviet Decisionmaking in the Yom Kippur War," in Jiri Valenta and William Potter, eds., *Soviet Decisionmaking for National Security* (London: Allen & Unwin, 1984), pp. 185–217; Bradford Dismukes and James McConnell, *Soviet Naval Diplomacy* (New York: Pergamon Press, 1979), p. 203.

35. On October 22, a Soviet merchant ship passed through the Bosphorous with radiating material on board. Yona Bandmann and Yishai Cordova, in an analysis of the incident, argue that the first reports of a neutron-radiating cargo reached Washington only on 25 October, when the crisis was over. "The Soviet Nuclear Threat towards the Close of the Yom Kippur War," *Jerusalem Journal of International Relations* 5, 1 (1980), pp. 94–110. Garthoff asserts that the reports reached Washington before the decision to alert nuclear and conventional forces was made, but that this was not a serious consideration at the meeting when American officials decided to alert U.S. forces. See Raymond L. Garthoff, *Détente and Confrontation: American-Soviet Relations from Nixon to Reagan* (Washington, D.C.: The Brookings Institution, 1985), p. 378, n. 69. Similarly, Dowty, citing interviews with Thomas Moorer, chairman of the Joint Chiefs of Staff, William Colby, director of the Central Intelligence Agency, and Helmut Sonnenfeldt of the National Security Council staff, concludes that the information was available to American leaders by 24 October but that it was not given great importance. Alan Dowty, *Middle East Crisis: U.S. Decision-Making in 1958, 1970, and 1973* (Berkeley: University of California Press, 1984), p. 275.

36. There is some controversy as to how many airborne divisions were moved to the status of ready-to-move that day. All seven divisions had been on alert since 11 October, but some analysts claim that only one airborne division moved to ready-to-move status on 24 October. See Garthoff, *Détente and Confrontation*, pp. 377–78, n. 68. Hart maintains that three of the seven divisions were placed on ready-to-move status on 10 October and the remaining four early on 24 October. See Douglas M. Hart, "Soviet Approaches to Crisis Management: The Military Dimension," *Survival* 26, no. 5 (September-October 1984), pp. 214–22.

37. Hart, "Soviet Approaches to Crisis Management."

38. Interview, Victor Israelian, State College, Pa., 8 January 1992. Evgueny Pyrlin confirms that during the October War, "Grechko frequently replied to questions from his Politburo colleagues, 'I just informed Comrade Brezhnev about this,' and all questions became useless." *Some Observations (Memoirs) About the Arab-Israeli War (1973)*, unpublished memorandum commissioned for this project, Moscow, August 1992, p. 5.

39. Interview, Andrei M. Alexandrov-Agentov, Moscow, 19 August 1992. Alexandrov was a career diplomat whom Brezhnev had borrowed from the Ministry of Foreign Affairs when he became Chairman of the Presidium of the Supreme Soviet.

40. Pyrlin, *Some Observations (Memoirs) About the Arab-Israeli October War (1973)*, p. 2.

41. Personal communication from Victor Israelian, 9 March 1992.

42. Interview, Victor Israelian, State College, Pa., 8 January 1992.

43. Victor Israelian, *The Kremlin: October 1973*, unpublished monograph, p. 22.

44. Ibid., p. 23.

45. Ibid., p. 21; personal communication, 9 March 1992.

46. Israelian, *The Kremlin: October 1973*, p. 23.

47. Interview, Aleksandr Kislov, Moscow, 18 May 1989.

48. See the statements by Secretary of State William Rogers in the *Department of State Bulletin*, 1 February 1971, pp. 134–35 and 29 March 1971, p. 444. See also *New York Times*, 17 March 1971, p. 18.

49. Interviews, Vadim Zagladin, then deputy director of the International Relations Department of the Central Committee, Moscow, 18 May 1989, and a consultant to the State Department who participated in some of the negotiations in 1971, Washington, D.C., March 1990.

50. Kissinger, *Years of Upheaval*, p. 583.

51. Interview, Victor Israelian, State College, Pa., 8 January 1992.

52. Interview, Vadim Zagladin, Moscow, 18 May 1989.

53. Interview, Aleksandr Kislov, Moscow, 18 May 1989.

54. Interview, Anatoliy Gromyko, Moscow, 18 May 1989.

55. Interview, Gen. Yuri Yakovlevich Kirshin, Moscow, 17 December 1991.

56. Interview, Anatoliy Dobrynin, Moscow, 17 December 1991.

57. Zamyatin was with Brezhnev throughout most of the October War, but not on 24 October. "When Kissinger came to Moscow to negotiate the cease-fire, I was in the room all night with Kissinger and Brezhnev. Brezhnev kept all the conference rooms very cold for his health reasons. It was 14 degrees Celsius and freezing. The next day I became ill and missed the rest of the crisis because I was in the hospital with pneumonia." Interview, Moscow, 16 December 1991.

58. Interview, Leonid Zamyatin, Moscow, 16 December 1991.

59. Interview, Georgiy Kornienko, Moscow, 17 December 1991.

60. Interview, Victor Israelian, State College, Pa., 8 January 1992.

61. Israelian is not certain how this last sentence was inserted. "It is difficult for me to say to whom this idea belonged originally. It is possible that it was born during one of Brezhnev's lobby interviews with his closest colleagues from the Politburo and was immediately put into the message." Israelian, *The Kremlin: October 1973*, p. 24.

62. Interview, Victor Israelian, State College, Pa., 8 January 1992.

63. Israelian, *The Kremlin: October 1973*, p. 21.

64. Kissinger, *Years of Upheaval*, p. 570.

65. Nixon, *RN: Memoirs of Richard Nixon*, p. 936.

66. In his conversation with Soviet chargé Yuli M. Vorontsov, Kissinger made it clear that he expected the argument about the location of the cease-fire line to be prolonged: " 'We want you and us to be slow about that debate,' I said. Vorontsov seemed eager to enter into the spirit of my approach. 'Let them argue but just not fight.' " Cited by Kissinger, *Years of Upheaval*, p. 572.

67. Kissinger, *Years of Upheaval*, pp. 572–73.

68. Cited in Kissinger, *Years of Upheaval*, p. 578.

69. Interview, Georgi Arbatov, Moscow, 19 May 1989.

70. Cited by Kissinger, *Years of Upheaval*, p. 580; Interview, Anatoliy Gromyko, Moscow, 18 May 1989.

71. Interview, Aleksandr Kislov, Moscow, 18 May 1989.

72. See the speeches by Grechko, *Pravda*, 7 October 1973 and *Krasnaia zvezda*, 12 October 1973; Shelepin, *Trud*, 17 October 1973. See also Karen Dawisha, "Soviet Decision-Making in the Middle East: The 1973 October War and the 1980 Gulf War," *International Affairs* (London) 57, 1(Winter 1980/1981), pp. 43–59, at p. 57.

73. Interview, Victor Israelian, State College, Pa., 8 January 1992.

74. Interview, Vadim Zagladin, Moscow, 18 May 1989.

75. Aleksandr Shelepin, who had been marginalized by Brezhnev in 1967, nevertheless remained an important competitor. Richard D. Anderson, *Visions of Socialism: Competitive Politics and the Dynamics of Soviet Global Policy*, unpublished manuscript, 1990, suggests that until 1975, Shelepin remained the principal alternative to Brezhnev, "a shadow Secretary-General who might take power if Brezhnev stumbled." Boris Rabbot contends that after the passage of the Jackson-Vanik amendment in the United States in December 1974, Shelepin charged that détente had failed and challenged Brezhnev directly. See "Détente: The Struggle within the Kremlin," *Washington Post*, 10 July 1977, B1. This account has never been confirmed by Soviet officials or scholars.

76. Israelian, *The Kremlin: October 1973*, p. 22.

77. Interview, Victor Israelian, State College, Pa., 8 January 1992.

78. Israelian notes that "People started talking about the chance of an Israeli breakthrough to Cairo along the highway from Suez to Cairo." Israelian, *The Kremlin: October 1973*, p. 22.

79. Interview, Victor Israelian, State College, Pa., 8 January 1992.

80. Interview, member of President Sadat's office, Cairo, April 1988. In their correspondence with Kissinger during the war, Hafiz Isma'il and President Sadat referred as well to "guarantees." Cited by Kissinger, *Years of Upheaval*, pp. 574–75.

81. Interview, Anatoliy Gromyko, Moscow, 18 May 1989.

82. Ibid.

83. Kissinger, *Years of Upheaval*, pp. 578–9; Interview, Aleksandr Kislov, Moscow, 18 May 1989.

84. Muhammad Hassanan Haykal, *The Road to Ramadan* (New York: Quadrangle, 1975), p. 251. Haykal, ibid., p. 253, then reports a conversation between Presidents Sadat of Egypt and Assad of Syria that confirms the spirit of his interpretation and simultaneously reveals the confusion and poor communication among the two Arab principal belligerents.

> President Assad sent a message [on 24 October] to President Sadat, asking him if the Soviet Union was going to send "personnel" but the same word in Arabic (*quwat*) can mean "personnel" or "forces" and though it was in the first sense that President Sadat used the word, the authorities in Cairo thought it possible that President Assad might be using it in the larger sense. Egypt knew the Syrians were complaining that the Iraqis were refusing to accept the cease-fire and threatening to withdraw all their troops, and thought it conceivable that the Syrians might be wanting some Soviet forces to plug the gap left by the Iraqis. So President Sadat's reply was: "The Soviet Union has told me that they have sent seventy observers. I understand your position, and accept that you may think it necessary to request Soviet troops if you think the situation calls for them."
>
> Exchanges between the two Presidents continued as follows—President Assad: "When I asked you to inform me about Soviet forces coming to the area, I thought these were as a result of a request by you. I called the Soviet Ambassador to Damascus and informed him about the Soviet forces to be sent to Egypt, but I have never requested a Soviet force for Syria." President Sadat: "I understand from your message that the demand for Soviet troops was for Syria and I

accepted this as far as it was made necessary by the situation on your front. We ourselves have never requested Soviet forces but only Soviet observers to take part in supervision of the cease-fire. The Soviet Union has already sent seventy observers. I have so informed [Secretary-General of the United Nations, Kurt] Waldheim."

The Arabic records of the Security Council meeting of 24 October show clearly that Egypt did use the term *"quwat,"* which is conventionally understood and translated in the official English record as "forces." Dr. el-Zayyat requested that the forces "supervise" the commitment by Israel to cease-fire and secure its duration and respect (*Al-Ahram*, 25 October 1973). Although Haykal is technically incorrect in that the conventional meaning of *"quwat"* is forces rather than personnel, he correctly captures the spirit of Sadat's request.

Kissinger, in his memoirs, equivocates on the crucial issue of whether Sadat, in his message to President Nixon on the afternoon of 24 October, asked for troops or observers: "Sadat . . . then agreed to what we had *not* offered: the immediate dispatch of American observers or troops for the implementation of the Security Council cease-fire resolution on the *Egyptian* side. . . . Sadat told us that he was 'formally' issuing the same requests to the Soviets. Shortly after Sadat's private message, I learned through a news bulletin that Cairo had announced publicly that it was calling for a Security Council meeting to ask that American and Soviet 'forces' be sent to the Middle East." Kissinger, *Years of Upheaval*, p. 579. Kissinger's careful use of language hints at some ambiguity in the Egyptian request, at least in the minds of American officials.

85. Interview, senior Egyptian military officer, Cairo, April 1988. The officer was at Central Headquarters from 22–30 October, 1973.

86. Interview, Victor Israelian, State College, Pa., 8 January 1992.

87. Interviews, Aleksandr Kislov, Moscow, 18 May 1989, senior officer in the Crisis Operations Center, Cairo, May 1987.

88. Interview, Victor Israelian, State College, Pa., 8 January 1992.

89. Ismail Fahmy, *Negotiating for Peace in the Middle East* (London: Croom Helm, 1983), p. 30.

90. Interview, Andrei Gromyko, *London Observer*, 2 April 1989. When asked about Brezhnev's alcoholism, Gromyko answered: "It was perfectly obvious that the last person willing to look at this problem was the general secretary himself." Asked if Brezhnev personally had a drinking problem, Gromyko paused and then said: "The answer is: Yes, yes, yes."

91. Interview, Anatoliy Gromyko, Moscow, 18 May 1989.

92. Interview, Henry Kissinger, New York, 19 June 1991.

93. Interview, Georgi Arbatov, Moscow, 19 May 1989.

94. Interview, Vadim Zagladin, Moscow, 18 May 1989.

95. *Anatomiya blizhnevostochnogo konflikta* [The Anatomy of the Near East Conflict] (Moscow: Nauka, 1978), p. 173.

96. Interview, Anatoliy Dobrynin, Moscow, 17 December 1991.

97. Kissinger, *Years of Upheaval*, p. 581.

98. Cited by Kissinger, *Years of Upheaval*, p. 582.

99. Interview, Victor Israelian, State College, Pa., 8 January 1992.

100. Israelian, *The Kremlin: October 1973*, p. 22.

101. Ibid., p. 27.

102. Ibid., p. 23.

103. Interview, Aleksandr Kislov, Moscow, 18 May 1989.

104. Interview, Gen. Aleksandr Ivanovich Vladimirov, Moscow, 18 December 1991. William Colby, director of the CIA in 1973, insists that Soviet forces did not need much coordination with Egypt to deploy. "They had a mission there. All they needed was landing times at Cairo West and they could have gotten those at the last moment." Interview, 11 January 1992. On the other hand, Adm. Nikolai N. Amelko, deputy chief of the navy in 1973, argued that the deployment of paratroopers would have required air, logistical, and marine support which would have required some coordination and time. No such request was made to the Soviet navy in October 1973. Interview, Adm. Nikolai Amelko, Moscow, 18 December 1991.

105. Personal communication from Raymond Garthoff, 9 July 1992. Garthoff estimates that it would have taken considerable time to move the full four divisions.

106. Interview, Anatoliy Gromyko, Moscow, 18 May 1989.

107. Interview, Aleksandr Kislov, Moscow, 18 May 1989 and Moscow, 16 December 1991.

108. Interview, Victor Israelian, State College, Pa., 8 January 1992.

109. Interview, Aleksandr Kislov, Moscow, 18 May 1989. Garthoff, *Détente and Confrontation*, p. 383, concurs with this interpretation of Brezhnev's intentions.

110. Kissinger, *Years of Upheaval*, p. 580.

111. Interview, Vadim Zagladin, Moscow, 18 May 1989.

112. Interview, Aleksandr Kislov, Moscow, 18 May 1989.

113. Pyrlin, *Some Observations (Memoirs) About the Arab-Israeli October War (1973)*, p. 1.

114. Seven COSMOS satellites were launched between 3 and 27 October. On 24 October, COSMOS 599 and 602 were in orbit over the battlefield. *World Armaments and Disarmament, SIPRI Yearbook of World Armaments, 1974* (Stockholm: SIPRI, 1974), p. 295; David Baker, *The Shape of Wars to Come* (Cambridge, Mass.: Patrick Stephens, 1981), p. 77.

115. Interview, senior official of the State Department, Washington, D.C., 19 February 1988. Kissinger confirms that by 8:00 P.M. Washington time on 24 October, his best information was that *no* fighting was going on in the Middle East. Kissinger, *Years of Upheaval*, p. 582.

116. In none of their communications to Nixon and Kissinger did Brezhnev or Dobrynin raise the question of the provision of food and medical supplies to the Third Army. Kissinger, *White House Years*, pp. 570–80.

117. Kissinger suggested to the prime minister that, to conform to the resolution to be passed by the United Nations that evening, Israel pull back a few hundred yards from wherever it was and call it the old cease-fire line: " 'How can anyone ever know where a line is or was in the desert?' I said. Golda's melancholy at my obtuseness was palpable even at a distance of six thousand miles. She replied: 'They will know where our present line is, all right.' Now I understood. Israel had cut the last supply route to the city of Suez. The Egyptian Third Army on the east bank of the Canal was totally cut off." Kissinger, *Years of Upheaval*, p. 571.

118. Ibid., p. 575.

119. Ironically, some officials in Israel thought that the Soviet Union would resupply the Third Army. Abba Eban, Israel's foreign minister at the time, recalls in his memoirs: "It was believed that the Soviet Union would not hesitate to land supplies by helicopter to relieve the Third Army. The Soviet Union would then be physically

involved in the war against Israel, and it would become necessary for the United States to think long and hard about its own commitment to regional stability and Israel's security. . . . When we knew that the United States had decided on a deterrent alert, we were profoundly heartened and impressed." Abba Eban, *Abba Eban: An Autobiography* (New York: Random House, 1977), p. 535.

120. Israel had turned back three convoys of food and medical supplies sent by the Egyptian Red Crescent and the International Red Cross.

121. Present as well in the Situation Room of the White House were the Deputy Assistant to the President for National Security Affairs, Gen. Brent Scowcroft, and Comdr. Jonathan T. Howe, the military assistant to the Secretary of State at the National Security Council.

122. *Inquiring Into the Military Alert Invoked on October 24, 1973* (Washington, D.C.: 93d Cong., House of Representatives, Report 93–970, U.S. Government Printing Office, 14 April 1974, 74–09780), p. 3. Nixon writes in his memoirs that "When Haig informed me about this message [from Brezhnev], I said that he and Kissinger should have a meeting at the White House to formulate plans for a firm reaction to what amounted to a scarcely veiled threat of unilateral Soviet intervention. Words were not making our point—we needed action, even the shock of a military alert." Nixon, *RN: Memoirs of Richard Nixon*, p. 938. Alexander Haig, who was with the president that night, recalls that

> When I took this ultimatum [Brezhnev's letter], for that was what it amounted to, to the President, he greeted it with a remark and an order. "We've got a problem, Al," he said. "This is the most serious thing since the Cuban Missile Crisis. Words won't do the job. We've got to act." Nixon ordered me to convene a meeting with Kissinger and the other members of the Washington Special Action Group for the purpose of formulating a response to the Soviet challenge. . . . When I passed on the substance of this conversation [with Kissinger about the location of the WSAG meeting] to Nixon, he nodded in approval but expressed no enthusiasm for attending the meeting in person. . . . Besides, he was tired. . . . With a wave of the hand, he said, "You know what I want, Al; you handle the meeting." We all knew what he wanted: a worldwide military alert of United States military forces tied to a strong reply to Brezhnev.

Alexander M. Haig, Jr., with Charles McCarry, *Inner Circles: How America Changed The World, A Memoir* (New York: Warner Books, 1992), pp. 415–16. The president's records show that he spoke to Haig for about twenty minutes around 10:30 P.M. This was the only time he communicated with his advisers until the next morning. See William B. Quandt, *Peace Process: American Diplomacy and the Arab-Israel Conflict since 1967* (Washington, D.C.: The Brookings Institution, 1993), p. 173.

123. Kissinger, *Years of Upheaval*, p. 581.

124. Cited in Kissinger, *Years of Upheaval*, p. 581.

125. Kissinger carefully words his memoirs to avoid highlighting the president's absence. He asked Alexander Haig twice that evening whether the president should be awakened. The first time Haig replied with a curt "No," and the second time, at 10:20 P.M., suggested that the meeting to discuss the appropriate response to Brezhnev's letter should be held in the White House. Haig agreed to handle "internal White House notification." Kissinger subsequently says: "I did not know what con-

versations Haig had with Nixon in the early hours of the morning." Kissinger, *Years of Upheaval*, pp. 581, 585, 587, 593. When asked directly whether Nixon was drunk, Kissinger refused to comment. Interview, New York, 19 June 1991.

In his biography of Haig, Roger Morris writes: "Eagleburger and other Kissinger aides later told a frightening story of Nixon upstairs drunk at the White House slurring his words and barely roused when Haig and Kissinger tried to deal with him in the first moments of the crisis. . . . Returning to his State Department office in the predawn hours, Kissinger gave Eagleburger an account of the drunken Nixon. . . . The aide and one-time Haig rival later told friends that it had been an appalling night in the White House." Roger Morris, *Haig: The General's Progress* (New York: Seaview Books, 1982), pp. 257–59.

There had been earlier incidents in which Nixon reportedly drank heavily during a crisis. On 24 April 1970, when Nixon was considering an invasion of Cambodia, the president went to Camp David with Charles (Bebe) Rebozo, an old personal friend. When he called Kissinger, he was slurring his words and shouting obscenities. Kissinger, in private conversations with his aides Anthony Lake and Winston Lord, subsequently described the president as a "basket case" and "drunk." Walter Isaacson, *Kissinger: A Biography* (New York: Simon & Schuster, 1992), pp. 259, 263, citing interviews with Anthony Lake, 11 January 1990, and Winston Lord, 2 November 1989. See also Fawn M. Brodie, *Richard Nixon: The Shaping of His Character* (New York: Norton, 1981), p. 477.

Nixon apparently had a very low tolerance for alcohol and would begin to slur his words after only one or two drinks. Interview, senior official in the State Department in 1973, Washington, D.C., 2 May 1991.

126. Bruce G. Blair, "Alerting in Crisis and Conventional War," in Ashton B. Carter, John D. Steinbruner, and Charles A. Zraket, eds., *Managing Nuclear Operations* (Washington: The Brookings Institution, 1987), pp. 75–120, at pp. 85, 89.

127. Barry M. Blechman and Douglas M. Hart, "The Political Utility of Nuclear Weapons: The 1973 Middle East Crisis," *International Security* 7, 1 (Summer 1982), pp. 132–156, at p. 136; Garthoff, *Détente and Confrontation*, p. 379; and Kissinger, *Years of Upheaval*, pp. 587–89. As well, at 3:30 A.M., sixty B-52 bombers were ordered back to the United States from Guam. This had been a long-standing objective of the Pentagon, but the State Department had objected to a visible reduction of the American commitment in southeast Asia. Under the rubric of the DEFCON III alert, the Pentagon ordered their return.

128. Interview, William Colby, 11 January 1992.

129. "Statement by President Richard M. Nixon," *Department of State Bulletin* 69, 12 November 1973, p. 581.

130. Transcript of Haig-Kissinger telephone conversation, October 24, 1973, cited by Isaacson, *Kissinger: A Biography*, p. 530.

131. Cited by Kissinger, *Years of Upheaval*, p. 585.

132. Kissinger, *Years of Upheaval*, p. 587.

133. Interview, Henry Kissinger, New York, 19 June 1991.

134. Steven Spiegel, *The Other Arab-Israeli Conflict: Making America's Middle East Policy from Truman to Reagan* (Chicago: University of Chicago Press, 1985), citing his interview with Secretary Schlesinger, p. 264. In a press conference given the day after the alert, Schlesinger spoke of the "mixed reactions and different assessments" of Soviet intentions among members of the National Security Council immediately before their decision to alert U.S. forces. See "Secretary of Defense Schlesin-

ger's News Conference of October 26," *Department of State Bulletin* 69, 19 November 1973, p. 622.

135. Interview, William Quandt, Washington, D.C., 7 December 1988.

136. Kissinger, *Years of Upheaval*, p. 508.

137. Ibid., p. 510.

138. Interview, William Quandt, Washington, D.C., 7 December 1988.

139. Kissinger, *Years of Upheaval*, p. 579; Interview, Henry Kissinger, New York, 19 June 1991. Kissinger, ibid., p. 584, elaborated on this reasoning in his memoirs:

> If we agreed to a joint role with the Soviet Union, its troops would reenter Egypt with our blessing. Either we would be the tail to the Soviet kite in a joint power play against Israel, or we would end up clashing with Soviet forces in a country that was bound to share Soviet objectives regarding the cease-fire. . . . But the impact would go far beyond Egypt. If Soviet forces appeared dramatically in Cairo with the United States as an appendage, our traditional friends among Arab moderates would be profoundly unnerved by the evident fact of US-Soviet condominium. The strategy we had laboriously pursued in four years of diplomacy and two weeks of crisis would disintegrate: Egypt would be drawn back into the Soviet orbit, the Soviet Union and its radical allies would emerge as the dominant factor in the Middle East.

140. Kissinger, *Years of Upheaval*, p. 482.

141. Spiegel, *The Other Arab-Israeli Conflict*, citing interview with Schlesinger, p. 264. William Colby confirmed that "Nobody had any problems. Schlesinger and Moorer went along. They had no problems with it." Interview, William Colby, 11 January 1992.

142. Kissinger, *Years of Upheaval*, p. 585, emphasis added. Scott Sagan cites an interview of an official of the State Department who remarked candidly: "You know, it didn't make any difference if you thought they [the Soviets] would intervene or not. A threat had been made. The United States had to react." "Lessons of the Yom Kippur Alert," *Foreign Policy*, no. 36 (Fall 1979), pp. 160–77, quotation on pp. 171–72.

143. Kissinger, *Years of Upheaval*, p. 509.

144. Ibid., p. 584.

145. The full text of the letter has not been declassified. Kissinger, *Years of Upheaval*, p. 591, and Nixon, *RN: Memoirs of Richard Nixon*, pp. 939–40, revealed some of its contents in their memoirs.

> Mr. General Secretary: I have carefully studied your important message of this evening. I agree with you that our understanding to act jointly for peace is of the highest value and that we should implement that understanding in this complex situation. I must tell you, however, that your proposal for a particular kind of joint action, that of sending Soviet and American military contingents to Egypt is not appropriate in the present circumstances. We have no information which would indicate that the cease-fire is now being violated on any significant scale. . . . In these circumstances, we must view your suggestion of unilateral action as a matter of gravest concern, involving incalculable consequences. It is clear that the forces necessary to impose the cease-fire terms on the two sides would be massive and would require closest coordination so as to avoid bloodshed. This is not only clearly infeasible, but it is not appropriate to the

situation. . . . The United States approves and is willing to participate in an expanded United Nations truce supervisory force composed of noncombat personnel. It would be understood that this is an extraordinary and temporary step solely for the purpose of providing adequate information concerning compliance by both sides with the terms of the cease-fire. If this is what you mean by contingents, we will consider it. Mr. General Secretary, in the spirit of our agreements this is the time for acting not unilaterally, but in harmony and with cool heads. I believe my proposal is consonant with the letter and spirit of our understandings and would ensure prompt implementation of the cease-fire. . . . You must know, however, that we could in no event accept unilateral action. . . . As I stated above, such action would produce incalculable consequences which would be in the interest of neither of our countries and which would end all we have striven so hard to achieve.

146. Joseph J. Kruzel, "Military Alerts and Diplomatic Signals," in Ellen Stern, ed., *The Limits of Military Intervention* (Beverly Hills, Calif.: Sage, 1977), pp. 83–100, quotation on p. 95.

147. Scott Sagan, "Nuclear Alerts and Crisis Management," *International Security* 9, 4 (Spring, 1985), pp. 99–139, at p. 128.

148. Blair, "Alerting in Crisis and Conventional War," p. 115.

149. Sagan, "Nuclear Alerts and Crisis Management," citing an interview of Adm. Moorer, 10 April 1984, p. 128, n. 83. CINCSAC recalled that he was told that he was not supposed to do anything that cost money. Personal communication from Bruce Blair to authors, Washington, D.C., 10 January 1992.

150. The message read as follows:

1. Most recent communication with Soviets contains request that US join them in more forceful enforcement of Israel/Arab cease-fire by introduction of both US/Soviet forces. Soviets further state intentions to consider unilateral action if US declines. 2. Our reply not final at this point but, as you have noted, US response includes signal of elevation in force readiness, i.e., DEFCON Three worldwide, alerting of 82nd Airborne, more eastward movement of carriers in Med, and redeployment of SAC forces from the Pacific. 3. I am in session with SECDEF and Chiefs and will keep you advised.

Joint Chiefs of Staff message, JCS 250737Z OCT 73, 25 October 1973 (declassified 1984).

151. Ironically, its visibility at home was its greatest drawback. As we shall see, because the alert was picked up so quickly in the United States and made public, the costs to the Soviet Union of refraining from action grew.

152. Kissinger, *Years of Upheaval*, p. 587; Blechman and Hart, "The Political Utility of Nuclear Weapons," p. 145.

153. Sagan, "Nuclear Alerts and Crisis Management," p. 124, reports that two competing positions were aired in the meeting that night in the White House Situation Room. The first advocated an alert of conventional forces, arguing that an alert of nuclear forces would not be credible. The second argued for a global alert, including strategic forces, in order to shock the Soviet leadership. This is the only report, however, that suggests that a conventional and strategic alert were considered as alternatives. Participants in the meeting, interviewed subsequently, recall no such careful distinction.

154. Interview, William Quandt, Washington, D.C., 7 December 1988.

155. These options are identified by Kruzel, "Military Alerts and Diplomat Signals," p. 95. He suggests, for example, that to convey a more precise signal, airborne divisions could have been alerted but bomber crews given the day off to demonstrate that any retaliation would be limited to the conventional level.

156. Blechman and Hart, "The Political Utility of Nuclear Weapons," p. 145.

157. Interview, Vice Adm. Daniel Murphy by Bruce Blair, personal communication from Blair to authors, Washington, D.C., 10 January 1992.

158. Blechman and Hart, "The Political Utility of Nuclear Weapons," p. 145.

159. Cited by Dowty, *Middle East Crisis*, p. 275.

160. Cited by Elmo R. Zumwalt, Jr., *On Watch: A Memoir* (New York: Quadrangle, 1976), p. 446.

161. Statement to the Southern Governors Conference, June 1975, cited in Richard Valeriani, *Travels with Henry* (Boston: Houghton, Mifflin, 1979), pp. 181–82.

162. John Steinbruner notes that at the beginning of the war, U.S. naval strength was somewhat larger than usual whereas Soviet deployments were smaller than the norm. When the war began, the United States was in the process of relieving one of the two carriers normally stationed with the Sixth Fleet. Because it was easy to recall the third carrier task force, the United States was stronger than usual in the naval strength at its disposal in the eastern Mediterranean. In contrast, Soviet naval strength was somewhat below its normal level because the *Nikolaev* left the Mediterranean through the Bosphorous on the day before the war started. Because of the transit regulations through the straits, the Soviet Union could not bring its navy up to strength as rapidly as the Americans. Nonetheless, the Soviets doubled the number of their combat ships from seventeen to thirty-six by the end of the war. "An Assessment of Nuclear Crises," in Franklyn Griffiths and John C. Polanyi, eds., *The Dangers of Nuclear War: A Pugwash Symposium* (Toronto: University of Toronto Press, 1979), pp. 34–49; and Zumwalt, *On Watch*, pp. 447ff. The total number of Soviet ships deployed in the eastern Mediterranean by the end of October was eighty, an increase of about twenty from their normal deployment. The U.S. Sixth Fleet deployed approximately sixty ships. However, as Vice Adm. Daniel Murphy, the commander of the Sixth Fleet at the time, pointed out, the numerical difference is misleading because forty percent of the Soviet fleet consisted of support ships in comparison to only twenty percent of the Sixth Fleet. See *New York Times*, 9 November 1973.

163. Bradford Dismukes and James McConnell, *Soviet Naval Diplomacy* (New York: Pergamon Press, 1979), p. 203, suggest that the deployment may have been designed to counter movement of the U.S. Sixth Fleet toward Egypt and protect Soviet air and sea lines if they were preparing to deploy troops.

164. Robert G. Weinland, "Superpower Naval Diplomacy in the October 1973 Arab-Israeli War," Professional Paper 221 (Arlington, Va.: Center for Naval Analysis, 1978). For a detailed analysis of U.S. and Soviet naval forces in the Mediterranean, see Joseph F. Bouchard, *Command in Crisis: Four Case Studies* (New York: Columbia University Press, 1991).

165. Adm. Nikolai N. Amelko explained that the Soviet fleet in the Mediterranean was reinforced in response to the entrance of several American carriers into the Mediterranean. Interview, Moscow, 18 December 1991. After the DEFCON alert, the Soviet navy deployed all three of its combat groups southeast of Crete and on 26 October, began large-scale anticarrier warfare exercises that continued for the next eight days. The new posture of the Soviet navy was also designed to deter any at-

tempted intervention ashore by the Sixth Fleet. A full surface action group was assigned to cover the amphibious units of the United States. Adm. Worth Bagley reported that the Soviet navy deployed their ships and submarines to target U.S. naval forces from multiple points. See *US News and World Report*, 24 December 1973. In addition, several units of the Soviet fleet were relocated north of the Nile Delta to interpose Soviet ships between the Sixth Fleet and the battle zone. See Weinland, "Superpower Naval Diplomacy," p. 54; and Stephen S. Kaplan, *Diplomacy of Power: Soviet Armed Forces as a Political Instrument* (Washington, D.C.: The Brookings Institution, 1981), pp. 458–60.

166. Thomas Schelling, *The Strategy of Conflict* (Cambridge, Mass.: Harvard University Press, 1960) analyzes that kind of strategy.

167. For an interpretation of American strategy as a deliberate "manipulation of risk," see Blechman and Hart, "The Political Utility of Nuclear Weapons."

168. Interview, William Colby, 11 January 1992.

169. Kissinger, *Years of Upheaval*, p. 591.

170. For Kissinger's analysis of the alert in 1970, see *White House Years* (Boston: Little, Brown, 1979), pp. 605–31.

171. The aircraft carriers *Saratoga* and *Independence* were deployed off the coast of Lebanon, *John F. Kennedy* was dispatched to join the Sixth Fleet, and an amphibious task force was positioned thirty-six hours away. Four additional destroyers were authorized to leave the United States for the Mediterranean, and two attack submarines were scheduled to pass through the Straits of Gibraltar. An airborne brigade in Germany was recalled from maneuvers to its base embarkation point, one of its battalions was ordered to prepare for an airdrop, and the Eighty-Second Airborne Division was put on full alert.

172. Sagan, "Nuclear Alerts and Crisis Management," p. 124, reports that two competing positions were aired in the meeting that night in the White House Situation Room. The first advocated an alert of conventional forces, arguing that an alert of nuclear forces would not be credible. The second argued for a worldwide alert, including strategic forces, in order to shock the Soviet leadership. If this discussion did take place, then Kissinger should have been aware that strategic forces were being alerted worldwide. However, Kissinger makes no reference to any such discussions in his reconstruction of the meeting and then proceeds to draw a strikingly inappropriate analogy to a selective alert, which involved no strategic forces.

173. Interview, Henry Kissinger, New York, 19 June 1991.

174. Interview, Peter Rodman, Washington, D.C., 24 April 1991.

175. Interview, William Quandt, Washington, D.C., 7 December 1988.

176. Cited by Isaacson, *Kissinger: A Biography*, pp. 531–32.

177. Kissinger, *Years of Upheaval*, p. 591.

178. Interview, James Schlesinger by Walter Isaacson, 17 November 1989, cited by Isaacson, *Kissinger: A Biography*, p. 532.

179. Interview, Henry Kissinger, New York, 19 June 1991.

180. Interview, William Colby, 11 January 1992.

181. Recounted by Secretary of Defense James Schlesinger in an interview with Steven Spiegel, *The Other Arab-Israeli Conflict*, p. 265.

182. Interviews, Adm. Moorer and Gen. George Brown, cited by Dowty, *Middle East Crisis*, p. 276, n. 130.

183. Sagan, "Nuclear Alerts and Crisis Management," p. 128, n. 4, citing interviews of participants.

184. Sagan, "Nuclear Alerts and Crisis Management," p. 125.

185. A senior Pentagon official suggested subsequently that Secretary Schlesinger as well did not understand the operational requirements of the alert. Cited by Dowty, *Middle East Crisis*, p. 276, n. 129.

186. Interview, Peter Rodman, Washington, D.C., 24 April 1991.

187. Blechman and Hart, "The Political Utility of Nuclear Weapons," p. 151.

188. There was the remote possibility that had the United States gone up to DEFCON II, the Soviet Union might have felt compelled to respond with an alert of its strategic forces. Normally, Moscow maintains its strategic forces at a lower level of readiness than does the United States. See Kruzel, "Military Alerts and Diplomatic Signals," pp. 86–90, for a comparison of the normal conditions of Soviet and American strategic forces. In 1973, the Soviet Union maintained enough ICBMs and warheads on ready status to discourage preemption by the United States, but Soviet leaders might have been sufficiently alarmed—or provoked—by any further increase in the level of the American alert that they would have responded in kind. Given the far tighter coupling of the nuclear and response systems of both superpowers in 1973, tension could have escalated dangerously.

189. Kissinger, *Years of Upheaval*, p. 589.

190. Interviews, William Quandt, Washington, D.C., 7 December 1988, and Roy Atherton, Washington, D.C., 15 March 1990.

191. Kissinger, *Years of Upheaval*, p. 593.

192. Interview, Henry Kissinger, New York, 19 June 1991.

193. Interview, Peter Rodman, Washington, D.C., 24 April 1991.

194. Some Soviet officials remain convinced that Kissinger deliberately deceived them. Aleksandr Kislov, for example, was interviewed twice for this project. In the first interview in Moscow in May 1989, he alleged that Kissinger had engaged in deliberate deception. During the second interview in Moscow on 16 December 1991, he was told of Kissinger's account of his meetings in Tel Aviv. Kislov replied: "I didn't believe Kissinger then, I don't believe Kissinger now, and I will continue to disbelieve him no matter what he says."

195. Interview, William Quandt, Washington, D.C., 7 December 1988.

CHAPTER ELEVEN
The Crisis and Its Resolution

1. Henry Kissinger, *Years of Upheaval* (Boston: Little, Brown, 1982), p. 980.

2. Interview, Georgi Arbatov, Moscow, 19 May 1989.

3. John Steinbruner, "An Assessment of Nuclear Crises," in Franklyn Griffiths and John C. Polanyi, eds., *The Dangers of Nuclear War: A Pugwash Symposium* (Toronto: University of Toronto Press, 1979), pp. 34–49, makes this argument persuasively. See also Richard Ned Lebow, *Nuclear Crisis Management: A Dangerous Illusion* (Ithaca, N.Y.: Cornell University Press, 1987), pp. 17, 38, 40, 71–72.

4. Lebow, *Nuclear Crisis Management*; Paul Bracken, *The Command and Control of Nuclear Forces* (New Haven, Conn.: Yale University Press, 1983); Ashton Carter, John Steinbruner, and Charles Zraket, *Managing Nuclear Operations* (Washington, D.C.: The Brookings Institution, 1987).

5. On 6 October, the Soviet Fifth Eskadra (Mediterranean Squadron) consisted of about 57 ships: 11 submarines (2 with antiship cruise missiles), 1 Sverdlov-class cruiser, 3 Kashin-class and 2 Kotlin-class guided-missile destroyers, 2 Kotlin-class

destroyers (guns only), 9 frigates and corvettes, 2 Polnocny-class medium landing ships, 2 minesweepers, and several auxiliary vessels.

The United States had 48 ships in the Mediterranean. Task Force 60, the carrier strike force, had 2 attack carrier task groups and Task Force 61 consisted of a helicopter carrier and 9 other amphibious ships. A Marine battalion landing team, with additional troops for an exercise, totaling 3,000 men, was in the amphibious group. The Sixth Fleet flagship, USS *Little Rock*, was at sea south of Crete. Four nuclear-powered attack submarines were on patrol in the Mediterranean. For a detailed analysis of U.S. naval operations in the 1973 war, see Joseph F. Bouchard, *Command in Crisis: Four Case Studies* (New York: Columbia University Press, 1991), pp. 160–87.

6. Interview, Aleksandr Kislov, Moscow, 16 December 1991.

7. Kissinger said: "We would have put down the Eighty-Second Airborne if the Soviets had sent forces." Interview, New York, 19 June 1991.

8. We are grateful to Tom McNaugher of the Brookings Institution for these comments.

9. "Agreement Between the Government of the United States of America and the Government of the Union of Soviet Socialist Republics on the Prevention of Incidents on and over the High Seas," *World Armaments and Disarmament: SIPRI Yearbook, 1973* (New York: Humanities Press, 1973), pp. 36–39; "Protocol to the Agreement Between the Government of the United States of America and the Government of the Union of Soviet Socialist Republics on the Prevention of Incidents on and over the High Seas," signed 25 May 1973, *United States Treaties and Other International Agreements*, vol. 24, part I, 1973 (Washington, D.C.: U.S. Government Printing Office, 1974), pp. 1063–64.

10. In the words of Vice Adm. Daniel Murphy, commander of the Sixth Fleet: "The Sixth Fleet was directed to continue routine, scheduled operations and to avoid overt moves which might be construed as indicating that the United States was preparing to take an active part in the conflict." Cited in Elmo R. Zumwalt, Jr., *On Watch: A Memoir* (New York: Quadrangle, 1976), p. 435.

11. Bouchard, *Command in Crisis*, p. 169.

12. Zumwalt, *On Watch*, pp. 300–301.

13. Bouchard, *Command in Crisis*, p. 172.

14. Ibid., p. 173; Zumwalt, *On Watch*, p. 436.

15. Bouchard, *Command in Crisis*, p. 177.

16. Ibid., p. 182; Zumwalt, *On Watch*, p. 447; James Schlesinger, "Secretary of Defense Schlesinger's News Conference of October 26," *Department of State Bulletin* 69, 19 November 1973, p. 621.

17. Zumwalt, *On Watch*, p. 446–47.

18. Cited in Zumwalt, *On Watch*, p. 447.

19. Interview, Adm. Nikolai Amelko, Moscow, 17 December 1991.

20. Interview, Leonid Zamyatin, Moscow, 16 December 1991.

21. Interview, Georgiy Kornienko, Moscow, 17 December 1991.

22. The capacity of the United States to communicate with its naval forces in the Mediterranean had improved significantly since 1962, largely as a result of automated message processing at communications centers ashore and satellite communications. Nevertheless, the president did not have the capability for real-time communication. Bouchard, *Command in Crisis*, pp. 163–64.

23. Bouchard, *Command in Crisis*, makes this argument, p. 177.

24. Ibid., p. 183.

25. Kissinger, *Years of Upheaval*, p. 980.

26. For an explicit version of this argument, see Barry M. Blechman and Douglas M. Hart, "The Political Utility of Nuclear Weapons: The 1973 Middle East Crisis," *International Security* 7, 1 (Summer 1982), pp. 132–56, at pp. 151–52.

27. Victor Israelian, *The Kremlin: October 1973*, unpublished monograph, pp. 5–6.

28. Ibid., pp. 13–14.

29. Ibid., p. 29.

30. Interview, Victor Israelian, State College, Pa., 9 January 1992.

31. Ibid.

32. Ibid.

33. Israelian, *The Kremlin: October 1973*, p. 26.

34. Interview, Georgi Arbatov, Moscow, May 19, 1989. Kissinger, too, had worried about the impact of Watergate, but for quite different reasons. At the meeting in the Situation Room of the White House on the night of 24 October, he and his advisors speculated about whether the Soviet Union would have challenged a "functioning" president. His concern about the weakness of the president made Kissinger all the more intent on signaling resolve through a worldwide alert. "We are at a point of maximum weakness," Kissinger said, "but if we knuckle under now we are in real trouble. . . . We will have to contend with the charge in the domestic media that we provoked this. The real charge is that we provoked this by being soft." Kissinger, *Years of Upheaval*, p. 589. It was not only the American media but most of the Soviet leadership that accused Nixon and Kissinger of manipulating domestic politics. The Politburo, however, did not see the domestic crisis in Washington as a weakness to exploit, but as a source of American irresponsibility.

35. Interview, Georgiy Kornienko, Moscow, 17 December 1991.

36. Interview, Anatoliy Dobrynin, Moscow, 17 December 1991.

37. Some experts did not take the alert seriously for different reasons. Anatoliy Gromyko emphasized the consequences of the frequent use of alerts by the United States in the past: "The Americans put forces on alert so often that it is hard to know what it meant." Interview, Moscow, 18 May 1989. Aleksandr Kislov made the same point: "Mr. Nixon used to exaggerate his intentions regularly. He used alerts and leaks to do this. I personally was not excited by the alert." Kislov observed that American and Soviet approaches are diametrically opposed. "We have tried consistently to understate our military intentions. The Americans do the reverse." Interview, Moscow, 18 May 1989.

38. Others drew a misleading and incorrect analogy to the American alert in September 1970. Georgi Arbatov, a sophisticated student of the United States, and a close advisor of Brezhnev at the time, considered the two alerts comparable. "Because the naval forces that were alerted in the Mediterranean carried nuclear weapons," he explained, "the alert in 1970 was also a strategic alert." Interview, Moscow, 19 May 1989. He did not distinguish between a selective alert of conventional forces and naval units, some of which were equipped with nuclear weapons, and a worldwide alert of the entire American military establishment, including land-, sea-, and air-based tactical and strategic nuclear forces. Arbatov was insensitive to the signal that Kissinger and Schlesinger thought would make such a dramatic impact in Moscow.

39. Interview, Anatoliy Dobrynin, Moscow, 17 December 1991. In the most striking comment made by a Soviet expert, Aleksandr Kislov remarked: "It was a third-degree alert, not a first or a second." Interview, Moscow, 18 May 1989.

40. Interview, Victor Israelian, State College, Pa., 9 January 1992.

41. Interview, Anatoliy Dobrynin, Moscow, 17 December 1991.

42. The Soviet alert system is designed to allow conventional alert readiness to be raised to a high level without alerting any strategic nuclear forces. Joseph J. Kruzel, "Military Alerts and Diplomatic Signals," in Ellen P. Stern, ed., *The Limits of Military Intervention* (Beverly Hills, Calif.: Sage, 1977), pp. 83–99, at p. 98.

43. Israelian, *The Kremlin: October 1973*, p. 27.

44. Ibid.

45. Ibid.

46. Ibid., p. 28; Interview, Victor Israelian, State College, Pa., 9 January 1992.

47. Israelian, *The Kremlin: October 1973*, p. 28. Gromyko, too, did not want to go to Washington.

48. Ibid., p. 29.

49. Ibid.

50. Ibid., pp. 13–14.

51. Interview, Aleksandr Kislov, Moscow, 18 May 1989.

52. Israelian, *The Kremlin: October 1973*, p. 28, and cited by Kissinger, *Years of Upheaval*, p. 608.

53. Kissinger, *Years of Upheaval*, p. 582.

54. Ibid., p. 587.

55. The proposed plan was a variant of a disengagement plan that had failed in 1971. The IDF would withdraw ten kilometers east of the canal in exchange for a complete evacuation of the Egyptian army from the east bank and its redeployment ten kilometers from the canal on the western side. A buffer zone of twenty kilometers between the two armies would be created. See Kissinger, *Years of Upheaval*, p. 588.

56. The Cabinet began meeting at 4:00 P.M. Tel Aviv time on 24 October, or 8:00 A.M. Washington time, ten hours before Kissinger learned from Dobrynin of the impending letter from Brezhnev.

57. Kissinger, *Years of Upheaval*, p. 590. His response early on the morning of 25 October was very different than it had been forty-eight hours earlier when Kissinger had agreed in conjunction with Moscow to press Israel to withdraw while insisting that the line would be difficult to establish.

58. Kissinger, *Years of Upheaval*, p. 590.

59. Interview, David Elazar, Tel Aviv, 14 May 1974.

60. Interview, Henry Kissinger, New York, 19 June 1991.

61. Interview, Peter Rodman, Washington, D.C., 24 April 1991.

62. Interview, William Quandt, Washington, D.C., 7 December 1988.

63. Interview, Joseph Sisco, Washington, D.C., 17 April 1991, emphasis in conversation.

64. Interview, Simcha Dinitz, Jerusalem, 7 January 1989.

65. Interviews, Ministry of Foreign Affairs, Jerusalem, June 1989. Moshe Dayan subsequently described the pressure on Israel *after* the crisis between Moscow and Washington was resolved as "brutal." Interview, Tel Aviv, 3 May 1975.

66. Moshe Dayan, *Moshe Dayan: Story of My Life* (London: Weidenfeld & Nicolson, 1976), p. 447, emphasis added; Interview, Tel Aviv, 3 May 1975.

67. Abba Eban, the foreign minister, is the only official in either Washington or Tel Aviv to assert that Kissinger pressed Israel to resupply the Third Army as a result of the Soviet threat. He writes in his memoirs that "Brezhnev's warning of unilateral action had impelled the United States to move on two fronts. Every pressure would be put on Israel to stabilize the cease-fire and to open a supply line to the Third Army; at the same time the threat of Soviet intervention would be met by a tough American posture." Abba Eban, *Abba Eban: An Autobiography* (New York: Random House, 1977), p. 536. Eban continued: "In Israel we had no doubt about the reality of Soviet danger. There was no reason to question the American warning that if the Soviet Union dropped supplies to the Egyptian Third Army, the United States could not oppose its action. We unanimously decided to open a controlled supply line through the United Nations checkpoints, enabling the Third Army to receive humanitarian aid while ensuring that no weapons would pass through."
Eban's account is contradicted by the record of Israel's Cabinet meetings. The most likely explanation of the inconsistency is that Eban did not distinguish carefully among the three meetings of Israel's Cabinet. The Cabinet met three times, on 24 October, late on the night of 25 October through to the next morning, and again on the evening of 26 October. In all likelihood, Eban is referring to the Cabinet meeting that did not begin until late at night on 25 October and met throughout the night until 4:00 A.M. Tel Aviv time, on 26 October. Eban subsequently refers to "the Cabinet meeting of the 25th [which] lasted until 04:00 in the morning [of the 26th]." Interview, Abba Eban by M. Brecher, 15 July 1974, cited in Michael Brecher with Benjamin Geist, *Decisions in Crisis: Israel, 1967 and 1973* (Berkeley: University of California Press, 1980), p. 227.

68. Alexander M. Haig, Jr., with Charles McCarry, *Inner Circles: How America Changed the World, A Memoir* (New York: Warner Books, 1992), p. 417.

69. Kissinger, *Years of Upheaval*, p. 592.

70. Ibid.

71. Brecher with Geist, *Decisions in Crisis*, p. 226. Brecher also reports a telephone conversation between Prime Minister Meir and President Nixon. Interview, U.S. Embassy officials by M. Brecher, 12 August 1974, cited in *Decisions in Crisis*, p. 226.

72. Kissinger, *Years of Upheaval*, p. 601.

73. Moshe Dayan, Public Lecture, 19 December 1974, *Ma'ariv*, 27 December 1974. He does not repeat the threat that the United States would resupply the Third Army in his memoirs. Plans for a U.S. resupply of the Third Army were confirmed in interviews of senior intelligence officials in Washington. See Alan Dowty, *Middle East Crisis: United States Decision-Making in 1958, 1970, and 1973* (Berkeley: University of California Press, 1984), p. 297, n. 48. Kissinger reports that the Defense Department had developed a plan for resupplying the Third Army with American C-130 aircraft. Kissinger, *Years of Upheaval*, pp. 602, 604, 623.

74. Dayan, *Story of My Life*, p. 448.

75. Kissinger, *Years of Upheaval*, p. 604.

76. Ibid., p. 602.

77. Ibid., pp. 604–5.

78. Ibid., p. 607.

79. Cited by Kissinger, *Years of Upheaval*, p. 607.

80. Ibid.

81. Ibid., pp. 608–9.

82. Ibid., p. 609.

83. The prime minister wrote: "I have no illusions but that everything will be imposed on us by the two big powers. . . . There is only one thing that nobody can prevent us from doing and that is to proclaim the truth of the situation; that Israel is being punished not for its deeds, but because of its size and because it is on its own." Cited by Kissinger, *Years of Upheaval*, p. 610.

84. Ibid., p. 610. Prime Minister Golda Meir made precisely that argument to Israel's Cabinet. See Golda Meir, *My Life* (Jerusalem: Steimatzky's, 1975), pp. 371–72.

85. Ibid.

86. Garthoff concurs that the alert and the Brezhnev letter that prompted it did not end the crisis or resolve the situation. He argues that the Brezhnev letter did not serve to reinforce U.S. readiness to curb Israel, which was in any case the product of American policy, but slowed it down. See Raymond Garthoff, *Détente and Confrontation: American-Soviet Relations from Nixon to Reagan* (Washington, D.C.: The Brookings Institution, 1985), pp. 380, 383.

87. Haig, *Inner Circles*, pp. 413–14.

88. On 23 October, Nixon and Kissinger had decided to prevent the destruction of the Third Army, and Kissinger had so informed Israel. Kissinger, *Years of Upheaval*, pp. 571, 573; William Quandt, *Decade of Decisions: American Policy Toward the Arab-Israel Conflict* (Berkeley: University of California Press, 1977), p. 194.

89. Interview, Victor Israelian, State College, Pa., 9 January 1992.

90. Kissinger, *Years of Upheaval*, p. 602.

91. Interview, Georgi Arbatov, Moscow, 19 May 1989.

92. Interview, Anatoliy Gromyko, Moscow, 18 May 1989.

93. Israelian, *The Kremlin: October 1973*, pp. 29–30.

94. Nixon writes that "We have no information which would indicate that the cease-fire is now being violated on any significant scale." Richard M. Nixon, *RN: Memoirs of Richard Nixon* (New York: Grosset and Dunlap, 1978), p. 939.

95. Nixon added, "It would be understood that this is an extraordinary and temporary step solely for the purpose of providing adequate information concerning compliance by both sides with the terms of the cease-fire. If this is what you mean by contingents, we will consider it." Nixon, *RN: Memoirs of Richard Nixon*, p. 939; Kissinger, *Years of Upheaval*, p. 591.

96. Israelian, *The Kremlin: October 1973*, p. 30.

97. Kissinger, *Years of Upheaval*, p. 592. Garthoff, *Détente and Confrontation*, pp. 380ff also suggests that Sadat's action helped to resolve the crisis.

98. Cited by Kissinger, *Years of Upheaval*, p. 588.

99. Ibid., p. 592.

100. Ibid.

101. Interview, senior member of President Sadat's office, Cairo, 3 April 1988. The only example of quick and easy compellence throughout the war and the crisis occurred between the United States and Egypt.

102. Israelian, *The Kremlin: October 1973*, p. 25.

103. Ibid., p. 27.

104. Ibid., p. 29.

105. Ibid., p. 26.

106. Ibid.

107. Interview, Victor Israelian, State College, Pa., 8 January 1992.

108. Interview, Leonid Zamyatin, Moscow, 16 December 1991.

109. Israelian, *The Kremlin: October 1973*, pp. 28–29.

110. Ibid., p. 29.

111. Arbatov added, "I was writing a speech for Brezhnev to give to the World Peace Congress in the conference room next door to where Brezhnev and Kissinger were meeting [three days before the crisis]. There was then a constant uninterrupted dialogue between the two countries. We knew the situation so well, what the United States would say and do." Interview, Moscow, 19 May 1989.

112. Israelian, *The Kremlin: October 1973*, p. 29.

113. Interview, Aleksandr Kislov, Moscow, 18 May 1989.

114. Interview, Victor Israelian, State College, Pa., 9 January 1992.

115. Israelian, *The Kremlin: October 1973*, p. 26.

116. Blechman and Hart, "The Political Utility of Nuclear Weapons."

117. In his press conference on 25 October, Kissinger said: "The United States and the Soviet Union are, of course, ideological and, to some extent, political adversaries. But the United States and the Soviet Union also have a very special responsibility. We possess—each of us—nuclear arsenals capable of annihilating humanity. We—both of us—have a special duty to see to it that confrontations are kept within bounds that do not threaten civilized life. Both of us, sooner or later, will have to come to realize that the issues that divide the world today, and foreseeable issues, do not justify the unparalleled catastrophe that a nuclear war would represent." Kissinger, *Years of Upheaval*, p. 594.

118. For an analysis of the impact of loss aversion on political choice, see Janice Gross Stein and Louis Pauly, eds., *Choosing to Cooperate: How States Avoid Loss* (Baltimore: Johns Hopkins University Press, 1993).

119. Kissinger, *Years of Upheaval*, p. 602.

120. Interview, Henry Kissinger, New York, 19 June 1991.

121. Interview, Georgi Arbatov, Moscow, 19 May 1989. Victor Israelian drew a similar conclusion. Interview, State College, Pa., 8 January 1992.

122. Kissinger, *Years of Upheaval*, p. 475.

123. Cited in Richard Valeriani, *Travels with Henry* (Boston: Houghton, Mifflin, 1979), pp. 181–82.

124. Bouchard, *Command in Crisis*, p. 182.

125. Interview, Aleksandr Kislov, Moscow, 18 May 1990.

126. Interview, Victor Israelian, State College, Pa., 8 January 1992.

127. Blechman and Hart, "The Political Utility of Nuclear Weapons," p. 150, n. 21.

128. William Odom, "C3I and Telecommunications at the Policy Level," *Incidental Paper* (Harvard University: Program on Information Resources Policy, Seminar on Command, Control, Communications, and Intelligence, 1980), cited by Scott Sagan, "Nuclear Alerts and Crisis Management," *International Security* 9, 4 (Spring, 1985), pp. 99–139, quotation on p. 130. Odom was head of the National Security Agency under President Reagan.

129. Garthoff, *Détente and Confrontation*, and Richard K. Betts, *Nuclear Black-mail and Nuclear Balance* (Washington, D.C.: The Brookings Institution, 1987) are outstanding exceptions.

130. For penetrating critiques, see Kruzel, "Military Alerts and Diplomatic Signals"; Douglas M. Hart, "Soviet Approaches to Crisis Management: The Military Dimension," *Survival* 26, 5 (September/October 1984), pp. 214–22.

131. Steinbruner, "An Assessment of Nuclear Crises," p. 46.

132. Cited by Betts, *Nuclear Blackmail and Nuclear Balance*, p. 125. Betts also reports interviewing one of Kissinger's principal aides who remembers Kissinger saying at the time: "This is the last time we'll ever be able to get away with this." William Odom drew a similar conclusion in the early 1980s: "I don't think, with the changed balance of forces today, that I would feel very comfortable about going all the way up and saying, okay, we are going to bargain down. I have a feeling that they would go up with us. Considering current Soviet force structure, if I were advising . . . [Soviet leaders] I think I would feel confident about staying in the bargaining all the way up a little longer than before. So that raises real questions about whether we can continue to behave the way we have in the past." "C3I and Telecommunications at the Policy Level."

133. Betts makes this argument in *Nuclear Blackmail and Nuclear Balance*, p. 125.

134. Interview, Vadim Zagladin, Moscow, 18 May 1989.

135. *Izvestiya*, 1 December 1973.

136. *Sovetskaia Belorussia*, 15 November 1973.

137. Interview, Aleksandr Kislov, Moscow, 18 May 1989.

138. Interview, Georgi Arbatov, Moscow, 19 May 1989.

139. Interview, Victor Israelian, State College, Pa., 8 January 1992.

140. The role of détente in the crisis at the end of the October War was discussed at the Central Committee plenary meeting held in December. As Garthoff notes, although Brezhnev continued to defend détente and prevailed, the crisis increased skepticism about détente in the collective judgment of Soviet leaders. Garthoff, *Détente and Confrontation*, p. 396. Those who had opposed détente also became more strident in their criticism. See the speech of Vladimir Suslov, *R. Vilnius*, 28 November 1973, reported in *Foreign Broadcast Information Service* (FBIS), 29 November 1973. See also George Breslauer, *Khrushchev and Brezhnev as Leaders: Building Authority in Soviet Politics* (London: Allen & Unwin, 1982), pp. 179–83; and Franklyn Griffiths, "The sources of American conduct: Soviet perspectives and their policy implications," *International Security* 9, 2(Fall, 1984), pp. 3–50.

141. Franklyn Griffiths notes: "One may therefore think in terms of a rolling consensus that shifted leftward to the advantage of reformative views after December 1969, halted its leftward movement as of October 1973, and swung back to the right and a renewed expansionist emphasis as of December 1974 [the passage of the Jackson-Vanik amendment in the U.S. Congress]. The overt consensus rolled primarily in response to change in the operative consensus of the collective leadership as it dealt with adjustments of power among oligarchs and processed a never-ending sequence of foreign and domestic issues." Franklyn Griffiths, "Attempted Learning: Soviet Policy Toward the United States in the Brezhnev Era," in George W. Breslauer and Philip Tetlock, eds., *Learning in U.S. and Soviet Foreign Policy* (Boulder, Colo.: Westview Press, 1991), pp. 630–83, quotation on p. 652.

142. Interview, Victor Israelian, State College, Pa., 8 January 1992.

CHAPTER TWELVE
How Crises Are Resolved

1. "Remarks made at press conference," John F. Kennedy School of Government, 21 October 1987.

2. Henry M. Pachter, *Collision Course: The Cuban Missile Crisis and Coexistence* (New York: Praeger, 1963); Albert and Roberta Wohlstetter, "Controlling the Risks in Cuba," *Adelphi Paper* no. 17 (London: International Institute for Strategic Studies, 1965); Elie Abel, *The Missile Crisis* (Philadelphia: Lippincott, 1966); Arnold L. Horelick and Myron Rush, *Strategic Power and Soviet Foreign Policy* (Chicago: University of Chicago Press, 1966); Thomas Schelling, *Arms and Influence* (New Haven, Conn.: Yale University Press, 1966); Graham T. Allison, *Essence of Decision: Explaining the Cuban Missile Crisis* (Boston: Little, Brown, 1971); Alexander L. George and Richard Smoke, *Deterrence in American Foreign Policy: Theory and Practice* (New York: Columbia University Press, 1974); Raymond L. Garthoff, *Reflections on the Cuban Missile Crisis*, rev. ed. (Washington, D.C.: The Brookings Institution, 1989).

3. William W. Kaufmann, *The Requirements of Deterrence* (Princeton, N.J.: Center for International Studies, 1954); Schelling, *Arms and Influence*, pp. 97–99; Bernard Brodie, *War and Politics* (New York: Macmillan, 1973), p. 416. For a critical review of this literature see Robert Jervis, "Deterrence Theory Revisited," *World Politics* 31, 2(January 1979), pp. 289–324, and chapter 14 for an additional empirical assessment.

4. Herman Kahn, *On Escalation: Metaphors and Scenarios* (New York: Praeger, 1965), pp. 74–82; Schelling, *Arms and Influence*, pp. 80–83; Albert and Roberta Wohlstetter, *Controlling the Risks in Cuba*, p. 16. For Taylor's views, see his interview with Richard Neustadt, reprinted in part in David A. Welch, ed., *Proceedings of the Hawk's Cay Conference on the Cuban Missile Crisis, 5–8 March 1987* (Cambridge, Mass.: Harvard University, Center for Science and International Affairs, Working Paper 89–1, 1989), mimeograph, pp. 72–74, hereafter cited as *Hawk's Cay Conference*. Curtis LeMay expressed similar views in the Sloan Foundation interviews, cited in Gregg Herken, *Counsels of War* (New York: Alfred Knopf, 1985), p. 168; Gen. William Y. Smith, Transcript of "Cuba Between the Superpowers," Antigua, 3–7 January 1991, mimeograph, p. 112, forthcoming as James G. Blight, David Lewis, and David A. Welch, eds., *Cuba Between the Superpowers: The Antigua Conference on the Cuban Missile Crisis* (Savage, Md.: Rowman and Littlefield, in press), hereafter cited as *Antigua Conference*, commenting on the views of the joint chiefs of staff.

5. Henry Kissinger, "Reflections on Cuba," *Reporter*, 22 November 1962, pp. 21–24.

6. McGeorge Bundy, *Danger and Survival: Choices About the Bomb in the First Fifty Years* (New York: Random House, 1988), pp. 446, 453. See also Maxwell D. Taylor, "General Taylor Reflects on Lessons from the Cuban Missile Crisis," *International Herald Tribune*, 13 October 1982, p. 6.

7. Cited by Richard Betts, *Nuclear Blackmail and Nuclear Balance* (Washington, D.C.: The Brookings Institution, 1987), p. 125.

8. William Odom, "C3I and Telecommunications at the Policy Level," (Cambridge, Mass.: Harvard University, Program on Information Resources Policy, 1980), cited by Scott Sagan, "Nuclear Alerts and Crisis Management," *International Security* 9, 4 (Spring 1985), pp. 99–139, at p. 130.

9. Raymond Garthoff, "Transcript of the Proceedings of the Havana Conference on the Cuban Missile Crisis, January 9–12, 1992," mimeograph, p. 184, forthcoming as James G. Blight, Bruce J. Allyn, and David A. Welch, eds., *Cuba on the Brink: Castro, the Missile Crisis, and the Soviet Collapse* (New York: Pantheon Books, in press), hereafter cited as *Havana Conference*, revealed that the Defense Department rushed some missiles into readiness during the crisis. By 31 October, the United States had 172 operational ICBMs and 1,450 bombers on alert and 144 Polaris missiles at sea on station for a total initial salvo of 2,952 weapons. Central Intelligence Agency, "Soviet Military Buildup in Cuba, 21 October 1962," Mary S. McAuliffe, *CIA Documents on the Cuban Missile Crisis 1962* (Washington, D.C.: History Staff, Central Intelligence Agency, October 1992), pp. 247–59, estimated that the Soviet Union had only 60–65 ICBM launchers. For the administration's awareness of the balance, see Scott D. Sagan, "SIOP-62: The Nuclear War Plan Briefing to President Kennedy," *International Security* 12, 1(Summer 1987), pp. 22–51; David A. Welch, ed., *Proceedings of the Cambridge Conference on the Cuban Missile Crisis, 11–12 October 1987* (Cambridge, Mass.: Harvard University, Center for Science and International Affairs, April 1988), final version, mimeograph, pp. 25–26, 44, 51, hereafter cited as *Cambridge Conference*; Bruce J. Allyn, James G. Blight, and David A. Welch, eds., *Back to the Brink: Proceedings of the Moscow Conference on The Cuban Missile Crisis, January 27– 28, 1989*, CSIA Occasional Paper no.9 (Lanham, Md.: University Press of America, 1992), pp. 23–24, 27–29, 38–39, 44–45, 63–64, hereafter cited as *Moscow Conference*; Raymond L. Garthoff, "Intelligence Assessment and Policymaking: A Decision Point in the Kennedy Administration," Staff Paper (Washington, D.C.: The Brookings Institution, 1984).

10. Interview, Georgiy Shakhnazarov, Cambridge, Mass., 12 October 1987.

11. Dimitri Volkogonov, *Moscow Conference*, pp. 52–53.

12. Dean Rusk as told to Richard Rusk, *As I Saw It*, Daniel S. Papp, ed. (New York: Norton, 1990), p. 250.

13. Gen. Anatoliy Gribkov, "Operation 'Anadyr,' " *Der Spiegel*, no. 16, 1992, pp. 152–54, and comments of Sergei Khrushchev, *Moscow Conference*, pp. 37–38.

14. Interview, Fedor Burlatsky, Cambridge, Mass., 12 October 1987.

15. N. Khrushchev, *Khrushchev Remembers*, Strobe Talbott, trans. and ed. (Boston: Little, Brown, 1970), p. 498; "Khrushchev Letter of October 30, 1962," English and Russian language texts in *Problems of Communism*, special edition, 41 (Spring 1992), pp. 62–73; Gribkov, "Operation 'Anadyr,' " Part II, *Der Spiegel*, no. 17, 1992, p. 205.

16. Oleg Darusenkov, *Antigua Conference*, pp. 135–36; Gen. Anatoliy Gribkov, *Havana Conference*, pp. 24–25, reports that if Cuba had been occupied, Soviet forces planned to join remnant Cuba forces in guerilla units.

17. John A. McCone, "Memorandum on Cuba," 20 August 1962; Ray S. Cline, Memorandum for Acting Director General of Intelligence, "Recent Soviet Military Activities in Cuba, 3 September 1962"; "Soviet Military Buildup in Cuba, 21 October 1962"; Central Intelligence Agency, Memorandum, "Deployment and Withdrawal of Soviet Missiles and Other Significant Weapons in Cuba, 29 November 1962," *CIA Documents on the Cuban Missile Crisis 1962*, pp. 19–20, 35–38, 357–60. The 29 November Memorandum estimated that there was enough equipment in Cuba for four Soviet armored-combat groups. According to Raymond L. Garthoff, *Havana Conference*, p. 113, the final CIA estimate in 1963 was twenty-two thousand Soviet military personnel.

18. John A. McCone, "Memorandum for the File, 19 October 1962," describing that day's Ex Comm meeting, *CIA Documents on the Cuban Missile Crisis*, pp. 183–86, for Kennedy's concern about Berlin. James Blight interview with Robert S. McNamara, Washington, D.C., 21 May 1987, in James G. Blight and David A. Welch, *On the Brink: Americans and Soviets Reexamine the Cuban Missile Crisis* (New York: Hill and Wang, 1989), p. 192; McNamara was even more definite in his estimate: "I cannot believe," he said, "that there would not have been a Soviet military response somewhere in the world." *Moscow Conference*, pp. 98–99.

19. John A. McCone, "Memorandum of Meeting with the President, Attorney General, Secretary McNamara, Gen. Taylor, and Mr. McCone, 10:00 A.M.—10/21/62," *CIA Documents on the Cuban Missile Crisis*, pp. 241–42; Theodore C. Sorensen, *Kennedy* (New York: Harper & Row, 1965), p. 684; Arthur M. Schlesinger, Jr., *A Thousand Days: John F. Kennedy in the White House* (Boston: Houghton, Mifflin, 1965), p. 759.

20. Gribkov, *Havana Conference*, p. 23. According to Robert McNamara, *Antigua Conference*, p. 131, the CIA was also uncertain about the presence of nuclear warheads in Cuba, including warheads for the longer range MRBMs and IRBMs.

21. FROG is the American designator for the *Luna* missile. Othon Montero, *Antigua Conference*, pp. 147–48; Gribkov, *Havana Conference*, pp. 16–21, for the Soviet order of battle in Cuba.

22. Gribkov, *Havana Conference*, p. 29. Khrushchev gave assurances to William E. Knox during the crisis that "all sophisticated military equipment were [sic] under direct 100 percent Soviet control." These weapons would only be used in defense of Cuba and then only on the "personal instructions from Khrushchev himself as Commander-in-Chief of the Armed Forces." The Cubans, he told Knox, were too "temperamental" to be given nuclear weapons. Roger Hilsman to the Secretary of State, "Khrushchev's Conversation with Mr. W. E. Knox, President, Westinghouse Electrical International, Moscow, October 24."

23. Sergo Mikoyan, "The Crisis of Misperceptions: One More Retrospective Appraisal of the Missile Crisis," in James A. Nathan, ed., *The Cuban Missile Crisis Revisited* (New York: St. Martin's Press, 1992), p. 67.

24. Gribkov, *Havana Conference*, pp. 23, 29–30, 278, and "Operation 'Anadyr,'" Part II, pp. 198–99 and A. Dokuchayev, "100-dnevnyi Yadernyi kruiz" [The Hundred-Day Nuclear Cruise], *Krasnaya zvezda*, 6 November 1992, p. 2; "Karibskii krizis" [The Caribbean Crisis], *Voenno-istorcheskii Zhurnal* [Military History Journal] part 3, no. 12 (December 1992), pp. 38–45, and part 4, no. 1 (January 1993), pp. 38–43; Fidel Castro, *Havana Conference*, pp. 33–34, citing Article 10 of the Soviet-Cuban Agreement.

25. John Newhouse, "A Reporter At Large: Socialism or Death," *New Yorker*, 27 April 1992, citing a Soviet General Staff retrospective on the Caribbean crisis; Dokuchayev, "100-dnevnyi' yadernyi kruiz" [The Hundred-Day Nuclear Cruise], p. 2; Gribkov, "Karibskii krizis" [The Caribbean Crisis].

26. On 29 October, Adm. Robert L. Dennison, CINCLANT, reported that Soviet forces in Cuba had FROG launchers and requested permission to equip U.S. forces with nuclear-capable Honest Johns. McNamara and the chiefs turned him down on the grounds that there was no evidence that there were any nuclear warheads in Cuba for the FROGs. Maj. Gen. John A. Heintoks, "Memorandum for the Special Assis-

tant to the Secretary of Defense, 29 December 1962," describing CINCLANT's request to have tactical nuclear weapons available for the invasion force. McNamara, *Havana Conference*, pp. 271–72.

27. Herken, *Counsels of War*, p. 168; Arthur Schlesinger, Jr., *Robert Kennedy and His Times* (Boston: Houghton, Mifflin, 1978), p. 524. The footnote offers no citation for Gen. LeMay's reported plea to Robert Kennedy: "Why don't we go in and make a strike on Monday anyway."

28. Sloan Foundation interviews, cited in Herken, *Counsels of War*, p. 168.

29. Dean Acheson, "Dean Acheson's Version of Robert Kennedy's Version of the Cuban Missile Affair: Homage to Plain Dumb Luck," *Esquire*, February 1969, pp. 76–77, 44–46.

30. Edward Weintal and Charles Bartlett, *Facing the Brink: An Intimate Study of Crisis Diplomacy* (New York: Charles Scribner's Sons, 1967), pp. 54–55.

31. Interview, C. Douglas Dillon, 15 May 1987; Blight and Welch, *On the Brink*, pp. 152–53.

32. Interview, Maxwell C. Taylor by Richard E. Neustadt, Washington, D.C., 28 June 1983, in *Hawk's Cay Conference*, p. 72; Maxwell D. Taylor, "General Taylor Reflects on Lessons from the Cuban Crisis," *International Herald Tribune*, 13 October 1982, p. 6, offers a more charitable view of the administration and its policies. He argues that nuclear weapons were irrelevant to the outcome because neither side could use them, but that the United States' conventional advantage was critical.

33. "Extracts from the record of a conversation between Anastas Mikoyan and Fidel Castro. . . . on November 3, 1962 at Fidel Castro's residence," *International Affairs* (Moscow), no. 10 (October 1992), p. 116, and the comments of Sergo Mikoyan, *Cambridge Conference*, p. 122. It is possible that the elder Mikoyan exaggerated the likelihood of war to convince Castro that the Soviet Union had no choice but to reach an accommodation with the United States.

34. Interview, Sergei Khrushchev, Moscow, 17 May 1989.

35. Interview, Sergo Mikoyan, Moscow, 17 May 1989.

36. Oleg Troyanovsky, "The Caribbean Crisis: A View from the Kremlin," *International Affairs* (Moscow) 4–5 (April-May 1992), p. 156. Khrushchev confided to his son-in-law, Aleksei Adzhubei, that American military action anywhere would place him in an extraordinarily difficult situation. He did not want to think about how he would respond. Interview, Aleksei Adzhubei, Moscow, 15 May 1989; N. Khrushchev, *Khrushchev Remembers: The Glasnost Tapes*, trans. and ed. Jerrold L. Schechter with Vyacheslav V. Luchkov (Boston: Little, Brown, 1990), p. 8. Sergei Khrushchev concurs. There were a few high-level meetings between the defense ministry and the defense chiefs to explore retaliatory options. "But as far as I know, none was accepted for further serious elaboration, because Khrushchev hoped for a peaceful resolution of the crisis." Sergei Khrushchev, *Antigua Conference*, p. 128.

37. For example, Bruce Bueno de Mesquita, *The War Trap* (New Haven, Conn.: Yale University Press, 1981).

38. Janice Gross Stein, "Calculation, Miscalculation, and Conventional Deterrence I: The View from Cairo," in Robert Jervis, Richard Ned Lebow, and Janice Gross Stein, *Psychology and Deterrence* (Baltimore: Johns Hopkins University Press, 1985), pp. 34–59, at p. 47.

39. For arguments that strategic parity complicates crisis prevention and management, see Gilbert R. Winham, "Introduction," in Winham, ed., *New Issues in*

International Crisis Management (Boulder, Colo.: Westview Press, 1988), pp. 1–10, at p. 9 and Alexander L. George, "U.S.-Soviet Global Rivalry: Norms of Competition," in Winham, ed., *New Issues in International Crisis Management*, pp. 67–89.

40. The point is also made by Robert Jervis, *The Meaning of the Nuclear Revolution: Statecraft and the Prospect of Armageddon* (Ithaca, N.Y.: Cornell University Press, 1989), p. 104.

41. Cited by Betts, *Nuclear Blackmail and Nuclear Balance*, p. 125.

42. Statement to the Southern Governors Conference, June 1975, cited in Richard Valeriani, *Travels with Henry* (Boston: Houghton, Mifflin, 1979), pp. 181–82.

43. Elmo R. Zumwalt, Jr., *On Watch: A Memoir* (New York: Quadrangle, 1976); Joseph B. Bouchard, *Command in Crisis: Four Case Studies* (New York: Columbia University Press, 1991).

44. Kaufmann, *The Requirements of Deterrence*; Schelling, *Arms and Influence*; Jervis, "Deterrence Theory Revisited."

45. Arthur M. Schlesinger, Jr., *A Thousand Days: John F. Kennedy in the White House* (Boston: Houghton, Mifflin, 1965), p. 811.

46. Schelling, *Arms and Influence*, pp. 92–99.

47. Robert F. Kennedy, *Thirteen Days: A Memoir of the Cuban Crisis* (New York: Norton, 1969), p. 93.

48. White House Tapes, "Transcript of 27 October 1962," pp. 1, 20; Roger Hilsman, *To Move A Nation: The Politics of Foreign Policy in the Administration of John F. Kennedy* (Garden City, N.Y.: Doubleday, 1967), p. 220; Kennedy, *Thirteen Days*, p. 94.

49. White House Tapes, "Transcript of 27 October 1962," pp. 2, 13; *Department of State Bulletin* 47, no. 1220, 12 November 1962, pp. 741–43, reprinted in David L. Larson, ed., *The "Cuban Crisis" of 1962: Selected Documents, Chronology and Bibliography*, 2d ed. (Lanham, Md.: University Press of America, 1986), pp. 183–86; Kennedy, *Thirteen Days*, pp. 196–201.

50. White House Tapes, "Transcript of 27 October 1962," pp. 81–82.

51. Kennedy, *Thirteen Days*, p. 97.

52. Sorensen, *Kennedy*, p. 714.

53. *Hawk's Cay Conference*, pp. 66–67; Douglas Dillon voiced this fear at the 27 October Ex Comm meeting. He speculated that Khrushchev's most recent public statement, in which he took a harder line, might be a stalling tactic to provide the Soviets with the time they needed to prepare for a full-fledged military confrontation. *Summary Record of NSC Executive Committee Meeting*, no. 7, 27 October 1962, 10:00 A.M.

54. Rusk, *As I Saw It*, p. 238. At the first Ex Comm meeting, Kennedy exclaimed: "If he [Khrushchev] wants to get into a war over *this*, uh . . . Hell, if it's war that's gonna come on this thing, or if he sticks those kinds of missiles in, it's after the warning, and he's gonna, and he's gonna get into a war for, six months from now or a year from now, so . . ." "Transcript of Ex Comm Meeting, 16 October 1962, 6:30–7:55 P.M.," p. 25.

55. "Letter from Premier Khrushchev to President Kennedy, 26 October 1962," *Department of State Bulletin*, 69, 19 November 1973, pp. 640–43. Reprinted in Larson, *The "Cuban Crisis" of 1962*, pp. 175–80, p. 180.

56. Hawk's Cay Conference, author's record.

57. Kennedy, *Thirteen Days*, p. 93.

58. Interview, Dean Rusk, Athens, Ga., 21 September 1987.

59. According to Ambassador Dobrynin, "The Washington embassy held an emergency meeting and as a precaution, of course, we were alerted. But there was no panic so as to drive us to burn papers. That did not occur." *Moscow Conference*, pp. 78–79; Interviews, Anatoliy Dobrynin and Georgiy Kornienko, Moscow, 17 December 1991. Garthoff, *Reflections on the Cuban Missile Crisis*, p. 89, points out that it is possible that the preparatory measures Soviet diplomats admit taking included procedures for burning papers if the crisis led to war. There is one report that papers were burned. János Radványi, *Hungary and the Superpowers: The 1956 Revolution and Realpolitik* (Stanford: Stanford University Press, 1972), p. 131, the Hungarian ambassador in Washington at the time, contends that on 26 October Dobrynin announced at a gathering of Warsaw Pact diplomats "that the Soviet embassy was this very moment burning its archives."

60. Interviews, Leonid Zamyatin, Anatoliy Dobrynin, and Georgiy Kornienko, Moscow, 16–17 December 1991.

61. Hilsman, *To Move A Nation*, p. 220; Comments by President Kennedy and Secretary of State Rusk, White House Tapes, "Transcript of 27 October 1962," pp. 129, 131, make reference to a single ship approaching the blockade line. There is an earlier reference, on Friday, to the forward movement of *Grozny* in Bromley Smith's "Summary Record of NSC Executive Committee Meeting no. 6, October 26, 1962, 10:00 A.M." The "Summary Record of NSC Executive Committee Meeting no. 10, October 28, 1962, 11:10 A.M." indicates that *Grozny* had stopped and was holding a course outside the blockade line.

62. Interviews, Leonid Zamyatin, Anatoliy Dobrynin, Georgiy Kornienko, and Adm. Nikolai Amelko, Moscow, 16–18 December 1991.

63. Interview, Oleg Grinevsky, Stockholm, 26 April 1992; The same claim is made by the less reliable Fedor Burlatsky, *Cambridge Conference*, pp. 106–7, and interview, Cambridge, Mass., 13 October 1987.

64. "Yesterday," he admonished Castro, "you shot down one of these . . . provocative flights." Nikita Khrushchev to Fidel Castro, 28 October 1962.

65. Khrushchev, *Khrushchev Remembers*, p. 499; and *The Glasnost Tapes*, p. 178. Sergei Khrushchev reported that he edited out many of the most sensitive revelations of his father's memoirs before sending them to the West for publication. This probably accounts for the discrepancy between the two versions. In 1970, Sergei Khrushchev was unprepared to have it known that it was Soviet, not Cuban gunners, who shot down the U-2.

66. *Moscow Conference*, pp. 30–31.

67. Aleksandr Alekseev, "The Caribbean Crisis: As It Really Was," *Ekho Planety*, no. 33 (November 1988), p. 32, and *Havana Conference*, p. 93; Sergo Mikoyan, *Cambridge Conference*, pp. 105–7, 110; Anatoliy Gribkov, *Havana Conference*, pp. 74–75, 78.

68. Fidel Castro, *Havana Conference*, p. 79.

69. Malinovsky sent a curt telegram to Gen. Pliyev in Cuba: "You hastily shot down the U.S. plane, and agreement for a peaceful way to deter an invasion of Cuba was already taking shape." Comments of Aleksandr Alekseev and Dimitri Volkogonov, *Moscow Conference*, pp. 30–31; Gen. Sergio del Valle, *Antigua Con-*

ference, pp. 121–22; Oleg Darusenkov, *Antigua Conference*, pp. 135–36; Anatoliy Gribkov, *Havana Conference*, pp. 87–88. Khrushchev's confusion probably derived from Malinovsky's silence. Because Khrushchev believed that the Cubans were responsible, his defense minister was in no rush to tell him the unpleasant truth that Soviet military officers in Cuba had exceeded their authority. It was not until many years later, Sergo Mikoyan explained, that Soviet political officials found out that the U-2 had been destroyed by a Soviet SAM. Khrushchev may have only learned the truth in retirement. He could not have sent a cable to Pliyev, as he maintains in *The Glasnost Tapes*, because he did not know that the military had violated his orders. His memory probably played a trick on him when he dictated his memoirs, and led him to conflate what he knew at the time with what he knew in 1962. *Cambridge Conference*, p. 110. Oleg Troyanovsky, "The Caribbean Crisis," p. 153, offers a different view. He contends that Khrushchev was "seriously worried" by a report that reached the Kremlin that the surface to air missile that had destroyed the U-2 had been fired on the initiative of a middle-rank Soviet officer. None of the other Soviets who have spoken about the incident remember any such report.

70. Bundy, *Danger and Survival*, p. 426.

71. Interview, Dean Rusk by James Blight, Athens, Ga., 18 May 1987.

72. Interview, Dean Rusk, 21 September 1987; Rusk, *As I Saw It*, pp. 238, 240–41.

73. Interview, Robert McNamara, Cambridge, Mass., 12 October 1987.

74. Franklyn Griffiths, "The Sources of American Conduct: Soviet Perspectives and Their Policy Implications," *International Security* 9, 2(Fall 1984), pp. 3–50.

75. After the crisis, Khrushchev wrote to Kennedy: "I take the liberty to think that you evidently held to a restraining position with regard to those forces which suffered from militaristic itching." "Khrushchev Letter of October 30, 1962."

76. White House Tapes, "Transcript of 27 October 1962," p. 89.

77. "We'll have to put . . . pressure on the Israelis or we are going to risk Soviet intervention." Alexander M. Haig, Jr., with Charles McCarry, *Inner Circles: How America Changed the World, A Memoir* (New York: Warner Books, 1992), pp. 413–14.

78. Henry Kissinger, *Years of Upheaval* (Boston: Little, Brown, 1982), p. 576.

79. Interview, Peter Rodman, Washington, D.C., 24 April 1991.

80. Interview, Henry Kissinger, New York, 19 June 1991. See also Kissinger, *Years of Upheaval*, p. 593.

81. See, for example, Barry M. Blechman and Douglas M. Hart, "The Political Utility of Nuclear Weapons: The 1973 Middle East Crisis," *International Security* 7, 1 (Summer 1982), pp. 132–56, 151–52.

82. Interview, Victor Israelian, State College, Pa., 9 January 1992.

83. Interview, Georgi Arbatov, Moscow, 19 May 1989.

84. Interview, Victor Israelian, State College, Pa., 8 January 1992.

85. Victor Israelian, *The Kremlin: October 1973*, unpublished monograph, p. 26.

86. Glenn H. Snyder and Paul Diesing, *Conflict Among Nations: Bargaining, Decision Making, and System Structure in International Crises* (Princeton, N.J.: Princeton University Press, 1977), pp. 189–90; Jonathan Wilkenfeld and Michael Brecher, "Superpower Crisis Management Behavior," in C. W. Kegley and P. J. McGowan,

eds., *Foreign Policy: US/USSR, Sage International Yearbook of Foreign Policy Studies*, vol. 7 (Beverly Hills, Calif.: Sage, 1982), pp. 185–212. Snyder and Diesing (p. 248) find that in ten of their fourteen cases that did not lead to war, the accommodative process was mostly one-sided. Wilkenfeld and Brecher find that in crises in which the United States or the Soviet Union was involved, victory or defeat occurred twice as often as compromise or stalemate.

87. George and Smoke, *Deterrence in American Foreign Policy*, pp. 550–61; Stephen Maxwell, "Rationality in Deterrence," *Adelphi Paper* no. 50 (London: International Institute for Strategic Studies, 1968); Betts, *Nuclear Blackmail and Nuclear Balance*, p. 134.

88. Alexander L. George, David K. Hall, and William E. Simons, *The Limits of Coercive Diplomacy: Laos, Cuba, Vietnam* (Boston: Little, Brown, 1971), pp. 217–18; George and Smoke, *Deterrence in American Foreign Policy*, pp. 558–61; Glenn Snyder, "'Prisoner's Dilemma' and 'Chicken' Models in International Politics," *International Studies Quarterly* 15, 1(March 1971), pp. 66–103; Robert Jervis, "Bargaining and Bargaining Tactics," in J. Roland Pennock and John Chapman, eds., *Coercion*, NOMOS, vol. 14 (Chicago: Aldine, Atherton, 1972), pp. 272–88, and *The Meaning of the Nuclear Revolution*, pp. 30–31; Robert Powell, "Crisis Bargaining, Escalation, and MAD," *American Political Science Review* 81, 3(September 1987), pp. 717–35, and "Nuclear Brinkmanship with Two-Sided Incomplete Information," *American Political Science Review* 82, 1(March 1988), pp. 155–78.

89. Robert Jervis, *The Meaning of the Nuclear Revolution*, p. 30. Jervis, pp. 243–47, suggests that a state's resolve to defend its interests will also be influenced by its leaders' judgment of how strongly motivated its adversary is to prevail. He reasons that when both sides have core concerns at stake they will be highly motivated to prevail but that even small concessions in this circumstance can significantly affect the balance of motivation. The bargaining advantage can be expected to shift in the favor of the state making the concession because its remaining interests are likely to be more important. Jervis deduces a series of propositions about the frequency, intensity, and outcome of challenges between nuclear adversaries based on the reality of mutual assured destruction and the political importance and acceptability of the status quo.

90. Remarks of Secretary of State Dean Rusk before an Executive Session of the Senate Foreign Relations Committee, Subcommittee on American Republics Affairs, 1 May 1961, in *Executive Session of the Senate Foreign Relations Committee (Historical Series)*, vol. 13, part 2, Washington, 1984, pp. 327–76.

91. Alekseev, "The Caribbean Crisis," p. 27.

92. Ibid., p. 29.

93. Betts, *Nuclear Blackmail and Nuclear Balance*, p. 134, also argues that the balance of interests may have been perceived differently by Moscow and Washington. In his view, it "is quite possible that while the U.S. perception of the balance of interests determined U.S. leaders' resolve to run the military risks of a nuclear threat, the Soviet perception of the balance, in itself, gave Moscow's leaders no obvious reason to cave in."

94. Interview, Sergo Mikoyan, Moscow, 17 May 1989.

95. Theodore C. Sorensen, *The Kennedy Legacy* (New York: Macmillan, 1969), p. 187.

96. Bundy, *Danger and Survival*, p. 416.

97. *Hawk's Cay Conference*, p. 15.

98. Alekseev, "The Caribbean Crisis," p. 29.

99. Nikita Khrushchev to John F. Kennedy, 30 October 1962, *Problems of Communism*, pp. 62–73, indicates his belief that the blockade was the result of pressure from right-wing, militarist forces, and his fear that these forces would compel Kennedy during the crisis to invade Cuba.

100. Norman Cousins, "The Cuban Missile Crisis: An Anniversary," *Saturday Review*, 15 October 1977, p. 4, quoting from his interview with Khrushchev.

101. Kennedy, *Thirteen Days*, pp. 63, 65–66; Comments of Anatoliy Dobrynin, *Moscow Conference*, pp. 78–84, 142–45.

102. Anatoliy Dobrynin, "The Caribbean Crisis: An Eyewitness Account," *International Affairs* (Moscow), 8 August 1992, pp. 52–53.

103. Khrushchev, *The Glasnost Tapes*, p. 178.

104. Cited in Kissinger, *Years of Upheaval*, p. 578.

105. Raymond Garthoff, *Detente and Confrontation: American-Soviet Relations from Nixon to Reagan* (Washington, D.C.: The Brookings Institution, 1985), pp. 382–83 makes a similar argument.

106. Interview, Victor Israelian, State College, Pa., 9 January 1992.

107. Interview, William Colby, 11 January 1992.

108. Kissinger, *Years of Upheaval*, p. 594.

109. Ibid., p. 584.

110. Interview, William Quandt, Washington, 7 December 1988.

111. Snyder and Diesing, *Conflict Among Nations*, p. 248.

112. Interview, Aleksei Adzhubei, Moscow, 15 May 1989.

113. Khrushchev, *The Glasnost Tapes*, p. 179.

114. Robert Jervis, letter to authors, 14 September 1992, suggests that there may have been some motivated bias in Kennedy's upgrading of the possible benefits of concession once he saw it as necessary.

115. *Hawk's Cay Conference*, p. 101.

116. Israelian, *The Kremlin: October 1973*, p. 28.

117. Richard M. Nixon, *RN: Memoirs of Richard Nixon* (New York: Grosset & Dunlap, 1978), pp. 939–940; Kissinger, *Years of Upheaval*, p. 591.

118. See Richard Ned Lebow, *Between Peace and War: The Nature of International Crisis* (Baltimore: Johns Hopkins University Press, 1981); Jervis, Lebow, and Stein, *Psychology and Deterrence*; Richard Ned Lebow and Janice Gross Stein, "Beyond Deterrence," *Journal of Social Issues* 43, no. 4 (1987), pp. 5–71; Janice Gross Stein, "Extended Deterrence in the Middle East: American Strategy Reconsidered," *World Politics* 39, 3(April 1987), pp. 326–52, and "The Wrong Strategy in the Right Place: The United States in the Gulf," *International Security* 13, 3(Winter 1988–89), pp. 142–67.

119. For an analysis of Saddam Hussein's calculations, see Janice Gross Stein, "Deterrence and Compellence in the Gulf, 1990–91: A Failed or Impossible Task?" *International Security* 17, 2(Fall 1992), pp. 147–179.

120. For an analysis of Munich and Hitler's preferences, see Richard Ned Lebow and Janice Gross Stein, "Review of the Data Collections on Extended Deterrence by Paul Huth and Bruce Russett," in Kenneth A. Oye, ed., *Specifying and Testing Theories of Deterrence* (Ann Arbor: University of Michigan Press, in press).

CHAPTER THIRTEEN
Deterrence and Crisis Management

1. Television and radio interview: "After Two Years—A Conversation with the President," 17 December 1962, *White House Press Release*, 29 December 1962.

2. Among the most prominent early examples are Thomas Schelling, *Arms and Influence* (New Haven, Conn.: Yale University Press, 1966); Oran Young, *The Politics of Force: Bargaining During International Crises* (Princeton, N.J.: Princeton University Press, 1968); Dina A. Zinnes, Robert C. North, and Howard E. Koch, Jr., "Capability, Threat and the Outbreak of War," in James N. Rosenau, ed., *International Politics and Foreign Policy: A Reader in Research and Theory* (New York: Free Press, 1969), pp. 469–82; Coral Bell, *The Conventions of Crisis: A Study in Diplomatic Management* (New York: Oxford University Press, 1971); Ole R. Holsti, *Crisis, Escalation, War* (Montreal: McGill-Queen's University Press, 1972); Philip Williams, *Crisis Management: Confrontation and Diplomacy in the Nuclear Age* (New York: Wiley, 1972).

3. In addition to Schelling, *Arms and Influence*, see Albert and Roberta Wohlstetter, "Controlling the Risks in Cuba," *Adelphi Paper* no. 17 (London: International Institute for Strategic Studies, 1965); Arnold L. Horelick, "The Cuban Missile Crisis: An Analysis of Soviet Calculations and Behavior," *World Politics* 16, 3(April 1964), pp. 363–89; Alexander L. George and Richard Smoke, *Deterrence in American Foreign Policy* (New York: Columbia University Press, 1974).

4. Richard Ned Lebow, *Between Peace and War: The Nature of International Crisis* (Baltimore: Johns Hopkins University Press, 1981) and *Nuclear Crisis Management: A Dangerous Illusion* (Ithaca, N.Y.: Cornell University Press, 1987); Paul Bracken, *The Command and Control of Nuclear Forces* (New Haven, Conn.: Yale University Press, 1983); John Steinbruner, "Nuclear Decapitation," *Foreign Policy* no. 45 (Winter 1981–82), pp. 16–28; Gilbert R. Winham, ed., *New Issues in International Crisis Management* (Boulder, Colo.: Westview Press, 1988); Kurt Gottfried and Bruce G. Blair, *Crisis Stability and Nuclear War* (New York: Oxford University Press, 1988); Alexander L. George, ed. *Avoiding War: Problems of Crisis Management* (Boulder, Colo.: Westview Press, 1991).

5. Edward Martin, then assistant secretary of state for Inter-American affairs, "Transcript of the Proceedings of the Havana Conference on the Cuban Missile Crisis, January 9–12 1992," mimeograph, p. 120, forthcoming as James G. Blight, Bruce J. Allyn, and David A. Welch, eds. *Cuba on the Brink: Castro, the Missile Crisis, and the Soviet Collapse* (New York: Pantheon Books, in press), hereafter cited as *Havana Conference*, revealed that on Monday night, 22 October, as the president delivered his television address announcing the quarantine, he delivered a speech to the Washington Newspaper Correspondents Association on Cuba in which he declared that there was no chance that the Soviets would take the risks involved in deploying nuclear weapons in Cuba. The speech had been cleared without objections by State, Defense, and CIA. Ray S. Cline, the CIA's deputy director of intelligence, periodically briefed the president about the Soviet military buildup in Cuba. "I can tell you," he insisted, "—and I talked to President Kennedy most of that summer about the evidence we found—that he did not anticipate that Khrushchev would put the missiles in Cuba." *Havana Conference*, pp. 114–15.

6. McCone, who invariably expected the worst from Soviet leaders, took the prospect of a secret missile deployment seriously. He gave great weight to what he

considered Khrushchev's far-reaching aggressive goals and his disturbing propensity for risk taking. On 22 August, McCone warned Kennedy, McNamara, and Rusk that Khrushchev might be preparing to introduce ballistic missiles into Cuba. McNamara and Rusk disagreed and insisted that there was no evidence in support of McCone's suspicion. In early September, in Paris on his honeymoon, McCone pressed his case with McGeorge Bundy. He argued that the volume of material going into Cuba was too large and expensive, and was inconsistent with any other explanation. Interview, John A. McCone by Joe D. Frantz, 19 February 1970, John F. Kennedy Library; Arthur Krock, 30 November 1962, "Confidential Memo," on John McCone's suspicions about a Soviet missile deployment in Cuba; Arthur Krock, *Memoirs: Sixty Years on the Firing Line* (New York: Funk & Wagnalls, 1968), pp. 378–80; Ray S. Cline, *Havana Conference*, p. 115; Theodore C. Sorensen, *Kennedy* (New York: Harper & Row, 1965), p. 670; Edward Weintal and Charles Bartlett, *Facing the Brink: An Intimate Study of Crisis Diplomacy* (New York: Charles Scribner's Sons, 1967), pp. 60–61; McGeorge Bundy, *Danger and Survival: Choices About the Bomb in the First Fifty Years* (New York: Random House, 1988), pp. 419–20; Dino A. Brugioni, *Eyeball to Eyeball: The Inside Story of the Cuban Missile Crisis* (New York: Random House, 1990), pp. 96–98.

7. The CIA also erred because it underestimated the size and nature of the Soviet buildup. On 19 September, the Special National Intelligence Estimate, 85-3-62, reported that the Soviet Union had deployed 4,000–4,500 military personnel in Cuba, most of them technicians. By 22 October, the day the president announced the naval quarantine, CIA estimates of Soviet military personnel in Cuba had risen to 8,000–10,000. This figure was off by a factor of four; Moscow had sent four fully armed regiments comprising 42,000 men. The Soviet military thought such a large force was necessary to protect the missiles and their warheads. By failing to comprehend the scope and military capabilities of the Soviet forces in Cuba, American intelligence missed an important clue about the purpose of these forces. Special National Intelligence Estimate 85–3-62, offered as evidence the seeming failure of the Soviet Union to deploy a sizeable military force in Cuba in support of their estimate that no missiles would be sent. More information about the CIA's underestimates of Soviet conventional forces in Cuba can be found in Senate Committee on Armed Services, *Investigation of Preparedness Program, Interim Report by Preparedness Investigating Subcommittee: The Cuban Military Buildup.* 88th Cong., 1st sess., 1963, p. 8, and U.S. Congress. House Committee on Appropriations, Subcommittee on Department of Defense Appropriations. "Statement of John McCone," *Hearings*, 88th Cong., 1st sess., 1963, pp. 51–53.

8. The Special National Intelligence Estimate, 85-3-62, "The Military Buildup in Cuba," 19 September 1962; Special National Intelligence Estimate 85-2-62, "The Situation and Prospects in Cuba," 1 August 1962, noted that it was unlikely because the Soviet Union had never deployed nuclear weapons outside its territory. "The Military Buildup in Cuba," an 11 July 1961 report prepared by an ad hoc committee of the United States Intelligence Board, concluded that Soviet support for the Castro regime was part of a political effort to isolate the United States and to destroy its influence throughout the world. In keeping with this objective, Cuba was to be made a base for propaganda and subversion in Latin America. The Current Intelligence Memorandum, no. 3047/62, 22 August 1962, "Recent Soviet Military Aid to Cuba," p. 4, prepared by the CIA Office of Current Intelligence, concluded that the Soviet military buildup was designed to strengthen the position of the Communist regime in Cuba.

9. Quoted in Brugioni, *Eyeball to Eyeball*, p. 147.

10. For a discussion of the intelligence problem and an evaluation of the intelligence community's performance, see Roger Hilsman, *To Move A Nation: The Politics of Foreign Policy in the Administration of John F. Kennedy* (Garden City, N.Y.: Doubleday, 1967), pp. 160–92; Graham T. Allison, *Essence of Decision: Explaining the Cuban Missile Crisis* (Boston: Little, Brown, 1971), pp. 118–23; Brugioni, *Eyeball to Eyeball*, pp. 116–18, 135–40, 154–55, 159–60, 182–86.

11. Interview, McGeorge Bundy, New York City, 27 April 1989. The political motive behind Cuban surveillance is also noted by Theodore Sorensen, "Oral History Interview with Theodore C. Sorensen, March 26, 1964, by Carl Kaysen," pp. 46–47, John F. Kennedy Library; Brugioni, *Eyeball to Eyeball*, pp. 168–72.

12. Janice Gross Stein, "Calculation, Miscalculation, and Conventional Deterrence I: The View from Cairo," in Robert Jervis, Richard Ned Lebow, and Janice Gross Stein, *Psychology and Deterrence* (Baltimore: Johns Hopkins University Press, 1985), pp. 34–59.

13. Cited by Henry Kissinger, *Years of Upheaval* (Boston: Little, Brown, 1982), p. 461. Kissinger also asked for a contingency plan should an Arab-Israeli war occur. The task fell to a junior State Department official who never completed the report. See William B. Quandt, *Peace Process: American Diplomacy and the Arab-Israeli Conflict since 1967* (Washington, D.C.: The Brookings Institution, 1993), p. 149.

14. Cited by Kissinger, *Years of Upheaval*, p. 462. See also Ray S. Cline, "Policy Without Intelligence," *Foreign Policy* 17 (Winter 1974–75), pp. 121–36.

15. Kissinger, *White House Years* (Boston: Little, Brown, 1979), p. 459.

16. Cited by Kissinger, *Years of Upheaval*, p. 464. A comprehensive analysis of American intelligence performance is found in the report of the House Select Committee on Intelligence, chaired by Representative Otis Pike. See *U.S. Intelligence Agencies and Activities: The Performance of the Intelligence Community*, Hearings before the Select Committee on Intelligence, 11, 12, 18, 25, 30, September, 7, 30, 31 October 1975, 94th Cong., 1st sess. (Washington, D.C.: Government Printing Office, 1975).

17. Kissinger, *Years of Upheaval*, p. 464.

18. Ibid., p. 465.

19. Ibid., p. 464.

20. Ibid.

21. Interview, Henry Kissinger, New York City, 19 June 1991.

22. Lebow, *Between Peace and War*, chap. 4; Lebow, "Conclusions," *Psychology and Deterrence*, pp. 203–32.

23. Alan Bullock, *Hitler: A Study in Tyranny*, rev. ed. (New York: Harper & Row, 1964), pp. 490–562; Gerhard Weinberg, *The Foreign Policy of Hitler's Germany*, 2 vols. (Chicago: University of Chicago Press, 1970–1980), II, pp. 535–656; Anna M. Cienciala, *Poland and the Western Powers, 1938–1939* (London: Routledge & Kegan Paul, 1968).

24. "Transcript of Off-the-Record Meeting on Cuba, 11:50 A.M.–12:57 P.M.," p. 15, John F. Kennedy Library. Special National Intelligence Estimate 11–18–62, "Soviet Reactions to Certain US Courses of Action on Cuba, 19 October 1962" (Excerpt), Mary S. McAuliffe, ed., *CIA Documents on the Cuban Missile Crisis 1962* (Washington, D.C.: History Staff, Central Intelligence Agency, October 1992), pp. 197–202, indicates that this was also the view of the intelligence community.

25. R. E. Nisbett and L. Ross, *Human Inference: Strategies and Shortcomings of Social Judgment* (Englewood Cliffs, N.J.: Prentice-Hall, 1980); Daniel Kahneman,

Paul Slovic, and Amos Tversky, *Judgment Under Uncertainty: Heuristics and Biases* (Cambridge: Cambridge University Press, 1982); Susan T. Fiske and Shelley E. Taylor, *Social Cognition* (Reading, Mass.: Addison-Wesley, 1984), 72–99.

26. The fundamental attribution error is a well-documented cognitive predisposition. We surmise that it is also influenced by affect and more likely in interactions where the actor has strong negative affect toward the other party. In such interactions, cognitive processes combine with motivated biases to support the contrasting stereotypes of a benign self and malign adversary.

27. The "proportionality" bias is probably a common cognitive failing, although not one that psychologists have explicitly examined. It is probably a second-order derivative from the anchoring and availability biases: people infer the values of the goals associated with the actions of others by "anchoring" the costs of these actions in a readily "available" criterion—their immediately available experiences and their consequences—and then conclude that the greater the costs, the greater the stakes. See Amos Tversky and Daniel Kahneman, "Availability: A Heuristic for Judging Frequency and Probability," *Cognitive Psychology* 5, 1(1973), pp. 207–32; Fiske and Taylor, *Social Cognition*, pp. 250–56, 268–75.

28. Experimental studies indicate that people determine the motives of a donor by how much a gift costs the giver in marginal utility; the greater the relative cost, the more sincere the giver. Stuart S. Komorita, "Concession-Making and Conflict Resolution," *Journal of Conflict Resolution* 17, 4(December 1973), pp. 745–62; Dean G. Pruitt, *Negotiation Behavior* (New York: Academic Press, 1981), pp. 124–25.

29. Carter and his advisors estimated the costs of the invasion to be high: it would end détente, make arms control difficult if not impossible, antagonize the Third World, and provoke stiff guerrilla resistance by Afghanis. These costs only made sense if Afghanistan was the prelude to an attack against Iran with the goal of controlling its oil fields and gaining access to a warm-water port. See Richard Ned Lebow and Janice Gross Stein, "Explaining Foreign Policy Change: The Carter Administration and Soviet Intervention in Afghanistan," in Daniel Caldwell and Timothy J. McKeown, eds., *Force, Leadership, and Diplomacy: Essays in Honor of Alexander L. George* (Boulder, Colo.: Westview Press, 1993), pp. 95–128.

30. Interview, Robert S. McNamara by James Blight, 21 May 1987, Washington, D.C., in James G. Blight and David A. Welch, *On the Brink: Americans and Soviets Reexamine the Cuban Missile Crisis* (New York: Hill and Wang, 1989), p. 193.

31. Kissinger, *Years of Upheaval*, p. 509.

32. Acute stress makes people feel apprehensive, tense, and helpless. It can induce headaches, indigestion, palpitations, insomnia, irritability, and interfere with concentration. Highly stressed people are likely to be indecisive, mistrustful of their own judgment, and easily influenced by the views of others. Their ability to perform complex tasks will decline. Joseph de Rivera, *The Psychological Dimension of Foreign Policy* (Columbus, Ohio: Bobbs-Merrill, 1968), pp. 150–51; Dean G. Pruitt, "Definition of the Situation as a Determinant of International Action," in Herbert C. Kelman, ed., *International Behavior: A Social-Psychological Analysis* (New York: Holt, Rinehart & Winston, 1965), pp. 391–432; Ole R. Holsti and Alexander L. George, "The Effects of Stress on the Performance of Foreign Policy-Makers," in C. P. Cotter, ed., *Political Science Annual: An International Review*, vol. 6 (Indianapolis: Bobbs-Merrill, 1975), pp. 255–319; Irving L. Janis, *Psychological Stress* (New York: Wiley, 1958); Irving L. Janis and Leon Mann, *Decision Making: A Psy-*

chological Analysis of Conflict, Choice, and Commitment (New York: Free Press, 1977); Yaacov Y. I. Vertzberger, *The World in Their Minds: Information Processing, Cognition, and Perception in Foreign Policy Decisionmaking* (Stanford: Stanford University Press, 1990).

33. Alexander L. George, "The Impact of Crisis-Induced Stress on Decision Making," in Frederic Solomon and Robert Q. Marston, eds., *The Medical Implications of Nuclear War* (Washington, D.C.: National Academy Press, 1986), pp. 529–52.

34. Holsti and George, "The Effects of Stress on the Performance of Foreign Policy Makers,"; George, "The Impact of Crisis-Induced Stress on Decision Making"; Janis and Mann, *Decision Making*; Irving L. Janis, *Groupthink: Psychological Studies of Policies, Decisions, and Fiascoes* (Boston: Houghton, Mifflin, 1982); Thomas C. Wiegele, "Decision-Making in an International Crisis: Some Biological Factors," *International Studies Quarterly* 17, 3 (September 1973), pp. 295–335; Lebow, *Between Peace and War*, pp. 171–72, 268–73 and *Nuclear Crisis Management*, pp. 104–56; Ole R. Holsti, "Crisis Decision Making," in Philip E. Tetlock, Jo L. Husbands, Robert Jervis, Paul C. Stern, and Charles Tilly, eds., *Behavior, Society, and Nuclear War*, vol. I (New York: Oxford University Press, 1989), pp. 8–84.

35. Michael Brecher and Jonathan Wilkenfeld, *Crisis, Conflict, and Instability* (Oxford: Pergamon Press, 1989), pp. 178–93; Michael Brecher, *Crises in World Politics: Theory and Reality* (Oxford: Pergamon Press, 1993).

36. This kind of stress can culminate in projection and acute denial through severe dissociative reactions in people with unstable personality structures. The classic description of defense mechanisms is Sigmund Freud, "The Neuro-Psychoses of Defense" (1894) and "Further Remarks on the Neuro-Psychoses of Defense," *The Standard Edition of Complete Psychological Works of Sigmund Freud*, ed. James Strachey (London: Hogarth, 1962), vol. 3, pp. 43–68, 159–85; Anna Freud, *The Ego and The Mechanisms of Defense* (originally published in 1936) (New York: International Universities Press, 1953). See also Norman A. Cameron, "Paranoid Conditions and Paranoia," in Silvano Arieti and Eugene B. Brody, eds., *American Handbook of Psychiatry: Adult Clinical Psychiatry*, vol. 3, 2d. ed. (New York: Basic Books, 1974), pp. 676–93; Abraham Kardiner and H. Spiegel, *War, Stress, and Neurotic Illness* (New York: Harper & Row, 1941); Charles D. Spielberger and Irving G. Sarason, eds., *Stress and Anxiety*, 2 vols. (Washington, D.C.: Hemisphere, 1975); Harold I. Kaplan and Benjamin Saddock, "Dissociative Disorders," in *Synopsis of Psychiatry*, 6th ed. (Baltimore: Williams & Wilkins, 1991), pp. 428–37; Lebow, *Between Peace and War*, pp. 115–19, for a brief overview of the relevant psychiatric concepts and related literature.

37. Dean Rusk as told to Richard Rusk, *As I Saw It*, Daniel S. Papp, ed. (New York: Norton, 1990), pp. 535–36.

38. Interview, Joseph Sisco, Washington, D.C., 17 April 1991.

39. See especially, Janis and Mann, *Decision Making*, pp. 57–60, 74–95, 107–33.

40. Ibid.

41. Quandt explained the order as a result of the stress and urgency in the White House that night: "You must remember, we were under considerable pressure. We felt there was some urgency, and we were tired, fatigued that night." Interview, William Quandt, Washington, D.C., 7 December 1988.

42. Kissinger, *Years of Upheaval*, p. 593.

43. "Transcript of Off-the-Record Meeting on Cuba, October 16, 1962, 11:50 A.M.–12:57 P.M.," p. 27, John F. Kennedy Library.

44. Oral History Interview with Roswell L. Gilpatric by Dennis O'Brien, 5 May 1970, p. 50, John F. Kennedy Library.

45. "Excerpts from Off-the-Record Meeting on Cuba, 16 October 1962, 11:50 A.M.–12:57 P.M.," *International Security* 10, 1(Summer 1985), pp. 171–94.

46. Even if Kennedy had not issued his September warnings, he would have confronted more or less the same dilemma given his assumptions about Khrushchev and the likely consequences of tolerating Soviet missiles in Cuba. As we argued in chapter 4, the September warnings did make the expected domestic and foreign costs of tolerating the missiles more severe.

47. The breakdowns of Wilhelm, Stalin, and Nehru are described in Lebow, *Between Peace and War*, pp. 135–45, 283–85.

48. Interview, Ray S. Cline, Washington, 13 May 1992.

49. Arthur M. Schlesinger, Jr., *A Thousand Days: John F. Kennedy in the White House* (Boston: Houghton, Mifflin, 1965), p. 734.

50. George Ball in David A. Welch, ed., *Proceedings of the Hawk's Cay Conference on the Cuban Missile Crisis, 5–8 March 1987* (Cambridge, Mass.: Harvard University, Center for Science and International Affairs, Working Paper 89–1, 1989), p. 12, hereafter cited as *Hawk's Cay Conference*. Interview, Dean Rusk, Athens, Ga., 21 September 1987; Robert McNamara, "Presentation to the Crisis Stability Project," Cornell University Peace Studies Program, 21 August 1985, mimeograph, p. 2; Interview, McGeorge Bundy, Cambridge, Mass., 12 October 1989.

51. Janis and Mann, *Decision Making*, pp. 74–79.

52. N. G. Kuznetsov, "At Naval Headquarters," I. V. Tuilenev, "At Moscow District Headquarters," in Seweryn Bialer, ed., *Stalin and His Generals: Soviet Military Memoirs of World War II* (New York: Pegasus, 1969), pp. 189–200, 200–203; A. M. Nekrich, "June 22, 1941," in Vladimir Petrov, *June 22, 1941: Soviet Historians and the German Invasion* (Columbia: University of South Carolina Press, 1968), pp. 240–45; Nikita S. Khrushchev, *Khrushchev Remembers*, ed. and trans. Strobe Talbott (Boston: Little, Brown, 1970), pp. 126–35, 166–87; Georgii Zhukov, *The Memoirs of Marshal Zhukov* (London: Cape, 1971), pp. 234–38.

53. Oleg Troyanovsky, "The Caribbean Crisis: A View from the Kremlin," *International Affairs* (Moscow) 4–5 (1992), pp. 147–57.

54. "Notes on Remarks by President Kennedy before the National Security Council, Tuesday, January 22, 1963."

55. Acute stress is most likely in those crises where time pressure, and the situational and personality triggers of stress interact. It is understandable that statistical analyses of large numbers of crises provide little evidence of stress. The findings of these studies and those of case studies that document the debilitating role of stress are not incompatible. Although it is far from a ubiquitous phenomenon, the problem of stress in crisis is nevertheless troubling because it is most likely in war-threatening crises—these are the crises in which the threat of loss is the greatest. When leaders cope with stress by bolstering, or adopt more extreme defense mechanisms to protect their personality structures, their ability to resolve these confrontations will be seriously impaired.

56. Kissinger, *Years of Upheaval*, p. 589.

57. Ibid.

58. Ibid., p. 596; Richard M. Nixon, *RN: Memoirs of Richard Nixon* (New York: Grosset & Dunlap, 1978), p. 940.

59. Similar processes seemed to be at work in Soviet public opinion in 1990. During the crisis but before the war in the Gulf, Prime Minister Nikolai Ryzhkov said that he did not believe the Soviet Union should send troops to the Gulf: "This is my personal opinion. I have said it before and I will say it again. We should not under any circumstances take part, not by sending troops, and not by any other means. We do not need to do this. Afghanistan was enough for us." Remarks to Soviet reporters, *Pravda*, 3 December 1990.

60. Janice Gross Stein, "Deterrence and Compellence in the Gulf: A Failed or Impossible Task," *International Security* 17, 2(Autumn 1992), pp. 147–179.

61. Lebow, *Between Peace and War*, pp. 281–91, and *Nuclear Crisis Management*, chap. 3.

62. Robert F. Kennedy, *Thirteen Days: A Memoir of the Cuban Missile Crisis* (New York: W. W. Norton, 1969), p. 98.

63. H. R. Haldeman with Joseph DiMona, *The Ends of Power* (New York: Times Books, 1978), p. 93, reports that Power told a subordinate: "Make a little mistake. Send a message in the clear." Scott Sagan, "Nuclear Alerts and Crisis Management," *International Security* 9 (Spring 1985), pp. 99–139; Raymond L. Garthoff, *Reflections on the Cuban Missile Crisis*, rev. ed. (Washington, D.C.: The Brookings Institution, 1989), p. 62, n. 101, reports that he learned of Power's decision to "rub it in" to the Soviets from Maj. Gen. (then Col.) George J. Keegan, Jr. in SAC intelligence, who was present when the alert order was sent out. Interviews of participants at the Hawk's Cay Conference indicated that the president's advisors had no knowledge of Power's action.

64. Many SAC officers were dismayed when the Kennedy administration failed to seize the opportunity provided by the crisis to eliminate the threat posed by the Soviet Union. After it was over, Gen. Power delivered a tirade to a shocked audience at RAND about Kennedy's cowardice and his failure to use the crisis as a pretext to destroy the Soviet Union. Interview, former RAND analyst, May 1989. Gregg Herken, *Counsels of War* (New York: Alfred Knopf, 1985), pp. 168, 364, citing videotape interviews conducted by the Alfred Sloan Foundation with participants in the Cuban missile crisis, reports that LeMay was also unhappy with the Kennedy administration's handling of the crisis. He is alleged to have complained that only unnecessary presidential caution had prevented the Air Force from proceeding with the air strikes against Cuba *after* the Soviets had capitulated.

65. See Allison, *Essence of Decision*, pp. 127–31; Richard K. Betts, *Soldiers, Statesmen, and Cold Warriors* (Cambridge, Mass.: Harvard University Press, 1977), pp. 12–15; Lebow, *Between Peace and War*, pp. 285–88, and *Nuclear Crisis Management*, chap. 3.

66. Kennedy and McNamara devoted a lot of attention to the blockade, where they rightly worried that bad judgment by a ship captain could start a war. Their supervision of the blockade was meticulous and thoughtful, and was intended to ensure that any Soviet ship that approached the picket line would be given every opportunity to comply with American procedures before force was used. They stipulated that only minimal force was to be used: a warning shot across the bow, and if that failed, ships were to be disabled by firing at their rudders. McNamara asked the navy to provide Russian-language translators to ships on the blockade line and make sure that their captains were provided with a detailed set of instructions covering as many contingencies as they could envisage. On the blockade, see Atlantic Command, Headquarters of the Commander in Chief, *CINCLANT Historical Account of*

Cuban Crisis–1963, 29 April 1963; Joseph F. Bouchard, *Command in Crisis: Four Case Studies* (New York: Columbia University Press, 1991), chap. 4; Comments of Robert McNamara, *Hawk's Cay Conference*, pp. 53–54.

On the evening of 23 October, in response to a suggestion from British Ambassador David Ormsby-Gore, Kennedy ordered McNamara to have the navy narrow the blockade radius from 800 to 500 miles from Cuba. He would give Khrushchev more time to reflect on the consequences of a military encounter at sea. Kennedy, *Thirteen Days*, p. 67. One prominent study charges the navy with having disobeyed McNamara's order. Allison, *Essence of Decision*, pp. 129–30. This allegation is convincingly refuted by Dan Caldwell, "A Research Note on the Quarantine of Cuba, October 1962," *International Studies Quarterly* 22, 4(December 1978), pp. 625–33. Declassified naval records indicate that the blockade was initially established at 500 miles, not at 800 miles as reported by Robert Kennedy. On the advice of the navy, McNamara decided to leave it at 500 miles to protect ships from attack from aircraft based in Cuba. Bouchard, *Command in Crisis*, chap. 5, citing especially the diary of Chief of U.S. Atlantic Fleet (CINCLANTFLT) Adm. Alfred G. Ward.

The navy has also been accused of carrying out dangerous antisubmarine warfare (ASW) operations without presidential knowledge or consent. It is alleged to have used depth charges to force Soviet submarines in the Caribbean to surface. Allison, *Essence of Decision*, p. 130; Sagan, "Nuclear Alerts and Crisis Management," p. 117. In reality, the navy developed special procedures, including the use of depth charges, to signal submerged submarines and did its best to inform the Soviet navy about them in the hope of preventing an incident. Bouchard, *Command in Crisis*, chap. 5. The navy not only carried out all the directives it received from the secretary of defense, but naval commanders on the picket line frequently sought additional instructions on how to handle a possible encounter with Soviet merchant vessels or submarines. Many officers were terrified that they would make some mistake that would start a war.

67. Interview, Dean Rusk, Athens, Ga., 21 September 1987; President Kennedy thought that the missiles were under American control but was informed by McNamara on Saturday that Turkey owned and controlled them but that the warheads were in American custody. White House Tapes, "Transcript of 27 October 1962," p. 17. Rusk also revealed that Kennedy was sensitive to the problem of the Jupiters and had ordered their warheads removed during the crisis as a signal to the Soviet Union.

68. Interview, Oleg Grinevsky, Vienna, 11 October 1991.

69. Roy Medvedev, *All Stalin's Men*, trans. Harold Shukman (New York: Doubleday, 1982), p. 52. As we noted in chapter 6, Medvedev's account of Khrushchev's behavior cannot be accepted at face value.

70. Coordination problems continued to plague the administration after the crisis subsided. Top defense and intelligence officials were so preoccupied by the crisis that they forgot about the stepped-up sabotage missions against Cuba that had been authorized in September. Task Force W still planned to infiltrate ten six-man sabotage teams into Cuba. On 30 October, the administration discovered that Operation Mongoose was still in full swing and ordered all of its missions aborted. Gen. Edward Lansdale was sent to Miami to supervise the dismantling of Task Force W. By then, three teams had left for Cuba, and on 8 November, one of them blew up a factory. News of the bombing never reached the White House because the CIA withheld the information. Garthoff, *Reflections on the Cuban Missile Crisis*, p. 89; Arthur Schlesinger, Jr., *Robert Kennedy and His Times* (Boston: Houghton,

Mifflin, 1978) pp. 533–34; John Prados, *Presidents' Secret Wars: CIA and Pentagon Covert Operations since World War II* (New York: William Morrow, 1986), p. 214; U.S. Congress, Senate, *Alleged Assassination Plots Involving Foreign Leaders: An Interim Report of the Senate Select Committee to Study Governmental Operations with Respect to Intelligence Activities*, 94th Cong., 1st sess., Senate Report 94–965, pp. 147–48.

The Soviets almost certainly knew about the incident from Castro. On 28 October, the Cuban leader had communicated his terms for a modus vivendi with Washington to United Nations Secretary General U Thant. Fidel Castro to U Thant, 28 October 1962, United Nations General Assembly Document A/5271, 1–2, reprinted in David L. Larson, ed., *The "Cuban Crisis" of 1962: Selected Documents, Chronology and Bibliography*, 2d ed. (Lanham, Md.: University Press of America, 1986), pp. 197–98. One of Castro's five conditions was the cessation of American sabotage operations against Cuba. He rushed to tell Moscow about the most recent American-sponsored sabotage because it supported his contention that Washington would not honor any agreement it made about Cuba. Interview, Oleg Grinevsky, New York, 10 November 1991.

71. U.S. Alaskan Air Defense Command, "Air Defense Operations," December 1962.

72. Defense Department Chronology, p. 14; Interview of Col. John A. Des Portes, Maj. C. B. Stratton, Gen. David Power, Lt. Col. A. Leatherwood, and Col. J. R. King by Ron Caywood, Headquarters, Strategic Air Command, 25 May 1965, p. 56; Hilsman, *To Move A Nation*, p. 221 and "The Cuban Crisis: How Close We Were to War," *Look* 28, 25 August 1964; Garthoff, *Reflections on the Cuban Missile Crisis*, p. 89, n. 154, reports that the U.S. interceptors were armed with nuclear air-to-air missiles.

73. Hilsman, *To Move A Nation*, p. 221.

74. "Letter from Chairman Khrushchev to President Kennedy, 28 October 1962," *Department of State Bulletin* 47, 12 November 1962, pp. 743–45. Reprinted in Larson, *The "Cuban Crisis" of 1962*, pp. 189–93, p. 192.

75. The naval chain of command went from the president, to the secretary of defense (James Schlesinger), to the unified commander (USCINCEUR), to the component commander (CINCUSNAVEUR), to the fleet commander (commander Sixth Fleet), to the task force commander, to the task group commander, and finally to individual ships. Adm. Thomas H. Moorer was chairman of the Joint Chiefs of Staff, Adm. Elmo R. Zumwalt, Jr., was chief of Naval Operations, Adm. Worth H. Bagley was CINCUSNAVEUR, and Vice Adm. Daniel J. Murphy was commander, Sixth Fleet.

76. Elmo R. Zumwalt, Jr. described the extraordinarily close control: "[T]he orders were extremely rigid. They specified latitudes and longitudes and gave Dan [Vice Adm. Murphy] little or no room for tactical maneuvers aimed at making his mission easier to carry out or his forces easier to protect or, optimally both. Several times . . . Dan asked permission of the JCS . . . to move these ships. . . . Each request was turned down by Adm. Moorer, acting, he told me, on instructions from the White House." *On Watch: A Memoir* (New York: Quadrangle, 1976), p. 436. See also the letter from Vice Adm. Engen to Joseph Bouchard, 25 April 1988, cited in Bouchard, *Command in Crisis*, p. 164, pp. 177–78.

77. Zumwalt, *On Watch*, p. 436. Vice Adm. Donald D. Engen described Washington's control of the Sixth Fleet as very restrictive. Letter from Vice Adm. Donald

D. Engen to Joseph Bouchard, cited by Joseph B. Bouchard, *Command in Crisis*, p. 164.

78. Bouchard, *Command in Crisis*, pp. 173–74, at p. 178.

79. Zumwalt, *On Watch*, p. 446; Bouchard, *Command in Crisis*, p. 179.

80. Bouchard, *Command in Crisis*, p. 179.

81. Scott Sagan, "Nuclear Alerts and Crisis Management," *International Security* 9, 4 (Spring 1985), pp. 99–139, citing an interview of Adm. Moorer, 10 April 1984, p. 128, n. 83.

82. The message read as follows: "1. Most recent communication with Soviets contains request that US join them in more forceful enforcement of Israel/Arab cease-fire by introduction of both US/Soviet forces. Soviets further state intentions to con-sider unilateral action if US declines. 2. Our reply not final at this point but, as you have noted, US response includes signal of elevation in force readiness, i.e., DEFCON Three worldwide, alerting of 82nd Airborne, more eastward movement of carriers in Med, and redeployment of SAC forces from the Pacific. 3. I am in session with SECDEF and Chiefs and will keep you advised." Joint Chiefs of Staff message, JCS 250737Z OCT 73, 25 October 1973 (declassified 1984).

83. *Hawk's Cay Conference*, p. 62.

84. Hawk's Cay Conference, author's record; Douglas Dillon thinks that Mc-Namara thought about it too much! "With more experience under his belt, McNamara might have worried less about accidents and things like that." Interview, C. Douglas Dillon by James Blight, New York, 15 May 1987, in Blight and Welch, *On the Brink*, p. 154.

85. Interview, Peter Rodman, Washington, D.C., 24 April 1991.

86. In an effort to improve crisis management, the Department of Defense devel-oped a sophisticated worldwide communications network. It promised the president instant communication with American forces and embassies anywhere in the world. Despite improved communications, the danger of loss of control increased in the last decades of the Cold War. The nuclear alert and response systems of both superpow-ers were tightly coupled. The latest generation of strategic weapons put enormous stress on these systems. Submarine-launched missiles were capable of striking an adversary's political leadership and military forces in a matter of minutes instead of hours. They were also less tolerant of error, because missiles, unlike the relatively slow bombers of 1962, could not be recalled. Moreover, the alert and warning sys-tems of both superpowers were plagued by technical and organizational problems and functioned in ways that were poorly understood by their operators, and even less by the political leaders who would have had to rely on them in an acute crisis. Lebow, *Nuclear Crisis Management*, explores these problems and the ways in which they could have caused an inadvertent war.

87. Sophisticated command and control aircraft have been grounded, submarine patrols have been reduced, and deep cuts have been made in nuclear arsenals.

88. Fidel Castro to Nikita Khrushchev, 28 October 1962, *Granma*, 2 December 1990, p. 3.

89. "With the Historical Truth and Morale of Baraguá," *Granma*, 2 December 1990, p. 2; Gen. Sergio del Valle, "Transcript of Cuba Between the Superpowers," Antigua, 3–7 January 1991, mimeograph, p. 122, forthcoming as James G. Blight, David Lewis, and David A. Welch, eds., *Cuba Between the Superpowers: The An-tigua Conference on the Cuban Missile Crisis* (Savage, Md.: Rowman and Littlefield, in press), hereafter *Antigua Conference*; Fidel Castro, *Havana Conference*, pp. 34,

76–78. American military records indicate that Cuban forces had begun to shoot at American aircraft on Friday. That afternoon, two low-level reconnaissance planes had been fired at by light antiaircraft and small arms. White House Tapes, "Transcript of 27 October 1962," pp. 30–31; Central Intelligence Agency, National Indications Center, *The Soviet Bloc Armed Forces and the Cuban Crisis: A Chronology, July-November 1962*, 18 June 1963, p. 7, claims that Cuban patrol ships fired on a U.S. Navy patrol plane over international waters on 30 August.

90. Nikita Khrushchev to Fidel Castro, 28 October 1962, *Granma*, 2 December 1990, p. 3, and *Khrushchev Remembers: The Glasnost Tapes*, trans. and ed. Jerrold L. Schechter with Vyacheslav V. Luchkov (Boston: Little, Brown, 1990), p. 178; Sergei Khrushchev in Bruce J. Allyn, James G. Blight, and David A. Welch, eds., *Back to the Brink: Proceedings of the Moscow Conference on The Cuban Missile Crisis, January 27–28, 1989*, CSIA Occasional Paper no. 9 (Lanham, Md.: University Press of America, 1992), mimeograph, hereafter cited as *Moscow Conference*, pp. 37–39, said: "I remember when the information arrived that this action had taken place. Nikita Sergeevich was very upset and considered it a big mistake on our part, which is confirmed by the cable sent by Marshal Malinovsky." Castro, *Havana Conference*, p. 80, reports that "for some time Khrushchev believed that we had shot down the plane. He was confused."

91. Fidel Castro to Nikita Khrushchev, 31 October 1962, *Granma*, 2 December 1990, p. 3.

92. "Extracts from the Record of a Conversation Between Anastas Mikoyan and Fidel Castro . . . on 3 November 1962 at Fidel Castro's Residence," *International Affairs* (Moscow), 10 (October 1992), pp. 108–44; comments of Sergo Mikoyan and Georgiy Shaknazarov, David A. Welch, ed., *Proceedings of the Cambridge Conference on the Cuban Missile Crisis, 11–12 October 1987* (Cambridge, Mass.: Harvard University, Center for Science and International Affairs, April 1988), final version, mimeograph, pp. 82, 102, hereafter cited as *Cambridge Conference*; Comments of Aleksandr A. Alekseev, "The Caribbean Crisis," pp. 27–37; Interview, Fidel Castro by Maria Schriver, broadcast on NBC "Sunday Today," 28 February 1988.

93. Tad Szulc, *Fidel: A Critical Portrait* (New York: Morrow Books, 1986), p. 649.

94. Bernd Greiner, "The Soviet View: An Interview with Sergo Mikoyan," *Diplomatic History*, 14 (Spring 1990), p. 219.

95. Garthoff, *Reflections on the Cuban Missile Crisis*, pp. 100–101, especially n. 175, reporting on his private discussions with Soviet participants at the Moscow Conference who admitted that Cuban forces had appeared at the bases on the twenty-eighth but denied that they had been ordered to surround them. Garthoff convincingly argues that Ambassador Alekseev's explanation that the Cuban forces were deployed to provide perimeter security makes no sense because these forces were sent *after* the crisis had in principle been resolved. Cuban officials claim that their forces were deployed around antiaircraft missiles to prevent a surprise American air strike.

96. Fidel Castro, *Havana Conference*, pp. 206, 221, 223, 236.

97. "Extracts from the Record of a Conversation Between Anastas Mikoyan and Fidel Castro," provides excerpts from these talks.

98. Rusk, *As I Saw It*, p. 245.

99. Aleksandr Alekseev, "The Caribbean Crisis: As It Really Was," *Ekho Planety*, no. 33, November 1988, pp. 31–36; Garthoff, *Reflections on the Cuban Missile*

Crisis, pp. 97–129, for the most authoritative secondary account of the postcrisis negotiations.

100. During the war, some "hotheads" in the Soviet Ministry of Defense, acting at the request of the Egyptian military command, urged that Egypt be authorized to use Soviet-made R-17 missiles to attack the airbase at El-Arish in the Sinai where equipment being airlifted to Israel by the United States was being unloaded. The Soviet chief of staff prepared a draft cable for Egypt authorizing an attack on the airbase, but Gromyko refused to approve the action. Soviet defense officials were displeased by the rejection of their proposal, but were told that according to Soviet-Egyptian agreements, the Egyptian military could not use the R-17 missile without the approval of the Soviet leadership. Although they were displeased, Soviet generals did act properly through channels. Evgueny D. Pyrlin, *Some Observations (Memoirs) About the Arab-Israeli October War, 1973*, unpublished paper, pp. 5–6.

101. Quoted by Coral Bell, *The Conventions of Crisis: A Study in Diplomatic Management* (New York: Oxford University Press, 1971), p. 2.

102. *Hawk's Cay Conference*, p. 94, and *Havana Conference*, for similar remarks. At the *Cambridge Conference*, p. 129, McNamara confessed that only in retrospect had he come to appreciate the risks of inadvertent war in the Cuban crisis.

103. Richard Ned Lebow and Janice Gross Stein, "Beyond Deterrence," *Journal of Social Issues* 43, 4 (Winter 1987), pp. 5–71.

Chapter Fourteen
Nuclear Threats and Nuclear Weapons

1. In keeping with the theological quality of the debate, followers of the "war-fighting" sect of deterrence had a sacred text: *Voyenaya mysl'*, the Soviet *Journal of Military Thought*. Many of the professional Soviet military discussions of the contingent uses of military power were misused to infer and attribute offensive military intentions to the Soviet Union.

2. McGeorge Bundy, *Danger and Survival: Choices About the Bomb in the First Fifty Years* (New York: Random House, 1988).

3. Richard K. Betts, *Nuclear Blackmail and Nuclear Balance* (Washington, D.C.: The Brookings Institution, 1987).

4. Harry Truman claimed to have compelled the Soviet Union to withdraw from Iran in 1946, but no documentary record of a nuclear threat can be found. See Betts, *Nuclear Blackmail and Nuclear Balance*, pp. 7–8; Richard Ned Lebow and Janice Gross Stein, "Review of the Data Collections on Extended Deterrence by Paul Huth and Bruce Russett," in Kenneth A. Oye, ed., *Specifying and Testing Theories of Deterrence* (Ann Arbor: University of Michigan Press, in press); and Richard W. Cottam, *Iran and the United States: A Cold War Case Study* (Pittsburgh: University of Pittsburgh Press, 1988).

5. John E. Mueller, *Retreat from Doomsday: The Obsolescence of Modern War* (New York: Basic Books, 1989). Kenneth N. Waltz, *Theory of International Politics* (Reading, Mass.: Addison-Wesley, 1979), also disparaged the role of nuclear weapons and argued that bipolarity was responsible for the long peace. Waltz, "The Emerging Structure of International Politics," paper prepared for the August 1990 Annual Meeting of the American Political Science Association, subsequently acknowledged nuclear weapons as one of "the twin pillars" of the peace. See Richard Ned Lebow, "Explaining Stability and Change: A Critique of Realism," in Richard

Ned Lebow and Thomas Risse-Kappen, eds., *International Relations Theory and the End of the Cold War*, forthcoming, for a critical examination of the realist position on the long peace.

6. Richard Ned Lebow, "Conventional vs. Nuclear Deterrence: Are the Lessons Transferable?" *Journal of Social Issues* 43, 4 (1987), pp. 171–91.

7. McGeorge Bundy, "To Cap the Volcano," *Foreign Affairs*, 48, 1 (October 1969), pp. 1–20; Harvard Nuclear Study Group, *Living With Nuclear Weapons* (Cambridge, Mass.: Harvard University Press, 1983); Klaus Knorr, "Controlling Nuclear War," *International Security* 9, 4 (Spring 1985), pp. 79–98; Michael Mandelbaum, *The Nuclear Question: The United States and Nuclear Weapons, 1946–76* (New York: Cambridge University Press, 1979); Robert W. Tucker, *The Nuclear Debate: Deterrence and the Lapse of Faith* (New York: Holmes & Meier, 1985).

8. For example, Raymond Aron, *The Great Debate: Theories of Nuclear Strategy*, trans. Ernst Pawel (Garden City, N.Y.: Doubleday, 1965); Stanley Hoffmann, *The State of War: Essays on the Theory and Practice of International Politics* (New York: Praeger, 1965), p. 236; Betts, *Nuclear Blackmail*; Bundy, *Danger and Survival*; Robert Jervis, *The Meaning of the Nuclear Revolution: Statecraft and the Prospect of Armageddon* (Ithaca, N.Y.: Cornell University Press, 1989).

9. For the evolution of McNamara's strategic thinking, see Desmond Ball, *Politics and Force Levels: The Strategic Missile Program of the Kennedy Administration* (Berkeley: University of California Press, 1980), especially pp. 171–93; Lawrence Freedman, *The Evolution of Nuclear Strategy* (New York: St. Martin's Press, 1983), pp. 331–71.

10. For war-fighting critics of MAD, see Daniel Graham, *Shall America Be Defended?: SALT II and Beyond* (New Rochelle, N.Y.: Arlington House, 1979); Colin S. Gray, *Nuclear Strategy and National Style* (Lanham, Md.: Hamilton Press, 1986); Colin S. Gray and Keith B. Payne, "Victory is Possible," *Foreign Policy* 39 (Summer 1980), pp. 14–27; Albert Wohlstetter, "Between an Unfree World and None," *Foreign Affairs* 63, 5 (Summer 1985), pp. 962–94; Fred Hoffman, "The SDI in U.S. Nuclear Strategy," *International Security* 10, 1 (Summer 1985), pp. 13–24.

11. Morton H. Halperin, *Nuclear Fallacy: Dispelling the Myth of Nuclear Strategy* (Cambridge: Ballinger, 1987); Adm. Noel Gayler, "The Way Out: A General Nuclear Settlement," in Gwyn Prins, ed., *The Nuclear Crisis Reader* (New York: Vintage Books, 1984), pp. 234–43.

12. Graham, *Shall America Be Defended?*; Gray, *Nuclear Strategy and National Style*; Wohlstetter, "Between an Unfree World and None."

13. Robert S. McNamara, "The Military Role of Nuclear Weapons: Perceptions and Misperceptions," *Foreign Affairs* 62 (Fall 1983), pp. 59–80, at p. 68; Jervis, *The Meaning of the Nuclear Revolution*, pp. 34–38; Alexander L. George, David K. Hall, and William E. Simons, *The Limits of Coercive Diplomacy: Laos, Cuba, Vietnam* (Boston: Little, Brown, 1971); Betts, *Nuclear Blackmail*.

14. This distinction was introduced by Patrick M. Morgan, *Deterrence: A Conceptual Analysis* (Beverly Hills, Calif.: Sage, 1977).

15. Arthur Schlesinger, Jr., *A Thousand Days: John F. Kennedy in the White House* (Boston: Houghton, Mifflin, 1965), pp. 347–48. This point is also made by Alexander L. George and Richard Smoke, *Deterrence in American Foreign Policy: Theory and Practice* (New York: Columbia University Press, 1974), pp. 429, 579.

16. On the Warsaw Pact, see Robin Allison Remington, *The Changing Soviet Perception of the Warsaw Pact* (Cambridge, Mass.: MIT Center for International

Studies, 1967); Christopher D. Jones, *Soviet Influence in Eastern Europe: Political Autonomy and the Warsaw Pact* (New York: Praeger, 1981); David Holloway, "The Warsaw Pact in Transition," in David Holloway and Jane M. O. Sharp, eds., *The Warsaw Pact: Alliance in Transition?* (Ithaca, N.Y.: Cornell University Press, 1984), pp. 19–38.

17. Interview, Leonid Zamyatin, Moscow, 16 December 1991; Sergei Khrushchev, *Khrushchev on Khrushchev: An Inside Account of the Man and His Era*, trans. William Taubman (Boston: Little, Brown, 1990), pp. 156–57; Oleg Troyanovsky, "The Caribbean Crisis: A View from the Kremlin," *International Affairs* (Moscow) 4–5 (April/May l992), pp. 147–57, at p. 149.

18. See Richard Ned Lebow, *Between Peace and War: The Nature of International Crisis* (Baltimore: Johns Hopkins University Press, 1981), pp. 82–97, for a discussion of the four traditional prerequisites of deterrence. For discussion of the conditions essential to deterrence success, see Richard Ned Lebow and Janice Gross Stein, *When Does Deterrence Succeed and How Do We Know?* (Ottawa: Canadian Institute for International Peace and Security, 1990), pp. 59–69.

19. Chapter 3 reviews this debate.

20. Janice Gross Stein, "Calculation, Miscalculation, and Conventional Deterrence I: The View from Cairo," in Robert Jervis, Richard Ned Lebow, and Janice Gross Stein, *Psychology and Deterrence* (Baltimore: Johns Hopkins University Press, 1985), pp. 31–59.

21. Henry Kissinger, *Years of Upheaval* (Boston: Little, Brown, 1982), p. 508.

22. Ibid., p. 510.

23. "United States Objectives and Programs for National Security," (NSC 68) (14 April 1950), *Foreign Relations of the United States, 1950*, vol. I (Washington, D.C.: Government Printing Office, 1977), p. 264; Vernon Aspaturian, "Soviet Global Power and the Correlation of Forces," *Problems of Communism* 20 (May-June 1980), pp. 1–18; John J. Dziak, *Soviet Perceptions of Military Power: The Interaction of Theory and Practice* (New York: Crane, Russak, 1981); Edward N. Luttwak, "After Afghanistan What?" *Commentary* 69 (April 1980), pp. 1–18; Richard Pipes, "Why the Soviet Union Thinks It Could Fight and Win a Nuclear War," *Commentary* 64 (July 1977), pp. 21–34; Norman Podhoretz, "The Present Danger," *Commentary* 69 (April 1980), pp. 40–49.

24. There is also some evidence that the fear of war influenced Soviet behavior in Korea. Joseph Stalin authorized Kim Il Sung to attack South Korea in June 1950 in the expectation that the United States would not intervene. When Washington did intervene, Stalin, afraid that the North Korean attack would provoke a Soviet-American war, quickly signaled interest in a cease-fire. N. Khrushchev, *Khrushchev Remembers: The Glasnost Tapes*, trans. and ed. Jerrold L. Schecter with Vyacheslav L. Luchkov (Boston: Little, Brown, 1990), pp. 144–47.

25. Oleg Grinevsky contends that Stalin feared that even a few atomic bombs dropped on Moscow would have destroyed the communist experiment. Interview, Oleg Grinevsky, Stockholm, 24 October 1992.

26. David A. Welch, ed., *Proceedings of the Hawk's Cay Conference on the Cuban Missile Crisis, 5–8 March 1987* (Cambridge, Mass.: Harvard University, Center for Science and International Affairs, Working Paper 89–1, 1989), mimeograph, pp. 81–83, hereafter cited as *Hawk's Cay Conference*.

27. Ibid., pp. 83ff.

28. Hawk's Cay Conference, author's record.

29. Ball, *Politics and Force Levels*, pp. 171–93; Freedman, *The Evolution of Nuclear Strategy*, pp. 331–71.

30. See Graham, *Shall America Be Defended?*; Gray, *Nuclear Strategy and National Style*; Gray and Payne, "Victory is Possible"; Wohlstetter, "Between an Unfree World and None."

31. Interview, Gen. Dimitri A. Volkogonov by Raymond L. Garthoff, Moscow, 1 February 1989; Anatoliy Gribkov, "Transcript of the Proceedings of the Havana Conference on the Cuban Missile Crisis, January 9–12 1992," mimeograph, in James G. Blight, Bruce J. Allyn, and David A. Welch, eds., *Cuba on the Brink: Castro, the Missile Crisis, and the Soviet Collapse* (New York: Pantheon Books, in press), pp. 18–21, hereafter cited as *Havana Conference*.

32. "Retrospective on the Cuban Missile Crisis," 22 January 1983, Atlanta, Ga. Participants: Dean Rusk, McGeorge Bundy, Edwin Martin, Donald Wilson, and Richard E. Neustadt (hereafter referred to as Retrospective), p. 6.

33. *Hawk's Cay Conference*, pp. 9–10.

34. Interview, Robert McNamara, Hawk's Cay, Fla., 6 March 1987.

35. Retrospective, p. 40.

36. Garthoff, *Reflections on the Cuban Missile Crisis*, 2d ed. rev. (Washington, D.C.: The Brookings Institution, 1989), pp. 158–86, on Soviet lessons from the crisis; Interviews, Leonid Zamyatin and Anatoliy F. Dobrynin, Moscow, 16–17 December, 1991.

37. The assertion that the Soviet Union could only be constrained by superior military power became something close to dogma in the United States government. It received its most forceful expression in National Security Council Memorandum (NSC) 68, written on the eve of the Korean War in 1950. NSC 68 is generally recognized as the most influential American policy document of the Cold War. See John L. Gaddis, *Strategies of Containment: A Critical Appraisal of Postwar American National Security Policy* (New York: Oxford University Press, 1982), chap. 4; Paul Y. Hammond, "NSC-68: Prologue to Rearmament," in Warner R. Schilling, Paul Y. Hammond, and Glenn H. Snyder, eds., *Strategy, Politics, and Defense Budgets* (New York: Columbia University Press, 1962), pp. 267–338; "United States Objectives and Programs for National Security," pp. 234–92.

38. Soviet leaders, with a mirror image of their adversary, made the same assumption about American foreign policy. Khrushchev put missiles in Cuba in part to achieve psychological equality and constrain American foreign policy.

39. The accepted strategic wisdom, reflected in our analysis, holds that the United States had a decisive strategic advantage throughout the 1950s. It possessed an expanding capability to attack the Soviet Union with nuclear weapons without the prospect of direct retaliation. The Strategic Air Command had a large and growing fleet of strategic bombers based in the United States, Western Europe, and North Africa. This strike force was supplemented by carrier and land-based aircraft deployed along the Soviet periphery. The Soviet Union's bomber force was small, shorter range, and technologically primitive.

The relative military balance changed in the 1960s when both superpowers began to deploy ICBMs. In 1962, at the time of the Cuban missile crisis, the United States had some 3,500 warheads against approximately 300 for the Soviets. Only 20 of the Soviet warheads were on ICBMs. See Sagan, "SIOP-62: The Nuclear War Plan Briefing to President Kennedy," *International Security* 12, 1 (Summer 1987), pp. 22–51; David A. Welch, ed., *Proceedings of the Cambridge Conference on the Cuban*

Missile Crisis, 11–12 October 1987 (Cambridge, Mass.: Harvard University, Center for Science and International Affairs, April 1988), final version, mimeograph, pp. 52, 79, hereafter cited as *Cambridge Conference*. By the end of the 1960s, the Soviet Strategic Rocket Forces had deployed enough ICBMs to destroy about half of the population and industry of the United States. It had achieved the capability that McNamara considered essential for MAD.

Some time in the 1970s the Soviet Union achieved rough strategic parity. This balance prevailed until 1991, although some analysts have argued that one or the other possessed some margin of advantage. American missiles were more accurate throughout the 1970s. The United States was also the first to deploy multiple independently targeted reentry vehicles (MIRVs). It put three warheads on Minuteman missiles, and fourteen on submarine-launched ballistic missiles (SLBMs). The Soviet Union began to deploy MIRVs in the late 1970s and, in the opinion of some analysts, gained a temporary strategic advantage because of the greater throw weight of their ICBMs. The SS-18 could carry thirty to forty MIRVs, but in practice was deployed with a maximum of ten.

40. Soviet aggressiveness is a subjective phenomenon. To measure it, we polled a sample of international relations scholars and former government officials. They were carefully chosen to ensure representation of diverse political points of view. These experts were given a list of events that could be interpreted as Soviet challenges to the United States, its allies, or nonaligned states. They were asked to rank them in order of ascending gravity. The survey revealed a surprising concurrence among experts. A description of the survey and its results appears in Richard Ned Lebow and John Garofano, "Soviet Aggressiveness: Need or Opportunity?" mimeograph.

41. This kind of need-based explanation of aggression provides a convincing explanation of both Soviet and American foreign policy in the Cold War since the Khrushchev and Kennedy years. See Richard Ned Lebow, "Windows of Opportunity: Do States Jump Through Them?" *International Security* 9 (Summer 1984), pp. 147–86.

42. McNamara, "The Military Role of Nuclear Weapons"; Jervis, *The Meaning of the Nuclear Revolution*; George, Hall, and Simons, *The Limits of Coercive Diplomacy*; Betts, *Nuclear Blackmail*.

43. Albert and Roberta Wohlstetter, "Controlling the Risks in Cuba," *Adelphi Paper* no. 17 (London: International Institute for Strategic Studies, 1965), p. 16. See also, Herman Kahn, *On Escalation* (New York: Praeger, 1965), pp. 74–82; Thomas Schelling, *Arms and Influence* (New Haven, Conn.: Yale University Press, 1966), pp. 80–83.

44. McNamara, "The Military Role of Nuclear Weapons"; Jervis, *The Meaning of the Nuclear Revolution*, pp. 34–38.

45. Years later, in an offhand comment, Kissinger claimed that he would not have felt secure enough to choose an alert if the Soviet Union had had a marked strategic advantage. Cited by Betts, *Nuclear Blackmail*, p. 125. This kind of indirect and fragmentary evidence fits best with the arguments of the war-fighters, largely because Kissinger thought very much as they did. It is of course debatable whether Kissinger would have acted differently had the United States been in a position of relative inferiority; the proposition has never been put to the test. Given Kissinger's heavy emphasis on reputation and resolve, it seems unlikely that he would have complied even if the Soviet Union had had a relative strategic advantage. Proponents of finite

deterrence and MAD would argue that Soviet compellence was unlikely to succeed even if the Soviet Union had had a marked advantage because the interests at stake were not sufficiently important.

46. This theme is developed at length in Richard Ned Lebow, *Nuclear Crisis Management: A Dangerous Illusion* (Ithaca, N.Y.: Cornell University Press, 1987).

47. By 2003, if the cuts proposed in the START II treaty are implemented, Russia will cut its missiles to 504 and its warheads to 3,000 and the United States will reduce its missiles to 500 and its warheads to 3,500.

POSTSCRIPT
Deterrence and the End of the Cold War

1. Interview, Mikhail S. Gorbachev, Toronto, 1 April 1993.

2. Tom Wicker, "Plenty of Credit," *New York Times*, 5 December 1989, p. A35, points to the irony that those who for years argued that a Communist-led Soviet Union could not be reformed, now claim credit for *perestroika* and the Soviet retreat from Eastern Europe.

3. Interview, Mikhail S. Gorbachev, Toronto, 1 April 1993.

4. Ibid.

5. Ibid. See also the comments by Soviet Foreign Minister Aleksandr Bessmertnykh and Anatoliy S. Chernyaev, advisor to President Gorbachev on foreign affairs, 1986–1991, "Retrospective on the End of the Cold War," Conference sponsored by the John Foster Dulles Program for the Study of Leadership in International Affairs, Woodrow Wilson School, Princeton University, 25–27 February 1993.

6. Interview, Mikhail S. Gorbachev, Toronto, 1 April 1993, and comments by Aleksandr Bessmertnykh, "Retrospective on the End of the Cold War."

7. Thomas Risse-Kappen, *The Zero Option: INF, West Germany, and Arms Control* (Boulder, Colo.: Westview, 1988); Richard Eichenberg, "Dual Track and Double Trouble: The Two-Level Politics of INF," Peter Evans, Harold Jacobsen, and Robert Putnam, eds., *Double-Edged Diplomacy: International Bargaining and Domestic Politics* (Berkeley: University of California Press, in press); Fen Osler Hampson, Harald von Reikhoff, and John Roper, eds., *The Allies and Arms Control* (Baltimore: Johns Hopkins University Press, 1992); Don Oberdorfer, *The Turn: From the Cold War to a New Era, The United States and The Soviet Union, 1983–1990* (New York: Poseidon Press, 1991), pp. 169–74.

8. Interview, Mikhail S. Gorbachev, Toronto, 1 April 1993. See also the comments by Bessmertnykh, "Retrospective on the End of the Cold War."

9. Interviews, Fedor Burlatsky, Cambridge, 12 October 1987; Vadim Zagladin, Moscow, 18 May 1989; Oleg Grinevsky, Vienna and New York, 11 October and 10 November 1991.

10. The arms proposal that Gorbachev tabled at Reykjavik was the Soviet analogue to Reagan's "double zero" proposal. Oleg Grinevsky, interview, Stockholm, 25 April 1992, reports that before the summit, Gorbachev asked his chief arms-control advisors, Viktor Karpov, Yuli Kvitinsky, and Oleg Grinevsky to prepare proposals for arms control. Defense Minister Dmitri Yazov and Chief of the General Staff Sergei Akhromeyev learned about the preparation of new proposals and strongly opposed the initiative because they were convinced that any likely arms-control agreement would be unfavorable to the Soviet Union. They went to see Gorbachev and asked if he was seriously interested in deep cuts in the arsenals of both

superpowers. When he responded affirmatively, they advised him that any proposal prepared by professional arms controllers would be overly conservative and require elaborate negotiations of definitions and verification. Yazov and Akhromeyev told a gullible Gorbachev of their abhorrence of nuclear weapons—they made conventional wars difficult, if not impossible to fight—and offered to prepare proposals for Reykjavik that would represent a serious step toward nuclear disarmament. Gorbachev immediately transferred responsibility for preparation of arms-control proposals for the summit to Yazov and Akhromeyev. They prepared the proposal that Gorbachev presented at Reykjavik, convinced that President Reagan and his advisors would reject it out of hand. Yazov and Akhromeyev were astonished when Reagan expressed serious interest.

11. Franklyn D. Holzman, "Politics and Guesswork: CIA and DIA Estimates of Soviet Military Spending," *International Security* 14 (Fall 1989), pp. 101–31; Central Intelligence Agency and Defense Intelligence Agency, "Beyond Perestroika: The Soviet Economy in Crisis," paper prepared for the Technology and National Security Subcommittee of the Joint Economic Committee, U.S. Congress, 14 May 1991.

12. The Soviet government reported that overall output declined by 2 percent in 1990 and by 8 percent in the first quarter of 1991. Big cuts in defense spending began in 1989, and the annual decline has been on the order of about 6 percent. Because the economy is declining more rapidly than defense expenditure, defense as a percent of gross national product has increased. "Beyond Perestroika," pp. iv, 1, 11–12.

13. For criticism of the powerful role of the "defense lobby" under Brezhnev by younger officials and scholars, see Stephen F. Cohen and Katrina vanden Heuvel, *Voices of Glasnost: Interviews with Gorbachev's Reformers* (New York: Norton, 1989) and Georgi Arbatov, *The System: An Insider's Life in Soviet Politics* (New York: Random House, 1992).

14. For discussion of logrolling under Brezhnev, see Jack Snyder, *Myths of Empire* (Ithaca, N.Y.: Cornell University Press, 1991) and Richard Anderson, *Competitive Politics and Soviet Foreign Policy: Authority-Building and Bargaining in the Brezhnev Politburo*, Ph.D. diss., University of California, Berkeley, 1989.

15. The command economy cannot be attributed to the Nazi threat because Stalin promulgated the first five-year plan in 1929 and collectivized agriculture in the early 1930s, before Hitler's rise to power.

16. Analysts of Soviet politics, writing in late 1989, argued that "new thinking" was limited to a few central Soviet leaders and advisors. A. Lynch, *Gorbachev's International Outlook: Intellectual Origins and Political Consequences*, Institute for East-West Security Studies, Occasional Paper no. 9 (Boulder, Colo.: Westview, 1989), p. 53.

17. For an explanation of "new thinking" and the political debate it provoked, see Janice Gross Stein, "Cognitive Psychology and Political Learning: Gorbachev as an Uncommitted Thinker and Motivated Learner," in Richard Ned Lebow and Thomas Risse-Kappen, eds., *International Relations Theory and the Transformation of the International System*, forthcoming.

18. See Sarah E. Mendelson, "Internal Battles and External Wars: Politics, Learning, and the Soviet Withdrawal from Afghanistan," *World Politics* 45, 3 (April 1993), pp. 327–60; Jeff Checkel, "Ideas, Institutions, and the Gorbachev Foreign Policy Revolution," *World Politics* 45, 2 (January, 1993), pp. 271–300.

19. Interviews, Fedor Burlatsky, Cambridge, 12 October 1987; Vadim Zagladin, Moscow, 18 May 1989; Oleg Grinevsky, Vienna and New York, 11 October and 10

November 1991; Georgi Arbatov, Ithaca, N.Y., 15 November 1991; Anatoliy Dobrynin, Moscow, 17 December 1991.

20. See Mikhail Gorbachev, *Pravda*, 21 October 1986 and speech to the United Nations General Assembly, 7 December 1988, *Novosti*, no. 97, p. 13; and speech by Eduard A. Shevardnadze, in *Vestnik Ministerstva Inostrannykh Del USSR* 15, 15 August 1988, p. 33.

21. For Western discussion of "new thinking" in foreign policy, see David Holloway, "Gorbachev's New Thinking," *Foreign Affairs* 68 (Winter 1988–89), pp. 66–81; Robert Legvold, "The Revolution in Soviet Foreign Policy," *Foreign Affairs* 68, 1 (America and the World 1988/89), pp. 82–98; Stephen M. Meyer, "The Sources and Prospects of Gorbachev's New Political Thinking on Security," *International Security* 13, 2 (Fall 1988), pp. 124–63.

22. Mikhail Gorbachev, "Speech to the United Nations."

23. Mikhail Gorbachev, *Perestroika: New Thinking for Our Country and the World* (New York: Harper & Row, 1987), p. 187; Holloway, "Gorbachev's New Thinking."

24. By 1987, Gorbachev insisted that the unforgiving realities of the nuclear age demanded new concepts and new policies, independent of *perestroika* at home: "Some people say that the ambitious goals set forth by the policy of *perestroika* in our country have prompted the peace proposals we have lately made in the international arena. This is an oversimplification. . . . True, we need normal international conditions for our internal progress. But we want a world free of war, without arms races, nuclear weapons, and violence; not only because this is an optimal condition for our internal development." Gorbachev, *Perestroika*, p. 11.

25. Stephen F. Cohen, "Soviet Domestic Politics and Foreign Policy," in Robbin F. Laird and Erik P. Hoffman, eds., *Soviet Foreign Policy in a Changing World* (New York: Aldine, 1986), pp. 66–83; Jerry F. Hough, "Soviet Succession: Issues and Personalities," *Problems of Communism* 31 (September-October 1982), p. 20–40; Raymond L. Garthoff, *Détente and Confrontation: American-Soviet Relations from Nixon to Reagan* (Washington, D.C.: The Brookings Institution, 1985); Jack Snyder, "International Leverage on Soviet Domestic Change," *World Politics* 42 (October 1989), pp. 1–30.

26. Aleksandr Yanov, *The Drama of the Soviet 1960s: A Lost Reform* (Berkeley, Calif.: Institute of International Studies, 1984), pp. 97–98, 103–6; Timothy J. Colton, "The Changing Soviet Union and the World," in Laird and Hoffman, *Soviet Foreign Policy in a Changing World*, pp. 869–89.

27. This was also the original idea behind George Kennan's policy of containment; Richard Pipes, "Can the Soviet Union Reform?"; Laird and Hoffman, *Soviet Foreign Policy in a Changing World*, pp. 855–68; Harry Gelman, *The Brezhnev Politburo and the Decline of Detente* (Ithaca, N.Y.: Cornell University Press, 1984). For a good critique, see Matthew Evangelista, "Sources of Moderation in Soviet Security Policy," in Philip E. Tetlock, Jo L. Husbands, Robert Jervis, Paul C. Stern, and Charles Tilly, eds., *Behavior, Society, and Nuclear War*, II (New York: Oxford University Press, 1991) 2 vols., pp. 254–354. Evangelista argues against a mechanistic formulation of the relationship between Soviet and American foreign policies.

Robert Kennedy's meeting with Anatoliy Dobrynin on Saturday evening has been the subject of great controversy. Did the attorney general present the Soviet ambassador with an ultimatum? Did he offer to remove the American Jupiter missiles in Turkey in return for the withdrawal of the Soviet missiles in Cuba? Did he warn of a possible American military coup? Documentation of the meeting was unreliable or unavailable. Robert Kennedy's account of the meeting, published in his memoir of the crisis, was edited before publication by Theodore Sorensen. The original manuscript is missing. Until 1989, the only Soviet account was Khrushchev's memoirs, and his description of the meeting was strikingly at odds with the information provided by former members of the Kennedy administration.

At the Moscow Conference on the Cuban Missile Crisis in 1989, Anatoliy Dobrynin and Georgiy Kornienko, in 1962 his assistant in the Washington embassy, spoke about the several Kennedy-Dobrynin meetings that had taken place during the crisis. Both ambassadors elaborated on their remarks in subsequent interviews with the authors. Our analysis and reconstruction of the meeting on Saturday evening draws on those interviews because Dobrynin's reporting on this meeting cable was not yet available. It has only recently been declassified and is reproduced in full in this appendix. The cable confirms the accounts of Dobrynin and Kornienko and sheds new light on the dramatic and partially secret dénoument of the crisis.

The cable testifies to the concern of John and Robert Kennedy that military action would trigger runaway escalation. Robert Kennedy told Dobrynin of his government's determination to ensure the removal of the Soviet missiles in Cuba, and his belief that the Soviet Union "will undoubtedly respond with the same against us, somewhere in Europe." Such an admission seems illogical if the administration was using the threat of force to compel the Soviet Union to withdraw its missiles from Cuba. It significantly raised the expected cost to the United States of an attack against the missiles, thereby weakening the credibility of the American threat. To maintain or enhance that credibility, Kennedy would have had to discount the probability of Soviet retaliation to Dobrynin. That nobody in the government was certain of Khrushchev's response makes Kennedy's statement all the more remarkable.

It is possible that Dobrynin misquoted Robert Kennedy. However, the Soviet ambassador was a careful and responsible diplomat. At the very least, Kennedy suggested that he thought that Soviet retaliation was likely. Such an admission was still damaging to compellence. It seems likely that Kennedy was trying to establish the basis for a more cooperative approach to crisis resolution. His brother, he made clear, was under enormous pressure from a coterie of generals and civilian officials who were "itching for a fight." This also was a remarkable admission for the attorney general to make. The pressure on the president to attack Cuba, as Kennedy explained at the beginning of the meeting, had been greatly intensified by the destruction of an unarmed American reconnaissance plane. The president did not want to use force, in part because he recognized the terrible consequences of escalation, and was therefore requesting Soviet assistance to make it unnecessary.

This interpretation is supported by the president's willingness to remove the Jupiter missiles as a *quid pro quo* for the withdrawal of missiles in Cuba, and his brother's frank confession that the only obstacles to dismantling the Jupiters were political. "Public discussion" of a missile exchange would damage the United States' position in NATO. For this reason, Kennedy revealed, "besides himself and his brother, only 2-3 people know about it in Washington." Khrushchev would have to cooperate with the administration to keep the American concession a secret.

Most extraordinary of all is the apparent agreement between Dobrynin and Kennedy to treat Kennedy's de facto ultimatum as "a request, and not an ultimatum." This was a deliberate attempt to defuse as much as possible the hostility that Kennedy's "request" for an answer by the next day was likely to provoke in Moscow. So too was Dobrynin's next sentence: "I noted that it went without saying that the Soviet government would not accept any ultimatum and it was good that the American government realized that."

Prior meetings between Dobrynin and Kennedy had sometimes degenerated into shouting matches. On this occasion, Dobrynin indicates, the attorney general kept his emotions in check and took the ambassador into his confidence in an attempt to cooperate on the resolution of the crisis. This two-pronged strategy succeeded where compellence alone might have failed. It gave Khrushchev positive incentives to remove the Soviet missiles and reduced the emotional cost to him of the withdrawal. He responded as Kennedy and Dobrynin had hoped.

•

NOTE: In this telegram, Dobrynin makes references to his last conversation with RFK, which supports the assertion that there was no intervening "mystery" meeting.

MID # 5
From A.F. Dobrynin's telegram to MID USSR
October 27, 1962

Late tonight R. Kennedy invited me to come see him. We talked alone.

The Cuban crisis, R. Kennedy began, continues to quickly worsen. We have just received a report that an unarmed American plane was shot down while carrying out a reconnaissance flight over Cuba. The military is demanding that the President arm such planes and respond to fire with fire. The US government will have to do this.

I interrupted R. Kennedy and asked him what right American planes had to fly over Cuba at all, crudely violating its sovereignty and accepted international norms? How would the USA have reacted if foreign planes appeared over its territory?

"We have a resolution of the Organization of American States that gives us the right to such overflights," R. Kennedy quickly replied.

I told him that the Soviet Union, like all peace-loving countries, resolutely rejects such a "right" or, to be more exact, this kind of true lawlessness, when people who don't like the social-political situation in a country try to impose their will on it—a small state where the people themselves established and maintained [their system]. "The OAS resolution is a direct violation of the UN Charter," I added, "and you, as the Attorney General of the USA, the highest American legal entity, should certainly know that."

R. Kennedy said that he realized that we had different approaches to these problems and it was not likely that we could convince each other. But now the matter is not in these differences, since time is of the essence. "I want," R. Kennedy stressed, "to lay out the current alarming situation the way the president sees it. He wants N.S. Khrushchev to know this. This is the thrust of the situation now."

"Because of the plane that was shot down, there is now strong pressure on the president to give an order to respond with fire if fired upon when American reconnaissance planes are flying over Cuba. The US can't stop these flights, because this is the only way we can quickly get information about the state of construction of the missile bases in Cuba, which we believe pose a very serious threat to our national security. But if we start to fire in response—a chain reaction will quickly start that will be very hard to stop. The same thing in regard to the essence of the issue of missile bases in Cuba. The US government is determined to get rid of those bases—up to, in the extreme case, of bombing them, since, I repeat, they pose a great threat to the security of the USA. But in response to the bombing of these bases, in the course of which Soviet specialists might suffer, the Soviet government will undoubtedly respond with the same against us, somewhere in Europe. A real war will begin, in which millions of Americans and Russians will die. We want to avoid that any way we can, I'm sure that the government of the USSR has the same wish. However, taking time to find a way out [of the situation] is very risky (here R. Kennedy mentioned as if in passing that there are many unreasonable heads among the generals, and not only among the generals, who are 'itching for a fight'). The situation might get out of control, with irreversible consequences."

"In this regard," R. Kennedy said, "the president considers that a suitable basis for regulating the entire Cuban conflict might be the letter N. S. Khrushchev sent on October 26 and the letter in response from the President, which was sent off today to N. S. Khrushchev through the US Embassy in Moscow. The most important thing for us," R. Kennedy stressed, "is to get as soon as possible the agreement of the Soviet government to halt further work on the construction of the missile bases in Cuba and take measures under international control that would make it impossible to use these weapons. In exchange the government of the USA is ready, in addition to repealing all measures on the "quarantine," to give assurances that there will not be any invasion of Cuba and that other countries of the Western Hemisphere are ready to give the same assurances—the US government is certain of this."

"And what about Turkey?" I asked R. Kennedy.

"If that is the only obstacle to achieving the regulation I mentioned earlier, then the president doesn't see any unsurmountable difficulties in resolving this issue," replied R. Kennedy. "The greatest difficulty for the president is the public discussion of the issue of Turkey. Formally the deployment of missile bases in Turkey was done by a special decision of the NATO Council. To announce now a unilateral decision by the president of the USA to withdraw missile bases from Turkey—this would damage the entire structure of NATO and the US position as the leader of NATO, where, as the Soviet government undoubtedly knows very well, there are many arguments. In short, if such a decision were announced now it would seriously tear apart NATO."

"However, President Kennedy is ready to come to agree on that question with N. S. Khrushchev, too. I think that in order to withdraw these bases from Turkey," R. Kennedy said, "we need 4–5 months. This is the minimal amount of time necessary for the US government to do this, taking into account the procedures that exist within the NATO framework. On the whole Turkey issue," R. Kennedy added, "if Premiere N. S. Khrushchev agrees with what I've said, we can continue to exchange opinions between him and the president, using him, R. Kennedy and the Soviet ambassador. "However, the president can't say anything public in this regard about Turkey," R. Kennedy said again. R. Kennedy then warned that his comments about

Turkey are extremely confidential; besides him and his brother, only 2–3 people know about it in Washington.

"That's all that he asked me to pass on to N. S. Khrushchev," R. Kennedy said in conclusion. "The president also asked N. S. Khrushchev to give him an answer (through the Soviet ambassador and R. Kennedy) if possible within the next day (Sunday) on these thoughts in order to have a business-like, clear answer in principle. [He asked him] not to get into a wordy discussion, which might drag things out. The current serious situation, unfortunately, is such that there is very little time to resolve this whole issue. Unfortunately, events are developing too quickly. The request for a reply tomorrow," stressed R. Kennedy, "is just that—a request, and not an ultimatum. The president hopes that the head of the Soviet government will understand him correctly."

I noted that it went without saying that the Soviet government would not accept any ultimatums and it was good that the American government realized that. I also reminded him of N. S. Khrushchev's appeal in his last letter to the president to demonstrate state wisdom in resolving this question. Then I told R. Kennedy that the president's thoughts would be brought to the attention of the head of the Soviet government. I also said that I would contact him as soon as there was a reply. In this regard, R. Kennedy gave me a number of direct telephone line to the White House.

In the course of the conversation, R. Kennedy noted that he knew about the conversation that television commentator Scali had yesterday with an Embassy advisor on possible ways to regulate the Cuban conflict [whited out]

I should say that during our meeting R. Kennedy was very upset; in any case, I've never seen him like this before. True, about twice he tried to return to the topic of "deception," (that he talked about so persistently during our previous meeting), but he did so in passing and without any edge to it. He didn't even try to get into fights on various subjects, as he usually does, and only persistently returned to one topic: time is of the essence and we shouldn't miss the chance.

After meeting with me he immediately went to see the president, with whom, as R. Kennedy said, he spends almost all his time now.

A. Dobrynin
October 27, 1962